The Soviet Crucible

The Soviet System in Theory and Practice

Fifth Edition

edited with introductory notes and an afterword by
Samuel Hendel
Professor Emeritus, The City College of The City University of New York
Professor Emeritus, Trinity College

Duxbury Press, North Scituate, Massachusetts

To Clara, with love

The Soviet Crucible: The Soviet System in Theory and Practice, 5th edition was prepared for publication by the following people:

Production Editor: Robine Storm van Leeuwen
Copy Editor: Rebecca Dorfman
Cover Designer: Delia Higgs

Duxbury Press
A Division of Wadsworth, Inc.

Library of Congress Cataloging in Publication Data

Hendel, Samuel, 1909- ed.
The Soviet crucible.

Bibliography: p.
1 Russia—Politics and government—1917-
2 Russia—Economic conditions—1918-
3 Communism—Russia. I. Title.
JN6511.H4 1980 320.447 80-14249
ISBN 0-87872-256-4

Printed in the United States of America
1 2 3 4 5 6 7 8 9 - 84 83 82 81 80

CONTENTS

PART FOUR: DICTATORSHIP SECURED

PART FIVE: THE SOVIET CONSTITUTIONAL AND POLITICAL SYSTEMS

PREFACE

It will, I hope, not be considered immodest for me to say that the high regard with which previous editions of *The Soviet Crucible* were received justifies retaining its basic structure and emphases. Unfortunately, however, printing costs have so increased that to incorporate materials dealing with important developments in the USSR since publication of the fourth edition required some painful deletions or telescoping. Compensation will be found, I am confident, in the additions, which include the Soviet Constitution of 1977 (see Appendix) and the differing opinions of John J. Abt and Robert Sharlet on its meaning and significance; a new topic on political participation in the Soviet Union, with the sharply contrasting views of Jerry F. Hough and Donald Barry; Roy Medvedev's analysis of the judicial system and the security forces; Tamara Deutscher's discussion of intellectual opposition in the USSR; Soviet and non-Soviet views on the strength and weakness of the USSR's economy; similarly contrasting views on the USSR's living standards; and new material on the position of women. It is particularly noteworthy, too, that nine of the contributions that appeared in the fourth edition have been updated, including those by Richard C. Gripp, Harold J. Berman, Harry G. Shaffer, Alec Nove, and your editor.

More than sixty years have passed since the Bolshevik Revolution of November 1917—an event not simply earthshaking in its immediate impact on war-torn and ravaged Russia, but whose reverberating effects were felt and are likely to continue to be felt throughout a considerable part of the world. The Revolution unleashed forces far deeper, raised hopes far higher, and engendered conflicts far more violent than any other upheaval of modern times. It is appropriate, therefore, to give consideration to the philosophical and historical background and the nature of this Revolution, and more particularly to its aftermath—its achievements, challenges, failures, problems, and prospects.

The task of comprehension and evaluation, however, is a formidable one. Books on Soviet theory and practice are "as the sands of the seashore." Those conforming to official Soviet explanations and rationalizations are uncritically laudatory and often involve distortions of historical fact. At the other extreme are the reports of critics of the USSR who picture communism as "a gigantic chamber of intellectual and moral horrors." To be sure, the story abounds in horror. "But this," as Isaac Deutscher wrote, "is only one of its elements; and even this, the demonic, has to be translated into terms of human motives and interests." Moreover, consideration should proceed with understanding and appreciation of the special history, geography, and circumstances which—to an important degree—shaped Soviet policies and institutions.

But even the serious and fair-minded student of Russian affairs confronts many difficulties. For one, prerevolutionary Russian history is little known in the West. For another, Marxist-Leninist theory, which purports to be the basis of Soviet practice, is ambiguous and inconsistent in significant respects and is seldom read except in crudely excerpted form; and the extent of its real influence on Soviet practice is seriously controverted.

Other difficulties derive from the complexity and dynamism of the Soviet system, which extends over a vast land mass of more than 8 million square miles and encompasses a great variety of peoples who number over 260 millions. Moreover, in its many years of history, the Soviet Union has passed through several more or less clearly differentiated phases of development in economic, military, religious, minority, and educational policies and programs—to name but a few. Then, too, close and detailed knowledge of the background, experience, thinking, and motivations of Soviet leaders is not generally available as it is in respect to their Western counterparts.

Secrecy and censorship (as well as expunging and distortion) continue to impede the process of gathering reliable information about the Soviet system. On the other hand there has been some noteworthy improvement in these areas in recent years. In general, in fields having little or no military significance, there is little doubt that much official Soviet information is substantially complete and accurate. (A note on the reliability of Soviet statistics—particularly economic statistics—appears in this volume.)

Notwithstanding formidable difficulties it is, I believe, fair to say that the extent to which Russian policy, and hence Russia itself, is "a riddle wrapped in a mystery inside an enigma," is greatly exaggerated. Even Churchill, who used the phrase with respect to Soviet foreign policy, added "but perhaps there is a key. That key is Russian national interest." Apart from the proceedings at high levels, which are shrouded in great secrecy, there is a considerable body of dependable knowledge and information about many aspects of Soviet life. This is, in no small part, due to the work of devoted scholars, journalists, diplomats, and many others who brought to their writing and comments about the USSR a high degree of intellectual integrity and objectivity.

This is all the more noteworthy since so much Soviet writing about American life is a distortion of reality. Of course Americans, with far greater access to diverse information about the Soviet Union, sometimes set up their own barriers to understanding. These derive at times from deliberate falsification or oversimplification, but more often perhaps from a yearning, sometimes unconscious, for tidy and simplistic explanation and categorization. It is a false conception, Harold Berman wrote, which assumes that men who believe in "evil doctrines" cannot at the same time, work to accomplish great humanitarian benefits. While, therefore, complete objectivity may in fact be a dream, the conscientious student will take account of his bias and preconceptions (whether positive or negative) and seek to discover and pursue the truth wherever it may lead.

As for the presuppositions and premises that in general guided the process of selection, it must be said, to begin with, that wide differences of opinion—often tenably supported—exist among scholars and writers regarding the development, nature, and prospects of the Soviet system. A basic premise from which this book proceeds is that understanding is likely to be enhanced by recognizing and giving consideration to variant positions on complex and controversial issues affecting the USSR.

Another premise is that both the form and substance of Soviet rule in the USSR were considerably affected and influenced by *peculiarly Russian* history and circumstances. One selection, therefore, deals with the Tsarist heritage generally, and another, in more detailed fashion, with the period from about the end of serfdom to the Bolshevik Revolution.

This book also reflects the assumption that a knowledge of Marxist and Leninist theory is of great importance for a true understanding of the Soviet order. Although Leninist theory, in vital respects, departed from Marxist theory, and Marxist-Leninist theory has, in fundamentals, been attenuated or discarded in Soviet practice, nevertheless theory played an important role in organizing the Bolshevik Revolution and state and is part of the ethos of Soviet society. As Edward Hallett Carr has written, it has "the status of a creed which purports to inspire every act of state power," so that even its emasculation requires appropriate genuflection. Certainly, Marxist-Leninist theory, however distorted, continues to inspire Communist-led revolutionary movements. Moreover, Marxist-Leninist theory merits evaluation as a body of doctrine claiming scientific validity and universal applicability.

The selection of these readings was further guided by the conviction that the foundation for the oligarchical character of Soviet institutions was significantly laid by the end of 1921—however unwittingly on the part of some who participated in the process—with the failure of the world revolution, the loss by the Bolsheviks of even militant working-class support, the destruction of all opposition parties, and the outlawry of factions within the Communist party. Certainly this dictatorial and essentially totalitarian character was fairly definitively formed by the end of 1928 when Stalin, after a series of internecine party struggles, had obtained a position of almost unchallengeable power (although its apogee was probably not reached until some years thereafter). Accordingly, the process by which the Bolshevik Revolution "went wrong" and abandoned so-called proletarian democracy and then intra-Party democracy is closely analyzed. This is followed by an examination of the uses of terror as a system of power, particularly in the hands of Stalin, and a general analysis of the development and evolution of the Soviet system from Stalin to Brezhnev.

With the completion of the primarily theoretical and historical survey, the book shifts to largely contemporary analyses and appraisals of the

Soviet constitutional, political, economic, and social systems. Apart from limitations of space, which preclude detailed chronological treatment, this shift is in accord with the intended emphasis on the fundamental character and spirit of Soviet institutions. Little or no attention is devoted to details of organization and structure of Soviet institutions—details of real importance to the specialist, but not basic to understanding of the Soviet system or likely to be long remembered by the nonspecialist.

The Soviet constitutional and political systems are examined from several focal points of interest: the meaning and significance of the Constitutions of 1936 and 1977; the nature of "socialist democracy"; the extent of political participation and the role of pressure groups; the system of justice, particularly affecting dissidents; intellectual dissent; and who governs in Soviet society.

In a thoroughly planned economy, there is an interrelationship and interdependence between politics and economics beyond anything known under capitalism. The fact is, too, that the apparent belief of Soviet leaders in the ultimate triumph of socialism throughout the world is based, in major part, upon its alleged superiority over capitalism as an economic system. The Soviet economic system—its historic development, priorities, organization, successes, failures, projections, and prospects—are rigorously considered, analyzed, and evaluated.

Among the proudest claims of the Soviet Union are that it has "solved the national question" and accorded essential equality to all nations, races, and people and otherwise created a highly egalitarian and advanced society; achievements allegedly reflected, *inter alia,* in the equality of women and general access to social welfare benefits, most notably in respect to improved living standards, health care, social security, housing, and education. The final section of this volume, entitled "The Soviet Social System: Community, Equality, Welfare," gives close attention to both the bases and support for these claims and qualifications of and reservations and challenges to them. The Afterword is an attempt on my part to assess the overall impact of Marxist theory upon Soviet practice.

The book contains no treatment of Soviet foreign policy or of American foreign policy concerned with the USSR. In light of the need to make choices, this omission proved unavoidable. Although Soviet internal policy is unquestionably affected by external policy, to do justice to foreign policy—its history, motivations, and limitations—would require another volume.

It is not pretended that the use of diverse sources on many aspects of Soviet theory and practice suggests neutrality. The book reflects a strong personal bias in favor of democracy and against dictatorship. Nevertheless, the attempt has been made to set forth, so far as practical, significant and divergent opinions, including the official Soviet view, on many of the great issues discussed. Inevitably, this has meant the inclusion of some of the most distinguished as well as authoritative writers in the Soviet field. It is hoped that the varied and conflicting opinions—sometimes among seminal scholars—will make clear the complexities of the subject matter, encourage wider reading, and tend to raise the level of discourse about the USSR to a more informed and sophisticated plane.

I am, of course, tremendously indebted to the authors and publishers whose materials are reprinted in this volume. Acknowledgment of permission is specifically made at appropriate points in this book. Separate mention must be made, however, of permission to quote the following: Ivan Turgenev's "The Threshold," from *A Treasury of Russian Life and Humor,* edited by John Cournos, published by Coward-McCann, Inc., 1943; Alexander Pushkin's "To Chaadayev," from *The Poems, Plays and Prose of Pushkin,* edited by Avrahm Yarmolinsky, published by Random House, Inc., 1936; and Vladimir Kirillov's "We," from *Russian Literature Since the War,* edited by Joshua Kunitz, and published by Boni & Gaer, Inc., 1948. I also want to express sincere appreciation to Robine Storm van Leeuwen of Duxbury Press for her help and cooperation.

I am grateful to my students at Trinity College, at The City College of The City University of New York, and at Claremont Graduate School, who, over a period of many years, subjected the ideas in my courses on the USSR to critical examination and raised challenging questions. I am also grateful to the many scholars and teachers in the Soviet field who were kind enough to give me their suggestions, advice and, in many instances, the benefit of their experience in using *The Soviet Crucible.*

I owe special thanks to Mrs. Marion Maxwell, who assisted with many of the typing chores, and to my research assistants at Trinity College, Richard S. Elliott and, more particularly, Paul J. Pantano, Jr., who for months made a preliminary examination and evaluation of hundreds of books and journals in the quest for suitable materials.

I am also indebted to the library staffs of Trinity College, *New World Review,* New York University, and The International Institute for Strategic Studies in London for their cooperation and assistance.

The help and support of my wife, Clara, was invaluable throughout the whole process of evaluating and organizing materials for publication—for which I am deeply grateful.

Samuel Hendel

PART ONE

THE HERITAGE

To Chaadayev

Not long we basked in the illusion
Of love, of hope, of quiet fame;
Like morning mists, a dream's delusion,
Youth's pastimes vanished as they came.
But still, with strong desires burning,
Beneath oppression's fateful hand,
The summons of the fatherland
We are impatiently discerning;
In hope, in torment, we are turning
Toward freedom, waiting her command. . . .
Thus anguished do young lovers stand
Who wait the promised tryst with yearning.
While freedom kindles us, my friend,
While honor calls us and we hear it,
Come: to our country let us tend
The noble promptings of the spirit. . . .
Comrade, believe: joy's star will leap
Upon our sight, a radiant token;
Russia will rouse from her long sleep;
And where autocracy lies, broken,
Our names shall yet be graven deep.

Alexander Pushkin

Chapter 1

THE TSARIST HERITAGE

The form and content of Soviet rule in the USSR were considerably affected and influenced by peculiarly Russian history and circumstances —this is undeniable. Can it be doubted, for example, that had a proletarian revolution come to England it would have established institutions and pursued internal policies different in fundamental respects from those which were, in fact, established and pursued in Russia? Early in the twentieth century, England was a country with a powerful industrial base, a large middle class, a mature proletariat, a high degree of literacy, and a developed tradition of democracy. Russia, on the other hand, was then a relatively backward, predominantly agricultural, and largely illiterate country with a long history of despotism and fanaticism—whose Fundamental Laws proclaimed the monarch an "unlimited autocrat" to whom obedience was "ordained by God himself."

This history gave substance to Alexander Herzen's prophetic comment in 1851 that "communism is the Russian autocracy turned upside down," and to the statement of William Henry Chamberlin that "the monarchical absolutism of Nicholas I was the natural parent of the revolutionary absolutism of Lenin." That is not to say that choices made and fortuitous circumstances could not and did not alter the course of Soviet history. It is only to suggest that events must be appraised in the context of the historic background in which they occurred. Some light is shed on that historic background in the broad canvas spread by William Henry Chamberlin and in the detailed story, beginning in 1857, told by George Vernadsky. Historians differ, of course, in their interpretations of Tsarist history but few challenge Mr. Chamberlin's *basic* thesis. Some of Professor Vernadsky's characterizations of leading figures and policies meet with greater dissent.

The Soviet Union Cannot Escape Russian History

William Henry Chamberlin

The Soviet Union cannot escape Russian history. . . . From the moment when the Russians emerge on the historical stage one finds them engaged in grim struggles, first for existence, then for the realization of certain goals of expansion.

Geographically, Russia was a bulwark of Europe against Asia and it bore some of the hardest blows inflicted by nomadic invaders from the East. In the early Kiev period of Russian history, in the tenth, eleventh and twelfth centuries, there are records in the old chronicles of constant fighting with the wandering peoples of the steppe, the Polovtsi and Pechenegi.

Russia was submerged in the flood of Tartar conquest in the thirteenth century. The Tartar rule was gradually shaken off during the fourteenth and fifteenth centuries. But Russian history for centuries was an almost continuous series of wars, regular and irregular, declared and undeclared, now with Oriental peoples like the Turks and the Tartars, now with the Western neighbors, Swedes, Poles, Lithuanians, who barred the Russian thrust towards the Baltic Sea.

These wars were an important cause of the wretched poverty of the Russian people. They strained to the limit the human and material resources of the medieval Muscovite state. "The state swelled and the people grew thin." In this brilliant phrase Klyuchevsky summarizes the results of Russia's slow and painful expansion of its frontiers during the seventeenth century. This expansion, like so many episodes in Russian history, was accompanied by a vast sacrifice of human lives. The last available penny was screwed out of the people in taxes, often with the aid of the knout, a peculiarly brutal Russian form of whip. A grotesque situation arose when people voluntarily wished to become serfs in order to escape tax obligations. This method of tax evasion became so prevalent that it was made punishable by whipping with the formidable knout. To be compelled to remain free by the threat of being beaten within an inch of your life if you preferred to become a serf: here was a characteristic, grim Russian paradox.

With most of its territory a vast plain, Russia lacked natural frontiers. It was always vulnerable to land invasion. On four critical occasions its national independent existence hung in the balance as a result of foreign war, sometimes complicated by domestic turmoil. . . . From 1240, when the wild Tartar horsemen of Baty slaughtered the people of Kiev, until 1941 and 1942, when Germans wrought the same scenes of carnage and destruction with modern weapons, Russia has always lived under the overhanging threat of war.

W.H. Chamberlin was a foreign correspondent in the USSR and is the author of many books on the Soviet Union, including Russia's Iron Age *and* The Russian Revolution. *This selection is reprinted from chapters 1 and 2 of* The Russian Enigma *by William Henry Chamberlin. Copyright 1943 by Charles Scribner's Sons, with permission of the publisher.*

There were some periods of fairly prolonged external peace, especially in the nineteenth century. But foreign war, actual or threatened, has always been a major force in Russian national development. This constant military pressure was not the only cause that made the Russian Tsar the most complete autocrat in Europe. But it was an important cause. And the organization of the country, almost on the basis of an armed camp, helped to clamp down the institution of serfdom in Russia. During the early Middle Ages, the Russian peasants could move freely, at stated times, from one landlord's estate to another. But during the sixteenth and seventeenth centuries, there was increasing pressure to attach the peasant to the service of a single master.

This was the result not only of the greed of the landlord class, but of the military exigencies of the time. The theory was put forward that, as the gentry had to fight in the Tsar's army, the peasants were under an obligation to support, or, in the old Russian phrase, to "feed" the gentry. Peter the Great lent a certain validity to this crude Russian conception of the "social contract" by issuing a series of regulations that added up to a national labor service act. This Tsar of unbounded energy demanded that every young noble should serve the state, either in the armed forces or in the civil administration. . . .

[By way of contrast] freedom from the threat of foreign invasion was not the only factor that made for the strengthening of American democracy and individualism. The inherited British tradition of political self-government and the sovereignty of law, the absence of any large, unassimilable, indigenous population, the high standard of literacy, all played their part. But the almost universal American assumption of political democracy and of respect for the constitutional rights of the individual would have been subjected to a much graver strain if our history had been heavily checkered with major wars. . . .

It is difficult for the American, accustomed to the ideas of separation of church and state, of freedom of opinion on religious questions, to understand either the curious mixture of state control and other-worldly mysticism in the Russian Orthodox Church or the doctrinaire atheism of the Communists. There is no parallel in American history for the passionate fanaticism that impelled tens of thousands of dissident Russian Old Believers, in the seventeenth century, to burn themselves alive as a protest against the wickedness of the world, and as a means of escaping from this wickedness and from the persecution of their belief. Both the absolutism of the autocracy and the absolutism of the revolutionary regime are alien to the Western mind, with its traditions of tolerance.

Russia, on its side, scarcely experienced the effect of three great movements which became part of the common heritage of Western Europe and America: the Renaissance, the Reformation and the French Revolution. Each of these movements, in its own way, contributed to the liberation of the human personality, to the strengthening of individualism. . . .

The roots of many Soviet actions and institutions may be sought and found in events and developments that occurred as far back as the days of Ivan the Terrible (1547–1584) and Peter the Great (1689–1725). There is historic justice and appropriateness in the fact that these two strongest figures in the long line of Tsars have been restored to official favor in the Soviet Union and commended to the admiration of the Russian people. Stalin was indebted to both these rulers for many models of policy, especially in such matters as carrying out a thorough liquidation of undesired or suspected individuals and classes.

If one were called to name a single dominant element in Russian history from the Middle Ages to the present time it would be the unlimited power of the ruler. The Russian Tsar was an autocrat in a measure unparalleled in European countries. He was absolute master of the lives and property of his subjects, like a Turkish Sultan or a Tartar Khan.

Of course, democracy, in the modern sense of the term, did not exist in medieval Europe. A network of privileges and distinctions separated the noble from the serf, the knight from the commoner, the wealthy merchant or master craftsman from the poorer classes in the cities. But in this European society there was a system of checks and balances, at least among the higher classes. The Church possessed independent authority and could sometimes bring the haughtiest monarch to his knees in repentance. The nobility often acted as a check on the Crown, the free cities on the nobility. The privileged orders were a counterpoise to each other and to the king. In the absence of any single all-controlling absolutism was the germ of future representative government.

Very different was the situation in Russia. No Tsar went to Canossa to perform public penance. No medieval Russian sovereign found himself obliged to limit his own authority by signing a charter at the demand of rebellious barons. No court would have protected a subject who refused to pay an exorbitant tax or to surrender a piece of property which the Tsar desired. Many Tsars were assassinated in palace conspiracies. But no Russian ruler was judged and sentenced to death by a revolutionary court of his subjects, like Charles I in England and Louis XVI in France.[1]

The last *zemsky sobor,* the Russian equivalent for a parliament, met in 1649. After that time no national representative assembly was held in Russia until 1906. The upsurge of the revolutionary movement in 1905 induced Nicholas II to promulgate a Constitution, which provided for a Duma, or elected parliament. But this body was quickly reduced to a pale and unrepresentative shadow by arbitrary changes in the election law as soon as the revolutionary tide subsided, and the autocracy again felt itself securely in the saddle.

It is not only in the retrospect of modern times that the Russian autocracy seems un-European in its unlimited power. A number of foreigners who visited Russia in the sixteenth and seventeenth centuries reported their impressions of a despotism that went far beyond anything with which they were familiar in their own countries. Ivan the Terrible made a show of his power to a visiting English merchant by ordering one of his courtiers to leap to certain death. When the Tsar asked whether the British sovereign (Queen Elizabeth) possessed similar power, the British visitor drily replied that Her Majesty had better use for the necks of her subjects.

There is little trace in Russian thinking of any idea that subjects possessed any rights against the Tsar until the great intellectual awakening and flowering of Russian culture in the nineteenth century.[2] And even then it was deeply significant for the future course of events that the majority of Russian revolutionary theorists were not so much interested in protecting the individual against the state as in using the power of the state to transform society along collectivist lines. Many of these theorists preached what Lenin practised: the remaking of the social order through the dictatorship of a picked revolutionary minority. Had it not been for the autocracy of the Tsars, with its blighting effect on the conception of individual rights and liberties, the dictatorship of the Communist Party might never have come into operation. The one was a natural sequel to the other.

What were the roots of this despotism, unlimited in theory until the Constitution of 1905, although it was moderated in practice by the emergence of a gradually enlarging, intelligent public opinion in the latter part of the nineteenth century? At the time when Kiev, the old city on the Dnieper, was the centre of Russian political life, in the tenth and eleventh centuries, Constantinople was the metropolis which the Russians knew best, through trade, through war and through religion. It was through the Greek Orthodox Church that the Russians were converted to Christianity. The Byzantine Empire was the state to which they naturally looked as a model.

And this Byzantine influence was entirely in favor of autocracy. The Byzantine Emperor was an absolute ruler, who was sometimes assassinated, but was never subjected to regular control by nobles, parliament or church. The Patriarch of Constantinople never assumed the independence of the Pope of Rome. This spiritual association with Constantinople was emphasized again at a later period. A Russian monk sent a message of greeting to Ivan III, who married a Byzantine Princess, and hailed him as sovereign of "the third Rome" that would never perish. Constantinople, the "second Rome," had just fallen to the Turks.

The Tartar conquest of the thirteenth century also worked in favor of the autocratic principle. Contrary to a general impression abroad, there was not much racial intermingling between Tartars and Russians. After the first orgy of killing and pillaging was over, the Tartar khans were satisfied if the Russian princes rendered tribute and paid occasional visits to the Tartar Court to render homage and seek confirmation of their titles. But the Asiatic despotism of the Tartar conquerors naturally had its effect upon the Russians. Moreover, the Tartar rule isolated Russia from the West and deepened the chasm between Russian and European civilization.

And in the further course of Russian history the forces that made for diversity of political life in Europe were blotted out. Russia became a primitive totalitarian state before the word was used in political terminology.

At one time there was a good deal of lusty, turbulent freedom in the two large trading towns of northwestern Russia, Novgorod and Pskov, which had belonged to the Hanseatic League. But eventually both sank to the level of ordinary provincial towns under the levelling despotism of the Muscovite Tsars. Ivan III took away the great bell that had once called the people of Pskov together for meeting, as a sign that such dangerous liberty was no longer to be permitted. Employing a method that has frequently been applied to undesired classes and groups in the Soviet Union, Ivan deported a considerable number of the Pskov citizens and replaced them with new settlers from Moscow. Ivan the Terrible mercilessly decimated the population of the two cities in reprisal for disloyalty, actual or suspected.

The boyars, as the older Russian nobles were called, also suffered at the hands of this stern Tsar. Ivan, who had been slighted by the boyars as a boy and nourished an implacable hatred for the whole order, built up a terrorist political police devoted to his service. Its members, the *oprichniki,* ranged over the country, clothed in black and displaying their formidable emblem, a dog's head and a broom. This symbolized their mission: to sniff out disloyalty and purge the land of treason.

There was no legal restraint on what the *oprichniki* could do. They were empowered to kill boyars suspected of treason (the word sabotage was not known in Ivan's day), to violate their wives and seize their estates. The result of this policy was to break the inherited power and prestige of the old nobility and to transfer much of the land, then the principal source of wealth, to a new class, selected by the Tsar for his personal terrorist service and completely dependent on him for favor and advancement. Stalin followed a similar policy, against a different political and social background, when he exterminated many of the surviving Old Bolsheviks and replaced them with henchmen of his own. . . .

Twenty years after Ivan's death, Russia was plunged into the crisis of the Troubled Times (1603–1613). The ruthless Ivan, as lustful as he was cruel, had married six times, in defiance of the canons of the Orthodox Church. He was succeeded by his son Fyodor, a weakling in body and mind. When Fyodor died childless, a cunning and ambitious boyar, Boris Godunov, had gained enough influence to insure his election as Tsar by a national assembly. A younger half-brother of the late Tsar Fyodor, named Dmitry, had died some years earlier. There was a strong suspicion that he had been murdered by order of Boris, in order to pave the way for the latter's succession to the throne.

But the ghost of Dmitry proved fatal to the ambition of Boris to found a dynasty of his own. A young adventurer who gave himself out as the escaped Dmitry found a hospitable reception and political support in Poland. He invaded Russia with a band of followers, accompanied by some Polish troops. This episode touched off the stormy decade of the Troubled Times (1603–1613). This is one of the most obscure and chaotic periods in Russian history. Every disintegrating force in the country was let loose. Cossacks swept up from the South to take part in pillage and devastation. Serfs rebelled and killed their masters. Swedes and Poles intervened. Rival Tsars were chosen and assassinated.

The existence of the Muscovite state seemed to be at stake. But the Russian people displayed their qualities of toughness, resilience, determination not to be ruled by foreigners. Bit by bit, order emerged from chaos. A movement to clear the country of the foreigners and restore a strong central government found leaders in Prince Pozharsky, an aristocrat, and Kuzma Minin, a man of the common people.

A national assembly, held in 1613, elected a new Tsar, Michael Romanov, first of a dynasty that endured for three centuries. Peace and the opportunity to recover from the ravages of the Troubled Times were purchased by the cession to Poland of some Russian territory in the neighborhood of Smolensk. But from that time on the balance of power, as between Russia and Poland, steadily inclined towards the former. The unlimited despotism of the Tsars was a blighting influence on many aspects of Russian life. But it was more conducive to military success and territorial expansion than the aristocratic anarchy of Poland, where the king was almost powerless and the peasants were held in serfdom. . . .

It is worth noting that periods of internal calm in Russian history are broken by terrific explosions of mass revolt. One such explosion began in 1669 under the leadership of Razin, a picturesque Robin Hood type of bandit whose memory is preserved in one of the most haunting of Russian folksongs. His forces rolled up the valley of the Volga, getting reinforcements of fugitive serfs. But he was defeated near Simbirsk, in the Middle Volga region. His motley hordes, with their ill-assorted arms, could not cope with the Government troops, which had received some training from European instructors. His final downfall was hastened by division among the Don Cossacks themselves. The wealthier disliked his primitive levelling tendencies. He was captured and executed in 1671.

Pugachev's revolt ran much the same course as Razin's, although it covered a wider area, including the valley of the Kama, the main tributary of the Volga. His rebellion foreshadowed the Bolshevik Revolution that was to occur a century and a half later inasmuch as it rallied the same forces of discontent that Lenin would mobilize in 1917. Along with discontented serf peasants, Pugachev found supporters among the early Russian "proletarians," the laborers in the ironworks of the Urals, and among the Bashkirs, Chuvashes and other non-Russian peoples who live in the valley of the Volga and in the land between the Volga and the Urals. But Pugachev was crushed by the trained soldiers of Catherine II, and after his defeat and execution, there were no more big serf revolts. . . .

When serfdom was abolished in 1861, it was not under the pressure of a peasant insurrection. It was better, as Tsar Alexander II told a gathering of reluctant landowners, that serfdom should be abolished from above than from below. Perhaps it was because serfdom was abolished in this way, and with a good deal of consideration for the interests of the landowners, that many peasant grievances remained unredressed. Russia, as the experiences of 1905 and 1917 proved, remained ripe for agrarian rebellion.

One very important element in Russia's past heritage is the marked time lag in the cultural development of the nation. No European country of corresponding population and political importance was so barren in free and questioning minds. During the centuries when religion was the first concern of men's minds in Europe, there was no Russian Thomas Aquinas, Loyola, Pascal, Luther, Calvin or Huss. The most serious schism in the Russian Church took place in the seventeenth century, when the Patriarch Nikon introduced changes in the prayer books and ritual to bring Russian practice into line with that of other churches of the Orthodox rite. These changes were stubbornly and suspiciously resisted by some of the clergy and parishioners, who were known as Old Believers. It is significant of the intellectual sterility of the time in Russia that no important question of theological belief or church organization was involved in this schism, although each side maintained its viewpoint with uncompromising determination and was prepared to give or receive the crown of martyrdom.

There was, to be sure, a certain psychological background for the schism. The Old Believers were averse to all the foreign innovations and administrative changes that took place in the latter part of the seventeenth century and reached their culmination in the reign of Peter the Great. Moussorgsky's magnificent opera, *Khovanstchina,* far too little known outside of Russia, gives an unforgettable imaginative picture of the clash between old and new in Russia on the eve of Peter's reforms and finds its climax in a scene of self-immolation on the part of the Old Believers.

The Russian Church was weakened by the schism. And it lost its last chance to function as even a modest counterpoise to the absolutism of the state when Peter the Great abolished the Patriarchate and placed the Church under the administrative authority of a layman, the Procuror of the Holy Synod.

So Russia did not share the mighty ferment of ideas that coincided in Europe with the struggle between Roman Catholicism and Protestantism. It also missed the humanistic culture of the Renaissance. Until the nineteenth century, Russia conveys the impression of a nation asleep, so far as cultural life is concerned. There is no fourteenth-century Russian Dante, no sixteenth-century Russian Shakespeare, no seventeenth-century Russian Newton, no eighteenth-century Russian Voltaire.

Now and then a European would bring into semi-Asiatic Russia some Western influence. Scotch and German soldiers of fortune helped to impart the elements of drill and discipline to the raw Russian levies. Italian architects, of whom Rastrelli was the most famous, designed churches and palaces. Skilled artisans were induced to come to Russia, especially in the time of Peter the Great, to teach industrial arts and crafts to the Russians. But there was only a very dim and pale Russian reflection of the humanist movement of the West, of the rediscovery of the Greek and Latin classics, because there were so few Russian scholars. Russia was a force to be reckoned with politically and militarily long before it was able to make a notable contribution to European culture. . . .

Russia was sufficiently part of Europe to be drawn into the wars of the French Revolution and of the Napoleonic period. But the French Revolution aroused no such response in Russia as in the countries of Western and Central Europe. The autocracy, the noble-serf social relation, remained unchanged. The most visible reflection of the influence of the French Revolution in Russia was the unsuccessful revolt of the Decembrists in 1825. They were a group of officers who had imbibed progressive ideas from service abroad in countries which had felt the impact of the French revolutionary changes.

The reign of Peter the Great (1689–1725) marked the transition from the Moscow to the St. Petersburg period in Russian history. That revolutionary autocrat shifted the capital from old, semi-Oriental Moscow to the new capital, which he built on the shore of the Gulf of Finland in the style of a European city and gave his own name. A giant of a man, gifted with enormous mental and physical energy, Peter strove mightily to debarbarize Russia, to bring it up to the level of the European civilization of the time. It was both a personal and perhaps a characteristic national tragedy that the means which he used to promote this debarbarization were often extremely cruel and oppressive and won him, in the eyes of some of his more conservative and superstitious subjects, the reputation of being the anti-Christ forecast in the Book of Revelations. . . .

Peter [the first Tsar who left his own country to travel in Europe] returned to Russia brimming over with plans for the modernization of the country. He encountered a mutiny of the *streltsi,* which he promptly quelled, cutting off the heads of the ringleaders with his own hand. There was nothing gentle about Peter. His son Aleksei, who did not sympathize with his innovating plans, died as a result of torture which was inflicted in order to make him disclose the accomplices in a suspected plot. V.O. Klyuchevsky, most eloquent and philosophical of Russian historians, sums up the paradox of Peter as reformer in the following sentences:

> His beneficent actions were accomplished with repelling violence. Peter's reform was a struggle of despotism with the people, with its sluggishness. He hoped through the threat of his authority to evoke initiative in an enslaved society, and through a slave-owning nobility to introduce into Russia European science, popular education, as the necessary condition of social initiative. He desired that the slave, remaining a slave, should act consciously and freely. The interaction of despotism and freedom, of education and slavery—this is the political squaring of the circle, the riddle which we have been solving for two centuries from the time of Peter, and which is still unsolved. . . .

Although Peter's quick and lively mind seized on many Western discoveries and methods of administration and adapted them for use in Russia, he made no attempt to introduce into Russia the element of individual freedom and initiative which contributed much to the scientific and technical progress of the West. The autocracy became stronger than ever. There was no loosening of the chains of serfdom. There was no experimenting with elected representative bodies. The Church was reduced almost to the status of a department of the state.

Throughout the eighteenth century the extension of Russia's frontiers proceeded with the inexorable finality of an expanding glacial ice cap. The growing weakness of Russia's neighbors, the Poles in the West, the Tartars and Turks in the South and Southwest, favored this extension. Under the reign of Peter's most distinguished successor, Catherine II, Russia reached its natural southern frontier, the Black Sea, and swallowed up the greater part of Poland. It maintained and somewhat improved its western boundary under the shock of the Napoleonic War. During the nineteenth century Russia made no very considerable territorial gain in Europe, but the Empire was rounded out with new conquests in the Caucasus and Central Asia.

More important than any political and military developments was the amazing cultural awakening of Russia in the nineteenth century. There was a flowering of imagination and of creative thought that is all the more impressive because of the previous sterile nature of the Russian intellectual soil. There were a few pioneers of the future Russian culture, like the poet-scientist, M.V. Lomonosov, who helped to establish the Russian literary language in the eighteenth century. But if everything written in Russian before 1800 (old sagas and folksongs excepted) were destroyed by some natural catastrophe, the loss would scarcely be perceptible, except to specialized students. Russia entered the nineteenth century with an intellectual past remarkably blank for a people so numerous and, as the future would show, so gifted artistically. There had been no achievements up to this time in literature or art (the inherited Byzantine ikon painting excepted), in science and philosophy that could challenge comparison with those of England and France, Germany and Italy. Several causes account for this retarded cultural growth.

There was the long sleep enforced by the Tartar Conquest. There was the chronic exhaustion of national strength and wealth by a long series of wars. The unlimited autocracy was itself no encouragement to free speculation. This might also be said of a state religion that was at once dogmatic and conservative. Cities are the centres of intellectual life, and Russia up to very modern times possessed very few genuine cities, only garrison towns and large trading villages.

The nineteenth century was an era of noteworthy cultural and material progress for all Europe. And Russia was caught up in the wave of this progress. Its two glowing lyric poets, Pushkin and Lermontov, rank with Byron and Shelley among the leading figures in the romantic movement. Both Russian poets found much of their inspiration in the life and legends of the Caucasus, with its magnificent mountain scenery and its medley of picturesque tribes.

In the field of the novel, Russia, with its four masters, Tolstoy, Dostoevsky, Turgenev, and Gogol, and its many lesser writers, such as Goncharov, Saltikov-Shchedrin, Chekhov, Gorky, Andreev, easily surpassed the contemporary achievement of any European country, with the possible exception of France. In music it achieved a position second only to Germany, with such composers as Tschaikovsky, Moussorgsky, Rimsky-Korsakov, Rubinstein, Borodin, Glinka and many others. Scientists, such as Metchnikov, Mendeleev and Pavlov, artists like Repin, historians ranging from the old-fashioned, courtly Karamzin at the beginning of the century to the brilliant and profoundly thoughtful Klyuchevsky at the end, all made their contribution to this great century of Russian cultural achievement.

This was no mere emergence of individual men of genius and talent. The Russian educated class steadily increased in numbers, although it remained relatively small because of the great masses of illiterate and semi-literate peasants and the still more backward non-Russian Oriental peoples of the Empire. But the quality of this young Russian intelligentsia was out of all proportion to its numbers. In breadth of intellectual interest, in spontaneity and keenness of literary and artistic appreciation, in receptivity to the new ideas, the Russian intellectual, the writer, teacher, physician, scientist, artist or student often compared very favorably with men and women of similar educational background in other countries. . . .

It is scarcely an exaggeration to say that only in the nineteenth century did Russians begin to come alive as human beings. The personalities of Tsars and Tsarinas, positive or negative, had always been important because of the absolutist character of the government. A few progressive-minded nobles and distinctive generals convey a sense of definite character. But until the nineteenth century the poverty of individual personality in Russia matched the poverty in cultural achievement. Then the ice that seemed to freeze the Russians of earlier generations commenced to crack. Figures of world significance began to emerge.

Perhaps the best known Russian of the last century was Count Leo Tolstoy. Descendant of an old aristocratic family, author of the two great novels, *War and Peace* and *Anna Karenina,* he attracted international attention by the philosophy of nonviolence, renunciation of wealth, abstinence and simple living which he preached and practised during the later period of his life. He was a successor of Rousseau and a precursor of Gandhi, with whom he had much in common spiritually and intellectually. In his attitude, bordering on anarchism, of rejecting the power of the state, in his repudiation of violence between man and man, Tolstoy expressed the unconscious aspirations of the peasants whom he knew on his estates, and who regarded taxes and military conscription as two of the principal curses of their lives.

Tolstoy escaped exile or imprisonment because of his aristocratic antecedents and because of his international prestige. But he was excommunicated by an officially controlled Church, although he might reasonably have been regarded as a most sincere Christian. Other independent minds were not so fortunate. Alexander Herzen, perhaps the most eloquent Russian publicist of his time, found that he could write freely only in London. N.G. Chernishevsky, a man who might have ranked with Mill and Spencer because of his encyclopedic learning and his fondness for social theory, was broken by a period of long exile in Siberia.

One of the most lovable figures in the revolutionary movement was Prince Peter Kropotkin. He gave up a promising scientific career to take up the hunted, persecuted life of the revolutionary. For a time he was imprisoned in the grim fortress of Peter and Paul, in St. Petersburg. His escape, after he had been transferred to a hospital, was one of the spectacular episodes of the struggle between the revolutionaries and the police. To Darwin's hard law of the survival of the fittest in a world of struggle, Kropotkin opposed a theory of mutual aid, for which he tried to find support in science and in history. Forced to live in exile for many years, Kropotkin returned to Russia, an old man, after the Revolution. He found a new form of dictatorial state instead of the voluntary association of free communes of which he had dreamed, and died, sad and disappointed, in 1921.

Another striking figure was Michael Bakunin. Like Kropotkin, he was an Anarchist by conviction. But, unlike the human and scholarly Prince, he reveled in violent action and was willing to resort to any kind of force and intrigue in order to gain his objective: the total overthrow of existing society and the substitution of anarchist communism. It is psychologically significant that this great Russian Anarchist, who yearned for the destruction of the state, as the source of all evil, who fought on more than one barricade in European insurrections, tried to create secret revolutionary organizations, based on the principle of absolute authority of the leaders. It was this very principle, successfully carried into practice by Lenin, that laid the foundation for the Communist dictatorship.

It was not only dangerous political thinkers like Herzen, Bakunin and Kropotkin who felt the stern hand of the Tsar's police. Authors like Dostoevsky and Turgenev also found themselves in difficulties. Because he had joined a discussion club which was suspected of seditious tendencies, Dostoevsky, under the reactionary rule of Nicholas I, was condemned to death. At the last moment the sentence was commuted to four years of penal servitude in Siberia. Curiously enough, Dostoevsky emerged from this experience not an embittered rebel, but a mystical Christian. His views became more conservative and nationalist in his later years and he satirized the revolutionaries savagely in his novel, *The Possessed.* The Westernized liberal Turgenev was so much harassed by police surveillance that he preferred to spend much of his life abroad.

Yet, although the autocratic system pressed heavily on the individual, especially upon the individual of liberal or radical views, the nineteenth century was still the freest and most progressive period in Russian history. No European country grew so visibly in mental stature between 1800 and 1900. No European land owes so large a part of its heritage of civilization to the effort of a single century. . . .

In the heritage of the Russian past one can find many seeds of the great revolution that was to shatter the political and social order, and many foreshadowings of the regime that was to emerge from that revolution. The traditional unlimited power of the government was an excellent preparation for the Communist dictatorship. The Russian folk pattern of bearing great poverty and hardship stoically over long periods of time and then flaring up in an outburst of wild revolt was favorable to the success of a group of determined revolutionaries who would take advantage of one of these moods of all-out rebellion and then lay a heavy yoke of their own on the masses of the people.

The essential newness of Russian conscious thinking on social and economic problems, the exclusion of most educated Russians from positions of practical responsibility, worked in favor of doctrinaire extremism. Russia had missed the individualist aspects of such movements as the Reformation, the Renaissance and the French Revolution. It was less touched than any large European power by the general trend towards parliamentarism and liberalism. Among the obvious causes of the Revolution were the intolerable strain and dislocation imposed by the First World War, the contrasts of wealth and poverty in the country, the hard living conditions of most of the industrial workers and peasants, the discontent of the non-Russian nationalities.

Less obvious, but no less important as a cause was the comparative absence, in Russian historical experience, of anything that would cultivate a strong sense of an individual's right to personal liberty and private property. No Russian was safe against arrest for political reasons. Only a minority of the peasants owned their land on an individual property basis. The number of persons with a conscious personal stake in the avoidance of violent change was smaller than in any other European country. On the very eve of its fall, the Tsarist system impressed most observers as a bulwark of conservatism and reaction. But it was also a powder-magazine of violent revolution. . . .

The Bolshevik Revolution made Russia more enigmatical than ever, in the eyes of the outside world. The downfall of Tsarism was generally welcomed in democratic countries. But many of the theories and acts of the victorious revolutionaries seemed harsh and repelling. The denial of political and civil liberties, the "liquidation" of whole classes of the population, the attempt to realize professedly humane ultimate ends by immediate means that were often ruthless and brutal, inspired doubts and questionings, even in the minds of many who were originally sympathetic with the Revolution.

Notes

1. *There might have been such a scene in Russian history after the Bolshevik Revolution if it had not been for the exigencies of the Civil War. Nicholas II, his wife, son and four daughters were simply butchered in the cellar of their place of confinement in Ekaterinburg (now Sverdlovsk) without any formalities of indictment and trial because it was feared that they might be rescued by the advancing anti-Bolshevik forces.*
2. *Peter the Great defined his own power in the following expansive terms: "His Majesty is an autocratic monarch, responsible to no one for his policies. He has power and authority to govern his state and lands as a Christian ruler according to his will and understanding."*

From 1857 to 1914

George Vernadsky

Alexander II [Emperor, 1855–1881]

The patriotic feelings of Alexander, as of many of his contemporaries, were deeply hurt by the outcome of the Crimean War [which ended in 1856]. Reforms in Russia seemed inevitable, as the old regime had proved itself incapable of organizing the defense of Russia. This was admitted prior to his death by Nicholas I, who told Alexander: "I am handing you command of the country in a poor state." The basic defect of the old regime was the institution of serfdom. It was consequently natural that the reforms of Alexander II should start with this matter, the more so because the solution of the question had been prepared during the reign of Nicholas I.

A decisive step was taken at the initiative of Alexander in the late summer of 1857, when the emperor authorized the governor-general of Vilna to organize "Provincial Committees" of the nobility in the Lithuanian provinces for the discussion of the terms of the proposed peasant reforms on December 2, 1857. Following this move there was no possibility of retreat; the reforms became inevitable. The nobles of other provinces were forced to request the Government's authorization to form similar committees. Their motives were clearly expressed in the famous speech of Alexander II to the nobility of Moscow: "Better that the reform should come from above than wait until serfdom is abolished from below." . . .

The basic principles of the reform were as follows: Household serfs were to be freed within a period of two years without redemption, but were to receive nothing on gaining their freedom. Peasant serfs were to receive not only their personal freedom, but also certain allotments of land. In determining the dimensions of each peasant's share, the amount of land worked by peasants for their own use under conditions of serfdom was taken into consideration. The serfs had worked both their own lands and the lands of their owner. The area of the allotments granted to the peasants following the reform was equal approximately to the area retained by the landowner. Thus, under the terms of the reform of 1861, the peasants received grants of land which, prior to the reform, had absorbed only half of their labor.

By the terms of the emancipation, the land which the peasants received did not become their private property. It continued to be regarded as the property of the landowner, but was held for the benefit of the peasant. The peasants, though now freedmen, were called upon to pay for the use of this land or to perform certain services for the landowner. The Government, however, was willing to help, if both the landowners and the peasants desired to terminate this relationship. Help was provided in the form of a long-term credit to purchase the land. In those cases where estate owners agreed to sell the land to their

George Vernadsky taught at Yale University and is the author of The Expansion of Russia; Lenin, Red Dictator; *and* Political and Diplomatic History of Russia. *This selection, somewhat rearranged, is from chapters 10, 11, and 12 of* A History of Russia, *Copyright 1929, 1930, and 1944, by Yale University Press. Used by permission.*

former serfs, the Government paid the landowners the cost of the land with an interest-bearing bond, and this sum was imposed upon the peasant in the form of deferred payments over a period of years. The cost was computed on the basis of the annual payment of the peasant, being worth 6 percent of the cost of the land. The deferred payments were added to the head tax of the peasant.

The appointed period was forty-nine years. Within twenty years following 1861, about 85 percent of landowners actually sold to the peasants their part of land in each estate with the above-mentioned assistance of the Government. Even in this case the peasant did not receive the land in complete personal ownership, but each peasant commune or village received the whole area of land in communal ownership under collective responsibility for the redemption payments of all the members of the commune. Special government agents named for the purpose of putting the reform into operation, called mediators, drew up charter deeds for the land in the name of a whole commune. The commune itself divided the land among its members according to the size of families. These subdivisions took place periodically every few years.

Thus, even following the reforms, the peasant did not become an individual property owner or an individual possessing full civil rights, but remained subject to the authority of the commune. Actually the peasants became dependent upon those government bureaucratic agencies which concerned themselves with peasant affairs. It is necessary to add that outside of the commune each peasant could purchase land on the basis of full ownership. This situation is important for the understanding of future events. It explains the continued juridical isolation of the peasants even following the reform. It also preserved in their consciousness the memory of serfdom. The firm bonds of the commune did not permit changes in the manner of owning land. The peasants never forgot that the commune had only half of the former estate. The reform of 1861 seemed incomplete and they dreamed of completing it. Another idea connected with the land commune was that the land was not the property of individuals but was granted in the form of an allotment to serve the uses of the individual. Thus, land within the whole state was regarded by the peasant as a fund which could be drawn upon for further allotments until it was used up. These were the embryonic ideas of the subsequent revolution.

The reform of 1861 was tragically inadequate. There were two ways of really solving the question finally. The first was to leave the possession as well as the ownership of the land with the landowner. The peasant in this case would have received merely his personal freedom. In the majority of cases, however, under the pressure of necessity, the landowner would have been forced to sell part of his land to his former serfs. The Government could have assisted in this transaction, in favor of the individual peasants, and not of the communes. The actual result would have been almost the same as it was by the reform of 1861, but the psychological results would have been quite different. Instead of thousands of peasant communes there would have been created millions of peasant landowners. The ideas of a "general fund" and of "allotments" would have been avoided. It was toward this result that the later reforms of Stolypin were directed, but the reforms of Stolypin came forty-five years too late (1906).

The other possibility, in introducing the reform of 1861, was to take all the land away from the estate owners and to divide it among the peasants. This would have been the simplest solution, which would have prevented all the later upheavals in Russia. If the partition of land had been completed in 1861, there would have been no need for it in 1918, and in that case, the Russian revolution would never have been accompanied by such riots as it actually was.

However, in spite of its incompleteness, the reform of 1861 was an ambitious effort which changed the whole old order. After the peasant reform, it seemed easier to start with other reforms which, taken together, completely changed the nature of the Russian state. The other leading "great reforms" of Alexander II were the reforms of the Zemstvo, the towns, the courts, and the military service.

The reform of the Zemstvo in 1864 created for the first time since that of the early Moscow state, real local self-government without regard to class. The basis of the reform consisted in granting to elected representatives of each county (Uyezd) control over the schools, medical affairs, and roads. The elective law provided for the division of electors into three *curias:* the private landowners (nobles and merchants); peasant communes; and townspeople. The representatives elected an "Executive Committee" known as the *Uprava* for a term of three years. The representatives of the Uyezd formed a provincial assembly which elected a provincial Zemstvo Committee (*Uprava*). Following the general spirit of the Zemstvo reforms, similar measures were introduced for town government in 1870. The electors were likewise divided into three *curias,* according to a property census; the amount of taxes paid was totaled and divided into three equal parts, each having an equal number of representatives. Both the Zemstvo and the town authorities succeeded in carrying out work of great cultural importance in Russia prior to the Revolution of 1917.

Of no less significance was the new judicial reform of 1864, of which S.I. Zarudny was the chief promoter. Its basic principles were: the improvement of court procedure; the introduction of the jury and the organization of lawyers into a formal bar. Despite some drawbacks of the Russian courts following 1864, they undoubtedly reached considerable efficiency, and in this respect, Russia could be favorably compared with the most progressive European countries. It is necessary, however, to note the difference between the facade and the foundation of the new Russian state. The peasants in the vast majority of small civil litigations did not use the new courts and had to be content with the "volost" courts, especially organized for them and, from the reign of Alexander III until 1912, they also had to accept the jurisdiction of the "Land Captains."

The last of the major reforms was the introduction of universal military service in 1874. The law of military service was practically the only one of the laws of this time which affected equally all the classes of the Russian people. Here there was no difference between the facade and the structure; it was profoundly democratic in spirit. The recruits were granted privileges only according to their family position. The only son, the only grandson, or only supporter of a family, received full privileges and were registered in the reserve of the second category, that is, in practice, prior to the World War, they were never called into service. With respect to the term of service and promotion, special privileges were recognized in favor of individuals having secondary education. Class differences were not in any way reflected in privileges of military service, with the exception of the selection of the Guards officers from the aristocratic circles of society. The society created by the reforms of Alexander II lasted in its general character until 1905, and in part until 1917. . . .

The internal policy of Alexander II did not bring about political peace in Russia. In spite of his far-reaching social and administrative reforms, he had to face bitter political opposition and direct revolutionary movements. The political opposition to the Government came primarily from the nobility. The idea was current that the nobility, having been deprived of its social and economic privileges, should receive in exchange political privileges, that is, a part of the governing power. This idea appeared during the preparation of the peasant reforms among members of the Provincial Committees who were discontented with the radicalism of the Revising Commission. In addition to the political programs of the nobles, other plans, looking to the reorganization of Russia along constitutional and democratic lines, were advanced, as a continuation of "Decembrist" tradition.

The revolutionary idea was chiefly current among the "Raznochintsi"—that is, individuals of no definite class: the children of peasants and merchants having received secondary or higher education; the children of the clergy who did not desire to enter the church; the children of small civil servants who did not desire to continue the vocation of their fathers; and the children of impoverished nobles. These Raznochintsi rapidly formed a new social class, the so-called "intelligentsia," which included many members of the nobility. The intellectuals grew rapidly with the reforms of Alexander II. The institution of the legal bar, the growth of newspapers and magazines, the increased number of teachers, etc., contributed to the growth. The intelligentsia consisted of intellectual people in general, but at first it consisted primarily of people connected with the publication of papers and magazines or connected with universities. The university students contributed the greatest number of radical and revolutionary leaders. The majority of the students consisted of men who had no means whatsoever. The average student lived in a state of semistarvation, earning his way through the university by giving lessons or by copying. The majority of the students had no notion of sport and no taste for it. Lack of physical exercise and consequent ill health had a crushing effect upon the psychology of the students.

The leaders of the intelligentsia desired not only radical political changes but also a social revolution, in spite of the fact that Russian industry was too underdeveloped to supply a firm basis for socialism. The Government was criticized for not being radical enough. The more moderate criticism was expressed in the legalized press, while the more bitter criticism appeared in revolutionary organs published abroad, the best known of which was *Kolokol* (The Bell), published by Herzen in London. Revolutionary propaganda against the Government immediately took a harsh tone. In 1862 there appeared a proclamation to the youth of Russia calling for terrorism and the murder of members of the Government and supporters of its policy. The appearance of this proclamation was contemporaneous with a number of cases of incendiarism in St. Petersburg. The Government took decisive steps; several individuals were arrested and exiled. . . .

A new wave of antigovernment activity arose in the 1870s. Among the liberal circles of society, the desire grew for elective representation not only in local self-government (Zemstvos and towns) but also in the central agencies of government. The institution of a parliament was to complete the unfinished reforms. This movement became particularly strong following the Turkish War of 1877–1878, when liberated Bulgaria received a constitution. The desire for a constitution in Russia became clearly expressed. The activity of the revolutionary organizations in Russia during this period likewise increased. Their activity may be divided into two periods. From 1870 to 1875 the radical intellectuals abstained from direct struggle against the Government, but undertook preparatory propaganda among the masses of the people. Many members of the intellectuals of that time went "to the people," living among the peasants and workmen, teaching school or becoming agricultural or industrial laborers.

The Government, fearing the results of the propaganda, oppressed the movement by arresting participants in it. At times the peaceful members of the movement suffered arrest together with the real propagandists. In many cases persons were tried and imprisoned or exiled on mere suspicion and action by the police. The Government's measures aroused the bitterest feeling among the radical intellectuals. In the middle of the 1870s, the revolutionaries began to use terrorism and to make attempts against members of the Government. In 1879, in Lipetsk in central Russia, the leaders of the revolutionary movement met in secret conference. An Executive Committee was elected at this meeting for the purpose of opposing the Government. This Executive Committee decided to abandon all attempts against individual members of the Government and to bend every effort toward assassinating the head of the Government, Emperor Alexander II. From that time on, Alexander II was the object of a manhunt by revolutionaries. Attempts were made in rapid succession, one after the other, but were without success until that made in St. Petersburg in the spring of 1881, which resulted in the death of Alexander II on March 13, 1881.

The assassination of Alexander II occurred on the very day when the emperor signed a *ukaz* calling for Representative Committees to advise the State Council. This was the "constitution" drawn up by Loris Melikov, the Minister of the Interior. Melikov's idea was that the revolutionary activity of the intellectuals could not be stopped by police measures alone. In his opinion the revolutionaries had the moral support of the moderate classes of society who were discontented with the autocratic policy of the Government. Melikov believed that the Government should placate the moderate elements of the opposition by granting a moderate constitution. This measure, he believed, would deprive the revolutionaries of the moral support of these classes. The assassination of Alexander II prevented the execution of this plan. His son and successor, Alexander III, withdrew the constitution of Melikov, and the *ukaz* signed by Alexander II was never published.

Alexander III [Emperor, 1881–1894]
and Nicholas II [Emperor, 1894–1917]

The impression made upon Alexander III by the assassination of his father lasted during his life. He retained a distrust for all popular movements and, influenced by Constantine Pobiedonostsev, expressed a firm belief in the infallibility of the principle of autocracy. The political program of Alexander III was extremely simple. It consisted in opposing all liberal and revolutionary movements in Russia and in satisfying, to a certain degree, the urgent economic demands of the Russian people. . . .

First of all, he sought to strengthen governmental control in all directions where free public opinion could be expected to manifest itself. Pursuant to this policy, the laws regarding local self-government were revised. The power of the Government, in the person of the provincial governors, was strengthened as against the power of the Zemstvos. According to the new laws of 1890, the peasants elected only candidates for the Zemstvo, while the governor chose representatives from among these candidates. This law was repealed in 1906. In order to extend governmental supervision over the peasants, the office of "Zemsky Nachalnik" or Land Captain, appointed by the Government from the nobility, was created in 1889. The Zemsky Nachalniks had administrative power in local affairs as well as the function of judge over the peasantry.

Many measures were also taken to repress the intellectuals. The universities were reorganized in 1884. Education became subject to government control. Censorship of the press was strengthened and the majority of newspapers and magazines became subject to the "preliminary censorship" of government agents. The political tendencies of the intellectuals became subject to redoubled watchfulness by the police. Persons who were suspected were subject to police supervision. Attempts at political conspiracies were mercilessly crushed. In 1887 the police discovered a plot to assassinate Alexander III. The guilty parties were executed, among them Alexander Ulianov, Lenin's eldest brother. In order to grant the police greater freedom, many provinces of Russia were declared in a state of "special protection." This enabled the administration to suspend the normal laws of procedure with respect to political prisoners. Several of the territories of Russia, inhabited by non-Russian peoples, also fell under suspicion. The Government began a policy of forcible "Russianization." This policy was applied particularly to Poland. Measures were also taken against the cultural dominance of the Germans in the Baltic provinces where they formed a minority of the population. Only the landowning class, the Barons, were Germans. Religious life was also subjected to restrictions. The Christian dissenters, the evangelical sects, Stundo-Baptists, and Catholics were equally affected. Particular suspicion was leveled against the Jews.

The Jewish question had arisen in Russia in the eighteenth century. A great many Jews had become subjects of the Russian state, following the division of Poland and the annexation of the southwestern Russian territories, which had a large Jewish population. According to the laws of 1804, the Jews were forbidden to settle in the central Russian provinces. The statutes fixed a "pale of settlement" where alone Jews could live. This included the western and southern provinces. Under Alexander III the conditions under which the Jews lived were subjected to further restriction. They were forbidden to settle outside the towns and villages, even within the territories which they might inhabit. The line of demarcation was further restricted in 1887 when the city of Rostov-on-Don was excluded from the pale. In 1891 seventeen thousand Jews were deported from Moscow. Furthermore, a quota of Jews, limited to their proportion of the population, was permitted in government educational institutions. With few exceptions the Jews were not admitted to government service.

These principles of policy were handed down by Alexander to his son Nicholas, who ascended the throne on the death of his father in 1894. It was only under the pressure of the Revolution of 1904–1905 that Nicholas agreed to grant a constitution; but up to the second revolution of 1917, and probably to his very death in 1918, Nicholas retained a belief in the principles laid down by his father. . . .

Seeking to hold the various classes under close observation, the Government searched for a group in society upon which it could itself depend. This group was the Russian nobility. During the reigns of Alexander III and Nicholas II, the Government attempted to secure the support of the nobility by granting it special privileges in respect to local self-government and local justice. In addition a number of financial privileges were granted to the nobility. The dependence of internal policy upon the nobility was a fatal political error. The Russian nobility was politically dead after the reforms of Alexander II and the beginning of the democratization of Russian life. The attempt to bring it back into political life was an attempt to revive a corpse. Even when the nobility had been a powerful force in Russia, in the eighteenth and the first half of the nineteenth century, the interests of the imperial power seldom agreed with those of the nobility. It was an act of political shortsightedness to seek to establish a close union between the Government and the nobility at a time when the nobility no longer possessed any vitality. This mistaken policy only brought about further discontent with the Government on the part of other classes.

However, it would be unjust to point only to the negative aspects of Russian policy in the last quarter of the nineteenth century for it must be admitted that the Government also carried out reforms improving the social and economic conditions of the majority of the people. Many measures were directed toward the improvement of the condition of the peasantry. First, early in 1882, a decree was issued ordering compulsory sale to peasants of land on those estates where the sale had not been completed following emancipation. Furthermore, the installments to be paid by the peasants for the land were lowered and the head tax was abolished (1886). New regulations were issued making it easy for peasants to rent government lands and aiding them to migrate to the free lands in the eastern part of the Empire. It was partly to further migration that the Siberian railroad was begun in 1892. The reign of Alexander III also marked the beginning of labor legislation in Russia. In 1882 government inspection of factories was instituted and the Government undertook to regulate the conditions of the workers. At the same time the working day of minors and women was limited by law. Labor legislation was continued during the reign of Nicholas II.

The Government also undertook financial reforms. The finances of Russia were greatly improved under Nicholas I, but since that time two wars and expensive internal reforms had succeeded in shaking them, and the currency had already depreciated. The Government was fortunate in having such a brilliant statesman as Witte. He succeeded in reorganizing Russian finances and in reintroducing gold into circulation in 1897.

All these government measures directed toward improving the economic conditions of the country could not, however, outweigh the irritation caused by the police supervision instituted by the Government. The internal policy of Alexander III succeeded in suppressing social discontent and political opposition only for a short time. Actually, in the course of the reign of Alexander III and the first half of the reign of Nicholas II, everything was quiet; but during the second half of the reign of Nicholas II, the accumulated social discontent expressed itself in a violent explosion. . . .

The war with Japan in 1904–1905 resulted in a series of defeats for Russia. The Japanese fleet showed itself to be considerably stronger than the Russian, whose vessels were less well constructed and had weaker armaments. The Japanese fleet soon succeeded in blockading Port Arthur. Shortly thereafter Japanese troops were landed on the mainland.

The Russian army was considerably stronger than the Japanese in numbers. As regards quality, the Russian troops were not inferior to the Japanese. Nevertheless, the war on land was as unfortunate for Russia as the war on sea. The first failures might be explained by the difficulty of rapidly concentrating Russian troops at the distant battlefield. The whole army depended upon the Siberian railway, which was not even completed. There was no line around Lake Baikal. But the subsequent defeats must be explained on psychological grounds. The Russian army went into battle without enthusiasm. The deep dissatisfaction of the Russian people with the Government could not fail to be reflected in the army. The war was unpopular in Russia from the very beginning. Its objects were not understood by the Russian people. It did not seem to them to affect the vital interests of the country. . . .

The revolutionary sentiments of the Russian people in 1904–1905 expressed themselves in the most diverse forms. The political activity of the intellectuals took the form of lectures on politics, the organization of societies of a semipolitical nature, and, in some cases, of riots on the part of students. The liberal landowners, members of the local (Zemstvo) administration, organized conferences to discuss reforms and a deputation from one of these congresses was sent to the emperor on June 19, 1905. The workers took recourse to strikes, the chief aims of which were political, rather than economic, reforms. The discontent of the peasantry found expression in agrarian riots, which resulted frequently in the destruction of landowners' houses or even in the murder of the landowners. Finally, following the termination of the Japanese war, disorder spread to the army. The soldiers were affected by socialist propaganda and in many cases revolted against their officers. Socialist agitators urged the formation of councils composed of soldiers, an idea which in 1917 proved fatal to the Russian army. Riots spread from the army to the navy, and on the battleship *Potemkin* the sailors succeeded in temporarily seizing control in June, 1905.

The whole period was characterized by a series of assassinations of governmental officials by terrorists. The Government first attempted to deal with the revolutionary sentiments of the people by suppressing disorders with armed force and by disrupting the revolutionary organizations. The Department of Police introduced secret agents in revolutionary organizations for the purpose of securing evidence against their leaders. The government agents sometimes became leaders of the revolutionary parties and took so active a part in the movement that it became impossible for the Government to determine where revolution began and where provocation ended. It was under circumstances of this kind that the Minister of the Interior, Plehve, was assassinated. The Department of Police also attempted to get control over the workers' movement by satisfying their economic demands and thus drawing them away from political activity. Zubatov, an agent of the secret police, succeeded in the spring of 1902 in organizing the workers along purely economic lines in Moscow and was ordered by Plehve to introduce his system all over Russia.

Following the death of Plehve and the dismissal of Zubatov, the workers' organization continued to develop of its own momentum. Its new leader, the priest Gapon, thought of petitioning the Tsar in person to effect the reforms demanded by the workers. On January 22, 1905, a huge crowd of workmen made their way to the Winter Palace in St. Petersburg to appeal to Nicholas II. The day had a tragic end, for, notwithstanding the fact that the workmen were peacefully inclined and unarmed, the crowd was dispersed by gunfire, as a result of which several hundred people were killed or wounded. "Bloody Sunday," as this day came to be called, became a decisive turning point in the history of the opposition of the working classes. It had as its immediate result their alliance with the socialist working class parties. The Government by this time realized that it had no plan to alleviate the situation and no firm support among the people. It consequently decided upon concessions in the matter of political reform. But even in this it moved unwillingly. On August 19, 1905, the order was given to call a national congress, the imperial Duma, which was to have deliberative, but not legislative, functions. This was, however, a half-measure which satisfied no one.

In the autumn of 1905, the situation became critical. A general strike was called throughout Russia. In the cities even the electricity and water supply were cut off; all railroads came to a standstill, with the exception of the Finland Railway. The leadership of the revolutionary group in St. Petersburg was taken by a special council composed of the leaders of the Socialist parties and representatives of the workers. This was the so-called Soviet of Workers' Deputies which was to take a prominent part in the events of 1917. At the first session of the Soviet the number of workers' representatives was only forty. It increased later to five hundred. The chairman of the Soviet was a lawyer, Khrustalev-Nosar, but the actual leader was the vice president Bronstein, subsequently known as Trotsky. It should be noted that the pseudonyms employed by many revolutionary leaders were assumed for self-protection against the espionage of the government police. All revolutionary instructions were signed by fictitious names.

The majority of the Soviet was in the hands of the Mensheviks, of whom Trotsky was a prominent member. The Bolsheviks failed to capture control of the first Soviet and regarded it with suspicion. Soviets were formed in some other cities, Moscow, Odessa, and elsewhere; but before they achieved any important results, the Government decided to make far-reaching political concessions. At the initiative of Count Witte, a manifesto, which amounted practically to capitulation by the Government, was issued October 30, 1905.

By this manifesto the imperial Government promised that it would grant to the Russian nation:

1. The fundamental principles of civil liberty—inviolability of person, and liberty of thought, speech, assembly, and organization;
2. Democratic franchise;
3. The principle that no law could henceforth be made without the consent of the Duma.

A new Prime Minister, Count Witte, with power to appoint assistants from opposition circles, was named to carry the manifesto into effect. This was the first time in Russia that a united cabinet was formed.

The manifesto was an embodiment of the principal demands of the liberal opposition. The hope was that it would stop the revolutionary activity of this opposition. In this regard the manifesto was an attempt to unite the Government and the Liberal parties against the imminent social revolution. For this reason leaders of the social movement who desired revolution at all costs were opposed to the manifesto. Their arguments were that the Government was not sincere in its promises, that it desired only to stop the revolutionary movement, and that as soon as conditions permitted, it would rescind the manifesto. The Government indeed did hope that the manifesto would stop the revolution; but it was not true that it wished to withdraw the concessions. In fact, it did not do so after its real victory over the revolutionaries. Count Witte, the head of the Government and the author of the manifesto, personally believed in the necessity for reform and had naturally no intention of retraction. Only the inexperience of the leaders of the Russian liberal movement can explain the decision of the liberal groups to decline all the invitations of Count Witte to enter his ministry. The result was that the manifesto of October 30 did not stop the revolutionary movement at once.

The Socialist parties desired only the triumph of their revolutionary doctrines. The leader of the Bolsheviks, Lenin, who came to Russia following the manifesto of October 30, became the staunchest opponent of the Government's policy. The strikes went on; a second railroad strike lasted from the end of November to the middle of December, and an armed insurrection occurred in Moscow at the end of December, 1905. The irreconcilable policy of the revolutionaries was not supported, however, by the majority of the people, who were fairly well satisfied with the program set forth in the manifesto. The Government was enabled to retake control of the situation. The Soviets were disbanded and the riots were suppressed by force. In several cities *pogroms* against Jews took place, organized by the so-called "Union of the Russian People," a reactionary group whose ideology was of the same pattern as that of German Nazism.

The insurrection at Moscow was not fully suppressed when the Government published a decree on December 24 on the procedure for elections. At the beginning of March, it issued a manifesto concerning the organization of the new Parliament, which was to be formed of two Houses; the state Duma and the state Council, the first consisting of members elected by the nation, and the second of members half of whom were appointed by the emperor and half elected by the nobility, Zemstvos, and university faculties. The electoral law gave the right of suffrage to the majority of the people, but it was neither equal nor direct. The voters were divided into groups: the workers in several large cities chose their electors to the Duma separately; the peasants chose electors who formed electoral colleges together with the electors chosen by the large landowners. These councils selected the deputies to the Duma. The electoral law artificially isolated the peasants and the workers and gave them a considerable role in the elections. This policy was prompted by the desire on the part of the Government to draw the peasants and the workers away from the opposition parties.

As a further means of appeasing the peasantry, Count Witte had the idea of expropriating the large estates and handing over the lands to the peasants. This project was developed by one of Witte's ministers, Kutler, who subsequently took a prominent part in the financial reorganization of the Soviet Government. The expropriation of large land holdings, however, was bitterly opposed by the estate owners. Witte did not have enough power to insist upon the measures he proposed, and was forced to cancel his project. This failure reacted upon the operation of the electoral law which was primarily a bid to the peasantry. Just as in the case of the earlier attempts to organize the workers in a manner favorable to the Government, it merely succeeded in stirring up social movements without either satisfying or being able to control them.

The elections to the first Duma took place in March, 1906. On May 10 the state Council and Duma were opened by Nicholas II. The majority of the Duma consisted of opposition deputies; of 490 members, 187 belonged to the Liberal party and 85 to the moderate labor group. The Constitutional Democrats, led by I. Petrunkevich (the other leader, P. Miliukov, being removed under a specious pretext from the list of voters), was the strongest party represented. The Socialist parties boycotted the elections, while the Nationalist and Conservative parties were defeated at the polls and secured only a small number of seats. The results of the elections were disappointing to the Government.

Finding a hostile group in control of the state Duma, Nicholas II immediately dismissed Count Witte and appointed Goremykin in his place. The new Prime Minister was a typical civil servant of the old regime. He was chosen, not because he had initiative and political convictions, but, on the contrary, because he lacked these qualities and was ready to execute the orders of the emperor. The appointment of Goremykin was a great political error. The relations between the Government and the Duma rapidly took on an unfriendly character.

The principal point of dispute between the Government and the Duma was the agrarian problem. Its discussion in the Duma aroused the passions of all groups. An agrarian bill, sponsored by the Constitutional Democrats, proposed the expropriation of the large estates and the transfer of land to the ownership of the peasants, granting compensation to the owners. This led to increased agitation against the Duma by the reactionaries. Nicholas II faced the problem of either submitting to the Duma and displeasing the nobility, or of dismissing it and provoking the hostility of the Liberals. On July 21 the Duma was dissolved. As a concession to the Liberals, Goremykin was dismissed and a new man, Stolypin, was appointed Prime Minister.

Stolypin had been Minister of the Interior in the Cabinet of his predecessor in office. He began his service to the Crown as a governor of one of the southern provinces. Before that he had managed his own estates. He had a profound comprehension of the agrarian problem in Russia and possessed the qualities of an outstanding statesman. He was firm, patriotic, and a man of ideas. The opposition parties did not support Stolypin and his program, but they were obliged to reckon with him. Following the dissolution of the Duma, the opposition groups were undecided as to their course. Their psychology was not that of peaceful parliamentary opposition, but of revolution. They dreaded the possibility of the

Government's canceling the whole program of reform and plainly distrusted the emperor. After the dissolution, members of the Duma issued an appeal to the Russian nation to resist the Government by refusing to pay taxes and to refuse conscription into the army. The appeal had no effect upon the people. Its only result was that its authors lost the right of voting in the subsequent elections.

Stolypin first tried to attract some of the leading members of the moderate liberal groups into his Cabinet. They refused to cooperate with him, and he was obliged to draw upon professional bureaucrats. His agrarian policy consisted primarily in destroying the communal ownership of land instituted by the reforms of 1861, and in encouraging peasant ownership of individual farms.

On November 22 the decree abrogating the peasant commune was published. Each peasant was given the right to receive his share of the common land in full ownership. Simultaneously, measures were taken to finance the purchase by the peasantry of Crown lands. Stolypin's measures were an attempt to repair the defects in the reform of 1861 and to create in Russia a new class of small landowners to form the basis for the new state. This program was deemed incompatible with the agrarian bill introduced by the first Duma. The expropriation of nearly all lands, the basis of that proposal, was calculated to solve the whole agrarian problem at one stroke. Stolypin's reform required a score of years to produce lasting results.

When the second Duma gathered on March 5, 1907, it proved to be even more hostile to the Government than was the first. The second Duma had a stronger left wing than the first one (180 Socialists); Lenin had abruptly changed his tactics, and the Socialists did not boycott the Duma. The conflict between the Government and the Duma in 1907 was more acute than in 1906. The Government now had a practical program of reform which the Duma did not possess. Fifty-five socialist deputies were charged with organizing a plot against the emperor and the second Duma was dissolved in June, 1907. In order to suppress similar expressions of opposition, the electoral law was changed. The large landowners were given preference over the peasants in selecting representatives to the electoral colleges. The third Duma, elected in November, 1907, had a membership different from that of its predecessors. The majority of deputies now belonged to parties of the right, and the liberal and socialist deputies were in the minority. The result of the two years of political conflict was the victory of Stolypin and the Moderate parties. . . . The third Duma sat without interruption through the whole period of its legal existence, from 1907 to 1912, and the elections of 1912 resulted in a triumph of the conservative nationalist groups.

While the political conflict between the Government and the Duma was temporarily solved by the reformed electoral law of 1907, there remained the more troublesome question of dealing with the aftermath of the revolutionary spirit of 1905. The dissatisfaction of that period found continued expression in a number of assassinations of prominent government officials. Premier Stolypin adopted a course of merciless suppression of revolutionary terrorism. Those accused of political crimes were subject to trial by a court-martial, and when found guilty were punished by death. Stoylpin's policy in this regard met with severe criticism from the opposition, but was supported by the majority of the conservative members of the Duma. The greatest number of executions during this period occurred in 1908, when the total number reached 782. After this year the number steadily decreased, and in 1911 seventy-three sentences were passed.

Just as political equilibrium seemed to have been reached, Stolypin was assassinated in September, 1911. His place was taken by the Minister of Finance, Kokovtsev. Like his predecessor, he was a Moderate Constitutionalist. He was faced with the constitutional problem of overriding the power of veto vested in the state Council organized at the same time as the Duma, and consisting only partially of elected members. One-half of the members of the Council were appointed by the emperor, and the Prime Minister had little influence in their selection. The Court circles of reactionary aristocrats were irreconcilably opposed to the Duma and succeeded in carrying out their policies without consulting the Prime Minister by direct influence upon the emperor. But notwithstanding irritating incidents of this kind, the Duma proved itself capable of bringing about many favorable changes in the country. Of great importance was the legislation concerning the peasantry, by which the precarious legal status of the peasants was done away with and their civil rights were equalized with those of other citizens.

The reform of local justice was an important measure in this connection. By virtue of the law of June 28, 1912, the general judicial system was to be gradually extended over the peasant population. The Land Captain was displaced in judicial matters by a justice of the peace. The Duma also undertook to organize the educational system and provided for an annual increase of 20,000,000 rubles in the educational budget, which grew steadily from 44,000,000 in 1906 to 214,000,000 in 1917. The number of pupils in the primary schools rose from 3,275,362 in 1894 to 8,000,000 in 1914. Thus, on the eve of the war, over half of all children of school age in Russia were receiving instruction. It was estimated by the educational committee of the Duma that universal education in Russia would be reached in 1922. The war and the revolution, however, prevented realization of this program. . . .

From the middle of the nineteenth century to the beginning of the twentieth century, the population of Russia doubled. During the first fifteen years of the twentieth century, the population increased 30 percent. In 1914 it totaled 175,000,000.

Particularly significant was the growth of city population. In 1851 there were less than three-and-a-half million people in the towns or less than 6 percent of the total population. In 1897 the town population had risen to sixteen and one-third million or 13 percent of the whole population, and in 1914 to 17.5 percent. These figures indicate the growth of the industrial population as compared with the agricultural. According to the census of 1897, 74.2 percent of the population was agricultural, and 13.3 percent industrial. Thus, in spite of the growth of the cities and of industry, about three-quarters of Russia's population before the First World War was occupied in agriculture. . . .

The ownership of land in Russia, following the peasant reforms of 1861, underwent great changes. Land rapidly passed into the ownership of the peasants. The peasantry not only retained the lands distributed in 1861, but also acquired new lands by purchase. Thus, simultaneous with the growth of the area under cultivation in Russia during the fifty years preceding the First World War, a radical change in the social structure of the agricultural population took place. As a result of the Stolypin reforms of 1906, the peasant communes began to disintegrate, and in 1911 six million households had acquired personal possession of the land. Russia was moving with great strides toward small landownership by citizens possessing equal rights with the rest of the population.

The industrialization of Russia which began in the second half of the nineteenth century increased rapidly until 1914, and in some branches of industry until 1917. We will trace this process briefly. . . . The Russian cotton industry, prior to the First World War, occupied fourth place in world production. It was exceeded only by Great Britain, the United States, and Germany. In 1905 the Russian cotton industry employed 7,350,683 spindles and 178,506 looms. By 1911 the productive forces of the industry had grown to 8,448,818 spindles and 220,000 looms. The increased production of Russian cotton factories was absorbed partly by the home market and partly by foreign trade. The increase of internal consumption may be illustrated by the fact that in 1890 the per capita consumption of cotton cloth in Russia was 2.31 pounds and in 1910, 4.56 pounds. . . . The metallurgical industries showed a similar development. In 1900, around 1,500,000 tons of pig iron were produced in Russia. By 1914 production had grown to over 3,500,000 tons. . . .

The growth of industrial production was reflected also in mining. Eighty-five percent of the coal used in Russia was of domestic extraction. The chief center of coal mining was the Donets basin which supplied 55 percent of Russia's needs for coal. In 1900, 11,000,000 tons were mined in the Donets basin and in 1913 the production rose to 25,000,000 tons.

The exploitation of forests served both domestic needs and foreign trade. In 1904, 13,200,000 rubles worth of lumber was exported. By 1913 exports reached 164,900,000 rubles. Of great importance also was the production of oil, chiefly in the neighborhood of Baku. In 1860 oil production in the Baku area hardly exceeded 160,000 tons. In 1905 production rose to over 7,000,000 tons and in 1913 to around 9,000,000 tons. . . .

Even more rapid than the expansion of industry was the development of railroads in Russia. In the middle of the nineteenth century, the total length of railroads in operation in Russia did not exceed 660 miles. In 1912 the Russian railroad system comprised 40,194 miles and was second only to that of the United States. The greatest achievement was the completion of the great Trans-Siberian Railroad, from 1892 to 1905. Its construction was one of the most daring railroad projects of our time. The length of the line from Moscow to Vladivostok is 5,542 miles. In the construction of this line it was necessary to overcome the greatest natural and technical difficulties—the frozen subsoil and the wildness of the territories penetrated. The cost of the Trans-Siberian Railroad exceeded $200,000,000. It was originally a single-track line, but during the First World War a second line was laid down.

The rapid expansion of Russian industry was accompanied by the creation of a working class on a scale previously unknown in Russia. . . . It was only in 1902 that the Government assented to the legislation [permitting] some unions, and it was only after the Revolution of 1905 that labor unions were permitted on a large scale by the Law of March 4, 1906.

The Government artificially retarded the development of labor unions and thereby unwittingly fostered the formation of illegal revolutionary organizations. But while restricting the development of labor unions, the Government made efforts to satisfy the principal needs of the workers by means of legislation. Labor legislation in Russia goes back to the 1880s in the reign of Alexander III. In 1897 day work was limited to eleven-and-a-half hours and night work to ten hours. Night work was forbidden for children under seventeen, and children under twelve were not allowed to engage in industrial work of any kind. The legislation of the twentieth century introduced workers' accident compensation in 1903, health insurance in 1912, and accident insurance in 1912. The condition of the working class gradually improved, thanks to increasing wages, particularly in Petrograd and Moscow. At the end of the nineteenth century, the average wage of the Russian worker was only 187 rubles a year. By 1913 it had risen to 300 rubles, and in some branches of industry in Petrograd and Moscow, to five times this sum. In many factories the low money wages were augmented by free lodgings, hospital services, and factory schools. . . .

Over two-thirds of the expenditures of the Zemstvos were for public health and education. The Zemstvo department of Public Health in 1914 expended 82,000,000 rubles. The rural population, prior to 1864 when the Zemstvos were introduced, was almost wholly lacking in medical care. Fifty years later, at the eve of the First World War, the Zemstvos had covered the rural territories with hospitals and dispensaries. The average radius of the medical districts was ten miles. . . .

The expenditure of the Zemstvos on public education in 1914 was 106,000,000 rubles. Most of these sums were expended upon primary schools. In 1914 there were fifty thousand Zemstvo schools with eighty thousand teachers and three million school children. The Zemstvos paid particular attention to the construction of new schools corresponding to modern pedagogical ideas and hygienic requirements. Besides primary education, the Zemstvos also organized their own system of secondary education for the training of teachers and organized courses for the improvement of teaching methods. The Zemstvos likewise organized extension courses and built libraries. In 1914 there were 12,627 rural public libraries in thirty-five of the forty-three Zemstvo [governmental districts].

PART TWO

THE THEORY

The Threshold

"To you who desire to cross this threshold, do you know what awaits you here?"

"I know," replied the girl.

"Cold, hunger, abhorrence, derision, contempt, abuse, prison, disease, and death!"

"I know, I am ready. I shall endure all suffering, all blows."

"Not from enemies alone, but also from relatives, from friends."

"Yes, even from them."

"Very well. You are ready for the sacrifice. You shall perish, and nobody will ever know whose memory to honor."

"I need neither gratitude nor compassion. I need no home."

"Are you ready to commit a crime?"

The girl lowered her head.

"I am ready for crime, too—"

The voice lingered for some time before resuming its questions.

"Do you know," it said at length, "that you may be disillusioned in that which you believe at present, that you may discover that you were mistaken, and that you ruined your young life in vain?"

"I know this, too."

"Enter!"

The girl crossed the threshold, and the heavy curtain fell behind her.

"Fool!" said someone, gnashing his teeth.

"Saint!" someone uttered in reply.

Ivan Turgenev

Chapter 2

MARXISM INTO LENINISM

It was Friedrich Engels who wrote, "People who imagined they had made a revolution always saw the next day that they did not know what they had been doing, and that the revolution they had made was nothing like the one they had wanted to make." The Bolshevik Revolution of November 1917, inspired by theories which Engels shared with Marx, was intended to put an end to the alleged economic, social, political, and even psychological evils and perversions engendered by an essentially exploitive, acquisitive and humanity-debasing capitalist system; a system controlled by and in the interests of a tiny minority concerned first and foremost with the maximization of private profit.

In the place of capitalism was to be built a socialist system in which the means of production would be owned in common, and production would be for the benefit of man rather than for private profit. Such a system, in the interests and commanding the support of the vast majority of the people, would require so little force that the state itself, the very embodiment of force, would wither away. In time, with the flowering of the productive forces, the elimination of all hostile classes, and the education of the people in communal living, a higher communist phase of society—stateless and classless—would emerge. This society would, for the first time in history, provide complete and genuine freedom, allow for the full and creative development of the individual, and proclaim the ultimate principle of equality: "From each according to his ability, to each according to his needs."

These expectations, it must in all fairness be noted, were predicated on the Marxist assumptions that a socialist revolution would first occur in a highly developed capitalist country with a massive and class-conscious proletariat (rather than in relatively backward and predominantly agricultural Russia) and, in any event, by force of momentum and example, would quickly touch off an international proletarian revolution. Nonetheless, since the claim is officially advanced that the USSR is a classless, highly democratic, and essentially Marxist society, it is reasonable and appropriate to consider the extent to which practice conforms to theory and to examine the events and explain the reasons which led to disparities.

Of specific importance in this connection are the alterations in Marxist theory made by Lenin, for his insistence upon his own rigid orthodoxy did not, in the judgment of Professor George Sabine, prevent him from being "responsible for the most considerable changes that any follower of Marx ever made in the master's teaching."

A major distinguishing characteristic that flowed from these changes lies in the enhancement of the role of the revolutionary party, which affected the means that the Bolsheviks—unlike, for example, the Mensheviks—were prepared to and did in fact use and justify to seize and hold power.

This material has more than just an historic importance. It was Lenin, above any other single individual, whose conceptions shaped the Bolshevik Party, who "made" the Bolshevik Revolution and supplied its theoretical justification; and it was his ideas and policies which often decisively shaped the Soviet system in a formative period with consequences that persist to this day. Soviet Russia is more in the image of Lenin than of Marx—especially when one considers some essential differences between Leninist theory (reflected for example in his *State and Revolution*) and postrevolutionary practice. The downgrading of Stalin and of subsequent Soviet leaders has served only to enhance Lenin's importance within the USSR and to Communist movements throughout the world. Lenin's ideas and practices merit, therefore, the most careful study.

Bolshevism before 1917

Merle Fainsod

An acute observer of Russian society in the late nineteenth and early twentieth centuries might have found the potential of revolution in every corner of the realm. Had he predicted that it would be the Bolsheviks who would ultimately inherit the Tsar's diadem, most of his contemporaries would probably have dismissed him as mad. Until 1917, the tiny handful of revolutionaries who followed the Bolshevik banner appeared to be swallowed in the vastness of Russia. Lenin, in a speech before a socialist youth meeting in Zurich on January 22, 1917, expressed strong doubts that he would "live to see the decisive battles of this coming revolution." The sudden rise of Bolshevism from insignificance to total power was as great a shock to the Bolshevik leaders as it was to those whom Bolshevism displaced.

Yet it would be the height of superficiality to treat the triumph of Bolshevism as a mere accident. The great crises of history are rarely accidents. They have their points of origin as well as their points of no return. The doctrine, the organizational practices, and the tactics which Bolshevism developed in its period of incubation enabled it to harness the surge of revolutionary energy released by deeper forces of social unrest and war. If in the process Bolshevism also succeeded in replacing the lumbering, inefficient police absolutism of Tsardom and the short-lived democratic experiment of the Provisional Government by the first full-scale venture in modern totalitarianism, that result, too, was implicit in the doctrinal, organizational, and tactical premises on which the structure of Bolshevism was built.

The Development of Doctrine

Until the 1880s the Russian revolutionary movement, as was natural in a country so predominantly agricultural, revolved around the peasant and his fate. Whatever may have been the tactical divergences among Narodnik intellectuals—whether they dedicated themselves to agitation or terror—their whole orientation was toward Ilya of Murom, the peasant hero of the folk poems (*byliny*), who, as Masaryk puts it, "when the country is in straits . . . awakens from his apathy, displays his superhuman energy, and saves the situation." Even the industrial awakening of the 1870s did little to disturb this fundamental preoccupation with the peasant and his destiny.

Narodnik philosophers, from Herzen to Lavrov and Mikhailovsky, were not unaware of Marx and Engels; indeed, the Narodniks were largely responsible for translating Marx and Engels into Russian and introducing them to a wide audience of the intelligentsia. For the Narodniks, however, the stages of industrialization and proletarianization which

The author was Professor of Government at Harvard University, author of Smolensk Under Soviet Rule; International Socialism and the World War; *and of many articles on the USSR. Reprinted by permission of the publishers from chapter 2 of Merle Fainsod's* How Russia Is Ruled *(Cambridge, Mass.: Harvard University Press, Copyright, 1953, by The President and Fellows of Harvard College). For footnote references, see original source.*

Marx and Engels described were dangers to be avoided rather than paths to be traversed. Nor were Marx and Engels themselves at first certain that the course of economic development in Russia would have to recapitulate that of the West. In a letter which Marx wrote in 1877 to a Russian publication, *Notes on the Fatherland,* he referred to this theory of capitalist development as not necessarily everywhere applicable and spoke of Russia as having "the best opportunity that history has ever offered to a people to escape all the catastrophes of capitalism." By 1882 Marx and Engels began to qualify their views on the possibility of Russian exceptionalism. In an introduction to a new Russian translation of the *Communist Manifesto,* they saw the capitalist system in Russia "growing up with feverish speed." They still thought, however, that the *mir* might "serve as a startingpoint for a communist course of development" but only "if the Russian revolution sounds the signal for a workers' revolution in the West, so that each becomes the complement of the other."

By 1892 Engels had in effect written off the *mir* as a Narodnik illusion. In a letter to Danielson, the Narodnik translator of *Capital,* Engels commented, "I am afraid that we shall soon have to look upon your mir as no more than a memory of the irrecoverable past, and that in the future we shall have to do with a capitalistic Russia." In a brief reference to earlier hopes, he continued, "If this be so, a splendid chance will unquestionably have been lost." To the end of their lives, Marx and Engels remained warm admirers of the Narodnaya Volya and its courageous, revolutionary Narodnik successors. Terror, for Marx and Engels, had a special justification in the struggle against Russian absolutism, and they deplored the efforts of their own Russian Marxist followers to discredit the Narodnik revolutionaries. Indeed, one of the last interventions of Engels in Russian affairs was his attempt in 1892 to arrange a merger of Narodniks and Marxists into a single party. The effort, needless to say, failed.

The Beginnings of Russian Marxism

Russian Marxism as an independent political movement originated in the split in 1879 of the Narodnik organization *Zemlya i Volya* (Land and Freedom). The seceders, who stood for propaganda and agitation as opposed to terrorism, established a rival organization, the *Chërnyi Peredel* (Black Repartition), to propagate their doctrines. One of their leaders was Plekhanov, soon to be known as the father of Russian Marxism, but then still clinging to the Narodnik belief in the peasant as the driving force of revolution. The roundup of revolutionaries, which followed the assassination of Alexander II in 1881, caused Plekhanov to flee abroad. His break with Zemlya i Volya on the issue of terror, the apparent bankruptcy of Narodnik policies in the reaction which followed 1881, and the manifest failure of the peasantry to respond either to agitation or terror impelled Plekhanov to reexamine his views. The search for a new faith led him to Marxism. In 1883 Plekhanov, Paul Axelrod, Leo Deutsch, and Vera Zasulich, all of whom had been members of the Chërnyi Peredel, joined in establishing the first Russian Marxist organization, the group known as Emancipation of Labor. Plekhanov from the beginning was the intellectual leader of the group. In a series of brilliantly written polemical works, he laid the doctrinal foundation for Russian Marxism.

Russian Marxism thus emerged out of disillusionment with the Narodnik infatuation with the peasantry. As a result, it quickly took on a strong anti-peasant orientation. "The main bulwark of absolutism," argued the 1887 program of the Emancipation of Labor group, "lies in the political indifference and the intellectual backwardness of the peasantry." In a later pamphlet by Plekhanov, *The Duty of the Socialists in the Famine,* the point was put even more strongly:

> The proletarian and the muzhik are political antipodes. The historic role of the proletariat is as revolutionary as the historic role of the muzhik is conservative. The muzhiks have been the support of oriental despotism for thousands of years. The proletariat in a comparatively short space of time has shaken the "foundations" of West European society.

Since peasant worship still exercised a powerful hold on the minds of the Russian revolutionary intelligentsia, the task of Plekhanov, and later of Lenin, was to undermine this faith and to turn the attention of the intellectuals from the village to the city, where capitalism was taking root and a new industrial proletariat was in process of creation. There, argued Plekhanov, was the coming revolutionary force. The challenge to the Narodniks was summed up in his famous dictum: "The revolutionary movement in Russia can triumph only as a revolutionary movement of the working class. There is not, nor can there be, any other way!"

The sharp antithesis which Plekhanov made between revolutionary worker and backward peasant had great polemical value in combating the influence of Narodnik ideology. But it also meant that the Social-Democratic movement turned its back on the countryside. Its long-term legacy was an attitude of suspicious distrust toward the peasantry which affected both the Bolshevik and Menshevik wings of Russian Social-Democracy and was never altogether extirpated. Even so perceptive and skillful a revolutionary engineer as Lenin did not really sense the revolutionary potential of the peasantry until the peasant risings of the 1905 revolution forced him to reexamine the tenets of his faith.

The first problem of the early Russian Marxists was to win acceptance for their proposition that Russia was launched on an irreversible course of capitalist development and that the Narodnik dream of skipping the stage of capitalism and leaping directly from the *mir* to socialism was nothing but a mirage. The struggle in its inception was a battle of books and pamphlets. The polemic of the Marxists against the Narodniks was even welcomed by the government, since in its eyes the Narodniks were still dangerous revolutionaries and the Marxists were viewed as essentially a rather harmless literary group. . . .

During this period, Plekhanov was still the master and Lenin the pupil. Both considered themselves orthodox Marxists. Marx's panorama of capitalist development seemed to imply that the socialist revolution stood its greatest chance of success in those countries in which the processes of industrialization were most highly advanced and in which the working class formed a substantial part of the population. How apply such a recipe for a successful socialist revolution to Russia with its nascent industrialism, its weakly developed proletariat, and its overwhelmingly peasant population? Confronted with Russia's industrial backwardness, both Plekhanov and Lenin agreed that the first order of business was to achieve a bourgeois-democratic revolution in Russia. With the further development of Russian capitalism, Russia would become ripe for a successful proletarian revolt. In this analysis they merely followed the familiar two-stage sequence laid down in the *Communist Manifesto.* Plekhanov, the theorist, was to remain loyal to this formulation for the rest of his life. Lenin, the activist, was to find it increasingly uncongenial, and though he continued for many years to pay it verbal tribute, his whole revolutionary career was essentially an escape from its confines.

The Problem of Industrial Backwardness

The question of the shape and pace of the Russian revolution was to produce furious controversies among Social-Democrats of all shades. The heart of the problem was Russia's industrial backwardness and the political consequences to be drawn from it. The Social-Democratic Labor Party based itself on a weak and still-undeveloped industrial proletariat. What was the role of the party to be? Should it attempt to seize power at the first promising opportunity or would it have to wait patiently until Russia's industrialization matched that of the most advanced Western nations? If it limited its immediate activities to organizing the proletariat and helping the bourgeoisie to overthrow the autocracy, would the party not be strengthening its most dangerous enemy by surrendering to it the power of the state? If, on the other hand, the party emphasized its hostility to the bourgeoisie and its role as capitalism's gravedigger, would the bourgeoisie not be driven to unite its fortunes with those of the autocracy? Questions such as these might be argued in terms of Marxian exegesis, but the answers that were evolved depended more on temperament than on theory.

The Menshevik wing of Russian Social-Democracy, with which Plekhanov was finally to ally himself, saw the arrival of socialism in Russia as the climax of a long process of development. The Menshevik response to the challenge of industrial backwardness was to preach the postponement of the socialist revolution until industrial backwardness had been overcome. Strongly influenced by orthodox Western Marxism and impressed by the weakness of the Russian industrial proletariat, the Mensheviks concluded that a socialist Russia was a matter of the distant future and that the immediate task was to clear the way for a bourgeois, middle-class revolution. Their first charge as good Marxists was to help the bourgeoisie to carry out its own historical responsibilities. They were therefore prepared to conclude alliances with liberal bourgeois forces who opposed the autocracy and to join them in fighting for such limited objectives as universal suffrage, constitutional liberties, and enlightened social legislation. Meanwhile, they awaited the further growth of capitalism in Russia to establish the conditions for a successful socialist revolution. Essentially, the Mensheviks had their eye on Western European models; they expected to march to power through legality and to be the beneficiaries of the spontaneous mass energy which the creation of a large industrial proletariat would release.

At the opposite extreme from the Menshevik conception was the theory of "permanent revolution" developed by Parvus and adopted by Trotsky during and after the 1905 revolution. For Parvus and Trotsky, the industrial backwardness of Russia was a political asset rather than a liability. As a result of backwardness and the large role played by state capitalism, the Russian middle class was weak and incapable of doing the job of its analogues in Western Europe. Thus, according to Parvus' and Trotsky's dialectic of backwardness, the bourgeois revolution in Russia could be made only by the proletariat. Once the proletariat was in power, its responsibility was to hold on to power and keep the revolution going "in permanence" until socialism was established both at home and abroad. The Russian revolution, Trotsky thought, would ignite a series of socialist revolutions in the West. This "permanent revolution" would offset the resistance which developed. Thus Trotsky's prescription for Russia's retarded economy was a new law of combined development. The two revolutions—bourgeois-democratic and proletarian-socialist—would be combined, or telescoped, into one. The working class would assert its hegemony from the outset and leap directly from industrial backwardness into socialism. Implicit in the Trotsky-Parvus formula was a clear commitment to the theory of minority dictatorship for Russia. An industrial proletariat which was still relatively infinitesimal in numbers was called upon to impose its will and direction on the vast majority of the population. Out of such theoretical brick and straw the edifice of Soviet totalitarianism was to be constructed.

The position of Lenin and the Bolshevik wing of the Russian Social-Democratic Party was much closer in spirit to Trotsky than to the Mensheviks, though the verbal premises from which Lenin started seemed indistinguishable from the Menshevik tenets. Like the Mensheviks, Lenin proclaimed that Russia was ripe for only a bourgeois-democratic revolution. His *Two Tactics of Social-Democracy in the Democratic Revolution* (1905) contained at least one formulation which Mensheviks would wholeheartedly have endorsed:

> The degree of economic development of Russia (an objective condition) and the degree of class consciousness and organization of the broad masses of the proletariat (a subjective condition inseparably connected with the objective condition) make the immediate, complete emancipation of the working class impossible. Only the most ignorant people can ignore the bourgeois nature of the democratic revolution which is now taking place. . . . Whoever wants to arrive at socialism by a different road, other than that of political democracy, will inevitably arrive at absurd and reactionary conclusions, both in the economic and the political sense. If any workers ask us at the given moment why not go ahead and carry out our maximum program, we shall answer by pointing out how far the masses of the democratically disposed people still are from socialism, how undeveloped class antagonisms still are, how unorganized the proletarians still are.

Again, in the same pamphlet, Lenin reiterated: "We Marxists should know that there is not, nor can there be, any other path to real freedom for the proletariat and the peasantry, than the path of bourgeois freedom and bourgeois progress."

While dicta such as these can be and have been cited to establish a basic area of agreement between Mensheviks and Bolsheviks on the two-stage perspective of the Russian revolution, the kinship was more illusory than real. Plekhanov summed up one of the important differences when he observed to Lenin, "You turn your behind to the liberals, but we our face." For Lenin, as for Trotsky, the bourgeois liberals were a weak and unreliable reed. Like Trotsky, Lenin came to believe that the proletariat would have to take leadership in completing the bourgeois revolution; but unlike both Trotsky and the Mensheviks, Lenin looked to an alliance with the peasantry to provide the proletariat with a mass base. In this rediscovery of the strategic significance of the peasantry, Lenin reclaimed the Narodnik heritage which both he and Plekhanov had done so much to repudiate in the nineties. In the essay on *Two Tactics,* Lenin declared:

> Those who really understand the role of the peasantry in a victorious Russian revolution would not dream of saying that the sweep of the revolution would be diminished if the bourgeoisie recoiled from it. For, as a matter of fact, the Russian revolution will begin to assume its real sweep . . . only when the bourgeoisie recoils from it and when the masses of the peasantry come out as active revolutionaries side by side with the proletariat.

The first task was to consolidate "the revolutionary-democratic dictatorship of the proletariat and the peasantry." After this was achieved, the socialist revolution would become the order of the day. Lenin's formula thus envisaged two tactical stages: first, the alliance of proletariat and peasantry to complete the democratic revolution, and second, an alliance of the proletariat and village poor to initiate the socialist revolution.

Given Lenin's activist temperament, it was inevitable that he should feel greater affinity for Trotsky's revolutionary dynamism than for the Mensheviks' passive fatalism. As the excitement of the 1905 revolution mounted, we find him speaking the language of Trotsky: "From the democratic revolution we shall at once, and just in accordance with the measure of our strength, the strength of the class-conscious and organized proletariat, begin to pass to the socialist revolution. We stand for uninterrupted revolution. We shall not stop halfway." Despite many intervening conflicts, the bond with Trotsky was to be sealed by the experiences of 1917. The dialectic of backwardness was "resolved" by the Bolshevik seizure of power.

Out of that adventure a new theory of revolution was to be developed with worldwide applications. Stalin has given it authoritative exposition:

> Where will the revolution begin? . . .
>
> Where industry is more developed, where the proletariat constitutes the majority, where there is more culture, where there is more democracy—that was the reply usually given formerly.
>
> No, objects the Leninist theory of revolution; *not necessarily where industry is more developed,* and so forth. The front of capitalism will be pierced where the chain of imperialism is weakest, for the proletarian revolution is the result of the breaking of the chain of the world imperialist front at its weakest link; and it may turn out that the country which has started the revolution, which has made a breach in the front of capital, is less developed in a capitalist sense than other, more developed countries, which have, however, remained within the framework of capitalism.

Thus Marx, who turned Hegel on his head, was himself turned on his head. Industrial backwardness was transformed from obstacle to opportunity. The concept of the dictatorship of the proletariat shifted from a weapon of the majority into a tool of minorities. Consciousness triumphed over spontaneity, and the way was cleared for the organized and disciplined revolutionary elite capable of transmuting the grievances of a nation into a new formula of absolute power.

Organization: The Elite Party

The organizational conception embodied in Bolshevism was essentially an incarnation of this elitist ideal. "Give us an organization of revolutionaries," said Lenin, "and we shall overturn the whole of Russia!" It was Lenin who forged the instrument, but the seeds of his conspiratorial conceptions were planted deep in Russian history and were nurtured by the conditions of the revolutionary struggle against the autocracy. Pestel among the Decembrists, Bakunin, Nechayev, Tkachev, and the Narodnik conspirators of the seventies and early eighties, all provided organizational prototypes of the professional revolutionary as the strategic lever of political upheaval. It was a tradition from which Lenin drew deep inspiration even when he found himself in profound disagreement with the particular programs which earlier professional revolutionaries espoused. His works are filled with tributes to the famous revolutionaries of the seventies (figures like Alekseyev, Myshkin, Khalturin, and Zhelyabov). In developing his own conceptions of party organization in *What Is to Be Done?* he refers to "the magnificent organization" of the revolutionaries of the seventies as one "which should serve us all as a model." Lenin's conviction that Russian Marxism could triumph only if led by a disciplined elite of professional revolutionaries was reinforced by his own early amateur experiences as a member of the Petersburg League of Struggle for the Emancipation of the Working Class. This organization was easily penetrated by the police, and the first effort of Lenin and his collaborators in 1895 to publish an underground paper—"The Workers' Cause"—resulted in the arrest of Lenin and his chief associates and a quick transfer of domicile to Siberia.

It is against this background that the organizational conceptions of Lenin took shape. By 1902, with the publication of *What Is to Be Done?*, they were fully developed. In this essay, the seminal source of the organizational philosophy of Bolshevism, Lenin set himself two main tasks: (1) to destroy the influence of Economism with its repudiation of revolutionary political organization and its insistence on trade unionism as the basic method of improving the welfare of the working class, and (2) to build an organized and disciplined revolutionary Marxist party which would insure the triumph of socialism in Russia. . . .

*[**Editor's note:** In* What Is to Be Done? *Lenin wrote: "The history of all countries shows that the working class, exclusively by its own efforts, is able to develop only trade-union consciousness (i.e., it may itself realize the necessity for combining in unions, to fight against employers and to strive to compel the government to pass necessary labor legislation, etc.)."*

As for socialist consciousness, that "could only be brought to [the working class] from without," that is to say, from those imbued with "the philosophic, historical and economic theories that were elaborated by the educated representatives of the propertied classes . . . the revolutionary socialist intelligentsia."

Lenin went on to assert that the workers' organizations must be "trade organisations" as wide open and public as possible. But "in a country with a despotic government," the organization of revolutionists "must be comprised first and foremost of people whose profession is that of revolutionists."

" 'Broad democracy' in party organisation," Lenin argued, "amidst the gloom of autocracy, and the domination of the gendarmes, is nothing more than a useless and harmful toy." In its place, he said, there would be a lively sense of "responsibility" on the part of the leaders because they "know from experience that an organisation of real revolutionists will stop at nothing to rid itself of an undesirable member."]

Democratic management, Lenin held, was simply inapplicable to a revolutionary organization. *What Is to Be Done?* disclosed the profoundly elitist and antidemocratic strain in Lenin's approach to problems of organization. It also made clear that in Lenin's new model party, leadership would be highly centralized, the central committee would appoint local committees, and every committee would have the right to co-opt new members. But it still left a precise blueprint to be worked out. This was the task which Lenin undertook to perform at the Second Party Congress of the Russian Social-Democratic Labor Party, which met in Brussels and then in London in the summer of 1903. Lenin prepared for this Congress with a meticulous attention to detail of which he alone among his revolutionary contemporaries was capable. His one desire was to construct a compact majority which would dominate the Congress and build a party willing "to devote to the revolution not only their spare evenings, but the whole of their lives."

The foundations seemed to be well laid. The rallying point of the "compact majority" was *Iskra* (The Spark), a journal which had been established abroad, in 1900, largely on Lenin's initiative. Wisely, Lenin and his young associates, Martov and Potresov, enlisted the cooperation of Plekhanov and other members of the Emancipation of Labor groups as coeditors. The association generated its own sparks; Lenin has provided a vivid record of the conflict in his "How the Spark Was Nearly Extinguished." But the quarrels for supremacy were composed; Lenin still needed the prestige of the older generation of revolutionaries in mobilizing adherents to the *Iskra* platform. Meanwhile, Lenin retained control of the secret agents who smuggled *Iskra* into Russia and maintained the closest connections with the underground organizations which distributed the journal. This organization of *Iskra* men was to provide the core of Lenin's majority at the Second Congress.

When the Second Congress assembled in Brussels in 1903, thirty-three votes, a clear majority of the fifty-one official votes, belonged to the *Iskra* faction. The remaining eighteen delegates represented a collection of Bundists (members of the All-Jewish Workers' Union of Russia and Poland), economists, and miscellaneous uncommitted representatives, whom the Iskraites described contemptuously as "the Marsh" because they wallowed in a quagmire of uncertainty. The Iskraites appeared to be in full control. They named the presidium and easily pushed through their draft program and various resolutions on tactics.

The next order of business was the adoption of the party rules, and here trouble developed. The Iskraites were no longer united; Lenin and Martov offered rival drafts. The initial issue was posed by the definition of party membership. Lenin's draft of Paragraph One read: "A Party member is one who accepts its program and who supports the Party both financially and *by personal participation in one of the Party organizations*." Martov's formulation defined a party member as "one who accepts its program, supports the Party financially and renders it regular personal assistance under the direction of one of its organizations." To many of the delegates, the difference in shading between the two drafts appeared slight, but as the discussion gathered momentum, the differences were magnified until a basic, and ultimately irreconcilable, question of principle emerged.

The issue was the nature of the party. Lenin wanted a narrow, closed party of dedicated revolutionaries operating in strict subordination to the center, and serving as a vanguard of leadership for the masses of workers who would surround the party without belonging to it. Martov desired a broad party open to anyone who believed in its program and was willing to work under its direction. Martov conceded the necessity of central leadership, but he also insisted that party members were entitled to have a voice in its affairs and could not abdicate their right to think and influence party policy.

As the debate raged, the *Iskra* group fell apart. Plekhanov rallied to Lenin's defense; the Leninist formula seemed to him admirably adapted to protect the party against the infiltration of bourgeoisie individualists. Axelrod and Trotsky supported Martov. To Axelrod it seemed that Lenin was dreaming "of the administrative subordination of an entire party to a few guardians of doctrine." And after the Congress had adjourned, Trotsky, in a sharp attack on Lenin, provided the classic formulation of the opposition. In Lenin's view, he pointed out, "the organization of the Party takes the place of the Party itself; the Central Committee takes the place of the organization; and finally the dictator takes the place of the Central Committee." It was to turn out a more somber and tragic vision of things to come than Trotsky realized at the time.

At the Congress, Martov's draft triumphed by a vote of twenty-eight to twenty-two. But Lenin had not yet shot his last bolt. He still retained the leadership of a majority of the Iskraites, though his group was now a minority in the Congress. This minority was soon transformed into a majority by a series of "accidents" to which Lenin's parliamentary maneuvering and planning contributed. When the Congress rejected the Bundist claim to be the sole representative of the Jewish proletariat, the five delegates of the Bund withdrew from the Congress. Their departure was followed by the withdrawal of the delegates from the League of Russian Social-Democrats, an Economist-dominated organization, which the Congress voted to dissolve on Lenin's motion. With the exit of these two groups, the *Iskra* majority became the Congress majority and proceeded to elect its representatives to the central party organs. It was this triumph which gave Lenin's caucus the title of Bolsheviks (the majority men), while his defeated opponents became known as Mensheviks (the minority men).

But the triumph was short-lived. The central party institutions elected by the Second Congress consisted of the editors of *Iskra,* the Central Committee in Russia, and a Party Council of five members (two representing *Iskra,* two the Central Committee, and a fifth elected by the Congress). The Board of Editors of *Iskra* was given power equal to and indeed above that of the Central Committee. Disputes between *Iskra* and the Central Committee were to be settled by the Party Council. Lenin, Plekhanov, and Martov were elected as editors of *Iskra*. Martov refused to serve unless the original editorial board, which included Axelrod, Zasulich, and Potresov, was restored. Lenin and Plekhanov were thus left in exclusive control. The Central Committee in Russia was composed entirely of Bolsheviks, and they were given power to co-opt other members. The party apparatus appeared to be safely in Bolshevik hands when Plekhanov, out of a desire to heal the breach with his old associates, acceded to Martov's conditions and insisted on the restoration of the original *Iskra* board. Lenin promptly withdrew, and at one stroke *Iskra* was transformed into an organ of Menshevism. . . .

Differences now began to develop in the Bolshevik Central Committee in Russia; a majority group emerged which advocated a policy of conciliation toward the Mensheviks. Three Mensheviks were co-opted into the Central Committee, and in the summer of 1904 this strategic power position, which Lenin had regarded as impregnable, passed over to the opposition. After all his careful planning and apparent triumph, Lenin was left isolated and alone, betrayed by his own nominees in Russia, alienated from the leading figures of the emigration, and the chief target of abuse in the party organ which he had been primarily instrumental in establishing.

After a temporary fit of utter discouragement, Lenin rallied and began once more to gather his forces. The remnants of the faithful in the emigration were welded into a fighting organization. Connections were reestablished with the lower party committees in Russia, and a new body, the Bureau of the Committee of the Majority, was established to coordinate the work of Lenin's supporters. Toward the end of 1904, a new paper, *Vperëd* (Forward), was founded as the organ of the bureau. A second effort to capture control of the party organization was now in the full tide of preparation. But this time the Mensheviks were wary and refused to attend the so-called Third Congress of the Social-Democratic Labor Party, which assembled on Lenin's initiative in London in May 1905. The Mensheviks met separately in Geneva.

The 1905 revolution brought Bolsheviks and Mensheviks closer together. Responding to the *élan* of the uprising, Mensheviks became more militant and Bolsheviks seemed to abandon their distrust of uncontrolled mass organization. As Lenin put it, "The rising tide of revolution drove . . . differences into the background. . . . In place of the old differences there arose unity of views." Joint committees were formed in many cities, and finally a Joint Central Committee was created on a basis of equal representation to summon a "Unity" Congress. Both parties were flooded with new members for whom the old quarrels were ancient history and the practical tasks of the moment were paramount. The misgivings of the leaders were swept aside in a widespread yearning for unity.

The Fourth so-called "Unity" Congress, which took place at Stockholm in 1906, reflected this surge from below. Thirty-six thousand workers took part in the election of delegates. Menshevism flourished on legality, and of the one hundred eleven voting delegates selected, sixty-two were Mensheviks and forty-nine Bolsheviks. As a result, the Mensheviks dominated the proceedings. They wrote the program and resolutions and controlled the leading party organs. The Central Committee elected by the Congress was composed of seven Mensheviks and three Bolsheviks; the editorial board for the central party newspaper (which never appeared) was composed exclusively of Mensheviks. Perhaps the most important organizational action taken at the Congress was the admission of the Bund and the Polish and Latvian Social-Democratic parties as constituent units in the united party. The Polish and Latvian parties joined as autonomous organizations operating in their respective territorial areas; the Bund renounced its claim to be the sole representative of the Jewish proletariat on the understanding that it would be permitted to retain its program of national cultural autonomy and to organize Jewish workers without respect to territorial boundaries. The admission of these groups introduced an additional complication into the power structure of the party. Given the relatively even distribution of strength between Mensheviks and Bolsheviks in this period, the balance of power now shifted to the Bund and the Polish and Latvian Social-Democrats, and their votes became of crucial significance in shaping the party's future course.

Although Lenin suffered defeat at the Stockholm Congress, he continued to maneuver for ascendancy. The Bolshevik factional apparatus was maintained, and funds to finance the apparatus were partly obtained through "expropriations" (robberies and holdups). The effort to capture local organizations was continued, and Menshevik policies were attacked with relentless ferocity. As a result of this activity, the Bolsheviks registered marked gains at the Fifth Congress, held in London in 1907. While the precise strength of the Bolshevik and Menshevik blocs is still in dispute, all accounts agree that the Bolsheviks achieved a slight preponderance over the Mensheviks at the Congress.

This did not mean, however, that the Bolsheviks controlled the Congress. The real power of decision rested with the Bund and the Polish and Latvian Social-Democrats, who exercised a role of balance between the conflicting Russian factions. On the whole, the Mensheviks attracted Bundist support, while the Bolsheviks were dependent on the Poles and Latvians for such majorities as they obtained. While the Bolsheviks failed to secure the support of the national delegates in their efforts to condemn the work of the Menshevik Central Committee and of the Duma fraction of the party, and were themselves condemned for their sponsorship of "expropriations," they were able to defeat the Mensheviks on a number of important resolutions. The Menshevik policy of cooperating with the Kadets was repudiated. The proposal of Axelrod and other leading Mensheviks to call a nonparty labor congress and to transform the Social-Democratic Party into a broad, open labor party was denounced by Lenin as "Liquidationism" and decisively rejected by the Congress. But the Bolsheviks were unable to achieve a dependable, monolithic majority, and the elections to the Central Committee yielded five Bolsheviks, and four Mensheviks, two Bundists, two Polish Social-Democrats, and one Latvian Social-Democrat.

During the period of reaction and repression which accumulated momentum after the London Congress, both Menshevik and Bolshevik segments of the party underwent a serious crisis. Party membership crumbled away, and police spies penetrated such remnants of the organizational apparatus as remained. The crisis was particularly acute for the Mensheviks. Potresov, in a letter to Axelrod toward the end of 1907, reflected an almost hopeless despondency:

> Complete disintegration and demoralisation prevail in our ranks. Probably this is a phenomenon common to all parties and fractions and reflects the spirit of the times;

but I do not think that this disintegration, this demoralisation have anywhere manifested themselves so vividly as with us Mensheviks. Not only is there no organisation, there are not even the elements of one.

The situation within Bolshevik ranks was not much better. "In 1908," notes the Bolshevik historian Popov, "the Party membership numbered not tens and hundreds of thousands, as formerly, but a few hundreds, or, at best, thousands." The plight of the Moscow organization was not atypical. From the end of 1908 to the end of 1909, membership declined from five hundred to one hundred fifty; in the next year the organization was completely destroyed when it fell under the control of a police spy. The Bolsheviks, by virtue of their conspiratorial traditions and tight discipline, made a better adjustment than the Mensheviks to the rigors of illegal existence, but even Bolshevik vigilance could not prevent the secret agents of the police from penetrating the underground hierarchy and rising to high places in the party apparatus. Meanwhile, the leaders of both the Bolshevik and Menshevik factions fled abroad once more where they were soon engaged in resurrecting old quarrels and giving birth to new differences.

Both factions fell victim to internal dissension. The Mensheviks divided between the "Liquidators" (as Lenin dubbed them), who counseled the abandonment of the underground party and concentration on legal work in the trade unions and the Duma, and the "Party" Mensheviks, who continued to insist on the necessity of an illegal organization. Bolshevism spawned in rapid succession a bewildering series of controversies. First, there were the "Duma Boycotters," led by Bogdanov, at that time one of Lenin's closest associates. On this issue Lenin joined with the Mensheviks and supported party participation in the election of the Third Duma. Then there were the "Otzovists" and "Ultimatumists," the former demanding the immediate recall or withdrawal of the Duma party delegation and the latter insisting that an ultimatum be dispatched to the delegation with the proviso that its members should immediately be recalled if the instructions contained in the ultimatum were rejected. Lenin again opposed both tendencies. Next came the philosophical heresies, the Neo-Kantian "Machism" of Bogdanov and the "God-Creator" religionism of Lunacharsky and Gorky. These were heresies that Lenin endured as long as the heretics were enrolled in his political camp; they became intolerable only when Bogdanov and the rest challenged his control of the party faction. Finally, there were the Bolshevik "Conciliators" who insisted that peace be made with the Mensheviks after Lenin had determined that a final split was essential.

In the parlance of latter-day Bolshevism, each of these "deviations" had to be "liquidated" if Lenin was to build the party in his own image. He was determined to accomplish precisely that task. The first act took place in the summer of 1909 at an enlarged editorial conference of *Proletarii,* the organ of the Bolshevik caucus. Again Lenin made careful advance preparations, and equipped with the necessary votes, he carried a resolution declaring that Boycottism, Otzovism, Ultimatumism, God-Construction, and Machism were all incompatible with membership in the Bolshevik faction. Over bitter protest, Bogdanov was ousted from the Bolshevik central leadership where he had been second only to Lenin, and he and his associates were declared "to have placed themselves outside the faction." Expelled from the fold, the dissidents proceeded to declare themselves "true Bolsheviks," established a new journal utilizing an old name, *Vperëd,* and became known during the next years as Vperëdist Bolsheviks.

Having disposed of the Vperëdists, Lenin confronted the new opposition of the so-called Conciliators, or Party Bolsheviks, who called for reconciliation with the expelled faction and unity with the Mensheviks. At a plenary session, held in January 1910, of the

Central Committee elected by the London Congress, Lenin received a sharp rebuff when the Conciliators turned against him. The conference voted to discontinue the Bolshevik paper *Proletarii* as well as the Menshevik *Golos Sotsial-Demokrata* (Voice of the Social-Democrat) and to replace both with a general party organ, *Sotsial-Demokrat,* which would have two Menshevik editors, Martov and Dan, two Bolshevik editors, Lenin and Zinoviev, and one representative of the Polish Social-Democrats, Warski, to break any deadlocks that might develop.

Again the attempt at "unity" miscarried. With the support of Warski, Lenin won control of the new party journal and denied the Menshevik editors the right to publish signed articles in what was supposed to be the organ of the united party. Martov replied by attempting to discredit Lenin through an exposure of the seamy side of Bolshevism—the holdups, the counterfeiting, and "expropriations" which Lenin had allegedly sanctioned and defended.

Lenin now moved toward an open and irrevocable break. Despite the protest of the Bolshevik Conciliators, he summoned an All-Russian Party Conference which met in Prague in January 1912 to ratify the split. Although the conference was dominated by a carefully selected group of Lenin's most reliable supporters, the uneasiness of the delegates in the face of Lenin's ruthless determination to move toward schism manifested itself in a belated decision to invite Plekhanov, Trotsky, and others to attend. To Lenin's great relief, both Plekhanov and Trotsky refused on the ground that the conference was too one-sided and imperiled party unity. Martov and the Menshevik Liquidators were not invited. The Bund and the Polish and Latvian Social-Democrats also stayed away.

The "Rump Parliament" proceeded to assume all the rights and functions of a party congress (indeed, Lenin called it The Sixth Congress of the Russian Social-Democratic Labor Party). The old Central Committee created by the London Congress was declared dissolved, and a new "pure" Bolshevik Central Committee was elected from which all Bolshevik Conciliators were excluded. The Prague Conference marked the decisive break with Menshevism and the turning point in the history of Bolshevism as an independent movement. There were to be many subsequent attempts to bring the Bolsheviks back into the fold of a united party, but all were doomed to failure. The last effort, sponsored by the International Socialist Bureau of the Second International, was slated to take place at the Vienna Congress of the Second International in August 1914. War intervened, and the congress was never held. By an ironical turn of events, the International which attempted to close the breach in the Russian party was itself split by the Bolsheviks whom it tried to bring to heel.

The early organizational history of Bolshevism, which has been briefly summarized here, holds more than historical interest. The experience of the formative years left an ineradicable stamp on the character and future development of the party. It implanted the germinating conception of the monolithic and totalitarian party. The elitism which was so deeply ingrained in Lenin, the theory of the party as a dedicated revolutionary order, the tradition of highly centralized leadership, the tightening regimen of party discipline, the absolutism of the party line, the intolerance of disagreement and compromise, the manipulatory attitude toward mass organization, the subordination of means to ends, and the drive for total power—all these patterns of behavior which crystallized in the early years were destined to exercise a continuing influence on the code by which the party lived and the course of action which it pursued.

*[**Editor's note:** It has been argued that some of Lenin's theories were radical alterations of Marxist theories verging on abandonment. Daniel Bell, for example, asked "if the intellectuals create the social*

ideology, while the workers left to themselves achieve only trade union consciousness . . . what, then, is the meaning of Marx's statement that existence determines consciousness, and that class fashions ideology."

"And still more difficult to understand," wrote George Sabine in A History of Political Thought, *"why should capitalist production, which creates the opposed bourgeois and proletarian classes and their ideologies, bring into existence a middle-class intelligentsia devoted to the task of making an ideology for the proletariat? Either the class struggle does not wholly determine the mentality of the class or else it produces in the middle class a perverted form of class-consciousness that devotes itself to the destruction of the class."*

So, also, George Sabine pointed out, "It was a settled principle of Marxism that any revolution, bourgeois or proletarian, occurs not through a sporadic application of force but must be prepared by the proper political and economic development. It followed [as Lenin for a long time believed] that the bourgeois revolution must be 'completed' before the proletarian revolution could properly be begun. It was this settled interpretation of Marxism that, to the astonishment of his followers and finally of Marxists everywhere, Lenin proceeded to set aside as antiquated." Taking account of the existence of dual power—that of the provisional government and the Soviets—and proposing to "telescope" the bourgeois and socialist revolutions in Russia, Lenin himself stated: "According to the old conception, the rule of the proletariat and peasantry, their dictatorship, can and must follow the rule of the bourgeoisie. In real life, however, things have already turned out otherwise; an extremely original, new, unprecedented interlocking of one and the other has taken place."]

State and Revolution

V.I. Lenin

This pamphlet, written during World War I and completed while Lenin was in exile following the March revolution, is presented here in abridged and rearranged form.

In his preface, dated August 1917, Lenin wrote: "The unheard-of horrors and miseries of the protracted war are making the position of the masses unbearable and increasing their indignation. An international proletarian revolution is clearly rising. The question of its relation to the state is acquiring a practical importance."

So far as the impact on the Russian revolution was concerned, with some ambiguity, he commented that "The Revolution is evidently completing the first stage of its development" and added, "but, generally speaking, this revolution can be understood in its totality only as a link in the chain of Socialist proletarian revolutions called forth by the imperialist war."

In this study, which contains perhaps the most authoritative left-wing critique of capitalist democracy, Lenin insisted upon the impossibility of overthrowing capitalism without a violent revolution. (Thus, he explicitly rejected Marx's "exceptionalism." Marx had said in 1872—a position later echoed by Engels—that "we do not deny that there are certain countries, such as the United States and England . . . in which the workers may hope to secure their ends by peaceful means.") Lenin also outlined in some detail the program to be followed by the proletarian state after the expected revolution. In this connection, it would be useful to compare Lenin's abstract conceptions with Soviet realities. It would also be useful to seek to understand how and why the disparities occurred.

Marx's doctrines are now undergoing the same fate which, more than once in the course of history, has befallen the doctrines of other revolutionary thinkers and leaders of oppressed classes struggling for emancipation. During the lifetime of great revolutionaries, the oppressing classes have invariably meted out to them relentless persecution, and received their teaching with the most savage hostility, most furious hatred, and a ruthless campaign of lies and slanders. After their death, however, attempts are usually made to turn them into harmless saints, canonizing them, as it were, and investing their name with a certain halo by way of "consolation" to the oppressed classes, and with the object of duping them; while at the same time emasculating and vulgarizing the real essence of their revolutionary theories and blunting their revolutionary edge. At the present time the bourgeoisie and the opportunists within the Labor Movement are cooperating in this work of adulterating Marxism. They omit, obliterate, and distort the revolutionary side of its teaching, its revolutionary soul, and push to the foreground and extol what is, or seems, acceptable to the bourgeoisie. . . .

The State as the Product of the Irreconcilability of Class Antagonisms

Let us begin with the most popular of Engels' works, *The Origin of the Family, Private Property, and the State*. Summarizing his historical analysis Engels says:

> The State in no way constitutes a force imposed on Society from outside. Nor is the State "the reality of the Moral Idea," "the image and reality of Reason," as Hegel asserted. The State is the product of Society at a certain stage of its development. The State is tantamount to an acknowledgment that the given society has become entangled in an insoluble contradiction with itself, that it has broken up into irreconcilable antagonisms, of which it is powerless to rid itself. And in order that these antagonisms, these classes with their opposing economic interests, may not devour one another and Society itself in their sterile struggle, some force standing, seemingly, above Society, becomes necessary so as to moderate the force of their collisions and to keep them within the bounds of "order." And this force arising from Society, but placing itself above it, which gradually separates itself from it—this force is the State.

Here, we have, expressed in all its clearness, the basic idea of Marxism on the question of the historical role and meaning of the State. The State is the product and the manifestation of the irreconcilability of class antagonisms. When, where and to what extent the State arises, depends directly on when, where and to what extent the class antagonisms of a given society cannot be objectively reconciled. And, conversely, the existence of the State proves that the class antagonisms *are* irreconcilable. . . .

According to Marx, the State is the organ of class *domination,* the organ of oppression of one class by another. Its aim is the creation of order which legalizes and perpetuates this oppression by moderating the collisions between the classes. But in the opinion of the petty-bourgeois politicians, the establishment of order is equivalent to the reconciliation of classes, and not to the oppression of one class by another. To moderate their collisions does not mean, according to them, to deprive the oppressed class of certain definite means and methods in its struggle for throwing off the yoke of the oppressors, but to conciliate it. . . .

But what is forgotten or overlooked is this: If the State is the product of the irreconcilable character of class antagonisms, if it is a force standing above society and "separating itself gradually from it," then it is clear that the liberation of the oppressed class is impossible without a violent revolution, and without the destruction of the machinery of State power, which has been *created* by the governing class in which this "separation" is embodied. . . .

Bourgeois Democracy

In capitalist society, under the conditions most favorable to its development, we have a more or less complete democracy in the form of a democratic republic. But this democracy is always bound by the narrow framework of capitalist exploitation, and consequently, always remains, in reality, a democracy only for the minority, only for the possessing classes, only for the rich. Freedom in capitalist society always remains more or less the same as it was in the ancient Greek republics, that is, freedom for the slave owners. The modern wage-slaves, in virtue of the conditions of capitalist exploitation, remain to such an extent crushed by want and poverty that they "cannot be bothered with democracy," have "no time for politics"; so that, in the ordinary peaceful course of events, the majority of the population is debarred from participating in public political life. . . .

Democracy for an insignificant minority, democracy for the rich—that is the democracy of capitalist society. If we look more closely into the mechanism of capitalist democracy, everywhere—in the so-called "petty" details of the suffrage (the residential qualification, the exclusion of women, etc.), in the technique of the representative institutions, in the actual obstacles to the right of meeting (public buildings are not for the "poor"), in the purely capitalist organization of the daily press, etc., etc.—on all sides we shall see restrictions of democracy. . . . Marx splendidly grasped the *essence* of capitalist democracy, when, in his analysis of the experience of the Commune, he said that the oppressed are allowed, once every few years, to decide which particular representatives of the oppressing class are to represent and repress them in Parliament! . . .

In a democratic Republic, Engels wrote, "wealth wields its power indirectly, but all the more effectively," first, by means of "direct corruption of the officials" (America); second, by means of "the alliance of the government with the stock exchange" (France and America). At the present time, imperialism and the domination of the banks have reduced to a fine art both these methods of defending and practically asserting the omnipotence of wealth in democratic Republics of all descriptions. . . .

We must also note that Engels quite definitely regards universal suffrage as a means of capitalist domination. Universal suffrage, he says (summing up obviously the long experience of German Social-Democracy), is "an index of the maturity of the working class; it cannot, and never will, give anything more in the present state." . . .

Take any parliamentary country, from America to Switzerland, from France to England, Norway and so forth; the actual work of the State is done behind the scenes and is carried out by the departments, the chancelleries and the staffs. Parliament itself is given up to talk for the special purpose of fooling the "common people." . . .

Two more points. First: when Engels says that in a democratic republic, "not a whit less" than in a monarchy, the State remains an "apparatus for the oppression of one class by another,'' this by no means signifies that the *form* of oppression is a matter of indifference to the proletariat, as some anarchists ''teach.'' A wider, more free and open form of the class struggle and class oppression enormously assists the proletariat in its struggle for the annihilation of all classes.

Second: only a new generation will be able completely to scrap the ancient lumber of the State—this question is bound up with the question of overcoming democracy, to which we now turn.

Dictatorship of the Proletariat

The forms of bourgeois States are exceedingly various, but their substance is the same and in the last analysis inevitably the *Dictatorship of the Bourgeoisie*. The transition from capitalism to Communism will certainly bring a great variety and abundance of political forms, but the substance will inevitably be the *Dictatorship of the Proletariat*. . . .

The State is a particular form of organization of force; it is the organization of violence for the purpose of holding down some class. What is the class which the proletariat must hold down? It can only be, naturally, the exploiting class (i.e., the bourgeoisie). The toilers need the State only to overcome the resistance of the exploiters, and only the proletariat can guide this suppression and bring it to fulfillment, for the proletariat is the only class that is thoroughly revolutionary, the only class that can unite all the toilers and the exploited in the struggle against the bourgeoisie, for its complete displacement from power. . . .

Together with an immense expansion of democracy—for the first time becoming democracy for the poor, democracy for the people, and not democracy for the rich—the dictatorship of the proletariat will produce a series of restrictions of liberty in the case of the oppressors, exploiters and capitalists. We must crush them in order to free humanity from wage-slavery; their resistance must be broken by force. It is clear that where there is suppression there must also be violence, and there cannot be liberty or democracy. . . . The replacement of the bourgeois by the proletarian State is impossible without a violent revolution. . . .

In the *Communist Manifesto* are summed up the general lessons of history, which force us to see in the State the organ of class domination, and lead us to the inevitable conclusion that the proletariat cannot overthrow the bourgeoisie without first conquering political power, without obtaining political rule, without transforming the State into the ''proletariat organized as the ruling class''; and that this proletarian State must begin to wither away immediately after its victory because in a community without class antagonisms, the State is unnecessary and impossible.

What Is to Replace the Shattered State Machinery?

In 1847 in the *Communist Manifesto,* Marx was as yet only able to answer this question entirely in an abstract manner, stating the problem rather than its solution. To replace this machinery by ''the proletariat organized as the ruling class,'' ''by the conquest of democracy''—such was the answer of the *Communist Manifesto*. . . .

Refusing to plunge into Utopia, Marx waited for the experience of a mass movement to produce the answer to the problem as to the exact forms which this organization of the proletariat as the dominant class will assume and exactly in what manner this organization will embody the most complete, most consistent ''conquest of democracy.'' Marx subjected the experiment of the [Paris] Commune, although it was so meagre, to a most minute analysis in his *Civil War in France*. . . .

> The Commune was the direct antithesis of the Empire. It was a definite form . . . of a Republic which was to abolish, not only the monarchical form of class rule, but also class rule itself.

What was this "definite" form of the proletarian Socialist Republic? What was the State it was beginning to create? The first decree of the [Paris] Commune was the suppression of the standing army, and the substitution for it of the armed people," says Marx. . . . But let us see how, twenty years after the Commune, Engels summed up its lessons for the fighting proletariat. . . .

> Against this inevitable feature of all systems of government that have existed hitherto, viz., the transformation of the State and its organs from servants into the lords of society, the Commune used two unfailing remedies. First, it appointed to all posts, administrative, legal, educational, persons elected by universal suffrage; introducing at the same time the right of recalling those elected at any time by the decision of their electors. Secondly, it paid all officials, both high and low, only such pay as was received by any other worker. . . .

Capitalist culture has created industry on a large scale in the shape of factories, railways, posts, telephones, and so forth: and *on this basis* the great majority of functions of "the old State" have become enormously simplified and reduced, in practice, to very simple operations such as registration, filing and checking. Hence they will be quite within the reach of every literate person, and it will be possible to perform them for the usual "working man's wage." . . .

The control of all officials, without exception, by the unreserved application of the principle of election and, *at any time,* recall; and the approximation of their salaries to the "ordinary pay of the workers"—these are simple and "self-evident" democratic measures, which harmonize completely with the interests of the workers and the majority of peasants; and, at the same time, serve as a bridge leading from capitalism to Socialism. . . .

To organize our whole national economy like the postal system, but in such a way that the technical experts, inspectors, clerks and, indeed, all persons employed, should receive no higher wage than the working man, and the whole under the management of the armed proletariat—this is our immediate aim. This is the kind of State and the economic basis we need. This is what will produce the destruction of parliamentarism, while retaining representative institutions. This is what will free the laboring classes from the prostitution of these institutions by the capitalist class. . . .

For the mercenary and corrupt parliamentarism of capitalist society, the Commune substitutes institutions in which freedom of opinion and discussion does not become a mere delusion; for the representatives must themselves work, must themselves execute their own laws, must themselves verify their results in actual practice, must themselves be directly responsible to their electorate. Representative institutions remain, but parliamentarism as a special system, as a division of labor between the legislative and the executive functions, as creating a privileged position for its deputies, *no longer exists*. Without representative institutions we cannot imagine a democracy, even a proletarian democracy; but we can and *must* think of democracy without parliamentarism, if our criticism of capitalist society is not mere empty words, if to overthrow the supremacy of the capitalists is for us a serious and sincere aim, and not a mere "election cry" for catching working men's votes. . . .

Again, during the *transition* from capitalism to Communism, suppression is *still* necessary; but in this case it is suppression of the minority of exploiters by the majority of exploited. A special instrument, a special machine for suppression—that is, the "State"—is necessary, but this is now a transitional State, no longer a State in the ordinary sense of the term. For the suppression of the minority of exploiters, by the majority of those who were *but yesterday* wage slaves, is a matter comparatively so easy, simple and natural that it will cost far less bloodshed than the suppression of the risings of the slaves, serfs or wage laborers, and will cost the human race far less. And it is compatible with the diffusion of democracy over such an overwhelming majority of the nation that the need for any *special machinery* for *suppression* will gradually cease to exist. The exploiters are unable, of course, to suppress the people without a most complex machine for performing this duty; but *the people* can suppress the exploiters even with a very simple "machine"—almost without any "machine" at all, without any special apparatus—by the simple *organization of the armed masses* (such as the Council of Workers' and Soldiers' Deputies, we may remark, anticipating a little).

Finally, only under Communism will the State become quite unnecessary, for there will be *no one* to suppress—"no one" in the sense of a *class,* in the sense of a systematic struggle with a definite section of the population. We are not utopians, and we do not in the least deny the possibility and inevitability of excesses by *individual persons,* and equally the need to suppress such excesses. But, in the first place, for this no special machine, no special instrument of repression is needed. This will be done by the armed nation itself, as simply and as readily as any crowd of civilized people, even in modern society, parts a pair of combatants or does not allow a woman to be outraged. And, secondly, we know that the fundamental social cause of excesses which violate the rules of social life is the exploitation of the masses, their want and the poverty. With the removal of this chief cause, excesses will inevitably begin to "wither away." We do not know how quickly and in what stages, but we know that they will be withering away. With their withering away, the State will also wither away.

The "Withering Away" of the State

Engels' words regarding the "withering away" of the State enjoy such a popularity, are so often quoted, and reveal so clearly the essence of the common adulteration of Marxism in an opportunist sense that we must examine them in detail. Let us give the passage from which they are taken.

> The proletariat takes control of the State authority and, first of all, converts the means of production into State property. But by this very act it destroys itself, as a proletariat, destroying at the same time all class differences and class antagonisms, and with this, also, the State.

Engels speaks here of the *destruction* of the capitalist State by the proletarian revolution, while the words about its withering away refer to the remains of a *proletarian* State *after* the Socialist revolution. The capitalist State does not wither away, according to Engels, but is *destroyed* by the proletariat in the course of the revolution. Only the proletarian State or semi-State withers away after the revolution. . . .

First Phase of Communist Society: Socialism

It is this Communist society—a society which has just come into the world out of the womb of capitalism, and which, in all respects, bears the stamp of the old society—that Marx terms the first or, lower, phase of Communist society.

The means of production are now no longer the private property of individuals. The means of production belong to the whole of society. Every member of society, performing a certain part of socially necessary labor, receives a certificate from society that he has done such and such a quantity of work. According to this certificate, he receives from the public stores of articles of consumption a corresponding quantity of products. After the deduction of that proportion of labor which goes to the public fund, every worker, therefore, receives from society as much as he has given it.

''Equality'' seems to reign supreme. . . . But different people are not equal to one another. One is strong, another is weak; one is married, the other is not. One has more children, another has less, and so on.

> With equal labor [Marx concludes] and, therefore, with an equal share in the public stock of articles of consumption, one will, in reality, receive more than another, will find himself richer, and so on. To avoid all this, ''rights,'' instead of being equal, should be unequal.

The first phase of Communism, therefore, still cannot produce justice and equality; differences and unjust differences in wealth will still exist, but the *exploitation* of man by man will have become impossible, because it will be impossible to seize as private property the *means of production*, the factories, machines, land, and so on. . . .

''He who does not work neither shall he eat''—this Socialist principle is *already* realized. ''For an equal quantity of labor an equal quantity of products''—this Socialist principle is also already realized. Nevertheless, this is not yet Communism, and this does not abolish ''bourgeois law,'' which gives to an unequal (in reality) amount of work, an equal quantity of products.

This is a ''defect,'' says Marx, but it is unavoidable during the first phase of Communism; for, if we are not to land in Utopia, we cannot imagine that having overthrown capitalism, people will at once learn to work for society *without any regulations by law*; indeed, the abolition of capitalism does not *immediately* lay the economic foundations for such a change. . . .

The State is withering away insofar as there are no longer any capitalists, any classes, and, consequently, any *class* whatever to suppress. But the State is not yet dead altogether, since there still remains the protection of ''bourgeois law,'' which sanctifies actual inequality. For the complete extinction of the State complete Communism is necessary.

The Higher Phase of Communist Society: Communism

Marx continues:

> In the higher phase of Communist society, after the disappearance of the enslavement of man caused by his subjection to the principle of division of labor; when, together with this, the opposition between brain and manual work will have disappeared; when labor will have ceased to be a mere means of supporting life and will itself have become one of the first necessities of life; when with the all-round development of the individual, the productive forces, too, will have grown to maturity, and all the forces of social wealth will be pouring an uninterrupted torrent—only then will it be possible

wholly to pass beyond the narrow horizon of bourgeois laws, and only then will society be able to inscribe on its banner: "From each according to his ability; to each according to his needs."

Only now can we appreciate the full justice of Engels' observations when he mercilessly ridiculed all the absurdity of combining the words "freedom" and "State." While the State exists there can be no freedom. When there is freedom there will be no State.

The economic basis for the complete withering away of the State is that high stage of development of Communism when the distinction between brain and manual work disappears; consequently, when one of the principle sources of modern *social* inequalities will have vanished—a source, moreover, which it is impossible to remove immediately by the mere conversion of the means of production into public property, by the mere expropriation of the capitalists.

This expropriation will make it possible gigantically to develop the forces of production. And seeing how incredibly, even now, capitalism *retards* this development, how much progress could be made even on the basis of modern technique at the level it has reached, we have a right to say, with the fullest confidence, that the expropriation of the capitalists will result inevitably in a gigantic development of the productive forces of human society. But how rapidly this development will go forward, how soon it will reach the point of breaking away from the division of labor, of the destruction of the antagonism between brain and manual work, of the transformation of work into a "first necessity of life"—this we do not and *cannot* know.

Consequently, we are right in speaking solely of the inevitable withering away of the State, emphasizing the protracted nature of this process, and its dependence upon the rapidity of development of the *higher phase* of Communism; leaving quite open the question of lengths of time, or the concrete forms of this withering away, since material for the solution of such questions is not available.

The State will be able to wither away completely when society has realized the formula: "From each according to his ability; to each according to his needs"; that is when people have become accustomed to observe the fundamental principles of social life, and their labor is so productive, that they will voluntarily work *according to their abilities*. "The narrow horizon of bourgeois law," which compels one to calculate, with the pitilessness of a Shylock, whether one has not worked half-an-hour more than another, whether one is not getting less pay than another—this narrow horizon will then be left behind. There will then be no need for any exact calculation by society of the quantity of products to be distributed to each of its members; each will take freely "according to his needs.". . . .

By what stages, by means of what practical measures humanity will proceed to this higher aim—this we do not and cannot know. But it is important that one should realize how infinitely mendacious is the usual capitalist representation of Socialism as something lifeless, petrified, fixed once for all. In reality, it is only with Socialism that there will commence a rapid, genuine, real mass advance, in which first the majority and then the *whole* of the population will take part—an advance in all domains of social and individual life.

*[**Editor's note:** In a critique of Lenin's* State and Revolution, *John Plamenatz maintained that Lenin never pondered the "curious" Marxist doctrine that "though the social classes [allegedly] have* irreconcilable *(and not merely different) interests, it is somehow possible to keep the peace between them." He added that "when classes are at peace and little force is required to keep that peace, surely the man who calls their interests 'irreconcilable' merely betrays his desire that there should be disputes where there are none, or that what disputes there are should be more bitter."]*

Communist Ethics

V.I. Lenin

First of all, I shall deal here with the question of Communist ethics. . . . But is there such a thing as Communist ethics? Is there such a thing as Communist morality? Of course there is. It is frequently asserted that we have no ethics, and very frequently the bourgeoisie makes the charge that we Communists deny all morality. That is one of their methods of confusing the issue, of throwing dust into the eyes of the workers and peasants.

In what sense do we deny ethics, morals? In the sense in which they are preached by the bourgeoisie, which deduces these morals from God's commandments. Of course, we say that we do not believe in God. We know perfectly well that the clergy, the landlords, and the bourgeoisie all claimed to speak in the name of God, in order to protect their own interests as exploiters. . . .

We deny all morality taken from superhuman or nonclass conceptions. We say that this is a deception, a swindle, a befogging of the minds of the workers and peasants in the interests of the landlords and capitalists.

We say that our morality is wholly subordinated to the interests of the class struggle of the proletariat. We deduce our morality from the facts and needs of the class struggle of the proletariat.

The old society was based on the oppression of all the workers and peasants by the landlords and capitalists. We had to destroy this society. We had to overthrow these landowners and capitalists. But to do this, organisation was necessary. God could not create such organisation.

Such organisation could only be created by the factories and workshops, only by the trained proletariat, awakened from its former slumber. Only when this class had come into existence did the mass movement commence which led to what we have today—to the victory of the proletarian revolution in one of the weakest countries in the world—a country which for three years has resisted the attacks of the bourgeoisie of the whole world. We see how the proletarian revolution is growing all over the whole world. And we can say now, on the basis of experience, that only the proletariat could have created that compact force which is carrying along with it the once disunited and disorganised peasantry—a force which has withstood all the attacks of all the exploiters. Only this class can help the toiling masses to unite their forces, to close their ranks, to establish and build up a definitely Communist society and finally to complete it.

That is why we say that a morality taken from outside of human society does not exist for us; it is a fraud. For us, morality is subordinated to the interests of the proletarian class struggle.

From a speech delivered at the Third All-Russian Congress of the Young Communist League of the Soviet Union on October 2, 1920.

On Violent Revolution

New Program of the Communist Party

It is important to take note of the contemporary views of the Soviet leadership on the necessity for violent revolution to overturn capitalism and achieve socialism—although obviously these had no bearing on the tactics pursued in the Bolshevik Revolution or on the theoretical position for years thereafter. The New Program of the Communist Party, adopted October 31, 1961, reads in part as below.

The working class and its vanguard—the Marxist-Leninist parties—seek to accomplish the socialist revolution *by peaceful means*. . . . In the conditions prevailing at present, in some capitalist countries the working class, headed by its forward detachment, has an opportunity to unite the bulk of the nation, win state power without a civil war and achieve the transfer of the basic means of production to the people upon the basis of a working class and popular front and other possible forms of agreement and political cooperation between different parties and democratic organizations. The working class, supported by the majority of the people and firmly repelling opportunist elements incapable of renouncing the policy of compromise with the capitalists and landlords, can defeat the reactionary, antipopular forces, win a solid majority in parliament, transform it from a tool serving the class interests of the bourgeoisie into an instrument serving the working people, launch a broad mass struggle outside parliament, smash the resistance of the reactionary forces and provide the necessary conditions for a peaceful socialist revolution. . . .

Where the exploiting classes resort to violence against the people, the possibility of a *nonpeaceful transition to socialism* should be borne in mind. Leninism maintains, and historical experience confirms, that the ruling classes do not yield power of their own free will. Hence, the degree of bitterness of the class struggle and the forms it takes will depend not so much on the proletariat as on the strength of the reactionary groups' resistance to the will of the overwhelming majority of the people, and on the use of force by these groups at a particular stage of the struggle for socialism. In each particular country the actual applicability of one method of transition to socialism or the other depends on concrete historical conditions.

It may well be that as the forces of socialism grow, the working-class movement gains strength and the positions of capitalism are weakened, there will arise in certain countries a situation in which it will be preferable for the bourgeoisie, as Marx and Lenin foresaw, to agree to the basic means of production being purchased from it and for the proletariat to "pay off" the bourgeoisie.

The success of the struggle which the working class wages for the victory of the revolution will depend on how well the working class and its party master the use of *all forms* of struggle—peaceful and nonpeaceful, parliamentary and extraparliamentary—and how well they are prepared for any swift and sudden replacement of one form of struggle by another form of struggle. . . . But whatever the form in which the transition from capitalism to socialism is effected, that transition can come about only through revolution.

*[**Editor's note:** Whether the present position of the Central Committee of the Communist Party of the Soviet Union represents a decisive break with Lenin on the necessity for violent overthrow of capitalism has been controverted. There are those who believe that the Communists are convinced of the superiority of*

socialism and of its ultimate appeal, that they appreciate the dangers of war and see prospects for the peaceful conquest of power through the policies and tactics of the Eurocommunists, especially in Italy and France, and therefore are prepared to eschew revolutionary methods. On the other hand, typical of an opposing view is that of Stefan T. Possony who wrote the following:

> The communists did not forswear violence at all, provided you go to the trouble of reading the fine print. . . . The need for the application of violence against bourgeois nations with strong military and police force was reaffirmed. On the assumption that the Communists will not succeed in talking the United States into dismantling its security forces, this country will remain a strong power. Hence it will have to be subjected to violence—or else the world revolution will have to be called off. The Communists continue to proclaim that the revolution will occur. Hence if logic means anything, nonviolent methods of revolution, while perhaps feasible in some countries without military and police forces, are not applicable to the United States.

On the question of violent revolution to achieve socialism, Morris Raphael Cohen wrote in "Why I am Not a Communist," Modern Monthly *(April 1934), that a "program of civil war, dictatorship, and the illiberal or fanatically intolerant spirit which war psychology always engenders may bring more miseries than those that the Communists seek to remove. . . . Communists ignore the historic truth that civil wars are much more destructive of all that men hold dearest than are wars between nations; . . . Civil wars necessarily dislocate all existing social organs and leave us with little social capital or machinery to rebuild a better society. The hatreds which fratricidal wars develop are more persistent and destructive than those developed by wars that terminate in treaties or agreements."*

Professor Cohen further maintained that "the Communist division of mankind into workingmen and capitalists suffers from the fallacy of simplism." He added that "if the history of the past is any guide at all, it indicates that real improvements in the future will come like the improvements of the past—namely, through cooperation among different groups, each of which is wise enough to see the necessity of compromising with those with whom we have to live together and whom we cannot or do not wish to exterminate." He considered that "sympathy with the sufferings of our fellow men is a human motive that cannot be read out of history. It has exerted tremendous social pressure. Without it you cannot explain the course of nineteenth-century factory legislation, the freeing of serfs and slaves, or the elimination of the grosser forms of human exploitation."]

PART THREE

TOWARD THE BOLSHEVIK TRIUMPH

We, the countless, redoubtable legions of Toil,
We've conquered vast spaces of oceans and lands,
Illumined great cities with suns of our making,
Fired our souls with proud flames of revolt.
Gone are our tears, our softness forgotten,
We banished the perfume of lilac and grass,
We exalt electricity, steam and explosives,
Motors and sirens and iron and brass. . . .
Our arms, our muscles cry out for vast labors,
The pain of creation glows hot in our breast,
United, we sweeten all life with our honey,
Earth takes a new course at our mighty behest.
We love life, and the turbulent joys that intoxicate,
We are hard, and no anguish our spirit can thaw.
We—all, We—in all, We—hot flames that regenerate,
We ourselves, to ourselves, are God, Judge, and Law.

Vladimir Kirillov

I am compelled to reject Bolshevism for two reasons: First, because the price mankind must pay to achieve Communism by Bolshevik methods is too terrible; and secondly because, even after paying the price, I do not believe the result would be what the Bolsheviks profess to desire.

Bertrand Russell

Instead of being a destructive force, it seems to me that the Bolsheviki were the only party in Russia with a constructive program and the power to impose it on the country.

John Reed in *Ten Days That Shook the World*

Chapter 3

WAR AND REVOLUTIONS

The First World War which linked Russia with the French and British democracies against imperial Germany at the outset aroused considerable support among the Russian people for their government. The detailed process by which enthusiasm turned to bitter discontent and then disaffection is traced by John S. Curtiss in the pages that follow.

The fundamental and historic backwardness and inequities of Russia's political, economic, and social structures and, more immediately, the privations of war, the inequalities of burdens, the incompetency and corruption of the imperial court, military inefficiency, and widespread agitation, culminated in March 1917 in the collapse of Tsardom in what has been called "one of the most leaderless, spontaneous, anonymous revolutions of all time"; "elemental, and for that reason all the more conclusive."

The Bolshevik Revolution, on the other hand, was carefully premeditated and planned. It is interesting to speculate on which of the decisions made during the war, and particularly after the March revolution, strengthened the Bolshevik position. (It is probably true that while the Bolsheviks did not command majority support at the time of the November revolution, "the active masses of workers and soldiers were, in the main, on the side of the coup, or at least regarded it with friendly neutrality"—as William Henry Chamberlin wrote.) Such speculation may provide some insight into Bolshevik success in Russia and have importance in relation to revolutionary movements and ferment elsewhere in the world.

The "indifference" with which the arbitrary dissolution of the Constituent Assembly was received by the nation after the freest and most equal election in all its history was further evidence of the people's lack of deep understanding of, or commitment to, democracy. The critical decision on land having apparently already been made, the majority of peasants were not prepared to fight to preserve democracy for, to them, as Michael T. Florinsky wrote, "freedom did not mean the introduction of parliamentary institutions about which they knew nothing, but the immediate division . . . of the landed estates in which they saw the real reason for their poverty and misery." That this "indifference" was to turn into "sullen discontent" with the program of collectivization did not alter the immediate situation.

The Russian Revolutions of 1917

John S. Curtiss

The Russian Empire in the First World War

Background of the War. . . . In June 1914, when the Austrian Archduke Francis Ferdinand was assassinated with the complicity of Serbian terrorists, the Russian government at first warned the Serbs to make amends. But then Austria-Hungary presented an ultimatum apparently designed to lead to war against Serbia, and when Vienna quickly declared war, Russia sought to protect her small ally against the Austrians. The Russians began partial mobilization against Austria, but then, under pressure from his generals, the Tsar reluctantly agreed to full mobilization, knowing that this might well lead Germany to declare war. Germany did so on July 19/August 1, 1914. From a Balkan quarrel the war had become a general one.

*[**Editor's Note:** The first named date is that under the old Russian calendar, the second is the same date under the new Soviet calendar, which is identical with that of the West.]*

The First Months of the War. When war came, Russia was stronger than ever before. There was considerable popular support for the government, and political conflict almost vanished. The Duma, in an outburst of patriotism, voted full support and gave the government a free hand. The people responded well to the call for mobilization. Even most of the socialists gave their support. As for the Bolshevik group in the Duma, who sharply opposed the war, it was quickly arrested and exiled to Siberia.

The Russian army, thoroughly reorganized after the Japanese war, had more artillery and machine guns than before, and an excellent spirit. But, in spite of belief in victory in a few months, the army was poorly prepared to fight the best military power in the world. The Russians had far fewer guns per division than the Germans, and no heavy field guns. Even worse, the Russians, with feeble facilities for making ammunition, had only 1,000 shells per gun, while the Germans had 3,000 per gun and ample capacity to make more. The Russians were also woefully lacking in machine guns, with only 4,100 in the whole army. Their supply and medical systems were primitive, their communications weak, and their aviation was far inferior to the Germans. Against the Austrians the Russians could more than hold their own, but from the beginning the Germans far outclassed them.

Even more disastrous, the Russian high command was poorly organized. It was only on the second day that the Grand Duke Nicholas, uncle of the Tsar, was named commander-in-chief, much to his surprise. He himself stated that at first he wept copiously because he did not know how to perform his new duties. Although he had some success,

J.S. Curtiss is Professor of History, Duke University. The selection is from pp. 21–87 of The Russian Revolutions of 1917 *(Princeton, N.J.: D. Van Nostrand Co., Inc., 1957). By permission of the publisher.*

his appointment was unfortunate. His chief-of-staff, General Ianushkevich, had had no field experience, and other high commanders were also poorly trained. V.A. Sukhomlinov, the Minister of War, was either extremely incompetent or a traitor. . . .

The Russian Disasters of 1915. By the spring of 1915, the Russians, in spite of heavy losses, had pushed to the crest of the Carpathians and even through some of the passes to the Hungarian plain. The Russians depended chiefly upon the bayonet, as their ammunition was almost gone. With their extended lines and almost silent cannons, the Russians invited a German counterstroke, which came suddenly in April 1915. With massed guns and heavy air attacks the Teutons cut the Russian army to pieces, whole units surrendering in confusion. The Germans pursued relentlessly, striking along the whole front, and threatened to entrap the Russians in Poland. The Russian cannons were limited at best to one shell per gun per day. Even the infantry lacked rifle ammunition, and reserve troops often had no rifles, but were forced to lie unarmed under fire until the rifles of the killed and wounded could be made available. Yet the Russian army held together under these demoralizing conditions, and late in the fall, the Germans halted their offensive on a line running from just west of Riga to the corner of Galicia.

Naturally, the Russian losses during this period were immense. At the height of the German drive, the killed and wounded numbered 235,000 per month, and 200,000 prisoners were lost each month. During 1915 alone, the Russians lost some 2,000,000 men killed and wounded, and 1,300,000 prisoners, bringing the total losses since the outbreak of the war to 4,360,000. It is no wonder that the British General Knox, who was with the Russian forces, stated that the army had come through a trial that "would have been fatal to most armies." The remnants of the army, although replenished in numbers, were inferior in quality, as the great quantities of regular officers and noncoms put out of action could never be replaced. Moreover, the morale of the Russians never could be restored.

Political Results of the Defeats. Inevitably, news of the difficulties of the army filtered back to the Duma as early as January 1915. At that time the members sharply questioned Sukhomlinov, the Minister of War, only to be told that the supply situation was satisfactory. The Duma could do nothing, even though it was sure that this answer was untrue. The leading political figures of the country met and repeatedly urged basic reforms in the government, only to be snubbed by the Tsar. The movement for reform grew, however, and early in the summer of 1915 two-thirds of the Duma organized the Progressive Bloc, headed by P.N. Miliukov, to ask necessary reforms and the "Ministry of Confidence" that was so widely demanded. When the Duma reconvened on June 19, 1915, there was a fierce attack upon the reactionary and incompetent ministers, who had opposed the mobilization of the public forces to support the war. As a result, the Tsar replaced three of the worst with able and respected conservatives. . . . The hopes of the Progressive Bloc were high.

The Sway of Rasputin. The Empress Alexandra, a fanatical believer in the autocratic power of the Emperor, had long been under the influence of Rasputin, who urged her to combat the progressive tendencies. She had already expressed her hatred for Guchkov. In August she and Rasputin persuaded the Tsar to dismiss the Grand Duke Nicholas, the commander-in-chief, and go to the front and take command himself. When the news leaked out, there was general consternation in the Duma, as the Tsar had no military training. Moreover, his absence from Petrograd would leave the government without a head. The feeling grew so strong that the ministers, under strong pressure from the Duma and the general public, on August 21 sent the Tsar a joint letter urging him to reconsider his decision. Only the aged Goremykin, the submissive Premier, opposed the protest. The letter, however, failed to deter the Tsar, who left for Headquarters on August 23. The ministers did not learn of his departure until two days later. By this act Nicholas cut himself off from the ministers. In reality, he turned over his political powers to the Empress, whom he encouraged to dabble in matters of state. The Empress, in turn, was firmly under the influence of Rasputin. And, thus, the great empire was dominated by a debauched and ignorant peasant, with whom no decent man could cooperate. The Empress, trusting firmly in him, threw herself into the work of running the state with dire results. The doom of the Empire was sealed.

The Brusilov Offensive in 1916. In spite of the fatal turn in political life, the Russian army made a remarkable recovery over the winter of 1915–1916. The troops were rested and reequipped, and heavy contingents of new men were added to the ranks. . . . But, as the German army also had improved greatly since 1914, the improved Russian army was even more inferior to the Germans than before. Nonetheless, it was decided to take the offensive in 1916, to relieve the Allies, hard-pressed in France, and especially to succor the Italians during an Austrian attack in the Tyrol.

The Russian commanders facing the Germans had little hope of success, but Brusilov, commander in Galicia, was sure of success against the Austrians and was given command of the offensive. Thanks to effective artillery fire and numerical superiority, the Russians quickly overwhelmed the Austrians on a wide front and captured 400,000 prisoners. But with German aid the Austrians again halted the Russians with heavy losses. The Russians had diverted large German forces from France and had saved Italy. Moreover, Brusilov's success had finally lured Rumania into the war on the allied side—although Rumania soon experienced disaster. But in spite of these successes, the offensive was unwise. In 1916 the Russians lost more than 2,000,000 men killed and wounded, and 350,000 prisoners. Even more important, the morale of the Russian army was ruined beyond repair, and its collapse seemed certain. The army was ripe for revolution.

Ministerial Leapfrog. After the Tsar had gone to the front, the internal situation worsened rapidly. The country's economy began to display alarming signs of weakness. Inflation, slow at first, soon gained momentum, and prices soared. For the swollen populations of the cities this brought great hardship, as wages, pitifully low at best, lost their purchasing power. The misery of the working people was intensified by a growing shortage of food. The peasants found it unprofitable to sell their grain for inflated money, especially as there were few manufactured goods to buy with it. In addition, the railroads proved unable to cope with the enormous problem of supplying the huge army as well as the civilian population and, often, available food supplies could not be transported. Food riots and strikes became more frequent, although the government dealt severely with the participants. A fuel shortage added to the woes of the urban inhabitants. As for the peasants, they were fairly docile, but they were more and more disgusted with the war, which had taken so many of their men and was constantly taking more.

Under these circumstances, able administration was imperative. It was not, however, supplied. Instead, the Empress, egged on by Rasputin, campaigned for the removal of the able men appointed by the Tsar in the summer of 1915. Two of them were dismissed in September, and a few months later two others went. Polivanov, the capable Minister of War, was especially hated by the Empress, who wrote to her husband: "A greater traitor than Sukhomlinov." When Nicholas finally gave in and removed him, she wrote: "Oh, the relief! Now I can sleep well." More and more the reputable men of Russia found it impossible to work under the influence of Rasputin, who, steeped in debauchery, was surrounded by a crowd of unprincipled adventurers. During the last eighteen months of the empire, the public was regaled with the spectacle of the "ministerial leap-frog," as one corrupt politician succeeded another in the positions of power, while Rasputin pulled the strings. In December 1915 Nicholas removed old Goremykin because of his inability to cope with the strong opposition to him. His successor, however, was Stürmer, a shady and disreputable politician for whom nobody had a good word. This appointment caused consternation at home and abroad, as he was incorrectly believed to be pro-German. He kept his post for almost a year. At first he posed as a friend of the Duma, to the great delight of the public.

But as the government scandals grew ever more noisome, and as the inability of the administration to deal with the food situation became more obvious, public opinion grew more and more vehement against Stürmer's government. Finally, the naming of A.D. Protopopov as Minister of Interior outraged Duma and public alike. Even the Tsar protested against him, but the urging of the Empress and Rasputin won out. It was not long before Protopopov's proven connections with Rasputin infuriated the citizenry, while his unbalanced mental state made him obviously unfit for the key post of Minister of Interior. Feeling ran so high that he did not dare appear before the Duma, over which he had once presided. In November 1916 the Tsar decided to dismiss him, but the Empress in despair fought for him, and Protopopov remained in power until the end.

The Rising Tide of Unrest. Protopopov failed signally in his efforts to control the situation. In October 1916 he sought to smash a city-wide strike in Petrograd by using two regiments of the garrison to reinforce the police. The troops, however, fired, not on the strikers, but on the police—an ominous note. Reports from the front frequently stressed that the soldiers wanted only peace and bread. Opposition to the war was so great that some officers feared to lead their troops in action lest they be shot by their own men. Protests demanding basic reforms were adopted by the *zemstvos* and the town governments, by the financial interests, by the nobility, and countless other organized groups. The situation grew so menacing that members of the Tsar's family met in secret to consider deposing the Tsar and the Empress as a means of avoiding the coming revolution. Generals and members of the Duma conferred concerning similar action, but nobody dared to take the lead.

On November 1, 1916 the Duma met for the first time in five months. Miliukov, leader of the Progressive Bloc, delivered a scathing attack on "the dark forces" around the throne, ending each part of his indictment with the question: "Is this stupidity or is it treason?" He was followed by several of the conservatives, who furiously denounced Rasputin and Stürmer. The latter, terrified, dared not challenge the Duma, in spite of the great wrath of the Empress. For once the Tsar acted independently by dismissing Stürmer and replacing him with a decent man, who insisted on removing Protopopov. The frantic Empress went to Headquarters, however, and secured the Tsar's promise to keep him, so that the dismissal of Stürmer brought little improvement. Fresh speeches in the Duma condemning Rasputin and his henchmen showed the enormous dissatisfaction of the Russian educated public, but produced no change in the government. The only result was further to infuriate the Empress, who demanded that the Tsar dismiss the Duma. "Russia loves to feel the whip."

One consequence of the speeches in the Duma was that several of the highest nobility of Russia decided to assassinate Rasputin in order to save the regime. Prince Yusupov, related to the Tsar by marriage, and the Grand Duke Dimitry, nephew of the Tsar, plied Rasputin with poisoned wine, and when that failed to take effect, he was shot and his body dumped into the river. When the corpse was recovered, the Tsar and the Empress attended his funeral upon the palace grounds. Rasputin's removal had no effect upon the political life of the land, which continued to drift toward revolution.

The First Revolutionary Months

The Mounting Crisis. In the first two months of 1917, dissatisfaction in Russia grew rapidly. The inflation advanced at a fast pace, with severe effects upon the working population, which showed its exasperation by an increasing number of strikes. The food shortages angered all, especially the women who had to wait in line for hours in the bitter cold, sometimes to find that there was no food to be had. In the rising popular fury the radical parties played little part, as the Mensheviks were still supporting the war and the Bolsheviks, with their chief figures in exile abroad or in Siberia, could accomplish little. The revolutionary movement was thus largely spontaneous and unexpected, even though it had long been foreseen. . . .

The Uprising. The insurrection began almost unnoticed. Early in March 1917 a strike of workers of Petrograd's great Pulitov Works turned thousands of men onto the streets, to demonstrate against the government and to appeal to the workers of other plants. March 8, International Woman's Day, regularly celebrated by the workers, brought thousands of women from the breadlines to swell the crowds. Red flags and banners with the slogan "Down with the Autocracy!" made their appearance. The police, however, had no great trouble in dispersing the crowds, and the unrest seemed no greater than on previous occasions. By the 9th there were nearly 200,000 strikers in the streets, demonstrating in the center of the city. Cossacks, called out to disperse the crowds, refused to charge them, and on one occasion they bowed to the crowd which applauded their inactivity. But the unrest apparently still was not threatening: the British ambassador cabled London: "Some disorders occurred today, but nothing serious."

On March 10 the movement grew in intensity, and the Tsar wired General Khabalov, commander of the garrison, to disperse the crowds with rifle fire. The next day preparations were made to subdue the demonstrations. Police with machine guns were placed in the upper stories of buildings overlooking main thoroughfares, and regiments of the garrison fired with considerable effect on crowds in several parts of the city. The government seemed to have won. But that night the troops in their barracks decided not to shoot down the crowds in the future. When ordered to march on the morning of the 12th, one of the regiments refused, shot the commander, and poured into the streets to join the crowds. Other regiments were quickly won over to the revolution. Together with the workers they hunted down the police and broke into the arsenals, where 40,000 rifles were captured and distributed to the workers. While these events were occurring, M.V. Rodzianko, President of the Duma, wired the Tsar, warning him of the seriousness of the situation and urging immediate reforms to avert a catastrophe. Nicholas said impatiently to his Court Chamberlain: "That fat Rodzianko has written me some nonsense, to which I shall not even reply."

Victory of the Revolution. By nightfall of March 12 it was all over. As the revolution surged ahead, General Khabalov sought to bring into play his special reserve of troops, but found himself able to collect no more than six companies. This force was sent to drive back the victorious crowds, but on contact with the insurrectionists they melted away, the men going over to the crowds, and the officers into hiding. Finally, late in the day, Khabalov, with less than two thousand men, took refuge in the Winter Palace, only to be asked to leave by the Grand Duke Michael. They went to the nearby Admiralty building, to disperse completely on the following day. The revolution was in full control of Petrograd. The overturn was marked by few excesses and by light casualties. Aside from burning the police stations and hunting down the police, the crowds shed little blood. In all, 1,315 persons, chiefly soldiers and citizens, were killed or wounded. In the rest of the vast Russian empire, the revolution spread rapidly, with little fighting. . . .

The Revolutionary Government. The Duma was in session when the disorders began, but on March 12 it was prorogued by order of the Tsar, prepared well in advance. The deputies hesitated whether to obey the order of dismissal, but after some thought they accepted it, lest they give aid and comfort to the revolutionaries. They moved from their official meeting place to a room across the hall, where they organized as an unofficial committee with the purpose "of restoring order and to deal with institutions and individuals." In the meantime, as early as March 9, some of the revolutionary leaders, with memories of 1905, suggested the election of a Soviet of Workers' Deputies, and several factories did hold elections. It was only on March 12, however, that the Soviet assembled in the Tavrida Palace, across the hall from the meeting of the Duma committee. After it had been joined by delegates from the garrison regiments, it changed its name to Soviet of Workers' and Soldiers' Deputies. Both the Soviet and the Duma were visited by hordes of workers and soldiers, who looked to them for leadership. The Soviet busied itself with the practical matters of the moment—patrolling the streets, feeding the soldiers who had joined the revolution, and similar matters, while the Duma leaders sought to preserve an effective government for the country.

Most of the Duma leaders were convinced monarchists, who felt that a Tsar was essential, even though the abdication of Nicholas II could not be avoided. So it was decided to send a delegation to the Tsar to ask him to abdicate, naming his brother Michael as regent. With some difficulty two of them made their way to the Tsar, who had come part way back to the capital. Before they arrived, Nicholas had heard from all the leading generals that his abdication was essential, so when the delegates appeared he surprised them by readily abdicating in favor of Michael. Back in Petrograd, however, the Duma leaders found it impossible to persuade the masses to accept *any* Tsar and barely escaped violence when they came out for Michael. Nevertheless, on March 16 a group of the Duma leaders, headed by Miliukov, visited Michael to urge him to take the throne. The Grand Duke, however, realizing the public hostility to a monarchy, refused to take the crown except from a Constituent Assembly. Hence, Russia became a republic *de facto,* although the formal declaration of the republic came much later.

Formation of the Provisional Government. The members of the Duma committee felt that they had no right to form a government, but as they realized that if they did not, the leaders of the Soviet, more radical in their outlook, would do so, they decided to take power, "otherwise others will take it, those who have already elected some scoundrels in the factories." Miliukov, especially, sought to establish the authority of the new government by negotiating with the leaders of the Soviet. The latter, however, did not desire to rule, as they were men inexperienced in governmental affairs. Moreover, they were moderate socialists, who believed that at this moment the revolution was bourgeois in character, as the workers were too weak to set up the dictatorship of the proletariat. Hence, the Soviet chiefs felt that power should be entrusted to the leaders of the bourgeoisie, drawn from the ranks of the Duma.

Consequently, on March 14 the leaders of the Duma and the Soviet conferred about the powers and program of the new government, which took office on March 16. The Premier of the Provisional Government was Prince G.E. Lvov, a noted liberal; Guchkov was Minister of War, and Miliukov was Foreign Minister. Alexander Kerensky took the post of Minister of Justice. He was nominally a right-wing Socialist Revolutionary, although he was basically conservative. But his enthusiasm for the revolutionary overturn and his inspiring speeches had made him a popular hero and had won him election to the Soviet. He joined the Provisional Government while retaining his membership in the Soviet for the purpose of serving as a link between the two bodies.

The program of the new regime, approved by the Soviet, provided for a full amnesty, broad civil liberties, and complete legal equality of all. Trade unions and strikes were declared legal. The manifesto promised immediate preparation for a constituent assembly, to be elected by universal, direct, equal, and secret voting. Local government was also to be elected. Finally, the soldiers were promised full civil rights, upon condition that firm discipline was observed. This program, which was necessarily a compromise between the Duma and the Soviet, said nothing about the vital issues: the war, and the distribution of land to the peasants. On these points no agreement was possible.

Like its program, the government itself was an uneasy compromise between the Soviet and the leaders of the former Duma. The latter, drawn from the middle-class parties, were quite conservative and instinctively distrusted the masses and the Soviet which represented them. For its part, the Soviet had no great confidence in the Provisional Government. Backed as it was by the vast majority of the workers and the soldiers of the Petrograd garrison, the Soviet undertook to support the Provisional Government only as long as the latter remained true to the cause of the revolution. It compelled the government to arrest the Tsar.

Order No. 1. One of the first acts of the Soviet was to issue its famous Order No. 1 to the troops, to ensure that they would not be used for counterrevolutionary purposes. It was drawn up on March 14 at the suggestion of some of the soldiers. It provided for the election of committees of soldiers in all army units, which were to obey the Soviet and were to keep control of the arms, which were not to be turned over to the officers. The troops were to obey their officers and the Provisional Government, but only insofar as their orders were not in conflict with those of the Soviet. Saluting off duty and elaborate honors to officers were abolished, and the officers were forbidden to be harsh toward their men. These instructions were in part a symptom of the distrust of the officers felt by the rank and file, who had seen that their officers had given no support to the revolution. Discipline in the army had begun to crumble well before the fall of the Tsar. Nevertheless, Order No. 1 doubtless contributed much to the further collapse of the authority of the commanders and of the discipline essential to any effective body of troops. Thus, the Provisional Government lacked effective military support and was dependent for its authority upon the backing of the Soviet.

An Era of Good Feeling. Although in the first weeks after the fall of the monarchy the dualism or divided control of the state held latent the seeds of conflict, matters for a time went fairly smoothly. The Soviet, which grew to over three thousand members, was dominated largely by the soldier delegates, who were usually noncommissioned officers, company clerks, or other partly educated persons, who were not especially radical in their views. Most of them were under the influence of the Socialist Revolutionaries, who supported the war and were not eager for further radicalism. For the most part the workers were led by the Mensheviks, who also supported the war. The latter were convinced that Russia was by no means ready for a proletarian dictatorship, so they were quite ready to let the upper classes represented by the Provisional Government run the country. Even the Bolsheviks did not take an extreme stand at this time.

Kamenev and Stalin, who returned from Siberia during these early days, in their *Pravda* editorials held that, while the war was imperialist in nature, until a general peace became possible there should be no attempt to make a separate peace, and the Russian army should continue to defend the country. And, indeed, even if the Bolsheviks *had* been inspired by the radical views of Lenin, who was fretting in exile in Switzerland, they were too few in numbers and too weak in influence to disturb the relative calm. . . .

The Moderate Attitude of the Masses. In general, the army, although it had long since lost any enthusiasm for the war, still thought along traditional lines of its duty to defend the country. . . .

As early as March 1917, the peasants began to call for peasant Soviets to consider the land question. Nevertheless, they still remembered their punishment in 1906 and 1907 too well to act rashly, and for a time they were willing to wait. The workers, who had immediately gained the eight-hour day as a result of the revolution, also were not yet ready for further insurrection. In March 1917 factory committees, elected by the workers, were set up to represent the workers in negotiating with the employers. Although there was much friction between committees and employers, in the early spring the committees were seeking higher wages for the employees rather than confiscation of the factories. As yet the moderate socialists had not been replaced by the militant Bolsheviks who later dominated the committees, and the workers were not in a revolutionary frame of mind.

The Rising Conflict over Foreign Policy. At first the Provisional Government took the position that the revolution had changed nothing in Russia's foreign policy. Miliukov, the Foreign Minister, hastened to assure the Allies that Russia stood by her treaty obligations and warmed their hearts by stating that the Tsar had been overthrown because his government had not been able to wage war with sufficient energy—a far from correct statement. Miliukov was especially interested in obtaining Constantinople and the Dardanelles for Russia, which had been promised by the secret treaties of 1915. The moderate socialists who dominated the Soviet, however, felt that the war was essentially imperialistic in character and hoped that the peoples of the other warring states would also overturn their governments and demand peace.

With this end in view, on March 27 the Soviet issued a "Manifesto to the Peoples of the World," calling on them to oppose actively the annexationist policies of their governments. The Russian democracy, the manifesto promised, would resist to the death all efforts of its ruling classes to pursue such a policy. The peoples of the West, especially in Germany, should rise in revolution against kings, landowners, and bankers, and thus bring about a revolutionary peace. But until this should happen, the Soviet declared, the Russian revolution would not retreat before conquering bayonets nor allow itself to be crushed by outside force. This manifesto was widely hailed by the socialist press, which strongly demanded a peace "without annexations and indemnities."

Miliukov, however, did not share this attitude. Early in April he issued a press interview stating that Russia was fighting to unite the Ukrainian parts of the Austro-Hungarian Empire with Russia and to gain Constantinople and the Straits. These objectives, he declared, could not be regarded as annexations. This utterance aroused a storm of protest. Conflict was averted, however, when the Provisional Government published a "Declaration on War Aims" renouncing annexations and upholding self-determination. It added, however, that Russia should not "emerge from the great struggle humiliated, undermined in her vital strength." The Provisional Government stated its determination "to protect national rights while strictly fulfilling the obligations assumed toward the Allies." In these vague phrases Miliukov saw support for his design to win Constantinople.

Lenin's Return. The news of the fall of the monarchy and the forming of the Provisional Government found Lenin in Switzerland, where he had spent much of the war years. During this period he had formulated his attitude toward the war. Capitalism, he held, must inevitably lead to imperialism, and imperialism is bound to produce war for the interests of the capitalists. In such a conflict the working class had no interest, but should strive to transform the war into a civil war. The socialists of Europe who had supported their nation's cause after Sarajevo were thus traitors to the proletariat. Only a true Marxist party could be trusted to end the war in the interest of the working class. . . .

Swiss socialist leaders arranged with the German government to let him and a number of other Russian exiles travel across Germany in a sealed car to Denmark; from there he made his way to Sweden and Finland, and on April 16 he reached Petrograd. Although he had expected to be arrested by the Provisional Government, to his surprise he was met by a deputation from the Soviet and a guard of honor at the Finland Station. He impatiently turned from his official welcome to address the throngs of people in a fiery speech ending with the words: "Long live the socialist revolution!"

The April Theses. On April 17, the day after his arrival, Lenin presented his revolutionary program to two gatherings: one of Bolsheviks, and the second of Bolsheviks and Mensheviks together. The program, known as the April Theses, contained ten points. It declared that the war was still an imperialistic one, to be ended by the overthrow of capitalism and fraternization of the soldiers with the enemy. The revolution, he held, should immediately take the power from the hands of the bourgeoisie and give it to the proletariat and poorer peasants. No support should be given to the Provisional Government, which should be replaced by the Soviet of Workers' Deputies. All large estates were to be nationalized and turned over to the Soviets of Farmhands' Deputies.

This program, in particular as it concerned the war, horrified even the Bolshevik leaders, who felt that it was utterly unrealistic. The Mensheviks regarded Lenin as so visionary as to be ludicrous and felt joy at his impracticability. His program was promptly rejected by the Bolsheviks, 12 to 2, and *Pravda* wrote that his proposals were based upon an incorrect analysis of the revolution. But Lenin was not dismayed by this reception. He pushed his program in incessant speeches to streams of men and women who came to hear him, and so simple and so logical did his points of "End the war" and "All land to the peasants'' seem that he won their complete support. His propaganda enjoyed such success among the masses that his party swung over to his side, and at an All-Russian Conference of Bolsheviks in May it strongly approved the program that it had rejected three weeks before. Thus, the lines began to form for a struggle between the Provisional Government and the masses, urged on by Lenin.

The Mounting Crisis

The Fall of Miliukov. Miliukov's trickery in attempting to cover his annexationist aims with vague words soon came out into the open. When it was discovered that the Allies had not heard of the ''Declaration of War Aims,'' there was a strong demand that he communicate it officially to them. He did so on May 1, but accompanied the Declaration with a covering note, in which he affirmed that Russia was determined to carry the war ''to a decisive conclusion,'' in order to obtain ''sanctions ad guarantees'' which would make new wars impossible. (''Sanctions and guarantees'' sounded ominously like annexations.) Finally, he again promised to ''fulfill Russia's obligations to her Allies.'' When, on May 3, this note became public, it was taken as a deliberate challenge to the wishes of the public. The people felt that their strivings for peace had been nullified by the obstinate Foreign Minister.

A crisis of extreme seriousness resulted, with mass demonstrations in front of the seat of the Provisional Government. Although some of the demonstrators supported Miliukov, most of them, including fully armed regiments, carried banners demanding peace without annexations and indemnities, the end of the war, and the dismissal of Miliukov. On the next day, there were even stronger demonstrations, in which there were demands for the end of the Provisional Government. General L.G. Kornilov, commander of the Petrograd garrison, wanted to use his troops to smash the demonstration, but severe bloodshed was averted by the Petrograd Soviet, which ordered that no regiment should come out into the streets without an order signed by the Soviet. Kornilov, angered by this check upon his authority, resigned his command and went to the front.

The demonstration was quickly checked by the orders of the Soviet. The Provisional Government hastened to calm the public by issuing its explanation of Miliukov's note, which it sent to the Allied ambassadors. It practically disavowed Miliukov's interpretation and repeated the pacifist phrases of the earlier declarations. As Miliukov held to his views, he now had to give up the Foreign Ministry, and he refused a lesser post. Likewise Guchkov, Minister of War, also resigned, in part because of poor health, and partly from despair with the trend of events. These resignations led to a reorganization of the Provisional Government, which reformed with nine ministers from the former Duma (chiefly Cadets), and six moderate socialists from the Soviet. It was hoped that this coalition would end the friction between the Soviet and the Provisional Government. The result, however, was to transfer the disharmony into the midst of the government itself. Probably the chief figure in the new regime was Kerensky, the Minister of War. . . .

The Lull before the Storm. The Provisional Government, and especially the Cadet party, which was rapidly absorbing the other conservative parties, seemed little concerned over the rise of the Bolsheviks. . . . The Bolsheviks, while growing, remained a considerable minority, while the moderate socialists remained in control of the Soviet. But here, too, the reality was not reassuring to the moderates. While the masses out of habit voted for socialists, at the same time they often would vote for Bolshevik resolutions. Nevertheless, when the First Congress of Soviets met on June 16, 1917, the Bolsheviks and allied groups had only 137 out of the 1,090 members. Tseretelli, a moderate leader of the Petrograd Soviet, was sufficiently encouraged by the lack of Bolshevik strength to declare in his speech that the government was secure, "as there is no political party in Russia which at the present time would say: 'Give us power'." But at this point Lenin spoke from his seat: "Yes, there is!" . . .

The Military Debacle. On July 1, 1917 the Russian offensive began in Galicia. The Russians, with great superiority in numbers and thanks to an unprecedented artillery preparation, penetrated the Austrian lines at several points near Lvov and took several thousand prisoners. Soon, however, they encountered unexpected resistance. The attack, which on other fronts had had no success, bogged down after twelve days. On July 19 the Germans and Austrians began a counterdrive which met almost no opposition as the Russians fled headlong. All discipline vanished and the rout intensified, accompanied by terrible outrages inflicted on the civilians as the troops fled. Finally the line stabilized after all Galicia had been given up; but it was the decision of the enemy rather than Russian resistance that ended the retreat. General Kornilov, who was appointed to command the Southwest Front on July 20, demanded the death penalty in the front areas, and immediately used machine guns and artillery on masses of deserters and mutineers. On July 25, the Provisional Government restored the death penalty and set up special military tribunals to deal with major offenses. But not even these measures accomplished much, for the morale of the army was ruined beyond repair.

The July Insurrection. While the Russian offensive was continuing, violence erupted in Petrograd. The masses of workers, already very hostile toward the Provisional Government, and the soldiers of the garrison, fearful that they might be sent to the front, grew impatient with the apparent timidity of the Bolshevik leadership. On July 16 the First Machine Gun Regiment, an especially radical unit, marched forth, although both the Soviets and the Bolsheviks sought to restrain them. The revolutionary call of the soldiers was eagerly obeyed by other troop units and by hundreds of thousands of workers, whom the Bolsheviks reluctantly led, in order to keep them from getting completely out of hand. On July 17 perhaps 500,000 in huge columns poured through the streets with banners demanding "All Power to the Soviets!" and "Down with the Provisional Government!" They converged on the Tavrida Palace, seat of the Central Executive Committee of the Soviets, to demand that this body assume power in place of the Provisional Government. Feelings ran extremely high, as the demonstrators, augmented by a large force of fierce sailors from Kronstadt armed to the teeth, streamed through the streets. Occasional shots were fired, at which the demonstrators, believing themselves under attack from neighboring buildings, broke into the houses to hunt for snipers. Several score of persons were killed, and over one hundred wounded. Some of the ministers had narrow escapes. Kerensky was almost captured on the first day, and Victor Chernov, the socialist Minister of Agriculture, escaped death at the hands of sailors only through the intervention of Trotsky.

In the meantime, in the palace, the Central Executive Committee, composed chiefly of Mensheviks and Socialist Revolutionaries, was beset by masses of furious armed men who demanded that they take power—something they refused to do. A stalemate developed as frustrated soldiers and workers threatened the frightened but stubborn leaders of the Soviet to induce them to take power. But the long discussions proved fruitless, and the Bolsheviks, who could easily have seized all Petrograd by giving the order, failed to do so, so that eventually the demonstrators grew weary and went home. The sailors boarded their ships and went back to Kronstadt, and the Central Executive Committee could breathe more freely.

Reaction against Lenin and the Bolsheviks. The tide of revolt receded as quickly as it had risen. Several of the Guards regiments, which had not taken part in the demonstration, were informed on July 17 that the Minister of Justice had documentary proof that Lenin was a German agent. The Guards, convinced by this, at once put themselves at the orders of the government and the Central Executive Committee. The danger was now over, and on the following day government forces raided and wrecked the offices and plant of *Pravda* and occupied without a struggle the Fortress of Peter and Paul and the Bolshevik headquarters. On July 19 a Bolshevik leaflet announced that the demonstration was at an end.

The documents charging Lenin and other Bolshevik leaders with treason were published in the newspapers, much to the annoyance of Kerensky, who claimed that this had prevented Lenin's capture and punishment. Other ministers were very dubious about the documents and their source. The middle classes, however, were easily convinced of the correctness of the charges, as they remembered that Lenin had left Switzerland in a German train. Warrants were issued for his arrest, and also for Zinoviev and Kamenev. But Lenin and Zinoviev hid, although they protested their innocence. Lenin at first wanted to stand trial, but as he was persuaded by his associates that he might be murdered in prison, he escaped to Finland, where the Russian police could not follow. He stayed in Helsingfors until autumn. Trotsky and several other Bolsheviks were arrested, but were soon released.

It is perhaps worth stating that most historians of repute do not believe that Lenin was a German agent, even though the Germans had enabled him to return to Russia. . . .

Government Policy after the July Days. The Provisional Government took advantage of its improved position to take further action. Legislation was adopted against incitement to mutiny. Regiments that had taken the lead in the uprising were disbanded and the men sent to the front, in some cases with the use of force. Several of the Bolshevik newspapers were closed and circulation of such publications among the troops was forbidden. . . .

The moderate and the conservative elements of Russia had been granted a new lease on life by the unexpected outcome of the July Days. Neither group, however, took advantage of the opportunity to satisfy the enormous popular demand for peace and land, which was the basis of the strength of the Bolsheviks. The moderate Left continued to advocate prosecution of the war to victory and urged that the land and other problems be deferred until the Constituent Assembly, which, it must be said, they did little to hasten. Thus, they did nothing of significance to win the masses from the Bolsheviks and, hence, remained without any real popular following. As for the Right—landowners, capitalists, army officers, and other upper-class elements—they had never accepted the revolutionary regime in their hearts, and now that the rabble had been subdued, they felt that they discerned the delightful possibility of a strong man—a military dictatorship—to sweep aside all this rubbish of socialists and soviets and to establish sound law and order again, as before the revolution.

The Kornilov Movement

The Illusion of Calm. Although the collapse of the July demonstration had apparently ended all danger from the Bolsheviks, the improvement in the government's position was largely on the surface, while underneath the situation grew worse. On instructions from Lenin, the Bolsheviks concentrated their efforts on the factory committees, which were becoming more and more aggressive. The factory workers found that the rapid inflation raised prices far more than they could raise their wages, and the poorer-paid were especially hard hit. The declaration of the textile workers that their children were dying like flies as a result of hunger was not entirely rhetoric. Hence, the lot of the workers became unbearable and they turned to the factory committees for redress and to the Bolsheviks for leadership. . . .

To add to the woes of the government, the national minorities became increasingly self-assertive. As Poland and most of the Baltic states were held by the Germans, they were not an active problem; but both Finland and the Ukraine were becoming restless. . . .

The Kerensky Government. The coalition formed after the July Days failed to endure, for on July 21 Prince Lvov resigned his post as Premier in disapproval of the socialist policy of Chernov, Minister of Agriculture, and others. Kerensky thereupon took office as Premier. After much negotiating and scheming a new government was installed in early August, with eleven socialists and seven nonsocialists. In spite of the preponderance of socialists, however, the new government was more conservative than its predecessor, as the socialists, frightened by the events of July, had lost all trace of revolutionary zeal. More and more, Kerensky dominated the scene. . . .

The Rise of General Kornilov. . . . General L.G. Kornilov, the new commander-in-chief, was a dashing soldier who had won great fame by his exploits in the war as well as by his spectacular personality. A Siberian, with somewhat Mongolian features, he was followed with devotion by a bodyguard of wild Caucasian cavalrymen, whose language he knew. In May, as commander of the Petrograd garrison, he had wished to smash the demonstration against Miliukov, and when the Soviet had prevented this he had resigned to go to the front. Kornilov's reputation as a Napoleonic figure had been further enhanced by his ruthless measures in dealing with the routed troops after the disastrous July offensive. He was greatly admired by Boris Savinkov, the former Socialist Revolutionary who had become head of the Ministry of War under Kerensky, and as Kerensky felt that Kornilov would be successful in reviving the fighting spirit of the army, the general had been named commander-in-chief on July 31. Kornilov's conditions for taking over this post, amounting to a virtual free hand with the army, as well as the extension of full military control to the rear military areas, indicated that he would be a difficult person to handle. The friction caused by this stand was soon eliminated when Kornilov agreed to a compromise, but the incident gave a hint of trouble to come.

Kornilov, who had little knowledge of politics, soon became a storm center. He was instinctively hostile to all socialists, whether extreme or mild, and he disliked Kerensky, although he promised to work with him. The Leftist press, which saw in him a danger to the revolution, attacked him strongly, asking that he be replaced by a general more in sympathy with the revolutionary cause. Conservatives and reactionaries became his enthusiastic allies. The Union of Cossack Troops warned that the consequences for the army would be disastrous if he were removed—an opinion voiced by other military organizations. . . .

Rodzianko, Miliukov, and other leaders of the Duma period, energetically enrolled landowners and financial magnets in well financed organizations to further the cause, while generals and officers built up organizations of officers and military cadets to support the march on Petrograd by uprisings at the right moment. Kornilov's chief-of-staff later claimed that there were thousands in Petrograd waiting to strike in support of the movement. On September 6, Savinkov, head of the War Ministry under Kerensky, with the latter's approval, visited Kornilov at Headquarters and approved the commander's demands for introducing the death penalty in the rear, Savinokov also told him that as a Bolshevik uprising was expected within a few days, he should send a cavalry corps to the capital to protect the Provisional Government.

This request, which Kornilov had already anticipated by sending troops, was part of the political scheme to which Savinkov was a party. Kerensky was to be invited to dismiss the government and form a new one in which he, Kornilov, and Savinkov would be the dominant figures. If Kerensky refused, the troops were to be brought into play. Unfortunately for the success of the scheme, V.N. Lvov, a lesser political figure, undertook to persuade Kerensky to cooperate, and thereby gave the Premier warning. Kerensky, realizing that if the scheme went through, his freedom, if not his life, would be in danger, at once took steps against the conspiracy. After arresting Lvov on September 9, he ordered Kornilov to resign and asked for support from the Soviet and from the ministers. The Soviet at once gave him full support, but the Cadet ministers resigned from the government, apparently hoping to cause its collapse. . . .

The Collapse of the Movement. Undismayed by Kerensky's opposition, Kornilov persisted in his undertaking, issuing a blast against the Provisional Government, charging it with collaborating with the Germans and ruining the army and the country. He appealed to the populace in a manifesto full of nationalist and religious phrases, which, however, had already lost their potency. With almost complete support from the Allies, and even aided by a British unit of armored cars whose men had donned Russian uniforms, he was certain of success. Most of the army leaders were with him, he was sure of the Wild Division and the Cossacks, and he counted on the aid of other disciplined troops. The garrison of Petrograd seemed to have no great enthusiasm for fighting for Kerensky. As for the Petrograd populace, he felt that they, unorganized and leaderless, would remain in sullen apathy, "an indifference that submits to the whip." General Krymov and the other field commanders were ordered to advance on Petrograd.

As soon as the Soviet in Petrograd realized the approaching danger, it hastened to act. Despairing of Kerensky's leadership, the Soviet leaders threw themselves into the work of defending the capital. On September 9 moderate socialists and Bolsheviks combined in a "Committee for Struggle against Counterrevolution" to defeat Kornilov. The garrison was put in a state of readiness, neighboring troops were called to their aid, and large numbers of eager sailors from Kronstadt arrived, with more coming from other parts of the fleet. Under Bolshevik leadership the Petrograd workers were mobilized. Trenches were dug, barbed wire was strung, barricades were built in the city streets. The Red Guards from the factories, who had been disarmed after the July Days, were again given weapons, and turned out, full of fight. Strong detachments were sent to break up the officers' organizations that had planned to rise as Krymov's forces approached. The conspiratorial center in the Hotel Astoria was taken without difficulty, and a sweeping series of arrests and searches eliminated other groups of plotters. A colonel sent by Kornilov to direct the movement fled to Finland. In all, some 7,000 arrests were made by the Soviet, thus ending all danger of an officers' uprising in Petrograd.

Not content to await the arrival of the attacking forces, the Soviet had sent word to the railway workers to impede the movement of the hostile troops. At the orders of their union the men cut telegraph wires, put locomotives out of commission, blocked tracks by tipping over freight cars, tore up rails. As the troop trains progressed, they were switched off in the wrong direction and finally halted isolated and helpless. . . .

Kerensky, who had been saved by the spontaneous action of the soviet and the Bolsheviks, was far from happy about his position after the episode. He now realized that, with the power of the Right destroyed, the Left had gained greatly in strength. Hence, he sought to use the remaining conservatives as a counterweight to the now rising popular forces. To replace Kornilov as commander-in-chief Kerensky named, not one of the generals in sympathy with the revolution, but General Alexeev, who had been hand in glove with Kornilov. Moreover, Kerensky ordered that, until Alexeev arrived at Headquarters, the army should continue to obey Kornilov's orders. Alexeev promptly cancelled the movement of strong revolutionary forces to subdue Kornilov's Headquarters garrison. It was only with the greatest reluctance that he had the insurgent general arrested on September 14, along with his most obvious supporters. The arrested men were transferred to a town in the Ukraine, where they were nominally imprisoned. The jailers were none other than Kornilov's devoted Caucasian bodyguard.

An extraordinary investigating committee was sent out to gather evidence against the conspirators, but they showed no willingness to take action and soon released all but the five chief participants. It was obvious that Kerensky's government was not willing to deal harshly with the insurgents. To the masses of soldiers and workers, who had been willing to risk their lives to suppress the Kornilov insurrection, this tenderness toward the defeated generals seemed as treasonable as the uprising itself.

The Aftermath of the Kornilov Affair

Another Chance for Kerensky. After the threat from Kornilov had been removed, Kerensky, although his prestige was badly shaken by his unwillingness to punish the rebels, still had an opportunity to bring the government into line with the aspirations of the people. It is conceivable that if he had accepted reality and had decided to support the demand for peace and had approved a land program satisfactory to the peasants, a more violent revolutionary outbreak could still have been avoided. A moderate democratic regime was perhaps still possible. Instead of making a sharp change in direction, however, the government remained much as before. It still depended on the old Central Executive Committee of the Soviet which had been elected in the earlier, conservative period and which did not represent the feelings of the masses. The Socialist Revolutionaries and the Mensheviks who composed it had been left behind by the rapid march of events. Beneath the surface the Soviets were beginning to swing to the Bolsheviks, while peasants and soldiers were no longer willing to support the war and to wait for a much-postponed Constituent Assembly to deal with the land problem. The appeal of the Right to counterrevolutionary force had made the masses far more impatient with the inaction of the government and more ready to decide the issue by a new resort to the enormous revolutionary force that still remained.

More than ever the government of Russia centered in Kerensky. After the crisis was over, the ministers, who had tendered their resignations, remained in office for a time on a day-to-day basis. On September 14 a Directory, or inner cabinet of five men, headed by Kerensky, was set up to determine policy. On the same day, Russia was proclaimed a republic. This step, which merely recognized what had long been obvious, met with strong opposition on the part of the conservatives, who asserted that it exceeded the powers of the Provisional Government. Many felt that beneath the legalistic basis for the protest there lingered a strong hope on the part of the conservatives that somehow the monarchy could be restored. . . .

The Failure of the Socialist Revolutionaries. Kerensky's failure to take advantage of the collapse of the Right was paralleled by the failure of his party—the Socialist Revolutionaries. This party, the largest political organization in Russia before the revolution, expanded enormously after the fall of the Tsar. It had long enjoyed the support of the teeming peasant millions, and now that many of these millions were in uniform and had rifles in their hands their political activity had greatly increased. They joined the Socialist Revolutionary party in such numbers that the party was not able to digest the huge mass. Several of its most effective leaders had died shortly before the revolution, leaving Victor Chernov, a theorist and writer rather than a practical politician, to deal with the vital problems of the times. Other Socialist Revolutionary leaders, especially those like Kerensky, who had represented the party in the Duma, became more and more conservative and lost touch with the masses. . . .

While the Socialist Revolutionary leaders for the most part were becoming more conservative, the rank and file were becoming more and more radical. In May 1917 the SR's held their Third All-Russian Congress, at which, in spite of a strong tendency of the Right faction to secede, Chernov's program was adopted, calling for a just and speedy peace and for a positive socialist policy of labor and agrarian legislation. This evidence that the bulk of the party wanted to follow a progressive policy was lost on the leaders, except Chernov, who before long was forced from power. . . .

The Breakdown of the Army and Navy. To the millions of Russian soldiers, suffering from hunger and cold in the trenches, the Kornilov insurrection added a new and more infuriating grievance. The soldiers had been distrustful of their officers, most of whom had taken no part in the struggle for the overthrow of the Tsar. The men were convinced that the war was an imperialistic struggle for Constantinople and Galicia, and when the July offensive was attempted, it confirmed these beliefs. Now they had seen their highest commanders, who had insistently demanded the death penalty as punishment for desertion and mutiny, rise in rebellion against the revolution. Many of the other officers had sought to aid the Kornilov mutiny and few had taken a stand against it. Moreover, after the rank and file of the army, together with the populace of Petrograd, had suppressed this revolt, it became clear that none of the guilty leaders—to say nothing of the lesser culprits—would pay with his life. . . .

Fraternization with the enemy became common—in part induced by Bolshevik or German propaganda, but often a spontaneous expression of distaste for the business of killing.

Any active measures against the enemy were bitterly opposed: when artillerymen, less infected with the mutinous spirit, opened fire on the enemy lines, thus inviting retaliation against the Russian trenches, the Russian infantry cut the telephone wires to the batteries and even beat the gunners if they persisted in firing. Violence against officers increased after the Kornilov affair. . . .

The Russian navy was an especially radical part of the armed forces. Kronstadt had become a hotbed of revolt early in the revolution and remained so, in spite of all that Kerensky could do. The naval bases at Helsingfors and Sveaborg were also radical. The crews of all the ships of the Baltic fleet were strongly behind the Bolsheviks and would have played a big role in the Kornilov affair if stubborn fighting had developed. The Black Sea fleet, on the other hand, for some time maintained its discipline under Admiral Kolchak, and in the spring of 1917 it even supported the war. But eventually it, too, succumbed to the revolutionary virus. By the middle of June the sailors began disarming their officers. Kolchak threw his sword into the sea rather than give it up and resigned his command in disgust. By October 1917 the Black Sea fleet was as radical as the Baltic fleet.

The Rising Peasant Movement. In the early days of the revolution the peasants had not taken the law into their own hands, but had apparently decided to wait for the Constituent Assembly to deal with the land problem. In the meantime, Chernov, Minister of Agriculture, took steps to prepare the basis for a future transfer of the land of the landowners to the peasants. But Chernov was forced from office with little to show for his efforts, and the Constituent Assembly was repeatedly postponed. The peasants, whose conviction remained firm that the land should go to him who tilled it, grew weary of waiting. . . .

In the autumn months of 1917 the climax was reached. More and more frequently the peasants marched in a body to the estate of the landowners, broke into the manor houses, and pillaged without mercy. If the gentry submitted without resistance, they were usually permitted to go in peace. The livestock, implements, furniture, and other useful articles, as well as the land, were divided up by the peasants, who then usually burned the manors and other buildings, to make sure that the owners would not return. Often much wanton damage was done: the leaves of fine library books were torn out for cigarette paper, and paintings by famous artists were cut from their frames to make canvas trousers. . . .

The Upsurge of the Workers. The factory workers had been, from the beginning of the revolution, the most radical element in Russia. Repeatedly, in Petrograd, the proletarians had given proof of their readiness to seek an extreme solution of their difficulties. After the frustration of the masses in the July Days, the workers had been somewhat subdued, and their units of Red Guards had been largely disarmed by the government. But their grievances had not been remedied, but rather had become more burdensome as the galloping inflation cut sharply into the buying power of their wages. Food riots grew increasingly frequent.

To make matters worse, after midsummer there were increasingly frequent closings of factories, which threw harassed men out of work. Probably, in most cases, these shutdowns were caused by such unavoidable factors as shortages of fuel or raw materials like steel, rubber, and cotton. But the desperate workers were always prone to think that the closings were lockouts intended to compel the workers to reduce their wage demands, especially as the employers were known to have expressed wrath on this score. The remark allegedly made by Riabushinsky, a great industrialist, rang from one end of Russia to the other: "Perhaps . . . we need the bony hand of hunger, the poverty of the people, which would seize by the throat all these false friends of the people, all those democratic Soviets and committees." Whether it was said or not, it was widely believed, and it infuriated the workers, who needed little to anger them . . . .

The Rising Power of the Bolsheviks. With soldiers, peasants, and workers in a militant frame of mind, the Bolsheviks found themselves in a steadily improving position. They could gain little support among the peasants, but the soldiers, both at the front and in the garrisons in the rear, were turning to them and rejecting less radical advisers. Likewise the workers, who had never believed the charges against Lenin, in the fall of 1917 almost completely gave their allegiance to the Bolsheviks. . . .

Control of the workers and the garrison troops led inevitably to control of the Soviets through their frequent elections. On September 12 the Bolsheviks obtained a majority in the Petrograd Soviet, and on October 8 it elected Trotsky as its president. The Moscow Soviet was won by the Bolsheviks on September 18, and many of the provincial Soviets were coming under their control.

The party of Lenin was strong not only in the two capitals, but also in the Volga towns, the industrial centers of the Urals, the Donets Basin, and in other industrial towns of the Ukraine. Moreover, the Bolsheviks had as allies the Left Socialist Revolutionaries, who had a considerable following in the army and among the peasants. Thus, the Bolsheviks had effective support in many important areas of Russia and no longer needed to fear that a Red Petrograd would be opposed by the rest of the country.

Lenin's Insistence on an Uprising. Lenin, still in Finland, was immensely cheered by the results of the Kornilov insurrection. In the latter part of September he wrote a letter to the Central Committee of the Bolshevik party demanding the seizure of power and reviving the slogan "All Power to the Soviets." This letter, however, was promptly rejected by the Central Committee as unrealistic. He followed this with two secret letters to the Central Committee saying that the time was ripe for seizure. His arguments, however, failed to sway the committee. . . .

Another letter, "The Crisis Is Ripe," repeated his earlier arguments that the Bolsheviks now had strong support from the masses and added a new argument: the revolution in Germany, he declared, was fast approaching and would back up the revolt in Russia. To show his sincerity and determination, Lenin offered his resignation to the Central Committee in order that he might have freedom of action. The offer was refused, but Lenin continued to oppose the decision of his party by writing to various local organizations of the Bolsheviks and to the populace to urge support for his program.

One of Lenin's most effective strokes was a pamphlet, *Can the Bolsheviks Hold State Power?* In it he strove to refute the arguments of some of the more moderate Bolsheviks who held that, even if an insurrection should prove successful, it would not be supported by the rest of the country and in the end would be drowned in a sea of blood. Lenin, however, argued that if a few hundred thousand landowners and Tsarist officials could rule Russia for centuries, the Bolsheviks, who already enjoyed the support of great masses of the people, could hold power. Especially, he stated, when the lowly and the poor began to see that the new Soviet government would suppress the rich and strip them of their wealth, which would be given to the needy poor, then "no power of the capitalists and kulaks . . . can conquer the people's revolution."

Gradually, Lenin's persistent urging won out over the doubts of his fellow Bolsheviks. On October 22 he returned to Petrograd in disguise and on the following day he spoke at a crucial meeting of the Central Committee. His passionate emphasis on the need for an uprising and his reproaches of "indifference" to this question turned the tide in his favor, albeit with difficulty. The vote was ten to two in favor of an insurrection, with Zinoviev and Kamenev opposed. The Central Committee also named a Political Bureau to carry out the preparations for the revolt. . . .

On October 29, Lenin again presented his arguments to an enlarged meeting of the Central Committee. He told the Bolsheviks that there would be either a dictatorship of the Right or the Left, and that the party should not be guided solely by the feelings of the masses, who were inclined to waver from one side to the other. He also expressed faith in the coming German revolution. Once more he won, but again Zinoviev and Kamenev voiced their doubts, which may have been shared by others present. Kamenev then resigned from the Central Committee. Two days later a letter from Zinoviev and Kamenev appeared in Maxim Gorky's *Navaia Zhizn,* announcing that the Bolsheviks were preparing an armed uprising, which the signers felt was a dangerous mistake. Lenin, infuriated, condemned their action as "strike-breaking" and "a crime." He followed this up with a letter to the Central Committee, which met without him on November 2, asking that the two be expelled from the party.

Nevertheless, an effort was made to patch the matter up. Kamenev resigned from the Central Committee, which enjoined the two members to refrain from further public opposition to the policy of the party. Lenin's demand for their expulsion from the party was not dealt with. Lenin seems to have been satisfied with the action taken, for on November 6, when the Central Committee met to prepare for the revolutionary action on the morrow, Kamenev resumed his seat as though he had never resigned. Lenin's policy was about to be applied.

The Overthrow of the Provisional Government

Bolshevik Preparations. The Bolshevik leaders, who, on October 23, had decided to undertake an armed insurrection, at first did little to prepare for it. On October 22, a proposal of the Mensheviks for the formation of a Military Revolutionary Committee to coordinate the defense of Petrograd, chiefly against the advancing Germans, offered a convenient way to organize the uprising. The Military Revolutionary Committee, as it was finally set up by the Petrograd Soviet, became a sort of general staff for the insurrection. Thanks to a boycott of the committee by the moderate socialists, the Bolsheviks completely controlled it. The Left Socialist Revolutionaries and Anarchists in the committee deferred to the Bolsheviks. Thus, the latter, headed by Trotsky, were able freely to prepare the troops of the garrison of Petrograd and of the surrounding towns, to expand and equip the Red Guards, and in other ways to get ready. . . .

The Fortress of Peter and Paul, which sprawled on the river bank across from the Winter Palace, appeared to be an obstacle to Bolshevik success. After many discussions as to how to win control of its neutral garrison, Trotsky, on November 5, casually went to the fortress and, finding a soldiers' meeting in progress, promptly addressed it. The soldiers, who were probably wavering already, needed little urging to join the insurrectionary forces. Thus, one of the government's main strongholds fell without a shot being fired. Moreover, the arsenal of Peter and Paul contained large stocks of rifles, which were promptly turned over to the Red Guards, who were among the most active forces at the disposal of the Military Revolutionary Committee. . . .

The Government Acts. Finally, in a meeting on November 5, the government decided to strike against the Bolshevik menace. The forces of junkers (military cadets) in Petrograd were to be called out to close the Bolshevik newspapers, to arrest the leading Bolsheviks, and to subdue the Military Revolutionary Committee. Reliable troops were to be brought to the capital, including junkers from the school at Oranienbaum, shock troops, and artillery. On November 6, the government forces moved. The junkers seized the printing shop where *Pravda* was published, scattered the type, and confiscated some 8,000 copies. The cruiser *Aurora,* anchored in the Neva near the Winter Palace, was ordered to put to sea for a training cruise. A Woman's Battalion of Death moved into the Winter Palace, the seat of the government, along with some junkers and a few Cossacks. Junkers seized and raised several of the main bridges and occupied important government buildings, including the main telephone and postal building. This show of force, like many of the actions of the Provisional Government, was both ineffectual and late. The reaction was immediate and strong.

The Attack on the Provisional Government. The Military Revolutionary Committee at once counterattacked. Troops were ordered to retake and guard the printing establishments, which by 11 o'clock were again in Red hands. The orders to the *Aurora* were countermanded, and it again dropped anchor. Sailors from its crew landed and helped the Red Guards seize and lower the bridges. . . .

At night the Red forces moved to attack, quickly overrunning the main railway stations and the remaining bridges. Torpedo boats from the Baltic fleet moved into the Neva to aid in the assault. On the morning of November 7, the State Bank and the main telephone station were taken, with very little bloodshed. The government now held little of the city but the Winter Palace. The vastly superior forces of the attackers and their high discipline had overwhelmed the weak and dispirited defenders. It must be said, however, that the Red forces were poorly led, as for hours they failed to make use of their opportunity to crush the defenders at once. But not even the gift of much precious time could save the government.

Kerensky's Flight. In the interim Kerensky was in the Winter Palace trying to obtain reinforcements. Several regiments of Don Cossacks promised their support, but failed to appear. When Kerensky telephoned them over a secret wire that was still functioning they repeatedly assured him that they "were getting ready to saddle the horses." But the horses were never saddled. Likewise, Kerensky's own party, the Socialist Revolutionaries, could provide him with no armed forces.

Eventually, therefore, the Premier realized that the government's position was hopeless and decided to flee Petrograd, hoping to bring back troops to retake the capital. One of his aides requisitioned a car belonging to a Secretary of the American Embassy, and thus, flying the American flag, Kerenksy escaped through the Bolshevik patrols to go for help.

The Fall of the Winter Palace. . . . The insurgents moved slowly toward the Winter Palace and, early in the evening, summoned it to surrender. Most of the military men there, realizing the hopelessness of the situation, urged acceptance, but the ministers refused to submit. They shut themselves up in the palace, defended by a small force of junkers and the Woman's Battalion of Death. Barricades of firewood were thrown up in the palace square, and the tiny force settled down for a seige. Part of the garrison had already slipped away, and the morale of those that remained was not high. . . .

For the most part the fighting consisted of rather aimless firing, while groups of men filtered in through the innumerable entrances to the palace. At first, the defenders were able to disarm the attackers, but as the latter increased in numbers they succeeded in disarming the garrison.

Finally, the last remnants of junkers sought to stand outside the inner room where the ministers were sitting, but they were quickly ordered to surrender. Antonov, the Red leader, promptly arrested the ministers and sent them off under guard to the Fortress of Peter and Paul. Passing through the infuriated crowd, they were almost lynched, but their guards succeeded in delivering them unharmed. A few days later they were put under house arrest in their homes, and before long they were given their freedom. The revolution was still relatively humane.

There was still opposition to the Bolshevik revolution in Petrograd. The moderate socialists—Mensheviks and Socialist Revolutionaries—resigned from the Congress of Soviets in protest against the overthrow of the government. After vainly trying a protest march, they withdrew to the city Duma, where, with delegates from the Council of the Republic and the old Central Executive Committee, they formed a Committee for the Salvation of the Fatherland and the Revolution. But it could do little but issue angry protests and appeal for support against the lawless action of the Bolsheviks. The new revolutionary regime held Petrograd. . . .

The Revolution in the Rest of Russia. In Moscow, in contrast to Petrograd, there was long and stubborn fighting. . . . In the rest of the country, especially in the main Russian areas, the change in power occurred more easily. Although in some places it took weeks, it was almost bloodless, as there were few to fight for the fallen government. In some of the minority areas, however, more enduring opposition regimes were set up. . . .

The attempt to use the army as a center of opposition failed. The Soviet government proceeded to establish complete control over all the command posts, so that a threat from that direction was no longer possible. Indeed, the army as an organized force was rapidly going out of existence, as a vast flood of deserters moved homeward. Only the Cossacks, the Georgians, and the [Ukrainian] *Rada* remained in defiance of the Soviet authorities. They, indeed, were too weak to be a threat, as they were menaced by attack from the sketchy Soviet military forces. The Soviet government was accepted throughout the rest of the vast territory of Russia, and no effective challenge to its power was visible anywhere in this expanse.

The First Measures of the Soviet Government

First Steps of the New Regime. On November 7, while the fighting for Petrograd was still going on, Lenin made his first public appearance before the Petrograd Soviet. To it he proclaimed in triumph the coming of "the workers' and peasants' revolution" which he had long predicted. He then sketched the immediate program of the victors: the destruction of the old governing machine and the creation of a new one, the immediate ending of the war, and the satisfying of the peasants by a decree wiping out the property rights of the nobility. Then, turning to the international scene, he hailed the movement of the workers "which is already beginning to develop in Italy, England, and Germany," and closed with the cry: "Long live the world socialist revolution!"

Secession of the Moderates. Lenin did not appear before the Second Congress of Soviets when it met that evening. As had been expected, it was predominantly Bolshevik: some 390 out of the total membership of 850 were followers of Lenin, with more than 100 of the Left Socialist Revolutionaries, who were allied with the Bolsheviks. There were not more than 80 Mensheviks, including members of the Jewish Bund, while the pro-Kerensky Socialist Revolutionaries had a mere 60 delegates. From the beginning, the moderates refused to accept the revolutionary overturn and bitterly denounced the insurrection as treason to the revolution. Representatives of the army joined the attack by terming the uprising a betrayal of the army and a crime against the people. The Mensheviks, the Socialist Revolutionaries, and the Bund followed these utterances by walking out of the Congress in protest against the revolt, whose cannon could be heard in the distance. . . .

Lenin's Proposals. Lenin, who had spent the night resting beside Trotsky, appeared before the Congress of the Soviets on November 8. After several preliminary speeches, Lenin rose to receive a loud ovation. He then read a "proclamation to the peoples and the governments of all the fighting nations." It contained a pledge to abolish secret diplomacy and to punish immediately the secret treaties with the Allies, as well as a renunciation of the special privileges granted to Russia. The proclamation went on to propose an armistice lasting three months, and appealed to the working people of England, France, and Germany to take "decisive, energetic, and persistent action" to bring about a successful peace and at the same time to achieve the liberation of the masses of exploited working people "from all slavery and exploitation." After a brief discussion the proposal was adopted with vast enthusiasm: one delegate who ventured to vote against it felt it safer to drop his opposition. The Congress then sang the "*Internationale,*" the anthem of international revolutionary socialism.

The next point on the agenda was land for the peasants. A short decree proposed by Lenin abolished private landholding at once and without compensation. Private, state, crown, and church lands were to be turned over to land committees and Soviets of Peasants' Deputies for distribution to the peasants. The rules for the distribution of the land were set forth in an Instruction appended to the decree. The Instruction, which Lenin had obtained from a compilation of peasant resolutions prepared by the Soviet of Peasants' Deputies, provided for a complete ban on private ownership of land, prohibition of the buying and selling of land, and for the use of the land solely by persons who would work it with their own and their families' labor. This measure, which would promote a mass of small peasant farms, was contrary to accepted Marxist views. Hence, there was some objection to it from Bolshevik members of the Congress. Lenin, however, frankly stated that this was a Socialist Revolutionary proposal which he felt it necessary to adopt in order to win the support of the peasant masses. On this basis, the Congress approved it.

The Formation of the Soviet Government. While the above measures were readily approved, it proved more difficult to form the revolutionary government. In spite of the secession of the moderate socialists and their opposition to the revolutionary overturn, the Left Socialist Revolutionaries and the Menshevik Internationalists were extremely eager to have a coalition of all socialist parties instead of a purely Leftist government. Likewise *Vikzhel,* the railway workers' union, insisted on a coalition, threatening to stop all rail traffic unless agreement were reached. The demand for an all-socialist government was also warmly endorsed by many of the Bolsheviks. Consequently, in spite of the scorn of Lenin and Trotsky for the moderates, it was necessary to try to form a coalition. But while this was being attempted a government was needed, and so an all-Bolshevik cabinet was set up. Several posts were offered to the Left Socialist Revolutionaries, but they refused to enter the government. So the Council of People's Commissars was approved, with Lenin as President, Trotsky as Commissar for Foreign Affairs, and Rykov as Commissar for Internal Affairs. Most of the other appointees were men who were not well known; among them was Joseph Stalin, Commissar for Nationalities.

A Coalition Government? The possibilities of a coalition regime were explored at length at a conference that met on November 11, 1917. The negotiations lasted for some time, but because of the stiff demands of the moderate socialists they produced no result. At first the socialists insisted that the Military Revolutionary Committee be dissolved and that Lenin and Trotsky be excluded from the government. Later, after the Bolsheviks had consolidated their power in both Moscow and Petrograd, there was less pressure for a coalition and Lenin was able to overcome the moderate Bolsheviks. Nevertheless, on November 17 five of the Bolsheviks of the Central Committee—among them Zinoviev, Kamenev, and Rykov—resigned in protest against the rejection of a coalition. There were also resignations from the cabinet over the same issue.

Lenin was not dismayed by this revolt within his party. He answered it with a furious manifesto from the Central Committee upholding his course and terming the dissenters "waverers and doubters." Such men counted for little, he said, when the Soviet government was supported by "millions of workers in the towns, soldiers in the trenches, peasants in the villages, ready to achieve at any cost the victory of peace and the victory of socialism." This ended the revolt.

Nonetheless, in November the Bolsheviks reached an understanding with the Left Socialist Revolutionaries, and 108 delegates from the Peasant Congress were added to the Soviet Executive Committee. On December 22 the Left Socialist Revolutionaries accepted three posts in the Council of People's Commissars. Thus, a coalition of a sort was finally established, although not so broad in its makeup as the one that had been demanded.

Miscellaneous Actions of the Soviet Government. From the first days of its existence, the new government wrestled with a whole series of problems and wrote a remarkable record of achievements—many of which, it must be said, existed only on paper. Almost immediately there was a sweeping strike of government workers, who refused to recognize the new order. For a regime without a shred of experience in governing, this proved most difficult, especially as the State Bank was among the striking institutions. For days the government could obtain no funds, and only the use of force and the opening of the vaults made money available to the Bolshevik rulers of Russia. On December 27, all banks were nationalized and occupied by forces of troops, while the vaults and safe deposit boxes were opened by a commissar. Eventually, the funds of the striking civil servants ran out and they returned to duty in January 1918.

Economic Measures. During the first few months decrees flowed forth in a rapid stream. One of the first was a decree directed to the working people, informing them that economic power had been transferred to them. The nationalization of banks was next, followed by a ban on dividends and securities. On February 10, 1918 a decree annulled all debts of the Russian government, including foreign debts. Contrary to Bolshevik doctrine, Lenin was in no hurry to nationalize industry and even wanted the managerial personnel to continue to work on fairly generous terms. Nevertheless, "workers' control" meant supervision and much outright interference by the workers, so that the conditions in the factories became chaotic. When this led to the shutting down of enterprises, the Supreme Economic Council, created on December 15, had the power to nationalize them.

There was a general levelling down of the standard of living—in part by the ever-rising inflation, and in part by decree: members of the Council of Commissars were restricted to 500 rubles per month, with allowances for dependents, and to one room for each member of the family. The ending of private ownership of multiple dwellings was another levelling measure. The city Soviets took them over and sought to equalize the housing facilities, often moving families from the slums into the half-empty apartments of wealthy citizens. The food situation proved to be the most insoluble problem. Try as they would, the Soviet authorities could not obtain more bread for the cities, and the amounts issued on rations fell drastically. To the hungry workers there was left only the consolation that the hated "bourgeois" were faring even worse than they.

Political and Social Legislation. Important political and social decrees were also issued during the first months. To cope with secret enemies of the regime, drunken mobs that invaded mansions in search of liquor, and food speculators, on December 20 Felix Dzerzhinsky, a fanatical Polish Communist, became head of the All-Russian Extraordinary Commission, whose name, abbreviated to *Cheka,* became dreaded throughout Russia. A system of revolutionary tribunals was set up to deal with political cases, while new, informal "people's courts" dispensed ordinary justice by common sense rather than law books. The Soviet legislators also found time to reform the Russian alphabet and the calendar. Sweeping new laws made marriage and divorce equally easy to obtain and legalized all children, whether born of registered or informal unions. The full legal equality of men and women was also proclaimed.

The Church and the Revolution. . . . Many of the measures of the new regime angered the churchmen, who hoped ardently for its overthrow, and on February 1, 1918, the Patriarch issued a pastoral letter to the people. It strongly indicted the Soviet leaders for having caused violence and outrages. "Your acts are not merely cruel, they are the works of Satan, for which you will burn in hell fire in the life hereafter. . . ." To this he added his anathema. To the believers, he issued a call to organize in defense of the church, for "the gates of Hell shall not prevail against it."

This, however, did not deter the Soviet authorities, who on February 5, 1918, published a law by which "the church was separated from the state, and the school from the church." Religion was made a private matter for the citizens, and no religious functions or ceremonies were permitted in any institution of government, whether national or local. Religious teaching was barred from all schools, public and private alike. Even the theological schools were ordered closed. The property of churches and religious societies was nationalized, although church buildings might be turned over to congregations of believers for free use for public worship.

This measure was strongly opposed by the leaders of the Orthodox church, but in spite of their angry protests, the government put it into effect. There were some demonstrations in opposition to it, and occasional riots, at times accompanied by bloodshed. But the government persisted in its purpose. Perhaps the fact that the churches remained open and no attempt was made to prevent divine worship explains why this legislation, which was unfavorable to the Russian church, did not produce any effective explosions of popular wrath.

The Problem of the Constituent Assembly. One of the worst dilemmas for the Bolsheviks was caused by the Constituent Assembly. The Provisional Government had promised to convene this body speedily, but nothing was done about it for months. Finally, the government set November 25 as the date for the elections. Thus, when the Bolsheviks took power they were in a quandary. Before they had seized power, one of their effective slogans had been for "Speedy Convocation of the Constituent Assembly!" But, while they were on record as wanting it to meet soon, Lenin and the other Bolsheviks had reason to believe that vast numbers of peasants as usual would vote for the Socialist Revolutionaries. It seemed likely that the new Soviet government would be challenged by a body in which the Bolsheviks would be only a minority. Lenin firmly held that the Soviets, which excluded the propertied classes, were a higher form of democracy than a body elected by universal suffrage. His solution was to postpone the elections, but it was decided to hold them and to convene the Assembly, which should, however, be dissolved if it proved troublesome.

The Result of the Elections. Although the Bolsheviks made no effort to dominate the elections, which began on November 25, the Cadet party was especially handicapped by the fact that many of their leaders were in hiding or in prison, and their newspapers were largely suppressed. The voting gave the Bolsheviks only 175 of the 707 elected members of the Constituent Assembly. The SRs (Socialist Revolutionaries) had 410—a substantial majority—and most of the other delegates were anti-Bolshevik. Yet the figures do not tell the whole story. The Bolsheviks were now in alliance with the Left SR's who had had a majority of the Peasant Congress. Although the Left SR's had only 40 out of the 410 SR delegates, it seems probable that their following in the country was far stronger than their representation in the Constituent Assembly.

Above all, the realities of power favored the Bolsheviks. They had full majorities in Petrograd and Moscow and their strength was great in other industrial centers. Their government had the positions of power in the cities and in the army, while the opposition's strength lay chiefly in the unorganized millions of peasants. Moreover, the Bolsheviks were united and determined, with a clearcut program which seemed to meet the needs of the people. The opposition was unorganized and lacked driving force. Also, it was unable to offer an alternative to the program that the Bolsheviks were already carrying out.

The Attitude of the Bolsheviks. The Bolsheviks, realizing that the Constituent Assembly would become the focal center for all anti-Bolshevik elements whether socialist or upper class, were determined not to permit it to play the counterrevolutionary role that the French National Assembly had played in 1848. On December 11, 1917 the Soviet government forcibly prevented an attempt of former ministers of the Provisional Government to convene the Assembly ahead of time. Shortly thereafter, Lenin wrote his "Theses on the

Constituent Assembly,'' published in *Pravda* on December 26, 1917. He stated that a Constituent Assembly had been highly desirable after the fall of the Tsar, when the revolution was still in its moderate or ''bourgeois'' stage. Now, however, the revolution was in its socialist stage, with the Bolsheviks establishing the dictatorship of the proletariat and its allies, the poorer peasantry. As for the bourgeoisie, they were in open counterrevolution. Hence, any attempt to treat the Constituent Assembly from a purely theoretical, legalistic point of view was treason to the proletariat. Either the Assembly would declare its acceptance of the Soviet government and its program, or else the crisis that would result ''can be solved only by revolutionary means.''

In order to cut the ground from beneath the feet of the Constituent Assembly, it was decided to have the Third Congress of Soviets meet three days after the opening of the Assembly, and the Congress of Peasant Deputies a few days later. On January 16 the Central Executive Committee drafted a Declaration of Rights of the Toiling and Exploited People, for adoption by the Assembly. It opened with a declaration that Russia was a republic of Soviets, to which all power belonged, and a statement that it was a ''free union of free nations, as a federation of national Soviet republics.'' There followed a long pronouncement for the Constituent Assembly to make, upholding Soviet policy and legislation. Finally, two paragraphs stated that, as the Constituent Assembly had been elected on the basis of party lists compiled before the changed situation after the fall of the Provisional Government, ''it would be basically incorrect to set itself up against the Soviet power. . . .'' Furthermore, the Assembly, supporting the Soviet regime, would recognize that its role was merely to be ''the general working out of the fundamental principles of the socialist reconstruction of society.''

The Dissolution of the Constituent Assembly. Lenin and his followers, then, had already made up their minds to deal rigorously with the Constituent Assembly unless it proved to be tame and toothless. Nevertheless, realizing that this body, advocated for decades by Russian liberals and revolutionaries, might enjoy immense prestige in the eyes of the populace, they did not want to shock public opinion by unnecessarily brutal treatment of it. It was permitted to meet, but the vicinity of the Tavrida Palace was surrounded by heavily armed troops, and the galleries were crowded with soldiers and sailors with rifles, pistols, and cartridge belts. For their part, the SR's had sought the support of some regiments, but as they refused to let them come out under arms, even those soldiers who sympathized with the moderates refused their appeal. A demonstration of civilian sympathizers with the Assembly—largely intellectuals and other white-collar workers—occurred, but it met the well-armed troops and was dispersed by gunfire, with some loss of life.

When the meeting opened, Sverdlov, a veteran Bolshevik, seized temporary control in order to read the Declaration of the Rights of the Toiling and Exploited People. After briefly urging the Assembly to adopt it, he withdrew to his seat. The big bloc of SR's now took over, electing Chernov as permanent chairman, in spite of Bolshevik warnings that they should support the program of active socialism. The session dragged on for almost twelve hours. At midnight the crucial vote was taken on the Bolshevik declaration, which lost, 237 to 138. Later, the Bolsheviks withdrew from the meeting, because of its ''counterrevolutionary majority.'' The Left SR's withdrew an hour later. Not long before daybreak the sailor in command of the guard, apparently under orders from Lenin, asked that the meeting adjourn ''because the guard is tired.'' There was a brief flurry of activity, during which a resolution on land and an appeal to the Allies for peace were read and declared approved. Neither of these differed greatly from the measures taken by the

Second Congress of Soviets after the fall of the Kerensky government. Then, a little before five in the morning, the meeting adjourned until late afternoon.

The Constituent Assembly never met again. The Central Executive Committee, after a strong speech by Lenin, declared that it was dissolved, and an armed guard at the doors prevented it from reconvening. There was scarcely any protest against the dissolution: The Constituent Assembly had given no heroic leadership to the people and had failed to gain effective support. Probably if it had been convened six months before, the result would have been far different.

Chapter 4

THE CRUSHING OF OPPOSITION

In the months following the Bolshevik Revolution, its leaders anticipated that the revolt in Russia would unleash a socialist revolution in the West. Pending this anticipated revolution, Lenin insisted that the government come to terms with the Germans. After some serious indecision and wrangling in the Party—which touched off a German military attack—Lenin finally won out and the Treaty of Brest-Litovsk was signed on March 3, 1918. Under this treaty, Russia lost more than 1¼ million square miles of territory containing a population of 62 million, half of her industrial plants, and a third of her best farm area. Three days later, Lenin stated:

> The revolution will not come as quickly as we expected. History has proved this, and we must be able to take this as a fact, we must be able to reckon with the fact that the world Socialist revolution cannot begin so easily in the advanced countries as the revolution began in Russia—the land of Nicholas and Rasputin, the land in which the overwhelming majority of the population was quite indifferent to the conditions of life of the people in the outlying regions. In such a country it was quite easy to start a revolution, as easy as lifting a feather.

Thereafter, however, Lenin alternated between optimism and pessimism on the prospects of revolution in the West.

The peace of Brest-Litovsk set off a chain of developments that almost encompassed the destruction of Bolshevik power. During the next few years the Soviets were engaged in civil war with forces ranging from the monarchist-restorationists at the extreme right to the left Socialist Revolutionaries. Many of these forces had the support—financial and otherwise—of Allied powers. And some of these powers, including Japan, Great Britain, France, and the United States sent military forces into Russia. The justification was the necessity of reestablishing an Eastern front in the desperate war against Germany, but the record is clear that other considerations—territorial spoils, fear of revolution, or detestation of the Bolsheviks—also played a part. Of course, the effort to destroy the Bolshevik regime was never massive and coordinated, and the Americans, particularly, did much to balk annexationist ambitions. The consequences, however, were to leave a residue of great bitterness in the USSR against the interventionist powers and create an encirclement psychosis which, whatever its uses for propaganda purposes, was also grounded in history.

During the period of civil war and intervention—which endured into 1922—the Bolsheviks outlawed all opposition parties (socialist as well as nonsocialist) and imposed a ban on factions within the Communist Party itself. Why? Marxist theory had not suggested that the dictatorship of the proletariat might be equated with the rule of one socialist party. And, according to Lenin, the dictatorship of the proletariat was to bring with it "a widening of the practical utilization of democracy by those oppressed by capitalism, by the laboring classes, as has never yet been seen in the whole world."

Many explanations have been offered for the failure of proletarian "democracy." One explanation placing responsibility on the internal and external foes of Bolshevism maintains that "Soviet 'totalitarianism' was not inevitable nor necessarily implicit in the Bolshevism of 1917–18 but was forced upon it, with death as the alternative, by the decisions of Russian democrats and the Western Democracies." Another, proffered by W.W. Rostow, suggests that "the maintenance of the internal power machine has had a clear priority over any other goal of Soviet policy." Still another may be inferred from Merle Fainsod's *Bolshevism before 1917*, in which he holds that "the early organizational history of Bolshevism . . . implanted the germinating conception of the monolithic and totalitarian party."

The democratic failure has been explained, additionally, for example, by the weakness and backwardness of the Russian economy and proletariat, and the basic incompatibility between large-scale economic planning and any form of democracy. In this latter vein, R.N. Carew Hunt wrote: "What Lenin early came to see was that a nationwide planned economy was incompatible with the parliamentary democracy of the West. If production is to be planned, some body of persons must do the planning, and this becomes impossible if the plan is liable to be reversed at any moment by a vote in a popular assembly." And, finally, there are the distinctive contributions made to this discussion in the following excerpts from the writings of Isaac Deutscher and Leonard Schapiro.

Varied explanations of the disparity between Marxist theory and Soviet practice have been alluded to in the hope that they will induce an appreciation of the complexities of judgment involved and encourage the reader to explore the problem further. It may be suggested, too, that important implications extending beyond the USSR may ensue from the acceptance of one or another explanation.

Defeat in Victory

Isaac Deutscher

The years of world war, revolution, civil war, and intervention had resulted in the utter ruin of Russia's economy and the disintegration of her social fabric. From a ruined economy the Bolsheviks had had to wrest the means of civil war. In 1919, the Red Army had already used up all stocks of munitions and other supplies. The industries under Soviet control could not replace them by more than a fraction. Normally, southern Russia supplied fuel, iron, steel, and raw materials to the industries of central and northern Russia. But southern Russia, occupied first by the Germans and then by Denikin, was only intermittently and during brief spells under Soviet control. When at last, at the end of 1919, the Bolsheviks returned there for good, they found that the coal mines of the Donets valley were flooded and the other industries destroyed. Deprived of fuel and raw materials, the industrial centres of the rest of the country were paralysed. Even towards the end of 1920, the coal mines produced less than one-tenth and the iron- and steelworks less than one-twentieth of their prewar output. The production of consumer goods was about one-quarter of normal.

The disaster was made even worse by the destruction of transport. All over the country railway tracks and bridges had been blown up. Rolling stock had not been renewed, and it had only rarely been kept in proper repair since 1914. Inexorably, transport was coming to a standstill. (This, incidentally, was one of the contributory causes of the Red Army's defeat in Poland. The Soviets had enlisted five million men, but of these less than 300,000 were actually engaged in the last stages of the Polish campaign. As the armies rolled onward, the railways were less and less capable of carrying reinforcements and supplies over the lengthening distances.) Farming, too, was ruined. For six years the peasants had not been able to renew their equipment. Retreating and advancing armies trampled their fields and requisitioned their horses. However, because of its technically primitive character, farming was more resilient than industry. The *muzhik* worked with the wooden *sokha,* which he was able to make or repair by himself.

The Bolsheviks strove to exercise the strictest control over scarce resources; and out of this striving grew their War Communism. They nationalized all industry. They prohibited private trade. They dispatched workers' detachments to the countryside to requisition food for the army and the town-dwellers. The government was incapable of collecting normal taxes; it possessed no machinery for doing so. To cover government expenses, the printing presses produced banknotes day and night. Money became so worthless that wages and salaries had to be paid in kind. The meagre food ration formed the basic wage. The worker was also paid with part of his own produce, a pair of shoes or a few pieces of clothing, which he usually bartered away for food.

Isaac Deutscher was the author of Stalin: A Political Biography; Soviet Trade Unions; *and* Russia in Transition. *This selection is from chapter 14 of* The Prophet Armed *(New York: Oxford University Press, Inc., 1954). Reprinted by permission of the publisher.*

This set of desperate shifts and expedients looked to the party like an unexpectedly rapid realization of its own programme. Socialization of industry would have been carried out more slowly and cautiously if there had been no civil war; but it was, in any case, one of the major purposes of the revolution. The requisitioning of food, the prohibition of private trade, the payment of wages in kind, the insignificance of money, the government's aspiration to control the economic resources of the nation, all this looked, superficially, like the abolition of that market economy which was the breeding ground of capitalism. The fully grown Communist economy about which Marxist textbooks had speculated, was to have been a natural economy, in which socially planned production and distribution should take the place of production for the market and of distribution through the medium of money. The Bolshevik was therefore inclined to see the essential features of full-fledged communism embodied in the war economy of 1919–20. He was confirmed in this inclination by the stern egalitarianism which his party preached and practised and which gave to war communism a romantic and heroic aspect.

In truth, war communism was a tragic travesty of the Marxist vision of the society of the future. That society was to have as its background highly developed and organized productive resources and a superabundance of goods and services. It was to organize and develop the social wealth which capitalism at its best produced only fitfully and could not rationally control, distribute, and promote. Communism was to abolish economic inequality once and for all by levelling up the standards of living. War communism had, on the contrary, resulted from social disintegration, from the destruction and disorganization of productive resources, from an unparalleled scarcity of goods and services. It did indeed try to abolish inequality; but of necessity it did so by levelling down the standards of living and making poverty universal.[1]

The system could not work for long. The requisitioning of food and the prohibition of private trade for the time being helped the government to tide over the direct emergencies. But in the longer run, these policies aggravated and accelerated the shrinkage and disintegration of the economy. The peasant began to till only as much of his land as was necessary to keep his family alive. He refused to produce the surplus for which the requisitioning squads were on the lookout. When the countryside refuses to produce food for the town, even the rudiments of urban civilization go to pieces. The cities of Russia became depopulated. Workers went to the countryside to escape famine. Those who stayed behind fainted at the factory benches, produced very little, and often stole what they produced to barter it for food. The old, normal market had indeed been abolished. But its bastard, the black market, despoiled the country, revengefully perverting and degrading human relations. This could go on for another year or so; but inevitably the end would be the breakdown of all government and the dissolution of society. . . .

Matters came to a head on 12 January 1920, when Lenin and Trotsky appeared before the Bolshevik leaders of the trade unions and urged them to accept militarization. Trotsky defended his own record. If his Commissariat, he said, had "pillaged" the country and exacted severe discipline, it had done so to win the war. It was a disgrace and a "sin against the spirit of the revolution" that this should now be held against him, and that the working class should be incited against the army. His opponents were complacent about the country's economic condition. The newspapers concealed the real state of affairs. "It is necessary to state openly and frankly in the hearing of the whole country, that our economic condition is a hundred times worse than our military situation ever was. . . . Just as we once issued the order 'Proletarians, to horse!', so now we must raise the cry

'Proletarians, back to the factory bench! Proletarians, back to production!.' '' The nation's labour force continued to shrink and degenerate. It could not be saved, reconstituted, and rehabilitated without the application of coercive measures. Lenin spoke in the same vein. Yet the conference almost unanimously rejected the resolution which he and Trotsky jointly submitted. Of more than three-score Bolshevik leaders, only two men voted for it. Never before had Trotsky or Lenin met with so striking a rebuff.

Trotsky's strictures on the complacency of his critics were not unjustified. The critics did not and could not propose any practical alternative. They, too, clung to war communism and disavowed only the conclusion Trotsky had drawn from it. He had little difficulty therefore in exposing their inconsistency. Yet there was a certain realism and valuable scruple in their very lack of consistency. Trotsky's opponents refused to believe that the wheels of the economy could be set in motion by word of military command, and they were convinced that it was wrong for a workers' state to act as a press gang towards its own working class. . . . They argued that compulsory labour was inefficient. ''You cannot build a planned economy,'' exclaimed Abramovich, the Menshevik, ''in the way the Pharaohs built their pyramids.'' Abramovich thus coined the phrase, which years later Trotsky was to repeat against Stalin. . . .

For a time the Polish war blunted the edge of this controversy. Peril from without once again induced people to accept without murmur policies which, before, had aroused their intense resentment. At the height of the war, Trotsky, surrounded by a team of technicians, made a determined effort to set the railways in motion. By this time the stock of locomotives had been almost entirely wasted. Engineers forecast the exact date—only a few months ahead—when not a single railway in Russia would be working. Trotsky placed the railway men and the personnel of the repair workshops under martial law; and he organized systematic and rapid rehabilitation of the rolling stock. He went into the repair workshops to tell the workers that the country was paying for their slackness in blood: the paralysis of transport had encouraged the Poles to attack. ''The situation of the worker,'' he declared, ''is grievous in every respect . . . it is worse than ever. I would deceive you if I were to say that it will be better tomorrow. No, ahead of us are months of heavy struggle until we can lift our country out of this terrible misery and utter exhaustion, until we can stop weighing our bread ration on the chemist's scales.'' When the railwaymen's trade union raised objections to his action, he dismissed its leaders and appointed others who were willing to do his bidding. He repeated this procedure in unions of other transport workers. Early in September he formed the *Tsektran,* the Central Transport Commission, through which he brought the whole field of transport under his control. The Politbureau backed him to the hilt as it had promised. To observe electoral rights and voting procedures in the unions seemed at that moment as irrelevant as it might seem in a city stricken with pestilence. He produced results and surpassed expectations: the railways were rehabilitated well ahead of schedule—''the blood circulation of the economic organism was revived''—and he was acclaimed for the feat.

But no sooner had the Polish war been concluded than the grievances and dissensions exploded anew and with greater force than before. He himself provoked the explosion. Flushed with success, he threatened to ''shake up'' various trade unions as he had ''shaken up'' those of the transport workers. He threatened, that is, to dismiss the elected leaders of the unions and to replace them by nominees who would place the nation's economic interest above the sectional interests of the workers. He grossly overstepped the mark. Lenin now bluntly dissociated himself from Trotsky and persuaded the Central

Committe to do likewise. The Committee openly called the party to resist energetically "militarized and bureaucratic forms of work" and it castigated that "degenerated centralism" which rode roughshod over the workers' elected representatives. It called on the party to reestablish proletarian democracy in the trade unions and to subordinate all other considerations to this task. A special commission was formed to watch that these decisions were carried out. Zinoviev presided over it, and, although Trotsky sat on it, nearly all its members were his opponents. . . .

The deeper ill which afflicted the whole system of government, and of which this tug-of-war was merely a symptom, lay in the frustration of the popular hopes aroused by the revolution. For the first time since 1917, the bulk of the working class, not to speak of the peasantry, unmistakably turned against the Bolsheviks. A sense of isolation began to haunt the ruling group. To be sure, the working class had not come to regret the revolution. It went on to identify itself with it; and it received with intense hostility any openly counterrevolutionary agitation. "October" had so deeply sunk into the popular mind that Mensheviks and Social Revolutionaries now had to preface their criticisms of the government with an explicit acceptance of the "achievements of October." Yet the opposition to current Bolshevik policies was just as intense and widespread. The Mensheviks and Social Revolutionaries, who in the course of three years had been completely eclipsed and had hardly dared to raise their heads, were now regaining some popular favour. People listened even more sympathetically to anarchist agitators violently denouncing the Bolshevik regime. If the Bolsheviks had now permitted free elections to the Soviets, they would almost certainly have been swept from power.[2]

The Bolsheviks were firmly resolved not to let things come to that pass. It would be wrong to maintain that they clung to power for its own sake. The party as a whole was still animated by that revolutionary idealism of which it had given such abundant proof in its underground struggle and in the civil war. It clung to power because it identified the fate of the republic with its own fate and saw in itself the only force capable of safeguarding the revolution. It was lucky for the revolution—and it was also its misfortune—that in this belief the Bolsheviks were profoundly justified. The revolution would hardly have survived without a party as fanatically devoted to it as the Bolsheviks were. But had there existed another party equally devoted and equally vigorous in action, that party might, in consequence of an election, have displaced Lenin's government without convulsing the young state. No such party existed. The return of Mensheviks and Social Revolutionaries would have entailed the undoing of the October Revolution. At the very least it would have encouraged the White Guards to try their luck once again and rise in arms. From sheer self-preservation as well as from broader motives, the Bolsheviks could not even contemplate such a prospect. They could not accept it as a requirement of democracy that they should, by retreating, plunge the country into a new series of civil wars just after one series had been concluded.

Nor was it by any means likely that a free election to the Soviets would return any clear-cut majority. Those who had supported Kerensky in 1917 had not really recovered from their eclipse. Anarchists and anarchosyndicalists, preaching a "Third Revolution," seemed far more popular among the working class. But they gave no effective focus to the opposition; and they were in no sense pretenders to office. Strong in criticism, they possessed no positive political programme, no serious organization, national or even local, no real desire to rule a vast country. In their ranks honest revolutionaries, cranks, and plain bandits rubbed shoulders. The Bolshevik regime could be succeeded only by utter confusion followed by open counterrevolution. Lenin's party refused to allow the famished and emotionally unhinged country to vote their party out of power and itself into a bloody chaos.

For this strange sequel to their victory, the Bolsheviks were mentally quite unprepared. They had always tacitly assumed that the majority of the working class, having backed them in the revolution, would go on to support them unswervingly until they carried out the full programme of socialism. Naive as the assumption was, it sprang from the notion that socialism was the proletarian idea *par excellence* and that the proletariat, having once adhered to it, would not abandon it. That notion had underlain the reasoning of all European schools of Socialist thought. In the vast political literature produced by those schools, the question of what Socialists in office should do if they lost the confidence of the workers had hardly ever been pondered.

It had never occurred to Marxists to reflect whether it was possible or admissible to try to establish socialism regardless of the will of the working class. They simply took that will for granted. For the same reason it had seemed to the Bolsheviks as clear as daylight that the proletarian dictatorship and proletarian (or Soviet) democracy were only two complementary and inseparable aspects of the same thing; the dictatorship was there to suppress the resistance of the propertied classes; and it derived its strength and historic legitimacy from the freely and democratically expressed opinion of the working classes. Now a conflict arose between the two aspects of the Soviet system. If the working classes were to be allowed to speak and vote freely they would destroy the dictatorship. If the dictatorship, on the other hand, frankly abolished proletarian democracy it would deprive itself of historic legitimacy, even in its own eyes. It would cease to be a proletarian dictatorship in the strict sense. Its use of that title would henceforth be based on the claim that it pursued a policy with which the working class, in its own interest, ought and eventually must identify itself, but with which it did not as yet identify itself. The dictatorship would then at best represent the idea of the class, not the class itself.

The revolution had now reached that crossroads, well known to Machiavelli, at which it found it difficult or impossible to fix the people in their revolutionary persuasion and was driven "to take such measures that, when they believed no longer, it might be possible to make them believe by force." For the Bolshevik party this involved a conflict of loyalties, which was in some respects deeper than any it had known so far, a conflict bearing the seeds of all the turbulent controversies and somber purges of the next decades.

At this crossroads Bolshevism suffered a moral agony the like of which is hardly to be found in the history of less intense and impassioned movements. Later Lenin recalled the "fever" and "mortal illness" which consumed the party in the winter of 1920–1, during the tumultuous debate over the place of the trade unions in the state. This was an important yet only a secondary matter. It could not be settled before an answer had been given to the fundamental question concerning the very nature of the state. The party was wholly absorbed in the controversy over the secondary issue, because it was not altogether clearly aware of the primary question and was afraid to formulate it frankly in its own mind. But as the protagonists went on arguing they struck the great underlying issue again and again, and were compelled to define their attitudes.

It is not necessary here to go into the involved and somewhat technical differences over the trade unions, although the fact that the drama of the revolution revealed itself in a seemingly dry economic argument significantly corresponded to the spirit of the age.[3] Suffice it to say that, broadly speaking, three attitudes crystallized. The faction led by

Trotsky (and later by Trotsky and Bukharin) wanted the trade unions to be deprived of their autonomy and absorbed into the machinery of government. This was the final conclusion which Trotsky drew from his conflicts with the trade unions. Under the new dispensation, the leaders of the unions would, as servants of the state, speak for the state to the workers rather than for the workers to the state. They would raise the productivity and maintain the discipline of labour; they would train workers for industrial management; and they would participate in the direction of the country's economy.

At the other extreme the Workers' Opposition, led by Shlyapnikov and Kollontai, protested against the government's and the party's tutelage over the unions. They denounced Trotsky and Lenin as militarizers of labour and promoters of inequality. In quasi-syndicalist fashion they demanded that trade unions, factory committees, and a National Producers' Congress should assume control over the entire economy. While Trotsky argued that the trade unions could not in logic defend the workers against the workers' state, Shlyapnikov and Kollontai already branded the Soviet state as the rampart of a new privileged bureaucracy.

Between these two extremes, Lenin, Zinoviev, and Kamenev spoke for the main body of Bolshevik opinion and tried to strike a balance. They, too, insisted that it was the duty of the trade unions to restrain the workers and to cultivate in them a sense of responsibility for the state and the nationalized economy. They emphasized the party's right to control the unions. But they also wished to preserve them as autonomous, mass organizations, capable of exerting pressure on government and industrial management.

Implied in these attitudes were different conceptions of state and society. The Workers' Opposition and the so-called *Decemists* (the Group of Democratic Centralism) were the stalwart defenders of "proletarian democracy" *vis-à-vis* the dictatorship. They were the first Bolshevik dissenters to protest against the method of government designed "to make the people believe by force." They implored the party to "trust its fate" to the working class which had raised it to power. They spoke the language which the whole party had spoken in 1917. They were the real Levellers of this revolution, its high-minded, Utopian dreamers. The party could not listen to them if it was not prepared to commit noble yet unpardonable suicide. It could not trust its own and the republic's fate to a working class whittled down, exhausted, and demoralized by civil war, famine, and the black market. The quixotic spirit of the Workers' Opposition was apparent in its economic demands. The Opposition clamoured for the immediate satisfaction of the workers' needs, for equal wages and rewards for all, for the supply, without payment, of food, clothing, and lodging to workers, for free medical attention, free travelling facilities, and free education. They wanted to see fulfilled nothing less than the programme of full communism, which was theoretically designed for an economy of great plenty. They did not even try to say how the government of the day could meet their demands. They urged the party to place industry, or what was left of it, once again under the control of those factory committees which had shown soon after the October Revolution that they could merely dissipate and squander the nation's wealth. It was a sad omen that the people enveloped in such fumes of fancy were almost the only ones to advocate a full revival of proletarian democracy.

Against them, Trotsky prompted the party to cease for the time being the advocacy and practice of proletarian democracy and instead to concentrate on building up a Producer's Democracy. The party, to put it more plainly, was to deny the workers their political rights and compensate them by giving them scope and managerial responsibility in economic reconstruction. At the tenth congress (March 1921), when this controversy reached its culmination, Trotsky argued:

> The Workers' Opposition has come out with dangerous slogans. They have made a fetish of democratic principles. They have placed the workers' right to elect representatives above the party, as it were, as if the party were not entitled to assert its dictatorship even if that dictatorship temporarily clashed with the passing moods of the workers' democracy. . . . It is necessary to create among us the awareness of the revolutionary historical birthright of the party. The party is obliged to maintain its dictatorship, regardless of temporary wavering in the spontaneous moods of the masses, regardless of the temporary vacillations even in the working class. This awareness is for us the indispensable unifying element. The dictatorship does not base itself at every given moment on the formal principle of a workers' democracy, although the workers' democracy is, of course, the only method by which the masses can be drawn more and more into political life.

The days had long passed when Trotsky argued that the Soviet system of government was superior to bourgeois parliamentarianism because under it the electors enjoyed, among other things, the right to reelect their representatives at any time and not merely at regular intervals; and that this enabled the Soviets to reflect any change in the popular mood closely and instantaneously, as no parliament was able to do. His general profession of faith in proletarian democracy now sounded like mere saving clauses. What was essential was "the historical birthright of the party" and the party's awareness of it as the "indispensable unifying element." Euphemistically yet eloquently enough he now extolled the collective solidarity of the ruling group in the face of a hostile or apathetic nation.

Lenin refused to proclaim the divorce between the dictatorship and proletarian democracy. He, too, was aware that government and party were in conflict with the people; but he was afraid that Trotsky's policy would perpetuate the conflict. The party had had to override trade unions, to dismiss their recalcitrant leaders, to break or obviate popular resistance, and to prevent the free formation of opinion inside the Soviets. Only thus, Lenin held, could the revolution be saved. But he hoped that these practices would give his government a breathing space—his whole policy had become a single struggle for breathing spaces—during which it might modify its policies, make headway with the rehabilitation of the country, ease the plight of the working people, and win them back for Bolshevism. The dictatorship could then gradually revert to proletarian democracy. If this was the aim, as Trotsky agreed, then the party must reassert the idea of that democracy at once and initiate no sweeping measures suggesting its abandonment. Even though the regime had so often resorted to coercion, Lenin pleaded, coercion must be its last and persuasion its first resort.

The trade unions ought, therefore, not to be turned into appendages of the state. They must retain a measure of autonomy; they must speak for the workers, if need be, against the government; and they ought to become the schools, not the drill-halls, of communism. The administrator—and it was from his angle that Trotsky viewed the problem—might be annoyed and inconvenienced by the demands of the unions; he might be right against them in specific instances; but on balance it was sound that he should be so inconvenienced and exposed to genuine social pressures and influence. It was no use telling the workers that they must not oppose the workers' state. That state was an abstraction. In reality, Lenin pointed out, his own administration had to consider the interests of the peasants as well as the workers; and the work was marred by muddle, by grave "bureaucratic distortions," and by arbitrary exercise of power. The working class ought therefore to defend itself, albeit with self-restraint, and to press its claims on the administration. The state, as Lenin saw it, had to give scope to a plurality of interests and influences. Trotsky's state was implicitly monolithic.

The tenth congress voted by an overwhelming majority for Lenin's resolutions. Bolshevism had already departed from proletarian democracy; but it was not yet prepared to embrace its alternative, the monolithic state.

While the congress was in session, the strangest of all Russian insurrections flared up at the naval fortress of Kronstadt, an insurrection which, in Lenin's words, like a lightning flash illumined reality.

The insurgents, sailors of the Red Navy, were led by anarchists. Since the end of February, they had been extremely restless. There had been strikes in nearby Petrograd; a general strike was expected; and Kronstadt was astir with rumours of alleged clashes between Petrograd workers and troops. The crews of the warship were seized by a political fever reminiscent of the excitement of 1917. At meetings they passed resolutions demanding freedom for the workers, a new deal for the peasants, and free elections to the Soviets. The call for the Third Revolution began to dominate the meetings, the revolution which was to overthrow the Bolsheviks and establish Soviet democracy. Kalinin, President of the Soviet Republic, made a flat-footed appearance at the naval base; he denounced the sailors as "disloyal and irresponsible" and demanded obedience. A delegation of the sailors sent to Petrograd was arrested there.

Soon the cry "Down with Bolshevik tyranny!" resounded throughout Kronstadt. The Bolshevik commissars on the spot were demoted and imprisoned. An anarchist committee assumed command; and amid the sailors' enthusiasm the flag of revolt was hoisted. "The heroic and generous Kronstadt," writes the anarchist historian of the insurrection, "dreamt of the liberation of Russia. . . . No clear-cut programme was formulated. Freedom and the brotherhood of the peoples of the world were the watchwords. The Third Revolution was seen as a gradual transition towards final emancipation; and free elections to independent Soviets as the first step in this direction. The Soviets were, of course, to be independent of any political party—a free expression of the will and the interests of the people."[4]

The Bolsheviks denounced the men of Kronstadt as counterrevolutionary mutineers led by a White general. The denunciation appears to have been groundless. Having for so long fought against mutiny after mutiny, each sponsored or encouraged by the White Guards, the Bolsheviks could not bring themselves to believe that the White Guards had no hand in this revolt. Some time before the event, the White emigre press had indeed darkly hinted at trouble brewing in Kronstadt; and this lent colour to the suspicion. The Politbureau, at first inclined to open negotiations, finally resolved to quell the revolt. It could not tolerate the challenge from the Navy; and it was afraid that the revolt, although it had no chance of growing into a revolution, would aggravate the prevailing chaos. Even after the defeat of the White Guards, numerous bands of rebels and marauders roamed the land from the northern coasts down to the Caspian Sea, raiding and pillaging towns and slaughtering the agents of the government. With the call for a new revolution, bands of famished Volga peasants had overrun the *gubernia* of Saratov, and later in the year, Tukhachevsky had to employ twenty-seven rifle divisions to subdue them. Such was the turmoil that leniency towards the insurgents of Kronstadt was certain to be taken as a sign of weakness and to make matters worse.

On 5 March Trotsky arrived in Petrograd and ordered the rebels to surrender unconditionally. "Only those who do so," he stated, " can count on the mercy of the Soviet Republic. Simultaneously with this warning I am issuing instructions that everything be prepared for the suppression of the mutiny by armed force. . . . This is the last warning." That it should have fallen to Trotsky to address such words to the sailors was another of history's ironies. This had been his Kronstadt, the Kronstadt he had called "the pride and the glory of the revolution." How many times had he not stumped the naval base during the hot days of 1917! How many times had not the sailors lifted him on their shoulders and wildly acclaimed him as their friend and leader! How devotedly they had followed him to the Tauride Palace, to his prison cell at Kresty, to the walls of Kazan on the Volga, always taking his advice, always almost blindly following his orders! How many anxieties they had shared, how many dangers they had braved together!

True, of the veterans few had survived; and even fewer were still at Kronstadt. The crews of the *Aurora,* the *Petropavlovsk,* and other famous warships now consisted of fresh recruits drafted from Ukrainian peasants. They lacked—so Trotsky told himself—the selfless revolutionary spirit of the older classes. Yet even this was in a way symbolic of the situation in which the revolution found itself. The ordinary men and women who had made it were no longer what they had been or where they had been. The best of them had perished; others had become absorbed in the administration; still others had dispersed and become disheartened and embittered. And what the rebels of Kronstadt demanded was only what Trotsky had promised their elder brothers and what he and the party had been unable to give. Once again, as after Brest, a bitter and hostile echo of his own voice came back to him from the lips of other people; and once again he had to suppress it.

The rebels ignored his warning and hoped to gain time. This was the middle of March. The Bay of Finland was still icebound. In a few days, however, a thaw might set in; and then the fortress, bristling with guns, defended by the whole Red Navy of the Baltic, assured of supplies from Finland or other Baltic countries, would become inaccessible, almost invincible. In the meantime even Communists joined in the revolt, announcing that they had left "the party of the hangman Trotsky." The fortress, so Trotsky (or was it Tukhachevsky?) resolved, must be seized before ice floes barred the approach. In feverish haste, picked regiments and shock troops were dispatched to reinforce the garrison of Petrograd. When the news of the mutiny reached the tenth congress, it aroused so much alarm and anger that most of the able-bodied delegates rushed straight from the conference hall in the Kremlin to place themselves at the head of the shock troops which were to storm the fortress across the Bay of Finland. Even leaders of the Workers' Opposition and *Decemists* who, at the congress, had just raised demands not very different from those the rebels voiced, went into battle. They, too, held that the sailors had no right to dictate, hands on triggers, even the justest of demands.

White sheets over their uniforms, the Bolshevik troops, under Tukhachevsky's command, advanced across the Bay. They were met by hurricane fire from Kronstadt's bastions. The ice broke under their feet; and wave after wave of white-shrouded attackers collapsed into the glacial Valhalla. The death march went on. From three directions fresh columns stumped and fumbled and slipped and crawled over the glassy surface until they too vanished in fire, ice, and water. As the successive swarms and lines of attackers drowned, it seemed to the men of Kronstadt that the perverted Bolshevik Revolution drowned with them and that the triumph of their own pure, unadulterated revolution was approaching. Such was the lot of these rebels, who had denounced the Bolsheviks for their harshness and whose only aim it was to allow the revolution to imbibe the milk of human kindness, that for their survival they fought a battle which in cruelty was unequalled throughout the civil war. The bitterness and the rage of the attackers mounted accordingly. On 17 March, after a night-long advance in a snowstorm, the Bolsheviks at last succeeded in climbing the walls. When they broke into the fortress, they fell upon its defenders like revengeful furies.

On 3 April Trotsky took a parade of the victors. "We waited as long as possible," he said "for our blinded sailor-comrades to see with their own eyes where the mutiny led. But we were confronted by the danger that the ice would melt away and we were compelled to carry out . . . the attack." Describing the crushed rebels as "comrades," he unwittingly intimated that what he celebrated was morally a Pyrrhic victory. Foreign Communists who visited Moscow some months later and believed that Kronstadt had been one of the ordinary incidents of the civil war, were "astonished and troubled" to find that the leading Bolsheviks spoke of the rebels without any of the anger and hatred which they felt for the White Guards and interventionists. Their talk was full of "sympathetic reticences" and sad, enigmatic allusions, which to the outsider betrayed the party's troubled conscience.

The rising had not yet been defeated when, on 15 March, Lenin introduced the New Economic Policy to the tenth congress. Almost without debate the congress accepted it. Silently, with a heavy heart, Bolshevism parted with its dream of war communism. It retreated, as Lenin said, in order to be in a better position to advance. The controversy over the trade unions and the underlying issue at once died down. The cannonade in the Bay of Finland and the strikes in Petrograd and elsewhere had demonstrated beyond doubt the unreality of Trotsky's ideas: and in the milder policies based on the mixed economy of subsequent years there was, anyhow, no room for the militarization of labour.

The controversy had not been mere sound and fury, however. Its significance for the future was greater than the protagonists themselves could suppose. A decade later Stalin, who in 1920–1 had supported Lenin's "liberal" policy, was to adopt Trotsky's ideas in all but name. . . .

Throughout the civil war the Bolsheviks had harassed the Mensheviks and Social Revolutionaries, now outlawing them, now allowing them to come into the open, and then again suppressing them. The harsher and the milder courses were dictated by circumstances and by the vacillations of those parties in which some groups leaned towards the Bolsheviks and others towards the White Guards. The idea, however, that those parties should be suppressed on principle had not taken root before the end of the civil war. Even during the spells of repression, those opposition groups which did not plainly call for armed resistance to the Bolsheviks still carried on all sorts of activities, open and clandestine. The Bolsheviks often eliminated them from the Soviets or reduced their representation by force or guile. It was through the machinery of the Soviets that Lenin's government organized the civil war; and in that machinery it was not prepared to countenance hostile or neutral elements. But the government still looked forward to the end of hostilities when it would be able to respect the rules of Soviet constitutionalism and to readmit regular opposition. This the Bolsheviks now thought themselves unable to do. All opposition parties had hailed the Kronstadt rising; and so the Bolsheviks knew what they could expect from them. The more isolated they themselves were in the nation, the more terrified were they of their opponents. They had half-suppressed them in order to win the civil war; having won the civil war, they went on to suppress them for good.

Paradoxically, the Bolsheviks were driven to establish their own political monopoly by the very fact that they had liberalized their economic policy. The New Economic Policy gave free scope to the interests of the individualistic peasantry and of the urban bourgeoisie. It was to be expected that as those interests came into play, they would seek to create their own means of political expression or try to use such anti-Bolshevik organizations as existed. The Bolsheviks were determined that none should exist. "We might have a two-party system, but one of the two parties would be in office and the other in prison"—this dictum, attributed to Bukharin, expressed a view widespread in the party.

Some Bolsheviks felt uneasy about their own political monopoly; but they were even more afraid of the alternative. Trotsky later wrote that he and Lenin had intended to lift the ban on the opposition parties as soon as the economic and social condition of the country had become more stable. This may have been so. In the meantime, however, the Bolsheviks hardened in the conviction, which was to play so important a part in the struggles of the Stalinist era, that any opposition must inevitably become the vehicle of counterrevolution. They were haunted by the fear that the new urban bourgeoisie (which soon flourished under the N.E.P.), the intelligentsia, and the peasantry might join hands against them in a coalition of overwhelming strength; and they shrank from no measure that could prevent such a coalition. Thus, after its victory in the civil war, the revolution was beginning to escape from its weakness into totalitarianism.

Almost at once it became necessary to suppress opposition in Bolshevik ranks as well. The Workers' Opposition (and up to a point the *Decemists* too) expressed much of the frustration and discontent which had led to the Kronstadt rising. The cleavages tended to become fixed; and the contending groups were inclined to behave like so many parties within the party. It would have been preposterous to establish the rule of a single party and then to allow that party to split into fragments. If Bolshevism were to break up into two or more hostile movements, as the old Social Democratic party had done, would not one of them—it was asked—become the vehicle of counterrevolution?

In the temper of the party congress of 1921 there was indeed something of that seemingly irrational tension which had characterized the congress of 1903. A split similarly cast its shadow ahead—only the real divisions were even more inchoate and confused than in 1903. Now, as then, Trotsky was not on the side of the controversy to which he would eventually belong. And now, as then, he was anxious to prevent the split. He therefore raised no objection when Lenin proposed that the congress should prohibit organized groups or factions within the party; and he himself disbanded the faction he had formed during the recent controversy. This was not yet strictly a ban on inner party opposition. Lenin encouraged dissenters to express dissent. He liberally invited them to state their views in the Bolshevik newspapers, in special discussion pages and discussion sheets. He asked the congress to elect the leaders of all shades of opposition to the new Central Committee. But he insisted that opposition should remain diffuse and that the dissenters should not form themselves into solid leagues. He submitted a resolution, one clause of which (kept secret) empowered the Central Committee to expel offenders, no matter how high their standing in the party. Trotsky supported the clause, or, at any rate, raised no objection to it; and the congress passed it. It was against Shlyapnikov, Trotsky's most immitigable opponent, that the punitive clause was immediately directed; and against him it was presently invoked. It did not occur to Trotsky that one day it would be invoked against himself.

The arrangement under which opposition was permitted, provided it remained dispersed, could work as long as members of the party disagreed over secondary or transient issues. But when the differences were serious and prolonged, it was inevitable that members of the same mind should band together. Those who, like the Workers' Opposition, charged the ruling group with being animated by "bureaucratic and bourgeois hostility towards the masses" could hardly refrain from concerting their efforts against what they considered to be a sinister and formidably organized influence within the party. The ban on factions could thus at first delay a split only to accelerate it later. . . .

When he was still at the threshold of his career, Trotsky wrote: "A working class capable of exercising its dictatorship over society will tolerate no dictator over itself." By 1921 the Russian working class had proved itself incapable of exercising its own dictatorship. It could not even exercise control over those who ruled in its name. Having exhausted itself in the revolution and the civil war, it had almost ceased to exist as a political factor. Trotsky then proclaimed the party's "historical birthright," its right to establish a stern trusteeship over the proletariat as well as the rest of society. This was the old "Jacobin" idea that a small, virtuous and enlightened minority was justified in "substituting" itself for an immature people and bringing reason and happiness to it, the idea which Trotsky had abjured as the hereditary obsession of the *Decembrists*, the *Narodniks*, and the Bolsheviks. This "obsession," he himself had argued, had reflected the atrophy or the apathy of all social classes in Russia. He had been convinced that with the appearance of a modern, Socialist working class that atrophy had been overcome. The revolution proved him right. Yet after their paroxysms of energy and their titanic struggles of 1917–21, all classes of Russian society seemed to relapse into a deep coma. The political stage, so crowded in recent years, became deserted and only a single group was left on it to speak boisterously on behalf of the people. And even its circle was to grow more and more narrow.

When Trotsky now urged the Bolshevik party to "substitute" itself for the working classes, he did not, in the rush of work and controversy, think of the next phases of the process, although he himself had long since predicted them with uncanny clear-sightedness. "The party organization would then substitute itself for the party as a whole; then the Central Committee would substitute itself for the organization; and finally a single dictator would substitute himself for the Central Committee."

The dictator was already waiting in the wings.

Notes

1. *The reader will find a detailed and instructive account of war communism in E.H. Carr,* The Bolshevik Revolution, *vol. ii.*
2. *Many Bolshevik leaders explicitly or implicitly admitted this. See Lenin,* Sochinenya, *vol xxxii, pp. 160, 176, 230 and* passim; *Zinoviev in* Desyatyi Syezd RKP, *p. 190. In a private letter to Lunacharsky (of 14 April 1926) Trotsky describes the "menacing discontent" of the working class as the background to the controversy of 1920–1.* The Trotsky Archives.
3. *A detailed account of the debate can be found in Deutscher,* Soviet Trade Unions (Their Place in Soviet Labour Policy), *pp. 42–59.*
4. *Alexander Berkman,* Der Aufstand von Kronstadt, *pp. 10–11.*

The Origin of the Communist Autocracy

Leonard Schapiro

Leninism Triumphant

. . . Before the revolution the conflict between the two wings of Russian social democracy had centered much more on questions of organization and method than on questions of theory. With the coming of the February Revolution, Bolsheviks and Mensheviks alike did not scruple to jettison theoretical principles to which each had previously adhered. The same process can be observed after the October Revolution, during the years of the civil war. Once again, it was much less dispute over the theory of Marxism which divided Bolsheviks and Mensheviks than questions of organization and method. The Mensheviks, in particular, had in practice abandoned, within a year of the revolution, the most cherished tenet of orthodox Russian Marxists, that a socialist revolution should only take place after a long period of "bourgeois" democracy, by conceding the "historical necessity" of the October Revolution. In introducing his New Economic Policy Lenin did little more than take over and put into practice a doctrine evolved by the Mensheviks—after first removing the Mensheviks from the political scene.

Even in the case of relations between the Bolsheviks and the Socialist Revolutionaries, it was to some extent true that what divided the two parties was more often disagreement over methods of government than widely divergent theoretical beliefs. The left wing of the Socialist Revolutionaries immediately accepted the Bolshevik Revolution, and only broke with the Bolsheviks on the question of the tactics to be adopted in preserving the revolutionary government in power. But even the rest of the party, who at first repudiated the Bolshevik Revolution, accepted it in the end when they found that their struggle against the revolutionary government was helping a counterrevolutionary government to power. The capitulation of many of their number to the Communists, and the hesitations of those who did not capitulate, proved this beyond doubt.

Lenin had in turn accepted, at any rate temporarily, the socialist revolutionary theory of land distribution to the peasantry, and had abandoned the Bolshevik programme of immediate nationalization. Once again, as before the revolution, the main source of conflict between Lenin and Russian socialism proved to be questions of organization and method—such as the *Vecheka,* the uncontrolled bureaucracy, or the subordination of the trade unions to centralized party control. Above all, the great majority of socialists were not prepared to tolerate the suppression of democratic liberties. The victory of the Bolsheviks over the socialists can of course in large measure be explained by the constant use of force. But there were other causes at work which were also of importance in helping to assure this victory. . . .

Reprinted by permission of the publishers from chapter 18 of Leonard Schapiro's The Origin of the Communist Autocracy *(Cambridge, Mass.: Harvard University Press, 1955); and also by permission of the London School of Economics and Political Science.*

[One] important [reason] for the victory of Bolshevism was the advantage which the Bolsheviks derived from the moral scruples of their socialist opponents. It is now commonplace to argue that the Provisional Government, headed by the socialist Kerensky, could easily have prevented the Bolshevik Revolution by taking effective and timely action against a mere handful of men and their skeleton organization. But, to argue thus is to look at the Bolsheviks through the eyes of 1921, or 1951, and not of 1917. In August or September 1917 the Provisional Government, largely composed of socialists and headed by a socialist prime minister, was understandably reluctant to use the methods of the overthrown autocracy against ostensibly socialist opponents, however extremist their views or actions. When it was goaded into taking some steps against the Bolsheviks after the abortive rising of July 1917, its measures were half-hearted and quite ineffective. It was not for nothing that the Bolshevik leaders subsequently maintained that their coup d'état in November 1917 had proved easy beyond expectation.

The hesitation of their political opponents to take up arms against the Bolsheviks played as great a part in their retention of power after 1917. The Mensheviks rejected armed opposition from the first, though a minority of the party was for a short time in favour of it, and a few individuals broke with their party and joined one or other of the anti-Bolshevik forces or conspiracies. As regards the party as a whole, such a course was foreign to their tradition, their temperament, and be it said their capabilities. The case of the Socialist Revolutionaries was different. They were neither a Marxist nor a proletarian party and the peasants whom they represented had given them an ostensible mandate in the elections to the Constituent Assembly against the Bolshevik usurpation of power. Unlike the Mensheviks, many of their number were in November 1917 anxious to fight to victory against Germany and the Central Powers, and the Bolshevik surrender outraged their patriotic sentiments. Even the internationalist Left Socialist Revolutionaries were not devoid of such sentiment. Their indignation at the treaty of Brest-Litovsk, though primarily due to what they regarded as the betrayal of the cause of world revolution, was not untinged with the romantic notions harboured by their intelligentsia of the enraged Slav masses rising against the invading West. Moreover, violence had always been an influential factor in socialist revolutionary tradition. Yet, the story of the Socialist Revolutionaries' struggle against the Bolsheviks is one of indecision, hesitation, disunity, and divided loyalty. The refusal of the Central Committee of the main party to take up arms in defence of the Constituent Assembly, at a time when there were still armed forces available to support the attempt, lost them an opportunity which never recurred, and dealt a great blow to their prestige.

The treaty of Brest-Litovsk goaded them at last into cooperation with the forces of the Western Allies and into an armed struggle against the Bolsheviks. But the weak governments which the Socialist Revolutionaries set up fell, and were replaced by military dictatorships. By November 1918 the ill-assorted partnership of inexperienced and doctrinaire socialists on the one hand, and politically illiterate and reactionary army officers on the other, had come to an end. The Socialist Revolutionaries' insistence on the adoption of a full socialist party in the midst of a civil war had contributed not a little to the debacle. Moreover, in November 1918 the defeat of Germany removed the circumstances which in the eyes of many Socialist Revolutionaries had alone justified armed struggle against the Bolsheviks. The fight against Lenin's government could now no longer be viewed as a means of restoring the Eastern front against Germany, but became open civil war. A number of the party capitulated to the Bolsheviks, preferring political extinction to a struggle which, though it might defeat the Bolsheviks, would do so at the cost of putting reactionary monarchists into power.

Within Russia the remnants of the party organization renounced recourse to arms for the duration of the civil war. From the end of 1918 onwards, the armed activity against the Communists by Socialist Revolutionaries inside Russia was limited to the participation of individuals in the fighting in the civil war and in a few conspiratorial organizations, while abroad groups of émigrés endeavored to enlist the support of the Western Allies for more effective intervention. The party organization waited to lead a popular rising on a national scale, which never came. Thus, of the opponents of the Bolsheviks during the years of the civil war, those who had moral authority to justify their resistance, the socialists, hesitated to use the method of the coup d'état. The reactionary White Armies, which remained in the field against the Bolsheviks, had no such scruples. But they, in turn, lacked the moral authority which could have won them popular support, and might have ensured their success.

These were the negative reasons for the Bolsheviks' success. There were positive reasons as well. In contrast to their socialist opponents, the Bolsheviks were resolute, and bold in decision. Under Lenin's leadership, and because of it, they were not afraid to jettison their doctrine where the all-important question of power was involved—not afraid, in fact, of that "opportunism" for which Lenin so frequently reviled his socialist opponents. Besides this, the personality of Lenin, his political skill as well as his clarity of thought and incisiveness in the analysis of a situation, were without rival anywhere on the Russian political scene. . . .

It will be recalled that the Russian social democrats, alone of all European Marxists, had accepted as an item of their programme the "dictatorship of the proletariat." Marx had used this phrase almost casually, on isolated occasions, to designate the temporary form which the struggle of the proletariat with its opponents would take immediately after its seizure of power. He had never defined or elaborated the shape which he thought a revolutionary government would assume in practice. But, since in Marx's conception the proletarian revolution was to take place at a moment when the vast exploited majority finally rose against a small minority of exploiters, it was plain that this dictatorship would be temporary and short-lived. Moreover, since the seizure of power by the proletariat would inaugurate the advent of the classless society, and since the state existed only as a device for preventing class conflict from erupting into violence, it followed, in Marxist analysis, that the state must begin to wither away progressively from the moment that the proletariat had seized and consolidated its power.

On the very eve of the Bolshevik Revolution Lenin still fully accepted this analysis. In his *State and Revolution,* written in August and September 1917 while he was in hiding—a work written with care and much thought, and a statement of principles to which he attached the utmost importance—Lenin fully accepted the classical Marxist analysis. "The proletarian state," he wrote, "will begin to wither away immediately after its victory, since in a society without class contradictions, the state is unnecessary and impossible." True, it would not, as the anarchists demanded, simply be abolished overnight. But neither, according to Lenin, would it resemble, while it lasted, the state which it had overthrown, with its police and other machinery of repression. Supported as it would be by the overwhelming mass of the population, it would enforce its will "almost without any special machinery."

These words, it should be emphasized, were not part of the demagogy with which the Bolsheviks captured the support of the masses between March and November 1917, since *State and Revolution* was not published until the spring of 1918. By the time Lenin's words were published, the *Vecheka* had been active for several months, and not even the most sanguine Marxist could have discerned any signs of the state beginning to wither away.

When the question of "withering away" came up in March 1918, at the Seventh Party Congress, Lenin now impatiently brushed it aside. "One may well wonder when the state will begin to wither away. . . . To proclaim this withering away in advance is to violate historical perspective." It was Bukharin, the Left Communist, who had raised the question. Many years passed before the question was raised again. The Left Communists, the Democratic Centralists, the Workers' Opposition—all accepted the need for the terror, the *Vecheka,* the unbridled powers of the executive. The reason was not, perhaps, far to seek. The Bolsheviks, so far from winning over the great majority of the country after they had seized power, as doctrine demanded, remained a small, unpopular minority, ruling by force. Their survival in sole power depended upon the state and the apparatus which they had created, and few Communists were prepared to question the necessity for this survival. . . .

Indeed, so little did questions of doctrine animate the Russian Communists for some time after the October Revolution, that the biggest departure from Marxism of all passed unnoticed. . . . The first impact of Lenin's unorthodox decision to seize power had thrown his followers into confusion. But the confusion did not last long. The unexpected failure of their opponents to rally and overthrow the new communist government was probably as powerful an advocate for the correctness of Lenin's decision as any theoretical doctrine. So long as war communism remained the official policy, the virtual one party state which existed in the country after the peace of Brest-Litovsk might have appeared to many to be justified as the correct political superstructure for the putting into effect of extreme socialist policies.

But by the spring of 1921 war communism had failed. It was now to be replaced by an economic system in which there would be room for private capitalist enterprise and interests. Marxist logic therefore demanded that the political machine corresponding to such an economic system should be composed of parties representing the interests of the various classes which were now to be tolerated, in a state which was no longer regarded even in theory as a one-class state. Lenin himself had conceded this theoretical necessity in 1905, when he had argued that so long as the revolution had not emerged from the democratic, and therefore multi-class stage, government should take the form of a coalition dictatorship of the peasantry and the proletariat. Yet, in 1921 no serious opinion within the communist party was prepared to challenge the monopoly of all political power by their own proletarian party, though many Communists were ready to criticize the abuses which proceeded from the monopoly. In this respect the simple mutineers at Kronstadt, who at all events demanded political freedom for all workers' and peasants' parties, may be said to have proved themselves better Marxists than the Communists.

The question can be looked at from another aspect in which Marxist theory plays no part. The Bolsheviks had never proclaimed the one party state as their avowed policy before the revolution. The seizure of power had been ostensibly accomplished in the name of the soviets in which several parties were represented. When Lenin's decision to govern alone became apparent immediately after the October Revolution, it even provoked a short-lived crisis inside the Bolshevik ranks. For some years to come the fiction that the Communists were but one party among many was maintained. The suppression of the socialists was, with the exception of the short period between June and November 1918, invariably bolstered by charges such as "counterrevolution," or speculation: it was not action openly taken against political opponents. The communist policy of defaming the political integrity of all socialists dates from this time. Up to 1921 it was not difficult for the Communists to justify to themselves their decision to take, and keep, power alone. The socialists had after all failed to achieve between March and November 1917 a solid and efficient government, and had then repudiated the Bolsheviks, who were at any rate prepared to take the responsibility for decisive action. The peace with Germany had been bitterly opposed by Mensheviks and Socialist Revolutionaries alike. Was it not logical that the Communists should take upon themselves the burden of government alone? The Socialist Revolutionaries had for a time even sided with the anti-Bolshevik forces in the civil war.

But all these factors had ceased to exist in 1921. The socialist parties inside Russia, or those of them who still had an opportunity of voicing their views, were vying with one another in their loyalty to the ideals of the revolution as such, while condemning the excess of the Communists. There was not the remotest threat of any right wing or counterrevolutionary restoration. Long after 1921, though deprived of all political power and though many of their number were in prison or exiled, the intelligentsia and the middle class continued to serve the Soviet state. The émigré socialists and *Kadety* even developed a whole philosophy of collaboration with the Communists in order to build up Russia, and many of them returned to implement what they considered to be their duty. There was opposition inside Russia, to be sure. But as the programme of the Kronstadt insurgents, which was typical of this opposition, shows, it was opposition not to Soviet government but to the Communists' monopoly of power, and to their party's illegal methods of preserving it.

Those, and there are many,[1] who justify the Communists' elimination of their socialist opponents in 1921 by the necessity of safeguarding the "revolution" from its enemies ignore two essential facts: first, that enmity against the Communists was not enmity against the revolution, i.e., the Soviet form of government, but against the methods of communist rule in the name of that revolution. It was therefore not only an enmity of the Communists' own creation, but one which it was in their power to remove without danger to the revolution, though with undoubted risk to their own monopoly of power. To be sure, Lenin and the Communists identified "the revolution" with themselves. But it was an identification made by them alone, which did not correspond to facts. Secondly, that a large number, perhaps even the majority, of the conscious proletariat, were in early 1921 menshevik or menshevik sympathizers. The revolutionary nature of this party's policy, which accorded political freedom to workers and peasants alone, and advocated large scale nationalization of industry and state control of foreign trade, cannot be conjured away, as is normally done by apologists of Lenin's policy, by describing it as "bourgeois." The socialists were not eliminated in 1921 because they were counterrevolutionary. They were described as counterrevolutionary in order to justify their elimination.

The fate of the socialists was sealed when it became apparent that in their criticism of communist methods they were speaking much the same language as the many malcontents inside the communist party. The realization of the extent of the support which the Kronstadt mutineers could muster, even inside the communist party within the naval garrison, had come as a grave shock. But different considerations applied to the Workers' Opposition. There was no vestige in their programme of any quarrel with the communist leaders for their treatment of socialist opponents, or of the peasantry. It was a mixture of the early syndicalism which the Communists had abandoned, utopianism, and nostalgia for the lost enthusiasm of the first months. They combined with it some well-founded criticism of the abuses of bureaucracy and of excessive party discipline and control. The communist leaders may have been right in seeing in the existence of this critical group a potential party split.

The moral case for the Workers' Opposition was perhaps not very strong. They demanded freedom for themselves, but had no thought of conceding it to others. When they complained of control by the centre over the communist committees in the trade unions, they did not pause to think that those same communist committees for which they demanded more freedom of action did not hesitate to impose their will on a trade union membership, some fourteen times their number, which was bitterly opposed to them. They accepted the state of affairs in which a party of a few hundred thousand could impose its will by force on millions of workers who did not support them. But they did not realize that if a minority party is to survive in sole power against the will of the great majority, it can only do so if it maintains the strictest discipline and control by its leaders over its own members. Once again the Kronstadt mutineers proved themselves more mature politicians than the Workers' Opposition. . . .

The balance sheet of political support was not an encouraging one for the communist party in March 1921. Among the peasantry it had lost most, if not all, of the support or at least neutrality which had once played an important part in achieving victory both in November 1917 and in the civil war. Even among the proletariat, dislike of the Communists had grown. With it grew the popularity of the socialist parties, notably of the Mensheviks. No communist leader could have had any doubt, and some, such as Zinoviev, openly admitted that in any free election to any soviet, or trade union committee, in March 1921, the number of communist candidates elected would have been small. It was true that much of this unpopularity was due to privations brought about by the civil war. But it was also true that much of it was due to the revolt of the Russian people against the unfairness, the violence, and the illegality with which the Communists suppressed all who did not accept their rule without question. The Kronstadt revolt proved this beyond any doubt.

In these circumstances there were only two policies open to Lenin. Either to resign himself to his failure to win over the majority, to moderate the policy by which his monopoly of power had been secured and to accept the consequent loss of that monopoly. Or, to preserve his monopoly of political power at all costs, and at the same time make the task of preserving it easier by removing, at the price of sacrificing communist doctrine, some of the economic causes of discontent. He chose the second course. But it was plain that this policy could only be successfully achieved by a disciplined party, united, if necessary by force, for the difficult task which now confronted it. There could be no room for party democracy. The trade union discussion, which had revealed the personal rivalries dividing the party as well as the wide divergence of view on fundamental questions of policy, had proved that. The views of the Democratic Centralists, of Preobrazhensky or Krestinsky, of Shlyapnikov or Kollontai, suffered from the contradiction that they stood for two incompatible aims: *both* a democratic communist party, *and* the exclusion of all other parties from power. It was this circumstance more than any other which determined their quick collapse at the Tenth Party Congress. . . .

It is plain that in 1921, as in 1917, many followed Lenin without completely realizing where he was leading them. The full significance of his policy then may have been no more apparent than had been the full significance of the seizure of power. In November 1917 a number of Bolshevik leaders cavilled when they discovered that what they had believed to be seizure of power by the soviets was in reality seizure of power by the Bolshevik party. In 1921 those who followed Lenin believed that what was being achieved was the consolidation of the power of the communist party. Many of them were to rebel once again, in 1923, when they discovered that what had really taken place was the consolidation in power of the central party apparatus. But it was then too late. . . .

In 1921 the fate of the country lay in the hands of Lenin. He had a chance of burying past enmities and of carrying the vast majority of the country with him in an attempt to build up ruined Russia on the basis of cooperation and legal order, and not of the dictatorship of an unpopular minority. It is difficult to escape the conclusion that a greater man than Lenin would have seized this chance. But Lenin's genius lay in the technique of grasping and holding power. He was a great revolutionary, but not a statesman. His conviction that he and his followers alone held the secret of successful rule in their hands was, to a large extent, the product of the struggle by which he had achieved his position. But from his fateful decision in the spring of 1921 flowed all the consequences of the one-party dictatorship which became apparent in the subsequent years of Soviet history.

Two main consequences derived from Lenin's political policy of 1921, both of enormous importance for the future history of Soviet Russia. The first was the emergence of what Engels has so well described as the "conventional hypocrisy." During the civil war there was at any rate some justification for the view that "he who is not with us is against us." In the heat of battle it was possible for the Communists to see in those socialists who were fighting against them enemies of the revolution, without seeming to do undue violence to truth. After 1921, the lumping together of Mensheviks, Workers' Opposition, serious theoretical critics, and malcontents inside the communist party as counterrevolutionaries was a falsification, and everyone knew it.

The acceptance of this official lie by almost the entire leadership of the communist party inevitably led to the result that whoever among them was strong enough to exploit it in his own interest had the rest of them at his mercy. What is the difference between the attempt by Lenin to expel Shlyapnikov, in 1921, and the expulsion of Trotsky six years later, if both can be justified by the same argument—that the stability of the dictatorship is the supreme law? But this, in turn, leads to the second main consequence of Lenin's policy. For, who has the power to decide by what faction the stability of the regime is to be best served? Clearly, he who manipulates the apparatus of the party, and can thereby ensure both the necessary majorities at the centre and implicit obedience to central orders throughout the country. The malignant figure of the General Secretary, Stalin, has become only too familiar in its portrayal by disappointed oppositionists, defeated by the apparatus which he controlled. But it was Lenin, with their support, who equipped him with the weapons, and started him upon his path.

Notes

1. *See, e.g., Deutscher,* Stalin, *p. 226, "It was true enough that concern for the revolution compelled Bolshevism to take the road chosen by the tenth congress . . . "; Carr,* The Bolshevik Revolution, *I, p. 183. The latter concludes that the demise of the legal opposition "cannot fairly be laid at the door of one party. If it was true that the Bolshevik regime was not prepared after the first few months to tolerate an organized opposition, it was equally true that no opposition party was prepared to remain within legal limits. The premise of dictatorship was common to both sides of the argument." This judgment ignores not only the Mensheviks, but most of the Socialist Revolutionaries as well. The premise of dictatorship was certainly common to both sides in Lenin's "argument" with Denikin. But what relation to fact does such an assertion bear in the case of Martov and the Mensheviks, whose policy was founded upon the need to "remain within legal limits"? Or in the case of the Samara Socialist Revolutionaries, who gave up the fight for fear it might assist the victory of a right wing dictatorship? The charge that the Mensheviks were not prepared to remain within legal limits is part of the Bolsheviks' case; it does not survive an examination of the facts.*

PART FOUR

DICTATORSHIP SECURED

During the time of the International, in my aversion from any cult of the individual, I never allowed the numerous manoeuvres of recognition by which I was molested from various countries to receive publicity; I never even answered them, except now and again with a rebuke. When Engels and I first joined the clandestine Communist League we did so only on condition that anything tending to foster irrational beliefs in authority should be expunged from the Rules.

Karl Marx

O great Stalin, O leader of the peoples,
Thou who broughtest man to birth,
Thou who fructifiest the earth,
Thou who restorest the centuries,
Thou who makest bloom the spring,
Thou who makest vibrate the musical chords.
Thou, splendor of my spring, O thou,
Sun reflected by millions of hearts. . . .

Translation of Uzbek poem in Pravda, *August 28, 1936*

Comrades! The cult of the individual acquired such monstrous size chiefly because Stalin himself, using all conceivable methods, supported the glorification of his own person. This is supported by numerous facts. One of the most characteristic examples of Stalin's self-glorification and of his lack of even elementary modesty is the edition of his Short Biography, *which was published in 1948.*

This book is an expression of the most dissolute flattery, an example of making a man into a godhead, of transforming him into an infallible sage, "the greatest leader," "sublime strategist of all times and nations." Finally no other words could be found with which to lift Stalin up to the heavens.

We need not give here examples of the loathsome adulation filling this book. All we need to add is that they all were approved and edited by Stalin personally and some of them were added in his own handwriting to the draft text of the book.

Nikita S. Khrushchev, *February 25, 1956*

Chapter 5

THE TRIUMPH OF STALIN

One of the more interesting and important questions is why and how Stalin was able to emerge from a position of relative obscurity to one of unexcelled power in the history of the modern world. (While it is probably true that Stalin was far abler than some critics have suggested, he was, when compared with certain other of the Bolshevik leaders, pedestrian and uninspired.) A more serious and related question is how did it happen that, under the aegis of a theory that was designed to liberate people from exploitation, so crass and pervasive a dictatorship could arise and develop. Relevant, of course, to these questions are the explanations considered or suggested in the previous section. But there are additional and variant explanations offered by Isaac Deutscher, Leon Trotsky and John Plamenatz in this section.

A few words should be added in regard to the historic circumstances under which Stalin consolidated his power—apart from those dealt with in the pages that follow. By 1928, under the New Economic Policy (NEP) (which abolished requisitioning from the peasantry and encouraged private trade and small-scale enterprise while the "commanding heights" of industry remained under state administration), productivity had been restored to prewar levels. However, the grain surplus available for urban consumption or export was only at one-third of prewar level. In the minds of Stalin and other Soviet leaders, NEP did not provide an adequate basis for large-scale investment in, and subsidization of, a massive industrialization. Moreover, a large class of peasant proprietors and business entrepreneurs presented at least a potential threat to the regime. Stalin decided to embark, therefore, upon wholesale collectivization of agriculture to support industrialization.

The first five-year plan, which went into effect on October 1, 1928, engendered tremendous enthusiasm and a spirit of sacrifice, particularly among the youth. On the other hand, it resulted in massive and sullen resistance by the kulaks who slaughtered cattle and refused to sow or reap. The immediate consequences were the deportation of hundreds of thousands of kulaks to the far reaches of Siberia and a famine in the Ukraine in 1932–33—which took at least a million and a half lives. In this situation, as difficulties developed, as suspicions, fears, and bitterness intensified, as arrests and executions of obstructionists, saboteurs, and scapegoats became commonplace, the dependence upon and power of Stalin grew mightily.

"Testament"

V.I. Lenin

By the stability of the Central Committee, of which I spoke before, I mean measures to prevent a split, so far as such measures can be taken. For, of course, the White Guard in *Russkaya Mysl* (I think it was S.E. Oldenburg) was right when, in the first place, in his play against Soviet Russia he banked on the hope of a split in our party, and when, in the second place, he banked for that split on serious disagreements in our party.

Our party rests upon two classes, and for that reason its instability is possible, and if there cannot exist an agreement between those classes its fall is inevitable. In such an event it would be useless to take any measures or in general to discuss the stability of our Central Committee. In such an event no measures would prove capable of preventing a split. But I trust that is too remote a future, and too improbable an event, to talk about.

I have in mind stability as a guarantee against a split in the near future, and I intended to examine here a series of considerations of a purely personal character.

I think that the fundamental factor in the matter of stability—from this point of view—is such members of the Central Committee as Stalin and Trotsky. The relation between them constitutes, in my opinion, a big half of the danger of that split, which might be avoided, and the avoidance of which might be promoted, in my opinion, by raising the number of members of the Central Committee to fifty or one hundred.

Comrade Stalin, having become General Secretary, has concentrated an enormous power in his hands; and I am not sure that he always knows how to use that power with sufficient caution. On the other hand, Comrade Trotsky, as was proved by his struggle against the Central Committee in connection with the question of the People's Commissariat of Ways and Communications, is distinguished not only by his exceptional abilities—personally he is, to be sure, the most able man in the present Central Committee—but also by his too far-reaching self-confidence and a disposition to be too much attracted by the purely administrative side of affairs.

These two qualities of the two most able leaders of the present Central Committee might, quite innocently, lead to a split; if our party does not take measures to prevent it, a split might arise unexpectedly.

I will not further characterize the other members of the Central Committee as to their personal qualities. I will only remind you that the October episode of Zinoviev and Kamenev was not, of course, accidental, but that it ought as little to be used against them personally as the non-Bolshevism of Trotsky.

In mid-December 1922, Lenin suffered a stroke and felt the nearness of death. On December 25 he dictated a memorandum to his secretary to be made known to the Party in the event of his death. On January 4, 1923, he dictated a postscript to his "Testament."

Subsequently, in the early months of 1923, when Lenin had recovered somewhat from his illness, he launched an open attack on Stalin. His March 4 article in Pravda, *without direct mention of Stalin, bitterly assailed the Workers' and Peasants' Inspectorate, which Stalin headed. The next day, Lenin "broke off" all personal relations with Stalin and prepared for his denunciation. But soon thereafter Lenin became incapacitated again. He died on January 21, 1924.*

The "Testament," although known to the Soviet leaders, was not published in the Soviet press until May 18, 1956, when a part of it first appeared in Komsomolskaya Pravda, *the Young Communist newspaper, to explain what was behind the attack on the "cult of the individual."*

Of the younger members of the Central Committee, I want to say a few words about Bukharin and Pyatakov. They are in my opinion, the most able forces (among the youngest) and in regard to them it is necessary to bear in mind the following: Bukharin is not only the most valuable and biggest theoretician of the party, but also may legitimately be considered the favorite of the whole party; but his theoretical views can only with the very greatest doubt be regarded as fully Marxist, for there is something scholastic in him (he never has learned, and I think never has fully understood, the dialectic).

And then Pyatakov—a man undoubtedly distinguished in will and ability, but too much given over to administration and the administrative side of things to be relied on in a serious political question.

Of course, both these remarks are made by me merely with a view to the present time, or supposing that the two able and loyal workers may not find an occasion to supplement their knowledge and correct their onesidedness.

December 25, 1922

Postscript: Stalin is too rude, and this fault, entirely supportable in relations among us Communists, becomes insupportable in the office of General Secretary. Therefore, I propose to the comrades to find a way to remove Stalin from that position and appoint to it another man who in all respects differs from Stalin only in superiority—namely, more patient, more loyal, more polite, and more attentive to comrades, less capricious, etc. This circumstance may seem an insignificant trifle, but I think that from the point of view of preventing a split and from the point of view of the relation between Stalin and Trotsky which I discussed above, it is not a trifle, or it is such a trifle as may acquire a decisive significance.

January 4, 1923

Stalin

Isaac Deutscher

Few important developments in history are so inconspicuous and seem so inconsequential to their contemporaries as did the amazing accumulation of power in the hands of Stalin, which took place while Lenin was still alive. Two years after the end of the civil war Russian society already lived under Stalin's virtual rule, without being aware of the ruler's name. More strangely still, he was voted and moved into all his positions of power by his rivals. There was to be an abundance of sombre drama in his later fight against

This selection is from chapter 7 of Stalin: A Political Biography *(New York: Oxford University Press, 1949). Reprinted by permission of the publisher.*

these rivals. But the fight began only after he had firmly gripped all the levers of power and after his opponents, awakening to his role, had tried to move him from his dominant position. But then they found him immovable.

Three of the offices he held immediately after the civil war were of decisive importance: he was the Commissar of Nationalities, the Commissar of the Workers' and Peasants' Inspectorate, and a member of the Politbureau.

As Commissar of Nationalities he dealt with the affairs of nearly half the population of the Russian Soviet Federative Socialist Republic, as the state that had replaced old Russia was now called. Sixty-five million of its 140 million inhabitants belonged to non-Russian nationalities. They represented every possible level of civilization, from the quasi-European way of life of the Ukrainians to the primitive, tribal existence of 25 million Turkmen-shepherds. Byelorussians, Kirghizians, Uzbeks, Azerbaidjans, Tartars, Armenians, Georgians, Tadzhiks, Buriats, and Yakuts, and a host of others for which there seem to be no names in the English tongue, found themselves in various intermediate phases of development between tribal community and modern society. Bolshevism, eager to attract all these nationalities and to wipe away their memories of Tsarist oppression, offered autonomy and self-government to all of them. Few such groups had any degree of "national" consciousness. Fewer still had acquired the minimum of education indispensable for self-government. For the management of their affairs they were dependent on help from outside—that is, from the Commissariat of Nationalities. To most of them the doctrinal problems of communism were as remote as the theories of Einstein were to the Khans of Bokhara. In their lands the revolution meant the freeing of the primitive communities from the dominance of Emirs, Khans, and Mullahs, and a degree of Europeanization.

Apart from the Ukraine, ruled by an independent-minded government under Christian Rakovsky, the Commissariat of Nationalities faced primarily Russia's vast, inert, oriental fringe. None of the leaders who had spent most of their adult life in western Europe was as fit to head that Commissariat as Stalin. His firsthand knowledge of the customs and habits of his clients was unsurpassed. So was his capacity to deal with the intricacies of their "politics," in which blood feuds and oriental intrigue mixed with a genuine urge towards modern civilization. His attitude was just that mixture of patience, patriarchal firmness, and slyness that was needed. The Politbureau relied on this and refrained from interfering.

The Asiatic and semi-Asiatic periphery thus became his first undisputed domain. Immediately after the revolution, when the leadership of the nation belonged to the turbulent and radical cities of European Russia, in the first place to Petersburg and Moscow, the weight of that periphery was not much felt. With the ebb of revolution, the primitive provinces took their revenge. They reasserted themselves in a thousand ways, economic political, and cultural. Their spiritual climate became, in a sense, decisive for the country's outlook. The fact that so much of that climate was oriental was of great significance. Stalin, who was so well suited to speak on behalf of Russian communism to the peoples of the oriental fringe, was also well suited to orientalize his party. During his years at the Commissariat he made and widened his contacts with the Bolshevik leaders of the borderlands, on whose devoted support he could count, and of whom so many were to be found in his entourage at the Kremlin later on.

He was appointed Commissar of the Workers' and Peasants' Inspectorate in 1919 on Zinoviev's proposal. The Rabkrin, as the Commissariat was called, was set up to control every branch of the administration, from top to bottom, with a view to eliminating the two major faults, inefficiency and corruption, which the Soviet civil service had inherited from its Tsarist predecessor. It was to act as the stern and enlightened auditor for the whole rickety and creaking governmental machine; to expose abuses of power and red tape; and to train an elite of reliable civil servants for every branch of the government. The Commissariat acted through teams of workers and peasants who were free at any time to enter the offices of any Commissariat and watch the work done there. In the end, teams of the Rabkrin regularly attended private departmental conferences and even the meetings of the Council of Commissars. This system was devised as a method of training an elite for the civil service; but as a result of it, the Rabkrin was able to keep its eye on every wheel of the governmental machine.

The whole bizarre scheme of inspection was one of Lenin's pet ideas. Exasperated by the inefficiency and dishonesty of the civil service, he sought to remedy them by extreme and ruthless "control from below," and the Commissariat was to be the means. The choice of Stalin for the job gives a measure of Lenin's high confidence in him, for the Inspectorate was to be a sort of a supergovernment, itself free from every taint and blemish of officialdom.

Lenin's cure proved as bad as the disease. The faults of the civil service, as Lenin himself frequently pointed out, reflected the country's appalling lack of education, its material and spiritual misery, which could be cured only gradually over the lifetime of at least a generation. The Rabkrin would have had to be a commissariat of angels in order to rise, let alone raise others, above the dark valley of Russian bureaucracy. With his characteristic belief in the inherent virtues of the working classes, Lenin appealed to the workers against his own bureaucracy. The mill of officialdom, however, turned the workers themselves into bureaucrats. The Commissariat of the Inspectorate, as Lenin was to discover later on, became an additional source of muddle, corruption, and bureaucratic intrigue. In the end it became an unofficial but meddlesome police in charge of the civil service. But let us not run ahead of our story. Suffice it to say here that, as the head of the Inspectorate, Stalin came to control the whole machinery of government, its workings and personnel, more closely than any other commissar.

His next position of vantage was in the Politbureau. Throughout the civil war, the Politbureau consisted of five men only: Lenin, Trotsky, Stalin, Kamenev, and Bukharin. Ever since the break between Bolsheviks and Social Revolutionaries, this had been the real government of the country. Lenin was the recognized leader of both government and party. Trotsky was responsible for the conduct of the civil war. Kamenev acted as Lenin's deputy in various capacities. Bukharin was in charge of press and propaganda. The day-to-day management of the party belonged to Stalin. The Politbureau discussed high policy. Another body, which was, like the Politbureau, elected by the Central Committee, the Organization Bureau (Orgbureau), was in charge of the party's personnel, which it was free to call up, direct to work, and distribute throughout the army and the civil service according to the demands of the civil war. From the beginning of 1919, Stalin was the only permanent liaison officer between the Politbureau and the Orgbureau. He ensured the unity of policy and organization; that is, he marshalled the forces of the party according to the Politbureau's directives. Like none of his colleagues, he was immersed in the party's daily drudgery and in all its kitchen cabals.

At this stage his power was already formidable. Still more was to accrue to him from his appointment, on 3 April 1922, to the post of General Secretary of the Central Committee. The eleventh congress of the party had just elected a new and enlarged Central Committee and again modified the statutes. The leading bodies of the party were now top-heavy; and a new office that of the General Secretary, was created, which was to co-ordinate the work of their many growing and overlapping branches. It was on that occasion, Trotsky alleges, that Lenin aired, in the inner circle of his associates, his misgivings about Stalin's candidature: "This cook can only serve peppery dishes." But his doubts were, at any rate, not grave; and he himself in the end sponsored the candidature of the "cook." Molotov and Kuibyshev were appointed Stalin's assistants, the former having already been one of the secretaries of the party. The appointment was reported in the Russian press without any ado, as a minor event in the inner life of the party.

Soon afterwards a latent dualism of authority began to develop at the very top of the party. The seven men who now formed the Politbureau (in addition to the previous five, Zinoviev and Tomsky had recently been elected) represented, as it were, the brain and the spirit of Bolshevism. In the offices of the General Secretariat resided the more material power of management and direction. In name, the General Secretariat was subordinate to the illustrious and exalted Politbureau. But the dependence of the Politbureau on the Secretariat became so great that without that prop the Politbureau looked more and more like a body awkwardly suspended in a void. The Secretariat prepared the agenda for each session of the Politbureau. It supplied the documentation on every point under debate. It transmitted the Politbureau's decisions to the lower grades. It was in daily contact with the many thousands of party functionaries in the capital and the provinces. It was responsible for their appointments, promotions, and demotions. It could, up to a point, prejudice the views of the Politbureau on any issue before it came up for debate. It could twist the practical execution of the Politbureau's decisions, according to the tastes of the General Secretary. Similar bodies exist in any governmental machinery but rarely acquire independent authority. What usually prevents them from transgressing their terms of reference is some diffusion of power through the whole system of government, effective control over them, and, sometimes, the integrity of officials. The overcentralization of power in the Bolshevik leadership, the lack of effective control, and, last but not least, the personal ambitions of the General Secretary, all made for the extraordinary weight that the General Secretariat began to carry barely a few months after it had been set up.

The picture would be incomplete without mention of another institution, the Central Control Commission, that came to loom large in Bolshevik affairs. Its role vis-à-vis the party was analogous to that of the Commissariat of the Inspectorate vis-à-vis the governmental machine: it audited party morals. It was formed at the tenth congress, in 1921, on the demand of the Workers' Opposition, with which the congress had otherwise dealt so harshly. It was in charge of the so-called purges. These, too, were initiated by the tenth congress, on the demand of the Opposition. They were intended to cleanse the party periodically of careerists, who had climbed the bandwagon in great numbers, of Communists who had acquired a taste for bourgeois life, and commissars whose heads had been turned by power. Lenin adopted the idea and intended to use it in order to stop his followers departing from the party's puritanic standards. But he also turned one edge of the purges against "anarcho-syndicalists," waverers, doubters, and dissidents, against the real initiators of the new practice.

The procedure of the purges was at first very different from what it became in later years. The purges were no concern of the judiciary. They were conducted by the party's local control commissions before an open citizen's forum, to which Bolsheviks and non-Bolsheviks had free access. The conduct of every member of the party, from the most influential to the humblest, was submitted to stern public scrutiny. Any man or woman from the audience could come forward as a witness. The Bolshevik whose record was found to be unsatisfactory was rebuked or, in extreme cases, expelled from the party. The Control Commission could impose no other penalties than these.

The original motive behind the purges was almost quixotic. It was to enable the people to crack periodically a whip over their rulers. But, since the ruling party was convinced that in all essentials of policy it could not really submit to popular control, these new devices for reviving popular control were *a priori* irrelevant and could not but prove ineffective. They illustrated the party's already familiar dilemma: its growing divorce from the people and its anxiety to preserve its popular character; the dilemma that underlay Lenin's pathetic experiments with his party in the last two years of his political activity. The purges were to serve as a substitute for real elections; they were to remove corrupted members, without removing the party, from power.[1]

The Central Control Commission in Moscow soon became the supreme court of appeal for the victims of the purges all over the country. Originally, it was to be independent from the Central Committee and the Politbureau. Later it was put on an almost equal footing with the Central Committee; and the two bodies regularly held joint sessions. The General Secretariat was the coordinating link between them. Thus, unofficially, Stalin became the chief conductor of the purges.

Lenin, Kamenev, Zinoviev, and, to a lesser extent, Trotsky, were Stalin's sponsors to all the offices he held. His jobs were of the kind which could scarcely attract the bright intellectuals of the Politbureau. All their brilliance in matters of doctrine, all their powers of political analysis would have found little application either at the Workers' and Peasants' Inspectorate or at the General Secretariat. What was needed there was an enormous capacity for hard and uninspiring toil and a patient and sustained interest in every detail of organization. None of his colleagues grudged Stalin his assignments. As long as Lenin kept the reins of government, they looked upon him merely as Lenin's assistant; and all of them readily accepted Lenin's leadership. Neither they nor Lenin noticed in time the subtle change by which Stalin was gradually passing from the role of assistant to that of coadjutor.

Less than two months after Stalin's appointment to the post of General Secretary, the reins of government slipped from Lenin's hands. By the end of May 1922, he suffered his first stroke of arteriosclerotic paralysis. Almost speechless, he was taken out of the Kremlin to the countryside, near Moscow. Not until the middle of the autumn did he recover sufficiently to return to office; and then his activity was very short. At the end of the autumn a second stroke put him out of action; and at the end of the winter, in March 1923, a third stroke removed him finally from the political scene, though his body still wrestled with death until 21 January 1924.

The impact of Lenin's illness on the Bolshevik leadership can hardly be exaggerated. The whole constellation ceased, almost at once, to shine with the reflected light of its master mind or to move in the familiar orbits. Lenin's disciples and satellites (only Trotsky belonged to neither of these categories) began to feel for their own, independent ways. Gradually they were shedding those characteristics of theirs that were merely imitative, their second, and better, nature. The negative side of Lenin's overwhelming and constant influence on his followers now became strikingly apparent. Just how overwhelming it had been can be seen from the circumstances, attested by Trotsky, that during the years of their apprenticeship with their leader, Zinoviev and Kamenev had acquired even Lenin's handwriting. They were now to go on using his handwriting without the inspiration of his ideas.

Stalin was in a sense less dependent on Lenin than were his colleagues; his intellectual needs were more limited than theirs. He was interested in the practical use of the Leninist gadgets, not in the Leninist laboratory of thought. His own behavior was now dictated by the moods, needs, and pressures of the vast political machine that he had come to control. His political philosophy boiled down to securing the dominance of that machine by the handiest and most convenient means. In an avowedly dictatorial regime, repression often is the handiest and most convenient method of action. The Politbureau may have been thrown into disarray by Lenin's disappearance; the General Secretariat was not. On the contrary, since it had no longer to account for what it did to the vigilant and astute supervisor, it acted with greater firmness and self-confidence. The same was true of the Workers' and Peasants' Inspectorate. . . .

It was about this time that a triumvirate, composed of Stalin, Zinoviev, and Kamenev, formed itself within the Politbureau. What made for the solidarity of the three men was their determination to prevent Trotsky from succeeding to the leadership of the party. Separately, neither could measure up to Trotsky. Jointly, they represented a powerful combination of talent and influence. Zinoviev was the politician, the orator, the demagogue with popular appeal. Kamenev was the strategist of the group, its solid brain, trained in matters of doctrine, which were to play a paramount part in the contest for power. Stalin was the tactician of the triumvirate and its organizing force. Between them, the three men virtually controlled the whole party and, through it, the Government. Kamenev had acted as Lenin's deputy and presided over the Moscow Soviet. Zinoviev was the chairman of the Soviet of Petersburg, soon to be renamed Leningrad. Stalin controlled most of the provinces. Zinoviev was, in addition, the President of the Communist International, whose moral authority in Russia was then great enough to make any pretender strive for its support.

Finally, the three men represented, as it were, the party's tradition. Their uninterrupted association with Bolshevism dated back to the split of 1903; and they held seniority in leadership. Of the other members of the Politbureau, apart from Trotsky, Bukharin was considerably younger, and Tomsky, the leader of the trade unions, had only recently become a member of it. Seniority carried with it the halo of a heroic past, distinguished by unflagging devotion to Bolshevism. The three men refused now to follow that "ex-Menshevik," Trotsky, who, after an association with the party which had lasted only five years, had come to be commonly regarded as Lenin's successor. This motive, the only one that made for their solidarity, impelled them to act in concert. As the other members of the Politbureau walked each his own way, the triumvirs automatically commanded a majority. Their motions and proposals, on which they usually agreed before every session of the Politbureau, were invariably carried. The other members were bound hand and foot by the discipline of the Politbureau—any attempt by one of them to discuss their inner controversies in public would have appeared as an act of disloyalty. . . .

Since the promulgation of the NEP in 1921, Russia's economy was beginning to recover. But the process was slow and painful. Industry was still unable to meet the country's most essential needs. It failed to supply the countryside with the goods that would induce peasants to sell food. Low wages, unemployment, and starvation were driving the working class to despair. Since trade unions refused to take up the workers' demands, discontent exploded in "unofficial" strikes. The restive mood penetrated into the ruling party. Clandestine opposition groups were discovered within its ranks. Some of these groups were half Menshevik; others were wholly Bolshevik and consisted of remnants of the oppositions that had been banned in 1921 as well as of new elements. Their main plank was the demand for freedom of criticism inside the party. Some of the dissenters were expelled, others imprisoned. These were the first instances of clandestine opposition among Communists. So far, the secret groups had acted without concert and lacked leadership. The triumvirs feared a linkup between their rivals and the discontented rank and file.

They reacted in 1923 to the crisis in a self-contradictory manner. They put before the Central Committee a motion about the need to restore democracy and freedom of discussion for the members of the party. On the other hand, they mobilized the political police against the secret oppositions. The police found that ordinary Bolsheviks often refused to cooperate in tracing the opposition groups. Dzerzhinsky asked the Politbureau to authorize the police to take action against uncooperative Bolsheviks, too. At this point the fight between Trotsky and the triumvirs entered a new phase. Without making it quite clear whether he thought that Dzerzhinsky's demand should be granted, Trotsky attacked the triumvirate. What had happened, he stated, was symptomatic of the party's state of mind, its sense of frustration, and its distrust of the leaders. Even during the civil war "the system of appointment [from above] did not have one-tenth of the extent that it has now. Appointment of the secretaries of provincial committees is now the rule." He granted that there was a grain of demagogy in the demands for a workers' democracy, "in view of the incompatability of a fully developed workers' democracy with the regime of the dictatorship." But the discipline of the civil war ought to have given place to "a more lively and broader party responsibility." Instead, "the bureaucratization of the party machine had developed to unheard of proportions; and criticism and discontent, the open expression of which was stifled, were driven underground, assuming uncontrollable and dangerous forms."

The triumvirs evaded the issues raised by Trotsky and charged him with malevolence, personal ambition, neglect of his duties in the Government, and so on. They accused him of trying to establish himself as Lenin's successor. This last charge was, in a sense, true, for the fight over the succession was inherent in the situation. Yet this, as well as the other charges, were beside the point, for the crisis in the party, as Trotsky diagnosed it, was a fact.

In the middle of this exchange forty-six prominent Communists issued a declaration the gist of which was identical with Trotsky's criticism. . . . It is not certain whether Trotsky directly instigated their demonstration. So far he had conducted his dispute with the triumvirs behind the closed doors of the Politbureau. The party at large was under the impression that he had all the time been wholeheartedly behind the official policy. He thus had the worst of both worlds: he had been burdened with responsibility for a policy to which he had been opposed; and he had done nothing to rally in time those who might have supported him.

In November the alarm caused by the crisis led the triumvirs to table a motion in favour of democratic reform in the party. As in the Georgian affair, so now Stalin agreed to make any verbal concession to Trotsky. The motion was carried by the Politbureau unanimously. Trotsky had no choice but to vote for it. On 7 November, the sixth anniversary of the revolution, Zinoviev officially announced the opening of a public discussion on all issues that troubled the Bolshevik mind. The state of siege in the party, so it might have seemed, was at last being lifted.

This was not the case. The state of affairs against which the opposition rose was not merely the result of Stalin's or the other triumvirs' ambition and ill will. It had deeper roots. The revolution had saved itself by building up a massive political machine. The apathy, if not the hostility, of the masses drove it to rely increasingly on rule by coercion rather than by persuasion. Who could say with any certainty that the time had now come to reverse all this, to scrap or even curb the political machine, and to rely on the soundness of popular opinion? Who could be sure that this would not have impaired the safety of the revolution? If a workers' democracy was needed, did that mean that the Mensheviks and the Social Revolutionaries were to be allowed to come back? Most of Stalin's critics, including Trotsky, agreed that the Mensheviks should remain outlawed. In their view, the time had not yet come to lift the state of siege in the republic—they wanted it to be lifted in the party only. But was it at all possible that the party should be an island of freedom in a society doomed, for good or evil, to dictatorial rule? Apart from all this, the massive dictatorial machine had now a vested interest in self-perpetuation, which it was able to identify with the broader interest of the revolution. Both sides in the dispute were aware of the dilemma; but while to one of them, the opposition, that awareness was a source of weakness, to the other it was a source of strength.

Trotsky consequently demanded not more than limited reform, to be promulgated from above, a degree of administrative liberalism. He had been careful so far to refrain from any appeal to public opinion, even Communist opinion, against the rulers. Yet he felt the need for bringing the dispute into the open. The official inauguration of a public discussion gave him the opportunity to do so, the opportunity, that is, to appeal to public opinion against the rulers and to do so with the rulers' own formal permission. His inconsistency, real or apparent, was dictated by deeper considerations. He believed that it should be possible to strike a balance between dictatorship and freedom, that it should be possible to restrict or broaden the one or the other, according to circumstances. He hoped that with Russia's economic recovery and the progress of socialism, the regime would be able to rely less and less upon coercion and more and more upon willing support. The revolution should be able to recapture its own youth. The divorce between the revolution and the people, he thought, was of a temporary character. The triumvirs, and especially Stalin, were far less hopeful.

Here we touch the root of most of the differences between Trotskyism and Stalinism. Both insisted on their basic loyalty to the Marxist outlook; and there is no reason to doubt the sincerity of their professions. For both factions to claim allegiance to Marxism and Leninism was as natural as it is for Protestants and Catholics to swear by Christianity. In the one case as in the other the professions of faith, common to both sides, offer almost no clue to their antagonism. What underlay Trotsky's attitude was a cautious and yet very real revolutionary optimism, a belief that, if only the rulers pursued the right Socialist policy, the working classes would support them. This belief had indeed been implicit in the Marxist philosophy; and Stalin never openly contradicted it. But between the lines of his policies there is always present a deep disbelief in the popularity of socialism, and even more than that: an essentially pessimistic approach to man and society. . . .

Meanwhile the one text of Lenin that might have removed the earth from under Stalin's feet, his will, was still unknown to the party and to himself. Only in May 1924, four months after Lenin's death, was it read out at a plenary session of the Central Committee, which was to decide whether the document should be made public at the forthcoming congress of the party. "Terrible embarrassment paralysed all those present," so an eyewitness describes the scene.[2] "Stalin sitting on the steps of the rostrum looked small and miserable. I studied him closely; in spite of his self-control and show of calm, it was clearly evident that his fate was at stake." In the atmosphere of the Leninist cult, it seemed almost sacrilegious to disregard Lenin's will. At this, for him, fateful moment he was saved by Zinoviev. "Comrades," so Zinoviev addressed the meeting, "every word of Ilyich [Lenin] is law to us. . . . We have sworn to fulfill anything the dying Ilyich ordered us to do. You know perfectly well that we shall keep that vow." (Many among the audience drop their eyes—they cannot look the old actor in the face.) "But we are happy to say that in one point Lenin's fears have proved baseless. I have in mind the point about our General Secretary. You have all witnessed our harmonious cooperation in the last few months; and, like myself, you will be happy to say that Lenin's fears have proved baseless."

Kamenev followed with an appeal to the Central Committee that Stalin be left in office. But if this was to happen it was not advisable to publish Lenin's will at the congress. Krupskaya protested against the suppression of her husband's testament, but in vain. Trotsky, present at the meeting, was too proud to intervene in a situation which affected his own standing too. He kept silent, expressing only through his mien and grimaces his disgust at the scene. Zinoviev's motion that the testament should not be published, but only confidentially communicated to picked delegates, was then passed by forty votes against ten. Stalin could now wipe the cold sweat from his brow. He was back in the saddle, firmly and for good.

The solidarity of the triumvirate stood this extraordinary test because both Zinoviev and Kamenev were as convinced that they had nothing to fear from Stalin as they were afraid of Trotsky. Zinoviev, the President of the Communist International, was still the senior and the most popular triumvir. Kamenev was conscious of his intellectual superiority over his partners. Both looked upon Stalin as their auxiliary; and, though they were sometimes uneasy about a streak of perversity in him, neither suspected him of the ambition to become Lenin's sole successor. Nor, for that matter, did any such suspicion enter the mind of the party as a whole.

It was not, on the other hand, very difficult to arouse in the party distrust of Trotsky. The agents of the triumvirate whispered that Trotsky was the potential Danton or, alternatively, the Bonaparte of the Russian revolution. The whispering campaign was effective, because the party had, from its beginnings, been accustomed to consult the great French precedent. It had always been admitted that history might repeat itself; and that a Directory or a single usurper might once again climb to power on the back of the revolution. It was taken for granted that the Russian usurper would, like his French prototype, be a personality possessed of brilliance and legendary fame won in battles. The mask of Bonaparte seemed to fit Trotsky only too well. Indeed, it might have fitted any personality with the exception of Stalin. In this lay part of his strength.

The very thing which under different circumstances would have been a liability in a man aspiring to power, his obscurity, was his important asset. The party had been brought up to distrust "bourgeois individualism" and to strive for collectivism. None of its leaders looked as immune from the former and as expressive of the latter as Stalin. What was striking in the General Secretary was that there was nothing striking about him. His almost impersonal personality seemed to be the ideal vehicle for the anonymous forces of class and party. His bearing seemed of the utmost modesty. He was more accessible to the average official or party man than the other leaders. He studiously cultivated his contacts with the people who in one way or another made and unmade reputations, provincial secretaries, popular satirical writers, and foreign visitors. Himself taciturn, he was unsurpassed at the art of patiently listening to others. . . .

Nor did Stalin at that time impress people as being more intolerant than befitted a Bolshevik leader. He was less vicious in his attacks on the opposition than the other triumvirs.

In his speeches there was usually the tone of a good-natured and soothing, if facile, optimism, which harmonized well with the party's growing complacency. In the Politbureau, when matters of high policy were under debate, he never seemed to impose his views on his colleagues. He carefully followed the course of the debate to see which way the wind was blowing and invariably voted with the majority, unless he had assured his majority beforehand. He was therefore always agreeable to the majority. To party audiences he appeared as a man without personal grudge and rancour, as a detached Leninist, a guardian of the doctrine who criticized others only for the sake of the cause. He gave this impression even when he spoke behind the closed doors of the Politbureau. In the middle of the struggle Trotsky still described Stalin to a trusted foreign visitor as "a brave and sincere revolutionary."[3] A few descriptions of scenes in the Politbureau give a vivid glimpse of Stalin, the good soul:

> When I attended a session of the Politbureau for the first time [writes Bazhanov] the struggle between the triumvirs and Trotsky was in full swing. Trotsky was the first to arrive for the session. The others were late, they were still plotting. . . . Next entered Zinoviev. He passed by Trotsky; and both behaved as if they had not noticed one another. When Kamenev entered, he greeted Trotsky with a slight nod. At last Stalin came in. He approached the table at which Trotsky was seated, greeted him in a most friendly manner and vigorously shook hands with him across the table.[4]

During another session, in the autumn of 1923, one of the triumvirs proposed that Stalin be brought in as a controller into the Commissariat of War, of which Trotsky was still the head. Trotsky, irritated by the proposal, declared that he was resigning from office and asked to be relieved from all posts and honours in Russia and allowed to go to Germany, which then seemed to be on the brink of a Communist upheaval, to take part in the revolution there. Zinoviev countered the move by asking the same for himself. Stalin put an end to the scene, declaring that "the party could not possibly dispense with the services of two such important and beloved leaders."[5]

He was slowly stacking his cards and waiting. The opposition, though again condemned by the thirteenth congress in May 1924, was still a factor to be reckoned with. The attitude of the Communist International had also to be considered. The leaders of European communism, Germans, Poles, and Frenchmen, had either protested against the discrediting of Trotsky or attempted to persuade the antagonists to make peace. It took Zinoviev a lot of wire-pulling to silence those "noises off." . . .

Dissension among the triumvirs was yet another reason for Stalin's caution. Not until a year later, in 1925, did they fall out; but even now personal jealousies troubled their relations. Zinoviev and Kamenev began to feel that Stalin was tightening his grip on the party machine and excluding them from control. Stalin was envious of their authority in matters of doctrine. Shortly after the condemnation of Trotsky, he made his first public attack, irrelevant in content, on Kamenev's doctrinal unreliability. Each of the triumvirs had enough ground to think that a split between them might drive one of them to join hands with Trotsky against the others. This motive did not impel Zinoviev and Kamenev, who eventually were to coalesce with Trotsky, to soften their attacks on him; but it did enter into Stalin's tactical calculations. As a tactician he proved himself superior to his partners.

Finally, he was still waiting for the adversary to make the blunders that were inherent in his attitude. Trotsky had accepted the Leninist cult, even though his rational mind and

European tastes were outraged by it. The uniform of Lenin's disciple was, anyhow, too tight for him. The Leninist *mystique,* however, had already grown too powerful for anybody who wanted to get the hearing of a Communist audience to ignore it, let alone challenge it. Trotsky thus involved himself in fighting on ground where he was weak. The triumvirs hurled at him old anti-Trotskyist quotations from Lenin and, what was even more embarrassing to him, his own strictures on Lenin which he had uttered twelve or fifteen years ago. In the mind of the young Communist, the selection of such quotations added up to a picture of Trotsky malevolently opposing Lenin at every turn of events, from the split in 1903 to the debates over Brest-Litovsk and the trade unions. In the light of the Leninist dogma, Trotsky stood condemned.

For Trotsky to reject the dogma would have meant to appeal against the party to noncommunist opinion. This was the one thing that Stalin could be quite sure Trotsky would not do. Outside the party, formless revolutionary frustration mingled with distinctly counterrevolutionary trends. Since the ruling group had singled out Trotsky as a target for attack, he automatically attracted the spurious sympathy of many who had hitherto hated him. As he made his appearance in the streets of Moscow, he was spontaneously applauded by crowds in which idealistic Communists rubbed shoulders with Mensheviks, Socialist Revolutionaries, and the new bourgeoisie of the NEP, by all those indeed who, for diverse reasons, hoped for a change. Precisely because he refused to rally in his support such mixed elements, he showed timidity and hesitancy in almost every move he made. He could not stop opposing the triumvirs who had identified themselves with the party; and yet even in his rebellion he still remained on his knees before the party. Every move he made was thus a demonstration of weakness. Stalin could afford to wait until his rival defeated himself through a series of such demonstrations.

It is here that the knot was tied which was to be cut only in the tragic purge trials twelve and thirteen years later. It is here, too, that the most important clue to the understanding of those trials is to be found. At the congress in May 1924, Trotsky, facing the implacably hostile phalanx of party secretaries, was on the point of surrendering to his critics and abjuring the opposition. Krupskaya, Radek, and others exhorted the antagonists to make peace. Zinoviev, however, was not to be persuaded. He demanded that Trotsky should surrender in this thoughts as well as in his deeds, that he should admit that he had been wrong in his criticisms. In the history of Bolshevism this was the first instance where a member of the party was vaguely charged with a "crime of conscience," a purely theological accusation. Its motive was tactical, not theological: Trotsky, submitting to party discipline but not recanting, still seemed to the triumvirs a formidable foe. Zinoviev therefore added to the terms of his submission an obviously unacceptable point, which would compel Trotsky to go on waging the unequal struggle. Thus, the first suggestion of a "crime of conscience" against the party was made by the man who, twelve years later, was to go to his death with appalling recantations of his own "crimes of conscience." Stalin, at least in appearance, had nothing to do with that. He repeatedly stated that the only condition for peace was that Trotsky should stop his attacks. He repeatedly made the gesture that looked like the stretching out of his hand to his opponent.

Trotsky's reply to Zinoviev was pregnant with the tragedy that was to overwhelm Zinoviev and Kamenev even more cruelly than himself:

> The party [Trotsky said] in the last analysis is always right, because the party is the single historic instrument given to the proletariat for the solution of its fundamental problems. I have already said that in front of one's own party nothing could be easier

> than to acknowledge a mistake, nothing easier than to say: all my criticisms, my statements, my warnings, my protests—the whole thing was a mere mistake. I, however, comrades, cannot say that, because I do not think it. I know that one must not be right *against* the party. One can be right only with the party, and through the party, for history has created no other road for the realization of what is right. The English have a saying: "Right or wrong—my country." With far greater historic justification we may say: right or wrong, on separate particular issues, it is my party. . . .[6]

These words of the leader of the opposition resembled less the words a patriotic Englishman might use than those of a medieval heretic, confessing his heresy, rueful and yet stubborn in his conviction, able to see no salvation beyond the Church and yet none in the Church either. Stalin sarcastically dismissed Trotsky's statement, saying that the party made no claim to infallibility. . . .

Stalin first formulated his ideas on socialism in one country in the autumn of 1924. Belief in socialism in one country was soon to become the supreme test of loyalty to party and state. In the next ten or fifteen years nobody who failed that test was to escape condemnation and punishment. Yet, if one studies the "prolegomena" to this article of Stalinist faith, one is struck by the fact that it was first put forward by Stalin almost casually, like a mere debating point, in the "literary discussion." For many months, until the summer of the next year, none of Stalin's rivals, neither the other triumvirs not Trotsky, thought the point worth arguing. Nor was Stalin's own mind fixed. In his pamphlet *The Foundations of Leninism*, published early in 1924, he stated with great emphasis that, though the proletariat of one country could seize power, it could not establish a Socialist economy in one country. . . .

He now stated [later in 1924] that the efforts of Russia alone would suffice for the *complete* organization of a Socialist economy. A Socialist economy—this had so far been taken for granted—was conceivable only as an economy of plenty. This presupposed a highly developed industry capable of ensuring a high standard of living for the whole people. How then, the question arose, could a country like Russia, whose meagre industry had been reduced to rack and ruin, achieve socialism? Stalin pointed to Russia's great assets: her vast spaces and enormous riches in raw materials. A proletarian government could, in his view, through its control of industry and credit, develop those resources and carry the building of socialism to a successful conclusion, because in this endeavor it would be supported by a vast majority of the people, including the peasants.

This, the most essential, part of Stalin's formula was very simple. It proclaimed in terms clear to everybody the self-sufficiency of the Russian revolution. It was true that Stalin begged many a question. He did not even try to meet the objections to his thesis that were raised later by his critics. One objection that most peasants, attached as they were to private property, were certain to put up the strongest resistance to collectivism, he simply dismissed as a heretical slander on the peasantry. Nor did he seriously consider the other argument that socialism was possible only on the basis of the intensive industrialization already achieved by the most advanced western countries; and that Russia by herself would not be able to catch up with those countries. According to his critics, socialism could beat capitalism only if it represented a higher productivity of labour and higher standards of living than had been attained under capitalism. The critics deduced that if productivity of labour and standards of living were to remain lower in Russia than in the capitalist countries then socialism would, in the long run, fail even in Russia. Nor did

Stalin ever try to refute their forecast that in an economy of scarcity, such as an isolated Russian economy would be, a new and glaring material inequality between various social groups was certain to arise.

But, whatever the flaws in Stalin's reasoning, flaws that were obvious only to the most educated men in the party, his formula was politically very effective. It contained, at any rate, one clear and positive proposition: we are able to stand on our own feet, to build and to complete the building of socialism. This was what made the formula useful for polemical and practical purposes. It offered a plain alternative to Trotsky's conception. For a variety of reasons, however, Stalin did not present his thesis in that plain and clearcut form. He hedged it round with all sorts of reservations and qualifications. One reservation was that the victory of socialism in Russia could not be considered secure so long as her capitalist environment threatened Russia with armed intervention. Socialism in a single state could not be beaten by the "cheap goods" produced in capitalist countries of which his critics spoke; but it might be defeated by force of arms. In the next few years Stalin himself constantly held that danger before Russia's eyes and thereby seemed to weaken his own case. Moreover, he went on to express, though with ever decreasing confidence, a belief in the proximity of international revolution. He proclaimed the absolute self-sufficiency of Russian socialism in one half of this thesis and disclaimed it in the other.

The strangeness of that passionate ideological dispute does not end here. As the controversy developed, Stalin ascribed to his critics the view that it was not possible to build socialism in Russia. He then presented the issue as one between those who believed in the "creative force" of the revolution and the "panic mongers" and "pessimists." Now the issue was not as simple as that. His critics were beyond question not guilty of the things imputed to them. They, too, asserted that it was possible and necessary to organize the country's economy on Socialist lines. Trotsky in particular had, since the end of the civil war, urged the Politbureau to begin gearing up the administration for planned economy; and in those early days he first sketched most of the ideas that were later to be embodied in the five-year plans.

The student of the controversy may thus often have the uncanny feeling that its very object is indefinable; that, having aroused unbounded passion and bitterness, it simply vanishes into thin air. Stripped of polemical distortions and insinuations, the debate seems in the end, to the student's astonishment, to centre on a bizarre irrelevancy. The point was not whether socialism could or should be built but whether the building could be *completed* in a single isolated state.

Notes

1. *The purges provided a good cover for all sorts of private vendettas. In May 1922, Lenin wrote in a letter to Stalin: " . . . the purging of the party revealed the prevalence, in the majority of local investigation committees, of personal spite and malice. . . . This fact is incontrovertible and rather significant." In the same letter Lenin complained about the lack of party men with "an adequate legal education . . . capable of resisting all purely local influences." See* The Essentials of Lenin, *vol. ii, p. 809.*
2. *B. Bazhanov,* Stalin, der Rote Diktator, *pp. 32–4.*
3. *M. Eastman,* Since Lenin Died, *p. 55.*
4. *B. Bazhanov,* Stalin, der Rote Diktator, *p. 21.*
5. *Ibid., p. 52.*
6. 13 Syezd Vsesoyuznoi Komunisticheskoi Partii, *pp. 166 and 245. See also M. Eastman,* Since Lenin Died, *pp. 88–9.*

The Revolution Betrayed

Leon Trotsky

The Soviet Thermidor

1. Why Stalin Triumphed. . . . A political struggle is in its essence a struggle of interests and forces, not of arguments. The quality of the leadership is, of course, far from a matter of indifference for the outcome of the conflict, but it is not the only factor, and in the last analysis is not decisive. Each of the struggling camps moreover demands leaders in its own image.

The February revolution raised Kerensky and Tseretelli to power, not because they were ''cleverer'' or ''more astute'' than the ruling tsarist clique, but because they represented, at least temporarily, the revolutionary masses of the people in their revolt against the old regime. Kerensky was able to drive Lenin underground and imprison other Bolshevik leaders, not because he excelled them in personal qualifications, but because the majority of the workers and soldiers in those days were still following the patriotic petty bourgeoisie. The personal ''superiority'' of Kerensky, if it is suitable to employ such a word in this connection, consisted in the fact that he did not see farther than the overwhelming majority. The Bolsheviks in their turn conquered the petty bourgeois democrats, not through the personal superiority of their leaders, but through a new correlation of social forces. The proletariat had succeeded at last in leading the discontented peasantry against the bourgeoisie. . . .

It is sufficiently well known that every revolution up to this time has been followed by a reaction, or even a counterrevolution. This, to be sure, has never thrown the nation all the way back to its starting point, but it has always taken from the people the lion's share of their conquests. The victims of the first reactionary wave have been, as a general rule, those pioneers, initiators, and instigators who stood at the head of the masses in the period of the revolutionary offensive. In their stead people of the second line, in league with the former enemies of the revolution, have been advanced to the front. Beneath this dramatic duel of ''coryphées'' on the open political scene, shifts have taken in the relations between classes, and, no less important, profound changes in the psychology of the recently revolutionary masses. . . .

A revolution is a mighty devourer of human energy, both individual and collective. The nerves give way. Consciousness is shaken and characters are worn out. Events unfold too swiftly for the flow of fresh forces to replace the loss. . . .

The axiomlike assertions of the Soviet literature, to the effect that the laws of bourgeois revolutions are ''inapplicable'' to a proletarian revolution, have no scientific content whatever. The proletarian character of the October revolution was determined by the world situation and by a special correlation of internal forces. But the classes themselves were formed in the barbarous circumstances of tsarism and backward capitalism, and

This selection is from chapter 5 and the appendix of the book by the same title, written by Trotsky in 1936 (New York: Pioneer Publishers, 1945). By permission of the publisher.

were anything but made to order for the demands of a socialist revolution. The exact opposite is true. It is for the very reason that a proletariat still backward in many respects achieved in the space of a few months the unprecedented leap from a semifeudal monarchy to a socialist dictatorship, that the reaction in its rank was inevitable. This reaction has developed in a series of consecutive waves. External conditions and events have vied with each other in nourishing it. Intervention followed intervention. The revolution got no direct help from the west. Instead of the expected prosperity of the country an ominous destitution reigned for long. Moreover, the outstanding representatives of the working class either died in the civil war, or rose a few steps higher and broke away from the masses. And thus after an unexampled tension of forces, hopes and illusions, there came a long period of weariness, decline and sheer disappointment in the results of the revolution. The ebb of the "plebeian pride" made room for a flood of pusillanimity and careerism. The new commanding caste rose to is place upon this wave.

The demobilization of the Red Army of five million played no small role in the formation of the bureaucracy. The victorious commanders assumed leading posts in the local Soviets, in education, and they persistently introduced everywhere that regime which had ensured success in the civil war. Thus on all sides the masses were pushed away gradually from actual participation in the leadership of the country.

The reaction within the proletariat caused an extraordinary flush of hope and confidence in the petty bourgeois strata of town and country, aroused as they were to new life by the NEP, and growing bolder and bolder. The young bureacracy, which had arisen at first as an agent of the proletariat, began now to feel itself a court of arbitration between the classes. Its independence increased from month to month.

The international situation was pushing with mighty forces in the same direction. As the Soviet bureaucracy became more self-confident, the heavier the blows dealt to the world working class. Between these two facts there was not only a chronological, but a causal connection, and one which worked in two directions. The leaders of the bureaucracy promoted the proletarian defeats; the defeats promoted the rise of the bureaucracy. The crushing of the Bulgarian insurrection and the inglorious retreat of the German workers' party in 1923, the collapse of the Esthonian attempt at insurrection in 1924, the treacherous liquidation of the General Strike in England and the unworthy conduct of the Polish workers' party at the installation of Pilsudski in 1926, the terrible massacre of the Chinese revolution of 1927, and, finally, the still more ominous recent defeats in Germany and Austria—these are the historic catastrophes which killed the faith of the Soviet masses in world revolution, and permitted the bureaucracy to rise higher and higher as the sole light of salvation. . . .

Two dates are especially significant in this historic series. In the second half of 1923, the attention of the Soviet workers was passionately fixed upon Germany, where the proletariat, it seemed, had stretched out its hand to power. The panicky retreat of the German Communist Party was the heaviest possible disappointment to the working masses of the Soviet Union. The Soviet bureaucracy straightway opened a campaign against the theory of "permanent revolution," and dealt the Left Opposition its first cruel blow. During the years 1926 and 1927 the population of the Soviet Union experienced a new tide of hope. All eyes were now directed to the East where the drama of the Chinese revolution was unfolding. The Left Opposition had recovered from the previous blows and was recruiting a phalanx of new adherents. At the end of 1927 the Chinese revolution was massacred by the hagman, Chiang-kai-shek, into whose hands the Communist International had literally betrayed the Chinese workers and peasants. A cold wave of disappointment swept over the masses of the Soviet Union. After an unbridled baiting in the press and at meetings, the bureaucracy finally, in 1928, ventured upon mass arrests among the Left Opposition.

To be sure, tens of thousands of revolutionary fighters gathered around the banner of the Bolshevik-Leninists. The advanced workers were indubitably sympathetic to the Opposition, but that sympathy remained passive. The masses lacked faith that the situation could be seriously changed by a new struggle. Meantime the bureaucracy asserted: "For the sake of an international revolution, the Opposition proposes to drag us into a revolutionary war. Enough of shake-ups! We have earned the right to rest. We will build the socialist society at home. Rely upon us, your leaders!" This gospel of repose firmly consolidated the *apparatchiki* and the military and state officials and indubitably found an echo among the weary workers, and still more the peasant masses. Can it be, they asked themselves, that the Opposition is actually ready to sacrifice the interests of the Soviet Union for the idea of "permanent revolution?" In reality, the struggle had been about the life interests of the Soviet state. The false policy of the International in Germany resulted ten years later in the victory of Hitler—that is, in a threatening war danger from the West. And the no less false policy in China reinforced Japanese imperialism and brought very much nearer the danger in the East. But periods of reaction are characterized above all by a lack of courageous thinking. . . .

Personal incidents were not, of course, without influence. Thus the sickness and death of Lenin undoubtedly hastened the denouement. Had Lenin lived longer, the pressure of the bureaucratic power would have developed, at least during the first years, more slowly. But as early as 1926 Krupskaya said, in a circle of Left Oppositionists: "If Ilyich were alive, he would probably already be in prison." The fears and alarming prophecies of Lenin himself were then still fresh in her memory, and she cherished no illusions as to his personal omnipotence against opposing historic winds and currents.

The bureaucracy conquered something more than the Left Opposition. It conquered the Bolshevik party. It defeated the program of Lenin, who had seen the chief danger in the conversion of the organs of the state "from servants of society to lords over society." It defeated all these enemies, the Opposition, the party and Lenin, not with ideas and arguments, but with its own social weight. The leaden rump of the bureaucracy outweighed the head of the revolution. That is the secret of the Soviet's Thermidor.

2. The Degeneration of the Bolshevik Party. The Bolshevik party prepared and insured the October victory. It also created the Soviet state, supplying it with a sturdy skeleton. The degeneration of the party became both cause and consequence of the bureaucratization of the state. It is necessary to show at least briefly how this happened.

The inner regime of the Bolshevik party was characterized by the method of *democratic centralism*. The combination of these two concepts, democracy and centralism, is not in the least contradictory. The party took watchful care not only that its boundaries should always be strictly defined, but also that all those who entered these boundaries should enjoy the actual right to define the direction of the party policy. Freedom of criticism and intellectual struggle was an irrevocable content of the party democracy. The present doctrine that Bolshevism does not tolerate factions is a myth of the epoch of decline. In reality the history of Bolshevism is a history of the struggle of factions. And, indeed, how could a genuinely revolutionary organization, setting itself the task of overthrowing the world and uniting under its banner the most audacious iconoclasts, fighters and insurgents, live and develop without intellectual conflicts, without groupings and temporary factional formations? The farsightedness of the Bolshevik leadership often made it possible to soften conflicts and shorten the duration of factional struggle, but no more than that. The Central Committee relied upon this seething democratic support. From this it derived the audacity to make decisions and give orders. The obvious correctness of the leadership at all critical stages gave it that high authority which is the priceless moral capital of centralism. . . .

In the beginning, the party had wished and hoped to preserve freedom of political struggle within the framework of the Soviets. The civil war introduced stern amendments into this calculation. The opposition parties were forbidden one after the other. This measure, obviously in conflict with the spirit of Soviet democracy, the leaders of Bolshevism regarded not as a principle, but as an episodic act of self-defense.

The swift growth of the ruling party, with the novelty and immensity of its tasks, inevitably gave rise to inner disagreements. The underground oppositional currents in the country exerted a pressure through various channels upon the sole legal political organization, increasing the acuteness of the factional struggle. At the moment of completion of the civil war, this struggle took such sharp forms as to threaten to unsettle the state power. In March 1921, in the days of the Kronstadt revolt, which attracted into its ranks no small number of Bolsheviks, the tenth congress of the party thought it necessary to resort to a prohibition of factions—that is, to transfer the political regime prevailing in the state to the inner life of the ruling party. This forbidding of factions was again regarded as an exceptional measure to be abandoned at the first serious improvement in the situation. At the same time, the Central Committee was extremely cautious in applying the new law, concerning itself most of all lest it lead to a strangling of the inner life of the party.

However, what was in its original design merely a necessary concession to a difficult situation, proved perfectly suited to the taste of the bureaucracy, which had then begun to approach the inner life of the party exclusively from the viewpoint of convenience in administration. . . . Of party democracy there remained only recollections in the memory of the older generation. And together with it had disappeared the democracy of the soviets, the trade unions, the cooperatives, the cultural and athletic organizations. Above each and every one of them there reigns an unlimited hierarchy of party secretaries. The regime had become "totalitarian" in character several years before this word arrived from Germany. . . . The prohibition of oppositional parties brought after it the prohibition of factions. The prohibition of factions ended in a prohibition to think otherwise than the infallible leaders. The police-manufactured monolithism of the party resulted in a bureaucratic impunity which has become the source of all kinds of wantonness and corruption.

The social meaning of the Soviet Thermidor now begins to take form before us. The poverty and cultural backwardness of the masses has again become incarnate in the malignant figure of the ruler with a great club in his hand. The deposed and abused bureaucracy, from being a servant of society, has again become its lord. On this road it has attained such a degree of social and moral alienation from the popular masses, that it cannot now permit any control over either its activities or its income. . . .

*[**Editor's note:** On this issue, Sidney Hook has written, contra Trotsky, that "the only controllable factor that led to the degeneration of the Russian Revolution and its Thermidorian regime was the abrogation of working-class democracy, signalized by the suppression of all other political parties and the concentration of all power in the hands of the Communist Party."*

He added that "It does not require much perspicacity to realize that the dictatorship of a political party cannot for long be effective without its own internal organization becoming dictatorial. The necessity of controlling *the mass of the population over whom the party wields a dictatorship, of effectively combating enemies, real and alleged, of imposing a uniform ideology, compels the party to assume a military, sometimes called monolithic, structure."]*

"Socialism, in One Country" . . .

In Lenin's "Declaration of the Rights of the Toiling and Exploited People"—presented by the Soviet of People's Commissars for the approval of the Constituent Assembly during its brief hours of life—the "fundamental task" of the new regime was thus defined: "The establishment of a socialist organization of society and the victory of socialism in all countries." The international character of the revolution was thus written into the basic document of the new regime. No one at that time would have dared present the problem otherwise! In April 1924, three months after the death of Lenin, Stalin wrote, in his brochure of compilations called *The Foundations of Leninism:* "For the overthrow of the bourgeoisie, the efforts of one country are enough—to this the history of our own revolution testifies. For the final victory of socialism, for the organization of socialist production, the efforts of one country, especially a peasant country like ours, are not enough—for this we must have the efforts of the proletarians of several advanced countries." These lines need no comment. The edition in which they were printed, however, has been withdrawn from circulation.

The large-scale defeats of the European proletariat, and the first very modest economic successes of the Soviet Union, suggested to Stalin, in the autumn of 1924, the idea that the historic mission of the Soviet bureaucracy was to build socialism in a single country. . . .

The "theory" of socialism in one country—a "theory" never expounded, by the way, or given any foundation, by Stalin himself—comes down to the sufficiently sterile and unhistoric notion that, thanks to the natural riches of the country, a socialist society can be built within the geographic confines of the Soviet Union. With the same success you might affirm that socialism could triumph if the population of the earth were a twelfth of what it is. In reality, however, the purpose of this new theory was to introduce into the social consciousness a far more concrete system of ideas, namely: the revolution is wholly completed; social contradictions will steadily soften; the kulak will gradually grow into socialism; the development as a whole, regardless of events in the external world, will preserve a peaceful and planned character. Bukharin, in attempting to give some foundation to the theory, declared it unshakably proven that "we shall not perish owing to class differences within our country and our technical backwardness, that we can build socialism even on this pauper technical basis, that this growth of socialism will be many times slower, that we will crawl with a tortoise tempo, and that nevertheless we are building this socialism, and we will build it." We remark the formula: "Build socialism even on a pauper technical basis," and we recall once more the genial intuition of the young Marx: with a low technical basis "only want will be generalized, and with want the struggle for necessities begins again, and all the old crap must revive. . . ."

Socialism must inevitably "surpass" capitalism in all spheres—wrote the Left Opposition in a document illegally distributed in March 1927—

> but at present the question is not of the relation of socialism to capitalism in general, but of the economic development of the Soviet Union in relation to Germany, England and the United States. What is to be understood by the phrase 'minimal historic peri-

> od'? A whole series of future five-year plans will leave us far from the level of the advanced countries of the West. What will be happening in the capitalist world during this time? . . . If you admit the possibility of its flourishing anew for a period of decades, then the talk of socialism in our backward country is pitiable tripe. Then it will be necessary to say that we were mistaken in our appraisal of the whole epoch as an epoch of capitalist decay. Then the Soviet Republic will prove to have been the second experiment in proletarian dictatorship since the Paris Commune, broader and more fruitful, but only an experiment. . . . Is there, however, any serious ground for such a decisive reconsideration of our whole epoch, and of the meaning of the October revolution as a link in an international revolution? No! . . . In finishing to a more or less complete extent their period of reconstruction [after the war] . . . the capitalist countries are reviving, and reviving in an incomparably sharper form, all the old pre-war contradictions, domestic and international. This is the basis of the proletarian revolution. It is a fact that we are building socialism. A greater fact, however, and not a less—since the whole in general is greater than the part—is the preparation of a European and world revolution. The part can conquer only together with the whole. . . . The European proletariat needs a far shorter period for its take-off to the seizure of power than we need to catch up technically with Europe and America. . . . We must, meanwhile, systematically narrow the distance separating our productivity of labor from that of the rest of the world. The more we advance, the less danger there is of possible intervention by low prices, and consequently by armies. . . . The higher we raise the standard of living of the workers and peasants, the more truly shall we hasten the proletarian revolution in Europe, the sooner will that revolution enrich us with world technique, and the more truly and genuinely will our socialist construction advance as a part of European and world construction.

This document, like the others, remained without answer—unless you consider expulsions from the party and arrests an answer to it. . . .

To be sure, the isolation of the Soviet Union did not have those immediate dangerous consequences which might have been feared. The capitalist world was too disorganized and paralyzed to unfold to the full extent its potential power. The "breathing spell" proved longer than a critical optimism had dared to hope. However, isolation and the impossibility of using the resources of world economy even upon capitalistic bases (the amount of foreign trade has decreased from 1913 four to five times) entailed, along with enormous expenditures upon military defense, an extremely disadvantageous allocation of productive forces, and a slow raising of the standard of living of the masses. But a more malign product of isolation and backwardness has been the octopus of bureaucratism.

The juridical and political standards set up by the revolution exercised a progressive action upon the backward economy, but upon the other hand they themselves felt the lowering influence of that backwardness. The longer the Soviet Union remains in a capitalist environment, the deeper runs the degeneration of the social fabric. A prolonged isolation would inevitably end not in national communism, but in a restoration of capitalism.

If a bourgeoisie cannot peacefully grow into a socialist democracy, it is likewise true that a socialist state cannot peacefully merge with a world capitalist system. On the historic order of the day stands not the peaceful socialist development of "one country," but a long series of world disturbances: wars and revolutions. Disturbances are inevitable also in the domestic life of the Soviet Union. If the bureaucracy was compelled in its struggle for a planned economy to dekulakize the kulak, the working class will be compelled in its struggle for socialism to debureaucratize the bureaucracy. On the tomb of the latter will be inscribed the epitaph: "Here lies the theory of socialism in one country."

Trotskyism

John Plamenatz

As an indictment of Stalinism, Trotsky's account of Soviet Russia is formidable. So much so, indeed, that some version or other of it has been adopted by nearly all Stalin's more plausible critics. But the account is not only an attack on Stalinism; it is also an apology for Trotsky and Lenin. For it was their revolution that Stalin betrayed, misunderstood and corrupted.

As an apology for the Bolshevik revolution, Trotsky's account is not impressive. It makes the assumption that Lenin made about the condition of western capitalism and the prospect of immediate world revolution. Trotsky, no more than Lenin, understood how it was that the German Social-Democrats, nourished on Marxism and enjoying in their own country incomparably greater working-class support than the Bolsheviks had ever done in Russia, could not make a proletarian revolution. He, too, spoke of treachery and corruption in a bourgeois environment. It never occurred to him that the German workers, knowing the "sham democracy" of the bourgeois better than he did, might have learnt to like it and to prize the benefits it brought them. Every sign of disorder in Germany seemed to him to announce the coming proletarian revolution in the West—the revolution so much needed by the Bolsheviks to justify their desperate hazard of 1917 but which the German workers felt they could do without. Blinded by Marxism, Trotsky even mistook the great and rapid increase in the number of civil servants in western countries for evidence that bourgeois repression was increasing as bourgeois predominance grew less secure. Though he survived Lenin by many years, he would not—perhaps because he dared not—recognize the emergence of the democratic welfare state. That state has, no doubt, inefficiencies and injustices peculiar to itself, but they are not faults that lead to proletarian revolution. The welfare state is no more bourgeois than the Communist state is proletarian. These old-fashioned categories no longer apply, but the Communist still believes that they do, and therefore systematically misdescribes the world he lives in.

The Bolshevik revolution was never betrayed, for both Lenin and Trotsky miscalculated when they made it. They quite misread the situation in the West; for there never was reasonable hope of proletarian revolution in Germany, or in any other major industrial country during or after the First World War. The Bolshevik revolution was premature and the coming of Stalinism, whose causes Trotsky described so well, was therefore (on Marxian premises) inevitable. If Marxism is true, not all the valiant efforts of Lenin and Trotsky could have prevented the emergence of some such system as Stalin later stood for. The "objective conditions" of his success were created by the Bolshevik revolution—which was itself a betrayal of Marxism but which no Marxist could betray. . . .

Moreover, most of the evil consequences of premature revolution were already apparent before Lenin died. They were, indeed, consequences of courses that the Bolsheviks had felt themselves driven to in their "valiant efforts" to retain power. They had had to fight hard to defeat numerous enemies, and most of the institutions that Trotsky after-

John Plamenatz is a Fellow of Nuffield College, Oxford. This selection is from pp. 303–05 of German Marxism and Russian Communism, *Longmans, Green & Co., Inc., 1954. By permission of the publisher.*

wards considered preclusive of socialism had been created to give victory to the Bolsheviks. After the civil war they had somewhat relaxed their hold on an almost stifled economy but had kept all their instruments of coercion; and Trotsky for one had never suggested that they could do without them. His strong dislike for these instruments was not evident until there was no longer a hope of his using them.

There can be no doubt that Stalin was right and Trotsky wrong in the dispute between them about the imminence of proletarian revolution outside Russia. There was not, after 1920, even the glimmer of a hope of it in any great industrial country. Had the Bolsheviks exerted themselves to stimulate it, they would have failed miserably and have united all the Powers against them. Western governments were willing enough to let the Bolsheviks play the masters in exhausted Russia, provided they kept their hands off the rest of Europe. It did not greatly concern them who killed whom, or how many millions starved, in so remote, impoverished and barbarous a country. They were too much occupied with their own quarrels and too little recovered from the effects of war to embark on new adventures in Russia. They had, for a time, while they thought the Whites might beat the Reds, thrust their little fingers just a short way into the Russian mess, but had got nothing for themselves or their friends by doing so. Russia, they now thought, was best left alone. She was the victim of a dreadful and catching disease, and should be kept away from other nations and allowed to cure herself as best she might. The western governments wanted to have as little to do with her as possible, and she was therefore safe from them. Only the reckless policy advocated by Trotsky could have caused them to change their minds, and drive the Bolsheviks out of Russia before they had time to make her and themselves formidable.

Chapter 6

THE ROLE OF TERROR

In the chapter titled "Marxism into Leninism," the discussion dealt primarily with the *theoretical* position of Lenin on the interrelationship between Marxist ends and revolutionary and violent means in the taking of power. In this section we are principally concerned with the *actual* uses of terror in the USSR as a means of securing, maintaining, and extending power—political and personal.

One of the most provocative explanations of the role of terror in a modern state appears in Barrington Moore, Jr., *Terror and Progress, USSR*. He suggests that organized terror

> does not stem from any particular type of economic structure, but from the attempt to alter the structure of society at a rapid rate and from above through forceful administrative devices. The essence of the situation appears to lie in the crusading spirit, the fanatical conviction of the justice and universal applicability of some ideal about the way life should be organized, along with a lack of serious concern about the consequences of the methods used to pursue this ideal. . . . The attempt to change institutions rapidly nearly always results in opposition by established interests. The more rapid and more thorough the change, the more extensive and bitter is the opposition likely to be. Hence organized terror becomes necessary. . . .
>
> If the socialists are content to take over the situation left by their predecessors without making fundamental changes, relatively little terror may be needed. This was the situation originally anticipated in Marxist theory, where terror would merely brush away the remnants of the old order. If, on the other hand, socialism is to be dynamic after it has come to power, it is likely to require the constant application of terror, both against the population at large and dissidents within its own ranks.

However, there is serious doubt whether the scope, intensity and duration of terror in the Soviet Union bear any relation to the continuance of socialist dynamism. Under Stalin, terror generated fear and immobilism and, in aid of communist objectives, was probably largely dysfunctional. It led to widespread famine and the killing or incarceration of millions, including many committed and competent Soviet leaders and supporters. It is surely tenable to maintain as Roy A. Medvedev does in *Let History Judge* (written by him in the USSR but published only in the West) that "The great transformation would have been effected much more quickly if Stalin had not destroyed hundreds of thousands of the intelligentsia, both old and new. Prisoners in

Stalin's concentration camps accomplished a great deal, building almost all the canals and hydroelectric stations, many railways, industrial plants, oil pipelines, even tall buildings in Moscow. But industry would have developed faster if these millions of innocent people had worked as free men. Likewise, the use of force against the peasantry slowed down the growth rate of agriculture, with painful effects on the whole Soviet economy to the present day." Would not, he asks, "the solidarity between the people and the government have been stronger had there been no mass repression?" And, specifically, "would not the war have ended much faster and with fewer losses if our finest officers had not perished before the war?" Another authority on Soviet purges, Robert Conquest, in his documented study, *The Great Terror,* concludes that whatever the ends in mind, "the casualties were too great for any attainable political or social objective."

What has happened to terror as a system of power in the USSR since the death of Stalin? There is fairly general agreement on the part of Kremlinologists that organized, systematic and pervasive terror does not exist in the Soviet Union today and is unlikely to recur. Alexander Dallin and George W. Breslauer, for example, in *Political Terror in Communist Systems,* conclude that "the dynamics of the system points in the opposite direction," that is, away from terror. Carl J. Friedrich, on the other hand, in *Totalitarianism in Perspective* argues that physical terror in the Soviet Union has to a considerable degree been replaced by sophisticated methods of psychic terror aided by the monopoly of mass communications. Terror of this kind, he writes elsewhere, "that forces people to see the error of their ways," remains highly functional in advancing the objectives of the regime.

Several other chapters in this book deal with or touch upon aspects of the role of terror in the Soviet Union; most notably those titled "Law and Politics" and "Intellectual Dissent."

Terror as a System of Power

Merle Fainsod

The Uses of Terror

The practice of totalitarian terror generates its own underlying theoretical justification. The role of terror in Communist ideology furnishes a prime example. Violence is accepted as implicit in the class struggle. As Lenin said in defending the dissolution of the Constituent Assembly, "Violence when it is committed by the toiling and exploited masses is the kind of violence of which we approve." This instrumental attitude toward violence prepares the way for its sanctification when employed by the Party in the name of the working class and by the Party leadership in the name of the Party.

The rationalization of terror embraces two central propositions. The first emphasizes the safety of the Revolution as the supreme law. In the words of Lenin, "The Soviet Republic is a fortress besieged by world capital. . . . From this follows our right and our duty to mobilize the whole population to a man for the war." The second emphasizes the intransigence of the enemies of the Revolution, the necessity of crushing them completely if the Revolution itself is not to be destroyed. . . .

The formula of capitalist encirclement proved elastic enough to embrace the enemy inside the Party as well as the enemy outside. . . . In his report to the Eighteenth Party Congress in 1939, Stalin addressed himself to the issue, "It is sometimes asked: 'We have abolished the exploiting classes; there are no longer any hostile classes in the country; there is nobody to suppress; hence there is no more need for the state; it must die away—Why then do we not help our socialist state to die away? . . . Is it not time we relegated the state to the museum of antiquities?' " Stalin rested his case for the retention of the terror apparatus on the allegation of capitalist encirclement:

> These questions not only betray an underestimation of the capitalist encirclement, but also an underestimation of the role and significance of the bourgeois states and their organs, which send spies, assassins and wreckers into our country and are waiting for a favourable opportunity to attack it by armed force. They likewise betray an underestimation of the role and significance of our socialist state and of its military, punitive and intelligence organs, which are essential for the defense of the socialist land from foreign attack.

Writing in 1950, after a considerable expansion of Soviet power as a result of World War II, Stalin remained committed to "the conclusion that in the face of capitalist encirclement, when the victory of the socialist revolution has taken place in one country alone while capitalism continues to dominate in all other countries, the country where the revolution has triumphed must not weaken but must strengthen in every way its state, state organs, intelligence agencies, and army if it does not want to be destroyed by capitalist encirclement." Behind these rationalizations was the crystallization of a system of govern-

Merle Fainsod was Professor of Government at Harvard University. Reprinted by permission of the publishers from chapter 13 of Merle Fainsod's How Russia Is Ruled *(Cambridge, Mass.: Harvard University Press, Copyright, 1953, by the President and Fellows of Harvard College). For footnote references, see original source.*

ment in which terror had become the essential ingredient. Defended originally as an expression of the class interests of the proletariat, its edge was first turned against all opponents of Communist ascendency and finally against any appearance of challenge to the domination of the ruling clique. . . .

*[**Editor's note:** Professor Fainsod then traces the development of the Bolshevik apparatus of terror from the first weeks after the seizure of power in 1917 to 1934. During this period, the most massive application of terror was directed against the kulaks. As he explains, "The commitment to collectivize and mechanize argiculture involved a decision to liquidate the kulaks as a class, on the ground that they were inveterate enemies of Soviet power and could be counted on to sabotage collectivization. . . . The OGPU was assigned the task of ejecting them from their land, confiscating their property, and deporting them to the north of Siberia. Some of the more recalcitrant were shot when they resisted arrest or responded with violence to efforts to dispossess them. The great majority became wards of the OGPU and were sentenced to forced labor in lumber camps or coal mines, or on canals, railroads, and other public works which the OGPU directed. At one stroke, the OGPU became the master of the largest pool of labor in the Soviet Union."]*

Before 1934 the victims of the OGPU-NKVD were largely former White Guards, the bourgeoisie, political opponents of the Bolsheviks, Nepmen, members of the old intelligentsia, and kulaks. During the late twenties and early thirties, some members of the Trotsky-Zinoviev and Right oppositions were also arrested by the OGPU and condemned to administrative exile or confinement in political *isolators;* but as Anton Ciliga, who was sentenced to one of the latter, records, the political prisoners received "special treatment," had books at their disposal, held meetings and debates, published prison news sheets, and lived a relatively privileged existence compared with the wretched inhabitants of the forced labor camps. Until 1934, the Party was largely exempt from the full impact of the OGPU-NKVD terror; the relatively few oppositionists who were confined in OGPU prisons were still treated with comparative humanity.

*[**Editor's note:** In July of 1934, the OGPU was transformed into the People's Commissariat of Internal Affairs or NKVD.]*

In December 1934, when Kirov was assassinated by Nikolayev, allegedly a former member of the Zinoviev opposition, a new era in NKVD history opened. The "liberal" regime which the imprisoned "oppositionists" enjoyed came to an abrupt end. The concentrated power of the NKVD was now directed toward uprooting all actual or potential opposition in the Party. For the first time, the Party felt the full brunt of the terror.

The murder of Kirov was followed by drastic reprisals. Nikolayev and a group of his alleged confederates were charged with having formed a so-called Leningrad Center to organize the assassination and were condemned to death. More than a hundred persons who had been arrested prior to Kirov's death as "counterrevolutionaries" were promptly handed over to military commissions of the Supreme Court of the USSR for trial, were found guilty of preparing and carrying out terrorist acts, and were instantly shot. This demonstrative massacre was accompanied by the arrest and imprisonment, on charges of negligence, of twelve high NKVD officials in Leningrad. In the spring of 1935, thousands and perhaps tens of thousands of Leningrad inhabitants who were suspected of harboring opposition sentiments were arrested and deported to Siberia. In the sardonic nomenclature of exile and concentration camp, they came to be referred to collectively as "Kirov's assassins."

Zinoviev, Kamenev, and all the principal leaders of the Zinoviev group were also arrested and transferred to the political *isolator* at Verkhne-Uralsk. During the summer of 1935, Zinoviev, Kamenev, and an assortment of lesser figures were secretly tried for plotting against the life of Stalin. According to Ciliga, "Two of the prisoners were shot: one collaborator of the G.P.U. and one officer of the Kremlin Guard. The others escaped with sentences ranging between five and ten years." . . .

The Great Purge reached its climax in the period 1936–1938. Its most dramatic external manifestation was the series of show trials in the course of which every trace of Old Bolshevik opposition leadership was officially discredited and exterminated. The first of the great public trials took place in August, 1936. Zinoviev, Kamenev, Ivan Smirnov, and thirteen associates were charged with organizing a clandestine terrorist center under instructions from Trotsky, with accomplishing the murder of Kirov, and with preparing similar attempts against the lives of other Party leaders. All sixteen were executed. In the course of the trial, the testimony of the accused compromised many other members of the Bolshevik Old Guard. A wave of new arrests followed. On August 23, 1936, Tomsky, hounded by a sense of impending doom, committed suicide.

In January 1937 came the Trial of the Seventeen, the so-called Anti-Soviet Trotskyite Center, which included such prominent figures as Pyatakov, Radek, Sokolnikov, Serebryakov, and Muralov. This time the accused were charged with plotting the forcible overthrow of the Soviet government with the aid of Germany and Japan, with planning the restoration of capitalism in the USSR, and with carrying on espionage, wrecking, diversive, and terrorist activities on behalf of foreign states. Again, the trial was arranged to demonstrate that Trotsky was the *éminence grise* who inspired, organized, and directed all these activities. The prisoners in the dock fought for their lives by playing their assigned role in a drama designed to destroy Trotsky's reputation. Radek and Sokolnikov were rewarded with ten-year prison sentences. Two minor figures were also sentenced to long prison terms. The remaining thirteen were shot.

On June 12, 1937, *Pravda* carried the announcement of the execution of Marshal Tukhachevsky and seven other prominent generals of the Red Army "for espionage and treason to the Fatherland." This time no public trial was held. The Party press merely declared that the executed generals had conspired to overthrow the Soviet government and to reestablish "the yoke of the landowners and industrialists." The conspirators were alleged to be in the service of the military intelligence of "a foreign government," to which they were supposed to have indicated their readiness to surrender the Soviet Ukraine in exchange for assistance in bringing about the downfall of the Soviet government. . . . The execution of Tukhachevsky and his associates was the prelude to a mass purge of the Soviet armed forces in the course of which the top commanding personnel was particularly hard hit.

The slaughter of the Old Guard continued with the Trial of the Twenty-One, the so-called Anti-Soviet Bloc of Rights and Trotskyites, in March 1938. Among the prisoners in the dock were Bukharin, Rykov, and Krestinsky, all former members of the Politburo; Yagoda, the former head of the NKVD; Rakovsky, the former chairman of the Council of People's Commissars in the Ukraine and Soviet ambassador to England and France; Rosengoltz, the former People's Commissar of Foreign Trade; Grinko, the former People's Commissar of Finance; and Khodjayev, the former chairman of the Council of People's Commissars of Uzbekistan. The indictment against them embraced the usual combination of treason, espionage, diversion, terrorism, and wrecking. The bloc headed by Bukharin and Rykov was alleged to have spied for foreign powers from the earliest days of the Revolution, to have entered into secret agreements with the Nazis and the Japanese to dismember the Soviet Union, to have planned the assassination of Stalin and the rest of the Politburo, and to have organized innumerable acts of sabotage and diversion in order to wreck the economic and political power of the Soviet Union. If the testimony of Yagoda is to be believed, he not only murdered his predecessor in office, Menzhinsky, but also tried to murder his successor, Yezhov; he facilitated the assassination of Kirov, was responsible for the murder of Gorky, Gorky's son, and Kuibyshev; he admitted foreign spies into his organization and protected their operations; he planned a palace coup in the Kremlin and the assassination of the Politburo.

If these lurid tales strain the credulity of the reader, they nevertheless represent the version of oppositionist activity which Stalin and his faithful lieutenants found it expedient to propagate. Without access to the archives of the Kremlin and the NKVD, it is doubtful whether the web of fact and fancy behind the show trials will ever be authoritatively disentangled. The hatred of the former leaders of the opposition for Stalin can be taken for granted. That their hatred carried them to the point of conspiring together to overthrow him is not unlikely, though the evidence adduced at the trials to support the charge is lame and unconvincing. What appears singularly implausible are the allegations that Old Bolsheviks who had given their lives to the Communist cause would plot with the Nazis to restore capitalism in the Soviet Union, would function as their puppets and espionage agents, and arrange to hand over large portions of the Soviet Union to them as compensation for dethroning Stalin. . . .

The crescendo of the Great Purge was reached in the second period, which extended from late September 1937, when Yezhov was appointed head of the NKVD, until the end of July 1938, when Lavrenti Beria was designated as Yezhov's deputy and eventual successor. The announcement of Yezhov's removal did not come until December, but meanwhile Beria assumed *de facto* command of the NKVD organization, and early in 1939, Yezhov disappeared and was probably liquidated.

The period of the Yezhovshchina involved a reign of terror without parallel in Soviet history. Among those arrested, imprisoned, and executed were a substantial proportion of the leading figures in the Party and governmental hierarchy. The Bolshevik Old Guard was destroyed. The roll of Yezhov's victims included not only former oppositionists but many of the most stalwart supporters of Stalin in his protracted struggle with the opposition. No sphere of Soviet life, however lofty, was left untouched. Among the purged Stalinists were three former members of the Politburo, Rudzutak, Chubar, and S.V. Kossior, and three candidate members, Petrovksy, Postyshev, and Eikhe. An overwhelming majority of the members and candidates of the Party Central Committee disappeared. The senior officer corps of the armed forces suffered severely. According to one sober account, "two of five marshals of the Soviet Union escaped arrest, two of fifteen army commanders, twenty-eight of fifty-eight corps commanders, eighty-five of a hundred and ninety-five divisional commanders, and a hundred and ninety-five of four hundred and six regimental commanders." The havoc wrought by the purge among naval commanding personnel was equally great. The removal of Yagoda from the NKVD was accompanied by the arrest of his leading collaborators. Agranov, Prokofiev, Balitsky, Messing, Pauker, Trilisser, and others. The Commissariat of Foreign Affairs and the diplomatic service were hard hit. Among the Old Guard, only Litvinov, Maisky, Troyanovsky, and a few lesser lights survived. Almost every commissariat was deeply affected.

The purge swept out in ever-widening circles and resulted in wholesale removals and arrests of leading officials in the union republics, secretaries of the Party, Komsomol, and trade-union apparatus, heads of industrial trusts and enterprises, Comintern functionaries and foreign Communists, and leading writers, scholars, engineers, and scientists. The arrest of an important figure was followed by the seizure of the entourage which surrounded him. The apprehension of members of the entourage led to the imprisonment of their friends and acquaintances. The endless chain of involvements and associations threatened to encompass entire strata of Soviet society. . . . Under the zealous and ruthless ministrations of NKVD examiners, millions of innocents were transformed into traitors, terrorists, and enemies of the people.

How explain the Yezhovshchina? What motives impelled Stalin to organize a blood bath of such frightening proportions? In the absence of revealing testimony from the source, one can only venture hypotheses. Stalin's desire to consolidate his own personal power appears to have been a driving force. The slaughter of the Bolshevik Old Guard may be viewed partly as a drastic reprisal for past insubordination; it was more probably intended as a preventive measure to end once and for all any possibility of resistance or challenge from this direction. The extension of the purge to the Stalinist stalwarts in the Party and governmental apparatus is much more difficult to fathom. It is possible that many fell victim to the system of denunciations in the course of which their loyalty to Stalin was put in question, that a number were still involved in official or personal relationships with former oppositionists, that some were liquidated because they displayed traces of independence in their dealings with the Supreme Leader, that others were merely suspected of harboring aspirations toward personal power, and that still others simply furnished convenient scapegoats to demonstrate the existence of a conspiracy that reached into the highest circles.

Implicit in any understanding of the Yezhovshchina is a theory of the role of terror in Stalin's formula for government. The consolidation of personal rule in a totalitarian system depends on the constant elimination of all actual or potential competitors for supreme power. The insecurity of the masses must be supplemented by the insecurity of the governing elite who surround the Supreme Dictator. The too strongly entrenched official with an independent base of power is by definition a threat to the dictator's total sway. The individuals or groups who go uncontrolled and undirected are regarded as fertile soil for the growth of conspiratorial intrigue. The function of terror thus assumes a two-fold aspect. As prophylactic and preventive, it is designed to nip any possible resistance or opposition in the bud. As an instrument for the reinforcement of the personal power of the dictator, it is directed toward ensuring perpetual circulation in the ranks of officeholders in order to forestall the crystallization of autonomous islands of countervailing force.

The manipulation of terror as a system of power is a delicate art. A dictator in command of modern armaments and a secret police can transform his subjects into robots and automatons, but if he succeeds too well, he runs the risk of destroying the sources of creative initiative on which the survival of his own regime depends. When terror runs rampant, as it did at the height of the Yezhovshchina, unintended consequences follow. Fear becomes contagious and paralyzing. Officials at all levels seek to shirk responsibility. The endless belt of irresponsible denunciations begins to destroy the nation's treasury of needed skills. The terror apparatus grows on the stuff on which it feeds and magnifies in importance until it overshadows and depresses all the constructive enterprises of the state. The dictator finds himself caught up in a whirlwind of his own making which threatens to break completely out of control.

As the fury of the Yezhovshchina mounted, Stalin and his intimates finally became alarmed. Evidence accumulated that the purge was overreaching itself and that much talent sorely needed by the regime was being irretrievably lost. . . . The third and final phase of the Great Purge involved the purging of the purgers. In late July 1938, Yezhov's sun began to set when Beria took over as his deputy. In December, Yezhov was ousted as head of the NKVD and appointed Commissar for Inland Water Transport, from which post he soon disappeared unmourned but not forgotten. During the same month came the sensational announcement of the arrest, trial, and shooting of the head of the NKVD of Moldavia and a group of his examiners for extracting false confessions from innocent prisoners. The enemies of the people, it now appeared, had wormed their way into the NKVD apparatus itself and had sought to stir up mass unrest and disaffection by their brutal persecution of the guiltless.

It was now the turn of Yezhov and his collaborators to play the role of scapegoat for the excesses of the purge. A wave of arrests spread through the NKVD organization. The prisons began to fill with former NKVD examiners; many prisoners who had been tortured by these same examiners had the welcome experience of greeting their former tormentors as cellmates in prisons and forced labor camps. The "Great Change," as it was soon to become known, was marked by a substantial amelioration in prison conditions and examining methods. According to Beck and Godin, "Prisoners were released by the thousands, and many were restored to their old positions or even promoted." A new era appeared to have dawned.

Stalin now presented himself in the guise of the dispenser of mercy and justice. Excesses of the purge were blamed on subordinate officials who had exceeded their authority, saboteurs who had tried to break the indissoluble link which bound Leader and people, and careerists and counterrevolutionaries who had insinuated themselves into the Party and NKVD organizations in order to subvert and undermine the Soviet regime. At the Eighteenth Congress in 1939, Zhdanov reeled off case after case of so-called slanderers and calumniators who had tried to advance themselves in the Party by wholesale expulsions of honest Party members. . . . Thus, the pressure of the purge was temporarily relaxed as Stalin sought to enlist the energies and loyalties of the new governing elite whom he had promoted to positions of responsibility over the graves of their predecessors. Again, as in the collectivization crisis earlier, Stalin demonstrated his remarkable instinct for stopping short and reversing course at the brink of catastrophe.

The full circle of the Great Purge offers a remarkable case study in the use of terror. Arrests ran into the millions. The gruesome and harrowing experiences of the victims blackened the face of Stalinist Russia. The havoc wrought in leading circles appeared irreparable. Yet despite the damage and the hatred engendered, the dynamic momentum of the industrialization program was maintained. The arrests of responsible technicians and officials frequently produced serious setbacks in production, but as their replacements acquired experience, order was restored, and production began to climb again. While many functionaries reacted to the purge by shunning all responsibility, others responded to the fear of arrest by working as they had never worked before. Terror functioned as prod as well as brake. The acceleration in the circulation of the elite brought a new generation of Soviet-trained intelligentsia into positions of responsibility, and Stalin anchored his power on their support. Meanwhile, Stalin emerged from the purge with his own position consolidated. The major purpose of decapitating the Boshevik Old Guard had been accomplished. Every rival for supreme power who was visible on the horizon had been eliminated. The Party and the nation were thoroughly intimidated. The purgers had been purged and the scapegoats identified. The ancient formula of protecting the infallibility of the Leader by punishing subordinates for their excessive ardor was impressively resurrected. . . .

As the Great Purge drew to a close, the major efforts of the NKVD were concentrated against elements which might prove unreliable in the event that the Soviet Union became involved in war. After the Soviet-Nazi pact and the partition of Poland, the NKVD undertook wholesale arrests in the newly occupied areas. The victims ran into the hundreds of thousands and included whole categories of people whose "objective characteristics" could be broadly construed as inclining them to anti-Soviet behavior. The great majority were deported to forced labor camps in the Soviet North, from which the survivors were amnestied by the terms of the Polish-Soviet pact concluded after the Nazi attack on the Soviet Union. The Soviet occupation of the Baltic States in June 1940 was also followed by large-scale NKVD arrests and deportations of so-called anti-Soviet elements.

After the Nazi invasion, the NKVD engaged in widespread roundups of former "repressed" people and others whose records aroused suspicion of disloyalty to the Soviet regime. The Volga-German Autonomous Republic was dissolved, and its inhabitants were dispatched to forced labor camps or exile in the far reaches of Siberia. With the turning of the tide at Stalingrad and the advance of the Soviet armies westward, the NKVD found new victims among the population of the reoccupied areas. Many were arrested on the ground of actual or alleged collaboration with the Germans, and the forced labor camps reaped a new harvest. A number of the national minorities served as a special target of NKVD retribution because of their alleged disloyalty. The Kalmyk and Chechen-Ingush Republics were dissolved. The Crimean Tatars were penalized for their "traitorous" conduct by the abolition of the Crimean Autonomous Republic. The Autonomous Republic of the Kabards and Bolkars was dismembered, leaving only the Kabardinian ASSR. Meanwhile German war prisoners accumulated, and the NKVD took over the responsibility of running the camps in which they were confined.

After the capitulation of the Nazis, the NKVD confronted the vast new assignment of sifting the millions of Soviet citizens who found themselves in Germany and Austria at the end of the war. Most of them were war prisoners and *Ostarbeiter* who had been shipped west by the Germans as forced labor. Some, however, had retreated with the German armies in order to escape Soviet rule. Others had fought in Nazi military uniform or in separate anti-Soviet military formations such as the Vlasov Army. The latter when caught received short shrift; the great majority were executed. All of these elements on whom the NKVD could lay its hands were rounded up at assembly points and subjected to intensive interrogations by the NKVD before being shipped back to the Soviet Union. The NKVD followed a calculated policy of treating the "returners" as contaminated by their contact with the West. In order to isolate them from the Soviet populace, large numbers were dispatched to forced labor camps on suspicion of disloyalty or traitorous conduct. . . . Large-scale deportations have been reported from the border areas of Esthonia, Latvia, Lithuania, Karelia, and the Western Ukraine; the native population has been shifted to remote areas in Siberia and replaced by Russians, frequently war veterans, brought in from other regions.

*[**Editor's Note:** Professor Fainsod points out that in 1948 Stalin touched off a campaign against Jews as "rootless cosmopolitans." This led to the destruction of virtually every distinctive institution of Jewish cultural life, brought the arrest of many Jewish writers and artists, dozens of whom were executed in 1952, and culminated in the charge, in January 1953, that a number of Kremlin doctors (mainly Jewish) had engaged in a plot to kill important Soviet leaders. Fortuitously, Stalin died on March 5, shortly after which, on April 4, the plot was officially denounced as a pure fabrication.]*

The Hazards of Terror

The reliance on terror as an instrument of dominion has its elements of danger. It is not easy to control. A secret police develops its own laws of growth. The more discord it discovers or develops, the more indispensable it becomes. Its tendency is always to extend its own sovereignty, to seek to emancipate itself from all external controls, to become a state within a state, and to preserve the conditions of emergency and siege on which an expansion of its own power depends. Once terror becomes an end in itself, there is no easy and natural stopping place. From the viewpoint of the leadership, there is an even greater worry, the fear that as the secret police apparatus emancipates itself from external controls, it becomes a menace to the security of the highest Party leaders themselves. It is a risk of which the Party leadership has been aware and against which it has taken precautions. . . .

Even if the Party leadership is successful in imposing its mastery on the secret police, there are other disadvantages in a regime of terror which are not so amenable to skillful manipulation. A system which relies on a large secret police as a basic core of its power is highly wasteful of manpower. The main occupation of the secret police is that of spying, investigating, examining, guarding, and controlling others. Large numbers of talented people are removed from productive work. There is always the hazard that the secret police will run amok and do serious and perhaps unintended harm to the productive and administrative machinery of the state. The atmosphere of universal suspicion which terror breeds is not ordinarily conducive to creative thinking and displays of individual initiative. If the weight of terror becomes too great and the penalty of any administrative failure or mistake is MVD detention, it becomes difficult to persuade people to take responsibility. (MVD was a successor to NKVD.) Even those driven by fear of the secret police to work as they have never worked before, begin to crack under the strain. It is no easy task to apply terror and at the same time to hold it in leash.

Perhaps the most subtle danger in a police regime of the Soviet type is its impact on the quality of political decisions at the very highest level. The MVD is one of the main pillars that sustains the regime. It is also a primary source of intelligence regarding both domestic and international developments. Since the MVD apparatus lives and grows on emergency and danger, its justification hinges upon the maintenance of a state of siege. Consequently, the intelligence that filters through the MVD to the top political leadership is apt, almost unconsciously, to emphasize the storms that are brewing, the plots against the regime, and sinister threats at home and abroad. The risk which the Party leadership faces is that it too will become the unconscious victim of the Frankenstein's monster which it has created. The ultimate hazard of terror as a system of power is that it ends by terrorizing the master as well as the slave.

*[**Editor's note:** On July 10, 1953, some few months after the death of Stalin on March 5, 1953, it was officially announced that Beria had been dismissed as head of the MVD and was being held for trial. On December 16, the Soviet State Prosecutor issued a statement that Beria (and accomplices) had confessed during the course of investigation to "having committed a number of State crimes." Among the crimes charged were that Beria had been "an agent of foreign capital, directed toward the subversion of the Soviet state" with links to foreign Intelligence services "as far back as the civil war"; had striven "to place the Ministry of Internal Affairs above the party and Government, to seize power and to liquidate the Soviet worker-peasant regime with a view to restoring capitalism and securing the revival of the bourgeoisie." It was also charged that Beria had attempted "to subvert the collective-farm system and to*

create food difficulties in our country" and "to sow hatred and discord between the peoples of the USSR."

On December 23, it was briefly announced that the accused had been tried (behind closed doors) before a tribunal headed by Marshal Ivan S. Konev, that all had been found guilty, and shot.]

Stalin and the Cult of the Individual

Nikita S. Khrushchev

---

*[**Editor's note:** This denunciation of Stalin and of "the cult of the individual" was delivered on February 24–25, 1956, before a closed session of the Twentieth Congress of the Communist Party of the Soviet Union and first published in the United States, after release by the United States Department of State, on June 4, 1956. Its authenticity has never been* officially *acknowledged. However, it has been widely credited in the Communist press of the world, and was implicitly acknowledged by Anastas I. Mikoyan, then First Deputy Premier of the USSR, on his visit to the United States. (See* New York Times, *January 19,1959.)*

In Russia itself, a long "Resolution of the Central Committee of the Communist Party of the Soviet Union," published in Pravda *on July 2, 1956, read in part: "For more than three years now our Party has been waging a consistent struggle against the cult of the person of J. V. Stalin, persistently overcoming its harmful consequences. Naturally this question occupied an important place in the work of the Twentieth Congress of the CPSU and in its decisions." The next day,* Pravda *commented editorially, "As is well known, at the Twentieth Congress of the Communist Party of the Soviet Union the question of the cult of the individual and its consequences was examined in detail."*

It may be said, finally, that during four visits made to the USSR by this editor, everyone with whom he raised the question was aware of the document and its general contents.]

Comrades! In the report of the Central Committee of the party at the 20th Congress, in a number of speeches by delegates to the Congress, as also formerly during the plenary

Khrushchev was First Secretary of the Communist Party of the Soviet Union and Chairman of the Council of Ministers of the USSR. The text of this speech is reprinted with permission in abridged form from the version published in The New Leader *on July 16, 1956, and in its pamphlet titled* The Crimes of the Stalin Era, *with the footnote annotations by Boris I. Nicolaevsky, author of* Letter of an Old Bolshevik *and coauthor of* Forced Labor in Soviet Russia.

CC/CPSU [Central Committe of the Communist Party of the Soviet Union] sessions, quite a lot has been said about the cult of the individual and about its harmful consequences.

After Stalin's death the Central Committee of the party began to implement a policy of explaining concisely and consistently that it is impermissible and foreign to the spirit of Marxism-Leninism to elevate one person, to transform him into a superman possessing supernatural characteristics, akin to those of a god. Such a man supposedly knows everything, sees everything, thinks for everyone, can do anything, is infallible in his behavior. Such a belief about a man, and specifically about Stalin, was cultivated among us for many years. . . .

Because of the fact that not all as yet realize fully the practical consequences resulting from the cult of the individual, the great harm caused by the violation of the principle of collective direction of the party and because of the accumulation of immense and limitless power in the hands of one person, the Central Committee of the party considers it absolutely necessary to make the material pertaining to this matter available to the 20th Congress of the Communist Party of the Soviet Union. . . .

Fearing the future fate of the party and of the Soviet nation, V.I. Lenin made a completely correct characterization of Stalin, pointing out that it was necessary to consider the question of transferring Stalin from the position of the Secretary General because of the fact that Stalin is excessively rude, that he does not have a proper attitude toward his comrades, that he is capricious and abuses his power.

In December 1922, in a letter to the Party Congress,[1] Vladimir Ilyich wrote: "After taking over the position of Secretary General, Comrade Stalin accumulated in his hands immeasurable power and I am not certain whether he will be always able to use this power with the required care." . . .

When we analyze the practice of Stalin in regard to the direction of the party and of the country, when we pause to consider everything which Stalin perpetrated, we must be convinced that Lenin's fears were justified. The negative characteristics of Stalin, which, in Lenin's time, were only incipient, transformed themselves during the last years into a grave abuse of power by Stalin, which caused untold harm to our party.

We have to consider seriously and analyze correctly this matter in order that we may preclude any possibility of a repetition in any form whatever of what took place during the life of Stalin, who absolutely did not tolerate collegiality in leadership and in work, and who practiced brutal violence, not only toward everything which opposed him, but also toward that which seemed, to his capricious and despotic character, contrary to his concepts.

Stalin acted not through persuasion, explanation and patient cooperation with people, but by imposing his concepts and demanding absolute submission to his opinion. Whoever opposed this concept or tried to prove his viewpoint and the correctness of his position was doomed to removal from the leading collective and to subsequent moral and physical annihilation. This was especially true during the period following the 17th Party Congress [1934], when many prominent party leaders and rank-and-file party workers, honest and dedicated to the cause of Communism, fell victim to Stalin's despotism.

We must affirm that the party had fought a serious fight against the Trotskyites, rightists and bourgeois nationalists, and that it disarmed ideologically all the enemies of Leninism. This ideological fight was carried on successfully, as a result of which the party became strengthened and tempered. Here Stalin played a positive role.

The party led a great political-ideological struggle against those in its own ranks who proposed anti-Leninist theses, who represented a political line hostile to the party and to the cause of socialism. This was a stubborn and a difficult fight but a necessary one, because the political line of both the Trotskyite-Zinovievite block and of the Bukharinites led actually toward the restoration of capitalism and capitulation to the world bourgeoisie. Let us consider for a moment what would have happened if in 1928–1929 the political line of right deviation had prevailed among us, or orientation toward "cotton-dress industrialization," or toward the kulak, etc. We would not now have a powerful heavy industry, we would not have the *kolkhozes,* we would find ourselves disarmed and weak in a capitalist encirclement. . . .

Worth noting is the fact that, even during the progress of the furious ideological fight against the Trotskyites, the Zinovievites, the Bukharinites and others, extreme repressive measures were not used against them. The fight was on ideological grounds. But some years later, when socialism in our country was fundamentally constructed, when the exploiting classes were generally liquidated, when the Soviet social structure had radically changed, when the social basis for political movements and groups hostile to the party had violently contracted, when the ideological opponents of the party were long since defeated politically–then the repression directed against them began.

It was precisely during this period (1935–1937–1938) that the practice of mass repression through the Government apparatus was born, first against the enemies of Leninism—Trotskyites, Zinovievites, Bukharinites, long since politically defeated by the party—and subsequently also against many honest Communists, against those party cadres who had borne the heavy load of the Civil War and the first and most difficult years of industrialization and collectivization, who actively fought against the Trotskyites and the rightists for the Leninist party line.

Stalin originated the concept "enemy of the people." This term automatically rendered it unnecessary that the ideological errors of a man or men engaged in a controversy be proven; this term made possible the usage of the most cruel repression, violating all norms of revolutionary legality, against anyone who in any way disagreed with Stalin, against those who were only suspected of hostile intent, against those who had bad reputations. This concept "enemy of the people" actually eliminated the possibility of any kind of ideological fight or the making of one's views known on this or that issue, even those of a practical character. In the main, and in actuality, the only proof of guilt used, against all norms of current legal science, was the "confession" of the accused himself; and, as subsequent probing proved, "confessions" were acquired through physical pressures against the accused. This led to glaring violations of revolutionary legality and to the fact that many entirely innocent persons, who in the past had defended the party line, became victims. . . . Mass arrests and deportations of many thousands of people, execution without trial and without normal investigation created conditions of insecurity, fear and even desperation. . . .

But can it be said that Lenin did not decide to use even the most severe means against enemies of the Revolution when this was actually necessary? No; no one can say this. . . . Lenin used severe methods only in the most necessary cases, when the exploiting classes were still in existence and were vigorously opposing the Revolution, when the struggle for survival was decidedly assuming the sharpest forms, even including a civil war.

Stalin, on the other hand, used extreme methods and mass repressions at a time when the Revolution was already victorious, when the Soviet state was strengthened, when the exploiting classes were already liquidated and socialist relations were rooted solidly in all phases of national economy, when our party was politically consolidated and had strengthened itself both numerically and ideologically. . . .

There was no matter so important that Lenin himself decided it without asking for advice and approval of the majority of the Central Committee members or of the members of the Central Committee's Political Bureau. In the most difficult period for our party and our country, Lenin considered it necessary regularly to convoke congresses, party conferences and plenary sessions of the Central Committee at which all the most important questions were discussed and where resolutions, carefully worked out by the collective of leaders, were approved. . . .

Whereas, during the first few years after Lenin's death, party congresses and Central Committee plenums took place more or less regularly, later, when Stalin began increasingly to abuse his power, these principles were brutally violated. This was especially evident during the last fifteen years of his life. Was it a normal situation when more than thirteen years elapsed between the 18th and 19th Party Congresses, years during which our party and our country had experienced so many important events? . . . It should be sufficient to mention that during all the years of the Patriotic War not a single Central Committee plenum took place. It is true that there was an attempt to call a Central Committee plenum in October 1941, when Central Committee members from the whole country were called to Moscow. They waited two days for the opening of the plenum, but in vain. Stalin did not even want to meet and talk to the Central Committee members. This fact shows how demoralized Stalin was in the first months of the war and how haughtily and disdainfully he treated the Central Committee members. . . .

The commission has become acquainted with a large quantity of materials in the NKVD archives and with other documents and has established many facts pertaining to the fabrication of cases against Communists, to false accusations, to glaring abuses of socialist legality, which resulted in the death of innocent people. It became apparent that many party, Soviet and economic activists, who were branded in 1937–1938 as "enemies," were actually never enemies, spies, wreckers, etc., but were always honest Communists; they were only so stigmatized and, often, no longer able to bear barbaric tortures, they charged themselves (at the order of the investigative judges—falsifiers) with all kinds of grave and unlikely crimes.

The commission has presented to the Central Committee Presidium lengthy and documented materials pertaining to mass repressions against the delegates to the 17th Party Congress and against members of the Central Committee elected at that Congress. These materials have been studied by the Presidium of the Central Committee.

It was determined that of the 139 members and candidates of the party's Central Committee who were elected at the 17th Congress, 98 persons (*i.e.*, 70 percent) were arrested and shot (mostly in 1937–1938). (*Indignation in the hall.*) What was the composition of the delegates to the 17th Congress? It is known that 80 percent of the voting participants of the 17th Congress joined the party during the years of conspiracy before the Revolution and during the civil war; this means before 1921. By social origin the basic mass of the delegates to the Congress were workers (60 percent of the voting members).

For this reason, it was inconceivable that a congress so composed would have elected a Central Committee a majority of whom would prove to be enemies of the party. The only reason why 70 percent of Central Committee members and candidates elected at the 17th Congress were branded as enemies of the party and of the people was because honest Communists were slandered, accusations against them were fabricated, and revolutionary legality was gravely undermined.

The same fate met not only the Central Committee members but also the majority of the delegates to the 17th Party Congress. Of 1,966 delegates with either voting or advisory rights, 1,108 persons were arrested on charges of anti-revolutionary crimes, (*i.e.*, decidedly more than a majority). This very fact shows how absurd, wild and contrary to common sense were the charges of counterrevolutionary crimes made out, as we now see, against a majority of participants at the 17th Party Congress. (*Indignation in the hall.*) . . .

While he still reckoned with the opinion of the collective before the 17th Congress, after the complete political liquidation of the Trotskyites, Zinovievites and Bukharinites, when as a result of that fight and socialist victories the party achieved unity, Stalin ceased to an ever greater degree to consider the members of the party's Central Committee and even the members of the Political Bureau. Stalin thought that now he could decide all things alone and all he needed were statisticians; he treated all others in such a way that they could only listen to and praise him.

After the criminal murder of Sergei M. Kirov, mass repressions and brutal acts of violation of socialist legality began. On the evening of December 1, 1934 on Stalin's initiative (without the approval of the Political Bureau—which was passed two days later, casually), the Secretary of the Presidium of the Central Executive Committee, Yenukidze, signed the following directive:

1. Investigative agencies are directed to speed up the cases of those accused of the preparation or execution of acts of terror.
2. Judicial organs are directed not to hold up the execution of death sentences pertaining to crimes of this category in order to consider the possibility of pardon, because the Presidium of the Central Executive Committee of the USSR does not consider as possible the receiving of petitions of this sort.
3. The organs of the Commissariat of Internal Affairs are directed to execute the death sentences against criminals of the above-mentioned category immediately after the passage of sentences.

This directive became the basis for mass acts of abuse against socialist legality. During many of the fabricated court cases, the accused were charged with "the preparation" of terroristic acts; this deprived them of any possibility that their cases might be reexamined, even when they stated before the court that their "confessions" were secured by force, and when, in a convincing manner, they disproved the accusations against them.

It must be asserted that to this day the circumstances surrounding Kirov's murder hide many things which are inexplicable and mysterious and demand a most careful examination. There are reasons for the suspicion that the killer of Kirov, Nikolayev, was assisted by someone from among the people whose duty it was to protect the person of Kirov.

A month and a half before the killing, Nikolayev was arrested on the grounds of suspicious behavior but he was released and not even searched. It is an unusually suspicious circumstance that when the Chekist assigned to protect Kirov was being brought for an interrogation, on December 2, 1934, he was killed in a car "accident" in which no other occupants of the car were harmed. After the murder of Kirov, top functionaries of the Leningrad NKVD were given very light sentences, but in 1937 they were shot. We can assume that they were shot in order to cover the traces of the organizers of Kirov's killing. (*Movement in the hall.*)

Mass repressions grew tremendously from the end of 1936 after a telegram from Stalin and [Andrei] Zhdanov, dated from Sochi on September 25, 1936, was addressed to

Kaganovich, Molotov and other members of the Political Bureau. The content of the telegram was as follows:

> We deem it absolutely necessary and urgent that Comrade Yezhov be nominated to the post of People's Commissar for Internal Affairs. Yagoda has definitely proved himself to be incapable of unmasking the Trotskyite-Zinovievite bloc. The OGPU is four years behind in this matter. This is noted by all party workers and by the majority of the representatives of the NKVD.[2]

. . . The mass repressions at this time were made under the slogan of a fight against the Trotskyites. Did the Trotskyites at this time actually constitute such a danger to our party and to the Soviet state? We should recall that in 1927, on the eve of the 15th Party Congress, only some 4,000 votes were cast for the Trotskyite-Zinovievite opposition while there were 724,000 for the party line. During the ten years which passed between the 15th Party Congress and the February-March Central Committee plenum, Trotskyism was completely disarmed; many former Trotskyites had changed their former views and worked in the various sectors building socialism. It is clear that in the situation of socialist victory there was no basis for mass terror in the country.

Stalin's report at the February-March Central Committee plenum in 1937 . . . contained an attempt at theoretical justification of the mass terror policy under the pretext that as we march forward toward socialism, class war must allegedly sharpen. . . .

Now, when the cases of some of these so-called "spies" and "saboteurs" were examined, it was found that all their cases were fabricated. Confessions of guilt of many arrested and charged with enemy activity were gained with the help of cruel and inhuman tortures. . . .

An example of vile provocation, of odious falsification and of criminal violation of revolutionary legality is the case of the former candidate for the Central Committee Political Bureau, one of the most eminent workers of the party and of the Soviet Government, Comrade Eikhe who was a party member since 1905. (*Commotion in the hall.*)

Comrade Eikhe was arrested on April 29, 1938 on the basis of slanderous materials, without the sanction of the Prosecutor of the USSR, which was finally received fifteen months after the arrest.

Investigation of Eikhe's case was made in a manner which most brutally violated Soviet legality and was accompanied by willfulness and falsification.

Eikhe was forced under torture to sign ahead of time a protocol of his confession prepared by the investigative judges, in which he and several other eminent party workers were accused of anti-Soviet activity.

On October 1, 1939 Eikhe sent his declaration to Stalin in which he categorically denied his guilt and asked for an examination of his case. In the declaration he wrote: "There is no more bitter misery than to sit in the jail of a government for which I have always fought." . . . On February 4 Eikhe was shot. (*Indignation in the hall.*) It has been definitely established now that Eikhe's case was fabricated; he has been posthumously rehabilitated. . . .

The vicious practice was condoned of having the NKVD prepare lists of persons whose cases were under the jurisdiction of the Military Collegium and whose sentences were prepared in advance. Yezhov would send these lists to Stalin personally for his approval of the proposed punishment. In 1937–38, 383 such lists containing the names of many thousands of party, Soviet, Komsomol, Army, and economic workers were sent to Stalin. He approved these lists.

A large part of these cases are being reviewed now and a great part of them are being voided because they were baseless and falsified. Suffice it to say that from 1954 to the present time the Military Collegium of the Supreme Court has rehabilitated 7,679 persons, many of whom were rehabilitated posthumously. . . .

Facts prove that many abuses were made on Stalin's orders without reckoning with any norms of party and Soviet legality. Stalin was a very distrustful man, sickly suspicious; we know this from our work with him. He could look at a man and say: "Why are your eyes so shifty today?" or "Why are you turning so much today and avoiding to look me directly in the eyes?" The sickly suspicion created in him a general distrust even toward eminent party workers whom he had known for years. Everywhere and in everything he saw "enemies," "two-facers" and "spies." Possessing unlimited power, he indulged in great willfulness and choked a person morally and physically. A situation was created where one could not express one's own will.

When Stalin said that one or another should be arrested, it was necessary to accept on faith that he was an "enemy of the people." Meanwhile, Beria's gang, which ran the organs of state security, outdid itself in proving the guilt of the arrested and the truth of materials which it falsified. And what proofs were offered? The confessions of the arrested, and the investigative judges accepted these "confessions." And how is it possible that a person confesses to crimes which he has not committed? Only in one way—because of application of physical methods of pressuring him, tortures, bringing him to a state of unconsciousness, deprivation of his judgment, taking away of his human dignity. In this manner were "confessions" acquired. . . .

The power accumulated in the hands of one person, Stalin, led to serious consequences during the Great Patriotic War. When we look at many of our novels, films and historical "scientific studies," the role of Stalin in the Patriotic War appears to be entirely improbable. Stalin had foreseen everything. The Soviet Army, on the basis of a strategic plan prepared by Stalin long before, used the tactics of so-called "active defense" (*i.e.,* tactics which, as we know, allowed the Germans to come up to Moscow and Stalingrad). Using such tactics, the Soviet Army, supposedly thanks only to Stalin's genius, turned to the offensive and subdued the enemy. The epic victory gained through the armed might of the land of the Soviets, through our heroic people, is ascribed in this type of novel, film, and "scientific study" as being completely due to the strategic genius of Stalin. . . . What are the facts of this matter?

*[**Editor's note:** Khrushchev proceeds to show that Stalin ignored repeated warnings of impending German attack and adds that "despite these particularly grave warnings, the necessary steps were not taken to prepare the country properly for defense and to prevent it from being caught unawares." As a consequence, "in the first hours and days the enemy destroyed in our border regions a large part" of our military forces and equipment. Furthermore, "Stalin's annihilation of many military commanders and political workers during 1937–1941 because of his suspiciousness and slanderous accusations had grievous consequences." This policy also "undermined military discipline" because soldiers were "taught to 'unmask' their superiors as hidden enemies." And, during the war, "the nervousness and hysteria which Stalin demonstrated, interfering with actual military operations, caused our Army serious danger" and the "tactics on which Stalin insisted" cost us "much blood."]*

All the more shameful was the fact that, after our great victory over the enemy which cost us so much, Stalin began to downgrade many of the commanders [including Zhukov] who contributed so much to the victory over the enemy, because Stalin excluded every possibility that services rendered at the front should be credited to anyone but himself. . . .

Comrades, let us reach for some other facts. The Soviet Union is justly considered as a model of a multinational state because we have in practice assured the equality and friendship of all nations which live in our great Fatherland. All the more monstrous are the acts whose initiator was Stalin and which are rude violations of the basic Leninist principles of the nationality policy of the Soviet state. We refer to the mass deportations from their native places of whole nations, together with all Communists and Komsomols without any exception; this deportion action was not dictated by any military considerations.

Thus, already at the end of 1943, when there occurred a permanent breakthrough at the fronts of the Great Patriotic War benefiting the Soviet Union, a decision was taken and executed concerning the deportation of all the Karachai from the lands on which they lived. In the same period, at the end of December 1943, the same lot befell the whole population of the Autonomous Kalmyk Republic. In March 1944 all the Chechen and Ingush peoples were deported and the Chechen-Ingush Autonomous Republic was liquidated. In April 1944 all Balkars were deported to faraway places from the territory of the Kabardino-Balkar Autonomous Republic and the Republic itself was renamed the Autonomous Kabardian-Republic.[3] The Ukrainians avoided meeting this fate only because there were too many of them and there was no place to which to deport them. Otherwise, he would have deported them also. (*Laughter and animation in the hall.*)

Not only a Marxist-Leninist but also no man of common sense can grasp how it is possible to make whole nations responsible for inimical activity, including women, children, old people, Communists and Komsomols, to use mass repression against them, and to expose them to misery and suffering for the hostile acts of individual persons or groups of persons. . . .

We must state that, after the war, the situation became even more complicated. Stalin became even more capricious, irritable and brutal; in particular his suspicion grew. His persecution mania reached unbelievable dimensions. Many workers were becoming enemies before his very eyes. After the war, Stalin separated himself from the collective even more. Everything was decided by him alone without any consideration for anyone or anything. . . .

Let us also recall the "affair of the doctor-plotters." (*Animation in the hall.*) Actually there was no "affair" outside of the declaration of the woman doctor Timashuk, who was probably influenced or ordered by someone (after all, she was an unofficial collaborator of the organs of state security) to write Stalin a letter in which she declared that doctors were applying supposedly improper methods of medical treatment.

Such a letter was sufficient for Stalin to reach an immediate conclusion that there are doctor-plotters in the Soviet Union.[4] He issued orders to arrest a group of eminent Soviet medical specialists. He personally issued advice on the conduct of the investigation and the method of interrogation of the arrested persons. He said that the academician Vinogradov should be put in chains, another one should be beaten. Present at this Congress as a delegate is the former Minister of State Security, Comrade Ignatiev. Stalin told him curtly, "If you do not obtain confessions from the doctors we will shorten you by a head." (*Tumult in the hall.*) Stalin personally called the investigative judge, gave him instructions, advised him on which investigative methods should be used; these methods were simple—beat, beat, and, once again, beat.

Shortly after the doctors were arrested, we members of the Political Bureau received protocols with the doctors' confessions of guilt. After distributing these protocols, Stalin told us, "You are blind like young kittens; what will happen without me? The country will perish because you do not know how to recognize enemies."

The case was so presented that no one could verify the facts on which the investigation was based. There was no possibility of trying to verify facts by contacting those who had made the confessions of guilt. We felt, however, that the case of the arrested doctors was questionable. We knew some of these people personally because they had once treated us. When we examined this "case" after Stalin's death, we found it to be fabricated from beginning to end. . . .

Comrades: The cult of the individual acquired such monstrous size chiefly because Stalin himself, using all conceivable methods, supported the glorification of his own person. This is supported by numerous facts. One of the most characteristic examples of Stalin's self-glorification and of his lack of even elementary modesty is the edition of his *Short Biography,* which was published in 1948. This book is an expression of the most dissolute flattery, an example of making a man into a godhead, of transforming him into an infallible sage, "the greatest leader, sublime strategist of all times and nations." Finally, no other words could be found with which to lift Stalin up to the heavens.

We need not give here examples of the loathesome adulation filling this book. All we need to add is that they all were approved and edited by Stalin personally and some of them were added in his own handwriting to the draft text of the book. What did Stalin consider essential to write into this book? Did he want to cool the ardor of his flatterers who were composing his *Short Biography*? No! He marked the very places where he thought that the praise of his services was insufficient. . . . Thus writes Stalin himself:

> Although he performed his task as leader of the party and the people with consummate skill and enjoyed the unreserved support of the entire Soviet people, Stalin never allowed his work to be marred by the slightest hint of vanity, conceit or self-adulation. . . .
>
> Stalin's military mastership was displayed both in defense and offense. Comrade Stalin's genius enabled him to divine the enemy's plans and defeat them. The battles in which Comrade Stalin directed the Soviet armies are brillant examples of operational military skill. . . .

Or let us take the matter of the Stalin Prizes. (*Movement in the hall.*) Not even the Tsars created prizes which they named after themselves. . . . And was it without Stalin's knowledge that many of the largest enterprises and towns were named after him? Was it without his knowledge that Stalin monuments were erected in the whole country—these "memorials to the living"? . . .

In speaking about the events of the October Revolution and about the civil war, the impression was created that Stalin always played the main role, as if everywhere and always Stalin had suggested to Lenin what to do and how to do it. However, this is slander of Lenin. (*Prolonged applause.*) I will probably not sin against the truth when I say that 99 percent of the persons present here heard and knew very little about Stalin before the year 1924, while Lenin was known to all; he was known to the whole party, to the whole nation, from the children up to the graybeards. (*Tumultuous, prolonged applause.*) . . .

We should also not forget that, due to the numerous arrests of party, Soviet and economic leaders, many workers began to work uncertainly, showed overcautiousness, feared all which was new, feared their own shadows and began to show less initiative in their work. . . .

Stalin's reluctance to consider life's realities and the fact that he was not aware of the real state of affairs in the provinces can be illustrated by his direction of agriculture. All those who interested themselves even a little in the national situation saw the difficult situation in agriculture, but Stalin never even noted it. Did we tell Stalin about this? Yes, we told him, but he did not support us. Why? Because Stalin never traveled anywhere, did not meet city and *kolkhoz* workers; he did not know the actual situation in the provinces. . . .

Some comrades may ask us: Where were the members of the Political Bureau of the Central Committee? Why did they not assert themselves against the cult of the individual in time? And why is this being done only now? First of all, we have to consider the fact that the members of the Political Bureau viewed these matters in a different way at different times. Initially, many of them backed Stalin actively because Stalin was one of the strongest Marxists and his logic, his strength, and his will greatly influenced the cadres and party work.

It is known that Stalin, after Lenin's death, especially during the first years, actively fought for Leninism against the enemies of Leninist theory and against those who deviated. Beginning with Leninist theory, the party, with its Central Committee at the head, started on a great scale the work of socialist industrialization of the country, agricultural collectivization and the cultural revolution.

At the time Stalin gained great popularity, sympathy and support. The party had to fight those who attempted to lead the country away from the correct Leninist path; it had to fight Trotskyites, Zinovievites and rightists, and the bourgeois nationalists. This fight was indispensable. Later, however, Stalin, abusing his power more and more, began to fight eminent party and Government leaders and to use terroristic methods against honest Soviet people. . . .

In the situation which then prevailed I have talked often with Nikolai Alexandrovich Bulganin; once when we two were traveling in a car, he said, "It has happened sometimes that a man goes to Stalin on his invitation as a friend. And, when he sits with Stalin, he does not know where he will be sent next—home or to jail."

It is clear that such conditions put every member of the Political Bureau in a very difficult situation. And, when we also consider the fact that in the last years the Central Committee plenary sessions were not convened and that the sessions of the Political Bureau occured only occasionally, from time to time, then we will understand how difficult it was for any member of the Political Bureau to take a stand against one or another unjust or improper procedure, against serious errors and shortcomings in the practices of leadership. As we have already shown, many decisions were taken either by one person or in a roundabout way, without collective discussion. . . .

Let us consider the first Central Committee plenum after the 19th Party Congress when Stalin, in his talk at the plenum, characterized Vyacheslav Mikhailovich Molotov and Anastas Ivanovich Mikoyan and suggested that these old workers of our party were guilty of some baseless charges. It is not excluded that had Stalin remained at the helm for another several months, Comrades Molotov and Mikoyan would probably have not delivered any speeches at this Congress. . . .

This question is complicated by the fact that all this which we have just discussed was done during Stalin's life under his leadership and with his concurrence; here Stalin was convinced that this was necessary for the defense of the interests of the working classes against the plotting of enemies and against the attack of the imperialist camp.

He saw this from the position of the interest of the working class, of the interest of the laboring people, of the interest of the victory of socialism and communism. We cannot say that these were the deeds of a giddy despot. He considered that this should be done in the interest of the party, of the working masses, in the name of the defense of the revolution's gains. In this lies the whole tragedy! . . .

We cannot let this matter get out of the party, especially not to the press. It is for this reason that we are considering it here at a closed Congress session. We should know the limits; we should not give ammunition to the enemy; we should not wash our dirty linen before their eyes. I think that the delegates to the Congress will understand and assess properly all these proposals. (*Tumultuous applause.*)

Comrades! We must abolish the cult of the individual decisively, once and for all; we must draw the proper conclusions concerning both ideological-theoretical and practical work. It is necessary for this purpose:

First, in a Bolshevik manner to condemn and to eradicate the cult of the individual as alien to Marxism-Leninism and not consonant with the principles of party leadership and the norms of party life, and to fight inexorably all attempts at bringing back this practice in one form or another.

To return to and actually practice in all our ideological work the most important theses of Marxist-Leninist science about the people as the creator of history and as the creator of all material and spiritual good of humanity, about the decisive role of the Marxist party in the revolutionary fight for the transformation of society, about the victory of communism.

In this connection we will be forced to do much work in order to examine critically from the Marxist-Leninist viewpoint and to correct the widely spread erroneous views connected with the cult of the individual in the sphere of history, philosophy, economy and of other sciences, as well as in literature and the fine arts. . . .

Secondly, to continue systematically and consistently the work done by the party's Central Committee during the last years, a work characterized by minute observation in all party organizations, from the bottom to the top, of the Leninist principles of party leadership, characterized, above all, by the main principle of collective leadership, characterized by the observance of the norms of party life described in the statutes of our party, and, finally, characterized by the wide practice of criticism and self-criticism.

Thirdly, to restore completely the Leninist principles of Soviet socialist democracy, expressed in the Constitution of the Soviet Union, to fight willfulness of individuals abusing their power. The evil caused by acts violating revolutionary socialist legality, which have accumulated during a long time as a result of the negative influence of the cult of the individual, has to be completely corrected.

Comrades! The 20th Congress of the Communist Party of the Soviet Union has manifested with a new strength the unshakable unity of our party, its cohesiveness around the Central Committee, its resolute will to accomplish the great task of building communism. (*Tumultuous applause.*)

And the fact that we present in all their ramifications the basic problems of overcoming the cult of the individual which is alien to Marxism-Leninism, as well as the problem of liquidating its burdensome consequences, is an evidence of the great moral and political strength of our party. (*Prolonged applause.*)

We are absolutely certain that our party, armed with the historical resolutions of the 20th Congress, will lead the Soviet people along the Leninist path to new successes, to new victories. (*Tumultuous, prolonged applause.*)

Long live the victorious banner of our party—Leninism! (*Tumultuous, prolonged applause ending in ovation. All rise.*)

*[**Editor's note:** After Stalin's death in 1953—both before and after Khrushchev's denunciation of Stalin in 1956—varied steps were taken to curb the terror-apparatus and mitigate its consequences. These include, to quote Merle Fainsod, "a wide-ranging series of reforms" involving "a curbing of the extrajudicial powers of the security police, a reassertion of Party control over the police, the dismantlement of the security police's economic empire, the release of hundreds of thousands of prisoners from the forced-labor camps, and the rationalization of the system of criminal justice." The last of these measures (i.e., the rationalization of the system of criminal justice), is the subject of detailed consideration in a subsequent chapter in this volume under the general title of "Law and Politics."]*

Notes

1. *The full text of this document is commonly known as "Lenin's Testament," although Lenin himself did not use that term. [It appears in this book.]*
2. *This telegram is an exceptionally important document, showing that Stalin felt that mass repressions within the Communist Party were four years overdue—that is, they should have begun in 1932, when Stalin first demanded execution of members of the opposition group headed by Ryutin, Gorelov and others but was defeated both in the Politburo and at the Central Committee plenum which met from September 28 to October 2, 1932. On Stalin's demand, Henry Yagoda was removed from the post of People's Commissar for Internal Affairs and, on September 26, 1936, replaced by Nikolai I. Yezhov.*
3. *Khrushchev does not mention two Soviet republics liquidated during the war on Stalin's orders whose populations were deported to Siberia and Kazakhstan (i.e., the autonomous Volga German and Crimean Republics).*
4. *The case of the "doctors' plot" was concocted on Stalin's orders in the winter of 1952–53 by the then Minister of State Security, S.D. Ignatiev, and his deputy, Ryumin. Several dozen of the leading doctors in Moscow were arrested, headed by the top specialists of the Kremlin hospital who treated Stalin and all the Soviet chieftains. They were officially charged with using improper medical techniques in order to murder their patients. Specifically, they were accused of having poisoned Andrei A. Zhdanov and Alexander S. Shcherbakov and of attempting to poison Marshals Konev, Vasilevsky, Govorov and others. . . .*

Chapter 7

EVOLUTION OF THE SOVIET SYSTEM AND THE PROBLEM OF SUCCESSION

Professors Robert V. Daniels and Sidney I. Ploss trace the evolution of the Soviet system from "the Stalin Revolution" to the rise and early role of Brezhnev. The following sections of this volume contain further—largely recent or contemporary—analyses and evaluations of Soviet political and economic policies and developments, particularly under the regimes of Khrushchev and Brezhnev.

The Stalin Revolution and Its Aftermath

Robert V. Daniels

It is easy to regard Soviet Russia since 1921 as a state permanently fixed in all its essentials. The continuities in the Soviet system are obvious—dictatorship, the political monopoly of the Communist Party, the official philosophy of Marxism-Leninism, the methods of the totalitarian police state. This continuity is emphasized by the Communist Party itself. The successive rulers of the USSR—Lenin, followed by Stalin, and then Khrushchev—have all claimed that they are carrying out the basic program of proletarian revolution. . . .

There are [however] a number of sharply distinct periods in the history of Soviet Russia. These periods are more than stages in the progress toward a previously defined goal, as the Communist line has always claimed. They constitute a sequence of widely different *directions* of policy and effort. The New Economic Policy, followed by the Stalin Revolution and the subsequent shifts and consolidation, not to mention the Khrushchev succession of the 1950s, all represent profound adjustments to the realities of Russian circumstances and the continuing changes in Russia's world environment. . . .

When Stalin got control of the Secretariat he used it to build a political machine of secretaries in the Party loyal to him. By 1923 he could control the election of a majority of the local delegates to the Party Congress and thus pack the Central Committee with his own supporters. In effect, Stalin controlled the body to which, as General Secretary, he was nominally responsible. It was only a matter of time and opportunity until he could remove all his rivals from the Party leadership and make himself the unchallenged boss of the Party and the country. Personal power achieved through the Party organization has ever since been the core of the Soviet dictatorship.

As long as Lenin lived, the Party and the country enjoyed a sort of collective leadership, not only in form but even to some extent in practice. Though Lenin was governmental head as Chairman of the Council of People's Commissars, there was no official chief of the Party above the Politburo. . . . Lenin did not behave as an absolute dictator within the Party. Genuine debate and voting continued in the Party's top organs until the succession problem raised the political stakes too high for Lenin's heirs to proceed in this fashion. . . .

The Stalin Revolution

The violent policy changes that Stalin initiated in 1929 wrought effects more profound, in many respects, than the Revolution of 1917. Stalin himself later described the period as a revolution from above. In the organization of industry, agriculture, and cultural life,

Robert V. Daniels is the author of The Conscience of the Revolution; The Nature of Communism; A Documentary History of Communism; *and many others. This selection is from chapter 4 of his book titled* Russia, *© 1964, and is reprinted by permission of Prentice-Hall, Inc., Englewood Cliffs, New Jersey. For footnotes, see the original source.*

and in the functioning of the Communist Party itself, the Stalin Revolution laid down the present foundation of the Soviet system. Violence and repression were stamped deep in the fabric of Soviet life. The country emerged from this era, on the eve of World War II, with untold millions of prisoners in the labor camps and most of its own Communist leadership dead at the hands of the secret police.

Stalin's most positive achievement was to initiate the five-year plans of industrial construction. Planning, of course, was already an accepted Communist doctrine, though Marx had said little about it because he had assumed that the industrial economy would be fully developed by capitalism before the proletariat took over. In 1920, the State Planning Commission (Gosplan) was established, and during the 1920s it set out to develop a science of economic planning. Ironically, Stalin found the scientific plans of Gosplan too cautious, and the plan he ordered into effect in the spring of 1929 was a set of target commands rather than a rational calculation of over-all achievement. For political effect the plan was made retroactive to the fall of 1928. At the end of 1932, Stalin proclaimed the First Five-Year Plan complete ahead of schedule: it had actually run only three years and eight months. The combined targets of the plan were well beyond the resources of the country, so that fulfillment of the plan by particular industries depended on the allocation of materials and funds. Such decisions always favored heavy industry; naturally, the plan of heavy industrial construction was fulfilled while small-scale and consumer goods industry fell far behind expectations. This deficiency was compounded by enormous waste of effort and materials because of Stalin's insistence on speed and quantity at all cost, and because funds were often allocated to unprofitable construction projects.

Despite all these defects, the First Five-Year Plan started a steady and decisive growth in Russia's economic potential. Steel production, to take the key indicator, rose from four and a half million tons in 1928 to six million in 1932, and then surged ahead to eighteen million tons in 1937, at the close of the Second Five-Year Plan. The total value of Soviet industrial output is difficult to measure because of errors in Soviet statistical procedures at that time, but the most plausible computation of output shows the index rising from the base of 100 in 1928 to 172 in 1932 and 371 in 1937.

Stalin's industrialization drive was accompanied by new measures of centralized economic control. Managers assumed even stronger authority and responsibility in their plants, but their freedom of action was limited by the new requirements of planning. Fulfillment brought them bonuses and promotions; underfulfillment meant demotion or even arrest on charges of sabotage. Even today, the Soviet planning system puts severe pressure on plant managers and other local officials, who have often responded by falsifying records, stealing materials, or committing other illegal actions.

The living and working conditions of industrial labor deteriorated sharply when the five-year plans began. The trade unions, which had concentrated on protecting the workers during the NEP, were now deprived of their autonomy and given responsibility for increasing the level of productivity. Labor discipline was tightened, and the incentive wage system became standard. Propaganda campaigns to increase productivity culminated in the celebrated Stakhanovite movement of 1935, named after a miner who performed prodigious feats of digging coal. Stalin dismissed the old ideal of equality as "a piece of reactionary bourgeois absurdity." Meanwhile, living standards for the average worker were depressed, because the government allowed prices to rise faster than wages and thus reduced real wages. City housing became extremely crowded—one room or less per family—because the building program fell far short of the need to accommodate the influx of peasants who came to work in the new industry.

Simultaneously with the First Five-Year Plan, the government determined to eliminate the areas of private enterprise that had been permitted during the NEP. The small-scale businesses of the Nepmen were all nationalized again, and most rural handicraft work was discouraged. The government has thus enjoyed a monopoly ever since in all forms of trade and industry, and this has permitted concentration on industrial and military expansion at the expense of consumer goods and services.

Stalin's drive for industrial construction had to have some source of financing that would channel the necessary labor and resources into capital investment. In Russia's development Stalin was playing the part that Marx, along with most of the classical economists, had ascribed to the private capitalists. However, Soviet socialism ruled out both native capitalists and foreign lenders as sources of capital. Stalin's only means of financing his drive for industrial construction was to resort to a system of forced saving and forced investment by the Soviet people themselves—the same approach that the Trotskyist economists had put forth during the 1920s. This was accomplished partly by underpaying the city workers and imposing a heavy turnover tax on their purchases. Another important source of capital was the exploitation of the peasants; this was the real economic purpose behind the new system of collective farms.

Collective agriculture, like economic planning, had been a vague but accepted Communist goal since the Revolution. The roots of the idea went far back in native Russian socialist thought of the nineteenth century. Some experimental farm communes had been set up during War Communism (some monasteries even tried to survive by declaring themselves communes), but during the 1920s, Russian agriculture became overwhelmingly individualistic. The collective farms of the 1930s were not a continuation of the old peasant commune but a new institution, justified in terms of the Russian tradition and Marxist doctrine but intended to guarantee the delivery of the grain supply to the state.

It is not certain that collectivization was the only way or the best way to support the industrialization drive, but it is fairly clear that Stalin became committed to both for political reasons. He began to put pressure on the kulaks in 1928, and in 1929 he ordered the wholesale collectivization of the Soviet peasantry. During the winter of 1929–1930, nearly half the peasants in the country were organized into collective farms, ostensibly by their own wishes. Kulaks were deliberately excluded from the farms, and then, because of their alleged resistance to collectivization, they were systematically dispossessed and deported. Literally millions of peasants—kulaks, suspected kulaks, or any who resisted—died in transit or languished in new "corrective labor camps" in Siberia. Violent peasant resistance frequently broke out, particularly in the Ukraine and the southeastern part of European Russia. These were the regions which the government tried to collectivize first and fastest because they were the main areas of surplus food production, but they were also the areas where the peasants were staunchly individualistic by tradition.

Collectivization did not actually mean relocation of the peasants, most of whom already lived in compact villages. It meant the confiscation of land, tools, and animals and the organization of collective village work in which the villagers were supposed to share. The advantage to the state lay in the direct taxes and fees for machinery that the collective farm had to pay and in the obligatory deliveries of specified quantities of produce that the farms had to supply at artificially low prices. Many villagers protested the collectives by slaughtering and eating their livestock. Soviet animal husbandry did not recover to the precollectivization level until after the death of Stalin, while the per capita supply of meat has not yet reached the NEP standard.

By the spring of 1930, Stalin recognized some of the harm that was being done, blamed his subordinates for the difficulties, and allowed a retreat. Half of the new collective farms were broken up. Then collectivization was resumed more gradually encompassing 50 percent of the peasants by the end of 1931, and 90 percent by 1936. Such damage had been done to farm capital and work routines, however, that the added impact of drought in 1932 caused the southern part of European Russia to suffer another devastating famine in the winter of 1932–1933. Deaths from hunger and malnutrition probably ranged into the millions; the figures are uncertain because the Soviet government never admitted the fact of the famine at all.

The effectiveness of collectivization as a system to guarantee cheap food for the government to sell expensively in the cities is demonstrated by the fact that the amount of grain collected by the government increased steadily right through the famine years even though the total grain crop fell disastrously. It was the peasants who had to bear the hardship. Thanks to the crisis of 1932–1933, however, the peasants did win a significant concession. Henceforth each peasant family was allowed to till its own private plot and market its produce freely—a limited return to the NEP compromise. Since then, most of the food for the peasants themselves and a large proportion of the vegetables and animal products for the cities have come from these plots.

The stresses that Russia experienced during the time of the First Five-Year Plan and the collectivization were so severe that political repercussions were felt even at the highest level of Stalin's political machine. Many Stalinists became alarmed, as the Bukharinists had been, that the inhuman rigors of Stalin's policy might cause the Soviet regime to be overthrown altogether. By the time of the famine, a moderate faction had taken shape in the Politburo under the leadership of the Leningrad party secretary, Sergei Kirov. Kirov had risen rapidly in the hierarchy, and after 1930 he was regarded as Stalin's second-in-command. Stalin yielded temporarily to the Kirov group, accepted the private-plot compromise in the collective farms, ended the food rationing that had been in effect since 1929, and agreed to a higher priority for consumers' goods in the Second Five-Year Plan set for 1933 to 1937.

The period of relaxation in 1933 and 1934 proved brief. In December 1934 Kirov was assassinated—with the complicity of the secret police and Stalin himself, it now appears. Nevertheless, Kirov's death was taken as the pretext for a sweeping roundup of suspected opponents of Stalin, and the four-year political convulsion of the Great Purge had begun. . . .

Just as the purges were getting under way Stalin took steps to make his regime look more respectable on paper. He had a new constitution for the USSR drawn up, and put it into effect in 1936. The principal change under this document was to eliminate the formal distinctiveness of the Soviets as a system of government, with their class representation and pyramid of indirect elections. The Congress of Soviets and the Central Executive Committee gave way to the present bicameral, directly elected Supreme Soviet. The local and regional Soviets were also to be directly elected. Class restrictions on voting were theoretically abolished. Executive power remained formally vested in the Council of People's Commissars, with Molotov as Chairman. In its reorganization of the Soviets, the Stalin Constitution abandoned the political forms on which the Communists had originally based much of their claim to revolutionary virtue, but these forms had already lost their meaning with the transfer of power to the Communist Party hierarchy. The purges accompanying the Stalin Constitution merely underscored the emptiness of that document as a promise of democracy.

Apart from the new constitution, Stalin made a number of pronouncements during the 1930s that served to bring Communist theory more in line with his own totalitarian practice. Back in 1924 he had already gone beyond most of his associates in spelling out the role of the Communist Party to lead and discipline the working class, not only to carry out revolution, as Lenin had stressed, but also "to maintain the dictatorship, to consolidate and expand it in order to achieve the complete victory of socialism," an end requiring "iron discipline" and "complete and absolute unity of action." Stalin was forced to concede at this time that "when classes disappear and the dictatorship of the proletariat withers away, the Party will also wither away." His actual conduct in power belied any early expectation of such "withering." In 1934 Stalin addressed himself to just this question, ridiculed the thought that the state could be dismantled while the "class struggle" was still going on, and asserted:

> We must realize that the strength and prestige of our party, state, economic, and all other organizations, and of their leaders, have grown to an unprecedented degree. And precisely because their strength and prestige have grown to an unprecedented degree, it is their work that now determines everything, or nearly everything. There can be no justification for references to so-called objective conditions. . . . The part played by so-called objective conditions has been reduced to a minimum; whereas the part played by our organizations and their leaders has become decisive. . . .

Here Stalin showed that he could change the most basic propositions of Marxian historical materialism to make the doctrine appear to square with the realities of the totalitarian state.

Stalin even tried to make the Great Purge square with Marxism. In 1937 he advanced the notion that:

> The more we move forward, the more success we have, then the more wrathful become the remnants of the beaten exploiter classes, the more quickly they turn to sharper forms of struggle, the more mischief they do the Soviet state, the more they grasp at the most desperate means of struggle, as the last resort of the doomed. . . .

This position was too much for Stalin's successors, and in 1956 they rejected it along with their repudiation of the purges. But Stalinist Marxism, with its emphasis on the role of leaders, organizations, and ideas rather than impersonal economic trends, is still the foundation of official Soviet thinking. Soviet ideas and Soviet policies over a wide range of matters ceased to be governed by the original meaning of Communist doctrine and conformed instead to a new amalgam of old and new beliefs which Stalin promulgated in the name of Marx.

The Transformation of Soviet Thought and Society

In the history of Soviet intellectual life and social policy the novelty of Stalinism stands out in sharp contrast to the original direction of the Revolution. Stalin turned the Soviet state into a unique structure serving rapid development and national power and gearing the individual to these overriding governmental objectives.

The present norms of Soviet social and cultural life were laid down somewhat later than the foundations of the totalitarian order in politics and economics. In the realm of intellectual and social policies, the Revolution lasted through a dozen years of innovation and liberation. This was followed during the time of the First Five-Year Plan by a transitional period when the machinery of totalitarian control over thought and social life was being erected. Finally, in the mid-1930s, came a series of policy changes and reversals under command from Stalin, with the net effect of a veritable counterrevolution in the intellectual requirements and social goals of the regime. The conservative line initiated by Stalin has been the basis of Soviet cultural standards and social legislation ever since.

The years of the Revolution and War Communism were a time of chaos in Russian society and of postponement in cultural creativity. Revolutionary experimentation in thought, the arts, education, and social norms flourished during the NEP, before the Communist Party contemplated imposing thought controls beyond the censorship of overtly anti-Communist political opinion. . . . Every conceivable variant of modernism or futurism was practiced in literature and the arts, each stylistic school claiming to represent the new "proletarian culture." In fact, the masses had little contact with the new art, for the country (particularly the peasants) still had to conquer illiteracy and gain an appreciation of the simplest classical culture.

Social thought in the 1920s displayed the same anomaly as the arts, in striving for the most advanced, liberating policies in a country whose masses were scarcely civilized. In the name of equality of the sexes, the intellectuals were proclaiming free love and the "postcard divorce," while the peasants were still treating their women as chattels. Communist educators endorsed progressive education with "learning-by-doing" and student democracy aimed at the eventual "withering away of the school," while in most of the country, there was no adequate schooling of any sort. Law and criminology sought to absolve the individual of guilt and blame the social heritage. Philosophy and psychology explained man in purely biological and deterministic terms. In sum, the revolutionary vision of man in society reaffirmed the hope of the eighteenth-century Enlightenment—in Marxist language—that human nature was naturally good, that evil came from class exploitation and oppressive institutions, and that all forms of authority and coercion would steadily wither away as Russia approached the classless society of free and equal citizens.

These hopes of the 1920s would have been utopian anywhere, let alone in Russia with its colossal problems of economic and cultural development. They were nonetheless genuinely held by the leading lights in most specialized fields of thought, though perhaps less by the political leadership in the Communist Party. But these revolutionary hopes, like most of Russian thought since the westernization in the eighteenth century, did not have a foundation in Russian society as a whole. Cultural unity could be gained only by pulling the masses up or pulling the thinkers down. Stalin undertook to do both.

Between 1929 and 1932 Soviet intellectuals for the first time felt the full force of totalitarianism. In one field after another, Stalin or his lieutenants intervened to impose their views of art or philosophy and give the nod to the Party faithful to enforce the ultra-Marxist line in each field. All art and literature had to be "proletarian" in a crudely propagandist way. All history had to be cast in the terms of economic determinism. Economics and political theory had to recognize the decisive role of the government and its leaders in building the industrial economy. "Party spirit"—i.e., abject justification of the dictator's preferences—became the standard in every field of thought. Objective respect for the truth was condemned by Stalin as "rotten liberalism." Nonconformists who tried to preserve old "bourgeois" views were purged, by censorship, unemployment, and imprisonment. . . .

The official organizations of writers and artists were purged between 1932 and 1934 and ordered to follow the line of Socialist Realism. Socialist Realism, "national in form and socialist in content," has been the official label for Social cultural policy ever since. In practice it means strictly classical forms, propagandist glorification of the leader, Party, and nation, and condemnation of all modernistic experimentation as "bourgeois formalism."

In the fields of social thought, Stalin's conservative shift was particularly striking. He condemned as "vulgar economic materialism" the ultra-Marxist writing of history that had been imposed by Mikhail Pokrovsky, and sanctioned a highly nationalistic approach to Russia's past—with Marxist terminology. Earlier efforts to cultivate the culture of the non-Russian minorities were rejected as "bourgeois nationalism" and supplanted by a pronounced favoritism for the Great Russians as the model nation in the USSR. The theory of the withering away of the state was revised to postpone its effect indefinitely and allow for the unabashed perfection of the totalitarian state and a bureaucratic society.

In line with his reinterpretation of Communist Party theory, Stalin heavily emphasized state authority and individual responsibility. Law, in both its theoretical and practical aspects, was rehabilitated as a permanent foundation of the Communist state. Criminology paralleled the purges by shifting the burden of guilt from corrupt society to rotten individual. The permissive attitude to relations between the sexes was repudiated as "bourgeois" and replaced by a rigid divorce code and a stifling public puritanism. Education was revamped to end the progressive approach of democratic self-expression and returned to the old disciplinary methods of authoritarian instruction and grading. For the sake of industrial productivity, labor relations were reorganized to stress individual responsibilities and material incentives.

In principle, Stalinism made no excuse for social conditions or class status. The individual was to be promoted and rewarded insofar as he availed himself of training and strove to serve the state. All special privileges for the proletariat were abolished, and what were in fact social classes were recognized as the "strata" of workers, peasants, and "toiling intelligentsia." For the upper officialdom, good pay, low taxes, rights to personal property, interest-bearing state bonds, and (after 1944) unrestricted inheritance became the rule to reward their efforts and loyalty.

One sphere of policy which did not evidence a clear shift was the area of religion. The Orthodox Church was persecuted periodically from the time of the Civil War, when it backed the Whites against Bolshevik secularism, up to the late 1930s. A notable shift by the Soviet government came in 1943, during World War II, when Stalin decided on an accommodation with the Church for its patriotic effect. The Church won *de facto* toleration and was allowed to revive the office of Patriarch in return for supporting the regime politically. For other faiths conditions became decidely worse after the purges because of their association with minority nationalism. . . .

Stalinism Triumphant

The new society that Stalin fashioned in the name of Marx and Lenin was harsh but stable. It met its test of life or death in the crucible of World War II and survived, after near disaster and unprecedented human loss at the hands of the German invaders. When peace came, Soviet Russia proved to have changed less politically and socially than any of the other belligerents, even though the physical and economic impact of the war was worse in Russia than anywhere outside Germany. Postwar Russia was still in spirit postpurge Russia, ruled by terror, shrouded from the outside world, guided by a crafty paranoid bent on the maximization of his power both at home and abroad. There was no relaxation until Stalin died in 1953.

In the Soviet leadership there was a surprising continuity from the late 1930s to 1953, in contrast to the political upheavals of the two preceding decades. Stalin, as General Secretary, had what was left of the Communist Party organization firmly in his grip, with the assistance of Georgi Malenkov as his Secretary for Personnel. Malenkov became a candidate member of the Politburo in 1941 and a full member in 1946. His chief rival as second-in-command and heir apparent to Stalin was Andrei Zhdanov, the Leningrad secretary, who advocated the aggressive expansion of international Communism and was responsible for a severe tightening of the controls over doctrinal discipline and cultural expression. Following Zhdanov's death in 1948, his followers in the Party hierarchy were purged in the so-called Leningrad Affair. Malenkov then moved up to the number two spot and seemed to have Stalin's blessing for the succession when the dictator died in 1953. . . .

The war, for all its rigors, caused little internal threat to the stability of Stalin's regime. He did relax the enforcement of Communist doctrinal discipline, and gained more than the equivalent in patriotic fervor. In the battle zone it was another matter. Soviet troops, badly deployed, their morale undermined by the experience of the purges, surrendered by the hundreds of thousands in the first months of the German attack. The civil population of occupied zones often welcomed the Germans as liberators, particularly in the Ukraine and the North Caucasus. Numerous Soviet prisoners of war volunteered for service with the Germans. General Andrei Vlasov, captured in 1942, was allowed to organize an Army of Liberation composed of some 50,000 anti-Stalin Russians, while over half a million Soviet nationals served under direct German command.

Had Germany used political warfare more effectively, there is little doubt that Stalin could have been defeated and overthrown in 1941 or 1942. . . . Such an eventuality was ruled out by German error. Hitler was so dedicated to the enslavement of the "inferior" Slavic peoples that he refused to make use of the political capital offered him by Russian surrenders and defections. Hundreds of thousands of Russian prisoners were systematically starved in the first winter of the war. Occupied Russia found that it had only exchanged native totalitarianism for foreign terror. Forced laborers were deported, and Jews and other condemned groups were hunted down and shot. Partisan groups controlled by Moscow began to wage guerrilla warfare behind the German lines and laid the basis for the restoration of Soviet authority in the German-occupied zones.

Soviet rule, for those to whom it returned and for the "displaced persons" who returned to it, was almost as severe as during the purges. Nazi collaborators or suspects were liquidated, and millions of people were sentenced to forced labor camps on charges of treason allegedly committed while they were under German control or imprisonment. The labor camp population, swelled also by captured Germans and deportees from the Soviet minorities, may have reached five to ten million or even more in the postwar years.

The rigors of the Soviet propaganda and intellectual controls of the 1930s were restored in 1946, as the gloomy clouds of the Cold War gathered. In literature and the arts, Zhdanov took the lead to reimpose the familiar line of Socialist Realism, with its conservative forms, Marxist vocabulary, and violently nationalistic and anti-Western content. With the ascendancy of Malenkov after 1949, the non-Russian minorities and particularly the Jews bore the brunt of an aggressive Russian nationalism which proclaimed the tsarist conquest to have been a benefit for all of Russia's borderlands. As for the natural sciences, some of the basic theories of modern physics and biology—Einstein's relativity and Mendelian genetics, for example—were condemned as "bourgeois idealism." Stalin's

Russia at the end of his career was a gray and frightened land of theory without meaning, where practical engineering, military and industrial, was almost the only avenue for the creative mind.

The one area of real accomplishment of Stalin's regime in the later years, as in the earlier, was the progress of heavy industry, though still at the expense of consumer goods and agriculture. On the eve of the war, midway in the Third Five-Year Plan, Soviet heavy industrial output had passed the British (in absolute but, of course, not per capita terms). The German invasion was economically catastrophic: half of Russia's prewar industry, including the Donets Basin and besieged Leningrad, was in the war zone. Some industrial equipment was evacuated to the east, and by cutting the civilian economy to the bone, the Soviet government was able to meet the basic manpower and munitions requirements of the army. The contrast with tsarist mismanagement in World War I was impressive. Anglo-American aid was an important supplement to the Soviets, particularly in automotive equipment and aircraft.

From a low in 1942, the Soviet econmomy was already partially restored by the end of the war, with steel production reaching 12 million tons in 1945. The five-year plans of expansion were resumed with the Fourth of 1946–1950 and the Fifth of 1951–1955, both of which put a premium on heavy industry. Thanks to this effort, industrial output rose at the impressive rate of nearly 20 percent a year, and when Stalin died, Russia had reached an annual steel production of 38 million tons. In those sectors of the economy which counted most in national military potential, Russia's industrial revolution was now virtually complete. The Soviet perfection of an atomic bomb in 1949 testified to this.

Living standards for the Soviet population improved only slowly during the postwar years. Most of the collective farm peasantry was dismally exploited and impoverished, with an average individual cash income of less than $100 per year. Famine struck again in 1946 and 1947. Further centralized control was the regime's only answer to the lack of progress in agriculture, but without incentives, the peasantry failed to respond. Factory labor was kept under the near-military discipline of wartime, and workers were virtually conscripted into the State Labor Reserves. The bad prewar housing situation was now far worse because of wartime destruction and the continuing lag of construction. The prewar standard of living for the average Soviet citizen was not achieved again until the early 1950s, and the NEP standard was not reached until the Khrushchev era.

In 1952 Stalin convoked the Nineteenth Party Congress, at which he marked Malenkov as his heir and tried to weaken the possibility of an opposition by enlarging the Politburo. (It was simultaneously renamed the Presidium, and the old Orgburo was abolished.) Then, in January 1953 came the bizarre announcement of a "Doctors' Plot," allegedly a plan to murder the whole Soviet leadership as part of a United States and Zionist conspiracy. Possibly a new general purge was in the offing. Such was the tense political atmosphere when Stalin's death by cerebral hemorrhage was announced on March 5, 1953.

The Succession and the Khrushchev Era

The death of Stalin signaled a new test of the regime he had constructed. It is a measure of the strength of the Stalinist system that in its fundamentals it survived a succession struggle and the personal repudiation of its own creator. With some amelioration, it remains the basis of Soviet political, economic, social, and intellectual life today.

No sooner was Stalin dead than his lieutenants undid most of the arrangements he had made for the succession. To be sure, Malenkov became government head as Chairman of the Council of Ministers, but he was forced to surrender direction of the Communist Party organization to Khrushchev. Khrushchev was probably the man least threatening to the other top leaders, but his position as First Secretary corresponded exactly to that of Stalin in 1922, and he was quick to capitalize on it. . . .

"Collective leadership" was proclaimed as the watchword of the new regime. Steps were quickly taken to repudiate the "Doctors' Plot" charges and to pardon many of Stalin's political prisoners. It seems possible that Beria took the lead in this direction, but his control of the police still posed a threat to his colleagues. In June 1953 they removed him from office—by shooting him on the spot, according to some reports. Then they split the police powers up and put them under the firmer control of the Party.

Along with the curb on police terror, the new leadership made substantial economic concessions to the population, with pay and pension raises for the workers and tax relief for the peasants. In intellectual life the "thaw" gradually opened some ground for artistic independence, and Marxist interference in natural science was largely abandoned. Even in foreign policy there were substantial moves toward more normal relations with the non-Communist world.

Between 1953 and 1956, Khrushchev rebuilt the Party Secretariat and secured his control over the regional Party organizations. Early in 1955, he moved against Malenkov on charges of mismanaging the economy and underrating heavy industry. Malenkov was compelled to resign as Chairman of the Council of Ministers in February 1955 and was relegated to the Ministry of Electric Power Stations. The premiership then went to Nikolai Bulganin, who was replaced as Minister of Defense by the World War II hero Marshal Georgi Zhukov. For the next two years, the Soviet leadership appeared to be a diarchy of Khrushchev and Bulganin.

In February 1956 the first post-Stalin Party Congress, the Twentieth, was held. Khrushchev chose this as the occasion for a remarkable political gamble, his "secret speech" (actually read all over the country by the Party "agitators") attacking Stalin's "cult of personality" record of paranoid despotism since the purges. The Stalinist victims of the purges (though not the old oppositionists) were posthumously "rehabilitated"—readmitted to history in a favorable light. Khrushchev lamely skirted his own role and that of his associates in the purges by pleading that Stalin had kept them in ignorance. He went on to condemn Stalin's methods of terror and torture and to promise that they would never be resumed. . . .

By the end of 1956 it appears that there was a movement afoot among the older Soviet leaders to unseat Khrushchev. Like the opposition of the 1920s against Stalin, the supporters of Malenkov and Molotov in the governmental hierarchy were stymied by Khrushchev's control of the Communist Party organization, which was now restored to the political preeminence it had enjoyed before Stalin's purges. Taking a leaf from Stalin's book, Khrushchev adopted a series of novel policies to provoke the opposition into an open fight: his virgin lands scheme of agricultural expansion, the radical decentralization of industrial administration, and overtures in foreign policy to such ostensible enemies as Tito's Yugoslavia, West Germany, and the United States. In June 1957 the opposition decided to strike. While Khrushchev was visiting Finland they convoked a meeting of the Presidium and voted to remove him from the post of First Secretary. He hurried back to summon the larger and theoretically more authoritative Central Committee and had it "democratically" override the Presidium. Khrushchev's victory was complete; not only did he stay in power, but he had Malenkov, Molotov, Kaganovich, and Saburov expelled from all their Party and governmental offices as an "anti-Party group." Marshal Zhukov supported Khrushchev decisively but showed too much strength; he was replaced as Defense Minister in the fall of 1957 by Marshal Rodion Malinovsky and consigned to obscurity. Finally, Khrushchev capped his victory by removing Bulganin as prime minister in 1958 and taking the post himself, thus acquiring all the formal power that Stalin had held. The individual succession had finally come to pass after all, though not with the man, manner, or policies intended by Stalin. . . .

During the first five or six years after Stalin's death, every current of change in the Soviet Union was for the better: steady industrial growth, improved living standards, more housing, less intellectual constriction, less international fear. Trouble began to appear in 1957 with Khrushchev's politically motivated interference in the top-heavy economic planning system, though Stalin's investment in technology paid off in that year with Russia's first successful launching of an artificial earth satellite or *sputnik*. By the fall of 1957, the Sixth Five-Year Plan was so badly disorganized that it had to be abandoned altogether; 1958 was the first peacetime year since 1928 that was not included in a long-term plan. Long-range planning was resumed with the Seven-Year Plan set to run from 1959 through 1965, but by this time the Soviet tempo of industrial growth had begun to decline appreciably. Khrushchev gave most of his attention to various experiments in the lagging field of agriculture but failed to correct the basic ills of overcentralized direction and insufficient peasant incentives. A crop failure in 1963 dragged the whole economy down to a net annual growth of about 3 percent, and forced the Soviet government to make large foreign grain purchases for the first time in its history. . . .

The post-Stalin thaw in cultural life proved to be limited in duration and scope. More rigorous controls were applied after the East European crisis of 1956, later eased up, then tightened again during the international crisis of 1962–1963. Yet certain truly basic changes in the attitude of the Soviet intelligentsia appear to have taken place since 1953: a restiveness, professional self-confidence, and passion for foreign contacts that the Party can defy only at a great price in morale and creativity. Writers, ranging from the old Boris Pasternak to the young Yevgeni Yevtushenko, tried to defy the regime's standards, while a true sign of change was the publication of Alexander Solzhenitsyn's fictional exposé of labor camp life under Stalin. Only in the realm of religion was Khrushchev harsher than Stalin: the Jewish faith was hounded with increasing cruelty, and even the Russian Orthodox Church encountered stiffer curbs on its propagation of the faith.

Khrushchev was sixty-four years old when he achieved supreme power in 1958, and he seemed content to make the most of the system he ruled without fundamental changes. In the new Communist Party Program, laid down at the Twenty-Second Party Congress in 1961, he undertook to claim for his regime a historic place in the realization of Marxist theory by announcing that Soviet Russia had entered the final lap on the path to the Marxist utopia—the phase of "building communism." The class struggle was now over, he contended, and class differences had ceased to exist (though differential rewards for individual effort and responsibility are likely to continue indefinitely). Accordingly, Khrushchev announced that the dictatorship of the proletariat was at an end and that the Soviet state was now a "state of all the people." This notion was a patent distortion of Marxist fundamentals—as the Chinese Communists were soon to point out—but it suited Khrushchev's interest in self-righteous stability. He declared that the function of the state from this time on would be to complete the construction of the "material and technical basis of communism"—i.e., more industry and more education.

To comply with Marx's prediction that the state would wither away, Khrushchev called for the step-by-step transfer of governmental functions to "non-governmental public organizations." In fact, however, this means only that the totalitarian state would continue under a different label, since the Communist Party would continue permanently as one of these "public organizations," with its familiar power to control all other activities in Soviet society. During the early 1960s, the Party assumed closer control of industry and agriculture, and now the trend seems to be for the Party to become everything that the government used to be. It is less certain that this will always be accepted as the last word in Marxism.

*[**Editor's note:** Some insight into the nature, implications, and consequences of the critical struggle for power within the Party in 1957 may be gleaned from Nikita S. Khrushchev's speeches to the Twenty-second Party Congress in October 1961. Khrushchev explained the reasons which had led to the denunciation of Stalin in 1956 as follows:*

> What would have become of the Party and the country had the cult of the individual not been condemned, had its harmful consequences not been removed and the Leninist standards of Party and government activity not been restored? The result would have been a cleavage between Party and people, grave violations of Soviet democracy and revolutionary legality, slower economic progress, a lower rate of communist construction and hence a deterioration of the people's standard of living. In the sphere of international relations, the result would have been a weakening of Soviet positions on the world scene and a worsening of relations with other countries, which would have had dire consequences. That is why criticism of the cult of the individual and the elimination of its consequences were of the utmost political and practical importance.

Khrushchev reiterated and elaborated on some of the charges made against Stalin in his 1956 "secret" speech. This time, however, his remarks were at open sessions and were published throughout the USSR. Also subjected to vitriolic denunciation and linked with Stalin's crimes—or, at the very least, with an unwillingness to expose them and alter Stalin's course—was "the anti-Party group headed by Molotov, Kaganovich and Malenkov."

During the proceedings, speaker after speaker mounted the rostrum and vied with each other in loosing fierce invectives against "the anti-Party group" which included senior Old Bolsheviks, two former Premiers, and a former Marshal of the Soviet Union. Typical remarks made to "stormy applause" were the following: "Molotov, Malenkov, and Kaganovich—these slugs—should not have been trusted"; "Kaganovich is a degenerate, in whom there has been nothing Communist for a long time"; "on Malenkov's conscience lie the deaths of totally innocent people and numerous repressions." They were called "swamp creatures . . . used to slime and mud," a "contemptible group of factionalists . . . and miserable clique of oppositionists." Although reference was made to a letter of Molotov's to the Congress, it was not published. Nor were members of the so-called anti-Party group permitted to present their case to the Congress or to the Russian people.

In October 1964, while Khrushchev was vacationing on the Black Sea, he was ousted as Premier and First Secretary of the Communist Party in a carefully organized, conspiratorial move by his Presidium colleagues. The "unanimous" vote in the Presidium in this instance (in contrast with what occurred in 1957) was upheld by the Party's Central Committee. In general, the attack on Khrushchev that ensued was much milder than that leveled at the "anti-Party group" but this time, with the tables turned, it was Khrushchev who was denied the opportunity to present his side of the case to the Russian people.]

From Khrushchev to Brezhnev

Sidney I. Ploss

The five years that have elapsed since Khrushchev's fall from power have seen the new Soviet leadership not merely slow down Russia's movement away from Stalinist iron rule but even, in some respects, reassert the dictatorial and militaristic traditions of Stalinism. Unlike Khrushchev, the majority of the present leaders have shown themselves disposed toward orthodox policies calculated to consolidate bureaucratic authority and to enhance the state's military power. They have been far less willing than Khrushchev to encourage academic theorists in devising sweeping changes in the management of the overly centralized planned economy. And the intellectuals have been obliged to desist from exposing the Stalinist system as the historical source of the moral corruption of the nation's political life.

Yet Khrushchev's downfall did not end the post-Stalin tension between reformist and conservative elements in the Kremlin. There is considerable evidence that the issues debated in the succession struggle of 1953–57 have reappeared in all their divisiveness. These issues apparently include choices between guns and butter in budgetary allocations and the related question of the proper Soviet posture in the costly nuclear arms race; the problem of how to gear the economic administration for greater efficiency; the historical evaluation of Stalin; and relationships between party organizers and the specialists of the state bureaucracy in the management of public affairs. In the climate of internal rivalry and intrigue in which Soviet leaders have always moved, these policy disputes have been associated with the power interests of various leadership factions.

The discussion that follows will first focus on how the present leadership under General Secretary Leonid Brezhnev and Premier Aleksei Kosygin has reversed or modified Khrushchev's policies in several key areas. This will be followed by an examination of the major issues on which there has been evidence of recurrent conflict among the different power groupings within the leadership. And finally some tentative conclusions will be offered as to the possible outcome of these conflicts and the implications it might have for future political evolution in the Soviet Union and the Soviet posture in world affairs.

Symptomatic of the return to orthodox policies and traditional roles for vested interests in the state and party bureaucracies was the prompt reversal of Khrushchev's party reforms once the First Secretary had been removed from power. This was a notable triumph for the full-time party workers who had come of age politically before World War II and did not share the widespread postwar hopes of a possible relaxation of the dictatorship. These technically unskilled stalwarts, fearing the rise of young technical and managerial cadres within the party, emphasized general supervision and thought-control in party activity.

Khrushchev had hoped to revitalize the party apparatus in order to make it a fit instrument with which to smash the barriers of bureaucratic opposition to his quick panaceas for

Sidney I. Ploss is the author of Conflict and Decision-Making in Soviet Russia, *and editor of* The Soviet Political Process. *This selection is reprinted from the author's "Politics in the Kremlin,"* in Problems of Communism, *vol. 19 (May–June 1970), pp. 1–14. For detailed footnote references see the original.*

the Soviet economy. To this end, he had proposed the division of the party apparatus into industrial and agricultural components to be charged with exercising practical economic leadership, and this reform had been decreed by a plenary session of the CPSU Central Committee on November 23, 1962. A direct consequence of the change was the career advancement of young, forward-looking party men. Whereas there were only two second secretaries of regional party committees in the Russian Republic under forty years of age before the reform, soon after the reform there were no less than fourteen second secretaries of industrial regional party committees and twenty second secretaries of agricultural regional party committees who were less than forty years old.

Khrushchev's action led the older political cadres to complain of the party's "depoliticization," while on the other hand state managers bemoaned the reform as a "reversal for the technocrats" which subjugated the government bureaucracy to party officials. The former group drew support from party secretaries Brezhnev and Mikhail Suslov; the latter from Kosygin and other high state officials. At the June 1963 Central Committee plenum, Khrushchev and his supporters had to counter outspoken criticisms emanating from the disgruntled groups. Their criticisms were directed at mounting crime, poor labor discipline and local nationalism—all matters which were normally the responsibility of the party apparatus—and thus constituted an implicit attack on the validity of the party reform.

It was these disparate elements who joined forces in October 1964 to oust Khrushchev. Drawn together by a common desire to restore the division of labor between party and state which had been an essential feature of bureaucratic life under Lenin and Stalin, they were determined to make one more stab at reconciling the ideal of total control of social processes with the pragmatic requirements of operating a modern industrial state. Khrushchev's involvement of the party in practical affairs was denounced as "commercialism" and "pure empiricism," and party spokesmen called for greater attention to party political training and indoctrination of the public. In mid-November 1964, one month after Khrushchev's dismissal, his party reform was swept away by the Central Committee after hearing a secret report by Nikolai Podgorny. Khrushchev's revamping of the party apparatus was condemned in the party press on the ground that it had caused "confusion of the functions, rights and duties of party, soviet and managerial agencies" and had "pushed party committees into taking the place of the managerial agencies."

Rehabilitation of Stalin

Also indicative of the new leadership's inclination toward more orthodox policies was its gradual movement away from destalinization, which had been the cornerstone of Khrushchev's domestic program. In part, the former First Secretary's moves to discredit Stalin—the symbol of mass discipline and administrative control from above—had been designed to promote a measure of self-assertiveness among the educated class and to instill a greater sense of responsibility in the half-million or so leading officials. However, the zigzag fashion in which this effort had been pursued reflected both Khrushchev's own concern lest things get out of hand and the misgivings of others in the top leadership who had a stake in the Stalinist political system.

Nevertheless, by 1964 Stalin had come to be treated in Soviet media as an arch-criminal and bungler who had brought the nation to the verge of disaster. The once-dreaded secret police were being held in check, and former inmates of Stalin's prison camps were encouraged to throw light on past infamies. Public attacks on Stalinist habits had indeed progressed so far that party officials were beginning to complain of a tendency on the part of ordinary citizens to be "insolent and insubordinate toward their leaders."

The men who wrested power from Khrushchev soon showed that they were anxious to halt the erosion of discipline resulting from his destalinization policies. The first clear indication of this was an unsigned *Pravda* article of April 29, 1965, which deplored "onesidedness" in the treatment of historical events and personalities. Although the new leaders did not go so far as to excuse Stalin's long reign of terror for fear that this would revive mass anxieties and possibly even lead to outbreaks of public disorder, they did call for a halt to emotional criticism of the late dictator.

While intensifying repressive measures against dissident writers and intellectuals, the new leadership took another step to dissociate itself from Khrushchev's destalinization policies with a *Pravda* editorial of January 30, 1966, which denounced Khrushchev's perjorative term "period of the cult of personality" on the ground that it demeaned "the heroic efforts of party and people in the struggle for socialism." Although Brezhnev himself failed to make any pronouncement on the Stalin issue at the subsequent 23rd Party Congress, which opened in March 1966, other speakers did praise the late dictator, and the Congress underlined continuity with the Stalin period by decreeing that the party Presidium should again be named the Politburo and that Stalin's title of party General Secretary should be resurrected.

The regime has since shown itself to be intent upon a limited rehabilitation of Stalin while retaining for itself a clear monopoly of the right to criticize various aspects of Stalinism. Thus, the Theses for the 50th Anniversary of the 1917 Revolution repudiated Stalin's domination of the Politburo and the blood purges; yet, on the other hand, Professor Aleksandr M. Nekrich was expelled from the CPSU for assailing Stalin's conduct of diplomatic and military affairs in the Second World War. Again, a *Pravda* article on the occasion of Stalin's 90th birth anniversary in December 1969 called the former leader a "great theoretician"—the highest tribute a Communist can receive—but also noted "theoretical and political errors that became serious in nature during the latter period of his life."

The members of the Central Committee Secretariat have been in the vanguard of the movement to revive latent pro-Stalin feelings in the ranks of officialdom. Brezhnev himself has freely used such Stalinist epithets as "two-faced people" and has consistently stood for the enforcement of Stalinist-type ideological orthodoxy and discipline both at home and in intrabloc relations. Piotr E. Shelest, Ukrainian party boss and a member of the CPSU Politburo, has also backed the use of Stalinist methods with hardline speeches and dogmatic press campaigns. Army generals, visibly distressed by the spread of pacifist sentiment among younger citizens, have tended as a group to favor a revival of Stalinist discipline, and judging from promotions of former or present security operatives and the popularization of counterespionage activities, police officials have likewise been active in engineering the retreat from destalinization.

Economic Recentralization

There has also been a clear-cut reversal of policy in the realm of economic administration. Whereas Khrushchev sought to remedy declining gains in industrial and agricultural output and productivity by promoting decentralization of economic planning and management, the Brezhnev-Kosygin leadership has in general brought economic reform back into a framework of bureaucratic centralism, notwithstanding some devolution of operational authority to managers of farms and industrial enterprises.

Khrushchev, it will be recalled, proposed in 1962 that the USSR State Planning Committee merely "dovetail" the economic plans of the union republics—an obvious departure from the traditional dictation of such plans from the center. Similarly, he gave his blessing to industrial reform at the July 1964 Supreme Soviet meeting and subsequently put forward concrete proposals for granting wide decision-making powers to factory directors. In agriculture, just prior to his ouster, he was contemplating a scheme for the assignment of kolkhoz land and machinery for long periods of time to small teams or "links" instead of the existing system of managing production through the larger field brigades. The goal was to inspire the collective farmers to identify more closely with the land and to develop a greater interest in its productivity, on which their income would be based. He also inspired a proposal that centralized procurement of certain foodstuffs be reduced in order to permit farms to market part of their crop commercially in the towns.

In contrast to Khrushchev's decentralization moves, his successors lost little time in moving to restrengthen central direction of the economy. The rebuilding of the state control hierarchy began with a party-state decree of March 1, 1965 restoring to the USSR Ministry of Agriculture its time-honored function of planning the production and sale of farm products. A decree of March 2 transformed into ministries several state committees concerned with defense technology and production. Moreover, the restored central bureaucracy continued to draw power away from republic agencies. By 1967, there were 25 all-union and 27 union-republic ministries in Moscow, with only 8 republic ministries in the Russian Republic which answered to no central body. (At the moment of Stalin's death there had been 30 all-union and 22 union-republic ministries.) . . .

The reform in economic management announced by Kosygin in the autumn of 1965 did, it is true, promise enterprise managers fewer planning orders from Moscow and the opportunity to dispose of increased sums of working capital, while plan fulfillment would be based on sales and profits rather than on physical volume of output. However, the ability of enterprises to make effective use of these new rights was hindered by the center's retention of control over investment and price policy, as well as over the physical distribution of 886 categories of producer goods. Kosygin also rejected a proposal that enterprises be permitted to fix their own wage funds because this would impair the state's authority to regulate purchasing power and the output of consumer goods. Moreover, the 1967 reform of wholesale prices gave little incentive to increase quality or improve production technology, still leaving managers without a reliable guide for production and investment decisions.

Khrushchev's recommendations for a basic reorganization of collective farm labor and greater flexibility in product marketing were still in the discussion stage when the change in leadership occurred, and they were left in abeyance for the time being. The new leadership confined itself to a series of stop-gap measures to halt deterioration of the national diet, including the easing of restrictions on private plots, the abolition of taxes on privately owned livestock, the release of reserve fodder to feed such livestock, and increased purchase prices for milk (without raising retail prices). At the March 1965 Central Committee meeting, Brezhnev further announced a doubling of state investments in agriculture during 1966–70 as compared with the total for the preceding five years, increases in crop delivery prices, and stable delivery quotas for several years. (As will be seen, the investment program ran into serious difficulties not long after its adoption.) Collective farmers were also offered a guaranteed monthly wage based on state-farm rates to replace the old system of deferring payment until crop deliveries were made to the state.

In any event, it is clear that Khrushchev's successors preferred to preserve the mechanism of central control rather than let economic development depend upon the responses of farm and enterprise managers to the desires of society at large. The economic cost of this reliance on power politics instead of on considerations of economic efficiency has been seen in gross waste, declining returns on capital investment, and a slowing annual growth rate—a modest 5.5 percent for 1966–69.

Shift in Priorities

Still another sphere in which the present Soviet leadership has veered sharply away from Khrushchev's policy intentions has been that of relative priorities in resource allocation as between defense and defense-related industry on the one hand, and the development of the light-industrial, consumer-goods sector of the economy on the other. Khrushchev's boast in *Izvestia* of September 20, 1964, that the Soviet Union possessed new and formidable weaponry was the last of many such avowals and carried the clear implication that Soviet military superiority made it possible to release investment funds from military projects to light-industrial development. Shortly thereafter, Khrushchev was reported (in *Pravda*, October 2) to have told a joint meeting of the CPSU Presidium and the Council of Ministers that, in drafting the 1966–70 economic plan, "it is essential to be guided by the fact that the main task . . . is the further improvement of the living standard of the people."

Speaking in Red Square only a few days after Khrushchev's dismissal, Brezhnev significantly modified the deposed leader's definition of the "main task":

> The party considers that its main task in the area of internal policy is the *development of the productive forces* of our society and unswerving improvement *on this basis* of the prosperity of the Soviet people. [Italics added]

In other words, there would be no shift of priorities in favor of consumer industry.

Although the 1965 state budget already prepared under Khrushchev, reduced declared defense outlays by 500 million rubles, the new leadership's intention to reverse this trend in favor of a determined effort to overtake the United States in the arms race was signaled at the end of 1965 when the 1966 budget programmed a 600–million ruble increase in declared defense spending. Additional increases followed: 1.1 billion rubles for 1967; 2.2 billion rubles for 1968; 1 billion rubles for 1969; and 200 million rubles for 1970. Declared defense expenditures, however, are but a part of overall investments in defense. Total Soviet investments in defense, space and nuclear energy programs in 1969 have been estimated at around $60 billion, or more than 13 percent of gross national product, representing a larger proportion of GNP than was spent on defense and defense-related programs by the United States last year. Western experts have reckoned that the Soviet stockpile of intercontinental missiles jumped from around 224 in 1965 to over 1,000 by 1969, while heavy expenditures are also believed to have been incurred in hardening Soviet missile-launching sites.

The increase in defense spending under the present Soviet leadership is thought to have entailed an appreciable slowdown of investment in the civilian sector of the economy. Total industrial investments, in constant prices of 1955, grew by 27.4 percent in the period 1961–64, as compared with only a 19.2 percent increase in the period 1965–68. While it is not possible to separate out consumer-industry investments, the continued underfulfillment of housing construction plans provides one indication that investments in the consumer sector have lagged behind. It is also surmised that at least $8 billion earmarked for farming in 1966–70 was redirected into defense-related projects. This was undoubtedly a factor in the decline of the agricultural sector after a brief period of improvement, and even though the situation did not deteriorate to the point of creating a grave economic emergency, it appears to have caused a number of the top Soviet leaders to develop second thoughts about sacrificing domestic programs, particularly those affecting agriculture, for the sake of accelerated military development.

The concern of the leadership over the deterioration in agriculture was reflected in a party-state decree of May 23, 1968, which ordered a doubling of the construction rate of new chemical fertilizer plants in 1969 and 1970. This move, in effect, revived Khrushchev's 1963 goal for fertilizer production and meant an annual increase of at least $1 billion in investment in the chemical industry. At a Central Committee meeting on October 30, 1968 Brezhnev himself took the lead in proposing even more ambitious plans for expanding the production of agricultural chemicals, and at the November 1969 All-Union Congress of Collective Farmers, he expressed himself in favor of increased government spending on agricultural irrigation and facilities for the production of farm machinery.

Although Brezhnev would thus appear to have been among those who had second thoughts in 1968 about channeling an excessive share of national resources into defense at the expense of vital domestic programs, there is little doubt that at first he, along with his Politburo and Secretariat colleagues, Mikhail Suslov and Andrei Kirilenko, had led the political forces championing first priority for the buildup of Soviet military might. After the change in leadership, Khrushchev's idea that the Soviet Union was already strong enough to permit economies in defense investments was quickly repudiated in organs mirroring the views of the Secretariat, and at the time the leap forward in nuclear armament began in 1965, Brezhnev, Suslov and Kirilenko were all speaking like devotees of military industrialization. (Brezhnev, it may be noted, has personal ties with army leaders dating back to World War II, as attested to in some military memoirs.) Kirilenko and Suslov continue to be staunch advocates of military claims on national resources, with the latter, in particular, frequently conjuring up the specter of global war. . . .

Collective Leadership Restored

Thus far, we have examined the major areas in which the acts, decisions, or pronouncements of the present Soviet leadership spelled a sharp deviation from the basically innovative policy initiatives of the Khrushchev regime. There is, however, abundant evidence to indicate that some of these, as well as other persistently recurring policy issues, have been the subject of renewed conflict between contending power and interest groups represented within the top leadership. Let us therefore look at the major issues which appear to have given rise to leadership dissension.

Investment Conflicts

First of all, questions involving priorities in the allocation of resources have apparently been the subject of high-level controversy on a number of occasions. One such dispute that came into the open in 1967 centered on the leadership's decision to cut back state investments in agriculture by 13 percent below the level targeted in the directives for the 1966–70 Five-Year Plan. Dmitri S. Polianski, the Politburo's agricultural specialist, had already warned publicly against such a cutback in a March 1967 statement in *Pravda* assailing "some people" who were "beginning to argue that collective and state farms can now develop even with less material aid," and that land reclamation work and deliveries of equipment and fertilizers to agriculture could be reduced. The 13-percent cut was nevertheless decided upon, and Polianski promptly voiced his opposition in an extraordinary article in *Kommunist* arguing for an "uninterrupted increase" in state investments in agriculture. Party and state leaders countered with a "letter" in *Pravda* (November 5, 1967) redefining the "main economic task" in terms that called for "unswerving growth of industry and agriculture" in place of the 1966 Five-Year Plan directives' primary emphasis on "high and stable rates of agricultural development."

The controversy over investment priorities intensified following a decision in late 1967 to commence work on the directives for the 1971–75 Five-Year Plan. Premier Kosygin and General Secretary Brezhnev took conflicting positions reminiscent of those taken, respectively, by Malenkov and Khrushchev in the immediate post-Stalin period. In a Kremlin address in December, Kosygin stressed the development of light and food industries and "satisfaction of the population's demand for a varied assortment of goods." Again, at a Minsk party rally the following February, he called for closing the gap between the slow growth rate of light industry and the rapid expansion of heavy industry, in order to solve the problem of providing the population with an "uninterrupted and varied supply of foodstuffs, clothing and other consumer goods." On the other hand, Brezhnev in the same month publicly urged "preserving the accelerated development of heavy industry as the basis of our industrial might" and called for a 22-million-ton increase in steel production over the next three years. In another statement in March, he seemed to take aim at Kosygin's emphasis on increasing the supply of consumer goods as a stimulant to labor productivity when he declared that "it would be wrong to reduce everything to material incentives; this would impoverish the inner world of Soviet man."

As a result of a combination of factors, including the need to ease inflationary pressures, the debate resulted in a compromise which leaned in favor of the advocates of consumer interests, as evidenced by the setting of slightly higher targeted growth rates for consumer goods output than for heavy industrial production in the 1968 and 1969 annual economic plans. . . .

The place of defense industry proper in the Soviet scheme of priorities became the focal issue of controversy later in 1969, on the eve of the Kremlin's decision to enter preliminary strategic arms limitation talks with the United States. On August 30, *Sovetskaia Rossiia* published an article by Marshal Nikolai I. Krylov, commander of Soviet missile forces, warning against attempts by "imperialist ideologists" "to lull the vigilance of the world's peoples by resorting to propaganda tricks and saying that there will be no victors in a future nuclear war." Krylov's remarks strongly implied that an "imperialist" (i.e., U.S.) attack on the USSR could not be ruled out, and that, instead of being complacent about the supposed balance of armaments, the Soviet Union should proceed with an even greater strategic buildup. The Soviet missile chief's call was echoed soon afterward by Major General A. Lagovsky, a retired professor of military science, writing in *Krasnaia zvezda* (September 25). Attributing "the greatest importance" to the "struggle for military-technical superiority," the author recalled Lenin's statement that an army is "unwise or even criminal" if it "does not train itself to master all arms, all means and methods of warfare that the enemy possesses, or may possess. . . . " He went on to draw special attention to the words "may possess"—seemingly a reference to U.S. development of multiple warhead missiles and new ABM defense systems.

But the tide seemed to be moving decisively against the army leaders' claims for a larger share of national resources. One indication that economic considerations played an important part in the Politburo's decision, announced in late October, to begin the preliminary SALT talks at Helsinki in November, was provided in an internal propaganda booklet circulated about this time. Holding up the earlier nuclear test-ban treaty and the agreement to halt the spread of nuclear weapons as examples of fruitful cooperation between the superpowers, the booklet stressed the "importance of partial agreements and compromises" in solving the problem of disarmament and went on to state:

> Experience has shown that only under conditions of a relaxation of tension is it possible to *concentrate a maximum of resources* on accomplishing the plans for the building of communism. [Italics added]

When the 1970 state budget was officially presented to the Supreme Soviet on December 16, following approval by the Central Committee, its contents did indeed suggest that the military lobby had failed to win majority support in the Politburo. Budgeted defense outlays were to increase by only 1.1 percent (200 million rubles) over 1969, as compared with a 6 percent increase in 1969, and a 15 percent increase in 1968. The targeted growth rate for steel production was also set lower than in the preceding two years, while that for consumer goods output continued to slightly exceed that for heavy industrial production. Significantly enough, *Pravda's* lead article on the budget, published on December 21, failed for the first time since 1964 to stress the importance of strengthening Soviet military power.

Economic Reforms

There have also been indications of recurring differences within the present leadership over the broad issue of reforms in economic management, both in agriculture and in industry. Generally speaking, the manner in which these differences were resolved suggests that the advocates of a conservative, centralist viewpoint prevailed.

The whole question of a restructuring of collective farm management was reopened in April 1969 with the publication of the proposed draft of a new Model Kolkhoz Charter, scheduled for submission to the Third All-Union Kolkhoz Congress the following November. For present purposes, it will suffice here to point to two specific issues on which there were strong evidences of leadership disagreement, with victory eventually going to the conservatives. Both issues involved proposals which had been put forward during Khrushchev's tenure but had not been promoted by his successors.

One was Khrushchev's idea of assigning land and machinery on the collective farms to small teams, or "links," for long periods of time, with remuneration to be based on unit productivity. The system was already being practiced on an experimental basis in parts of the USSR with good results, and the draft Charter posed the question of extending and formalizing it. In the course of the public debate, the proposal received strong support from Gennadi I. Voronov, Premier of the RSFSR and a member of the Politburo, in *Komsomolskaia pravda* (May 11, 1969), as well as from specialists writing in *Pravda* (August 26) and in letters published in *Sovetskaia Rossiia* (November 15–16). On the other hand, a *Pravda* discussion of agricultural issues on September 24 strongly suggested that conservative elements in the leadership opposed the "link" system on the ground that it would lead to the transformation of the kolkhozes into family-type farms.

Brezhnev eventually sided with the conservatives, presenting to the All-Union Kolkhoz Congress in late November a watered-down proposal for a network of collective-farm "councils" which would be staffed by kolkhoz chairmen and other agricultural specialists and would only be empowered to make recommendations to the government. The conservative victory was further underlined by the appointment of the incumbent USSR Minister of Agriculture, V.V. Matskevich, to the chairmanship of the newly established All-Union Collective Farm Council.

A recurrence of top-level disagreement likewise became apparent last year with respect to the future direction of industrial reforms. One clue was the highly unusual failure of the press, on two separate occasions in April and June, to publicize speeches delivered by Premier Kosygin at conferences of industrial workers. These incidents—suggestive of a deliberate press embargo—took on added significance when they were followed by a spate of attacks in the press directed at economic theorists who favored breaking fresh ground in planning reforms. These conservative arguments appeared mainly in organs of the party Secretariat and State Planning Committee.

Writing in *Pravda* (September 26), the deputy director of the USSR Academy of Sciences' Institute of Economics, D. Allakhverdian, rebuked economists who urged greater stress on profit as the key indicator of enterprise performance, as well as those who would switch to the free sale of almost all types of producer goods, or who favored Yugoslav-type regulation by the center through monetary methods rather than by fixing physical output parameters. He saw in all this a particular threat to the "observance of assigned ratios"—i.e., to continued preferential treatment of defense-related output. Behind Allakhverdian's criticism seemed to be the fear that increased professionalism in planning would tend to deprive the party apparatus of its role in implementing economic decisions.

In a similar vein, an article published in the November issue of the Gosplan organ *Planovoe khoziaistvo* censured Academician N.P. Fedorenko for espousing the formulation of plans in terms of prices calculated mathematically on the basis of relative scarcities—a proposal which, the author claimed, undermined state authority and introduced "drift" into plan fulfillment. Interestingly enough, the Soviet leaders only four and a half years before had honored four mathematical economists by awarding them Lenin Prizes.

A division of opinion over economic policy appears to have emerged anew at the December 1969 plenum of the Central Committee. Not only was General Secretary Brezhnev's speech at the December 15 session not made public (nor has it been since), but the communique issued at the close of the plenum conspicuously omitted the usual claim of unanimity in announcing the plenum's approval of Politburo policies. . . .

Party vs. State

Conflicts between party and state bureaucrats are endemic to the Soviet system of rule, and such conflicts are no less apparent under the present leadership than in the past. Broadly speaking, the interest of the party organizers lies in preserving their control of economic decision-making and bureaucratic appointments regardless of considerations of efficiency, while on the other hand the state technical experts seek the right to run the economy with minimal interference by party functionaries and to select personnel without regard to dogmatic political criteria. . . . These constant struggles for power have a significant bearing on policy in that the state officials' immersion in practical affairs disposes them toward a less doctrinaire approach to problems than that of the party apparatchiks. . . .

At the highest level, the party-state rivalry for power has manifested itself in an apparent attempt by Brezhnev and his supporters to increase the relative weight of the party secretariat in the central decision-making hierarchy. . . . With his secret speech to the Central Committee plenum last December, Brezhnev appears to have launched a new drive for rigorous control of the economy by party functionaries. This was evidenced by a key change in the Theses for the Lenin Centenary, published on December 23, 1969. The Theses affirmed that the party "accomplishes its tasks *both directly* and through the soviets, state bodies and public organizations" (italics added), thus nullifying the tactful formula of the 1967 Theses for the 50th anniversary of the 1917 Revolution, which had stated that the party fulfills its leading role in society "through the system of state and public organizations." In line with this change, a decree issued by the party center in January 1970 required party committees of the government's economic ministries to keep party headquarters informed of shortcomings in the work of the ministries. This, in effect, made the top state bureaucracy directly responsible to Brezhnev as well as to Kosygin and tended to violate the spirit of the collective leadership understanding reached upon the overthrow of Khrushchev.

*[**Editor's note:** Why should internecine struggles for power within the USSR interest and concern the Western student? The matter has, I believe, been well put by Robert Conquest in the final paragraph of his book* Power and Policy in the USSR. *He suggests that such study "gives us priceless insights into not only the nature of the Soviet political world but also the special characteristics of the members of the Soviet ruling group." Moreover, their "basic habits of thought and modes of action are likely to manifest themselves in international affairs as well."*

Harrison E. Salisbury, for one, explained what he regarded as a "fatal flaw in the Soviet system," namely, that Russia had developed no constitutional means resting on popular participation and consent for transmitting governmental power. He queried whether "a modern technological state" can afford "the fantastic price of a murderous struggle for power each time a transition in leadership is required." Howard R. Swearer, writing in 1965, in a more tentative view, asserted that "although a step in the direction of regularization of political succession may have been taken in October 1964 [on the occasion of Khrushchev's ouster], a closer look casts doubt that this serious problem, which has plagued the Soviet system from its inception, has really been overcome." However, he went on to argue that whether or not oligarchic rule continues for some time, the leadership and the party will have to reckon with the altered social environment and new demands.

More recently some scholars have maintained—most notably T.H. Rigby writing in Soviet Studies*—that while Khrushchev's successors "have acquiesced in the emergence of a 'pecking order' in the oligarchy, with Brezhnev as No. 1 to make it easier to achieve coherence and expedition in current policy-making and administration," at the same time "they have hedged the power and authority of individual leaders around with a number of quite formidable controls, with the object of preventing history from repeating itself, of obstructing a new drift to one-man rule." Specifically, he believed that an implicit compact entered into at the time of Khrushchev's ouster envisaged:*

1. *Keeping the two top posts in different hands.*
2. *Reducing opportunities for patronage.*
3. *Distributing among leaders seats in the Party Presidium (Politburo from April 1966), Presidium of the Council of Ministers, and Central Committee Secretariat in such a way as to avoid dangerous patterns of overlap.*
4. *Maintaining countervailing power between topmost leaders.*

Myron Rush, on the other hand, writing some time later, asserted that "the oligarchy that replaced Khrushchev has been slowly perverted and may be about to suffer the fate of its predecessors. . . . Although formidable obstacles remain, Leonid Brezhnev, General Secretary of the Central Committee, seems close to achieving personal rule."

Parenthetically, it is worthy of mention that recent ousters in the Soviet Union, while they may not have solved the problems of orderliness and legitimization of succession without the aspects of a coup, *have in the opinion of some scholars demonstrated the hegemony of the party and clearly made the secretarial machine of the party the central avenue of political succession in the Soviet Union.]*

PART FIVE

THE SOVIET CONSTITUTIONAL AND POLITICAL SYSTEMS

. . . [V] irtually every state sees its citizens either as slaves—or as enemies.

Joseph Brodsky

The truth is that all men having power ought to be distrusted.

James Madison

Nothing is gained, in any discussion of communism, by treating it as a wicked doctrine which would never have arisen if a handful of criminal adventurers had not devoted themselves to its propagation.

Harold J. Laski

Let us not, having criticized the Russian Communists all these years for being too totalitarian, pour scorn and ridicule upon them the moment they show signs of becoming anything else.

George F. Kennan

We are ruled not by a Communist or a fascist party, and not by a Stalinist party, but by a status quo party.

Lev Kopelev

Chapter 8

SOVIET CONSTITUTIONALISM

The first Soviet Constitution, which went into effect on July 19, 1918 on the eve of civil war and intervention, was limited in its application to the Russian Socialist Federated Soviet Republic (RSFSR). It affirmed that:

> The principal object of the Constitution of the RSFSR . . . consists in the establishment of the dictatorship of the urban and rural proletariat and the poorest peasantry, in the form of the strong All-Russian Soviet power, with the aim of securing the complete suppression of the bourgeoisie, the abolition of the exploitation of man by man, and the establishment of socialism, under which there shall be neither class divisions nor State authority.

Although it provided disproportionate representation for the proletariat, it made no mention of the Communist Party, which did not then enjoy a legal monopoly of power.

The first All-Union Constitution, which was approved by the Second All-Union Congress of Soviets on January 31, 1924, was closely patterned after the 1918 Constitution. The USSR was declared "a trustworthy bulwark against world capitalism, and a new decisive step along the path of the union of the workers of all countries in a World Socialist Soviet Republic." The Constitution stated that each Republic "retains the right of free withdrawal from the Union."

The 1924 Constitution was replaced by the "Stalin" Constitution, in effect on December 5, 1936, which eliminated all disproportionate representation and, on the other hand, accorded to the Communist Party a special position. Its basic principles are explained and acclaimed in the excerpt herein of a speech made by Stalin in 1936.

The Constitution of 1977, which appears in the Appendix, according to Brezhnev's Report before the Central Committee of the Communist Party of the Soviet Union (CPSU) on May 24, 1977, "on the one hand, sums up all the main features of the previous Soviet Constitution and, on the other, enriches these features with a new content corresponding to the requirements of the contemporary epoch." Analyses of its basic provisions from the divergent points of view of John J. Abt and Robert Sharlet appear in the pages that follow.

On the Soviet Constitution of 1936

Joseph V. Stalin

The main foundation of the draft of the new Constitution of the USSR is formed on the principles of socialism and its chief mainstays, already won and put into practice, namely, the socialist ownership of land, forests, factories, shops and other implements and means of production; abolition of exploitation and exploiting classes; abolition of poverty for the majority and luxury for the minority; abolition of unemployment; work as an obligation and duty and the honor of every able-bodied citizen according to the formula: "He who does not work, neither shall he eat," i.e., the right of every citizen to receive guaranteed work; the right to rest and leisure; the right to education, etc. . . .

The draft of the new Constitution of the USSR proceeds from the fact that antagonistic classes no longer exist in our society, that our society consists of two friendly classes: the workers and peasants, that precisely these toiling classes are in power, that the state guidance of society (dictatorship) belongs to the working class as the advanced class of society, that the Constitution is needed to consolidate the social order desired by and of advantage to the toilers. . . .

The draft of the new Constitution of the USSR is profoundly international. It proceeds from the premise that all nations and races have equal rights. It proceeds from the premise that color or language differences, differences in cultural level or the level of state development as well as any other difference among nations and races, cannot serve as grounds for justifying national inequality of rights. . . .

Finally, there is one other specific feature in the draft of the new Constitution. Bourgeois constitutions usually limit themselves to recording the formal rights of citizens without concerning themselves about the conditions for exercising these rights, about the possibility of exercising them, the means of exercising them. They speak about equality of citizens but forget that real equality between master and workman, between landlord and peasants, is impossible if the former enjoy wealth and political weight in society, while the latter are deprived of both; if the former are exploiters and the latter are exploited.

Or again: they speak of free speech, freedom of assemblage and of the press, but forget that all these liberties may become empty sound for the working class if the latter is deprived of the possibility of having at its command suitable premises for meetings, good printshops, sufficient quantity of paper, etc.

A specific feature of the draft of the new Constitution is that it does not limit itself to recording formal rights of citizens, but transfers the center of gravity to questions of the guarantee of these rights, to the question of the means of exercising them. It does not merely proclaim the equality of the rights of citizens but ensures them by legislative enactment of the fact of liquidation of the regime of exploitation, by the fact of liberation of citizens from any exploitation.

From a speech delivered to the Extraordinary Eighth Congress of Soviets on November 25, 1936.

It not only proclaims the right to work, but ensures it by legislative enactment of the fact of nonexistence of crises in Soviet society, and the fact of abolition of unemployment. It not merely proclaims democratic liberties but guarantees them in legislative enactments by providing definite material facilities. It is clear, therefore, that the democracy of the new Constitution is not the "usual" and "generally recognized" democracy in general, but socialist democracy. . . .

There is a group of critics which charges that the draft makes no change in the existing position of the USSR; that it leaves the dictatorship of the working class intact, does not provide for freedom of political parties, and preserves the present leading position of the Communist Party of the USSR. And, at the same time, this group of critics believes that the absence of freedom for parties in the USSR is an indication of the violation of the fundamental principles of democracy.

I must admit the draft of the new Constitution really does leave in force the regime of the dictatorship of the working class, and also leaves unchanged the present leading position of the Communist Party of the USSR. (*Loud applause.*)

If our venerable critics regard this as a shortcoming of the draft Constitution, this can only be regretted. We Bolsheviks, however, consider this as a merit of the draft Constitution. (*Loud applause.*) As for freedom for various political parties, we here adhere to somewhat different views.

The party is part of the class, its vanguard section. Several parties and consequently freedom of parties can only exist in a society where antagonistic classes exist whose interests are hostile and irreconcilable, where there are capitalists and workers, landlords and peasants, kulaks and poor peasants.

But in the USSR there are no longer such classes as capitalists, landlords, kulaks, etc. In the USSR there are only two classes, workers and peasants, whose interests not only are not antagonistic but, on the contrary, amicable. Consequently there are no grounds for the existence of several parties, and therefore for the existence of freedom of such parties in the USSR. There are grounds for only one party, the Communist Party, in the USSR. Only one party can exist, the Communist Party, which boldly defends the interests of the workers and peasants to the very end. And there can hardly be any doubt about the fact that it defends the interests of these classes. (*Loud applause.*)

They talk about democracy. But what is democracy? Democracy in capitalist countries where there are antagonistic classes is, in the last analysis, democracy for the strong, democracy for the propertied minority. Democracy in the USSR, on the contrary, is democracy for all. But from this it follows that the principles of democracy are violated not by the draft of the new Constitution of the USSR but by the bourgeois constitutions.

That is why I think that the Constitution of the USSR is the only thoroughly democratic constitution in the world.

The Soviet Constitution of 1977

John J. Abt

In the forty years since the 1936 Constitution proclaimed the victory of socialism, the Soviet Union has developed into a mature socialist society. Recovering from the incalculable losses of World War II, it has increased the overall volume of industrial production twenty-nine times until it stands at 85 percent of the U.S. level and has surpassed the latter in steel, coal, oil and other key indicators. In the same period, socialized agriculture has increased output 3.2 times. Per capita real income doubles every fifteen years and is more than five times higher than in 1936. Accompanying the betterment of the material conditions of the people has been a change in their social relations. Soviet society has become increasingly homogeneous as the differences in educational level and mode of life between town and country and between manual and intellectual workers have narrowed. Similarly, the equality of the nations comprising the Soviet Union, which the 1936 Constitution guaranteed as a matter of law, has now become equality in fact as affirmative action by the central government has raised the economic and cultural level of the formerly underdeveloped republics of Central Asia and elsewhere to a parity with what had been industrially advanced areas of the country.

As a result of these profound changes, the Soviet state is no longer characterized as a dictatorship of the proletariat but has developed into a form described as a state of the whole people.

The change in the international position of the Soviet Union has been no less far-reaching. No longer isolated by capitalist encirclement, it has become a member of a powerful socialist community. . . .

The draft of the new Constitution builds on the foundation laid by its predecessors, taking into account the tremendous advances of the last forty years in the life of the country and in the international arena. Like them, it is at once a programmatic document which sets forth the principles and goals applicable to the present stage of Soviet society and a codification of the nation's major social advances and political structure.

The draft's preamble characterizes the Soviet Union as a "developed socialist society" having "mature social relations" in which the state, after fulfilling the tasks of the dictatorship of the proletariat, "has become a state of the whole people" where "the law of life is the concern of all for the welfare of each and the concern of each for the welfare of all." Unlike any of its forerunners, the preamble then sets its sights on the transition to communism, the highest stage of socialist society. It states:

> The supreme purpose of the Soviet state is to build a classless communist society. The principle tasks of the state are: to build the material and technical basis of communism, to perfect socialist social relations, to mould the citizen of communist society, to raise the living standard and cultural level of the working people, to ensure the country's security, to help strengthen peace and to promote international cooperation.

John J. Abt is a prominent constitutional lawyer and counsel for the Communist Party, U.S.A. This excerpt from his "The New Soviet Constitution," which originally appeared in Marylyn Bechtel, David Laibman, and Jessica Smith, eds., Six Decades That Changed the World *©NWR Publications, Inc., 1978, is reproduced with the permission of the publisher and author.*

In his report on the draft to the Central Committee of the Communist Party, General Secretary Brezhnev who chaired the commission that prepared it, capsulized its new features by stating that, "the main trend of the new elements contained in the draft is towards broadening and deepening socialist democracy." This trend manifests itself on two levels: in the expansion of the basic guarantees of economic and cultural rights of the people embodied in the 1936 Constitution, and in the increasing involvement of the people in the economic management and political administration of the country.

The 1936 Constitution's guarantee of the right to work has been expanded to include the right of people to choose their profession, trade or occupation "in accord with their vocation, abilities, training, education, and with account of the needs of society." Closely associated with this right is the draft's guarantee of the right to free education at all levels, including free textbooks and the provision of scholarships, grants and other benefits to students. Universal ten-year education is made compulsory (up from eight years in the 1936 Constitution), and the "extensive development of vocational, secondary specialized and higher education" is ensured.

The article on the right to rest and leisure provides for a general forty-one-hour work week with shorter hours for onerous occupations, including mining, chemical and textiles; and reduced hours of night work, annual paid vacations, weekly days of rest, and "extension of the network of cultural, educational and health-building institutions, and development of sports, physical education and tourism on a mass scale."

The former right to free medical service has been materially extended to guarantee the "right to health protection" which includes "broad preventive measures and measures of environmental improvement; special care for the health of the rising generation," and "development and improvement of safety techniques and sanitation in production."

The right to maintenance in old age, sickness or disability without cost to the worker has been extended to include collective farmers and to cover partial disability and "disability or loss of breadwinner." Currently, legislation provides for pensions ranging from 50 to 75 percent of earnings at age 60 for men and 55 for women, reduced to 50 and 45 for certain hazardous occupations. Sick benefits are at the rate of 60 percent of wages for up to five years of service, 80 percent from five to eight, and 100 percent after eight.

The draft adds a new and important right—the right to housing at low rent. This guarantee has been made possible by the massive construction program which rehoused the 25 million people left homeless by World War II and went on from there until a solution of the housing problem is now in sight. In the period from 1971 to 1975, some 56 million people had their housing improved, and homebuilding is currently at the rate of 6,000 apartments a day, five times the growth rate of the population. Today, 90 percent of the people enjoy a separate apartment for each family at rents, stabilized at the 1928 level, of not more than 4 percent of average family income, utilities included. Next goal is an apartment with a room for each member of the family and beyond that, with an additional room for the family as a whole.

The draft guarantees equal rights for women, including equal opportunities for education, employment, remuneration and promotion. Unlike the proposed Equal Rights Amendment to the U.S. Constitution which lacks any safeguards, the draft ensures "special measures for the protection, material and moral support of mother and child, including paid leaves and other benefits to mothers and expectant mothers, and state aid to unmarried mothers." An additional article, not in the 1936 Constitution, provides for family aid by means of "an extensive network of child care institutions," extending and improving community services and public catering, and by allowances to families with many children.

As in the 1936 Constitution, all Soviet citizens are guaranteed equal rights, irrespective of nationality or race. And restriction of these rights and "any advocacy of racial or national exclusiveness, hostility or contempt'' is punishable. Incitement of hostility or hatred on religious grounds is likewise prohibited.

No capitalist state has ever provided its whole people with these, the most fundamental of all human rights, let alone guaranteed them in its constitution. Capitalism, by its very nature, is incapable of doing so. It is an achievement which only socialist society can make possible. In such a society, these rights carry with them correlative duties on the part of the citizen which are enumerated in the draft. Among them are observance of Soviet law and the rules of socialist behavior, conscientious labor in one's ''chosen socially useful occupation,'' the safeguarding of socialist property, respect for the national dignity and the rights of others, the protection of nature, the development of friendship with the peoples of other countries, defense of the motherland and service in its armed forces.

The draft contains guarantees of the freedoms of speech, press and assembly and the right of privacy when these are exercised ''in conformity with the interests of the working people and for the purpose of strengthening socialism.'' The quoted qualification is the Soviet equivalent of the ''clear and present danger'' limitation on the exercise of First Amendment rights in the United States, under which the advocacy of ideas may be restrained or punished if found to threaten the national security or the public peace. The difference is that the limitation is explicitly stated in the Soviet Constitution while, in this country, it has been supplied by a Supreme Court ''interpretation'' of the unconditional wording of the Amendment.

One may disagree with the extent of Soviet restraints on freedom of expression as excessive and lacking justification in any actual or threatened injury to the fabric of socialist society. But criticism must be tempered by the knowledge that from the moment of its birth, the Soviet Union has been the target of a conspiracy by the capitalist powers to overthrow, dismember or strangle it by every available means, including war, quarantine, ''containment,'' ''massive retaliation,'' ''positions of strength,'' subversion, and discriminatory trade practices, and that these policies have by no means been abandoned today.

''Our goal,'' Lenin wrote in 1918, ''is the unpaid fulfillment of government duties by every worker. . . . Only in this change is the guarantee of the final transition to socialism.'' The draft constitution confirms and codifies the measures taken for the attainment of this goal.

The composition of the Supreme Soviet of the USSR is modified to provide that the Soviet of Nationalities shall be elected by the voters of the constituent republics on the basis of thirty-two for each of the fifteen Union Republics, eleven for each of the twenty Autonomous Republics, five for each of the eight Autonomous Regions and one for each Autonomous Area established by the Supreme Soviet of the Union Republic of which it is a part. The Soviet of the Union will have the same number of deputies as the Soviet of Nationalities, elected by districts containing equal populations. The two chambers have equal rights, and all legislation requires the concurring votes of both.

The draft reduces the age of eligibility to office at all levels, including the highest, from 23 to 18 (the present voting age). It lengthens the terms of deputies to the Supreme Soviets of the USSR and constituent republics from four to five years and to other Soviets from two to two and one-half years. It provides that all deputies shall continue to work at their trades or professions but shall be released for the performance of their public duties and paid their average earnings for the time spent in doing so.

The right to nominate candidates for election as deputies may be exercised by public organizations such as the Communist Party, the trade unions, cooperatives and cultural organizations, as well as by collective farms and other collectives. Nominations are made at public meetings of the voters to whom the draft guarantees ''free and all-sided discussion of the political, professional and personal qualities of the candidates'' before nominations are made. Deputies are subject to recall by their electors who have exercised that right in some 4,000 cases over the past ten years.

A total of 2,200,000 deputies serve in Soviets from the city district or village level to the Supreme Soviet of the USSR. They represent more than 100 different nationalities. Workers or collective farmers make up 68 percent, nearly one-half are women, and one-third are young people. Two-thirds are not members of the Communist Party.

Their duties are not confined to the sittings of the Soviets for the enactment of legislation. For unlike our Congress, state legislatures and city councils, they exercise executive as well as legislative power. In the words of the draft, they ''resolve matters related to state, economic, social and cultural development, organize the execution of [their] decisions, and exercise control over the work of state organs, enterprises, institutions and organizations.'' In performing these functions, they serve on a wide variety of departments, boards and commissions covering every aspect of political and economic affairs within the jurisdiction of the particular Soviet. They are assisted in this work by 30 million volunteer ''activists'' so that one out of every eight Soviet citizens participates in administering the affairs of government.

Additionally, the draft provides for the formation of ''organs of people's control.'' It is their function to ''exercise control over the fulfillment of state plans and assignments, combat violations of state discipline, manifestations of parochialism, narrow departmental attitudes, mismanagement, wastefulness, red tape and bureaucracy, and help to improve the work of the state apparatus.'' Nine million people are already serving on these bodies.

Popular participation in government affairs is further ensured by four other provisions of the draft. First, every citizen is given the right to submit proposals to governmental bodies for improving their work and to criticize their shortcomings. Officials are obliged to examine these proposals and criticisms, reply to them ''and take due action.'' Second, the draft requires that the ''most important matters of state'' shall be submitted to a referendum vote of the people. Third, the draft provides that the right to initiate legislation shall be enjoyed not only by the Soviets and their deputies but by ''mass public organizations [such as the trade unions] represented by their all-Union organs.'' Finally, it is made the duty of all deputies to report to their constituents on their own work and that of the Soviets of which they are members. In 1976, report-back meetings of the local Soviets were attended by 130 million voters, the great majority of the voting population.

The draft includes a chapter on peace. It provides that ''war propaganda shall be prohibited by law,'' and states:

> The foreign policy of the USSR shall be aimed at ensuring favorable international conditions for the building of communism in the USSR, at strengthening the positions of world socialism, supporting the struggles of people for national liberation and social progress, preventing wars of aggression and consistently implementing the principle of peaceful coexistence of states with different social systems. . . .

This brief comparative survey of the four Soviet constitutions affords a perspective on the arduous but triumphant road which the Soviet people have travelled in the space of sixty short years, one-third of them disrupted by war and postwar recovery. The achievements of those years establish the immense superiority of a planned socialist society over capitalist exploitation and anarchy. . . .

The new constitution was adopted at a session of the Supreme Soviet of the USSR on October 7, 1977. Adoption followed four months of unprecedented nationwide discussion that involved over 140 million people, 1.5 million meetings and what President Brezhnev, in his report to the session, described as "an unending flow of letters from Soviet people." The discussion resulted in the submission to the Constitution Commission of some 400,000 proposals for amendments to the draft. After examining them all, the Commission recommended amendments to 110 of the 173 articles of the draft and the inclusion of one additional article.

Many of the amendments are of an editorial character. Others refine and clarify the draft. The preamble, for example, is amended by adding a definition of the "classless communist society," of which it speaks as one "in which there will be public, communist self-government."

Another amendment clarifies the role of the Communist Party. The draft describes it as, "the leading and guiding force of Soviet society" which "directs the great constructive work of the Soviet people, and imparts a planned, systematic and theoretically substantiated character to their struggle for the victory of communism." The amendment adds the proviso that, "All party organizations shall function within the framework of the Constitution of the USSR," making it explicit that the Communist Party, like all other organs or state bodies, is subject to and governed by the mandates of the Constitution.

Another series of amendments add further particulars to the rights guaranteed the people. Thus the special measures for the protection of women enumerated in the draft are enlarged to include "conditions enabling mothers to work," and "gradual reduction of working time for mothers with small children." The right of people to choose their trade or profession is based not only on "their abilities, training and education," as stated in the draft, but on their "inclinations" as well. And the list of measures that insures this right has been expanded to include "systems of vocational guidance and job placement." Again, an amendment adds "low charges for utility services" to the guarantee of housing at low rent.

Amendments likewise add specifics to the articles defining the duties of citizens. "Evasion of socially useful work" is declared to be "incompatible with the principles of socialist society." It is the duty of citizens "to make thrifty use of the people's wealth," "rational use of the land," "increase its fertility," and "take good care of the housing allocated to them." An amendment balances the obligation of citizens "to concern themselves with the upbringing of children" contained in the draft with the corresponding obligation of children "to care for their parents and help them."

Other amendments relate to people's deputies and judges. The age of eligibility for election to the Supreme Soviet of the USSR is raised to 21 years while remaining at 18 for all other offices. A new article provides that voters shall give mandates to their deputies which the latter are required to take into account, implement and report on to their constituents. The provision of the draft for referenda has been revised to provide that laws may be enacted "by a nationwide vote (referendum) held by decision of the Supreme Soviet" which may likewise submit an unresolved disagreement between its two chambers to a referendum of the people. Another amendment provides for the recall of judges by the voters or bodies that elected them.

As President Brezhnev's report emphasized:

> Millions upon millions of working people in town and country have supported the new Constitution by word and by deed. They compared every line of the Draft with their own practical work and with the work of their labor collectives. They made increased socialist pledges, amended production plans, discovered new reserves for enhancing production efficiency and improving work performance and met their new Constitution with great labor exploits. In short, our people have again shown themselves to be full masters of the socialist homeland.

The New Soviet Constitution

Robert Sharlet

In the wake of major leadership changes, the long-awaited draft of a new Soviet Constitution—now nearly twenty years in the making—finally has appeared. With little advance warning, impending publication of the document was announced at a Central Committee plenary session in late May. But the significance of this event was at once overshadowed by the simultaneously announced ouster of Nikolay Podgorny from the CPSU Politburo. Podgorny's dramatic exit from the party leadership and his "request" for retirement from chairmanship of the Presidium of the USSR Supreme Soviet paved the way for General Secretary Leonid Brezhnev to be elected to the Soviet "presidency" at the regular Supreme Soviet session in mid-June.

Thus, in the space of a few weeks, Brezhnev reached the summit of his political career. Having successfully engineered the fall of a reputedly major Politburo rival, he became the first CPSU leader to serve as not only de facto but also de jure head of state. . . .

The process of drafting a new Constitution was not a smooth one. The published Draft surfaced after nearly two decades of discussion and uncertainty—not just about its contents but about whether it would even appear at all. Entangled in the politics of destalinization the passage of the new Soviet Constitution through the more open, factionalized, and conflict-ridden policy-making process of the post-Stalin era proved a complex undertaking, requiring numerous changes and compromises to accommodate the diverse interests involved in such a broad, overarching document. . . .

Continuity and Change

In keeping with Brezhnev's political style, the Draft Constitution is a moderate, middle-of-the-road document, neither anti-Stalinist nor neo-Stalinist in its thrust, but rather a generally pragmatic statement of already existing practice and principle. Despite its association with the General Secretary's recent political triumphs, however, this Draft should not be regarded simply as a "Brezhnev Constitution." In the first place, as stressed in its Preamble, the 1977 Constitution displays much "continuity of ideas and principles" with the three previous constitutions. For example, most of the articles dealing with property and the economy (Chapter 2 of the Draft) and with the ordinary citizen's economic rights and duties (Chapter 7) date from the 1936 Constitution, in which they helped institutionalize and consolidate Stalin's "revolution from above." Moreover, Brezhnev himself made constitutional "continuity" a keynote in his plenum Report.

Second, and of much greater importance, the 1977 Constitution codifies major social and political changes which extend beyond the scope of Brezhnev's leadership alone. In

At this writing, Robert Sharlet is a professor of political science at Union College and an Associate of the Research Institute on International Change at Columbia University. This selection is excerpted from pages 1–24 of his article by the same title that appeared in Problems of Communism, *vol. XXVI (Sept.-Oct. 1977). For footnote references, please consult original source. Note that there is some variation in numbering of chapters between those set forth in the 1977 Constitution as finally adopted (see Appendix) and in the numbering of the draft of the Constitution with which Professor Sharlet dealt.*

the most general sense, this is demonstrated by the fact that Soviet authorities describe the Draft as the constitution of an advanced industrial society, one which, in Soviet parlance, has reached the stage of "developed socialism" (*razvitoy sotsializm*). In contrast, earlier constitutions were designed to serve a Soviet society at very different stages of revolutionary development or post-revolutionary consolidation.

More specifically, the new Constitution takes full account of the great volume of post-Stalin legislation that has affected nearly every branch and area of Soviet law. In fact, there are few points in the Draft which have not been raised or institutionalized already in code law, statutory legislation, or the scholarly juridical commentary explicating the extensive post-Stalin legal reforms. For example, the environmental protection clauses (Arts. 18 and 67), the foreign policy section (Arts. 28–30), and the constitutional prescription (and pun) of a forty-one-hour work week in Article 41 are all novel in comparison with the 1936 Constitution. But they break no new ground in terms of post-Stalin policy, practice, and legal development.

In broader terms, the Draft Constitution serves as a useful register of both the accomplishments and the limits of destalinization. In retrospect, it is clear that Khrushchev himself set out the boundaries of destalinization in his famous "secret speech" to the 20th Party Congress in 1956. Although he indicted Stalin for the "cult of personality" and its egregious consequences for the party and "socialist legality," Khrushchev also explicitly praised his predecessor for the latter's "great services to the party" in forging the socioeconomic foundations of the Soviet system, laid out in the course of the first Five-Year Plan.

One major aspect of destalinization affirmed in the proposed Draft is the constitutionally enhanced status of the individual in relation to the state, especially in criminal proceedings (Articles 150 and 159) but in civil matters as well (Article 58), (although, as we shall see, this is not the case with respect to the Soviet Union's political, religious, ethnic, and cultural dissidents). No less important is the formally institutionalized "leading role of the party" (Art. 6), a change in constitutional form that culminates the party's renaissance following the end of Stalin's personal dictatorship. At the same time, the moderate tone and obvious compromises in the Draft illustrate the consequences of post-Stalin leadership change, political factionalism, and interest group conflict.

The limits to change, however, are no less significant. Most important, the party has constructed in the Draft Constitution a political instrument for routinizing the governance process, but it has done so in such a manner as to leave sufficient ambiguity for a jurisprudence of political expediency to circumvent the system of "legality" (*zakonnost'*) when necessary. In fact, the party has merely "constitutionalized" the traditional dualism of law and extra-legal coercion. In this fundamental sense, the 1977 Constitution represents codification of the post-Stalin system as a party-led constitutional bureaucracy. . . .

A Soviet "Systems" Approach

As expressed by Soviet political and legal commentators, a major purpose of the new Soviet Constitution is to reflect the infrastructure of the Soviet system now, after sixty years of development. In particular, this means recording in constitutional language the most important and enduring political, legal, socioeconomic, and doctrinal changes since promulgation of the 1936 Constitution, and especially following Stalin's death. In this connection, the more dynamic, "systems" approach to sociopolitical structure that is contained in Part I of the Draft (Arts 1–32) stands in decided contrast to the static, state-society formula of its predecessor. . . .

One particularly notable feature of the post-Stalin "political system" is doctrinal evolution from the "dictatorship of the proletariat" to "the state of the whole people." Although Soviet jurists have failed to conceptualize this notion clearly since it first emerged under Khrushchev, the "state of the whole people," to a large extent, remains today—as earlier—a political metaphor signaling the leadership's interest in greater participation in the implementation of the party's policies by both mass organizations (Art. 7) and the public in general (Art. 5). These participatory declamations are in turn operationalized in Articles 111 and 112, which provide, respectively, for legislative initiative by mass organizations and for general discussion of draft legislation by the public as a whole. With regard to both, however, the new Constitution merely confirms existing practice.

Chapter 1 also includes a clause on the legal subsystem, a reference which points to another of the major changes in the post-Stalin period. The 1936 Constitution included a statement of the citizens' duty to obey the law, but the present document requires both the citizen (Arts. 59 and 65) and the state (Arts. 4 and 57) to observe the requirements of "socialist legality." Of course, the state's obligation to observe the law gives first priority to its function of protecting "law and order," a key slogan of the Brezhnev period.

Finally, Article 6 in Chapter 1 makes explicit a party-dominant political system. The Communist Party, which was mentioned twice in the 1936 Constitution and only in connection with the rights of mass organizations, has been institutionalized in the new Constitution as "the leading and directing force of Societ society, the nucleus of its political system"—finally in accord with its actual role during the past decades of Soviet history. Since the Preamble declares that the Soviet system will strive to build communism in the future, the party's role is described in the more functional terms of serving as the guiding source for the domestic and foreign policy of the USSR.

The chapter on the economy describes the same infrastructure of public and personal economy set forth in the 1936 Constitution but also consolidates those structural changes associated with post-Stalin economic development. Thus, Article 9 of the 1936 Constitution permitted the "small-scale private economy" of individual peasants and handicraftsmen; the corresponding Article 17 of the 1977 Draft Constitution allows "individual labor activity" (*individualnaya trudovaya deyatel' nost'*) in the delivery of "consumer services for the population." Trade union property has been added as a type of "socialist property" (Art. 9). This, of course, had been its de facto status for many years, a situation recognized formally in the 1961 Fundamental Principles of Civil Legislation. The planning clause (Art. 15) incorporates some of the features of "Libermanism" and the 1965 economic reforms with its reference to the "economic independence and initiative of enterprises, associations, and other organizations" and its explicit bow to the importance of profits, costs, and *khozraschët* (economic accountability). Article 28 declares the state's commitment to the protection and rational utilization of the environment, an injunction of both reflective and programmatic dimensions.

More purely programmatic is the consumption and labor productivity clause (Art. 14), which earmarks social production (*obshchestvennoye proizvodstvo*) for the satisfaction of people's wants and needs and charges the state with the task of raising labor productivity in order to fulfill this commitment. The prominence accorded consumer needs in Articles 13 and 14 of the Draft constitutes a marked departure from the corresponding passage in the "Stalin Constitution," which placed relatively greater stress on economic growth. Both the socialist emulation or competition technique, "inspired" by Stakhanov in the 1930s, and the more recently launched "scientific-technological revolution" are invoked in quest of higher labor productivity. In view of the questionable effectiveness of the former technique and widespread doubts regarding Soviet capacity to stimulate and manage innovation, Article 14 is likely to remain more programmatic than "reflective" for some time.

Finally, the 1936 exhortation to work has been softened somewhat in the new Constitution (Art. 13) but nonetheless ends on a phrase which maintains the spirit of the antiparasite legislation: "*socially useful* labor and its results shall determine a citizen's status in society" (italics added). This impression is strengthened by the more exhortative "rights and duties" section (Art. 60), in which "conscientious labor in one's chosen field of socially useful activity" is described as both a duty and a "matter of honor."

The chapter on the social subsystem consists largely of a set of programmatic directional signs on the road to communism, as Brezhnev acknowledged in his plenum report. Included are commitments to the enhancement of social homogeneity (Art. 19), the eventual abolition of manual labor through mechanization (Art. 21), and the development of consumer services (Art. 24)—all in connection with the long-standing commitment to encourage development of the "new man" (Art. 20). These social articles in the 1977 Constitution give rise to a sense of *déjà vu*—the rhetoric is reminiscent of Khrushchev's 1961 Party Program, minus the detail and accompanying timetable for the realization of specified goals. . . .

The Citizen and the State

The second main purpose of the new Constitution is to define the relationship between the state and the individual. This relationship can be divided, for analytic purposes, into the citizen's economic, civil, and participation rights and duties.

Economic rights. The economic rights need only brief review, since they are the same rights as those of the 1936 Constitution, albeit with a few additions and amplifications. A constitutional guarantee of housing (Art. 44) and the right to use the achievements of culture (Art. 46) have been added, while the 1936 Article on economic security has been expanded and divided in the Draft into two articles on health protection (Art. 42) and old-age maintenance (Art. 43). The right to work also has been enlarged to include the freedom to choose one's profession, occupation, or employment, provided the choice is consistent with society's needs (Art. 40), a constitutional "right" made possible by the higher level of economic development and general affluence of Soviet society today as compared with life in the mid-1930s. Indeed, while many of the economic rights were programmatic when first included in the "Stalin Constitution," they are now, for the most part, simply reflective of a highly developed welfare state.

At the same, time, the economic rights of the Soviet citizen are balanced by a basic economic "duty," also carried over from the 1936 Constitution. In this connection, the citizen's obligation to protect socialist property has been reaffirmed, although in destalinized form—that is, public property is no longer described as "sacred and inviolable," and persons who commit property crimes are no longer castigated as "enemies of the people." The property protection clause is already amply supported in the criminal codes of the various union republics. Yet, in view of the extent of economic crime and the scale of the "second economy" or "parallel market," it would seem fair to predict that countless Soviet citizens, from factory workers to enterprise directors, will continue to disregard this constitutional injunction.

Civil liberties. The civil rights clauses of the new Constitution, which should be judged together with the sections on justice (Chapter 20) and the Procuracy (Chapter 21), reveal much more about the citizen's status vis-à-vis the state and provide further evidence for assessing the current scope and limits of destalinization. Most important, the basic civil rights continue to be limited by the standard caveat that the rights of speech, press, association, assembly, public meetings, and demonstration are guaranteed to the citizen only "in conformity with the working people's interests and for the purpose of strengthening the socialist system" (Arts. 50–51). The same preference for the social over the individual interest also limits the new civil right of "freedom of scientific, technical, and artistic creation" (Art. 47). In fact, the new Constitution has two additional paragraphs that further emphasize the social limits on the citizen's rights to exercise his economic rights and his civil liberties. In the article introducing Chapter 7, on the "Basic Rights, Liberties, and Duties of USSR Citizens," Soviet citizens first are granted the "whole range of social, economic, political and personal rights and liberties" which follow—but under the condition of the closing injunction which points out that the "exercise of rights and liberties by citizens must not injure the interests of society and the state or the rights of other citizens" (Art. 39). The predominance of the prevailing social interests is reinforced in the "duty to obey" clause (Art. 59). The spirit and some of the language of this clause incorporate most of the antecedent article from the 1936 Constitution, although with an added phrase stressing the nexus between citizens' rights and their social obligations: "the exercise of rights and liberties is inseparable from the performance by citizens of their duties." Again, as with much of the Constitution's content, this concept of linkage does not represent an innovation in Soviet law. Moreover, it is relevant to all of the citizen's rights and obligations and is not addressed exclusively to the criminal justice process.

Turning now to the position of the individual in the criminal justice system, we find that the most significant aspects of post-Stalin legislation on criminal law and procedure also have been incorporated into the Draft Constitution. From arrest through appeal, the position of the individual in the Soviet criminal justice process has been considerably strengthened since enactment of the all-union Fundamental Principles of Criminal Procedural Legislation in 1958. A Soviet "due process" in *ordinary* (nonpolitical) criminal cases has developed and survived leadership turnover and the vicissitudes of Soviet politics. For the vast majority of individual citizens, this may have been the most important and durable accomplishment of destalinization.

Much of this change, of course, arose from post-Stalin reaction to the conditions of official lawlessness and terror that prevailed at the time of the adoption of the 1936 Constitution and that continued, though significantly reduced in scale, up to and even after Stalin's death in 1953. Although the current personal inviolability clause (Art. 54) resembles its 1936 antecedent, the injunction against arrests without either court order or approval of a procurator is now grounded in the operative legislation and codes on criminal procedure as well as in actual post-Stalin Soviet practice. After the arrest, contemporary Soviet justice is, in fact, "administered solely by the courts" (Art. 150). . . .

The citizen's right to defense has also been strengthened in the new Constitution in accordance with previous legislative development. The 1936 Constitution contained a "right to defense" clause, the language of which is nearly the same as that of the current clause (Art. 157). But the right to defense is now supported by constitutional recognition of the collegia of defense attorneys and by the right of mass organizations to assign a "social defender" to a case in support of one of its members (Art. 161). To be sure, the defense bar has existed for a long time, and the institution of citizen defenders is rooted in the earliest days of Soviet legal history. At the same time, the regime evidently has chosen to install these well-known institutions in the new Constitution as reaffirmation of the post-Stalin commitment to the Soviet version of due process. In this context, the "open court" clause (Art. 156), a carryover from the Stalin Constitution, is now more meaningful and less frequently violated.

The judiciary's constitutional monopoly over the administration of justice is explicitly reinforced in a clause that reflects post-Stalin dissolution of the notorious "special boards." The constitutional declaration that "no one can be adjudged guilty of committing a crime and subjected to criminal punishment other than by the verdict of a court and in accordance with criminal law" is both a reminder of and a response to the extralegal traditions of Stalinism as well as one of several "signals" in the current document that there will be no return to, what Brezhnev himself called in his May plenum report, "the illegal repressions" that "darkened" the years following ratification of the 1936 Constitution. Although the clause assuring judicial independence (Art. 154) still is liable to the party's contravention, there have been some indications, if difficult to document, that direct party interference in the work of the judiciary has abated since the Stalin years. . . .

With respect to the tiny minority of activist dissidents, however, both the personal security clauses and the formal rights accorded criminal defendants have been sorely abused by the regime, especially since the Sinyavskiy-Daniel trial in early 1966. In the endless stream of dissident cases reported in *samizdat*, there have been numerous recorded violations of the inviolability of the home (Art. 55) and of the confidentiality of correspondence and telephone conversations (Art. 56). In recent years, incidents of intimidation, mugging, physical assault, and, in a few instances, death under mysterious circumstances—all believed to have been provoked or even perpetrated by KGB personnel in mufti—indicate that for dissidents the "right to legal protection against threats against life and health, property and personal freedom, and honor and dignity" (Art. 57) is, for all practical purposes, a dead letter. If, as is often the case, the bureaucratic harrassment and administrative actions directed against dissidents have led to criminal prosecution for either a political offense or an ordinary crime, the dissident defendant routinely finds his due process rights violated both in the preliminary investigation and during the subsequent trial. In fact, the constitutional due process clauses in the present document are frequently inverted to the disadvantage of the dissenter. Instead of executing his responsibility to legally prevent the official capriciousness experienced by dissidents (Art. 163), the procurator usually shares complicity. Rather than benefit from a strengthened right to defense (Art. 157), the dissident's right to choose a defense counsel generally is subject to KGB interference and is frequently abridged. Finally, instead of enjoying equality before the law and the court (Art. 155), the dissident is classified as a "political case" and subjected systematically to a pattern of discrimination by the legal personnel formally involved and by the party and KGB officials who may discreetly direct the administration of political justice from behind the scenes. In effect, as Harold Berman has aptly pointed out, in political cases "socialist legality" breaks down into its constituent parts—socialism versus legality. . . .

Participatory rights. The Soviet citizen's economic rights and civil liberties have been supplemented in the new Constitution by an increased emphasis on his participatory rights. In theory, this is a result of the transition from a proletarian dictatorship to a "state of the whole people" (Art. 1). In structural terms, a greater scope and opportunity for citizen involvement in public life is outlined in the political and economic chapters of the Constitution reviewed above. The individual's specific participatory rights may be viewed as giving practical meaning to this enlargement of participatory space in the Soviet system. In general, the participatory rights are to be exercised mainly in the broad process of *policy implementation*, while the opportunity for greater citizen input into the *policy-making* process, as presented in the new Constitution, is confined at most to the arena of local government.

Thus, the new Constitution guarantees to the citizen the general right of public participation (Art. 48); the right to submit proposals and to criticize with impunity the performance of government agencies (Art. 49); the right to lodge complaints against public officials and, in some cases, to seek judicial remedy (Art. 58); and the right to sue government agencies and public officials for tort liability incurred by illegal actions causing the citizen-plaintiff damage (Art. 58). In regard to the citizens' slightly increased opportunities for participating in local policy-making, Chapters 14 and 19 of the Draft Constitution codify those post-Stalin changes in state law (*gosudarstvennoye pravo*) associated with the growth of the responsibilities of local soviets and of the powers of their deputies. In the spirit of the "all-people's state," the soviets of "working people's deputies" have been renamed soviets of "people's deputies" (Art. 88). And, consistent with the increased interest in citizen participation which began under Khrushchev and continues under Brezhnev, the new Draft Constitution was published in June 1977 for nationwide public discussion, as stipulated in its discussion clauses (Arts. 5 and 112). . . .

Participation and Public Discussion

. . . While an analogous "public" discussion preceded ratification of the 1936 Constitution, extensive public "commentary" on various legislative proposals has become, since Stalin's death, a much more common method of involving the average citizen in public affairs. In general, this involvement is circumstantial and very limited—usually to no more than suggesting changes in tone, wording, or emphasis in a given piece of legislation, for which the basic framework already has been set by party authorities. Public discussion has thus become an oft-used leadership technique for mobilizing the population and encouraging citizen participation in policy *implementation*, while the party uses the occasion for a mass political socialization campaign at the same time.

The 1977 constitutional discussion does stand apart from previous discussions of legal reform, at least in terms of its scope and duration. But it marks no obvious watershed in either the extent of public political participation or in the quality of regime-society relations. It is extremely doubtful that the ongoing public discussion will result in significant changes in the Constitution before its ratification. . . .

Commentary on certain issues remains proscribed. Thus, even passing remarks on the Draft articles concerning either the party's role or Soviet foreign policy have been exceedingly rare in the discussion published thus far. On the other hand, the discussion has brought forth a remarkable variety of proposals on a wide range of concerns. In a narrow sense, the discussion has afforded to individuals and groups an opportunity for self-advertisement and the promotion of group or institutional interests which might be advantaged by some constitutional modification. The discussion has also served, however, as a forum for individuals who are more interested in the Constitution itself and certain of its provisions. This second category of commentators seems to take rather seriously the normative potential of the Constitution, increasingly emphasized by Soviet legal scholars.

Chapter 9

SOCIALIST "DEMOCRACY": SOME CONTRASTING VIEWS

Speaking generally, the Soviet Constitutions of 1936 and 1977 would appear to be among the most advanced and forward-looking in the world. To what extent this is reality and to what extent myth, with special regard to the meaning and content of socialist "democracy," are discussed in the following pages by G.F. Aleksandrov, Richard C. Gripp, and this editor. The nature and reality of other constitutional guarantees are dealt with in various other sections of this volume.

The Pattern of Soviet Democracy

G.F. Aleksandrov

All the critics of Soviet democracy are united in one requirement that these people wish to set for so-called "pure," "genuine" democracy. The foreign press—not only newspapers and magazines, but a large number of the books issued in recent years—tiresomely poses one and the same question: if the Bolsheviks are right and they are indeed carrying out democratic principles, why is there only one political party in the Soviet Union? Is not the constant struggle of several parties the sign of "true" democracy? Is not freedom of speech, of assembly, of thought concerning the social system and government policy, not better assured if several political parties compete: if the government policy is carefully considered from the point of view of the interests of various social groups, various political principles and various parties?

This question, as is self-evident, presents several aspects: does the presence of two or more parties bespeak the democratic structure of society? Is the view, widely held today among bourgeois politicians, true that the more parties there are fighting for power, the more perfect and broader the democracy? And finally, do the arrows of the modern critics of Soviet democracy hit the mark when they consider it undemocratic for the people to have a single party?

As is known, the very concept of "democracy" means popular sovereignty in general. The majority of those discussing the question of democracy agree that by democracy is meant a system of political relations within society which assures the development of society and its institutions in the interests of the people and with the participation of the people itself. Glimmers of this thought shine through even the haziest reasoning of the most mystically inclined modern bourgeois philosophers. Consequently, from the historical and social points of view, the character of democracy is revealed not by whether the form of government and the state system are connected with the existence of one, two, or more parties, but by the content of political institutions, the nature of the state and the nature of the internal and foreign policies followed by the state and its governments. For example, who does not know of the abundance of political organizations and the existence of a sharp struggle among social classes and groups in Athens of the fifth and fourth centuries, B.C.? Or of the struggle of various social classes and cliques in ancient Rome? Yet who dares term these cities and the countries they represented, with their slave-holding system of life, examples of democratic organization of society, on the basis of the abundance of competing political groupings? . . .

English and American politicians and social scientists often cite their countries as examples for others, as countries of basically two parties and thereby, presumably, com-

At this writing, Mr. Aleksandrov was a member of the Academy of Sciences of the USSR and author of The History of Western Philosophy. *This selection is from pp. 21–26 of the translation by Leo Gruliow of a speech delivered at a session of the Academy of Sciences on December 4, 1946, and widely distributed in the USSR. Reprinted with the permission of the publisher, Public Affairs Press, Washington, D.C.*

pletely democratic. But in politics one cannot take reasoning of this sort on faith. Why, many labor members of Parliament themselves consider that the Labor and Conservative parties of England *do not differ in principle* on many quite important contemporary questions. Some call themselves Conservative and carry out a frankly imperialistic, expansionist policy; others call themselves Labor, socialists, the workers' party, but often, particularly in the field of foreign relations, carry out the very same policy.

The same can be said concerning the United States. More than thirty years ago Lenin pointed out that the two bourgeois parties in America were distinguished by particular stability and vigor after the Civil War over slavery in 1860–65. The party of former slaveholders is the so-called "Democratic party." The party of the capitalists, standing for emancipation of the Negroes, developed into the "Republican Party."

> After the emancipation of the Negroes, the difference between the two parties grew less and less. The struggle of these parties was conducted primarily over the question of higher or lower tariffs. This struggle did not *possess serious* significance for the masses of the people. The people were deceived and deflected from their vital interests by means of the effective and empty *duels* of the two bourgeois parties. This so-called "two party system" prevailing in America and England, was one of the most powerful means of hindering the rise of an independent workers', i.e., a truly socialistic, party.[1]

However, if the modern supporters of "two-party democracy" do not hesitate to put to us any—in their opinion—"tricky" questions, then, on the basis of mutual politeness and those same democratic principles, we Soviet people, in turn, would like to put a few questions to the variegated "specialists" in democracy, to those who love to pose questions: if the existence of two, three or more parties corresponds to a truly democratic way of life, then why, for instance, do the Laborites fight the Conservatives on questions, yet fly into a fury at the mere mention of the English Communists? If the existence of several parties is the real sign of genuine democracy, it would seem sensible and logical to encourage and support any opposition movement in England, and to afford an opportunity for free expression of the views of parties which have not obtained a majority in Parliament. Yet everybody knows that as a matter of fact the Laborites are not guided by this principle; as a matter of fact, they strive to dislodge the Conservative Party and, if they could, apparently they would be happy to obtain all the seats in Parliament now held by Conservatives, without particular concern that the existence of one party in Parliament would be a "violation" of democratic principles. No, apparently when the democratic or undemocratic character of the state is discussed, the question is not whether there is one or several parties. Who will believe that certain Laski-type theoreticians of the Labor Party and the other various lovers of "defending" democracy are interested in the existence of their political foes and extension of their foes activity? Yet only thus must one interpret the passionate argument for the necessity of preserving a system of two or more parties in order to preserve democracy! No, the point is merely that today the Laborites still lack the strength to finish off their political foes in the electoral struggle and to win over the whole of society to their side.

That is why it seems entirely probable that the thesis of identity between democracy and the struggle of two or more parties within society is the thesis of those who today are in no position to win over to their side the majority of society; the thesis of those who know that in the conditions of bourgeois society—that is, in the conditions in which society lives and develops on the basis of a struggle of diverse social classes—there can be no place for a single party which would express with equal success the interests of opposed social classes. As long as antagonistic class society exists, the struggle among various political parties, expressing the struggle of classes, is inevitable. In this, and only in this, lies the essence of the question so often asked in foreign literature: is democracy compatible with a one-party system? Is not the existence of several parties in society the sign of true, genuine democracy?

We Soviet people give a clear and unequivocal answer: no, it is not. The democratic or anti-democratic nature of public life, of a state, of a government's policy, is determined not by the number of parties but by the substance of the policy of this state, of these parties—by whether this or that policy is carried out in the interests of the people, in the interests of its overwhelming majority, or in the interests of its minority. That is how matters stand with regard to the first question—whether democracy coincides with the existence of one or several parties in society. . . .

Soviet democracy expresses the principles of a socialist society. As is known, socialist society begins where and when the exploiting classes—landowners, manufacturers, financial magnates, bankers, kulaks, speculators and other social groups living on unearned income—cease to exist, and society begins to develop on the basis of a friendly alliance of the workers, peasants and intelligentsia. As long as exploiting classes exist, they strive to protect their political interests in society, to create their political organizations and to have their own parties for the protection of their private interests and the subordination of the interests of society to the interests of the given clique or social group. But after the new social order, namely, the socialist order, triumphs in all fields, no place remains in society for the classes oppressing other classes: the time comes of a great concord of the people and the creation of the deepest unity of all society. In this period the former need and the former necessity for the existence of divergent political parties disappears.

That party which is best able to express the deepest fundamental interests of the whole of society and can point the way to the quickest practical plan for establishing the foundations of a new life—a life without exploiters and parasites; that party which, buy its organizational work, is able to rally around all of society, and lead it along the new paths of building communism; that party, finally, which by its devoted, self-sacrificing service to the people, has won unquestionable and undisputed authority throughout the whole of society—that particular party can express historically the deepest desires, life aims and ideals of the tremendous majority of the population of the country. It is precisely in this historical situation that the necessity and any possibility for the existence of divergent parties in society disappears completely. In the Soviet Union such a single party really exists and works for the welfare of the people—the party of the Communists, the Leninist party, guided by its leader, Comrade Stalin. The Soviet people have linked themselves with the party of the Bolsheviks and have adopted its program and ideas for their own.

Any other party that might arise in Soviet society could have only one program: a program of return to the past, to the old, to the life liquidated by our people: a program of struggle against socialism.

Notes

1. Lenin, Collected Works *(Russian Edition), vol. 16, p. 190.*

Politics and Power

Richard C. Gripp

The Electoral Process

Nominations of candidates to the national Supreme Soviet are made not by individuals, but by organized groups: Communist Party, trade unions, cooperatives, youth and cultural societies. In addition, workers at their factories, collective and state farmers at their farms, and soldiers and sailors in their military units can nominate candidates. Nominations are made at general meetings attended by interested persons who represent specific organizations.

So long as the nominees are sober, honest citizens, the party probably does not object to them being the "people's choice." After all, there are enough key local and regional party leaders elected to check any popular impetuosity in the various local, regional, and national soviets. Then too, the soviets as legislatures, do not possess policy-setting authority, so nothing is really left to chance by the regime. It must be assumed, of course, that all nominees have at least the tacit approval of the Communist Party in view of the responsibility which local party organs must bear for everything taking place in their areas.

As for Communist Party candidates, in the Supreme Soviet elections, party members and candidate members approximate 75 percent of all deputies nominated. The formally nominated candidates are now referred to as the "bloc of party and nonparty" people. The "bloc of party and nonparty" candidates now campaigns on a common platform of support for the regime.

In the election itself, the voter, upon identifying himself, receives his ballot and, according to the regulations, goes into a booth or special room where he crosses out the names of all candidates except the one he chooses—leaving untouched this name on the ballot. Regulations to the contrary, in fact only one name appears for each office, the voter upon receiving his ballot has merely to drop it untouched in the box—usually bypassing the privacy of the voting booth. If a voter so desires, he may vote against the single candidate by crossing out the candidate's name, an action of possible but rare occurrence. If the candidate receives a majority of votes in a district in which at least 50 percent of the eligible voters cast their ballots, that candidate is elected. If no such majority is received, a new election is called for within two weeks for that particular district. In each national election, a few voters do cross out the officially sponsored candidate and, occasionally, the candidate in a local election actually does not get the needed majority of votes and consequently fails to be elected.

Soviet voters have the right, by a simple majority vote, to recall deputies once elected. Although this right is very seldom taken advantage of, voters in the Ukraine recalled a deputy when, reportedly, they found him "incompetent" and "unsatisfactory." Simi-

Richard C. Gripp is a political scientist. This selection is from his Patterns of Soviet Politics, *© 1963 by the Dorsey Press, Inc. and is reproduced here by permission. The excerpt, drawn from various sections of the book, has been updated by the author, has been somewhat rearranged and, in the interest of readability, the usual indication of a break in the text is not shown. Footnotes have been omitted. The interested reader should consult the original.*

larly, a deputy to the Latvian Supreme Soviet was recalled for failing to carry out the voters' "mandate." And a deputy to the Belorussian Supreme Soviet was recalled because of "dishonest" practices.

Responsibilities and duties of deputies include representing their constituents in the government. Deputies are expected to meet the "lawful" complaints, needs, and requests of those whom they represent. One deputy relates how he helped his constituents get land to build houses after the city council originally had refused their request. The voters also complained to this deputy of inadequate electricity, which he remedied by getting the Ministry of Power Stations (since abolished) to send a portable power station to his city. One deputy of the Supreme Soviet has depicted his role as that of a connecting link between the local and the Supreme Soviet, where, in the latter body he represents the interests of the local soviet. In the local area, the deputy in turn serves as a representative of the Supreme Soviet. More importantly, deputies are expected to be leaders in promoting and carrying out directives of the Communist Party—to be, in fact, the functional link between the regime and the people. The "rights" of deputies include those of participating in legislative review such as it is, addressing inquiries to governmental officials, and enjoying immunity from arrest during sessions of the Supreme Soviet.

The theory of the Soviet electoral system is that it expresses unanimous popular ratification of the policies and actions of the regime. The nation as a body, through its elections, gives to Soviet leaders a legal mandate of approval and displays to both those at home and abroad the apparent unity and devotion which the Soviet people have for communism. The voting public—more than 99 percent of them—put themselves on record, formally, as approving and endorsing the Communist system.

*[**Editor's note:** According to official returns, in all elections to the Supreme Soviet between 1962 and 1979, over 99 percent of those eligible to vote did so, and of these eligible voters, over 99 percent cast their ballots for the named candidates.]*

In the frank words of the government's leading newspaper, elections to the Supreme Soviet express the people's "profound approval of the internal and foreign policies of the Communist Party and the Soviet government and demonstrate before all the world its firm solidarity, its supreme moral-political unity." This statement readily explains the why of Soviet elections; it shows the necessity for holding elections even when no contest for office exists, when no dissenting minority views of any sizeable proportions emerge, when results of the election can be safety predicted before the event actually takes place, and when the occupational and sex quotas for deputies seem to be preselected to achieve a certain desired percentage distribution. Regime leaders hope elections will legitimate their oligarchical rule. Apart from popular endorsement, Soviet elections give many citizens in the USSR the feeling of participating, however remotely, in the overall political process.

The Supreme Soviet

The national legislature in the USSR is the bicameral Supreme Soviet popularly elected for a four-year term. Officially, the Soviet is more than merely a legislative body. It is an organ invoked by the "will" of the entire Soviet people to preserve and to protect the interests of the workers and to reinforce and defend "victorious socialism." The two houses of the Supreme Soviet, enjoying equal power, are the Council of the Union and the Council of Nationalities.

The two houses, in joint session, elect a ruling Presidium to serve as the executive body of the entire Soviet. Its formal, constitutional powers include the ostensibly significant issuing of decrees, interpreting laws, dissolving the Supreme Soviet, and ordering new elections—given an impasse between the two houses—annulling illegal decisions of the Council of Ministers, appointing and removing the high command of the armed forces, proclaiming martial law, appointing and releasing members of the Council of Ministers when the Soviet is not in session (on the recommendation of the chairman of the Council), and declaring war under certain circumstances, ordering mobilization, and ratifying and denouncing international treaties.

The Council of Ministers is the operating executive branch of government and there is no record of the Supreme Soviet or its Presidium ever refusing to adopt a Council proposal. The Presidium seems to serve the purpose of having on hand a permanent organ of the duly elected legislature which can be readily available to give immediate, constitutional ratification to any and all decrees, resolutions, and draft laws issued by the Party Central Committee and the Council of Ministers.

Proceedings of the Supreme Soviet follow a rather standardized format of electing presiding officers and standing commissions, voting on the agenda for the session, hearing governmental reports, such as those from the chairman of the Council of Ministers and from the minister of finance. "Debate" among deputies takes the form of laudatory speeches extolling plan fulfillment in the deputy's own republic or region, but it occasionally injects mild criticism of second or lower echelon administrators. Finally, the Supreme Soviet approves interim decrees of its Presidium and passes sundry other resolutions, such as those favoring world disarmament, or world peace. Voting at a session of the Soviet gives the impression of being perfunctory, even mechanical, always unanimously in favor of all governmental proposals.

Apart from broad, noncommital resolutions, the chief functions of the Supreme Soviet are to appoint a government (Council of Ministers) and to ratify laws and decrees previously adopted by its Presidium. These laws, decrees, and resolutions include such matters as awarding medals and other honors to deserving citizens, approving personnel and organizational changes in the governmental apparatus, formally appointing the Council of Ministers and its chairman, electing the Presidium, electing a Supreme Court, and designating the Court's chief officer, the procurator-general, in addition to passing normal governmental laws.

In comparison to legislative bodies in Western governments, the Supreme Soviet, its commissions, and its directing Presidium cannot be considered as influential organs in Soviet policy formation for several reasons. The top Russian leaders occupy only a few important offices in either the Soviet or its Presidium. The Presidium is not staffed to be a policy-making organ. Moreover, there is no evidence available to indicate that the Presidium actually exercises any of its considerable rights (such as voiding decrees of the Council of Ministers). We do know that it gives its approval to governmental decrees, as drawn up by the Council of Ministers. Even this approval, however, might involve only the chairman and the secretary, both of whom sign documents for the Supreme Soviet.

Sessions of the Supreme Soviet meet only twice a year, for a total of twenty days or less. The bulk of this time is taken up with hearing reports from the government and party leaders. Moreover, the Soviet passed only some 130 laws in the twenty-year period, 1938–59. Modern governments in most other parts of the world, on the other hand, require the passage of literally hundreds of laws each year, all of which consume weeks, if not months, of legislative deliberation annually. Consequently, there must either be numerous laws (or decrees having legal force) which are secretly passed by the Supreme Soviet, or which are approved by party and governmental leaders without ever being referred to the Supreme Soviet. Of the two possibilities, the latter seems the more probable. Having on hand an interim Presidium that can approve laws—any laws—while the parent Supreme Soviet is not in session is itself disrespect for an elected legislature and can only testify to the emptiness of the Soviet legislature as a true law-making body.

Finally, there is no record, official or otherwise, of any serious debate taking place in any of the sessions of the Soviet, or of dissent on the part of any deputy to either laws that are presented or to programs that are recommended by party and governmental leaders. It can only be concluded, therefore, that the Supreme Soviet is the very epitome of a rubber stamp legislative body whose role and purpose in the Soviet governmental scheme are definitely not to take part in the formation of governmental policy.

The Supreme Soviet gives to the Russians, no doubt, a certain sense of participation in the governmental process. It also serves, as do Soviet elections, to put the people on record as approving past and future programs of the Communist Party and of the government. From superficial and perfunctory actions of their pseudo-legislature, the Soviet leaders lay claim to having a large, elected, democratic parliament which, they believe, will duly impress not only their own citizens but the rest of the world.

Communist Party Functions

The functions of the Soviet Communist Party are both varied and far-reaching. Indeed, they are as broad and extensive as is the Soviet political, governmental, economic, cultural, and social system itself. The party defines the goals and tasks and exercises leadership of the state "in all fields of it activity." The policy of the party "is the basis of the activity of the Soviet state." More than just the vanguard of the working class and the dictatorship of the proletariat, the Communist Party is the guiding compass for the conduct of virtually all organized activity in the USSR. The merging with, in effect taking over, of Soviet life on the part of the party is described by a famous Yugoslav Communist as a process in which the communist government constitutes, in practice, a party government; the communist army, a party army; and the state, a party state.

More specifically, the activities of the party include the following:

> Domestic: (1) Establish plans and broad policies for various aspects of Soviet life and to oversee their fulfillment; (2) Initiate all of the important governmental acts, decrees, reorganizations; (3) Supervise, at least indirectly, normal governmental functions (central-regional-local) throughout the nation; (4) Select the cadres for present and future officials in party government, industry, culture, education, and agriculture; (5) Establish the structural framework and operational guidelines for education, the economy, cultural life, and for such tasks as scientific investigations.

Party rules require the holding of at least one ordinary congress every four years and extraordinary congresses (such as the Twenty-first) on the call of the Central Committee, or on demand of at least one third of the party membership. Apart from the congresses, there was yet another type of broad meeting labeled the party conference.

In the Soviet regime's early years the party congresses and conferences were deliberating bodies for much of what became official policy. They constituted forums where the party as a whole—as represented by its elected delegates—dealt with matters of considerable importance. After the Fourteenth Congress in 1922, however, the general tenor of these gatherings changed. No longer did they seriously debate party affairs. No longer were they to any measureable degree originators or even interpreters of party policy. Instead their purpose now was simply to endorse and approve policy previously set by the top leadership. Although some debate was still permitted, even opposition views aired, party congresses and conferences became more perfunctory because they were now attended by selected representatives of the apparatus who were chiefly loyal to the party Secretariat and to its general secretary—Stalin. After 1922, virtually unanimous approval was given to the programs of the leadership by its faithful followers in the congresses and conferences. As Stalin's rule became more entrenched, even these modest party sessions were held less and less frequently. Only one conference was held after 1932—the one in 1941. In violation of party rules which called for a congress to be held at least every four years, Stalin allowed five years to pass between the Seventeenth and the Eighteenth Congress, and the Nineteenth Congress was convened thirteen and one half years after the Eighteenth. As congresses and conferences were allowed to atrophy in the latter part of Stalin's reign, so the same fate was suffered by the plenary sessions of the party's Central Committee.

There are no officially reported plenary meetings of the Central Committee for the years 1917–23 (although some probably occurred), and only two held between 1940 and 1953. Thus, for the years in which plenary meetings were officially reported, they averaged slightly more than two a year. Although there were six plenary meetings held in 1924 and five in 1927, they became fewer in direct relation to the increasing efficiency of Stalin's dictatorship. As with party congresses and conferences, Stalin had less and less need for plenary meetings of the Central Committee during the latter period of his reign. Following Stalin's death, congresses have been held more frequently (six in twenty-five years), and plenary meetings of the Central Committee have averaged more than two a year.

The subject matter of Central Committee plenums have included such matters as internal power struggles, governmental reorganizations, changes in both the top leadership and in existing party and government programs, domestic problems relating to industrial production and agricultural output, as well as certain questions of foreign policy. Although in 1957 and 1964 plenary sessions of the Central Committee decided the outcome of the power struggle between Khrushchev and his opponents, normally the plenums have nothing so important to rule on. The chief function of the plenums, as with party congresses, is to have at the call of the leaders a duly established and respected authoritative institution of the party which can give official approval—in the name of the whole party membership—to the programs and directions of the leadership. Similar functions are performed by congresses and central committee sessions of the union republic party organizations.

Local party organs hold conferences and plenary meetings which serve purposes similar to those on the regional and national levels. One plenary meeting of the Stalinsk Party Committee, which took place in a worker's club at a construction site, criticized party work in construction affairs and decided to send 300 Communists and 700 *Komsomol* members out to work on solving certain problems in construction. The party has regular duties to carry out then, based on its administrative divisions: union republic, *oblast*, *rayon*, and city. The party apparatus also assumes responsibilities for functions of a specific nature, such as industry and agriculture.

A recurring problem which has faced party leaders throughout most of Soviet history, is that of controlling industry. To what extent should party officials—particularly on the lower organizational echelons—within reason, interfere with economic administration? Should party representatives dictate to economic managers specific, technical decisions which are normally a part of professional administration? If so, what effects on industrial management will result from such technical decisions made, or at least strongly influenced, by members of the "political" apparatus? Or, should economic administrators alone make economic decisions? In this case, however, the Communist Party might risk losing control over operational decision making in industry. If the standard operating rule that the party must control all phases of Soviet life is adhered to in practice as well as in theory, what price can safely be paid in lost efficiency in order to ensure continuous political dominance of economic affairs? Soviet leadership, since 1917, has never resolved the dilemma, even to its own satisfaction. Direct party control over industrial decision making has waxed and waned over the years in response to current evaluations and reevaluations by the leadership as to whether economic administration was suffering from such close interference or whether party controls needed to be strengthened to ensure managerial loyalty to the regime.

Several broad tasks have been given to party organizations in industrial enterprises. These include helping to fulfill monthly production quotas, working to improve quality of output, using the reserves of production to maximum effect, "strengthening" labor discipline, striving for a smooth work flow within the enterprise, introducing new techniques of production and systematically controlling the "economic activity" of administrators. The most helpful type of party "leadership" over industry comes when party members contribute to the production process. A party bureau which recommended measures to increase mechanization in a given shop within a factory is cited as a healthy example of expected party-industry cooperation.

As in industry so in agriculture, the party seeks and plans not only to set overall policy but to control and shape the important managerial decisions. Soviet agricultural administration must not only be party oriented; it must be party guided, directed, and influenced. To accomplish these objectives a widespread party apparatus was established in rural areas as a necessary precondition to providing for party hegemony over agriculture.

Similar to its function in industry, the party apparatus in agriculture seeks to insure Communist Party domination as well as to increase the output of farm commodities. Specifically, party officials watch over fulfillment of higher party directives, conduct educational and propaganda courses, try to increase production and introduce new farming techniques, supervise all phases of agricultural administration, and serve as the clearing house for appointment of agricultural officials. . . .

Lethargy among collective farm workers coupled with a lack of initiative on the part of party members works to limit the overall effectiveness of party groups. One party secretary complained that only half of the 864 pig farms in his *oblast* had active party groups. In other cases there may be flurries of party meetings and conferences attended by most of the farm workers which may, however, have the adverse effect of interrupting rather than facilitating output. One *raykom*, in fact, held ten different conferences within a fifteen-day period and, in the process, interfered with the sowing of grain.

At other times, however, the party apparatus helps to raise output through its various efforts to stimulate agriculture. *Komsomol* members are occasionally sent to areas where agricultural production is lagging. Units of government and party committees from time to time are reorganized and key leaders, including those on the management staffs of collective and state farms, are shifted and changed in attempts to raise efficiency. Such party direction of agriculture at times results in the promotion of dubious plans, such as the rash and over-optimistic virgin lands program of the late 1950s. In some cases, it should be assumed, party direction probably improves the overall administration of agriculture.

A very important function of the Communist Party is to work toward achieving a high degree of ideological-cultural uniformity in the life of the nation—all in support of promoting and strengthening communism and of insuring the dominance of party rule.

Soviet history is an uneven record of periods of rather heavy party censorship of literature alternating with brief lapses of "thawing." Immediately after the Revolution Lenin shut down the anti-Bolshevik press in Russia, but by the early 1920s a relatively high degree of literary freedom existed. By late 1928 the party called for a mobilization of literature, theater, and movies to support communist viewpoints in culture. The year 1932 saw a last outbreak of literary protest against steadily increasing restriction under Stalinism. In 1934 the Union of Soviet Writers was formed, and by 1941 all other literary groups but this one had been dissolved. Meanwhile, party influence grew more firm. Although literary controls, among many others loosened during World War II the party tightened them up again immediately thereafter. In 1946 Politburo member Andrei Zhdanov took over concentrated and high-level control of all propaganda affairs. Zhdanov became the spokesman for an intensive effort to achieve ideological purity; this period is referred to as the "Zhdanovshchina."

Following Stalin's death, writers and artists cautiously began to criticize Stalinist "formalism." Two of the country's most eminent composers, Shostakovich and Khachaturyan, called for greater freedom in music. Although party leaders continued to insist on setting literary standards and on requiring artistic fidelity to "socialist realism," artists were permitted more leeway, for example, in choice of general themes and style. In 1956 Khrushchev's denigration of Stalin and Stalinism raised hopes among some Soviet citizens for even more literary freedoms. This year also saw publication of the novel *Not by Bread Alone* by a promising young Soviet writer; this work was a fictionalized though poignant criticism of some obvious weaknesses in party officialdom as these existed in the USSR. In late 1956 after the Hungarian Revolution, there followed increased controls over literary life and a rather broad reimposition of some of the older restrictions on Soviet literature.

By 1963 the party's censorship was called upon to discipline outbreaks in Ehrenburg's writing, Yevtushenko's poetry, Solzhenitsyn's writing, and abstract art, all of which were deemed too liberal. Khrushchev noted once again that writers, artists, composers, all creative workers in fact, are to use their talents in pursuit of the party's task of perfecting Marxism-Leninism; in short, to fight for communism and to oppose its enemies. In a further claim that abstract painting is a perversion in art, Khrushchev argued that there can be no peaceful coexistence of ideologies. Finally, he strongly implied that opposition to these views could in effect be treasonous.

The 1966 trial and conviction of the writers Siniavsky and Daniel for "anti-Soviet agitation and propaganda" signaled harsh supression of dissident literature as well as other forms of dissent. The official campaign against dissidents continues. Thus, if Soviet writers fail to win official approval for their work, these writers become criminals if their work is subsequently published or even disseminated either inside or outside the USSR.

As with literature, Soviet education also is closely watched over by the party apparatus. Both Lenin and Stalin viewed education chiefly as a weapon with which to further the development of communism. Their successors hold the same view. The whole system of education in the general "political-educational" sphere and in the particular realm of art, Lenin maintained, must be imbued with feelings for the class struggle of the proletariat, the abolition of exploitation, and the achievement of the aims of the dictatorship of the proletariat. The party, he continued, must actively lead in the entire activity of popular education. A more recent Soviet author has written: "The Party regarded the school not as a self-inclosed educational institution, but as an educational center, disseminating Communist ideology and Communist morality."

Organizationally, there is a section of the Central Committee apparatus for Science, Higher Educational Institutions, and Schools. In the Committee there is also a section for Science, Schools, and Culture which is attached to the Bureau for the RSFSR. All of the other fourteen union republics have similar sections in their respective central committees. The chiefs of the sections (both national and regional ones) are, at the same time, members of their respective republic central committees. To complete the tie-in of party controls, sizeable numbers of teachers and professors are party members. In 1961 there were an estimated 400,000 Communist teachers in the USSR and, in the great majority of schools, there were party organizers.

To gain power in 1917 the Bolsheviks needed, among other support, the active assistance of the bulk of the military forces. Since gaining that support, the communist leadership over the years has taken special pains, even some risk, to retain the unswerving loyalty of the military, security, and police forces—even at the cost of seriously decimating the trained officer class which has followed various purges. In building the Red Army, with few trained professionals, Trotsky early on faced the necessity of placing former tsarist officers in Red Guard units. At the same time Trotsky's military system was based on discipline, centralized political control, and orthodoxy of doctrine. More than that, the party leadership has steadfastly insisted on its unquestioning supremacy over the military high command in all matters whatsoever.

Functioning at present under the Central Committee's Chief Political Directorate for the Armed Forces, there are subordinate political directorates within military units. At each such unit the head of the party organization generally is the deputy commander for political affairs (*zampolit*). The *zampolit* is subordinate both to the regular commander of the respective unit and also to the *zampolit* of the next higher military unit who, in effect, appointed him. The main tasks of a *zampolit* are politically to "educate" officers and troops in official propaganda and to get them to support the Soviet system. The *zampolit*, according to one view, functions as a combination chaplain, information and education officer, special services officer, censor, and disciplinarian.

Party organization and activities within the military sphere, as might be anticipated, differ somewhat from party actions outside of the armed forces. Except for the lower echelons within the party hierarchy, the practice of election of party leaders is abandoned, and party organs are organized by military units rather than on a territorial basis. Although party leaders form a part of the general military hierarchy, the tasks of party organs very definitely do not include control over "production" matters—that is, over operational military rule by the authorized military commander.

The formal legal government in the Soviet Union, be it national, regional, or local is never far removed from supervision and control by the Communist Party. From the establishment of overall top policy, through review of yearly and quarterly plans, down to periodic checking on routine operations and selection of key governmental officials, the party unit at each stratum of the organization serves both as cornerstone and general guide for all governmental actions of any importance. Party policy for decisions on matters of industry becomes governmental policy, party programs for agriculture become governmental programs, party assignments whatever they may concern—such as education, culture, foreign policy, local industry—become, by definition, governmental responsibilities. This virtual merger of party and government is neither concealed nor rationalized by Soviet leaders. Rather, it is freely admitted and held up as a healthy example of the success and novelty of the Soviet political-governmental system. In fact, for many Soviet officials, especially those on the higher policy-forming levels, there is no practical difference between party and government. They function, when all is said and done, as one organ.

The problem of allowing lower party organs to exercise some democratic procedures while yet holding these organs strictly accountable to higher control has caused hope, expectation, frustration, and confusion among party units over the years. In local government, party and governmental officials overlap frequently enough to ensure dominant party influence within each governmental unit. Normally the heads of local governments at the same time are members of the guiding bureau of the respective local party committee, and first secretaries of the latter also are on the local government's executive committee. In addition, each governmental unit usually has a party cell, with its own elected secretary and which itself is subordinate to the party committee at the appropriate area level.

Obviously, freedom to criticize, supposedly guaranteed to communists by the Party Rules, does not mean, from the party's standpoint, freedom to speak against party policy or to express views which are "antiparty" or which are alien to "Marxism-Leninism." And yet, there are officials who complain about "undemocratic" procedures, however infrequently. This suggests that some improvements both from below and from above aimed at improving democratic methods may yet be forthcoming in Communist Party procedures. In 1956 the special representatives (party organizers) of the Central Committee which had been attached to important enterprises and organizations were withdrawn in favor of less national supervision and a bit more autonomy for the local party organs. In another vein, a collective farmer prided himself on the fact that on his farm secret balloting prevailed; there were even two or three candidates regularly nominated for the position of farm chairman. So far, these examples drawn from different spheres of party control may be but mere straws in the wind. They are too few to indicate any definite trend.

Political power within the USSR is concentrated and monopolized in the small ruling Political Bureau (Politburo) of the Communist Party. Thus, the Soviet political system is highly organized to ensure centralized leadership for pursuing the goal of building a communist society; all Soviet governmental institutions are expected to serve this goal.

On the Nature and Prospects of Soviet Democracy

Samuel Hendel

The Marxist-Leninist View

According to Marx and Engels, the destruction of capitalism would bring about the dictatorship of the proletariat, that is, "the proletariat organized as the ruling class," and "establish democracy." This, explained Lenin, while involving suppression of the bourgeoisie would at the same time lead to "an immense expansion of democracy" for the proletariat, that is to say, "democracy for the vast majority of the people." All officials without exception would be subject to election and recall. And from the time of its taking power, the proletarian state, as an instrumentality of force in the hands of the vast majority directed against a small minority, would begin to wither away until, after a protracted period of time, there would exist only a stateless, classless society.

More specifically, the dictatorship of the proletariat, as Lenin, the Bolsheviks, and Marxists generally conceived of it *before* the Bolshevik seizure of power in November 1917, would have permitted all leftist parties to compete for the support of the masses. No Marxist then thought of the dictatorship of the proletariat as equivalent to the dictatorship of one party and certainly not of any one group within a party. It is true that Lenin, with specific regard to Russia, "amid the gloom of autocracy," opposed the use of broad principles of democracy in the organization of the Russian socialist party in the *preparation and making* of the revolution. But for many years he was convinced that Russia, as a backward, agricultural country, *after* the revolution, would be ready only for a bourgeois, capitalist phase of development and probably would be governed by a coalition of parties, representing the proletariat, peasantry and sections of the bourgeoisie. Lenin, for example, had rejected the Parvus-Trotsky formula which had called for a minority dictatorship of the proletariat in Russia. While after April 1917 he came closer to accepting this formula, the fact is that even the revolutionary seizure of power in November 1917 was in the name of the Soviets in which several parties were represented.

Under Lenin, however, in the years that followed, the Bolsheviks suppressed all other working class and peasant as well as bourgeois parties and their press, and in addition, outlawed all organized "factions" within the Communist party itself. Lenin, to be sure, had proposed or agreed to these measures in the face of war, civil war, intervention, and desperate economic circumstances. While he lived, he and his ideas were openly criticized and attacked at Party congresses and conferences; on occasions, he was even outvoted.

In any event, whatever the explanation, the dictatorship of the proletariat became under Lenin the dictatorship of the Communist party and at times of the Politburo, a

This updated excerpt is from "The USSR After Fifty Years: An Overview" in Samuel Hendel and Randolph L. Braham, eds., USSR After Fifty Years: The Promise and the Reality *(Alfred A. Knopf, Inc., 1967), and appears here by permission.*

small group of Party leaders, while under Stalin it degenerated from a dictatorship of a small group of Party leaders into as thoroughgoing a dictatorship of one man as modern history has known. . . .

Soviet Socialist "Democracy"

In 1936, at the very apogee of Stalin's power, a new Soviet constitution was adopted and proclaimed by him to be "the only thoroughly democratic constitution in the world"; as one Soviet writer put it "a million times more democratic than that of the most democratic bourgeois republic." The Soviet people, asserted Khrushchev, "are the freest of the free in the world," and this view continues to be echoed by Soviet leaders and writers to this day.

The whole question of Soviet "democracy" might perhaps be dismissed with the statement that these affirmations rest on a particular definition and that the USSR is free to define democracy any way it pleases. But it is not a question of semantics. The concept of democracy corresponds to one of the deepest and noblest aspirations of mankind and has great attraction and appeal throughout the world. It is well to consider, therefore, whether the Russian claim can be supported by any meaningful, reasonable, and consistent definition of democracy—non-Marxist or Marxist.

To begin with, no honest observer could seriously maintain that Soviet practice conforms to the criteria suggested in the West, for example, by Ernest Barker, one of Britain's leading political philosophers, who wrote that democracy

> is not a solution, but a way of seeking solutions—not a form of State devoted to this or that particular end (whether of private enterprise or public management), but a form of State devoted, whatever its end may be, to the single means and method of determining that end. The core of democracy is choice, and not something chosen; choice among a number of ideas, and choice, too, of the scheme on which those ideas are eventually composed.

And to make those choices meaningful, as Professor Robert M. MacIver has insisted, it is a necessary condition of democracy that opposing doctrines remain free to express themselves, to seek converts, to form organizations, and so to compete for success before the bar of public opinion.

If these "Western" standards are not, what then *are* the bases upon which the claim of the Soviet regime to democracy is made to rest? Allegedly of particular importance are the provisions of Article 50 of the Soviet Constitution of 1977 (which, with slight modifications, reproduced the language of Article 125 of the 1936 Constitution) guaranteeing to Soviet citizens freedom of speech, press, assembly, and demonstrations, with the proviso that exercise of these political freedoms is assured "by putting public buildings, streets and squares at the disposal of the working people and their organizations, by broad dissemination of information, and by the opportunity to use the press, television, and radio."

But the fact is that the very provision granting these rights imposes the limitation that they must be exercised "in accordance with the interests of the people and in order to strengthen and develop the socialist system." And, what is more, a new article (number 39) in the 1977 Constitution requires that "enjoyment by citizens of their rights and freedoms must not be to the detriment of the interest of society. . . ."

Another new article (number 62) makes it the obligation of Soviet citizens not only to "safeguard the interests of the Soviet state" but "to enhance its power and prestige." In practice, the judgment of which freedoms serve the "interests" of the people, or are "detrimental" to their interests, or help to strengthen the socialist system, or enhance the power and prestige of the Soviet state rest, of course, not with the people themselves but with the Party or, more accurately, with the Party leaders.

Even before these constitutional guarantees of freedom of speech and related freedoms were adopted, *Pravda*, on June 2, 1936, warned that

> He who makes it his task to unsettle the socialist structure, to undetermine socialist ownership . . . is an enemy of the people. He gets not a scrap of paper, he does not set foot over the threshold of the printing press to realize his base designs. He gets no hall, no room, no cover to inject poison by word of mouth.

And, of course, the Party continues to exercise pervasive control over press, radio, television and other media of information and influence within the USSR.

A second basis upon which the USSR predicates its claim to democracy is the widespread participation of its people both in formal state elections and in the running of factories, farms and enterprises. Soviet writers have boasted that their turnout at the polls is much higher than in any nonsocialist country and that their representatives can "in all justice be called the elect of the people, because all the electors, with scarcely any exception, vote for them."

Now it must be conceded that on what Sir John Maynard years ago called "the lower planes of public affairs" there is a "kind of democracy which is altogether *sui generis*" in the sense that factories, farms and enterprises are run under the continual criticism of workers who freely express opinions and make suggestions. What is more, workers' dwellings are managed by committees chosen by and responsible to them. And it is true that on occasion the Party invites widespread public discussion of policies under consideration. Recent cases in point were widespread national discussion, debates and proposed modifications of a new family law, new model rules for collective farms, and the new Soviet Constitution. But to suppose that this enables the Soviet people to change its governors without force or the violation of law is plainly untrue. Furthermore, there is a clear and vital distinction between general freedom of criticism and of choice, and the opportunity for public discussion of policies selected, submitted, delimited and ultimately decided from above.

As for almost unanimous approval of the single slate of candidates offered to the Soviet voters, these "ritualistic exercises in unanimity," as they were called by a largely friendly observer of the Soviet scene, must inherently be viewed with suspicion. But, how is it possible, Soviet writer V. Denisov asks, "to force the people of a huge multi-national state to vote against their own will and interests, when there is universal and equal suffrage by secret ballot (whose existence none deny)?" "The question alone," he maintains, "demonstrates the absurdity of such allegations."

It may be asked in turn, how is it possible to explain that, in the 1938 election to the republican Supreme Soviet, 99.8 percent of the Volga Germans went to the polls, of whom 99.7 percent voted for the official list of candidates, while three years later the entire population was acused of harboring "tens of thousands of deviationists and spies" and deported *en masse* for disloyalty? How explain, in general, that although in the course of World War II seven nationalities were deported *en masse* for disloyalty, their votes in favor of the official list in the elections to the Supreme Soviet in 1937 were stated to have been well in excess of 90 percent? And is it credible that in the elections to the Supreme Soviet, in excess of 99.86 percent of the citizens of Lithuania, Latvia, and Estonia (most recently incorporated Soviet republics with a history of independence) freely voted for the official candidates?

Nor is the further argument of Soviet writers that "the genuine freedom of Soviet elections consists first and foremost in the fact that candidates are nominated by the workers themselves, from among themselves" any more persuasive. It is true that Article 100 of the Soviet Constitution vests the right to nominate candidates for all Soviets in the Communist Party, trade unions, Young Communist League, cooperatives and other public organizations, work collectives, and meetings of servicemen in their military units. However, while in theory this makes possible a number of candidates, in all elections thus far held to the Supreme Soviet (including that in 1979) the name of only one candidate has appeared on the ballot in each constituency. What is critical, therefore, is obviously the process of elimination of nominees. And this process designed to assure "dependable" candidates, it is clear, is carried on by and through the Communist party which is declared by the Constitution (Article 6) to be "the leading and guiding force of the Soviet system and the nucleus of its political system, of all state organizations and public organizations."

The leadership of the Communist party, in turn, although theoretically constituted on the basis of free elections in ascending hierarchies, in fact represented at the height of Stalin's power a virtual dictatorship of one man, and in more recent times continues to reflect a marked concentration of power. With few exceptions, since Lenin's death the leaders at the top of the hierarchy have been able to control and limit the discussion of policy at all lower levels and in all media, and determine or control the selection of personnel for all important positions. There is a vast difference, as Plekhanov once pointed out, between the dictatorship of the proletariat and of a group.

Another basis upon which the USSR claim to democracy is advanced is that under the leadership of the Communist party, in fundamental and far-reaching respects, the interests and the well-being of the Soviet peoples have been served and advanced. When, under such leadership, the means of production were turned into the property of the people, exploitation destroyed, poverty and unemployment eliminated, the Soviet peoples achieved *real* freedom. In this view, the existence of a democracy is determined, as G.F. Aleksandrov wrote, "by the substance of the policy pursued by the state, by whether this or that policy is carried out in the interests of the people, in the interests of its overwhelming majority, or in the interest of its minority." More recently, Brezhnev, in the Report of the CPSU Central Committee to the 25th Party Congress, commented "that for us the democratic is that which serves the people's interests, the interests of communist construction."

It cannot be denied that, under the domination of the Communist party, the USSR has made great advances in industrialization, in education, in cultural areas, and in the eradication of many forms of discrimination and inequality characteristic of the Tsarist period. Concomitantly, particularly in the process of rapid industrialization and collectivization, great hardships and burdens were imposed upon the Soviet people. But important as the benefits conferred and hardships imposed are for other purposes, they have little or no relevance to the existence or nonexistence of *political* democracy in the Soviet Union. The essence of democracy, in any meaningful sense, must surely lie in self-government rather than in service to the interests of the people (although it is, of course, probably true that in the long run self-government alone will provide good government). If democracy does not involve self-government, then the term not only loses all connection with its historic connotation but may be reduced to a manifest absurdity to describe the most thoroughgoing dictatorship provided only that it is benevolent or enlightened (or, perhaps, only claims to be so). What is more, to deny or denigrate self-government as the essence of democracy would be, as has been shown, to do violence not only to conceptions of capitalist democracy but to *Marxist* conceptions of socialist democracy as well.

But we are told that because of the "great concord" of the Soviet peoples and the absence of the hostile or antagonistic classes there is no need for Western indicia of self-government since "there are no grounds for the existence of several parties, and therefore for the existence of freedom of such parties in the USSR." "The Party and the people in our country are as one," said Khrushchev, "so why do the Soviet people need other parties? Or are they to be created especially for the people in capitalist countries who are not satisfied with the socialist system?" The Soviet people, Soviet writer D. Zemlyansky tells us, "are all united in a common purpose: the construction of a happy classless society, communism."

It is revealing that when a measure of opposition or dissent is permitted to find expression in the USSR, how quickly the notion of a "great concord" is dispelled. But even assuming the absence of antagonistic classes in the USSR and a great concord on Marxist *ends* (a large assumption), is it really possible to argue in light of the known facts of Soviet history that at all times the Soviet people were agreed on means? Were all "as one" on the tempo of industrialization and collectivization, on "socialism in one country," on aid to World Revolution, on the Nazi-Soviet pact, on the dissolution of the Comintern, and on official attitudes toward law, religion, art, and literature? Did (and do) good socialists disagree among themselves about these and myriad other questions—especially in light of occasional sudden and drastic shifts of policy—without finding any legal means to express dissent, except on those occasions when expression is invited or permitted from above? The answers to these questions are in part given by the official denunciation of the wanton purges of the 1930s based, concededly, in good part on nothing more than honest disagreement with Stalin.

It remains to deal with a recent conception of socialist democracy in the USSR. According to the New Program of the Communist party, adopted in October 1961 (only the third formal program in the history of the Party), the USSR, which "arose as a state of the dictatorship of the proletariat, has in the new, present stage turned into a state of the entire people, an agency expressing the interests and will of the people as a whole." This development, it is maintained, involves a comprehensive extension and perfection of socialist democracy, including active participation of all citizens in the administration of the state and management of the economy. And, it is contemplated, "As socialist democracy develops further, the agencies of state power will gradulaly be transformed into agencies of public self-government." . . .

But, it is abundantly manifest that "the state of the entire people" is not intended to interfere with the hegemony, power, and control of the Communist Party. The New Party Program, which proclaimed this stage, added that it "is characterized by a further *rise in the role and importance of the Communist Party* as the leading and guiding force of Soviet society." (Italics in original.) And that such a role is not to be limited to criminal, parasitic, and pro-capitalistic elements is evidenced, to cite an important example, by continuing close control (despite some relaxation) over the press and the arts. Speaking to the 23rd Party Congress in 1966 Brezhnev went to special pains to assert that the Party is "unswervingly guided by the principle of partymindedness in art, a class approach in the evaluation of everything that is done in the field of culture." At the 24th Party Congress in 1971 he reaffirmed that, in accordance with what he called "the Leninist principle of partisanship,'' the task is ''to direct the development of all forms of creative art towards participation in the people's great course of communist construction.''

And it is clear that there is no intention to allow open, public presentation of opposing positions nor factional organization within the Party. Khrushchev, on his ouster in 1964, for example, was afforded no opportunity to reply to his denunciation in *Pravda* for ''harebrained scheming, immature conclusions, hasty decisions, actions divorced from reality, bragging, phrase-mongering, and commandism.'' Of course, this was no worse than the fate meted out by Khrushchev to the so-called Anti-Party group in 1957, which included Malenkov, Molotov, and Kaganovich, who were subjected to even worse vilification without opportunity to respond.

The Widening Scope of Controversy

On the other hand, since the death of Stalin in March 1953, it cannot be doubted that there have been some highly significant changes in the USSR which, while they do not amount to a thoroughgoing democratization of Soviet society, do represent a substantial liberalization and widening of the scope of permissible controversy and dissent. These changes are reflected in virtually every facet of Soviet life including the economy, law, science, literature and art. . . .

It is true that in the years after Stalin's death and Khrushchev's ouster there have been marked swings of the pendulum involving greater restraint (as well as latitude), of which the trials of many dissidents and the forcible incarceration of some in mental hospitals, the foreign exiling of Solzhenitsyn, and the internal exiling of Sakharov are dramatic cases in point; and that the Party retains its hegemony and the legal basis to curb dissent. Article 62 of the new Soviet Constitution of 1977 provides that ''citizens of the USSR are obliged to safeguard the interests of the Soviet state, and to enhance its power and prestige,'' and it is a crime under Soviet law to carry on ''agitation or propaganda'' with the object of undermining or weakening state power or to disseminate or even possess materials of such defamatory nature. But reinstitution of systematic and pervasive terror, to assure the virtually total outward conformity and uniformity that marked long periods of Communist party rule, seems to me extremely unlikely for a variety of reasons.

The Soviet people know the massive, wanton, and often senseless cruelty which so poignantly affected so many of their lives, and they are likely to resist its recurrence. What is more, the Soviet leaders have come to recognize the personal risks involved in a restoration of the terror apparatus but, apart from concern for self-preservation, no doubt many of them recoil from the reimposition of the rule of terror as a matter of principle and, in any event, as inexpedient if the creative energies and initiative of the Soviet people are to be fully released.

It is I believe true, too, that the leadership which came to power with the ouster of Khrushchev shares power *collectively* to an extent unparalleled since the death of Lenin. It is possible of course, that in this instance, as in the past, collective leadership will prove only to have been a brief prelude to the emergence of a single peerless *Vozhd*; but it appears to me dubious that in the foreseeable and predictable future—barring a great catastrophe—any one man could arrogate to himself the plenitude of power of a Stalin or even of a Khrushchev. For one thing, each ouster, with its revelation of prior abuses, makes it more difficult to cloak a new leader with the necessary charisma and mantle of infallibility. For another, any attempt at organized and massive terror of the kind on which Stalin relied to curb all opposition, real, potential, and imagined, would undoubtedly meet with great resistance.

In all these circumstances, I conclude that while it is incorrect to suggest that political democracy in any thoroughgoing sense (Western or Marxist) exists in the USSR, a return to a prototype of Stalinist totalitarianism and terror seems to be excluded. What is more, at and near the top of the Party, government and other hierarchies there has been some diffusion of power and responsibility; and, at lower levels, increased participation and activity by the Soviet people in public affairs. In general, as Professor Frederick C. Barghoorn has written, "there has recently been an encouraging revival of rational and empirical thinking in many fields," and of "the rudiments of a free, critical public opinion" which, though shackled, is "almost unimaginable when measured by the Stalinist yardstick." The USSR continues to retain and foster slogans and appeals toward a more far-reaching and more genuine socialist democracy. Early in 1980 in the wake of the tension arising out of the Soviet invasion of Afghanistan, it seemed doubtful that in the immediate future the slogans and appeals would take on greater substance and reality.

*[**Editor's note:** Further discussion, reflecting a variety of viewpoints on the nature and significance of changes in the USSR since the death of Stalin, appears in several chapters but most particularly in the chapter immediately following.]*

Chapter 10

POLITICAL PARTICIPATION IN THE SOVIET UNION

As H. Gordon Skilling has pointed out, "the idea that interest groups may play a significant role in communist politics has, until recently, not been seriously entertained either by Western political scientists or by Soviet legal specialists." In fact, however, he maintains that since the death of Stalin, "In an increasingly vigorous debate on public policy, certain specialized elite groups were able to express their views and interests and to exert some influence on the ultimate decisions in areas such as education, military strategy, industrial management, legal reform, science, art, and literature." Milton Lodge, in an essay that appeared in 1968 in the *American Political Science Review,* concluded, from a detailed content analysis of articles in specialist elite journals serving the Central Party apparatus, the military, the legal profession, and the literary and economic elite, that "the general trend is toward specialist elite participation in the policy-making area," that "conflict characterizes Party-specialist elite relations," and "in sum, the Soviet political system is competitive." "This is not to deny," he wrote, "that the Party is more powerful than the elites, but rather that the Party is not omnipotent. Party-specialist elite interdependence, not Party dominance, characterizes Party-elite relations." Isaac Deutscher, in an even eralier analysis reproduced here, lent some support to these conclusions.

Professor Jerry Hough in his study entitled "The Brezhnev Era: The Man and the System" also found that "The broadening of participation in policy debates has been matched by an increase in the scale of participation in different types of groups and in voluntary work for governmental and other political institutions." While Hough is wary about judging the relationship between participation and power, he concludes that "certain types of decentralization of power clearly have occurred." Professor Donald Barry challenges some of Hough's basic theses and their implications, and Hough responds.

With particular regard to the military as an interest group in Soviet politics, a study by a leading Western authority, Roman Kolkowicz, finds that in the absence of a threat to its basic interests, which makes for its unity, "the military community has shown itself to be a veritable battleground of divergent ideas, interests and objectives." While, in general, he believes that "the military's influence and autonomy are enhanced by the mounting importance of its functions and expertise, and because of a certain dispersal of authority at the pinnacle of the party," he adds the comment that the military tended to "obtain important political influence [only] during periods of profound internal crises in the party when warring factions courted the military's support," but that otherwise it "failed to obtain any real and formal political influence in the decision-making bodies of the party and government."

Constellations of Lobbies

Isaac Deutscher

Khrushchev's successors are still assessing the legacy they have taken over, trying to find out how much of it they can preserve and how much they must discard. They are also rearranging, redistributing and overhauling the levers and instruments of power. For the second time since Stalin, an attempt is being made to separate to some extent the powers of party and state; the previous attempt was made in 1953, when Malenkov was Prime Minister and Khrushchev became First Secretary. Many Soviet citizens hope that much good may result from a relative duality of power; some see in it the precondition for a genuine growth of civil liberties. The idea has a long history: in the early days of Stalin's autocracy, N. Bukharin, the great theorist of the "Right Opposition," had reached the conclusion that "the root of all evil in our system of government is that party and state are so completely merged." It is remarkable that after nearly four decades people are now arriving at this conclusion quite independently, and are trying to get at that "root of all evil." Yet, while the prerogatives of party and state are being disentangled, each of the two machines of power is being remodeled and reintegrated so as to overcome the effects of some of Khrushchev's divisive arrangements. . . .

I do not propose to indulge in the Kremlinologists' favorite game and to discuss personalities and speculate on the chances of Messrs. Podgorny, Suslov or Voronov, and on their respective attitudes toward either Brezhnev or Kosygin. The hierarchy of these Kremlin stars is highly capricious and elusive. It is also largely irrelevant, as those who so recently saw Khrushchev as the irremovable dictator and Frol Kozlov as his heir apparent, should have learned by now. Far more stable, important and clear are the basic alignments on which the men of the Presidium depend, for neither the Presidium nor the Central Committee acts in a vacuum.

Within the Central Committee and around it there are powerful lobbies and pressure groups that represent multiple sectional interests in a perpetual interplay of conflict and common action. The spokesmen of the most powerful lobbies have direct access to the Presidium, whose sessions they often attend, if not as parties to conflicts, then as experts and consultants.

Here is a tentative listing of these lobbies and pressure groups in the approximate order of their importance:

1. Nuclear scientists, managers of nuclear plants, heads of the military nuclear services and the men in charge of outer space experiments. Compared with the other "conventional" pressure groups, they are a small, though growing, body; much younger than the others, more compact and quite exceptionally self-confident. As a group they handle between 10 and 15 percent of the net national income, or between 17 and 25 billion rubles that are annually allocated to scientific research, nuclear armament and outer space navigation. The members of this group are undogmatic, or they combine Marxism with an

Reprinted, with permission, from Isaac Deutscher, "Moscow: The Quiet Men," The Nation, *vol. 200, no. IX, April 5, 1965, p. 352 ff.*

ultramodern scientific outlook; they know how indispensable they are to party and state, and are completely unafraid of the party bosses. (It is, for instance, an open secret in Moscow that nuclear scientists are the chief patrons of the artistic avant-garde: they take under their wings the unorthodox poets; they buy abstract paintings and sculptures; and in this way they enable "modernistic" artists to stand up to the wrath of Ilyichev and the other art censors.)

2. The chief planners and managers of heavy industry and of engineering still represent the largest single economic interest in the state. The power of this lobby, however, has been weakened by the antagonism between its central Muscovite elements and the various republican and provincial managerial groups. The central managers suffered a signal defeat in 1957–58, when Khrushchev disbanded the All-Union economic Ministries; now the balance seems to be shifting back in their favor. The men of this lobby work through the Central Planning Commission, the Councils of the National Economy, and directly through the Central Committee.

3. The Trade Union lobby, organized in the All-Union Council of the Trade Unions, has an important say in economic planning as far as it concerns issues of social policy and of the national wage structure. Although the Trade Union bosses represent the interests of the employer-state vis-à-vis the workers, they must also, to some extent, voice the desires of their immense membership, which comprises about 70 million workers and employees. This lobby has been responsible over the last decade for narrowing the wide discrepancies in wages and salaries, and for shortening working hours in industry.

4. The lobby of municipalities partly overlaps the Trade Union lobby. Its importance arises from the fact that since Stalin's death, only twelve years ago, the urban population of the USSR has increased by about 50 million souls—as much as the entire population of Great Britain, or France or Italy. The demand for housing has grown incomparably faster than the housing space provided; and the municipalities and the trade unions have had to press the demand for living accommodations on the ruling group, especially in the last few years, when construction has been falling short of the Plan.

5. The agricultural interest is represented on the one hand by the well-organized and influential chiefs of the state-owned farms, the *Sovkhozy*; and, on the other, by the timid and rather unrepresentative spokesmen of the collective farms, the *Kolkhozy*. State farming had gained much from Khrushchev's decision to bring under the plough vast areas of virgin land—the new farms on those lands are state-owned. However, since the partial fiasco of the experiment, the *Kolkhoz* lobby has been gaining some ground; and it has been further strengthened since Khrushchev's departure.

6. It is not quite clear where exactly in this list the officers corps of the conventional military forces ought to be placed. Its influence has fluctuated violently in the post-Stalin era. Twice it reached peaks: at the moment of Beria's downfall, in the summer of 1953; and by the time of Molotov's and Kaganovich's demotion, in the summer of 1957. The phantom of a Soviet Bonaparte then hovered over the Russian scene; it was laid in the autumn of 1957 with Marshal Zhukov's eclipse. There are signs of a recent rise in its influence, possibly because the conventional forces are recovering part of their old strategic importance. However, for a variety of reasons (the continuing predominance of the nuclear services and the departure of the famous but aging marshals of the last war), this lobby is not likely to recapture the power it had between 1953 and 1957.

7. The leaders of the many academic institutes and their coteries derive much influence from the relevance of their research to issues of national economy. In combination with the nuclear scientists and advanced managers, this lobby has been pressing hard for

speeding the tempo of automation, for the modernization of planning techniques, for the extensive and systematic use of computers.

8. The journalistic and literary lobbies are important for propaganda, so the party leaders and the men of the party machine are sensitive to their pressure. But they are frightened by the dissent spreading among young writers. The power of that dissent showed itself lately in Moscow's Union of Writers, when in an election an overwhelming majority rejected the official candidates and elected "heretics" to the union's board.

Any classification and characterization of these lobbies is bound to be schematic; it cannot reproduce the immense reality of the pressures and counterpressures that are active in a quasi-Socialist state with nearly 230 million citizens. Across the lines of influence described here run the divisions between the geographic regions and the nationalities, Great Russian, Ukrainian, Byelorussian, Georgian, Armenian, Kazakh, Uzbek and others. All this produces an infinite complexity and variety of interests and aspirations acting on party and state from within and without. And the lobbies and pressure groups are themselves subjected to the pressures and counterpressures coming from the depth of society, from the mass of workers and peasants.

Khrushchev's overthrow was brought about by the exceptionally wide front which the lobbies and pressure groups had formed against him in the course of the last year of his government. Two major critical developments brought about this situation: the disastrous state of agriculture and the resultant scarcity of food; and the steep decline, in consequence of the Russo-Chinese feud, of the Soviet influence over the Communist camp. Another factor was the widespread and explosive discontent of the working class, caused in the main by the wage freeze which Khrushchev had been tacitly imposing on industry over a period of four or five years. The full impact of this factor is becoming apparent in the latest information from the USSR. According to certain Soviet opposition circles, which may be described as near Trotskyist, Khrushchev's downfall was preceded by a strike of all workers in Moscow's great ZIS motorcar factory and by many turbulent strikes all over the Donetz Coal Basin. In the Donetz Basin troops were allegedly brought out, and bloody clashes followed in which 200 strikers were killed or wounded. I cannot vouch for the accuracy of the reports about the events in the Donetz Basin, but I have reason to believe the information about the strike in Moscow. The strikes were economic, it seems, and with no political element in them. But they induced the Trade Union lobby to turn against Khrushchev and assist in his overthrow.

While the Soviet press has not given its readers any inkling of these events, Khrushchev's successors have had to begin their term of office by canceling quietly his wage freeze and promising an immediate and radical expansion of the housing program.

These are the real issues and pressures that shape Soviet policy. They are much larger and far more dramatic than any of the personal rivalries at the top of the party hierarchy which fascinate most Western Sovietologists. These fundamental issues decide the outcome even of the personal rivalries; they determine how, in what direction and in whose favor, the lobbies and pressure groups exercise their influence at the level of the Central Committee.

The Brezhnev Era and Citizen Participation

Jerry F. Hough

There has been such an incredible misunderstanding in the West about the nature of policy in the Brezhnev era that it is really best to begin with negatives—to state what policy has not been. The Brezhnev period has *not* been a period of growing repression of individual freedom; it has *not* been a period of declining citizen participation; it has *not* been a period of greater privileges accorded to the "New Class" in comparison with other strata of society; it has *not* been a period of neglect of the consumer; it has *not* been a period of recentralization of the Soviet political system. On the contrary, the trend in policy has been in the opposite direction in these areas. Indeed, the policies of the last decade in each of these areas have represented a continuation of those of the Khrushchev era. In this respect, then, the Brezhnev era has in fact been (to use the phrase of the mid-1960s) "Khrushchevism without Khrushchev."

The basic direction of policy on the questions mentioned in the last paragraph has been so clear that it should be a source of great wonderment that so many Westerners writing about the Soviet Union consider the statements of the last paragraph controversial or even incorrect. Perhaps the problem has been that many Westerners have come to identify so much with dissidents in the Soviet Union that they have judged the current regime by the standard of the hopes and rhetoric of the Khrushchev period rather than of its reality. Perhaps journalists as Adam Ulam suggests, have grown frustrated because they cannot collect "news" as it is understood in the West—"constant streams of revealing and often scandalous goings-on in high circles, spectacular crimes, and social disturbances"—and have let this frustration affect their judgment.[1] Perhaps, also, too few scholars have been conducting primary research on the Brezhnev period and have been relying on the journalists' reports or their own sense of the style of the present leadership.

Most probably, however, the problem in our understanding of the Brezhnev era has been confusion about the phenomenon of "conservatism." In style and rhetoric, Brezhnev and his associates have been much more "conservative" than Khrushchev. The new regime has likewise been much more "conservative" in the way that it tackles problems. No longer is policy implementation characterized by a succession of rather wild campaigns, and no longer is the governmental and party machinery subjected to drastic reorganization almost yearly. Moreover, as will be discussed later, the new leadership is also more "conservative" with respect to challenging the professional judgments of the various specialized establishments in the country.

In the foreign policy realm, the term "conservative" both can and does denote a real change in policy. Early in the Brezhnev era, the Khrushchev predilection for crises and for

At this writing, the author is a professor of political science at Duke University. He has written extensively on Soviet politics. This excerpt is from his article entitled "The Brezhnev Era: The Man and the System," which appeared in Problems of Communism *vol. XXV (March–April 1976), pp. 1–17. For complete footnote references, the reader should consult the original source.*

confrontations and near-ultimatums (as over Berlin) gave way to a tendency to mute conflicts and even to settle them in some cases. . . .

Yet, the word "conservative" can be highly misleading, especially in the realm of domestic policy. Certainly "conservative" in the sense of "cautious" does not necessarily mean "conservative" on freedom-of-speech or social-welfare issues. In the former sphere, the continuation of restrictions on dissent should not blind us to the fact that dissenters have been treated with considerably more gingerliness than they were in the Khrushchev era. (Our increased exposure to the dissenters has been one of the clearest indicators of this phenomenon. Paradoxically, however, we have interpreted the beginning of the visibility of dissent and its repression as the beginning of repression itself.) The variety of statements that can pass the censors into published works is greater than prior to 1964, and the debates are fuller and more wide-ranging. Even Soviet historians writing about the postrevolutionary period—persons widely thought to have suffered the greatest restriction during the Brezhnev period[2]—have generally been able to publish richer, more solid, and more objective work than had been the case earlier.

The broadening of participation in policy debates has been matched by an increase in the scale of participation in different types of groups and in voluntary work for governmental and other political institutions. The "populism" of Khrushchev did not disappear with him, and as Table 1 indicates, the rate of growth in political participation has been much more rapid than that in the size of the adult population. Even the much-discussed slowdown in the increase in party membership resulted less from a reversal of policy than from the movement of the small cohort of World War II babies through the age levels at which persons normally enter the party (see Table 2); certainly, the party has expanded much faster than the adult population.

*[**Editor's note:** The varied, extensive, and specific sources and analyses upon which Professor Hough drew in constructing Tables 1 and 2 are omitted. Interested students should consult the original article in* Problems of Communism *vol. XXV (March–April 1976).]*

The relationship between participation and power is always a peculiarly difficult thing to measure in any country, and one certainly should be wary of concluding that an increase in citizen participation in the Soviet Union automatically means an increase in citizen power. Yet certain types of decentralization of power clearly have occurred. However one wants to conceptualize or label the Soviet political system of the last decade, the General Secretary and/or the Politburo obviously have done much less to override the judgments of the relevant specialists (and power centers) in the various policy areas. Despite the unquestioned right of the Politburo to intervene, the actual exercise of power and influence has often drifted to lower levels of the hierarchy.

While, as will be discussed later, the most obvious decentralization of power has been to the specialized ministerial-party-scientific complexes centered in Moscow, there also seems to have been some de facto delegation of authority to the republic and regional levels as well. For example, an examination of the pattern of increase in hospital beds from region to region of the RSFSR strongly suggests that the effort to enforce rigid central norms slackened in the late 1960s and that local factors became more important in determining the pattern.[3] The degree of actual authority exercised at the republic level—and the degree of variation from republic to republic—has been studied far too little in the West, but the impression grows of greater autonomy (within, of course, well-defined limits).

TABLE 1 Political Participation in the USSR, 1954-76

Group	1954-55	% Increase 1954-63	1963-64	% Increase 1963-76	1975-76
Adult population[a]	120,751,000	16	140,000,000	17	163,510,389
Party members and candidates	6,864,864	51	10,387,196	51	15,694,000
Deputies to local soviets	1,536,310	27	1,958,565	13	2,210,932
Trade union members	40,240,000	60	68,175,600	57	107,000,000
Komsomol members	18,825,324	17	22,000,000	59	35,000,000
"Controllers"	apparently 0	—	4,300,000	118	9,370,000
Activists in "independent organizations"	?	—	20,000,000	55	31,000,000
People's auxiliary policemen (*druzhinniki*)	0	—	5,500,000	27	7,000,000

[a]The effective adult population is defined here in terms of the number of persons registered to vote in elections.

TABLE 2 CPSU Membership in Relation to USSR Population, by Age Groups

Age Group	1965 (%)	1967 (%)	1973 (%)
18-25	3.1	2.2	2.5
26-40	11.0	11.5	11.2
41-50	10.7	11.8	13.0
51+	5.5	6.5	8.0
Total	7.9	8.3	8.9

An outsider cannot judge whether these political changes have had an impact upon policy outcomes, but at a minimum it can be said that the improvement in the living conditions of the consumer, and particularly of the low-income citizens that began under Khrushchev, continued after 1964 as well. The average wage within the worker and employee category rose 62 percent between 1964 and 1975 (from 90 rubles to 146 rubles),[4] and the income of the collective farmer (excluded from the above category) increased even more rapidly. Table 3 indicates the improvement in diet that has accompanied the rise in incomes. The most dramatic change in living standards, however, has involved the acquisition of major appliances. In 1965, only 24 percent of Soviet families had a television set, but in 1974 this figure had reached 71 percent. The percentage of families owning refrigerators grew from 11 percent in 1965 to 56 percent in 1974, while the percentage of those owning washing machines increased from 21 percent to 62 percent.[5] The amount of living space available to the average urban dweller rose from 10.1 square meters in 1964 to 11.8 meters in 1973,[6] and by 1975 over 70 percent of worker and employee families lived in unshared apartments.[7]

Western newsmen going to the Soviet Union always seem to discover to their shock that income and privileges are distributed unevenly, but in reporting that "news," they have totally missed the real news of the last decade in this realm: a continuation of the sharp reduction that began after Stalin's death in the degree of inequality of incomes in the Soviet Union.[8] (After a most careful survey of the data, Peter Wiles asserts that "the

TABLE 3 Changes in Soviet Diet, 1958–73 (annual per capita consumption in kilograms)

Foodstuff	1958	1964	1973
Meat	36	38	53
Milk and dairy products	238	238	307
Eggs (units, not kilograms)	108	113	195
Vegetables	71	74	85
Potatoes	150	140	124
Grain products	172	159	143

Sources: Narodnoye khozyaystvo SSSR v 1965 g. (The National Economy of the USSR in 1965), Moscow, Statistika, 1966, p. 597; *Narodnoye khozyaystvo SSSR v 1973 g.* (The National Economy of the USSR in 1973), Moscow, Statistika, 1974, p. 630.

statistical record since Stalin is a very good one indeed. I doubt if any other country can show a more rapid and sweeping progress towards equality."[9] The ratio of the average earnings of the top 10 percent of Soviet workers and employees (collective farmers excluded) to the average earnings of the bottom 10 percent declined from 4.4 in 1956 to 3.7 in 1964 and to 3.2 in 1970; a ratio of 2.9 was planned for 1975.[10] (Wiles calculates an after-tax ratio of 6.7 for the United States in 1968 and roughly 3.0 for the Eastern European countries.[11] If the earnings of collective farmers were included in the calculation of the ratios (as they are in Eastern Europe), the ratios would be higher, but the rate of decline would also be greater. As Table 4 indicates, the rate of decline would also be greater if the party leadership could break out of its Marxist frame of mind and understand that white collar personnel, particularly in occupations staffed primarily by women, often belong to the truly oppressed strata of society. The wages of members of the working class have been growing much more rapidly than those in the managerial-professional class,

TABLE 4 Changes in Average Wages and in Pensions in the USSR, 1965–73

Group	1965 (in rubles)	1973 (in rubles)	Increase (in %)
Employees of the state apparatus	106	126	19
Industrial engineering-technical personnel	148	185	25
Education and culture employees	94	121	29
Trade and service employees	75	102	36
Industrial white-collar workers	86	119	38
Industrial workers	102	146	43
State-farm workers	72	116	61
Collective farmers	49	87	78
All workers and employees (excluding collective farmers)	97	135	39
	(in billions of rubles)		(in %)
Total budgetary expenditures on pensions	101	184	82

Sources: Most of the figures come from *Narodnoye khozyaystvo SSSR v 1973 g.* (The National Economy of the USSR in 1973), Moscow, Statistika, 1974, pp. 586–87. Those on pensions come from p. 780 of the same work. The figures for collective farmers were calculated by the author on the basis of a Soviet assertion (*Partiynaya zhizn'* [Moscow], no. 20, October 1975, p. 16) that the wages of the collective farmer were 68 percent of those of the state-farm worker in 1965 and 75 percent of them in 1974. It is conceivable that private-plot income for the collective farmer is not included in these figures.

and if the lowly-paid clerks were arbitrarily labeled proletariat and paid accordingly, the system might become considerably more egalitarian.[12]

The efforts of the Brezhnev regime to improve the situation in the countryside have been particularly noticeable. Investment in agricultural productive facilities, amounting to some 14 percent of total capital investment under Khrushchev, rose steadily thereafter to 20 percent in 1973.[13] The electrification program was pushed through to completion, so that 99 percent of peasant homes are now electrified and the amount of electricity used in agriculture has more than tripled in the last decade;[14] the wage policy toward agriculture is reflected in Table 4. Still other steps have been taken to benefit the peasant. Collective farmers were brought under a guaranteed-income system and made eligible for state pensions early in the Brezhnev period, and they were granted an unconditional right to a passport in late 1974. Moreover, the drive for universal secondary education is a program which has its greatest impact in the countryside, while the 1974 decision to step up agricultural production in the non-black-earth regions of the USSR brought about increased cultural as well as economic investment in one of the poorer rural areas of the country.

It should be emphasized once again that all the statements in this section have been comparative ones. The question asked has been: How do the trends in various Soviet policies during the Brezhnev era compare with those in the policies followed by Khrushchev and/or Western leaders? Nothing said here should be taken to imply that censorship has withered away or that certain types of dissent (particularly those of a nationalistic type) do not carry with them a very serious risk of prison. Obviously, top officials in Moscow retain powerful weapons if subordinates attempt to use any delegated authority "unwisely." Similarly, in the realm of social policy, any improvement in living standards continues to be limited by the continuing high rates of investment in heavy industry and the high levels of military expenditure. Conditions on the collective farms have scarcely reached a quality level which would stimulate a migration from the major cities. Yet if the question is the nature of the policy goals of the Brezhnev regime, and if the standard of judgment is not the utopian Marxist image of a Communist society but the performance of political leaders of other industrial countries grappling with the problems of industrial society, then trends in outcomes should be considered more important than the fact that the millenium has not been achieved.

Notes

1. *Adam B. Ulam, "Americans in Russia,"* Saturday Review *(New York), Feb. 7, 1976, p. 29.*
2. *In an article published in this journal in March–April 1972 ("The Soviet Political System—Petrification or Pluralism?"), the present author advanced such a position. Since then, he has had more opportunity to read Soviet histories on the prewar period and to discuss this question fully with a historian who is much more familiar with the subject (Sheila Fitzpatrick), and it seems clear to him that his earlier judgment, which reflected the conventional wisdom, was completely wrong. While current Soviet historians appear to be less free than previously to condemn the Soviet past, they are generally freer to describe sensitive aspects of it in neutral terms. [**Editor's note:** Professor Hough proceeds to list a large number of books published in the Soviet Union in support of his thesis, and concludes that "it should be emphasized that the titles in this list are merely a sample of those that could be given."]*
3. *Jerry F. Hough, "Centralization and Decentralization in the Soviet Administrative System," to be published in a collection of essays,* The Soviet Union and Social Science Theory, *Cambridge, Mass.: Harvard University Press, 1977.*

4. Narodnoye khozyaystvo SSSR v 1973 g. *(The National Economy of the USSR in 1973), Moscow: Statistika, 1974, p. 586;* Pravda, *Feb. 1, 1976, p. 2.*
5. Agitator *(Moscow), No. 23, December 1975, pp. 7 and 9;* Politicheskoye samoobrazovaniye *(Moscow), No. 10, 1975, p. 19. In 1960, 8 percent of Soviet families owned television sets, 4 percent owned refrigerators, and 4 percent owned washing machines. See G.S. Sarkisyan,* Uroven', tempy i proportsii rosta real'nykh dokhodov pri sotsializme *(Level, Rates, and Proportions of Growth of Real Income under Socialism), Moscow: Ekonomika, 1972, p. 103.*
6. *These figures were arrived at by dividing the total number of urban residents into the total fund of urban living space. See* Narodnoye khozyaystvo SSSR v 1964 g. *(The National Economy of the USSR in 1964), Moscow: Statistika, 1965, pp. 7 and 610;* Narodnoye khozyaystvo SSSR v 1973 g., *pp. 7 and 615.*
7. Sotsialisticheskiy trud *(Moscow), No. 9, 1975, p. 128.*
8. *Unfortunately, the two most recent books by reporters fit within this time-worn category. See Robert G. Kaiser,* Russia: The People and the Power, *New York, Atheneum, 1976; and Hedrick Smith,* The Russians, *New York, Quadrangle, 1976.*
9. *Peter Wiles,* Distribution of Income: East and West, *Amsterdam: North-Holland Publishing Company, 1974, p. 25.*
10. *Ibid., p. 25, Table IV, and Sarkisyan, op. cit., p. 132. Wiles, incidentally, draws his data from Sarkisyan, op. cit., pp. 125, 126, and 132.*
11. *Wiles, op. cit., p. 48, Table VIII.*
12. *In 1970, sales clerks were arbitrarily transferred from the category of "mental laborers" to that of "workers." Besides "improving" such statistics as the percentage of workers in the party, this change may also have had a real impact on the way sales clerks are treated by the regime. (Compare, e.g., their wage increases from 1965 to 1973, as shown in Table 4, with those of other "white collar" groups.)*
13. Narodnoye khozyaystvo v 1973 g., *p. 549.*
14. *Ibid., p. 195.*

A Criticism of Hough's Views

Donald Barry

All students of Soviet politics are in Jerry Hough's debt for his writings on the subject. We have come to expect from him a high level of analysis based on meticulous collection of data organized in fresh and original ways. His contribution to *Problems of Communism*, "The Brezhnev Era: The Man and the System" (March–April, 1976), fully lives up to expectations. But a few of his interpretations seem so at odds with generally accepted views (or at least with my personal reading of the situation) that they ought to be challenged in order to give Mr. Hough a chance to elaborate.

Hough says that "the Brezhnev period has *not* been a period of growing repression of individual freedom," which point he supplements by adding that "dissenters have been treated with considerably more gingerliness than they were in the Khrushchev era." Unless Hough is using "individual freedom" and "dissenters" in some highly idiosyncratic way, I can't see that the statements are reasonable at all. Although Khrushchev's actions may have sprung from his own tactical motivations, he allowed Solzhenitsyn to be published and permitted *Novyi mir* and other journals a degree of literary room for maneuver that hasn't been approached since. Although these and other examples from the Khrushchev era don't exactly amount to freedom of speech (Hough's context for the point about treatment of dissenters), they come much closer than what has followed. Khrushchev's actions ushered in two periods of post-Stalin thaw (1956–57 and 1961–62) that have no parallel since his ouster. The frankness and relative honesty of discussions of shortcomings during these periods and the proposals in open publications for *political* reform (as opposed to proposals for mere *policy* changes, which are more characteristic of the present period) are not to be found during the Brezhnev era.

We know considerably less about dissenters during the Khrushchev period than during the Brezhnev period. Certainly there were fewer during the former. It seems likely that the dissent movement grew in large part out of disappointment over the unrealized promise of the Khrushchev thaws. A major manifestation of this disappointment was *samizdat* and the protests associated with it. There was relatively little *samizdat* under Khrushchev. Most people agree that the protest movement received its real impetus from the repression of the purveyors of *samizdat* (or *tamizdat*) during the post-Khrushchev period. The Siniavskiy-Daniel trial in February 1966 is a particular watershed in this respect. In other words, the kind of repression of dissenters that has occurred during the post-Khrushchev era had no analogue when Khrushchev was in power.

Finally, the level of repression is probably judged best not by us on the outside but by those who experience it. My impression from discussions with Soviet friends during visits to Russia after 1964 is that in general the atmosphere has been more repressive than under Khrushchev. Further talks with numerous recent Soviet émigrés only support this point.

At this writing, the author is a professor of government at Lehigh University. He is a specialist in Soviet law and politics. His comment originally appeared in Problems of Communism *vol. XXV (Sept.-Oct. 1976), pp. 93–94.*

Acknowledging all of his faults, many émigrés comment on how people could breathe a bit easier and talk a bit more freely under Khrushchev (a number of comments to this effect may be found in Irina Kirk, ed., *Profiles in Russian Resistance,* New York: Quadrangle, 1975).

Part of Professor Hough's judgment about the differences between the Khrushchev and Brezhnev regimes is based on the data he has gathered on political participation. Hough's interest in participation will be familiar to those who have read certain of his earlier writings, one of which he cites here. Participation, for Hough, has two aspects: "the broadening of participation in policy debates" and "an increase in the scale of participation in different types of groups and in voluntary work for governmental and other political institutions." On the first mode of participation he states that "debates are fuller and more wide-ranging" under Brezhnev and that the top of the political hierarchy in recent years "has done much less to override the judgments of the relevant specialists (and power centers) in the various policy areas." These are extremely broad statements, and Hough offers only a few examples to support them. It would be my guess that the generalization could not be sustained over very many fields. It certainly isn't true, in my opinion, in the field of law, the subject that I follow most closely. But this is really somewhat beside the point because, as I shall argue below, these developments, even if they are as Hough has stated them, have little to do with "freedom of speech" and "repression of individual freedom," the yardsticks by which Hough in these passages set out to measure the Brezhnev regime.

On the second mode of participation, Hough cites published Soviet figures which show sizable increases over the last two decades in the number of party and Komsomol members, local soviet deputies, trade union members, *druzhinniki,* and members of other "voluntary" organizations. Hough calls this "political participation," but I find it hard to take this assertion seriously. Does it really make any sense to call Komsomol or trade union membership either "voluntary" or "political participation"? The very structure and ground rules by which these organizations (and some of the others cited by Hough) operate serve to deny the possibility of meaningful participation.

Approaching participation from another direction, Professor Walter Connor recently came to different (and in my mind, more persuasive) conclusions on the subject ("Generations and Politics in the USSR," *Problems of Communism,* September–October 1975). Connor argues that one of the main characteristics of current Soviet political culture is the apoliticality of the population. The educational system, communications media, and other extrafamilial socialization instruments, including the various collectives to which an individual may belong, serve to depoliticize the populace. They "assure the public that there *are* no more major domestic political issues." In other words, most of the organizations that Hough cites to demonstrate increased political participation don't engage in participation at all; at most they engage in a charade of participation. Most Soviet citizens understand this role and, because of their essential apoliticality, don't find it strange. "To them," according to Connor, "politics, insofar as its existence is perceived, is the business of the leaders, not of the common folk." Connor goes on to talk specifically about *genuine* political participation. Not surprisingly, he finds that (aside from what goes on in certain areas of party and governmental activity) the only participation worthy of the name that exists among members of the general populace is that practiced by the dissidents. In the eyes of the Soviet authorities, this is their "heresy," which is "rooted not so much in opposition as in laying claim to participation. To be a dissident is to enter politics without a license, to participate without official sponsorship. It is to attempt (as do the writings of the Solzhenitsyns, Medvedevs, and Sakharovs) to *restore* 'politics' as a weighing of alternatives. This is the major crime of the dissenters; their break with the apoliticality of the mass political culture.''

In sum, then, Hough cites figures showing the membership growth of certain organizations, but the participation he ascribes to these organizations is in large part sham participation at best. He argues that consultation among specialists is broader and more meaningful. But even if this is true, such consultation is carried out within strictly circumscribed rules of the game; and on a number of very important issues, not even the facade of such consultation is maintained. Finally, as suggested earlier, it is quite misleading to connect either of these developments with ''freedom of speech'' or ''individual freedom.'' Political participation, as defined by Hough, could easily coexist with increasing restrictions on these Soviet constitutional guarantees. That, in fact, is closer to what has been happening in recent years, in my opinion, than the picture Hough describes.

In Reply to Criticism

Jerry F. Hough

There seem to be several points of disagreement between Professor Barry and myself. The first involves trends in the Soviet Union over the last dozen years. Judgments about trends are, of course, based on judgments about both the beginning and the end of the period, and in this case the disagreement may be primarily about the former. I think Professor Barry has a far too rosy picture of the ''good old days'' under Khrushchev. It is absolutely clear that dissenters were ruthlessly suppressed under Khrushchev (see, for example, Chapter 1 in Pavel Litvinov's *The Trial of the Four*) and extremely unclear that the possibility of proposing political reform was so great.

The evidence on the Brezhnev era is voluminous, and since I have laid out much of it both in the *Problems of Communism* article and in ''Political Participation in the Soviet Union'' (*Soviet Studies*, January 1976), it seems inappropriate to do so again. I will only say that the vast majority of my research over the last eight years has centered on the question of participation in the Soviet Union and the West (indeed, one-quarter to one-third of my teaching has been on the subject), and while in an abstract way I will always admit that I can be wrong, I really have no personal doubts whatsoever that, on balance, freedom to participate and the extent of meaningful participation are greater in 1976 in the Soviet

Jerry F. Hough's reply appeared in Problems of Communism vol. XXV (Sept—Oct. 1976), pp. 94–95.

Union than they were in 1964. So far as the dissenters are concerned, clearly they have gotten away with more *samizdat* and especially with more transmission of documents to Western journalists—and for a longer period of time—than they would have under Khrushchev.

A second difference between us may be a methodological one. As I have argued in the political participation article and especially in "The Soviet Experience and the Measurement of Power" (*Journal of Politics*, August 1975), I think we give far too little attention to these matters. Even aside from more esoteric methodological points, it seems to me that we need to become much more rigorous in our assessment of émigré and dissenter evidence.

The Harvard Refugee Project back in the days of the so-called "cold-war" scholarship was extremely cautious in the type of questions it asked and the conclusions it drew. Now that we are dealing with an emigration that is *far* less random (indeed, one that comes in large part from a minority whose view must be shaped by the existence of antisemitism), we are no longer exercising as much care. Perhaps my skepticism has become too great because of my four years of experience at the University of Toronto listening to the New Left American émigrés as they told Canadian listeners about the true nature of the American system, but surely the question of collaborative and documentary evidence is one that a scholar must continually raise. The need for it is particularly great when any group—émigré or otherwise, Soviet or otherwise—begins talking nostalgically about the good old days when they were young. And this is especially true when we recall that good old Khrushchev was initiating the execution of people (primarily with Jewish names) for economic crimes, suppressing *Dr. Zhivago,* instituting exile of "parasites" by public meeting, and so forth.

The third major point of disagreement between Professor Barry and myself concerns the definition of "political participation." To say that the only political participation worthy of the name is that practiced by the dissidents is to use a definition of participation that is often found in Soviet studies, but that is highly idiosyncratic in the literature on political participation in general. Gabriel Almond considers even awareness of the existence of the national government a form of participation, while David Easton would say that a person who tells a friend that the government should do something about inflation is not only engaged in the input of a demand into the political system, but is serving as a gatekeeper.[1] American studies of membership in politically relevant groups invariably include church groups, sports clubs, fraternity organizations, the PTA, adult work in the Boy Scouts, and so forth. Precinct party work—often not all that different from Soviet propaganda and agitation—is considered a sign of a very high level of political activity. I find it wholly wrong to call the United States a participatory society on the basis of such phenomena and then to say that in the Soviet case only frontal attacks on the fundamentals of society constitute political participation.

Undoubtedly the American political system features types of political participation that are not found in the Soviet Union or are found there in very truncated form. But to say that the absence of *some types* of participation means the absence of participation in general is to throw the baby out with the bath water. Even if one wants to discount such activities as trade union and Komsomol membership, involvement in various Komsomol and trade union committees and commissions is far from involuntary, and there is much evidence to suggest that an individual can make an impact through it. The thought that the involvement of over 4 million deputies and nondeputies in work of the committees of the local soviets (which may meet a half-dozen times a year) has no meaning is as difficult for me to accept as the claim that the Soviet population is completely apolitical when 21–22 percent of all men between the ages of thirty and sixty are members of the Communist Party.

To neglect the participation that obviously goes on in the Soviet Union and to concentrate only on the limitations is to destroy the possibility of any meaningful comparisons between the Soviet Union and the West, for we have shifted our definition. Moreover, we have foreclosed the examination of a question of crucial theoretical importance: Of the various types of political participation that exist in the West, which do in fact have an impact upon the distribution of power and the nature of policy outcomes? As I tried to demonstrate in "The Soviet Experience and the Measurement of Power," the answers which we instinctively accept rest on little more than ideological faith.

Notes

1. *See Gabriel Almond and G. Bingham Powell Jr.,* Comparative Politics: A Developmental Approach, *Boston: Little, Brown and Co., 1966; and David Easton,* Systems Analysis of Political Life, *New York: John Wiley and Sons, 1965.*

Chapter 11

LAW AND POLITICS

In *Justice in the USSR*, published in 1963, Harold J. Berman dealt with arguments, on the one hand, that the Soviet legal system was a mere facade masking the rule of naked force and, on the other, that reforms since the death of Stalin (which he described in some detail) had securely established the rule of law. His comments encountered some sharp objections from a Soviet scholar, V.A. Tumanov, to which he subsequently responded.

In a postscript, written in 1979 especially for this volume, Professor Berman elaborates on the continuing tension between the strengthening of legality and the resort to arbitrary political action and force (which characterizes the Soviet system notwithstanding significant improvements noted in the earlier discussion herein of the New Soviet Constitution of 1977).

Roy Medvedev follows with an analysis of the "many serious shortcomings not only in the work of the various bodies concerned with the administration of justice but also in their very structure," particularly as they affect dissidents within the USSR, among whom he is one of the most prominent.

Justice in the USSR

Harold J. Berman

Law and Force

The term Soviet Law will at first seem to many people to be a self-contradiction. It is widely believed that the Soviet system is run solely by terror, the only principle of order being that of hierarchical subordination backed up by the secret police. From the proposition that the Soviet regime places heavy reliance on the use of force, it is often deduced that the Soviet legal system is merely windowdressing.

These are dangerous delusions, which in the long run only weaken us. They conceal the inner resources of the Soviet social order. The Soviets do have a working legal system, founded on rather definite principles of law and justice.

A system of law and a system of force exist side by side in the Soviet Union. There are certain areas into which law penetrates only slightly. For example, until 1953 a person who was suspected of antagonism to the regime could be picked up by the secret police, held incommunicado for a long period of time, tried secretly by an administrative board, and sentenced to hard labor—without benefit of defense counsel and without any possibility of appeal. On the other hand, there are other areas which even under Stalin were on the whole governed by well-defined legal standards. For example, crimes such as theft or assault or murder, suits between state business enterprises for breach of contract, disputes over rights of inheritance, workers' grievances against wrongful treatment by management, and many other types of conflict within the social order, were and are generally dealt with publicly by regular procedures and established norms.

One would suppose that political and ideological repression would undermine the legal system. How can there be respect for law when the most important political decisions are made secretly behind the scenes and when the rulers themselves have no qualms about resorting to force when they feel that the stability of the regime is threatened? The evidence tends to show a surprising degree of official compartmentalization of the legal and the extralegal.

In this connection we might recall the experience of the Roman Empire. The absolutism of the Imperial rule, and its brutality, did not prevent the coexistence of a legal system. A modern illustration may be found in the United States, where the fact that in some areas Negroes are often deprived of a fair trial and are sometimes victims of violence does not mean that law is nonexistent in those areas. In each of the examples cited, the acceptance of force and violence in certain types of situations undoubtedly has a deleterious influence on the legal system as a whole. But that influence may be a subtle one. . . .

Harold J. Berman is the James Barr Ames Professor of Law, Harvard Law School. He is the author of many books on Soviet law as well as on other subjects relating to comparative law, legal history, and legal philosophy. *This excerpt is reprinted by permission of the publishers from Harold J. Berman,* Justice in the USSR, *rev. ed., pp. 7–8, 67–88, 91–94, 165–167, 282–284, Cambridge, Mass.: Harvard University Press, © 1950, 1963 by the President and Fellows of Harvard College.*

Soviet Law Reform after Stalin

The attack upon Stalinist terror facilitated the introduction of wholesale reforms in almost every branch of Soviet law. Indeed, the law reform movement which started in 1953 and gathered increasing momentum throughout the following years may prove to have been the most significant aspect of Soviet social, economic and political development in the decade after Stalin's death.

In interpreting this reform movement, however, one must start with Stalin—however much his successors would have liked to expunge his name from the memory of their people. For despite the very substantial changes which they introduced, the Soviet legal system remained Stalinist in its basic structure and its basic purposes. The organization and functions of the lawmaking, law-enforcing, and law-practicing agencies—of the legislature, the Procuracy, the courts, the administrative organs, the bar—were not essentially different ten years later from what they were when Stalin died. The main outlines of Soviet criminal law and procedure, civil law and procedure, labor law, agrarian law, family law, administrative law, constitutional law, and other branches of the Soviet legal tree—remained basically the same as before.

Also, if one looks behind the structure to the purposes of Soviet law, it remained a totalitarian law, in the sense that it sought to regulate all aspects of economic and social life, including the circulation of thought, while leaving the critical questions of political power to be decided by informal, secret procedures beyond the scrutiny or control either of legislative or judicial bodies. It remained the law of a one-party state. It remained the law of a planned economy. It remained a law whose primary function is to discipline, guide, train, and educate Soviet citizens to be dedicated members of a collectivized and mobilized social order.

If this is so, it may be asked, what is the significance of the post-Stalin reforms? Indeed, many Western observers treated each successive development in Soviet law after Stalin's death as mere smoke without fire—or even as a smokescreen designed to conceal the absence of any fire. Others viewed the reforms as half-hearted concessions designed to appease the appetite of the Soviet people without really satisfying their hunger. The foreign journalist in Moscow—and the readers of his articles at home—tend to see a whirling, eddying stream. The only solution is to seek a composite picture, from various perspectives.

Such a composite picture would reveal at least seven major tendencies in Soviet law reform in the decade after March 1953:

First, there was a tendency toward the elimination of political terror.

Second, there was a tendency toward the liberalization both of procedure and of substantive norms.

Third, there was a tendency toward the systematization and rationalization of the legal system.

Fourth, there was a tendency toward decentralization and democratization of decision making.

Fifth, there was a tendency to introduce popular participation in the administration of justice.

Sixth, there was a tendency in 1961 and 1962 to threaten those who will not cooperate in building communism with harsh criminal and administrative penalties.

Seventh, there was developed a new Soviet theory of state and law which rejected some of the Stalinist innovations in Leninist doctrine.

The Tendency toward the Elimination of Terror

Important steps were taken after March 1953 to eliminate those features of the previous Soviet law which permitted the disguise of terror in legal form.

First, the Special Board of the Ministry of Internal Affairs was abolished. It was this Special Board which had been the chief instrument of terror. It was a three-man administrative committee—the Russians called it a troika—which was empowered by a 1934 statute to send people to labor camps without a hearing, in a secret administrative procedure, without right of counsel and without right of appeal.

Second, the security police were deprived of the power to conduct investigations of crimes under their own special rules without supervision by the Procuracy.

Third, the special procedures for court cases involving the most serious antistate crimes were abolished. The laws of 1934 and 1937 permitting persons charged with certain such crimes to be tried secretly, in absentia, and without counsel, were repealed.

Fourth, the military courts, which had previously had a wide jurisdiction over civilians, particularly in the case of political crimes, were deprived of all jurisdiction over civilians except for espionage.

Fifth, the law permitting punishment of relatives of one who deserts to a foreign country from the armed forces—though they knew nothing of the desertion—was abolished.

Sixth, Vyshinsky's doctrine that confessions have special evidentiary force in cases of counterrevolutionary crimes—based on the transparently false notion that people will not confess to such crimes unless they are actually guilty—was repudiated; confessions were now treated as having no evidentiary force in themselves, and the matter contained in a confession must be corroborated by other evidence.

Seventh, Vyshinsky's doctrine that the burden of proof shifts to the accused in cases of counterrevolutionary crimes was also repudiated. The new Soviet codes place the burden of proving the guilt of the accused squarely on the prosecutor. Although the phrase "presumption of innocence" is avoided in the codes, all that American jurists generally mean by that phrase is spelled out in Soviet law.

Eighth, Vyshinsky's broad definition of complicity, borrowed from the Anglo-American doctrine of conspiracy, was repudiated. Persons may no longer be held liable for acts of their associates unless they intended those acts to take place.

Ninth, the law on so-called "counterrevolutionary crimes" was slightly narrowed and made a little less vague. The term "counterrevolutionary" was eliminated and the term "state" (i.e., anti-state) substituted. The crime of "terrorist acts," which hitherto had been interpreted to include any violent act against a state or Party official, or, indeed, his close relatives, whatever the motive, was restricted to murder or serious bodily injury of the official himself committed for the purpose of overthrowing or weakening the Soviet authority. The law on state secrets was substantially relaxed—though it is still far wider in its scope than most Americans would consider tolerable—and a new list of information constituting a state secret was enacted which is less broad and more precise than the earlier list.

Finally, there took place from 1955 to 1957 a systematic reexamination of all cases of persons previously convicted of counterrevolutionary crimes and the release from labor camps of the overwhelming majority of such persons, with full rehabilitation.

The restoration of procedural due process of law in political cases is a signal achievement of the post-Stalin regime. The Soviet citizen is now protected against police terror, false charges and faked trials to a far greater extent than ever before in Soviet history. No longer need he fear the midnight knock on the door as a prelude to transportation to a Siberian labor camp without a fair hearing.

Yet one cannot speak of the total elimination of political terror so long as open opposition to Communist Party policy—the "Party line"—can lead to criminal sanctions, however "objectively" and "correctly" imposed. The 1958 Statute on State Crimes carries over from the earlier law on counterrevolutionary crimes the provision against "agitation or propaganda" directed against the Soviet system. To defame the Soviet political and social system, or even to possess written materials of such defamatory nature, if for the purpose of weakening Soviet authority, is punishable by deprivation of freedom of up to seven years.

The law of anti-Soviet agitation and propaganda is only one of many features which keep alive the fear of Soviet citizens that the terror may return. This fear, and the conditions which give rise to it, will be discussed more fully below. But it is important to stress at this point that the fear of a return to terror is itself a form of terror. Therefore, one must view the developments of the ten years after Stalin's death as reflecting only a tendency—though an extremely important tendency—toward the elimination of terror.

The Liberalization of Soviet Law

Even apart from political crimes, Soviet law underwent substantial liberalization after Stalin's death. It would be impossible to list the hundreds, indeed thousands, of needed reforms which were introduced. A brief account of some of the most important may suffice, however, to indicate the direction and scope of the tendency toward liberalization.

In criminal law and procedure, the "tightening up" of the rules with respect to burden of proof, the evaluation of confessions, and the doctrine of complicity gave increased protection to persons accused of other, as well as political, crimes. In addition, the right to counsel prior to trial, though still limited, was significantly extended; time for supervisory review of an acquittal in a criminal case, formerly unlimited, was reduced to one year; powers of search and seizure were somewhat restricted; the doctrine of analogy, whereby a person who committed a socially dangerous act not specifically made punishable by law could be sentenced under a law proscribing an analogous act, was finally eliminated; penalties were substantially lightened for many crimes—for example, new laws imposing lighter sentences for petty rowdyism ("hooliganism") and petty theft of state or public property removed the necessity of many long years in labor camps for such trivial offenses; some crimes were eliminated altogether—for example, abortion and also absenteeism from work and quitting one's job without permission. Large-scale amnesties of 1953 and 1957 released all except those sentenced for, or charged with, the most serious offenses.

With respect to the system of detention, a 1957 law eliminated the term "labor camp," substituting "labor colony" for all places of confinement (except prisons, which are used only for temporary detention or, very rarely, for the most serious crimes) and introduced a new regime for prisoners which permits far more leniency in their treatment. Those convicted of less serious crimes are permitted to have their wives (or husbands) visit and stay with them from time to time; they are paid substantial wages for their work and are required to send home allotments to their dependents. Also liberal parole provisions were introduced.

Liberalization was not confined to criminal policy. After 1953, and especially after 1955, there was a reexamination of every branch of law and a weeding out of many of the harshest features. For example, a new civil right was created to obtain a court order for public retraction of a newspaper libel. In labor law, the rights of trade unions were enhanced and the procedures for settlement of workers' grievances were improved. Similar examples could be multiplied from many other fields of law.

In 1961 and 1962 there was a contrary trend, away from liberalization, in certain areas. These backward steps, however, did not stop the liberal momentum of the post-Stalin reforms.

Systematization and Rationalization

The tendency toward liberalization of law generally is, of course, an important supporting buttress of the tendency toward elimination of political terror. For such tendencies to have permanence, however, deeper foundations are required in the legal system as a whole. From that standpoint, the efforts of the post-Stalin regime to systematize and rationalize the Soviet legal system are of great significance. . . . Only with the removal of the political and ideological pressure of Stalinist autocracy did it become possible to introduce new codes, and, together with them, a reorganization of the entire system of legal administration.

The first major event in this development was the adoption in August 1955 of a new Statute on Procuracy Supervision. The Procuracy is the cornerstone of the Soviet legal system. It combines functions of our Department of Justice, Congressional investigating committees, and grand juries. It not only investigates and prosecutes crimes, but it supervises the entire system of administration of justice, and has power to investigate and protest to higher authorities (whether administrative or judicial) any abuse of law which comes to its attention. Until 1955 it operated on the basis of a 1922 statute upon which were encrusted many legislative and administrative modifications. The 1955 statute clarified and consolidated its supervisory powers over judicial and administrative acts. Incidentally, the new statute also added sanctions against officials of the Procuracy for negligence in failing to expose illegal practices in places of detention of criminals.

The second major event was the removal of certain aspects of Ministry of Justice control over the courts and the reorganization of the Supreme Court of the USSR and of the republican and regional courts. This took place in 1956 and 1957. The result was a streamlining of the court system and an increase in its independence.

In December 1958 the Supreme Soviet of the USSR adopted a series of Fundamental Principles of various branches of law—Fundamental Principles of Criminal Law, Fundamental Principles of Criminal Procedure, and Fundamental Principles of Court Organization—together with new comprehensive Statutes on State Crimes, Military Crimes, and Military Tribunals. Subsequently, in December 1961, the Supreme Soviet adopted

Fundamental Principles of Civil Law and of Civil Procedure. As of 1962, Fundamental Principles of Family Law and of Labor Law were in preparation [and subsequently adopted]; indeed, a Statute on the Procedure for the Hearing of Labor Disputes adopted in 1957 was itself a systematization of many aspects of labor law.

On the basis of the various Fundamental Principles, the republics adopted their own new codes of criminal law and criminal procedure and in 1962 were in the last stages of work on new codes of civil law and civil procedure [also subsequently enacted].

Of the many other important pieces of legislation of the first post-Stalin decade, mention should also be made of the 1961 statute on administrative commissions of local municipal councils, which restricted the powers of administrative bodies to impose fines and established a procedure for appealing from such fines; the 1960 Statute on State Arbitrazh, which reorganized the procedures for hearing the hundreds of thousands of contract disputes which arise each year between state economic enterprises; and the new statutes on the organization of the legal profession in the various republics, which strengthen the independence of the advocate and his responsibility to his client. . . .

The systematization and rationalization of Soviet law is not something which can be accomplished in a few years. Indeed, it is something which must go on continually. The recognition of its importance, and the very great efforts devoted to it, are an encouraging sign of the determination of the post-Stalin regime to establish a far higher degree of legal security than that which existed in the past.

The Tendency toward Decentralization and Democratization

Implicit in the tendencies toward an all-embracing, liberalized and systematic legality is the belief in the possibility of a wide decentralization of decision-making and a still wider participation of the public in the formulation of issues for decision.

Two qualifications must be made at the outset, however, in discussing the tendency of the post-Stalin period of Soviet history toward greater decentralization and democratization. The first is that there has been no sign that the present Soviet leadership has any intention of allowing this tendency to go beyond its power to control it. The limits of decentralized decision-making and democratization are set by the central authorities. The second qualification is that this theory of "democratic centralism"—centralization of authority combined with decentralization of operations—was also Stalin's theory. The difference since his death is a difference in degree. . . .

The comprehensive legislation enacted in the late 1950s and early 1960s were worked on by representatives of hundreds, indeed thousands, of organizations. All the major governmental agencies expressed detailed views on their various provisions. There was endless discussion of them in the universities, in research institutes, in economic organizations of various kinds, in scholarly journals, and in the daily press. . . .

Of course it would be a mistake to suppose that Soviet federalism and Soviet democracy involve—as ours do—a struggle between opposing political units and groups, a competition for political leadership. In the Soviet Union all power resides in the Communist Party, which remains, as stated in the Constitution, the "central core" of all organizations, whether they be state organizations or social organizations. Despite the development of greater intra-Party democracy after 1953, the Party remains a disciplined elite, subservient to its leadership. Decentralization and democratization of decision-making in the spheres of government, law, and economic administration are not a threat to Party supremacy; indeed, they are required by the Party as a means of maintaining its supremacy.

Yet Party control is, in a much deeper sense, challenged by the development of autonomous centers of discussion and initiative, even though it remains the "central core" of such centers. The cohesion of Soviet jurists, for example, is striking. Whether they are judges, procurators, Ministry of Justice officials, law professors, research workers, legal advisers of state institutions and enterprises, advocates, or notaries, the seventy to eighty thousand jurists in the Soviet Union are bound together by the closest professional ties. They meet together in many different kinds of activity; they discuss and debate common problems; they work together; and they are bound not only by their common legal education but also by their common vested interest in the preservation of legality. As a class, they have grown greatly in importance during the years after Stalin's death.

Popular Participation in the Administration of Justice

No doubt both the leaders and the people are greatly relieved at the decrease in emphasis upon terror and coercion and the increase in emphasis upon the liberal, rational and democratic elements in their legal system. But these elements are not—for the leaders, at least—ends in themselves, but rather a means toward lifting their society to new heights of economic progress, political power and social solidarity.

Law is conceived as a major instrument for achieving these goals. Law is conceived, above all, as a means of educating Soviet people to be the type of socially conscious, dedicated members of society which are required if socialism is to be maintained and if communism is to be achieved. . . .

It is Soviet theory that under communism the functions of state organizations (which operate in part by coercion) will be turned over entirely to social organizations (which operate only by persuasion). In anticipation of this glorious day, the role of social organizations was greatly increased from about 1959 on. Neighborhood and factory meetings were convened for a variety of purposes and were given certain semijudicial functions. Also a voluntary auxiliary police force was organized—the so-called *druzhiny,* or bands—to help keep order; they direct traffic, take drunks into custody, and in general attempt to enforce law and order among the people on the streets. In addition many special volunteer commissions have been formed and given semiofficial status—to observe conditions in the labor colonies and to make recommendations, to report to municipal councils on housing questions, to report on local observance of "socialist legality," and for a host of similar purposes. Trade unions and the Young Communist League (Komsomol) are also considered to be social organizations, and their functions have been extended. . . .

For example, the Komsomol organizations in the universities call for student volunteers to work during the summer holidays in the so-called "virgin lands" of the East. The volunteers are recruited, however, by lists posted on bulletin boards, and refusal to go courts expulsion from the Komsomol and probably—at least it is so assumed by the students—from the university.

A second example may be found in the activities of the "Comrades' Courts," now operating under a 1960 statute, which meet in apartment houses or in factories to consider minor offenses committed by neighbors or fellow-workers. Their punitive powers are limited to a ten-ruble fine. Mostly they issue reprimands and warnings. However, they may also recommend eviction from the apartment or disciplinary action (including demotion but not discharge) by the factory management. Such eviction or disciplinary action may be resisted through regular court proceedings, but nevertheless the recommendation of the Comrades' Court is a serious matter.

One other example: Soviet courts sometimes go "on circuit," so to speak, to apartments or factories, to hear criminal cases involving persons in those places. The purpose is to demonstrate to the entire "collective" and to the public the social danger of the offenses charged and to educate people in the requirements of the law. But the tendency to convict and to mete out harsh punishment is very strong when such an educational purpose is in the forefront of the procedure itself.

Some Western students of the Soviet scene have exaggerated the evils of this kind of new "social justice." To evaluate them properly, one must put oneself in the Soviet situation, where true social cooperation in informal voluntary groups, entirely independent of the state, hardly exists. The Comrades' Courts in action have impressed outside observers by the good spirit with which they are received. Especially important is the fact that their powers are very limited and that these limits are enforced by the courts and by the legal system.

The great danger, of course, is the potentiality of abuse of these social organizations by the Communist Party and the state. The still greater danger is the dream of a far-off time when there will be no legal system and no state but only one vast social organization, one vast Communist Party. It is, no doubt, a dream which can never be realized; but so long as it is held it inhibits the achievement of true legal security.

The Return to Harsh Criminal and Administrative Penalties

A sixth major tendency in Soviet law in the post-Stalin period was the return in 1961 and 1962 to harsh criminal and administrative penalties against those who refuse to cooperate in building communism.

In May and June 1961, the three largest republics, comprising three-fourths of the Soviet population, finally enacted the notorious antiparasite law which had been first proposed for public discussion in 1957 and later adopted in the smaller republics during 1957 to 1960. This law, in its final form, provides for "resettlement" (*vyselenie*) in "specially designated localities," for two to five years, of persons who "are avoiding socially useful work and are leading an antisocial parasitic way of life." Money or property acquired by such persons "by nonlabor means" is subject to confiscation. Persons may be sentenced under this law by the judges of the regular courts in a summary procedure and without the usual guarantees of the criminal law and without right of appeal, or else by general meetings in the factories or collective farms with review by the local municipal council.

To a Western lawyer, and—judging from private conversations—to many Soviet lawyers as well, the antiparasite laws contradict the provision of the 1958 Fundamental Principles of Criminal Procedure that no person may be punished for a crime except by sentence of a court. Official Soviet doctrine, however, has reconciled these laws with the Fundamental Principles on the more-than-tenuous theory that the offender is not being punished for a crime, nor is he being confined; he is simply "resettled" in another place where he must take a socially useful job! This is considered an "administrative," not a "penal," measure.

In the first year of the operation of this law in the RSFSR, according to a statement made by the Minister of Justice at a public lecture in Moscow in May 1961, 10,000 people in Moscow were charged under the antiparasite law; 8,000, he said, received only warnings; 2,000 were sent out of Moscow; of these, only a small number were subjected to confiscation of property. It may be inferred from the relatively few instances of confiscation that the law is principally a device for getting rid of vagrants and putting them to work.

Also, the extension of the death penalty in 1961 and 1962 to a wide variety of crimes, many of them economic crimes not involving violence, reflected the regime's determination to take extreme measures against those who most flagrantly violate the tenets of communist morality. In May 1961, the death penalty (which had been abolished altogether in 1947, and restored in 1950 for treason, espionage, wrecking, terrorist acts and acts of banditry, and in 1954 for murder committed under aggravating circumstances) was extended to theft ("plunder") of state or social property in especially large amounts, counterfeiting money or securities for profit, and the commission of violent attacks in places of detention by especially dangerous recidivists or persons convicted of serious crimes. In July 1961, the death penalty was extended to speculation in foreign currency. In February 1962, it was extended to attempts upon the life of a policeman or volunteer auxiliary policeman (*druzhinnik*) on duty, to rape committed by a group or by an especially dangerous recidivist or entailing especially grave consequences or committed on a minor, and to the taking of bribes under aggravating circumstances by an official who holds a responsible position or who has been previously tried for bribery or has taken bribes repeatedly.

In a case tried in July 1961, the statute imposing the death penalty for foreign currency speculation was applied retroactively by a special decree of the Presidium of the Supreme Soviet authorizing the retroactive application "as an exception" in the specific case. (The decree was never published as it was not considered to be "of general significance.") There is reason to believe that there were other such cases of retroactive application of the death sentence, specially authorized by similar edicts. The 1961 law was the first example of a Soviet criminal law expressly made retroactive, so far as the author has been able to discover, since 1929.

Judging from Soviet press accounts of individual trials, probably over 250 Soviet citizens were executed for economic and other crimes in the year from May 1961 to May 1962, and probably an equal or greater number were executed from June to December 1962. One can only say "probably" because Soviet crime statistics are a state secret! (In 1961, 43 persons were executed in the United States.)

This harsh policy was also reflected in increased penalties for lesser crimes. Soviet jurists have publicly criticized the tendency of some procurators and courts to treat the imposition of the death penalty for serious crimes as a signal for reversing the entire trend toward liberalization.

What significance should we attach to these developments? As is so often the case with violations of basic principles of judicial procedure, the particular individual victims do not command our affection. They were, presumably, scoundrels. It is rather the abuse of the integrity of the legal process that concerns us, for one abuse suggests another.

During the years after Stalin's death much was heard of "the thaw"—to use the title of Ilya Ehrenburg's 1954 novel—that is, the unfreezing of Soviet life, the reduction of terror, the increased freedom to criticize, the greater encouragement of individual initiative, the relaxation of tensions. But the *long-range* problem of government in the Soviet Union is whether the Soviet leaders are willing and able to establish not merely a season, or a climate, or a policy, of freedom and initiative, but also a legal and institutional foundation which will make freedom and initiative secure from their own intervention. Until that problem is solved, the fear of a return to Stalinist terror will haunt the Soviet people, and especially the intellectuals. In research institutes and universities, as well as among educated people generally, debates rage over the "liquidation of the consequences of the cult of personality," which is Party jargon for preventing a recurrence not only of violence but also of all the rigidities that went with it. Nobody wants such a recurrence. But nobody can guarantee that it won't happen.

In 1957, Deputy Procurator General P.I. Kudriavtsev, responding to a series of questions on guarantees against a return to Stalinist terror, said to the author: "Do not forget that we have in the Soviet Union the dictatorship of the proletariat, and that law must serve the state authority." To the question: "Suppose the law conflicts with the interests of the state, which prevails?"—he replied, "The interests of the state." He amplified: "Compulsion may be necessary. The Special Board of the MVD was necessary in its time, in the 'thirties. Only it was later abused. The Cheka, which Lenin introduced, was entirely justified. No revolution is bloodless—ours is the most bloodless revolution in history, far more bloodless than the French or English revolutions." I asked: "When will your revolution be over?" He replied: "We live in an age of war and revolution. The revolution goes on." And then, to make crystal clear the connection between this basic historical perspective and the law reforms we had been discussing, he said: "If it becomes necessary we will restore the old methods. But I think it will not be necessary."

In addition to preserving the possibility of a return to physical terror "if it becomes necessary," Khrushchev replaced the Stalinist dualism of law and terror by a new dualism of law and social pressure: one is free from arbitrary arrest by the secret police, but one is not free from the social pressure of the "collective"—whether it be the more innocuous pressure of the collective of the neighbors in the crowded apartment houses or the less innocuous pressure of the factory, one's co-workers, or the local Party organization. The new dualism still stands in the shadow of the old.

Yet it would be a great mistake to assume that the "thaw" ended with the harsher methods adopted in 1961 and 1962. Such an assumption underestimates the importance of the legal and institutional changes which had in fact taken place. The law reforms had already counted. They had acquired a momentum which was hard to stop. A vast structure of procedures and rights had been built, and though its foundations needed to be greatly strengthened, it was not something which could easily be toppled.

The Reform of Soviet Theory of State and Law. . .

The theoretical question of the nature and functions of law during and after the period of transition to communism is one that has exercised the ingenuity of Soviet jurists. The definition of law given by Vyshinsky in 1938, which of necessity was accepted in all published legal writings thereafter, stressed three elements: the source of law in the will of the state (ruling class), the sanction for law in the coercive power of the state, and the nature of law as a body of rules. . . .

The question of the nature of law bears directly, of course, upon the role it is to play in a society conceived of as moving away from institutions of coercion toward institutions of persuasion and cooperation. If those who tend toward the narrower concept of law reflected in Vyshinsky's definition win the day, it would appear that law will continue to be under the theoretical cloud of the "withering away" doctrine. If the broader concept gains the favor of the Communist Party leadership, the sharp distinction between the coercive functions of law and the cooperative nature of the ideal society will be blunted and law will be considered to have not merely a temporary but a permanent value for communist society. . . .

However academic such a question may appear, it has a strong bearing on the attitudes of Soviet people—both leaders and led—toward the absolute value of law. If law is defined as norms enacted by the state and enforced by the coercive sanctions of the state, it is destined, like the state, to find its way ultimately into the "museum of antiquities" (to use Engels' phrase). If, however, law is defined as an institutional process of resolution of conflicts, based on general standards objectively applied—a definition which many Americans would endorse and toward which some Soviets are groping—then it is not inconsistent with the "unified, generally recognized rules of communist social life," observance of which will become the "inner need and habit of all people" under communism, according to the Party Program. . . .

Marxism and Socialist Law

Both partisans and antagonists of the Soviet system tend to view Soviet institutions in terms of the extent to which they embody Marxist theory. This frame of reference has served as a starting point for the present study. Marx said: Economics is basic; law is superstructure, designed to serve the interests of the ruling economic class. The Soviet leaders say: Within the Soviet Union we have eliminated class exploitation and antagonism; our law reflects the classless—or class-conflictless—socialist character of our planned economy. Having analyzed some of the features of Soviet law which stem from socialism, and in particular those aspects of the legal system which implement and protect the planned economy, we may inquire to what extent it is a concrete expression of Marxism.

Affirmatively, three outstanding features of Soviet law may be traced in part to its Marxist heritage. The first is its collectivist character. The Marxist principle of totality, of the basic unity of all social relations, finds expression in the integration of politics and economics and in the conscious treatment of legal problems as social problems. Even a lawsuit between two Soviet citizens has an explicit social character, since the state is interested in fixing responsibility. This is especially important in cases involving state economic enterprises, where Arbitrazh has the duty of "signalizing" gross misconduct on the part of directors to the appropriate administrative organ or to the prosecutor's office.

Second, the dialectical character of Soviet socialist law manifests its Marxist orientation. Despite the struggle for stability, Soviet law changes rapidly to meet changing conditions. It is not static or conceptual. It tolerates logical contradictions and inconsistencies even more readily than our law does. The emphasis on the social-economic purpose of rights is still strong, despite the restoration of the "formal-juridical"element as having equal importance. In particular, the administrative structure of industry undergoes almost continual change. The drive for strict legality is itself conceived in the interests of dynamic social development.

Third, the influence of Marxist theory may be seen in the Soviet emphasis on extra-legal and nonlegal means of social control, and the subordination of law to those extra- and nonlegal means. Marxism is a theory of power. Law is created by the social order, which itself, however, is considered to be based ultimately on force. When its existence is threatened, the social order may be compelled, for its own preservation, to abandon law and to revert to its ultimate sanction. Thus Soviet law is always precarious; the secret police may step in at any time. Marxism is also a theory of social harmony. The communist society, in its ideal form, requires only a minimum either of force or of law. In order to reach its goal, the socialist order therefore stresses the development of nonlegal social sanctions, especially those associated with membership in the Communist Party and with Party propaganda and agitation.

Despite these characteristics, the Soviet legal system, even in its socialist aspects, cannot be explained satisfactorily as a Marxist system. The very existence of "socialist law" is an innovation in Marxist theory, and a contradiction of the spirit of Marxism if not its letter. Moreover, many of the features of Soviet law which are considered by the Soviet rulers to be peculiarly socialist bear striking resemblance to the law of those societies which they condemn as capitalist.

In seeking to construct an affirmative theory of law, the Soviet rulers are handicapped by their Marxist heritage. The Marxist features of the Soviet legal system are limiting features. But in spite of Marxism, the Soviet rulers have found law necessary—necessary to the planned economy itself—not only because of the rationality and calculability which a legal system provides, but also because of the assurance which it gives to those who operate the economy that their acts will be judged according to some standard of rightness. The rational allocation of resources requires a reasonable adjudication of rights and duties. . . .

Law as a Teacher and Parent

Of course every system of law educates the moral and legal conceptions of those who are subject to it. In the *Digest of Justinian* it is explicitly recognized that the task of law is the moral improvement of the people. Thurman Arnold describes the judicial trial as a "series of object lessons and examples." "It is the way in which society is trained in right ways of thought and action, not by compulsion, but by parables which it interprets and follows voluntarily." Justice Brandeis was a leading exponent of the view that the courts should recognize the importance of their educational function.

Nevertheless, the educational role of law has not been traditionally regarded as central. Law has been conceived primarily as a means of delimiting interests, of preventing interference by one person in the domain of another, of enforcing rights and obligations established by the voluntary acts of the parties insofar as that is compatible with the social welfare. It has been assumed that the persons who are the subjects of law, the litigants or potential litigants, know their own interests and are capable of asserting them, that they are independent adults whose law-consciousness has already been formed. . . .

In the Soviet system, on the contrary, the educational role of law has from the beginning been made central to the concept of justice itself. Law still has the functions of delimiting interests, of preventing interference, of enforcing the will and intent of the parties—but the center of gravity has shifted. The subject of law, legal man, is treated less as an independent possessor of rights and duties, who knows what he wants, than as a dependent member of the collective group, a youth, whom the law must not only protect against the consequences of his own ignorance but must also guide and train and discipline. The law now steps in on a lower level, on what in the past has been a prelegal level. It is concerned with the relationships of the parties apart from the voluntary acts by which their alleged rights and duties were established; it is concerned with the whole situation, and above all, with the thoughts and desires and attitudes of the people involved, their moral and legal conceptions, their law-consciousness. Soviet law thus seeks not simply to delimit and segregate and define, but also to unite and organize and educate. The result is the creation of entirely new legal values within a framework of language and doctrine which otherwise appears conventional and orthodox.

It is apparent that the Soviet emphasis on the educational role of law presupposes a new conception of man. The Soviet citizen is considered to be a member of a growing, unfinished, still immature society, which is moving toward a new and higher phase of development. As a subject of law, or a litigant in court, he is like a child or youth to be trained, guided, disciplined, protected. The judge plays the part of a parent or guardian; indeed, the whole legal system is parental.

It should be understood that the words "parental" and "educational" as used in this context are morally inconclusive. The parent or guardian or teacher may be cruel or benevolent, angry or calm, bad or good. He may dislike the child. But he is responsible for the child's upbringing. To speak of "parental law" is therefore not so much to describe the state which proclaims and applies the law as to describe the assumptions which are made regarding the nature of the citizen and his relationship to the state. To say that under Soviet law the state has extended the range of its interests and its powers is not enough. The state has sought in law a means of training people to fulfill the responsibilities now imposed on them—and it has made this function of law central to the whole legal system.

"Parental law" may be implicit in the actual practice of socialism as such. It surely has deep roots in Russian history. Yet it is essential to isolate the parental features of Soviet law from both its socialist and its Russian background, for parental law is not restricted to socialism or to Russia. According to Karl Llewellyn, "our own law moves steadily in a parental direction."

A Criticism of Berman's Views

V.A. Tumanov

The basic ideas permeating [Harold Berman's] book are essentially a reflection in law of certain of the general theses of contemporary anticommunism. . . . The worn-out slogan of the alleged "incompatibility of socialism and law" has been paid homage to for many years in the West, and recently perhaps even more than before. . . .

At first glance, it may appear to a reader of Berman's book that its author is departing from this anticommunist stereotype. In fact, he calls it a "dangerous delusion" to deny the existence of law in Soviet society. "The Soviets do have a working legal system, founded on rather definite principles of law and justice," he writes.

However, it was not by accident that we employed the expression "at first glance." For, following this admission, the entire subsequent presentation of the book tends essentially to return to this same basic position, although perhaps in a somewhat more refined fashion.

Let us begin with the fact that Berman has long held that the existence of law under socialism contradicts, if not the letter, then the spirit of Marxism. In his new book he repeats once again that "the Soviet system cannot be explained satisfactorily as a Marxist system of law. The very existence of 'socialist law' is an innovation in Marxist theory." Essentially, Berman repeats, with respect to the law, a thesis common in the West that Soviet society has developed and is now developing "not according to Marx." . . .

It suffices to turn, in this connection, to Marx's well-known *Critique of the Gotha Programme*. Here Marx demonstrates clearly and precisely that, in the period of transition from capitalism to communism, the economic prerequisites for the abandonment of law do not yet exist, because distribution in society occurs not in accordance with needs, taking into account the actual differences that may exist in the situation of people, but in accordance with work performed. A characteristic of distribution in accordance with work is the fact that it cannot dispense with legal regulation of the measure of work and the measure of consumption. No law is needed for distribution in accordance with need, but it is still needed if distribution is in accordance with work. Marx not only does not cast doubt upon the need for law under socialism but, on the contrary, proceeds from this as a necessary condition.

It is well known that Marx's formulations in the *Critique of the Gotha Programme* were generalized and developed by Lenin in his famous *State and Revolution*. Lenin emphasizes over and over again that, during the period of transition from capitalism, law remains as a

V.A. Tumanov is a Soviet legal scholar. The article from which these excerpts are reproduced was published in the leading Soviet law journal, Sovetskoe Gosudarstvo i Pravo *("Soviet State and Law"), 1965, no. 8, pp. 64–72. It was translated in* Soviet Law and Government, *vol. IV (Winter 1965–1966), pp. 3–9, and is reproduced here with the permission of the International Arts and Sciences Press.*

regulator of the distribution of products and the distribution of work among members of society. Here Lenin also points to another social need for retaining law until full communism is attained. "Unless one yields to utopianism," he wrote, "one must not think that after capitalism has been overthrown, people will immediately start to work for society *without any norms of law. . . .*"

Thus, Berman understood little with respect to the relationship of socialism and law in Marxism. . . . However, something else is important in this connection: why was it necessary for Berman to erect a barrier between Marxist theory and socialist law? The answer to this question is not complicated. He attempts in this way to instill in the reader the idea that the creation and perfection of law, and also the strengthening of legality, is not a lawful development of socialist society but only pragmatic steps which at any moment may be renounced. In such a portrayal law and legality are not immanent in socialism but are accidental, occasional, and hence have a supposedly curtailed, imperfect character. All through the book, and in the most diverse connections, Berman never stops emphasizing that "Soviet law is always precarious," "the state of Soviet legislation is appallingly chaotic," and inasmuch as violence and terror are, above all, in accord with the spirit of Marxism and socialism, its "accidental" law and legality may be sacrificed at any time "in the interests of the dynamics of social development." . . .

However, even within the framework of his own book, Berman's concept comes into direct conflict with the factual material that, willy-nilly, he is compelled to present. This material, no matter how the author comments upon it, demonstrates that as early as five years after the October Revolution all the most important branches of law had been codified (there is no other case in modern history of such rapid codification after deep-going social change), that thereafter the most important institutions of this law were constantly being perfected, including those which had appeared for the first time in history (socialist property, planning, etc.). Finally, the reader learns something about the new codification of Soviet law after 1956. The reader cannot but wonder whether this does not add up to just too many "accidents" and "departures from theory." . . .

Another basic anticommunist stereotype consists in the affirmation that the individual is suppressed under socialism, that he is wholly and completely subordinated in all respects to the state, being under its complete, "total control." . . . [Berman] begins by declaring Soviet law to be "teacher and parent." This entire section of the book is termed "Parental Law." At first glance this might appear not to be negative, and even benevolent. For the fact is that law is called upon to teach many things to men. Marxist-Leninist theory has always emphasized the important educational role of socialist law, and conceptions reducing law solely to compulsion have been subject to criticism in the Soviet literature. But the essence of the matter is that Berman grossly distorts the educational role of socialist law. This is what it looks like in his interpretation: "The subject of law, legal man, is treated less as an independent possessor of rights and duties, who knows what he wants, than as a dependent member of the collective group, a youth, whom the law must not only protect against the consequences of his own ignorance, but must also guide and train and discipline."

Berman thus counterposes the educational role of law and the rights of the individual without any justification and for clearly biased purposes. According to Berman's logic, the greater the educational role of law, the less attention is given to the rights of the individual. The educational role of Soviet law provides Berman with the opportunity to present Soviet people in a remarkably caricatured and ridiculous light. While the American "legal man'' emerges in his writing as a hearty and independent personality who boldly disposes of his rights and duties, Soviet people are, as subjects in law or participants in trials, ''like children or juveniles'' under tutelage in every respect. . . .

When Soviet doctrine speaks of the educational role of socialist law, it has in mind a very specific range of questions, namely: the content of the law in effect (the principles and standards people learn from it); the clarity and accessibility of legislation to the broadest masses of the people; the importance of conscious, voluntary compliance with the law (and not under fear of punishment); the fact that regulation by law must, above all, persuade people of the need and desirability of precisely a certain and not another development of the given group of social relationships; and, finally, that the sanction in the application of a provision of law is not an end in itself, but primarily a means of education and of preventing similar violations. However, Berman prefers to keep silent about this true content of the problem. Instead he propounds another problem: ''tutelary law'' versus individual freedom. Berman attempts to create the impression that the ''tutelary'' role of law is so great that the personal freedom of the citizen is threatened. As Berman depicts it, Soviet people can be only objects of education or parental tutelage, and in turn they are alleged to be unable to influence the institutions and established order created by the state.

It is characteristic that it is precisely in connection with his ratiocinations about the ''tutelary'' role of Soviet law that Berman propounds the thesis that criminal law is the central branch of the Soviet legal system. He declares that it is precisely criminal law which ''receives more attention in Soviet legal literature than any other branch of law. Its constructs and postulates are basic to every other branch.'' It is not hard to understand the goal of this maneuver. Berman is attempting to impress upon his reader the notion that the ''tutelary'' role of Soviet law is related primarily to the function of repression of crime. By its very essence this maneuver is a double falsification.

In the first place, if we speak of the educational role of law, the development of this aspect of socialist law is associated precisely with the steady narrowing of the sphere of compulsion (and particularly the repression of crime). The greater and more effective the educational role of law, the greater the degree to which persuasion supplants compulsion. In Berman's eyes, the picture is the opposite: the ''tutelary'' or ''parental'' role of law turns out to be associated with the advancement of criminal law to a paramount position.

In the second place, criminal law has never been the central, principal branch of the system of Soviet law and has not been regarded as such in the Soviet literature. To pose the question in this manner would contradict the ABCs of Marxism, in accordance with that which is basic to any legal system are the production relations and their foundation—property relations—and consequently, those branches of law that express and reinforce the economic and political system of society (primarily state or constitutional law). Berman could have read this in any textbook on the general theory of state and law. And he would also have learned that there are no instances in Soviet law of the application of principles of criminal law in other branches of the law.

Let us summarize briefly the principal theses offered by Berman on Soviet law, which he, as an ''expert,'' puts before the American reader: Soviet law is a departure from Marxism; it is not stable and borders on tyranny; it lags behind Western systems; the influence of the traditions of old Russia cannot be extinguished; its educational role gives it a totalitarian and repressive character. Truly, an unsightly and, even more, a terrible picture! Fortunately, it has nothing in common with reality and falls entirely into the realm of fantasy.

A Reply to Criticism

Harold J. Berman

. . . Mr. Tumanov is right, of course, and it is also so stated in the book, that both Marx and Lenin foresaw a period of transition from socialism to communism, following the proletarian revolution, during which period the institutions of state and law would continue to exist. How then, Mr. Tumanov asks, can it be said that the existence of law under socialism—the first stage of communism—contradicts the spirit if not the letter of Marxism?

The answer is not hard to find in the writings of Marx, Engels, Lenin, and others, and it is stated—I think clearly enough—in *Justice in the USSR*. For Lenin, as well as for Marx, it is not "socialist law" but "bourgeois law" which will survive in the first phase of communism—as a necessary evil, or, as Lenin put it in *State and Revolution* (building on Marx's *Critique of the Gotha Program*), an "unavoidable defect." "Bourgeois law," Lenin emphasizes over and over, must continue to exist so long as class antagonisms exist—even under conditions of state ownership of the means of production when private property is replaced by public property.

It is no accident that the phrase "socialist law" is not to be found either in the *Critique of the Gotha Program* or in *State and Revolution*. . . . Since the mid-1930s, Soviet jurists have attributed a more lasting and more positive value to law, and have not hesitated to speak of "socialist law" as an instrument of justice in a society without class antagonisms. This represents a fundamental shift in the Marxist-Leninist theory of law. Law in this sense—the law of a "state of whole people," in which "the proletarian dictatorship has ceased to be a necessity" (to quote the 1961 Party Program)—is what contradicts the spirit if not the letter both of classical Marxism and of Leninism.

Soviet jurists still preach the eventual withering away (literally, dying out) of law under communism. So long as they do so, Soviet law will continue to be under a theoretical cloud and true security will be inhibited. This point, stated at various places in *Justice in the USSR* is not taken up by Mr. Tumanov. Would he agree that the continued existence of law in the final stages of communism—"communist law"—would require a revision of classical Marxist-Leninist theory?

Nevertheless, despite the negative implications of the dying-out theory, Soviet law has a high degree of stability and many strong points. Mr. Tumanov is apparently puzzled that such a conclusion can be reached by one who does not accept the view that Marxism-Leninism is an adequate theoretical foundation for a legal system. He believes that the author is attempting "to create in the reader the idea that [law and legality are] not a lawful development of socialist society but only pragmatic steps which at any moment may be renounced.". . . In fact, the implication is just the opposite. Soviet law has developed not as a matter of theory but as a matter of necessity. As stated in *Justice in the USSR,* Stalin

This excerpt is from Soviet Law and Government, *vol. IV (Winter 1965–1966), pp. 11–16, and reproduced here with the permission of International Arts and Sciences Press.*

learned through bitter experience that "without a legal system and a legal order—without Law with a capital L—he could neither control the social relations of the people nor keep the economy going nor command the political forces in the country as a whole. It was rediscovered that law is not a luxury but a necessity, that at the very least it satisfies a basic need for some outlet for the feelings of justice, of reward and punishment, of reciprocity, which exist in all people."

More than that, the very extension of state control over the economic life of the country, and the introduction of national economic planning, has made the strengthening of law and legality the "lawful development of socialist society." The Soviet law of planning, and of contracts between state enterprises—to which the first part of the book devotes much attention—is socialist law par excellence, not subject (in its main outlines) to the vagaries of theory, whether Marxist or non-Marxist, but a product of social, economic, and political necessity. I believe that this interpretation is actually more in the spirit of Marxism than Mr. Tumanov's, despite the fact that Marx himself did not foresee the development under socialism of a system of national economic planning. From the point of view of Marxism, whether or not Soviet law comforms to the theories and predictions of certain individuals who lived fifty or one hundred years ago should be a matter of very little importance. . . .

If the third part of the book had been confined to an elaboration of the Soviet emphasis on the educational role of law, Mr. Tumanov would apparently have been content. It goes further, however, and attempts to analyze the conception of man implicit in a legal system which makes the educational role of law central. Clearly, if the law is an educator, then the person to whom it is addressed, or whom it controls, is presumed to be in need of education; and in that sense he is conceived as young, dependent, growing, not yet mature. . . .

Perhaps it is an overstatement to say that criminal law receives more attention in Soviet legal literature than any other branch of law. I have, however, been struck by the extent to which Soviet legal literature concerning constitutional law, administrative law, contract law, and other branches of the Soviet legal system deal with the criminal-law aspects of those subjects. I think it is fair to say that almost every branch of Soviet law emphasizes duties, and sanctions for violations of duties, and in this connection inevitably builds on the constructs and postulates of criminal law. In this respect, too, Soviet law manifests, and carries farther, tendencies that are apparent in other legal systems as well.

Postscript

Harold J. Berman

The tension between the strengthening of legality, on the one hand, and the resort to arbitrary political action and to force, on the other, which is described above in the pages reproduced from the 1963 edition of *Justice in the USSR,* continued to play an important part in political, economic, and social life during the following decade and a half. The tendencies toward legality became more and more pronounced. At the same time, the tendencies toward illegal repression of political and ideological dissent also became more and more pronounced. In addition, the tensions between leniency and severity within the law, as well as between decentralization and centralization of decision making, continued to mount.

The strengthening of legality was greatly reinforced by the fact that the fear of a return to Stalinist terror, which remained strong until the mid-1960s, diminished greatly in the 1970s. This was due in part simply to the passage of time and the maturing of a generation that knew Stalinism only by hearsay. Soviet people seemed to become increasingly confident that if they did not violate the law, they would not be subjected to criminal sanctions. Secret administrative trials of persons suspected of opposition to the regime remained a thing of the past. People were not prosecuted merely on the ground that they were "enemies of the people," nor were they convicted without a trial or sentenced merely on the basis of denunciations.

On the other hand, the KGB not only continued, as it was authorized by law to do, to indict persons for committing crimes against the state, including the crime of circulating anti-Soviet statements, but also illegally manipulated the trials of such persons by giving secret instructions to judges, restricting the activities of defense counsel, manufacturing evidence, and so forth. Under Khrushchev, criminal prosecutions for political and ideological dissent ("anti-Soviet agitation and propaganda") had been carried on in the greatest secrecy and were hardly known about, either inside or outside the Soviet Union. Starting in 1966, however, with the case of the two writers Siniavsky and Daniel, such trials came to be held more or less openly. The accused were generally defended by counsel, and they often pleaded not guilty. Although the trials were usually rigged, and the accused were invariably convicted, the opportunity to speak in their own defense gave them the possibility to turn the trials into countertrials, in which they openly proclaimed their democratic, religious, nationalist, or other "dissident" views. Relatives and friends who were permitted to attend the trials then carried reports of the proceedings to others, who circulated them through unofficial typescripts (so-called *samizdat*, "self-publishing") and through foreign correspondents. Such unofficial circulation of factual information concerning arrests, trials, and sentences, is not prohibited by Soviet law and has not been in and of itself a ground for criminal prosecution. Eventually, the reports reached large Soviet audiences through Western radio broadcasts beamed to the Soviet Union. To listen to these is also not a violation of Soviet law.

This postscript was written by Professor Berman for this edition in 1979.

The very existence of a more or less legal *samizdat* and of more or less unjammed foreign radio broadcasts, as well as of more or less public trials, testifies to a certain relaxation of controls under Brezhnev and a greater freedom to express dissenting opinions. It may also testify to a greater respect for legality than existed under Khrushchev. On the other hand, crude violations of the legal rights of dissidents in some hundreds and perhaps even thousands of cases, including not only rigged trials but also illegal searches and seizures, illegal commitments to psychiatric institutions, illegal treatment of prisoners, and the like, testify to the difficulty of maintaining the integrity of the law when the law itself is intended to serve as a conscious instrument for preserving ideological unity.

With respect to nonpolitical crimes, the reformation of Soviet criminal law, which received its first great impetus in the late 1950s, continued throughout the 1960s and 1970s. On the one hand, penalties for more serious crimes were periodically increased, although in practice the wave of executions for large-scale economic crimes (currency violations, stealing state property, and bribery), which Khrushchev inaugurated in 1961 to 1964, substantially diminished; the death penalty for such crimes (when committed on a large scale) remained on the books, but was only occasionally invoked. In addition, various new crimes were created to catch types of misconduct that escaped the meshes of the codes as originally drafted. On the other hand, penalties for less serious crimes were drastically reduced, and in 1977 a new and much milder sanction was introduced for many types of offenses committed for the first time: namely, suspension of sentence coupled with mandatory assignment to work for the period of the sentence. Such mandatory work assignment is to be supervised and carried out without deprivation of freedom. Also various minor offenses were, in effect, decriminalized by being subjected to mild administrative penalties (chiefly fines).

Also, the "anti-parasite laws" introduced by Khrushchev, which authorized administrative exile ("resettlement") of persons living on "nonlabor" income and pursuing an "antisocial parasitic way of life," were changed to conform to higher standards of procedural justice. Only a court could sentence, and only after administrative authorities found appropriate work for the accused and issued a warning of failure to report for such work.

In the late 1960s and early 1970s, many Western observers, striving to perceive substantial differences between the policies of the Khrushchev and Brezhnev regimes, seized upon widespread criticisms in Soviet legal literature concerning the operation of the Comrades' Courts. These criticisms generally focused on the excessive optimism concerning popular justice that had been displayed in the past and on resulting abuses of rights of individuals. Despite some curtailment of their activity, however, the Comrades' Courts continued to play an important role. In 1977 a new Comrades' Court statute was enacted that was not essentially different from the 1961 statute; its most important changes were to eliminate the power of the Comrades' Court to recommend eviction of tenants from their apartments, the elimination of the catch-all jurisdiction over "other antisocial offenses not subject to criminal punishment," somewhat better protection of procedural rights of persons charged, an increase in the amount of the fines that Comrades' Courts may impose for petty criminal acts, and an expansion of their jurisdiction over petty crimes committed for the first time.

The preservation of the Comrades' Courts is linked with the continued emphasis on the role of social organizations and other forms of popular participation in the administration of justice and in legal decision making generally. Here, too, the contrast drawn by some Western observers between a more "democratic" or "liberal" Khrushchev era and a more "autocratic" or "conservative" Brezhnev era seems entirely misplaced.

Perhaps the most significant of the post-Khrushchev developments in the sphere of legality was the increase in the role of law and of lawyers in the economy and especially in the industrial sector. Contracts assumed increased importance in the transfer of goods between state enterprises. The officially reported number of lawyers increased from about 100,000 in 1965 to 188,300 in 1976; of these about 50,000 were said to be lawyers for state enterprises ("jurisconsults"). Although decentralization of planning and of operations, which was promised in the economic reform program of the mid-1960s, proceeded only at a snail's pace, the legal machinery to implement such a decentralization was made available.

Finally, mention must be made of the adoption of a new Constitution in 1977, replacing the 1936 "Stalin" Constitution. Khrushchev had announced his intention to adopt a new Constitution as early as 1962, and had appointed a large committee to undertake the task of drafting it. The propitious time, however, only arrived fifteen years later under his successor. The new Constitution, containing 174 articles, did not change any preexisting Soviet laws. It made a strong statement of the rights and freedoms of Soviet citizens. However, these rights and freedoms were presented as grants by the State and not as limitations upon the powers of the State, and they were expressly conditioned upon their exercise in accordance with the aims of Soviet socialism. In this way, the 1977 Constitution was in the tradition of previous Soviet Constitutions. Indeed, the 1977 Constitution went farther than the 1936 "Stalin" Constitution in emphasizing the social responsibilities of citizens. It also went farther in identifying the Communist Party as "the leading and guiding force of Soviet society."

Perhaps the most significant aspect of the new Constitution is its confirmation of basic changes that have taken place during the past twenty-five years in various branches of the Soviet legal system, including not only criminal law and procedure but also civil and economic law, family law, land law, environmental law, and others. On the basis of the Constitution, Soviet jurists have been mobilized to systematize existing legislation and to remove obsolete provisions from it. Such stabilization and systematization of the legal system is both a reflection and an instrument of increased political stability as well.

The Judicial System and the Security Forces

Roy Medvedev

In a socialist democracy, it is crucially important that the legal system (courts, procuracy,* and lawyers) and state security services function correctly. To quote from a leading article in *Kommunist*: "It should be a matter of deepest concern not only for the government but also for party, trade union, and Komsomol organizations to reinforce the concept of law and order and to see that the workers have a better knowledge of the law. It is vital that we reach a stage where respect for the law has become the personal concern of every individual and is reflected in every action of people in authority."

This same point is emphasized in the Central Committee's report to the Twenty-fourth Party Congress: "Attempts to deviate from the law, whatever the motive, cannot be tolerated under any circumstances. Similarly, infringements of the rights of the individual and encroachments on the dignity of citizens must not be tolerated. It is a question of principle for us as communists, as supporters of the highest ideals of humanitarianism."

Unfortunately it must be noted that at the present time there are many serious shortcomings not only in the actual work of the various bodies concerned with the administration of justice but also in their very structure. Our law courts, for example, are still insufficiently democratic. Deficiencies in the system of election to the Soviets also apply to elections for the People's Courts†—there is no element of contest and little contact between "people's judges" and their electors. "People's assessors" are elected in factories, institutions, etc.; but the selection of candidates is generally done in a bureaucratic manner and discussion of the nominations at workers' meetings is superficial and lacks any element of real debate.

At the lowest level a court consists of a judge, who has specialized legal training, and two assessors, each with one vote. The verdicts of the court are reached by simple majority. This system has been subject to well-founded criticism in the press on a number of occasions (for example, in *Literaturnaya Gazeta*). It has been pointed out that the usual number of assessors is too small to justify the term "People's Court." There should,

* *Soviet procurators have a dual function. They prosecute in criminal cases but also are charged with defending the rights of the accused as part of their responsibility for the observance of the law throughout the judicial and penal system.—Trans.*

†*People's Courts have first-instance jurisdiction for all civil and criminal cases (except where codes of procedure indicate otherwise) and are set up in towns, municipal and rural districts. Their judges are elected by the inhabitants of their area of jurisdiction for five-year terms. (Judges of higher-level courts are elected by the appropriate Soviet.) Assessors are laymen chosen from a panel to which they have been elected. They have equal authority with the judge in passing verdict and sentence, but in present practice it is virtually unknown for them to disagree with the judge.—Trans.*

Roy Medvedev is a prominent dissident and leading proponent of socialist democracy within the Soviet Union and author of Let History Judge. *This excerpt is drawn from chapter VIII of* On Socialist Democracy, *translated by Ellen de Kadt.* *For detailed footnote references, see the original.*

therefore, be a larger number of assessors with verdicts reached by a two-thirds or three-fourths vote rather than by simple majority. Under the jury system used in other countries, complete unanimity is generally required for a verdict of guilty.

The status of the legal profession in the Soviet Union is very low. In accordance with the Code of Criminal Procedure, a defense lawyer is admitted to a case only after the preliminary investigation has been completed and the case for the prosecution has been drawn up. Such a way of doing things is completely incompatible with the adversary nature of legal procedure. It is not only that the defense has far less time than the prosecution to prepare its case; the fatal defect of this system is that in the majority of cases the defense lawyer is deprived of the opportunity to give the accused an explanation of his rights as a person who is presumed to be innocent. The lawyer has no chance of challenging the investigating officials' decision to order the detention of the accused before he is brought into court nor is he able to follow the course of the interrogation and prevent possible abuses (which unfortunately are by no means infrequent). For example, the majority of citizens who are faced with prosecution for the first time are ignorant of their right to refuse to make statements as laid down in the Code of Criminal Procedure. The same is true of persons detained on suspicion—although it is in violation of the Code, they are often interrogated as witnesses (who do not have the right to refuse to make statements). Clearly our system of legal representation, a vital element in the protection of the rights of the individual, is very much behind that of the bourgeois democracies. This situation is totally unacceptable in a socialist state.

Soviet citizens still have no means of legal redress in cases where they feel actions by state officials or organizations have been improper or illegal. Their only possible course is to protest through administrative channels, something that rarely results in a satisfactory response. Lenin wrote in 1903: . . . "We will only have redress against officials when every person in Russia has the right to complain to an elected court, talk freely about his grievances or write to the newspapers, as happens in all other countries." Unfortunately, for the most part such a right does not yet exist.

We still have many cases of illegal interference by local or higher state and party bodies in court proceedings. There are also breaches of the rule that deliberations between the judge and assessors concerning the verdict must not be divulged to outsiders. Sometimes during the actual consideration of a verdict or in the intervals between court sessions judges even call the district party committee or some other nonjudicial body to ask for advice or for approval of a particular verdict.

It is quite intolerable that political cases should be heard in semiclosed or in effect fully closed courtrooms, when it is just these cases that arouse the greatest interest among the Soviet and foreign public. A good example of this was the trial of Sinyavsky and Daniel, which caused such a stir in 1966 and which was the first in a whole series of similar political trials. The courtroom was packed with hand-picked "members of the public," many of whom came not on their own initiative but under orders. But a number of writers and scientists who made persistent requests to be allowed to attend were not admitted, nor were foreign journalists—not even communists. Although "public accusers"* were there to testify, no "public defenders" were invited. It is hardly surprising, therefore, that both the proceedings and the verdict quite justifiably attracted much unfavorable comment both in the Soviet Union and abroad.[1]

**A "public accuser" is a person who supports the prosecution case on behalf of a "public organization" (e.g., the Writers Union, as in this case).—Trans.*

The trials of Khaustov and Bukovsky in 1967 were also semiclosed, as were those of Litvinov, Bogaraz, and others (1968), Ginzburg, Galanskov, and others (1968), Grigorenko (1969), Gorbanevskaya (1970), Pimenov and Vail (1970), Amalrik (1970), Bukovsky (1972), and many similar trials which have taken place in recent years in Moscow, Leningrad, Sverdlovsk, Kaluga, and other cities. The trials of various groups of Crimean Tartars accused of breaches of the peace, as well as of Ukrainians, Armenians, and Estonians, charged with nationalist activities were to all intents and purposes completely closed. The same was true of the trial in Leningrad (1970) where a group of persons, mostly of Jewish origin, were accused of planning to hijack a civil aircraft in order to flee the country. Such cases not only arouse skepticism among the public about the way in which political trials are conducted but also undermine confidence in the legal system as a whole. Public opinion is alarmed not so much by the fact of the trials themselves as by the numerous infringements of legal procedure, by the secrecy, and by the one-sided and extremely incomplete reporting in our press. A short time before the trial of Ginzburg, Galanskov, Lashkova, and Dobrovolsky it became widely known in the Soviet Union and abroad that a group of thirty-one eminent members of the Soviet intelligentsia had signed a letter demanding that the case be heard in public. However not one of the signatories was allowed to attend the trial. Friends of the accused were also kept out, and the court even refused to admit a number of people whom the defense wished to call as witnesses. Furthermore there was no mention of the trial in the press until it was over; then several tendentious and misleading accounts finally appeared. . . .

There are also serious and well-founded misgivings about certain pieces of legislation that are very relevant to the problem of socialist democracy. For example, under our present laws, persons can be held criminally liable for "anti-Soviet agitation and propaganda." These are defined as activity "carried out with the purpose of subverting or weakening Soviet power or of committing particularly dangerous crimes against the state, disseminating for the said purposes slanderous fabrications which defame the Soviet state and social system, as well as circulating, preparing, or harboring for the said purposes, literature of similar content" (Article 70 of the Criminal Code).

Obviously every country must protect its citizens against slander and prosecute persons who incite others to commit particularly dangerous crimes against it. But the terms of Article 70 are extremely vague and imprecise: they are frequently applied to works containing even completely justified criticism of particular aspects of the political structure, usually survivals from the Stalin years which contravene the basic principles of socialism and the Soviet system. Materials intended to strengthen socialist democracy are thus denounced as "anti-Soviet agitation and propaganda." Similarly, entirely reasonable spoken or written criticisms of the various shortcomings of Soviet life are made out to be "slanderous fabrications." Even a historical study of the abuses of power under Stalin was not long ago condemned in the following irresponsible way by certain very senior party authorities: "Under the pretext of criticizing the cult of Stalin the author has slandered the Soviet social and state system." In other words, the author should be arrested and tried under Article 70 of the Criminal Code.

Legal comment on Article 70 qualifies it in a number of important respects. For example: "A person can only be convicted of anti-Soviet agitation and propaganda when he has deliberately spread slanderous or defamatory views about the Soviet state and social order which he knows to be false. . . . There shall be no grounds for conviction if the person is honestly misguided in his interpretation of some aspect of Soviet reality or in his appraisal of various political institutions, etc. Such misguided judgment may, for example, be the result of misinformation. . . . An important criterion for the correct definition of 'anti-Soviet agitation and propaganda' is the subjective element, the presence of deliberate and specific intent on the part of the accused to undermine and weaken Soviet power. Intent is determined by the fact that the accused is aware of the danger to society and the possible consequences of his actions and was deliberately attempting to undermine or weaken Soviet power. . . . The absence of such awareness precludes the possibility of a successful prosecution under Article 70.''

These qualifications are evidence that Soviet jurisprudence has come a long way since the days when our prevailing legal theory maintained that there was no difference between objective and subjective behavior or activity. In other words, during the Stalin period, whether or not a person was in his own mind completely loyal to the Soviet system was irrelevant in the courtroom. If in the view of the party leadership he had in some way done harm to the dictatorship of the proletariat or supposedly aided the enemies of the country by means of an actual or alleged theoretical or practical error, then he should be made to answer for it no matter what his subjective intention.

Unfortunately, however, progress in legal theory is not always matched by corresponding improvements in the functioning of the legal system. During most of the political trials of recent years the courts have paid little attention to evidence concerning motivation. As a result people have been condemned almost entirely for views and convictions, arbitrarily and wrongly branded as anti-Soviet.

Public opinion has been severely critical of Paragraphs 1 and 3 of Article 190, recently introduced into the Criminal Code. Paragraph 1 is very much the same as Article 70. It is again a question of ''the systematic dissemination of fabrications known to be false discrediting the Soviet state and social system.'' In legal comment on this article we read: ''Isolated or repeated (not systematic) instances of dissemination of information known to be false which discredits the Soviet political and social system does not constitute a crime but rather provides grounds for intensifying political education of a preventive character.'' . . .

Unfortunately, for all practical purposes this commentary has been ignored during most of the trials held in recent years under Article 190 (1). People have been convicted in spite of their sincerely held belief that the information or materials circulated by them were truthful and accurately reflected the facts of Soviet life whether past or present. There have also been convictions where the accused had not *systematically* disseminated information found by the court to be slanderous.

Paragraph 3 of Article 190 clearly contradicts the Constitution of the USSR. This paragraph defines as a crime ''the organizing of or active participation in group actions which result in flagrant violation of public order or are combined with arrant refusal to comply with the lawful demands of representatives of authority or which entail a disruption of transport services, or the work of state or public enterprises or institutions.'' The adoption of this article in effect means a legal ban on any public demonstration involving several people which has not received previous sanction from the authorities. Even if a demonstration does not involve a ''disruption of transport services'' or ''flagrant violation of the public order,'' it is always possible to charge people with ''arrant refusal to comply with the lawful demands of representatives of authority.''

Soviet legislation with regard to hooliganism also leaves much to be desired from a legal point of view. Abuses can easily occur because of the extremely summary way in which cases are heard without even the benefit of people's assessors. The police often bring a charge of ''hooliganism'' in order to obtain a rapid conviction under this simplified procedure where cases of a totally different kind are involved—such as attempts by Soviet citizens to enter the embassy of a capitalist country.

Our so-called "parasite" laws also give grounds for disquiet. Much of the wording of the Special Decree of the Presidium of the Supreme Soviet (May 4, 1961) is so vague that it has become the basis for a series of abuses. The most scandalous of these was probably the case of Joseph Brodsky in 1964, a gifted poet without regular employment who was sent to a northern region of the country where he was put to compulsory work. Unfortunately the new version of the law on parasites—the Decree of the Presidium of the Supreme Soviet of February 25, 1970—also has a number of serious flaws, following particularly from the fact that the term "parasite" remains exceedingly ill-defined from a legal point of view.

An extremely unfortunate aspect of our legal system is the legislation regulating the activities of psychiatric institutions. Psychiatric measures against dissenters—the certification of sane people as mentally ill or "psychopathic" and their consequent forcible committal to psychiatric hospitals of a general or special type—are nowadays resorted to more and more frequently. There are also cases in which the medical history of a person who may have sufferered in the past from a relatively mild form of mental disturbance is deliberately misinterpreted to justify his committal to a psychiatric institution. According to my information, several dozen people have been illegally committed during the last few years. It is evident that forced hospitalization has become one of the authorities' favorite repressive measures against persons who have incurred their displeasure—a means of discrediting and intimidating dissidents. This abuse of psychiatry makes it possible to avoid normal court proceedings, the provision of evidence, and so forth. It is all too obvious that the use of psychiatry for political purposes poses an enormous threat to the future of socialist democracy in our country. . . .

Up to 1960 the Criminal Code contained special articles that made doctors and psychiatrists liable to prosecution for ordering improper or groundless committal to a psychiatric hospital. This enabled relatives or the injured party himself to apply to the courts for redress. During the preparation of the new code in 1961, however, these articles were dropped, and since that time there has been no way to lodge complaints about psychiatrists (or their superiors) in the courts. It can be done only through administrative channels via the district health department and eventually up to the Ministry of Health of the RSFSR and the USSR. Needless to say such an arrangement makes it very much harder to prevent or rectify cases of malpractice. And indeed, when some of the victims tried to complain to the courts about their illegal detention in mental hospitals, their applications were invariably rejected with the explanation that the actions of the psychiatrists or institutions concerned could only be challenged by an appeal to the Ministry of Health through normal channels.

At the end of 1961 the Ministry of Health in collaboration with the Ministry of Internal Affairs and the Procurator's Office adopted a special directive called "The Emergency Hospitalization of Mentally Ill Persons Who Are a Public Danger." Its basic provisions lay themselves open to severe criticism.

The directive appeared only in a specialized legal publication which was not made available to the general public. In all cases of compulsory hospitalization known to me, the Health Department concerned has refused to show it either to the "patient" or to his relatives. Interested parties are also prevented from seeing many other directives, such as those regulating compulsory treatment, the procedure for psychiatric examinations, etc. This makes it all the easier to violate official regulations, and certain psychiatric institutions take every advantage of the possibility. It should of course be pointed out that the documents themselves are highly dubious from both medical and legal points of view.

None of them, for example, specifically defines what is meant by an action that constitutes a public danger. This gives rise to many abuses: "public danger" is applied to actions that do not constitute a direct threat to the life of the "patient" himself or those around him, but are perfectly normal manifestations of a critical spirit, such as the writing of dissident manuscripts, the putting up of posters, taking part in demonstrations, expressing the wish to emigrate to another country, attempting to publish one's work abroad, etc. What is more, the medical reasons mentioned in the directive as grounds for emergency committal are deliberately couched in vague terms which admit of a very arbitrary interpretation. This most important section of the directive amounts to only *twelve lines!* Among the symptoms indicating compulsory committal are the following: "(c) a systematic syndrome of delusions with chronic deterioration if this results in behavior dangerous to the public; (d) a hypochondriac delusional condition causing an irregular and aggressive attitude in the patient toward individuals, organizations, or institutions." One does not have to be a psychiatrist to understand the inadmissibility of such imprecise language. What exactly is a "hypochondriac delusional condition"? Who can possibly establish what constitutes an "irregular and aggressive attitude toward individuals, organizations, or institutions"? If a Soviet citizen criticizes an institution, takes it to court, exposes improper activities on the part of those in charge of it—is this not likely to cause the institution in question to turn to psychiatrists for help? Yet the authors of the directive apparently felt that even in such vague form the grounds for hospitalization still did not offer enough scope, and they therefore added the following caveat: "The grounds for compulsory hospitalization enumerated above are not exhaustive but only a list of the most frequently encountered morbid states that present a public danger. . . . The morbid conditions enumerated above which can undoubtedly constitute a danger to the public may be accompanied by externally correct behavior and dissimulation." What this means, in effect, is that with the aid of the police, psychiatrists may forcibly commit people to hospital for reasons other than those listed in the directive! The opportunities for abuse are appallingly obvious—it becomes possible for any unscrupulous psychiatrist to maintain that a seemingly "normal" citizen is in fact mentally ill and only simulating "normality."

One is also bound to have very serious misgivings about Special Order No. 345/209 dated May 15, 1969, "Measures for the prevention of socially dangerous actions by mentally ill persons," signed by the Minister of Health, B. Petrovsky, and the Minister for Internal Affairs, P. Shchelokov. This order empowers both the police and psychiatric institutions to give a very broad interpretation of what constitutes a "socially dangerous act." The order notes that insufficient use is being made of the 1961 directive and urges that it be applied to "prevent dangerous actions by mentally ill persons." This means that since May 1969, not only *improper behavior* but even the *possibility* of improper behavior has been sufficient cause for compulsory hospitalization. As for persons who have already perpetrated socially dangerous acts (in the opinion of the police and the doctors), the new order makes it possible for psychiatric institutions to continue treatment even after the court order for committal has expired and to brush aside all attempts by relatives to secure the patient's discharge from hospital. The order introduces a new concept—"socially dangerous tendencies"—which is in no way defined or interpreted. It is not surprising that during 1969–70, after this order had been issued, there was an increase in the number of cases involving the abuse of psychiatry for obviously political reasons.

It is particularly important for the healthy functioning of a socialist democracy that the role and responsibilities of the security forces be correctly defined. After an unlimited expansion had in effect placed them above all other state and party bodies, their power was in fact substantially reduced in the post-Stalin period. The security services were put under the control of the party, which meant that they ceased to have a punitive function—this was now made the sole prerogative of the judiciary. . .

The restriction of the KGB's functions led quite naturally to a cutting down of its staff and the liquidation of some of its lower-level divisions. For example, formerly each Moscow district had its own KGB section but these were now abolished. Two years ago, however, these district sections in Moscow were reconstituted, and their subordinate network of special departments in factories and institutions was again enlarged. To a great extent the KGB is now entrusted with the struggle against "ideological subversion," as it is called. In fact we are once more observing a growth of the staff and functions of the security services, but this is certainly not a response to any increase in foreign espionage activities.[2] Rather it is a question of internal processes, particularly the development of various political trends and the activities of certain groups of dissidents. . . . Because there is too little democracy in our country, the security organs have been given greater powers and larger staff—measures that will only perpetuate the situation.

Obviously those in power should pay close attention to the development of political moods and trends within a country. This is one of the basic and obvious responsibilities of a political party. Lenin, we may recall, wrote that communists "should live in the midst of the masses and know their every mood." Under present conditions in our country, however, where many elementary democratic freedoms are absent or at best extremely limited—i.e., first and foremost freedom of speech, freedom of the printed word, freedom of assembly, and the freedom to demonstrate and organize—the study and analysis of political moods and trends become exceedingly difficult. New ideas evolve secretly, out of sight, and opinion is formed somewhere far away from public meetings and the official press. In this situation it is impossible for party bodies to study moods and opinions at various levels of the community in the normal way, or to find out the attitudes of various groups of workers toward important pieces of legislation—in short, they simply cannot keep abreast of basic social trends. . . .

A *samizdat* author has written, not without justification, that "first we spend vast sums of money to prevent citizens from openly expressing their opinions and then spend just as much trying to find out what they are actually thinking and what they really want." The security services are gradually becoming involved in the surveillance and study of developing trends not only outside the party but inside as well. I believe this is the major reason behind their renewed expansion in recent years. For the time being this process is still under the control of central and regional party bodies. Eventually, however, when the struggle between the various new trends is reflected at the higher levels of the party, the security organs could once more break loose and achieve an independent position which would put them above both party and government.

Since the well-being of a socialist democracy depends on the nature of its judicial system and security services, it is particularly important to consider how it might be possible to improve their functioning. Here I shall discuss only some of the measures that could be taken.

It would seem desirable, for example, to increase the power and independence of judicial bodies and the procuracy. The Soviet Constitution states that judges are independent and subordinate only to the law; it also lays down that procurators shall be independent of all local authorities and answerable only to the procurator general. In practice, however, these provisions of the Constitution tend to be ignored and local organs exert considerable influence on both judges and procurators at the district level, even more so at the regional level—and at the republican level it is evidently overwhelming. . . .

It is vital that there be strict observance of the provisions of the Constitution requiring court cases to be heard in public. Sessions should be held *in camera* exclusively at the request of the defendant or the defense counsel, and even then only if the case touches on extremely intimate problems. But whenever it is a question of a political case, the trial must be absolutely open and take place in full public view. . . .

M. Lebedev stresses the need as well to strengthen the supervisory powers of the procurator's office over central government departments, public organizations, and officials in very powerful positions. In Lebedev's opinion the procuracy "should be given the right to challenge all administrative acts that contravene the law."

There is a need to substantially extend the competence of the courts to deal with infringements of civil rights, particularly on the part of the authorities. As things stand at present, Soviet citizens have no right to turn to the courts over a wide range of important matters such as those involving pensions, residence permits, illegal committal to mental hospitals, etc., but may only complain through administrative channels. . . .

Several authors have discussed the question of creating a special Constitutional Court whose function would be to determine the legality, from the constitutional point of view, of measures taken by higher executive organs. The Crimean Tartars, for example, could ask a court of this type to reestablish their own national republic and make it possible for all those wishing to return to do so.

It is also necessary to make a number of radical changes in our statute books. For example, it is evident that the article making psychiatrists criminally liable for professional misconduct as described above should be reinstated in the Criminal Code.

Though it goes without saying that the interests of the state must be protected by law, nevertheless Articles 70 and 190 (1) and (3), so imprecise and open to abuse, should certainly be rescinded; or at least until this happens, examination of the accused in court should be concerned not only with objective facts but also with subjective intent. There are certain other articles of the law that need to be formulated in more rigorous language.

As regards the state security services, I believe it is quite possible to reduce the scope of their activities to a reasonable level while at the same time extending freedom of expression and access to information. In any event the intellectual world of Soviet citizens, their political views and convictions, their thoughts and opinions should not be the concern of the organs of state security. Other ways (research institutes, polls, etc.) must be found for the study of public opinion.

Notes

1. *For example, in a letter to the Central Committee by a group of Soviet philosophers on the lessons of the Sinyavsky Daniel affair, we read: "In the history of the Soviet state there has never been a single case of a writer's being arrested and openly tried for anti-Soviet or anti-state activity as expressed in a work of literature, whether written and published in the Soviet Union or abroad. . . . Furthermore, so far as we know this never happened in tsarist Russia nor has it happened in Europe, America, Asia, or Africa in modern times. . . .*

   "Not one foreign correspondent was admitted to the courtroom. Not even the foreign communist press. . . . Anti-Soviet critics were thus given the chance to remind us of the presence of foreign correspondents during the political trials of 1936–38, and to ask, 'Why not now? Surely foreign communist journalists would not slander the Soviet Union.' . . .

"Furthermore, there was no stenographic report of this unusual trial in our press or even a detailed account of the proceedings, making it impossible to counter reports in bourgeois newspapers. And so the bourgeois propaganda machine was able to do its work." . . .

2. *Western espionage services now acquire their basic information about our military objectives through analysis of intercepted radio messages, the press, the use of spy satellites, etc., and not from the reports of agents.*

Chapter 12

INTELLECTUAL DISSENT

"Literature always anticipates life," said a distinguished writer. While this is an exaggeration, there can be little doubt that the state of freedom or unfreedom in a nation is largely explained by the status of writers and more specifically by the degree to which they may use their talents to express themselves, unfettered by intimidation and censorship. This is what gives a special cogency to the appeal of Aleksandr Solzhenitsyn (here presented) against censorship in the USSR which "imposes a yoke on our literature and gives people unversed in literature arbitrary control over writers." Tamara Deutscher, in more general terms, discusses the emergence, diversity, impact, and prospects of dissidents and dissident opinion in the USSR. Leonid Brezhnev, the head of the Communist Party in the Soviet Union, presents the official current position of the Party leadership on literature and art.

Censorship and Creativity

A.I. Solzhenitsyn

To the Presidium and the delegates to the Congress, to members of the Union of Soviet Writers, and to the editors of literary newspapers and magazines:

Not having access to the podium at this Congress, I ask that the Congress discuss:

I. The no longer tolerable oppression, in the form of censorship, which our literature has endured for decades, and which the Union of writers can no longer accept.

Under the obfuscating label of Glavlit,* this censorship—which is not provided for in the Constitution and is therefore illegal, and which is nowhere publicly labeled as such—imposes a yoke on our literature and gives people unversed in literature arbitrary control over writers. A survival of the Middle Ages, the censorship has managed, Methuselah-like, to drag out its existence almost to the twenty-first century. Of fleeting significance, it attempts to appropriate to itself the role of unfleeting time—of separating good books from bad.

Our writers are not supposed to have the right, are not endowed with the right, to express their cautionary judgments about the moral life of man and society, or to explain in their own way the social problems and historical experience that have been so deeply felt in our country. Works that might express the mature thinking of the people, that might have a timely and salutary influence on the realm of the spirit or on the development of a social conscience, are proscribed or distorted by censorship on the basis of considerations that are petty, egotistical, and—from the national point of view—shortsighted. Outstanding manuscripts by young authors, as yet entirely unknown, are nowadays rejected by editors solely on the ground that they "will not pass." Many members of the [Writers'] Union, and even many of the delegates at this Congress, know how they themselves have bowed to the pressures of the censorship and made concessions in the structure and concept of their books—changing chapters, pages, paragraphs, or sentences, giving them innocuous titles—just for the sake of seeing them finally in print, even if it meant distorting them irremediably. It is an understood quality of literature that gifted works suffer [most] disastrously from all these distortions, while untalented works are not affected by them. Indeed, it is the best of our literature that is published in mutilated form.

Meanwhile, the most censorious labels—"ideologically harmful," "depraved," and so forth—are proving shortlived and fluid, [in fact] are changing before our very eyes. Even Dostoevsky, the pride of world literature, was at one time not published in our country (still today his works are not published in full); he was excluded from the school curriculum, made unacceptable for reading, and reviled. For how many years was Yesenin

***Editor's note:** Glavlit (Main Administration for Literary Affairs and Publishing) was established on June 6, 1922.*

A.I. Solzhenitsyn, a Soviet Nobel Prize-winning writer, is author of One Day in the Life of Ivan Denisovich, The Cancer Ward, August 1914, *and* Gulag Archipelago. *This appeal was addressed to the Fourth Congress of Soviet Writers which met in May 1967.*

considered "counterrevolutionary"?—he was even subjected to a prison term because of his books. Wasn't Maiakovsky called "an anarchistic political hooligan"? For decades the immortal poetry of Akhmatova was considered anti-Soviet. The first timid printing of the dazzling Tsvetaeva ten years ago was declared a "gross political error." Only after a delay of twenty to thirty years were Bunin, Bulgakov, and Platonov returned to us. Inevitably, Mandelshtam, Voloshin, Gumilev and Kliuev will follow in that line—not to mention the recognition, at some time or other, of even Zamiatin and Remisov.

A decisive moment [in this process] comes with the death of a troublesome writer. Sooner or later after that, he is returned to us with an "explanation of [his] errors." For a long time the name of Pasternak could not be pronounced out loud; but then he died, and since then his books have appeared and his verse is even quoted at ceremonies.

Pushkin's words are really coming true: "They are capable of loving only the dead."

But the belated publication of books and "authorization" [rehabilitation] of names does not make up for either the social or the artistic losses suffered by our people as a consequence of these monstrous delays and the suppression of artistic conscience. (In fact, there were writers in the 1920s—Pilniak, Platonov, Mandelshtam—who called attention at a very early stage to the beginnings of the cult [of personality] and the peculiar traits of Stalin's character; but these writers were silenced and destroyed instead of being listened to.) Literature cannot develop in between the categories of "permitted" and "not permitted," "about this you may write" and "about this you may not." Literature that is not the breath of contemporary society, that dares not transmit the pains and fears of that society, that does not warn in time against threatening moral and social dangers—such literature does not deserve the name of literature; it is only a facade. Such literature loses the confidence of its own people, and its published works are used as wastepaper instead of being read.

Our literature has lost the leading role it played at the end of the last century and the beginning of this one, and it has lost the brilliance of experimentation that distinguished it in the 1920s. To the entire world the literary life of our country now appears immeasurably more colorless, trivial and inferior than it actually is—[or] than it would be if it were not confined and hemmed in. The losers are both our country—in world public opinion—and world literature itself. If the world had access to all the uninhibited fruits of our literature, if it were enriched by our own spiritual experience, the whole artistic evolution of the world would move along in a different way, acquiring a new stability and attaining even a new artistic threshold.

I propose that the Congress adopt a resolution which would demand and ensure the abolition of all censorship, open or hidden, of all fictional writing, and which would release publishing houses from the obligation to obtain authorization for the publication of every printed page.

II. The duties of the Union towards its members.

These duties are not clearly formulated in the statutes of the Union of Soviet Writers (under "Protection of copyrights" and "Measures for the protection of other rights of writers"), and it is sad to find that for a third of a century the Union has not defended either the "other" rights or even the copyrights of persecuted writers.

Many writers have been subjected during their lifetime to abuse and slander in the press and from rostrums without being afforded the physical possibility of replying. More than that, they have been exposed to violence and personal persecution (Bulgakov, Akhmatova, Tsvetaeva, Pasternak, Zoshchenko, Platonov, Aleksandr Grin, Vassili Grossman). The Union of Writers not only did not make its own publications available to these writers for purposes of reply and justification, not only did not come out in their defense, but through its leadership was always first among the persecutors. Names that adorned our poetry of the twentieth century found themselves on the list of those expelled from the Union or not even admitted to it in the first place. The leadership of the Union cravenly abandoned to their distress those for whom persecution ended in exile, labor camps, and death (Pavel Vasilev, Mandelshtam, Artem Veseley, Pilniak, Babel, Tabidze, Zabolotsky, and others). The list must be cut off at "and others." We learned after the 20th Party Congress that there were more than 600 writers whom the Union had obediently handed over to their fate in prisons and camps. However, the roll is even longer, and its curled-up end cannot and will not ever be read by our eyes. It contains the names of young prose writers and poets whom we may have known only accidentally through personal encounters and whose talents were crushed in camps before being able to blossom, whose writings never got further than the offices of the state security service in the days of Yagoda, Yezhov, Beria and Abakumov.

There is no historical necessity for the newly-elected leadership of the Union to share with its predecessors the responsibility for the past.

I propose that all guarantees for the defense of Union members subjected to slander and unjust persecution be clearly formulated in Paragraph 22 of the Union statutes, so that past illegalities will not be repeated. . . .

I am of course confident that I will fulfill my duty as a writer under all circumstances—even more successfully and more unchallenged from the grave than in my lifetime. No one can bar the road to truth, and to advance its cause I am prepared to accept even death. But may it be that repeated lessons will finally teach us not to stop the writer's pen during his lifetime?

At no time has this ennobled our history.

A.I. Solzhenitsyn
May 16, 1967

Intellectual Opposition in the USSR

Tamara Deutscher

In "The Autocracy is Wavering," written in 1903, Lenin observed that "there is no more precarious moment for a government in a revolutionary period than the beginning of concessions, the beginning of vacillation."[1] The Soviet hierarchy is, of course, perfectly well aware of the dangers of "vacillation." Yet, since the death of Stalin, and especially since the 20th Congress—now two decades in the past—it has been granting innumerable concessions to its critics and opponents. Not that the concessions go far enough: on the contrary, they are disappointingly meagre, and the method of granting them has been desperately inconsistent and whimsical, testifying not to a coherent policy or well-thought-out programme of gradual change, but precisely to vacillation and uncertainty. This is not the place to survey at length the enormous transformation that the Soviet Union has undergone during the last two decades: the power of the political police has been broken, the *univers concentrationnaire*—the Gulag Archipelago—has been largely dismantled. The old days when any Soviet citizen, any member of the Politbureau or Central Committee (except Stalin), could be taken from his home and shot in the dead of night are over. True, there is a lack of freedom, there is persecution, there are psychiatric prison-hospitals and horrors of all kinds, perpetrated on a smaller scale than before, but not therefore any the less reprehensible. But half-hearted and miserable as the concessions have been, they have nevertheless created conditions in which the emergence of a vague, unformed and unorganized opposition has become possible. This opposition has found its voice in *Samizdat*, compilations of uncensored literature circulating in typescript, in innumerable copies.

The Emergence of *Samizdat*

Samizdat began to appear around 1964, and initially took the form of a protest against conformism in Soviet letters. After Khrushchev's dismissal, however, these underground writings acquired a more political tone. Half-hearted and halting though Khrushchev's destalinization was, his fall provoked fears that the hard-liners, the Stalinists, would regain the upper hand. *Samizdat's* writers attempted to analyze the course of events which led from the 20th Congress, with its denunciation of Stalin, to the efforts (sometimes quite successful) to rehabilitate the dead dictator. This led them further back into history to an analysis of the years of Stalin's ascendancy, of his victory over all oppositions and the establishment of his undisputed autocracy. In the course of this exploration, many facts of history were revealed, either in the writings of historians who in one way or another gained access to historical documentation or, quite often, in the reminiscences of the few witnesses of 1917 and the early post-revolutionary years, who had survived, as if by a mir-

This excerpt from the article by the same title, © Tamara Deutscher, which appeared in New Left Review, *March-April 1976, pp. 101–113, is reprinted with the permission of the author.*

acle, all the horrors of concentration camps. The politicization of *Samizdat* was further stimulated in 1968 by the invasion of Czechoslovakia. This does not mean that literary topics have been abandoned. These still take up a considerable amount of space in underground publications, because no novel or poem betraying any sign of originality or "modernism" can find its way to approved journals, and also because, as has always been the case in Russia, literary writings are more often than not marked by political undertones.

The scale of *Samizdat* is truly staggering. Heavy volumes like *The Gulag Archipelago* or Medvedev's *Let History Judge* are not alone in having large "editions" and circulating in thousands of copies; the regular bulletins are also quite impressive in size. Two volumes of Roy Medvedev's *Political Diary* have now appeared in the West. Excerpts from only nineteen of the bulletins which he issued monthly during the years 1964–71 fill nearly 2,000 printed pages[2]. . . .

For the Soviet reader the most revealing writings must be those of eyewitnesses of the revolution who after twenty or twenty-five years in camps have still preserved the memory of the past. Old Menshevik M.P. Yakubovich was a Soldier Deputy in 1917. Later he left the Mensheviks and worked in a Soviet trade agency. Arrested as a "wrecker," he spent twenty-five years in camps. At the age of seventy-five he wrote admiringly about Zinoviev, Kamenev, and other "unpersons." In 1967 he engaged in an acrimonious exchange of letters with Solzhenitsyn. No less curious is the exchange of letters between an old revolutionary, Professor Dashkovsky, and a radio commentator, Stepanov. Dashkovsky just "could not believe his ears" when he heard on the radio remarks about Trotskyism as an "anti-Leninist tendency" and about Trotsky himself as an opponent of Lenin during the July Days. Dashkovsky's protest against this distortion of truth was made directly to the appropriate governmental authority. Stepanov answered and tried to prove his point. But Dashkovsky replied bluntly: you have not done your homework. You have not even read Lenin. And all your adjectives and epithets about Trotskyism "are taken from the arsenal of the era of the personality cult." No wonder that your mind is such a hotchpotch of erroneous ideas. Another old Bolshevik, V. Gromov, also writes about Trotsky and presents him as a complicated character, full of contradictions, but a great revolutionary. "Do not believe what Stalin wrote about Trotsky," who was "perhaps the only opponent who did not try to evade the struggle which Stalin imposed on him. . . ."[3]

The Diversification of the Opposition

When uncensored activity began there seemed to be near-unanimity among the writers: they all denounced Stalin with equal vehemence, all protested against persecution and fought to get out of the straitjacket of conformity, attacking officialdom with its uncomprehending ossified "line" on how literature should be written and history interpreted.

They all demanded more freedom and greater opportunity to influence domestic and foreign policy. More freedom—but for what? To influence their government—but in what direction, towards what goal? Inevitably, quite considerable differences of opinion emerged very soon, and were reflected not only in divergent views of the future of the Soviet Union—which features of the regime should be preserved and which discarded, in what form should the Soviet Union survive and should it survive at all, what tactics should be adopted to introduce the necessary changes—but also in contrasting appraisals of the past. Was Stalin a new, cruel and willful Tsar who destroyed Russia, or does he deserve some credit for modernizing it? Was Lenin responsible for Stalinism? What was the role of Trotsky and the Opposition in the crucial years before the war? And last but not least: was the revolution an unmitigated disaster, or has it brought some benefits which should still be salvaged?

Before I try to summarize the attitude of the various groups of writers to all these problems, it may be useful broadly to define the tendencies which have recently emerged in the uncensored literature. Our usual concepts of Left and Right apply to the Russian scene only to a limited extent. In the language of the dissidents, the Stalinist wing of the hierarchy and its supporters are termed "conservative dogmatist." The Sakharov school of thought is seen as pro-Western and antisocialist while those disciples of Solzhenitsyn who remain faithful to him are regarded as "religious mystics" and Slavophiles. Another religious opposition, slightly more modern in its outlook, formed itself into an "all-Russian Social Christian Union for National Liberation" and disseminated the ideas and writings of Djilas and Berdyaev. There is also, of course, opposition among the various nationalities of the Soviet Union: among the Ukrainians, Lithuanians, Estonians and Jews, Crimean Tartars and Volga Germans, whose national rights have been trampled upon and to whom Russification has been deeply offensive. They now demand greater autonomy, more freedom and less dependence on Moscow. Some are moved by purely nationalistic considerations, others combine with them socialist aspirations. How difficult it is to draw a line dividing the first from the second is perhaps best illustrated by the fact that it was General Grigorenko and Alexei Kosterin—both men with undoubted socialist credentials—who most ardently embraced the cause of the Crimean Tartars.

The State of the Marxist Opposition

Most classifications, even those which dissenters themselves adopt, seem to lack precision. Although Medvedev defines himself as a Marxist, his approach to most contemporary problems is a distinctly gradualist one. For him Grigorenko, with his advocacy of workers control and management of industry and of the immediate abolition of existing bureaucratic institutions, seems an old-fashioned, even dangerous, "anarcho-communist of 1918–1920." Nor can Medvedev agree with Kosterin, whose wholesale condemnation of the Soviet Communist Party in 1968 seemed to him "too emotional" and "exaggerated." Alexei Kosterin was a unique figure on the Soviet scene. Born in 1896, he was a member of the Bolshevik Party from 1916 onwards and a veteran of the Civil War. Arrested in 1938, he spent seventeen years in concentration camps. Released and rehabilitated, he became active in the opposition, representing the Marxist trend of thought: ". . . with the party card or without, I was, I am, and I shall remain a Marxist–Leninist, a communist, a Bolshevik. This is my life from early youth to the grave," he wrote when returning his *partbilet* two weeks before his death.[4] In the early sixties, Kosterin gathered around him a small circle of devoted friends and disciples of whom the most prominent was General Grigorenko. In his numerous writings, he tried to keep alive the traditions of the Bolshevik Old Guard and was calling for a return to the pristine ideas of the pre-Stalinist epoch. His daughter, Nina, fought as a partisan and perished behind the enemy lines at the age of twenty, in the years when her father was languishing in Kolyma. Her diary, an extremely moving and tragic document, was discovered after the war and published in the period of The Thaw, before Khrushchev's demotion. In 1968, along with

Grigorenko and Yakhimovich, Kosterin protested openly against the invasion of Czechoslovakia. Shortly afterwards the party committee of the Union of Writers expelled him from the CPSU. Before the final decision was communicated to him, he had resigned from the Party which, as he said, "does not allow [its members] to reason and think independently" and in which people remain out of sheer opportunism.

Kosterin died in November 1968. His funeral became the first, since 1927, open demonstration of the opposition. Between 300 and 400 people gathered at the cemetery, where, in spite of chicanery and harassment by the police, the valedictory speeches went on for half an hour before the gathering was brutally dispersed.[5] However, the occasion gave the participants a sense of their own strength, and stimulated the formation of the Group for the Defence of Civil Rights, in which at that time Yakir and Petrovsky were active. Searches, arrests and trials followed. Grigorenko paid heavily for his involvement with long years in a psychiatric prison-hospital. Arrested in 1969, he was not released until 1975. He has remained a communist, but has somewhat revised his oppositionist tactics. In his *Diary from Prison* he maintains that his future task lies not in creating conspiratorial organizations, but in "open, bold attacks on obvious tyranny, falsehood and hypocrisy"; not in revolutionary action for the overthrow of the regime, but in open struggle "within the framework of the law" for democratization and "constitutional rights."[6] It is difficult to judge what made Grigorenko change his views and his tactics. In the sixties, when he set up the "Union for the Revival of Leninism," his call was "for a return to the point at which Lenin left off." But this was a period at which some stirring "from below" could be clearly heard.

Already in 1957 at Moscow University there was so much ferment and unrest that a number of students were arrested. Boris Levitsky, who left the Soviet Union a few years ago, reports that between 1964 and 1971 there used to appear in various parts of the country groups of students and workers acting, or attempting to act, under slogans such as "All Power to the Soviets."[7] In Leningrad, some Komsomol members who organized a "Union of Communards" were sentenced to long terms of imprisonment and exile. In Alma Ata in 1967, members of the Marxist circle "The Young Worker" were arrested; the same fate befell a number of young communists in Ryazan, Saratov and Petrozavodsk. In Voroshilovgrad the authorities uncovered a secret organization called "For the Reality of Leninist Ideas." In 1971, a group of political prisoners smuggled an open letter to the Danish Communist Party in which they drew the attention of all fraternal parties to their plight. *The Chronicle of Current Events* reported a trial of one Fedorov who tried to set up a "Union of Communists." This incredibly courageous individual is reported to have stated in court: "I have been and I remain a communist. Only love for my country and for socialism led me to the dock. Even were I to be sentenced ten times, as long as my strength allows me, I shall defend communist ideals."

There is disaffection among Komsomol members at large. Medvedev reports that there are about 400 secret youth groups, circles and organizations; but one has reason to think that the proportion of Marxists among them is very small. While the big names among the dissidents are protected from repression by their standing and fame, young unknown oppositionists are quite helpless. Moreover, the Soviet security organs pounce with perhaps greater speed and ferocity upon these "extremist" dissidents than on any others. They have no chance to engage in any activity, not least because they are the most impatient to act. Levitsky's report compels one to the sad conclusion that the so-called communist Left is mostly in camps and prisons.

Solzhenitsyn and Reactionary Dissent

If the communist Left is in camps and prisons, the extreme, reactionary Right is in voluntary or involuntary exile. Writers like Solzhenitsyn and Maximov are now active abroad and are grouped around the journal *Kontinent*.

The birth of *Kontinent* was accompanied by something of a literary scandal. Günther Grass, an implacable critic of the Soviet brand of communism, had been asked for a statement welcoming the new journal. In reply he drafted a harsh and blunt Open Letter to Solzhenitsyn and Sinyavsky denouncing the financial dependence of *Kontinent* on the extreme right-wing Springer Press, "the fascist Beelzebub" with the help of which the dissidents want to fight the "communist devil." By taking Springer money, said Grass, the sponsors of *Kontinent* had opted for western totalitarianism and forfeited the right to present themselves as fighters for democracy. However, *Kontinent* percolates into Russia and is read by the opponents of the regime as well as by high-ups in the hierarchy. Solzhenitsyn remains the central theme of many whispered political and literary debates. His revelations of the horrors of the Stalin era have been for a long time the only source of much information—and some misinformation—which continues to be completely excluded from all official publications. His pioneering role in stirring the conscience of a society in whose name terrible crimes have been perpetrated, in showing the darkest side of Soviet reality, is widely recognized. His religious ideas appeal to people bewildered by their past and uncertain of their future: "Religion is, indeed, the sigh of the oppressed creature . . . the heart of a heartless world, the soul of soulless conditions; it is the opium of the people." His political precepts, however, seem far-fetched, too retrograde even for those who hanker after the good old prerevolutionary times. His denunciation of modern civilization, Western and Russian alike, his call for the "construction of more than half our state in a fresh place," that is in the wastes of the North East, finds no echo in a population craving for the minimal solace of material goods for so long denied. His Great-Russian chauvinism, extolling Russia's "spiritual peculiarities and folk traditions" offends small nationalities—under Stalin's rule, there had been an equality of suffering from which non-Russian citizens were not exempt. The vision which Solzhenitsyn offers of a Russia which "for the foreseeable future" is "destined to have an authoritarian order" frightens some and repels others. Although there is no doubt that there are many lesser Solzhenitsyns who have remained in the Soviet Union, the great exile himself has few followers to endorse his political programme.

The Role of the West: Sakharov and Medvedev

This programme has been subjected to respectful but remorseless criticism, by another famous dissident, Academician Sakharov. For Sakharov the scientist, Solzhenitsyn's way of thinking is hopelessly irrational and even dangerous. Stagnation and retrogression in the development of science, economy, and technology—not progress, as Solzhenitsyn supposes—are the evils from which his country suffers. Far from admiring the "spiritual peculiarities and folk traditions" of Old Mother Russia, Sakharov is full of admiration for the "progressive" West and for western science and technology. He is an internationalist in so far as he feels an affinity, a common bond of brotherhood, with western scientists. He would like to see the Soviet Union reconstructed on the model of western democracies. True, some of the changes brought about by the revolution are irreversible: agriculture can be only partially decollectivized, and denationalization of heavy industry would be impracticable. But some kind of neo-NEP would "restore social and psychological health," especially to rural areas which are now, says Sakharov, "under the threat of a complete lapse into drunkenness and torpor." For this state of affairs he blames Marxism, socialism, Leninism and Stalinism, identifying them completely and wasting little time on any social analysis of either present-day Russia or of postrevolutionary developments. Unlike Solzhenitsyn, who condemns all revolutions whenever and wherever they may have occurred, Sakharov makes no excursions into history. With science and technology strangled by the dead hand of stupid and obdurate bureaucracy, Russia is now in an impasse, he concludes.[8]

What, according to Sakharov, are the forces that could pull the Soviet Union out of that impasse and set it on the road to further development? He does not seem to search for such forces within the country. It is from the outside, from the democratic West, that help may come. For this the capitalist bloc must be strong and united: "Unity requires a leader. And that leader, both by right and by virtue of its great responsibilities is the United States. . . . " The United States and its allies should use all peaceful means at their disposal to press for reform in Russia. The United Nations should demand the right to inspect Soviet prisons and camps. Foreign policy and trade should be used as levers to extract from the Soviet rulers the maximum concessions for their citizens: civil rights, release of political prisoners, freedom to emigrate. Russia needs trade, credits, and détente in international relations. All these should be made conditional on the internal liberalization of the regime. The pressure of Western public opinion and its expressed outrage at the worst features of lingering Stalinism are of considerable help to Sakharov and his allies in the civil rights movement.

The historian Roy Medvedev also attaches the greatest importance to the pressures coming from the West, but in a perspective quite different from that of Sakharov. No matter how urgently the Soviet government needs American trade and credits, the threat to withhold them will not induce it to change its domestic legislation or essentially to modify the internal policy of the Soviet Union. And in any case, Medvedev argues European countries in their economic crisis also need commerce with Russia which they are not likely to forego for the sake of democratization in the Soviet Union. In opposition to Sakharov, Medvedev is a fervent advocate of détente between East and West, maintaining that in a less tense atmosphere demands for reform will have a greater chance of success. It is, of course, a debatable point: Will international détente lead to the relaxation of the regime at home and to a more liberal "exchange of goods, people, and ideas"; or should détente be the prize granted to Russia for a relaxation of its internal regime? On this point the difference between Sakharov and Medvedev seems to be one of tactics, not strategy.

But there is a wider gulf between them. Medvedev is not an unconditional admirer of European democracies, let alone the United States. He criticizes Sakharov for appealing to the reactionary politicians in the United States Congress, who are not in the least concerned with the democratization of the Soviet Union, but oppose the "exchange of goods, people and ideas" only because they—just like their counterparts, the Soviet "conservative dogmatists"—fear that such an exchange would not be beneficial for their country. To exchange "people for dollars," says Medvedev, to link trade with emigration, is immoral. To humiliate the Soviet leaders by too brutal an interference in what they regard as their internal affairs is counterproductive and only strengthens the hand of the hard-liners in Moscow. Neither Senator Jackson nor Senator Buckley, he adds, are really affected by the tragedy of Soviet Jews when they discuss Soviet emigration laws, nor do they care whether intellectuals in Moscow or Leningrad are free to voice their opinions. Soviet intellectuals should, according to Medvedev, appeal not to right-wing, anti-Soviet American politicians, but to all progressive forces, to the broad Left, to the Communist Parties which are effectively shaking off Stalinist tutelage. The pressure from the Left is less humiliating for the Soviet leaders.[9] It is also more moral and more sincere, because it comes from people concerned with freedom and socialism not only in the Soviet Union but also in their own far from perfect bourgeois countries. Medvedev does not identify Stalinism with Marxism, and firmly believes that the cause of socialism will be considerably strengthened once the cancer of Stalinism has been removed. He attributes the degeneration of the "First Workers' State" to social conditions and historical circumstances which made the rise of Stalinism possible, without, however, exonerating Leninism completely. Lenin was aware that dark forces were pushing the young Soviet state in the wrong direction and, had he lived, would have been able to reverse the trend, argues Medvedev. Even now, after the terrible holocaust, the Soviet Union is still alive. True, Stalin's epigones are strangling science, stifling freedom of expression and hampering economic development. Yet, contrary to Sakharov's contention, the Soviet Union is not in a hopeless impasse. The standard of living is rising, and although the productivity of labour is much lower than in the West, the Soviet worker is at least not haunted by the spectre of mass unemployment. "Soviet society can and will develop even within the existing political structure and in existing economic conditions." Once the Stalinist monolith has been broken, the pressure of socialist forces from without as well as from within the country will break it even further and gradual reforms will release the grip which the bureaucracy still holds on the country. Even the Communist Party of the Soviet Union, compromised as it is, is not beyond reform and renovation. . . .

The Intellectuals, the Masses and the State

It has been remarked, not without reason, that the dissidents—or at least those of whom we know—are elitists, that they are preoccupied only with their own intellectual freedoms, that they completely disregard the working masses, and are even "antagonistic to them."[10] Instead of appealing to United States Congressmen or left-wing bourgeois circles, should the dissidents not try to involve their own working class in the struggle for freedom? Surely the liberation of the Soviet people should be the task of the Soviet peoples themselves? There is indeed a curious dichotomy in the attitude of people like Medvedev and his cothinkers to the broad masses of the population. There is not the slightest desire that *the people* should take it upon themselves to overthrow the existing order. On the contrary, there is fear of an uncontrollable outburst from below which might bring upon the country a new *Smutnoye Vremia—The Times of Troubles* which followed the death of Ivan the Terrible. . . .

No doubt, chaos and violence from below would endanger the privileged position of the intelligentsia. The life of a Soviet intellectual is brighter and easier than the life of a worker or peasant, in spite of lack of freedom, persecution and harassment. The authorities do not yet feel threatened enough by the intellectual opposition to silence it completely by means too harsh and brutal. At the top of the far from monolithic hierarchy, there obviously are some individuals who sympathize with its aims and perhaps even stealthily collaborate with it. The more progressive wing of the ruling group may view the dissenters as welcome though still illegitimate allies. The more conservative hard-liners realize that too much in the running of the state depends on cooperation of the technical and scientific intelligentsia to risk a head-on collision. True, the intelligentsia cannot feel comfortable between the bureaucracy, which can still apply pressure from above, and the working mass, which it feels might upset the stability of the whole state from below. The intelligentsia wants, therefore, to avoid any crisis, any drastic deterioration in the economic situation of the masses which might push them on the road to an "uncontrollable" emotional outburst against the regime.

It is tempting to any Marxist to see in an alliance between the dissenting libertarian intelligentsia and the workers the best, and even the only way to salvation. This would indeed be a neat classical pattern, but until we know a little more about the Soviet working masses and can make contact with them, the actual prospects for a "classical" relationship of this type will remain difficult to assess. We do know that the standard of living of the Soviet worker is rising steadily though slowly. No matter how lyrically a Maximov or a Solzhenitsyn may describe prerevolutionary Russia, the Soviet worker is convinced that it was Lenin—not the Tsar or the Church—who brought about the Great Change. If he was not caught in the purges, if he had not infringed the draconian Stalinist labour code, the Soviet worker knew very little about concentration camps; and even if he learns about them now, he treats them as past history. Whatever doubts he may have, he views Stalin as a successor to Lenin. He identifies Leninism, Stalinism, and the regime under which he lives with socialism. Still burdened by the memory of the last war in which 20 million of his brethren perished, he is anxious to live in peace and quiet, leaving the affairs of the state to those on top with whom he has no violent quarrel.

A Russian Spring?

This picture may, however, be deceptive. One might have had a similar impression of the Portuguese masses right up to the very eve of the 1974 upheaval. All seemed quiet in Czechoslovakia in 1967, and yet the thaw was already on the way. The Prague Spring aroused great hopes: here was a country within the Soviet orbit and in the grip of Stalinism which suddenly rejected the Soviet brand of Communism. But one must not forget that the first impulse came from within the hitherto meek and obedient party and only later spurred the whole population to revolt. Can the Czechoslovak experience be regarded as a pointer to future developments in the Soviet Union? . . .

It is, of course, possible that the Soviet working masses too may rise in revolt.[11] If a war were to break out, if there were an economic catastrophe, a series of calamitous harvests with no help from abroad, a complete breakdown in the functioning of the state—if, in other words, the conditions of life were to become much more wretched than they are now—then there might indeed come an "uncontrollable burst of dissatisfaction" sweeping away all authority for a time. But can we at all take it for granted that such a revolt of the masses would be carried out in the name of socialism?

Arguments are advanced on the revolutionary Left in the West that since the Soviet ruling party is "unreformable," and since the intellectual dissidents are "antagonistic to the working classes," the only hope lies in an "upheaval from below."[12] By now one can have no illusions: antisocialist and anti-Marxist sentiments prevail among the most articulate opponents of the regime. How can we assume that the Soviet masses will not be moved by similar sentiments?

True, the worker at the factory bench in Moscow, Leningrad, Petrozavodsk or Magnitogorsk describes himself, not without pride, as a "Soviet worker": *Ya Sovietskii rabochyi*. He is still proud of "his" revolution, of its tremendous achievements, of space flights and supersonic airliners, of the network of schools and social services. Yet this pride is mixed with disillusionment and weariness. He has waited for a long time for a brighter tomorrow. Today his life is still a grinding drudgery with periodic shortages of basic necessities, with queues in the shops, shoddy goods, uninspiring TV programmes, and dull daily papers at which he glances in his painfully overcrowded home. He knows that even so, he is "better off" than he was. He knows that the revolution has transformed his backward country into one of the world's superpowers, and he is proud of this too. Yet his own misery seems to mock the splendour of the Soviet achievement and this feeling cannot but breed malaise and resentment, which may turn into anger at the ineptitude of the ruling party which feeds him with big words and slogans and small supplies of earthly goods, with restricted living space and even more restricted freedom to vent his anger.

Blaming the present rulers for economic bungling and incompetence, the Soviet worker seems to have no alternative to turn to: no other programme of action is presented to him; no other party exists; there is no organized opposition to the existing regime, nor has there been one within his memory. The more enlightened and intellectually awake worker may ponder the continuities and discontinuities between the CPSU as he sees it at present and the party that initiated the Great October Revolution. But for this he knows too little of his country's past, and the *Short Course* gives him no clue. (Incidentally, the writings of dissident historians are not too helpful either.) His pride in the Soviet socialist achievement on the one hand and, on the other, his anger at the misery of daily life seem for the time being delicately balanced. But it cannot be excluded that anger, which is not conducive to rational thinking, may come to the fore; the discontent which, at the beginning of the century, was the motive force of progress may, as it nears its end, pave the way for reaction and retrogression.

We might have expected that the Soviet intelligentsia would be able to see the extent to which Stalin was the perverter of Marxism, and what a tremendous and bloody gulf separates the pristine ideas of socialism from the fraudulent version of it which for decades has been presented from Moscow to the whole world. For over half a century the Soviet worker identified his regime with socialism. Should a calamity strike his country, might he not try to throw this very socialism overboard? Might not the very socioeconomic bases of the workers state be destroyed in the process of such an upheaval? Might such an upheaval not put power into the hands of black reaction and the Greek Orthodox Church, more obscurantist than any other, bringing to the surface those dark forces of moral and spiritual restoration in which Solzhenitsyn sees salvation?[13]

It may be that, in spite of everything, the Soviet worker will remain attached to socialism, no matter how his confidence in the present regime is shaken. The present malaise may find rational expression, and stimulate the formation of a truly revolutionary movement capable of releasing the latent creative potentialities of a people who are, after all, heirs to the Great October Revolution. The latter development may not be so improbable as a purely internal analysis of Soviet society might suggest. For just as, half a century ago, the rising tide of counterrevolution left the new workers state stranded and alone, so now the current resurgence of working-class struggles in Western and Southern Europe may yet inspire the growth of authentically revolutionary mass movements capable of overturning the bureaucracies of the Soviet Union and Eastern Europe. Should that occur, future socialist development in those countries will no longer be obliged to suffer stunting isolation within restrictive national boundaries, behind a *cordon sanitaire* or iron curtain; strengthened and enriched by membership of the community of their European siblings, they will find their way to a truly socialist order.

For the time being, the Soviet ruling group seems firmly in control, and can still afford to make minor concessions. "The precarious moment" of which Lenin wrote has not yet arrived, perhaps because the Soviet Union has not yet entered its "revolutionary period." We can only hope that tragedy will not occur, and that a future upheaval will not initiate a "counterrevolutionary period."

Notes

1. *Lenin,* Polnoye Sobranie Sochinenii, *5th Russian edition, Vol. 7, pp. 123–8.*
2. Politicheskii Dnevnik, *ed. Roy & Zhores Medvedev, Vol. I and II, Amsterdam, 1975.*
3. Politicheskii Dnevnik, *Vol. I, p. 376.*
4. Politicheskii Dnevnik, *Vol. II, p. 369.*
5. *For a description of the Kosterin funeral see Tamara Deutscher "Soviet Oppositions,"* NLR *60.*
6. Voices of the Soviet Opposition, *ed. George Saunders, New York 1974, p. 357.*
7. Politique Aujourd'hui, *August 1975.*
8. *A Sakharov,* My Country and The World, *London 1975.*
9. *Roy Medvedev,* A Lesson for Both Sides, *as yet unpublished in the West.*
10. *M. Cox, "The Politics of the Dissenting Intellectual,"* Critique *5.*
11. *The oppositionist Leonid Plyushch, recently released from psychiatric hospital and allowed to leave the Soviet Union, commented, in an interview given to* Informations Ouvrières *(Paris),* inter alia *on the following sentence in the programme of the Fourth International: "Only the victorious revolutionary uprising of the oppressed masses can revive the Soviet regime and guarantee its further development towards socialism." "I wonder about this," remarked Plyushch. "The masses have no political consciousness whatsoever. A revolutionary situation takes form when 'the masses can no longer live as they have before.' But in the Soviet Union living conditions are improving. It is a slow process but real. There might be a chance if there were a war. But war is too monstrous and it would not bring democratization." (Translation in* Intercontinental Press, *22 March 1976.)*
12. *Cox, op. cit.*
13. *"It is inconceivable that Russia should ever call back the Romanovs, even if only to overthrow them for a second time." Isaac Deutscher,* The Unfinished Revolution, *p. 4. "But although restoration [in previous revolutions] was a tremendous setback, indeed a tragedy, to a nation that succumbed to it, it had its redeeming feature: it demonstrated to a people disillusioned with the revolution how unacceptable the reactionary alternative was." Ibid., p. 105.*

The "Leninist" Principle of Partisanship

Leonid Brezhnev

Comrades, with our society's advance along the road of communist construction a growing role is played by *literature and art* in moulding the outlook, moral convictions and spiritual culture of Soviet people. Quite naturally, therefore, the Party continues, as it has always done, to devote much attention to the ideological content of our literature and art and to the role they play in society. In line with the Leninist principle of partisanship we believe that our task is to direct the development of all forms of creative art towards participation in the people's great cause of communist construction.

During the past five years our literature, theatre, cinema, television, fine arts and music have given Soviet people many new, interesting and talented works. New works and productions have appeared which deal with our people's past and present realistically, from Party positions, without embellishment and without playing up shortcomings, and concentrate attention on truly important problems of communist education and construction. These works are further confirmation that the closer the artist is to the many-faceted life of the Soviet people the surer is the road to creative achievement and success.

During the period under review a prominent place in literature and art was held by the Lenin theme. A number of interesting novels, plays and films about Lenin, all of them permeated with revolutionary passion and the grandeur of devotion to Leninism, were brought out.

A highly satisfying fact is that literature and art are fruitfully developing in all our republics, in dozens of languages of the peoples of the USSR, in the vivid diversity of national forms.

The congresses held in recent years by the unions of writers, artists, composers and film-makers of our country have been noteworthy landmarks in the development of Soviet art. They mirrored the indisputable growth of the ideological and political maturity of our creative intelligentsia, and of their responsibility for the content and artistic value of the works created by them.

Thus, much has been done in recent years by workers in Soviet art. Our people highly value their achievements, which are noteworthy contributions fostering communist consciousness in Soviet people.

However, it cannot be said that all is well in the realm of artistic creative work, particularly as regards quality. It would not be amiss to note here that we are still getting quite a few works that are shallow in content and inexpressive in form. We sometimes even get cases of works being dedicated to a good, topical theme but giving the impression that the artist has taken too insubstantial an approach to his task, that he has not put all his effort,

Leonid Brezhnev is General Secretary, Central Committee of the Communist Party, and chairman of the Presidium of the Supreme Soviet, of the USSR. This is Brezhnev's complete statement on literature and art that appeared in his lengthy Report for the Central Committee delivered at the 24th Party Congress of the CPSU on March 30, 1971.

his talent into it. It seems to me that we all have the right to expect workers in art to be more demanding of themselves and of their colleagues.

The achievements of Soviet literature and art would have been unquestionably greater and shortcomings would have been eradicated quicker if our literary-art criticism pursued the Party line more vigorously, adopted a more principled stand and combined exactingness with tact and a solicitous attitude to the creators of artistic values.

Furthermore, sight must not be lost of the fact that in the development of our art there were complicating factors of another order. There were some people who sought to reduce the diversity of present-day Soviet reality to problems that have irreversibly receded into the past as a result of the work done by the Party to surmount the consequences of the personality cult. Another extreme current among individual men of letters was the attempt to whitewash past phenomena which the Party had subjected to emphatic and principled criticism, and to conserve ideas and views contravening the new, creative elements which the Party had introduced into its practical and theoretical work in recent years.

Essentially, both these cases were attempts to belittle the significance of what the Party and the people had already accomplished, and divert attention from current problems, from the Party's constructive guideline and the creative work of Soviet people.

Workers in literature and art are in one of the most crucial sectors of the ideological struggle. The Party and the people have never reconciled nor will ever reconcile themselves to attempts, no matter who makes them, to blunt our ideological weapon and cast a stain on our banner. If a writer slanders Soviet reality and helps our ideological adversaries in their fight against socialism he deserves only one thing—public scorn.

We mention these negative phenomena not because they have become appreciably widespread. The Central Committee feels that the Party's frank and principled attitude towards these phenomena helps writers and artists to work with greater confidence and conviction in the general direction of the development of Soviet literature and art in which they have been fruitfully working during the past five years.

Soviet writers and artists have been educated by the Communist Party. They draw their inspiration from the deeds and thoughts of their people, and their creative destiny is inseparable from the interests of the socialist motherland.

We are for an attentive attitude to creative quests, for the full unfolding of the individuality of gifts and talents, for the diversity and wealth of forms and styles evolved on the basis of the method of socialist realism. The strength of Party leadership lies in the ability to spark the artist with enthusiasm for the lofty mission of serving the people and turn him into a convinced and ardent participant in the remaking of society along communist lines.

Chapter 13

THE GOVERNORS AND THE GOVERNED

Few serious students of Soviet affairs would maintain that significant political power resides in the mass of the Russian people—except in an inchoate sense—or even in the millions of Communist Party members as a whole. While E.H. Carr and Milovan Djilas, in the excerpts that follow, both see power concentrated in a ruling group which, in Carr's phrase, "finds its institutional embodiment in the Party," they disagree on whether there may be said to be a ruling *class* in Russia and on the extent to which there is fluidity in Soviet society and the ruling group. On this issue, dissident Roy Medvedev, in his *On Socialist Democracy,* supports Carr. "Although," he writes, "there are groups within Soviet society that might with some justification be regarded as a bureaucratic elite, they do not constitute a class in the socioeconomic sense of the word. It is perfectly obvious that they do not own the means of production or the land, and they are not able to bequeath their rights, privileges, or positions to their children." In respect to mobility, he comments that "It is important to note that in our socialist society, the growing ranks of the intelligentsia are recruited not from certain privileged sections of the community but from among the people as a whole."

What has been the impact of the system upon the values, beliefs, loyalties, habits, and social behavior of the Soviet people? This, in essence, is the broad question to which Wright Miller addresses himself in this section.

Who Rules in Soviet Society?

E.H. Carr

The victors of 1917 thought they were establishing a dictatorship of the proletariat, or, a shade more realistically, a dictatorship of the proletariat and the peasantry. Just as the peasants were encouraged to seize the land, so the workers were encouraged to take over the factories. "Workers' control" was the slogan of the hour. Workers' control did not work, and without it the dictatorship of the proletariat ceased to be a reality and became a symbol. It was replaced by what? The answer is clear. By the dictatorship of the party (a phrase used at the time by Lenin and others, though afterwards rejected as heretical) and later by the dictatorship of the party machine. In other words, if we want to identify the ruling group in Soviet society, we have to look not for a class but for a party.

The Marxist class analysis of society was a product of the nineteenth century. Few people are convinced by the famous generalization with which the Communist Manifesto opens, that all history has been the history of class struggles. Marx took what he correctly diagnosed as the most significant feature of contemporary society in Western Europe and sweepingly extended it to other periods, where its application was by no means so clear. Marx never explained what he meant by a class: it probably seemed so obvious a phenomenon of the world in which he lived as not to require definition. But I will take Lenin's definition: "Classes are groups of people of such a kind that one group can appropriate the labor of another, thanks to the difference of their position in the specific structure of the social economy."

This takes account of the two cardinal factors in class. Class is primarily based on common economic interest, but it also acquires a quasi-permanent character conferred on it by social tradition or convention. I have never been altogether happy about the application of the class analysis to countries like the United States where, for historical reasons, this quasi-permanent character is weak or nonexistent, or to countries like Czarist Russia where the major divisions of society were not economic, but legal and constitutional; and I feel sure that it is altogether misleading as an explanation of the structure of Soviet society. There is no ruling class in Soviet Russia. There is a ruling group which finds its institutional embodiment in the party.

This is, I think, significant. A class is an economic formation, a party a political formation. I shall not argue that economic factors play a smaller role in the life of society than in the nineteenth century. But what I would maintain is that the clear-cut line of demarcation between economics and politics which dominated all economic thinking in the nineteenth century, including that of Marx, is out of date. In Soviet Russia, at any rate, economics means politics, and the structure of Soviet society must be analyzed in terms not of economic class but of political party.

As I have said, the dictatorship of the proletariat was replaced by the dictatorship of the party when workers' control collapsed in the factories. And workers' control collapsed because the workers lacked the necessary technical engineering and managerial skills. One

E.H. Carr is the author of the monumental A History of Soviet Russia; Studies in Revolution; The Soviet Impact on the Western World, *and many scholarly articles on Soviet affairs. The selection is from* The Nation, *vol. 181 (October 1, 1955), pp. 278–80. Reprinted by permission.*

of the first tasks of the party, of the ruling group, was to find the technicians and white-collar workers of all grades to put industry back into production; and the attitude to be adopted by these "specialists," as they were called, was a constant preoccupation of party literature. And when, a few years later, the even more desperate problem was tackled of mechanizing agriculture and introducing modern methods of cultivation, the difficulty once more was to provide not only machinery but skilled personnel to use it and organize its use. It was precisely those specialists who, being indispensable to the regime, came to occupy a leading—and sometimes equivocal—position in the ruling group of what was still called a workers' state; and to study the party's attitude toward them is an important part of the analysis of Soviet society.

From the outset the attitude of the party toward specialists was utterly different from its position on the nepman. The nepman, and *a fortiori,* the *kulak*, was *ex hypothesi*, an enemy of the regime, pursuing aims incompatible with it, tolerated only so long as he had to be. A loyal nepman or a loyal *kulak* was an impossibility; no nepman or *kulak* could conceivably be admitted to the party. The specialist, on the other hand, though by his origins he might be a class enemy like the nepman, was pursuing the aims of the regime whose servant he was. His origins might make him suspect. But he could be, and often was, loyal; and as time went on, more and more specialists became party members. Thus, for the specialist, origin was not the determining factor. He might be bourgeois by origin but he was not bourgeois in function. He did not enjoy the economic independence of the *entrepreneur*. On the contrary, he was politically dependent on the government and on the party. If he was successful, success was rewarded not by increased profits, but by promotion to a bigger and better job. The soft-pedalling of world revolution, the proclamation of "socialism in one country," and the policy of industrialization, eased the process of assimilation for the specialist. By the end of the nineteen-twenties he had become, by and large, a loyal servant of the regime; the avenues of promotion and of party membership were wide open to him.

I do not think that up to this time the specialist had any important influence on decisions of policy. These were still taken by the old party leadership, by the survivors of the prerevolutionary party intelligentsia. But in the nineteen-thirties, when a new generation grew up which had never known prerevolutionary Russia, and when sons of workers had clambered up the educational ladder to the top, the distinctions began to fade. The taint of bourgeois origin was no longer acutely felt; and the whole group of white-collar workers—party officials, government officials, managers, technicians, teachers, doctors, lawyers, and intellectuals of all kinds—began gradually to coalesce. Official pronouncements began to extol the member of this new intelligentsia; the Stalin constitution enfranchised him irrespective of his origin; the party statute of 1939 gave him a status in the party side by side with the worker and the peasant.

It is in this new intelligentsia, recruited from different class origins, and not constituting a class in the Marxist or Leninist sense of the term, that we must look for the ruling group in Soviet society. This is the group which has substituted itself for the dictatorship of the proletariat; the only theoretical justification for the substitution is that its *raison d'être* and its purpose—the cementing force which holds it together—is the industrialization of the country. In this respect, it still carries the dynamic of the proletarian revolution; and to this long-term purpose the immediate welfare of the worker, to say nothing of the peasant, will be ruthlessly sacrificed. The ruling group remains pledged to the eradication of everything bourgeois from Soviet society. If it still tolerates a handful of nepmen, it tolerates them because it must. It is engaged in a desperate uphill struggle to turn the *kolkhoz* worker into a good Socialist—a struggle only halted by the still more desperate need to induce him to feed the towns for a meager return in the form of consumer goods. This is the core of the problem which any ruling group that stands for industrialization has to face.

One more question: How far does this ruling group constitute a closed and privileged social order? . . . Every ruling group looks after its own, including its own children; and, when good educational facilities are scarce, it will see to it that its children get the best. But the essential facts about Soviet society are that it is the society of an expanding economy; and educational facilities, too, are expanding rapidly. In an expanding society, policies of exclusion do not work and do not last. The child of the worker does not, it is true, start level with the child of the party official or of the industrial manager. But the gulf is not unbridgeable, and it seems likely to narrow if the Soviet economy continues to expand at anything like its present rate. So long as this goes on, Soviet society and the ruling group will remain fluid and we shall see further changes. Meanwhile, we only confuse ourselves by attempting to equate the present regime in Russia with anything we have seen in the past—whether with a Czarist autocracy or with a Victorian bourgeoisie. It is a new phenomenon in history, with new merits and new vices, and we had better try to see it for what it is.

The New Class

Milovan Djilas

Everything happened differently in the USSR and other Communist countries from what the leaders—even such prominent ones as Lenin, Stalin, Trotsky, and Bukharin—anticipated. They expected that the state would rapidly wither away, that democracy would be strengthened. The reverse happened. They expected a rapid improvement in the standard of living—there has been scarcely any change in this respect and, in the subjugated East European countries, the standard has even declined. In every instance, the standard of living has failed to rise in proportion to the rate of industrialization, which was much more rapid. It was believed that the differences between cities and villages, between intellectual and physical labor, would slowly disappear; instead these differences have increased. Communist anticipations in other areas—including their expectations for developments in the non-Communist world—have also failed to materialize.

Milovan Djilas was a Partisan leader during the war and Vice-President of Yugoslavia under Tito. He broke with Yugoslav Communism, was expelled from the Party in 1954, and was subsequently imprisoned for a number of years. This selection is from the book and chapter titled The New Class *(New York: Frederick A. Praeger, Inc., 1957). By permission of the publisher.*

The greatest illusion was that industrialization and collectivization in the USSR, and destruction of capitalist ownership, would result in a classless society. In 1936, when the new Constitution was promulgated, Stalin announced that the "exploiting class" had ceased to exist. The capitalist and other classes of ancient origin had in fact been destroyed, but a new class, previously unknown to history, had been formed. . . . The roots of the new class were implanted in a special party, of the Bolshevik type. Lenin was right in his view that his party was an exception in the history of human society, although he did not suspect that it would be the beginning of a new class.

To be more precise, the initiators of the new class are not found in the party of the Bolshevik type as a whole but in that stratum of professional revolutionaries who made up its core even before it attained power. . . . The once live, compact party, full of initiative, is disappearing to become transformed into the traditional oligarchy of the new class, irresistibly drawing into its ranks those who aspire to join the new class and repressing those who have any ideals.

The party makes the class, but the class grows as a result and uses the party as a basis. The class grows stronger, while the party grows weaker; this is the inescapable fate of every Communist party in power. . . . The movement of the new class toward power comes as a result of the efforts of the proletariat and the poor. These are the masses upon which the party of the new class must lean and with which its interests are most closely allied. This is true until the new class finally establishes its power and authority. Over and above this, the new class is interested in the proletariat and the poor only to the extent necessary for developing production and for maintaining in subjugation the most aggressive and rebellious social forces. The monopoly which the new class establishes in the name of the working class over the whole of society is, primarily, a monopoly over the working class itself. . . .

As defined by Roman law, property constitutes the use, enjoyment, and disposition of material goods. The Communist political bureaucracy uses, enjoys, and disposes of nationalized property. If we assume that membership in this bureaucracy or new owning class is predicated on the use of privileges inherent in ownership—in this instance nationalized material goods—then membership in the new party class, or political bureaucracy, is reflected in a larger income in material goods and privileges than society should normally grant for such functions. In practice, the ownership privilege of the new class manifests itself as an exclusive right, as a party monopoly, for the political bureaucracy to distribute the national income, to set wages, direct economic development, and dispose of nationalized and other property. This is the way it appears to the ordinary man who considers the Communist functionary as being very rich and as a man who does not have to work. . . .

Membership in the Communist Party before the Revolution meant sacrifice. Being a professional revolutionary was one of the highest honors. Now that the party has consolidated its power, party membership means that one belongs to a privileged class. And at the core of the party are the all-powerful exploiters and masters. . . .

In Stalin's victory Trotsky saw the Thermidoric reaction against the revolution, actually the bureaucratic corruption of the soviet government and the revolutionary cause. Consequently, he understood and was deeply hurt by the amorality of Stalin's methods. Trotsky was the first, although he was not aware of it, who in the attempt to save the Communist movement discovered the essence of contemporary Communism. But he was not capable of seeing it through to the end. He supposed that this was only a momentary cropping up of bureaucracy, corrupting the party and the revolution, and concluded that the solution was in a change at the top, in a "palace revolution." When a palace revolution actually took place after Stalin's death, it could be seen that the essence had not changed; something deeper and more lasting was involved. The Soviet Thermidor of Stalin had not only led to the installation of a government more despotic than the previous one, but also to the installation of a class. . . .

Without relinquishing anything it created under Stalin's leadership, the new class appears to be renouncing his authority for the past few years. But it is not really renouncing that authority—only Stalin's methods which, according to Khrushchev, hurt "good Communists." . . . In view of the significance of ownership for its power—and also of the fruits of ownership—the party bureaucracy cannot renounce the extension of its ownership even over small-scale production facilities. Because of its totalitarianism and monopolism, the new class finds itself unavoidably at war with everything which it does not administer or handle, and must deliberately aspire to destroy or conquer it. . . .

The fact that the seizure of property from other classes, especially from small owners, led to decreases in production and to chaos in the economy was of no consequence to the new class. Most important for the new class, as for every owner in history, was the attainment and consolidation of ownership. The class profited from the new property it had acquired even though the nation lost thereby. The collectivization of peasant holdings, which was economically unjustified, was unavoidable if the new class was to be securely installed in its power and its ownership. . . .

The establishment of the ownership of the new class was evidenced in the changes in the psychology, the way of life, and the material position of its members, depending on the position they held on the hierarchical ladder. Country homes, the best housing, furniture, and similar things were acquired; special quarters and exclusive rest homes were established for the highest bureaucracy, for the elite of the new class. The party secretary and the chief of the secret police in some places not only became the highest authorities but obtained the best housing, automobiles, and similar evidence of privilege. Those beneath them were eligible for comparable privileges, depending upon their position in the hierarchy. The state budgets, "gifts," and the construction and reconstruction executed for the needs of the state and its representatives became the everlasting and inexhaustible sources of benefits to the political bureaucracy. . . .

Open at the bottom, the new class becomes increasingly and relentlessly narrower at the top. Not only is the desire necessary for the climb; also necessary is the ability to understand and develop doctrines, firmness in struggles against antagonists, exceptional dexterity and cleverness in intraparty struggles, and talent in strengthening the class. . . .

Just as under Stalin, the new regime, in executing its so-called liberalization policy, is extending the "socialist" ownership of the new class. Decentralization in the economy does not mean a change in ownership, but only gives greater rights to the lower strata of the bureaucracy or of the new class. If the so-called liberalization and decentralization meant anything else, that would be manifest in the political right of at least part of the people to exercise some influence in the management of material goods. At least, the people would have the right to criticize the arbitrariness of the oligarchy. This would lead to the creation of a new political movement, even though it were only a loyal opposition. However, this is not even mentioned, just as democracy in the party is not mentioned. Liberalization and decentralization are in force only for Communists; first for the oligarchy, the leaders of the new class; and second, for those in the lower echelons. This is the new method, inevitable under changing conditions, for the further strengthening and consolidation of monopolistic ownership and totalitarian authority of the new class. . . .

The new class instinctively feels that national goods are, in fact, its property, and that even the terms "socialist," "social," and "state" property denote a general legal fiction.

The new class also thinks that any breach of its totalitarian authority might imperil its ownership. Consequently, the new class opposes *any* type of freedom, ostensibly for the purpose of preserving "socialist" ownership. Criticism of the new class's monopolistic administration of property generates the fear of a possible loss of power. . . . In defending its authority, the ruling class must execute reforms every time it becomes obvious to the people that the class is treating national property as its own. Such reforms are not proclaimed as being what they really are, but rather as part of the "further development of socialism" and "socialist democracy." . . .

This is a class whose power over men is the most complete known to history. For this reason it is a class with very limited views, views which are false and unsafe. Closely ingrown, and in complete authority, the new class must unrealistically evaluate its own role and that of the people around it. Having achieved industrialization, the new class can now do nothing more than strengthen its brute force and pillage the people. It ceases to create. Its spiritual heritage is overtaken by darkness.

While the new class accomplished one of its greatest successes in the revolution, its method of control is one of the most shameful pages in human history. Men will marvel at the grandiose ventures it accomplished, and will be ashamed of the means it used to accomplish them. When the new class leaves the historical scene—and this must happen—there will be less sorrow over its passing than there was for any other class before it. Smothering everything except what suited its ego, it has condemned itself to failure and shameful ruin.

Russians as People

Wright Miller

The Russian town scene is today an index, among other things, of the driving power which the Soviet Government, despite all repressions, has been able to generate in its subjects, and it is a measure, too, of the belief and trust in the future which has superseded so much of the old hopelessness and lethargy. The attraction of the expanding urban life is such that the Government has long ago prevented peasants, in general, from taking town jobs except through official channels, though a good many still seem to get themselves recruited unofficially. One may hear townspeople speak of what is "peasant" as *ipso facto*

Wright Miller is the author of five books, two bibliographies, and many articles on the USSR. He has visited the Soviet Union numerous times since 1934 and lived there almost three years. This excerpt is from pp. 61–69, 114–115, 183–202 of Russians as People *© by the author, and published by E.P. Dutton & Co. Inc., 1961. It is reproduced here by permission.*

dirty and to be swept away in due course, like the ikons which, for years after the Revolution, used to sit at every street corner, slobbered and dripping with hearty moujik kisses. Under the latest reforms peasants are a great deal better off than they used to be, and some town workers consider them "privileged," yet they are still coarsely dressed, are short of public services and entertainment, and have a much slenderer assortment of goods on the boards of the village co-op than they can see in the city stores.

Some townspeople have been heard to speak of "common people who live like animals." Yet these are only the crude and brash among the town-dwellers, the newly urbanized, who have kept a peasant coarseness and lost the peasant sense of brotherhood. The fact is that the countryside, for nearly all Russian townspeople, is at most only one generation away. It is where parents or uncles and aunts live, to visit whom is often the only chance of a holiday. The contrast between the material standards of town and peasant is new and striking, but there is still a great continuity between town and country, an inheritance of social ways and upbringing which is powerful in spite of being often unrealized or even superficially rejected by the new generation in town. . . .

Only one must not judge the peasants too much, as one would judge in Western Europe, by what they make of their surroundings. If there is little sweetness in huts or gardens, the sweetness is there in the people—in the warm hospitality, in the good nature of the peasant crowds however thick they throng in trains or markets, in the old country nannies who attach themselves to hundreds of modest city families as well as privileged ones, in the beautiful courtesy of so many of the old. . . .

And if the sweetness is to be seen in human relationships rather than in the work of men's hands, then it seems to me that, with every material shortage and hardship allowed for, the bias must be deeply significant of something in the Russian character. External appearances in Russia are far less informative than in the West. . . .

It is [a long time] since I first visited Russia, but the dominant characteristics of the people still seem to me the same as they did then—the strong, largely unconscious sense of community, and the naturalness and truth-to-feeling of individual behavior. . . .

Government, in Russia, is not traditionally expected to derive its sanction from the governed, from which it follows that government, though unloved, is respected according to its efficiency and even sometimes according to its ruthlessness. But that does not imply that one cooperates with it. Russian history is full of revolts against landowners and officials. . . . And today only a slight experience of Russian life will disabuse a foreigner of the idea that Russians have any natural tendency to do as they are ordered—still less that they feel the need, to which some Germans will confess, of actually preferring to receive orders.

Soviet power is a great deal more efficient than Tsarist power ever was, and yet the average Russian reaction to the orders of officials other than the political police is still to cajole or to argue. And this includes the ordinary policeman— the "militiaman" in Soviet terminology. There are few more instructive sights than the little crowd which can gather in protest around a militiaman dragging away a drunk who cannot keep his feet; the comrade militiaman (who can hardly keep his) is being far too rough with the citizen drunk! . . .

In the early days of the Revolution the country naturally seethed with political discussion, and some discussion of policy, so long as it was Communist policy, went on well into the time of the First Five-Year Plan. But the purges of 1935–38 put an end to all that. The discussion of policy as a matter of pro and con became too dangerous, and the Party rules forbid it even in Party branch meetings. Since only a handful of Soviet citizens play any part in deciding policy there seems no reason why discussion of this kind should revive unless in the greatest privacy. The "line" is laid down through the press, radio, schools, and public lectures, and it is so universally publicized that when people read the newspaper it is significant that they very often turn to the foreign news page first; they know only too well what the rest of the paper will contain.

Yet though Russians have to accept policy, and political discussion in the Western sense is almost excluded, they are far from being passive in their attitudes to their Government and its policies. Their first reaction to any new policy is—"What is behind it? What is safe for us to do?" These, it is reported, were the questions people asked each other when Stalin died; they were also the questions asked when one of the nineteenth-century Tsars died. Russians have become adept at reading between the lines of communiqués, and they can estimate impending policy changes by noticing the dropping of a slogan or the nonappearance of a familiar Kremlin figure at an important gathering.

When Russians attend meetings they are not as emotionally exploitable as one might expect. They show enthusiasm for processions, they cheer in the right places but not too much, and they never give that impression which one used to get from Fascist crowds—of atoms ready to be burned up into one great molecule. . . . Russians are not usually people who like accepting discipline more than is absolutely necessary. They have always been quick to take advantage of loopholes and quick to sense which officials or which orders need not be taken too seriously. Even a foreigner will come across instances. He is sure to overhear some of the long arguments about queues and exits and entrances; in a café he may notice the public turning a completely deaf ear to the "agitator" at the bar who is making a speech to recruit volunteers for military training; or he may witness such incidents as the "home guard" drilling of Bolshoi Theatre dancers which I saw in wartime in the public square at Kuibyshev, where the ballerinas, giggling and fooling, made the young officer blush and turned the whole thing into a farce.

As for discipline which cannot be so openly flouted, it is well known what ingenuity the Russians have shown in what they call *kombinatsia*—arrangements arrived at by persuasion of the right persons, with or without a bribe. When the "norms" were too high for the average worker to achieve, a good-natured foreman would discover "conditions of special difficulty" demanding a lower norm, or a bookkeeper might manipulate the returns. . . . The whole system of under-the-counter deals, illegal exchanges, and oiling of palms is known collectively as *blat*, and *blat* flourished, of course, long before the Revolution. In Soviet times we know of it not only from the report of refugees but from the thousands of instances which are exposed in the Soviet press and radio as examples for punishment, and from Soviet plays and films which are devoted to the exposing of these abuses, implying at the same time that there must be a great deal to expose. . . .

And all this has gone on while the Soviet nation as a whole—including all the people involved in *blat*—has built up a production of pig-iron 10 times, of oil 12 times, of coal 16 times, and of electric power 123 times the prerevolutionary figures,* besides defeating the Germans, making good most of the damage they inflicted, and maintaining peacetime armaments on a huge scale. The whole stupendous achievement is a tribute partly to dictatorship, partly to genuine enthusiasm among a large minority, partly to education, but partly also to an extraordinary fact about the Russian people—extraordinary, that is, to

***Editor's note:** *In a letter to this editor dated November 18, 1966, Mr. Wright Miller updated his statement to read that production of pig-iron increased 15 times, of oil 22 times, of coal 17 times, and of electric power 230 times the prerevolutionary figures. More recent figures appear in the section on "The Soviet Economic System."*

most people from the West, though it does not strike Russians as extraordinary. It is this—that in spite of all the oppression, individual suffering, and shortages, in spite of all the shifts people have been put to to satisfy their simplest needs, basically they have nearly all of them retained the sense of belonging to one great Russian community, and they have in a rough way identified their community with the State. Many of the people who have suffered most, and most unjustifiably, at the hands of the Soviet system, have distinguished themselves later by their patriotism and self-sacrifice for the nation, as though they were obliged to convince themselves that Russia, after all, was in the right. An intellectual who spent six years in a labour camp for an almost unidentifiable "political offense" told me: "The thing on which I concentrated most when I was away was to convince myself that my incarceration was not the fault of our Government, but only of certain individuals."

This remarkable loyalty to the common cause is not incompatible with *blat*, because *blat* seems to arise mostly from the pressure of situations rather than from officials who are abusing their position in order to enrich themselves (though there is naturally a minority who try to do just this). . . .

The blend of mass loyalty and *blat* shows how far most Russians are from wanting or even understanding a system of representative government of Western form. To a limited extent they do choose their own representatives, but they choose them as men and women and not as supporters of policies. They choose their representatives at the lowest levels in trade union and Party branches and local Soviets, and though so far as one can hear they very rarely choose them by a vote between two or more candidates, their choice is in fact sifted through communal feeling until it reaches the point where one nomination seems obvious, in the same way that things were done in the *Mir*. Russians account this system a choice, and when the candidate is eventually nominated it is always possible to vote against him. The Government attaches great importance to this "selection of representatives from below," and the press sometimes reports cases of new elections being ordered where the nominated candidate was found to have been imposed by a higher authority and not "chosen from below." Soviet citizens also vote in larger units for their representatives in the Supreme Soviet, the Soviet of their Republic, and so forth, but here they have much less chance of acquaintance with persons who might win the nomination. . . .

The sophisticated idea of the seesaw between parties seems beyond the grasp of all but a few Russians, probably because they have no experience in their own history of a change of government other than by force. Most of them seem to think of political parties—if they think about them at all—as bodies determined to achieve power by fair means or foul, or else as the tools of some other power seekers. In either case it seems to them irresponsible to put the government of one's country at the mercy of a popular choice between such factions. It was a Tass correspondent long established in London, and familiar with parliamentary debates, who expressed to a Swedish correspondent his opinion that British party strife was merely a farce—not because the party policies were so similar, but because when the Opposition was defeated on any important issue "it did not proceed to sabotage."

The Communist Party of the Soviet Union is not, of course, a political party in the sense in which parties are understood by people who are not Communists. In 1917, though not yet counting on majority support, it suppressed all the other political parties in Russia, and the last thing likely in the most liberal possible future would be that other parties should be allowed to rise again. The Communist Party's task now is to govern the country and bring about Communism. It is meant to be an organizational and propaganda elite, spreading all over the country not only geographically but through branches or cells in every work unit and every other form of organization. Its work can appeal only to a minority, and most Soviet citizens are not members of the Communist Party. You cannot join simply by virtue of approving of Party aims and being willing to pay your subscription and attend a few meetings. The people wanted as members are Nature's organizing secretaries, troubleshooters, club leaders, propagandists, and scoutmasters, and if you are not prepared to put your leisure and convenience entirely at the service of the Party, and to be sent away for months on special duties, you are unlikely to be accepted as a member. Once you have joined you cannot resign from the Party, though you may be expelled, and at intervals there have been mass expulsions of the careerists, the power-seekers, or "those who joined because they couldn't do any other job," as I have heard Russians express it. Many people look down on Party members because of this element among them, or because they just do not like being chivvied, but some of the finest people in the country are also members and [if not], especially if they are already popular among their fellows, are frequently pressed by the Party to join. Over the last twenty years or so the total Party membership has varied between about 3 percent and about 5 percent of the population, and this proportion is apparently thought satisfactory. The other 95–97 percent describe themselves for political purposes by some such phrase as "non-Party sympathizers." Only Party members are normally referred to as "Communists."

However, this terminology should not be taken to imply that any large proportion of the Soviet people are privately out of sympathy with Communism. If a foreigner bluntly asks Soviet citizens what they think of Communism he will get one or two violently antipathetic replies (assuming the time and place of his question are discreetly chosen), but he would be unwise to attach much political significance to them. People who are opposed to Communism are in fact the very ones most likely to seek out a foreigner. But other persons, if approached, may point out that "Communism," as Communists understand the term, is a state of things to be reached in the future; it does not yet exist anywhere. "Building Communism" is one of the most widely-used propaganda phrases, and it is a utopian slogan which seems to inspire a fair number of Soviet citizens.

To ask the ordinary person what he thinks of the present state of "Communism" is too general a question altogether. He may approve of the new school his children attend, or the new goods in the shops; he may speak of sputniks or recall that Soviet power defeated the Germans (though he, like many Russians, privately feared that this could not happen); he may recall the seven price cuts since the war, or if he is old enough he may recall the village where peasants used to eat with their fingers from a common bowl and now, though living in the same huts, most of them have TV sets. On the other hand he may pass a sardonic comment, as an old peasant did to me in 1959, about his "local Party secretary who misappropriated 30,000 rubles"; he may recall half a dozen friends who were hauled off to Siberia and died there, or the brutal questioning he had himself to endure from Soviet security police when his home town was recaptured by Soviet troops; or if he is an intellectual he may rail at the dogma he has to teach. He is surrounded by Communist features or features which have undergone Communist influence, but he has other things to think of than the quite theoretical possibility that an alternative "system" might suit him better. . . .

It is most important for the foreigner to appreciate how universally the "Communist" label is applied in the Soviet Union; it is used not only to describe the typically Communist features of the economic and political system, but also to describe attitudes—in the realm of morals, for instance—which may be almost identical with what is considered admirable by non-Communist peoples. . . .

It can be regarded ideally as "Communist" to be sincere and discriminating when one is attracted by a woman, it is "Communist" also to be loyal to wife or husband or respectful to parents—and it is "Communist," too, to suppress all political opposition. Respect for the marriage tie or for parents, it would be said, is part of the basis of Soviet society, and to suppress political opposition must be necessary because, among other reasons, no other political system could secure the triumph of the moral values which, it is maintained, are so typically "Communist."

The Communist Party can thus attract the young by means of the moral image of a good Communist, as well as by the opportunities it can offer for social service, for vigilance against the capitalist foe, or for exercise of power. . . . The Soviet Union owes much to the enthusiasm of such young men. But it is not surprising that more sophisticated citizens, without being at all anti-Soviet, may pay only lip service to the Communist label and will turn away contemptuously from all the "clenched-fist-in-air" type of propaganda. The nation in general has been outgrowing some of its naiveté, and one of the striking features of the recent political relaxation is that the whole business of banners and slogans is much less than it used to be, and the clumsiest kinds of propaganda are particularly reduced. Political formulations remain blunt, even savagely simple on the whole, but it is easier for people to ignore them than it used to be.

The relaxed conditions since 1956 or so are of the greatest interest for what they reveal or confirm about the Russian people, as well as for the possibilities which they have revealed in the Soviet system of government. It should be noted, however, that nothing fundamental has been changed in the Communist system of economic and political control; there is nothing in that system to guarantee that another Stalin might not arise, or that all the old machinery of police spying and labour camps might not be started up again. It seems rather unlikely that this would happen, because such good progress is being made without it, but the possibility is still there. . . .

The limits within which public criticism is permissible have also been much relaxed. Even Ministers are now criticized by individuals through the normal channels of the trade unions, the press, or Party branches. They may be criticized, that is, on the usual Soviet grounds of not having carried out policy adequately. But at lower levels popular opinion is being allowed to develop into what might be considered as a fragmentary criticism of policy itself, or even into suggestions for formulation of policy. . . .

So long as material prosperity continues to increase, and so long as control by the political police does not resume its old severity, the Soviet Government is obviously going to have much more popular support—more, probably, than it has ever had. People may demand still more liberty of criticism and still more voice in formulating the detail and sometimes perhaps the methods of policy, but one can scarcely hear of any evidence that they will demand a voice in determining basic policy, and there is no sign that the Government would yield to such a demand if it were made.

PART SIX

THE SOVIET ECONOMIC SYSTEM

It is not technical and economic innovations but the human aspects of a society that matter.

Karl Kautsky

Without freedom, heavy industry can be perfected but not justice or truth.

Albert Camus

A very long road, a road drenched in the blood of fighters for the people's happiness, a road of glorious victories and temporary setbacks was traversed before communism, which once seemed a mere dream, became the greatest force of modern times and a society that is being built up over vast areas of the globe.

From the *Program of the Communist Party of the USSR, 1961.*

Chapter 14

THE ECONOMY IN PERSPECTIVE

By way of introduction to the several chapters concerned with the Soviet economic system, it must be emphasized that there is in the USSR a close interdependence and interrelationship, both in theory and practice, between economics and politics—beyond anything known to the capitalist world. It must be said, too, that the belief of Russian leaders (and of many Russian people) in the ultimate triumph of socialism throughout the world is predicated, in major part, upon what they regard as the demonstrated superiority—and, hence, the ultimate irresistible appeal—of the socialist economic system over capitalism. Typical, for example, was the statement made by Khrushchev in an interview with the correspondent of *Figaro*:

> We, Communists, are convinced that mankind's only right path is the path of socialist development. Socialism expresses the vital interests of the people, of all men and women who live not by exploiting working people, but by their own labor. It brings the peoples' deliverance from social and national oppression, from the horrors of unemployment and the arbitrary rule of a handful of monopolists who usurped all the wealth of a country. We are convinced that the peoples of all countries will come to socialism, to Communism, but when and how—this is the internal affair of each people.

This confidence is predicated on the claim made by Leonid Brezhnev in November 1977, in celebrating the sixtieth anniversary of the Bolshevik Revolution, that "no other society anywhere on earth has done or could have done so much for the masses . . . as socialism has done."

In the process of analysis, what reliability may be attached to official Soviet statistics? This does not admit of an easy answer. Since the death of Stalin a great volume of statistical information has been published, but there are still some conspicuous gaps. Alec Nove, a distinguished authority on Soviet economics, identified the more important of these as follows:

> Output figures for some *industrial products* are missing, among them nonferrous metals, ships, aircraft, many chemicals, some machines, as well as military weapons.
>
> While more is now appearing about the breakdown of the *labor force*, including agriculture and the military services, numbers in particular industries are not given in detail.

While since 1964 we have had some average wage statistics, there is nothing about average pay in different industries, or as between different categories of workers, and hardly anything at all about actual earnings of peasants.

There is no information given on the composition of turnover tax revenue, and only a few actual rates of tax are published.

There are other problems with Soviet statistics according to Alec Nove, Naum Jasny, Robert Campbell, Gregory Grossman, Keith Bush, and others. These include:

The need for more refined and rational indexes particularly in their weighting of prices and new products and in the treatment of national income data.

Ambiguities of definition.

Aggregation of nonhomogeneous commodities under a single statistical head.

Padding below to realize the benefits of plan fulfillment.

Concealment of output below to enable enterprises to hoard extra supplies.

Inability of statistics to reveal quality.

Having said all this it is pertinent to point out:

In the Soviet Union, as Gregory Grossman has written, "since the middle of 1948, concern with the reliability of statistical information has been openly and frequently expressed in the specialized literature." And it is noteworthy that Soviet authorities have taken vigorous action to improve reliability. One of the leading analysts and a severe and skeptical critic of Soviet statistics, Naum Jasny, as early as 1958 categorically asserted that "the bulk of Soviet statistics, so far as they are released at all, are correct." The truth is, too, that some difficulties in achieving statistical accuracy derive from the complexities involved—a truism for the West as well as the East.

There is no evidence that central Soviet statistical agencies concoct figures to order. No such evidence has been given by various Soviet officials who defected.

There is no reason to believe that the Soviet Union, which must have reliable data for internal purposes, maintains two sets of books. Evidence to the contrary is provided by an official Soviet security document captured by German forces during World War II. Although the document was clearly not intended for publication because, as later pointed out by our State Department, it "disclosed the part played by forced labor in the economic life of the country on the eve of World War II," it confirmed the reliability of nonsecret statistical data published by the USSR.

With respect to the rate of growth in the USSR, in industry at least, Alec Nove has demonstrated that unless it can be shown that the extent of exaggeration changes from year to year, there is no long-range impact of falsification from below because of the "law of equal cheating."

This chapter presents the viewpoints of two economists who describe and analyze Soviet economic problems and development in broad historic terms, Professor Harry G. Shaffer of the University of Kansas and Alexander Guber, a Soviet economic specialist. Both writers emphasize Soviet accomplishments in the face of herculean difficulties. The following chapter largely focuses on deficiencies of the Soviet centrally planned economic system.

Soviet Economic Performance in Historical Perspective

Harry G. Shaffer

To evaluate Soviet economic performance under the previous highly centralized, and the now somewhat modified planning apparatuses, one must look at this country's economic achievements and shortcomings in light of its own goals and not in light of what Western value judgment may consider desirable. In the case of the USSR, the leadership was motivated primarily by the aspiration of transforming the country into a military power capable of warding off any attackers and into an economic power second to none. Hence, rapid industrialization became the paramount economic goal from the very outset. Priority was therefore given to the industrial rather than the agricultural sector, and within the former to the producers' goods rather than the consumers' goods subsector. Only in recent years has greater allowance been made for the needs of agriculture and of the consumer. . . .

Economic Performance under the Plan: The USSR

During its sixty-one years of existence, the Soviet economy has had to operate under unusually severe handicaps. At the outset, an economy badly disrupted by World War I, with a population ill-equipped by background or education to meet the challenges of industrialization; further disruption caused by years of revolution, civil strife, and military intervention by several of the leading Western powers including the United States; years of virtually total economic blockade by all the major industrial nations of the world that deprived the country of the benefits of substantial foreign investments and of extensive foreign trade which had so greatly facilitated industrialization in the United States; a devastating war that destroyed much of Soviet productive capacity; a prolonged period of cold war with its concomitant military expenditure that represented a drain on resources which could have been devoted to the more rapid development of productive facilities; and throughout the entire period, operation under an economic system untried in the history of industrialization. (On the plus side, one should point out, the Soviets did have the advantage of being able to utilize the technological know-how of already developed countries and to exact reparations, especially from East Germany, which offset a small part of the incredibly high costs of World War II.)

In spite of all handicaps, the Soviet Union has advanced from a relatively backward and predominantly agricultural country to an economic power second only to that of the United States. When using official Soviet statistical releases in one's evaluation, one may question the methodology employed in computing official Soviet aggregate output data:

At this writing, Harry G. Shaffer is Professor of Soviet and East European Studies at the University of Kansas and author of many studies on the USSR. This excerpt from the author's "Economic Performance Under the Plan: The Soviet Union and East Europe," published in 1972 in Revue de l'Est *(Paris) and revised by the author for this book is reproduced with permission.*

one may challenge the accuracy of certain Soviet claims (for instance indexes for long-run increases in real income); one may take exception to the use of certain weights (for instance 1926–27 prices which, in the opinion of Western economists, tend to overstate subsequent Soviet growth rates); but after all caution has been applied, figures computed by Western economists—though as a rule considerably lower than those released by the Soviets—still spell remarkable economic success in terms of overall, and even more in terms of industrial, development. It is probably fair to say that in spite of all the shortcomings of the Soviet economic system one can point to, the annals of no other country show such rapid industrialization and such high growth rates sustained for so long a period of time.

From Tsarist Russia to the First Five-Year Plan. During the quarter of a century preceding the outbreak of World War I, manufacturing and mining in Tsarist Russia grew at an average annual rate of about 5 percent—fairly high but far below average rates achieved by the Soviet Union during the more than six decades of her existence. Overall national income, unfavorably affected by the relative inertia of the agricultural sector, grew much more slowly, perhaps at an average rate of 2.5 to 3 percent per year between 1860 and 1913. In 1894, Russia's per capita income was far below that of not only the United States but also of all major European powers, and there is strong evidence that it fell farther behind during the next two decades. [See Table 1.]

The first steps towards industrialization were taken in the pre-Soviet era; but in 1913, the high point of pre-World War I economic development, Tsarist Russia was far behind the leading industrial powers of the world. Agriculture, according to Soviet sources, accounted for more than 57 percent of Russia's GNP in that year, for more than 75 percent of those engaged in productive activities, and, together with industrial raw materials, for over 94 percent of her total exports. Only one-tenth of Russia's population was engaged in industrial pursuits and per capita industrial output was 13 times higher in Germany, 14 times higher in England, and more than 21 times higher in the United States than in Russia.

Russia's economic condition left much to be desired in 1913; and it deteriorated considerably during the subsequent seven years. As a consequence of the World War, the Revolution, the Civil War, and the concurrent and subsequent economic disorganization, the Soviet Union's industrial output had, by 1921, dropped to a small fraction of what Russia's had been before 1917, and amounted to only about one-half of one percent of the industrial output of the world. When after three or four years of War Communism, and

TABLE 1 National Income

	1894 (rubles per capita)	1913 (rubles per capita)	Growth (percent)
United Kingdom	273	463	70
France	233	355	52
Italy	104	230	121
Germany	184	292	58
Austria-Hungary	127	227	79
Russia (in Europe)	67	101	50

Source: From Alec Nove, *An Economic History of the USSR,* Allen Lane, The Penguin Press, London, 1969, pp. 12–15. (Originally published in *Opyt ischisleniya narodnovo dokhoda v Evropeiskoi Rossii,* Moscow, 1918.)

some seven years of a "New Economic Policy" (NEP) the first five-year plan was introduced in 1928, the Soviet economy had barely recovered from its pre-World War I level.

1928–1940: The First Three Five-Year Plans. The introduction of the first five-year plan in 1928 ushered in the era of detailed economic planning from the center. The years that followed were years of ruthless mobilization of resources, of extraordinarily high rates of forced savings and investment, and of primary concentration on heavy industry at the expense of the agricultural and consumers' goods sectors. Much has been written about Stalin's inhumanity and about the great suffering of the Soviet people and especially the peasants during that era. Unfortunately, human suffering is not easily measurable so that it would be difficult to determine whether or not it exceeded the suffering of British laborers, of slaves in the American South, or of immigrant workers in the New England textile mills during the first half of the 19th century when England and the United States were in the throes of early industrialization. In any case, the industrially advanced Western countries all paid their price for industrialization in terms of hard labor and of consumers' goods foregone so that efforts could be channeled into the erection of an industrial base. Yet, most Western analysts consider the price exacted from the Soviet populace in the pre-World War II era unnecessarily excessive. But while one may reject the cold-blooded ruthlessness of the Stalin era, one can hardly deny the economic achievements. While the West lingered under the harrowing experience of a prolonged and exceedingly severe depression, the Soviet economy continued to make rapid economic progress. The increase in heavy industrial production during the "first dozen years of forced industrialization," writes a well-known American Sovietologist [Stanley H. Cohn, *Economic Development in the Soviet Union,* 1970] "was unprecedented in international historical experience for a time period of this length. From a basically agricultural economy the USSR was catapulted into the first rank of industrial powers."

Official Soviet statistics claim an almost fourfold increase in national income for the period of the first two five-year plans, from 1928 to 1937, and a more than fivefold increase from 1928 through 1940. The third five-year plan (1938–42) had called for national income to be doubled. But under strained prewar conditions, growth rates fell off and, moreover, appear to have been quite uneven. The output of capital goods, Soviet sources have it, rose by 53 percent from 1938 to 1940; but oil production increased by only 9 percent, iron and steel production by 3 percent, and the output of the electrical goods, automotive, tractor, transport, and the road building and construction-machinery industry was actually lower in 1940 than in 1937. Agricultural output increased but slightly during the three years preceding World War II.

Western sources, using less favorable weights and prices than those used in official Soviet indexes, see aggregate Soviet output as having roughly doubled between 1928 and 1940—much less spectacular an accomplishment than that depicted by official Soviet figures, but still highly respectable. [Unless otherwise stated, Western computations, throughout this paper, are in terms of GNP or (where it says "excluding capital consumption" as in Table 2) in terms of NNP, thus including direct services. Soviet figures, on the other hand, are for national income or net material product, which in Soviet national income accounting excludes capital consumption *and* direct services.]

In terms of the goals of the Soviet leadership at the time, overall growth was of much less import than the growth of the industrial sector. According to Soviet sources, industrial output increased almost sixfold between 1928 and 1940. Western estimates vary, but even the most conservative among the well-known ones grants a more than two and a half-

TABLE 2 Growth of Soviet Output, 1928-1940 (1928 = 100)

	1940
Official Soviet[1]	513
Bergson,[2] 1937 prices	197.2
1950 prices	188.0
Moorsteen-Powell,[3] 1937 weights	
excluding capital consumption	196.1
including capital consumption	202.4
Kaplan,[4] basic index, 1937 weights	
excluding capital consumption	201.5
including capital consumption	206.2
basic index, 1955 weights	
excluding capital consumption	180.2

[1]*Strana Sovietov za 50 let,* Statistical, Moscow, 1967, p. 29.

[2]Abram Bergson, *The Real National Income of Soviet Russia Since 1928,* Harvard University Press, Cambridge, Mass. 1963, pp. 128, 149, and 303.

[3]Richard Moorsteen and Raymond P. Powell, *The Soviet Capital Stock, 1928-1962,* Richard D. Irwin, Homewood, Ill. 1966, pp. 622-24.

[4]Norman Kaplan, *The Record of Soviet Economic Growth, 1928-1965,* The Rand Corporation, Santa Monica, Cal., pp. 5, 99, 100, 110, and 112.

fold increase while some others come closer to Soviet figures than to those of their Western colleagues. (By the way, extraordinarily high rates of industrial growth were acknowledged by most Western specialists for the period of the first two five-year plans; but for 1937–40, industrial growth was deemed much less impressive.) Agriculture, languishing under the dual impact of enforced collectivization and priority for heavy industry, grew but slowly during the twelve-year period. . . .

1941–1945: Four Years of War. On June 22, 1941, Nazi Germany launched the largest land invasion and the most devastating war in history against the Soviet Union. By November, the German armies occupied territory roughly equal to the land area of the United States east of Chicago. On this occupied territory lived ten out of every twenty-five Soviet citizens and it accounted for 63 percent of all Soviet coal production, 68 percent of pig iron output, 58 percent of steel, 60 percent of aluminum, 38 percent of grain, 84 percent of sugar, and 41 percent of railroad lines. The four years of war cost the Soviet Union some twenty million dead, thirty million injured, and left many of her cities and towns and much of her agriculture, industry, and transportation system in shambles. Soviet statistics show staggering economic losses: Some 1,700 cities and some 70,000 villages and other small inhabited communities were fully or partially wrecked and burned; destroyed were some 4,700,000 houses, 127,000 schools, universities, and public libraries, 31,850 industrial enterprises, 15,800 locomotives, 428,000 railroad cars, and 65,000 miles of railroad track; some 100,000 collective and state farms were wrecked and plundered; and the invaders slaughtered or shipped to Germany 7,000,000 horses, 17,000,000 cattle, 20,000,000 pigs, and over 100,000,000 chickens. Much of Soviet industry that miraculously survived the original German onslaught was systematically destroyed by the Russians in their "scorched earth" policy, by Soviet partisans during the Nazi occupation, or by the retreating Germans towards the end of the war, including, for instance, the Donets basin in which three-fourths of the Soviet mining potential prior to the War had been concentrated, and the Dnieper power works, pride of the first five-year plan. A recent Soviet estimate by Nikolai Baibakov, Chairman of the Soviet State Planning Committee and Vice-Chairman of the USSR Council of Ministers, to the effect that World War II delayed Soviet economic development by eight to ten years, appears to be rather conservative. . . .

1946–1950: The Reconstruction Era. The period of the fourth five-year plan, 1946–50, witnessed exceedingly rapid restoration of the Soviet Union's war-torn economy. According to officially released Soviet statistics, the 1940 output of electricity was surpassed in 1946, of coal in 1947, of steel and cement in 1948, of pig iron and oil in 1949; in the war-devastated regions, the harvest of grain, sugar beets, flax, sunflowers, potatoes and other crops exceeded pre-war levels in 1949; and by the end of that year, 90 percent of all town houses destroyed during the war were said to have been restored. Gross agricultural output, Soviet figures have it, reached the pre-war level in 1950, and national income and gross industrial product in that year reportedly exceeded planned targets and were almost two-thirds and three-fourths respectively above their 1940 levels. Western estimates, though lower, also show considerable progress. Keeping in mind that overall production in 1945 was well below that of 1940, the first five postwar years were indeed years of highly creditable economic progress. . . . American economist Norman Kaplan, for instance, estimates Soviet GNP for 1950 as less than 18 percent above 1940; but according to his own computations, this represents a more than 50 percent growth for the five-year period 1945–50. . . .

1950–1980: The Last Three Decades. During the 1950s industrial output and national income continued to increase rapidly. Even agricultural production, after 1951, rose every year, jumping drastically to an all-time high in 1958. Consequently, towards the end of the decade, an exhilarated and overoptimistic Soviet leadership began to prepare a highly unrealistic twenty-year plan. Adopted under Khrushchev's leadership by the 22nd Party Congress in October, 1961, the plan predicted, for instance, that by 1970 Soviet industrial output would have surpassed that of the United States and labor productivity would be twice as high in the USSR as in the United States. According to that long-range plan, the Soviet Union would, by 1980, "occupy first place in the world in per capita production."

When sharply dropping growth rates reached a low in 1963, a year of bad crop failure, it became evident that the forecasts of the 1961 twenty-year plan far exceeded the realm of possible achievement. But, on the other hand, those in the West who described the situation in terms of crisis or stagnation were obviously in error: the setback was but temporary. Although the Soviets could report only a 14 percent increase in agricultural output for the period of the seven-year plan, 1959–65, they claimed increases of 53 percent in national income, of 60 percent in sales of goods through state and cooperative retail outlets, and of 84 percent in industrial output. Western estimates, as usually somewhat lower, still show considerable progress. (See Table 3.)

After 1963, industrial and overall growth rates recovered from their 1962–63 lows. Although not as impressive as during previous decades, they were again highly creditable. Agricultural output, so greatly dependent on weather conditions, had its ups and downs, rising somewhat faster during the second than during the first half of the 1960s, with growth rates oscillating (according to Soviet data) between a 10 percent increase in 1966 and a 3.2 percent drop in 1969.

TABLE 3 Soviet Economic Growth 1950-80 (in percent)

	National Income or Product		Industrial Output		Agricultural Output	
	Official Soviet[1]	Western Estimate[2]	Official Soviet[3]	Western Estimate[4]	Official Soviet[5]	Western Estimate[6]
1951-55	70.4	42.4	84.8	62.4	23.7	26
1956-60	54.6	38.1	63.7	49.7	32.4	19
1961-65	37.1	29.9	51.0	37.5	12.4	14
1966-70	41.0	30.5	50.0	38.9	21.0	24.6
1971-75	34.0	20.7	45.0	34.1	13.0	−3.4
1976-80 (plan)	24-28	23.5	35-39	39.4	14-17	14.5
1976[7]	5.0	3.7	4.8	3.8	4.0	6.2
1977[7]	3.5	—	5.7	—	3.0	—

[1]Figures for 1951-55, 1956-60, and 1961-65 from Communication from Central Statistical Office of USSR, Moscow, in *UN Yearbook of National Accounts,* United Nations, New York, 1968, p. 692; for 1966-70 from *Directives of the Five-Year Economic Development Plan of the USSR for 1971-1975,* Novosti Press Agency Publishing House, Moscow, 1971, p. 8; for 1971-75 and 1976-80 (plan) from A.N. Kosygin, *Guidelines for the Development of the National Economy of the USSR for 1976-1980, XXVth Congress of the CPSU,* Novosti Press Agency Publishing House, Moscow, 1976, pp. 11 and 29; for 1976 from *Pravda,* Jan. 23, 1977; for 1977 from *Pravda,* Jan. 28, 1978.

[2]Through 1965 derived from Kaplan, op. cit., (see source reference 4 to Table 2); for 1966-70 and 1971-75 from Rush V. Greenslade, "The Real Gross National Product of the USSR, 1950-1975," *Soviet Economy in a New Perspective,* A Compendium of Papers submitted to the Joint Economic Committee, Congress of the United States, Government Printing Office, Washington, 1976, p. 273; for estimate for 1976-80, from Donald W. Green, Gene D. Guili, Herbert S. Levine, and Peter Miovic, "An Evaluation of the 10th Five-Year-Plan Using the SRI-WEFA Econometric Model of the Soviet Union," in *ibid*, p. 311; and for 1976, *Handbook of Economic Statistics, 1977,* Central Intelligence Agency, Washington, Sept. 1977, p. 24.

[3]Through 1957 derived from *Narkhoz,* 1960, p. 219; 1958-65 from *Narkhoz,* 1965, p. 121; for subsequent years and five-year plan periods, same as in source reference 1 above.

[4]Through 1965, derived from Moorsteen and Powell, op. cit., (see source reference 3, Table 2); for subsequent years and five-year plan periods, same as in source reference 2 above, except in *Handbook* . . . etc., op. cit., it is p. 39.

[5]Through 1965, derived from *Narkhoz,* 1965, pp. 295-60; for subsequent years, same as in source reference 1 above, except in *Directives,* . . . etc., op. cit., it is p. 9.

[6]Through 1965 derived from Douglas B. Diamond, "Trends in Output, Inputs, and Factor Productivity in Soviet Agriculture," *New Directions in the Soviet Economy,* Studies Prepared for the Subcommittee on Foreign Economic Policy of the Joint Economic Committee, Congress of the United States, Government Printing Office, Washington, 1966, Part II B., p. 380; for 1966-70 and 1971-75, from David W. Carey, "Soviet Agriculture: Recent Performance and Future Plans," *Soviet Economy in a New Perspective,* op. cit., (see source reference 2 above), p. 280; for estimate for 1976-80, from Green and others, op. cit., (see source reference 2 above), p. 311; for 1976, from *Handbook* . . . etc., op. cit., (see source reference 2 above), p. 40.

[7]Percent change over preceding year.

Imperfections and Economic Reforms. Soviet leaders have long pointed with pride to the economic achievements of the USSR. Yet, after economic growth slowed down at the end of the 1950s, they began to encourage "constructive criticism"; and during the early 1960s they themselves repeatedly expressed deep dissatisfaction with the efficacy of the planning apparatus and asked for alterations to improve economic performance. Apart from the general slowdown in growth rates, Soviet leaders showed concern, for instance, over the decrease in the rate of growth of labor productivity, and they called for steps to improve the situation.

According to official Soviet sources, labor productivity in industry increased 16.5 times between 1913 and 1968; and an unofficial Soviet computation by the Soviet Union's most famous statistician, the late S. Strumilin (who admits that his calculations are necessarily "far from perfect"), arrives at a 22.8-fold increase in the productivity of Soviet labor during the first half a century of Soviet power, achieved with only a five-fold increase in the capital-labor ratio. But at the 23rd Party Congress in 1966, Kosygin reported that labor productivity had increased by an annual average of only 4.6 percent between 1961 and 1965 as compared with 6.5 percent during the preceding five-year period, and he demanded that "we must do everything we can to overcome the lag." Some non-Soviet sources show even lower increases in Soviet labor productivity in the early 1960s (although the rates are higher than those given for the United States), and there was apparently no improvement in 1968 and 1969.

Numerous other shortcomings became ever more apparent during the first half of the 1960s. The consumers' goods sector, for instance, continued to show a lack of variety and an inadequacy of quality often contrary to the intentions of the planners; insufficient supplies of certain inputs repeatedly caused production bottlenecks; the hoarding of scarce capital goods by some enterprises interfered grossly with their optimum utilization, etc. Convinced that economic performance could be greatly improved, the Soviets frankly recognized and openly discussed existing inadequacies; to correct them, they started to introduce drastic changes in their system of economic planning and administration.

A system of detailed command planning from above and of highly centralized and strictly enforced administration of economic activities is particularly well suited for harnessing unused resources, for imposing forced savings, for bringing about expansion primarily by net additions to plant, equipment, and to the industrial labor force; it is particularly well suited, in other words, to a relatively less developed economy embarked on a crash industrialization program.

But by the onset of the 1960s the situation had changed. The number of economic decisions to be made had increased gigantically; the single predominant priority goal (rapid industrialization) had been replaced by a great number of goals with equal or similar priority rankings; the era of sellers' markets had drawn to a close in many sectors of the economy with the Soviet consumer, much choosier than before, no longer willing to accept whatever was available on the shelves. And probably most important, the epoch of "extensive" economic growth had virtually come to an end. Henceforth, growth would have to be attained increasingly not by adding inputs of labor and machinery but by modernizing production facilities and techniques, by improving enterprise planning and organization, by economizing on inputs, by a more rational division of labor—in other words, by enhancing economic efficiency at the micro level.

The old system of planning and administration seemed ill-equipped to cope with economic conditions in an advanced socialist economy. It had become obsolete, a victim of its own successes. The Soviet leadership therefore found it necessary to introduce far-reaching economic reforms aimed at extensive decentralization of economic decision making at the micro level and at making increased use of market forces in resource allocation. This, however, did not mean that Brezhnev and Kosygin were about to preside over the dismantling of their socialist economy. There was nothing in the economic reforms that would imply the return of the means of production to private enterprise. The center has retained control, via the central plan, over the major economic proportions and, as a matter of fact, over virtually all macroeconomic decisions.

Actually, the Soviet Union proceeded very cautiously with the revamping of her planning and administrative machinery, more cautiously than envisaged in the early 1960s when growth rates were less satisfactory than in subsequent years. Soviet economic reforms have surely been much more limited in scope than those introduced in some of the East European countries. In recent years, moreover, many industrial enterprises have been grouped together into enterprise associations; and some economic functions and varying degrees of power to make economic decisions, bestowed upon the enterprises in the late 1960s, have now been transferred to the management of these enterprise associations.

During the period of the ninth five-year plan, 1971–75, Soviet industrial growth rates continued their steady decline; and overall growth rates dropped even more (see Table 3 above). But it ill behooves us to be overcritical of Soviet economic progress. While most of the Western world has been suffering from both inflation and unemployment, and while the United States in addition has had to cope with severe deficits in her international balance of trade and with a steady decline in the value of her currency in international markets, the Soviet Union has continued to make substantial economic progress, albeit in many areas more slowly than in the past. According to official Soviet sources, as compared with the preceding five-year period, national income increased by 34 percent, industrial output by 45 percent, retail trade turnover by 40 percent, the productivity of labor in industry by 84 percent, wages and salaries of industrial and office workers by 20 percent and those of collective farmers by 25 percent. Even her much maligned agricultural sector, very unfavorably affected by adverse weather conditions in 1972 and 1975, has by now well recovered; in four of the five years from 1973 to 1977, Soviet grain output reached record heights. (Continued grain imports from the West, it should be pointed out, are devoted primarily to livestock feed in an effort to further improve the citizens' diet—for it takes between seven and fourteen pounds of grain to produce one pound of meat.) And the U.S. Central Intelligence Agency gives the per capita GNP of the USSR for 1976 as $3,590 (computed in 1976 U.S. dollar purchasing power equivalents). While this is still less than half that of the United States, it is, for instance, higher than that of Italy, almost three times that of Mexico, and more than ten times that of mainland China, and it places the Soviet Union squarely among the affluent nations of the world. Living standards, although rapidly rising during the 1970s, appear somewhat lower than would seem to be indicated by this figure of per capita GNP. This is so partly because in housing and in much of the durable consumers' goods sector the Soviet Union can catch up, but gradually, with what the industrially advanced countries of the West have built up over decades and, in some respects, over centuries. And secondly, the USSR does devote a much larger part of her GNP than most Western countries to the capital goods sector.

The 1976–80 five-year plan is not a repetition of the overoptimistic plans of the Khrushchev era. Adopted under the Brezhnev-Kosygin leadership by the 25th Congress of the CPSU in early 1976, it is conservative, realistic, and will in all probability be largely fulfilled. (For planned increases in national, and in industrial and agricultural, output, see Table 3.)

Soviet Economic Performance: An Assessment. As has been shown, Soviet economic growth has been quite uneven. The previously mentioned estimate by Strumilin asserted a 238-fold increase in the output of the means of production during the first half century of Soviet history, from 1917 to 1967, a less than 38-fold increase in the output of consumers' goods, and a mere tripling of agricultural production. Since then, in spite of greater emphasis on the consumers' goods sector, the output of capital goods has continued to rise somewhat more rapidly; and overall industrial growth rates have on the average been several times higher than growth rates in the agricultural sector. But outstanding as the record has been in the capital goods sector on which most efforts have been concentrated, it has obviously not been unimpressive in the consumers' goods sector either. Even in agriculture, where Soviet growth experience has left much to be desired, considerable progress has been made. Per capita growth in all sectors has necessarily been smaller than aggregate development. But since population has increased by only some 83 percent between 1917 and 1977, growth of per capita production has still been high throughout, even per capita agricultural output has doubled over the past six decades. In this connection, it should perhaps still be mentioned, that in the process of industrialization the structure of the labor force has so vastly changed that the 1977 agricultural output (allegedly four times that of 1913) was produced with less than 25 percent instead of the prerevolutionary 75 percent of the working population—a considerable improvement even since 1960 when still more than 46 percent of all gainfully employed persons were engaged in agricultural pursuits.

The Soviets claim to have achieved a gigantic 21-fold increase in per capita national income between 1928 and 1966; a Western computation, using different weights and base years, shows Soviet GNP, per capita, in 1965 as merely somewhat more than three and one-half times that of 1928. Even accepting the Western estimate, it should be emphasized that this increase was achieved over a period of only thirty-seven years, interrupted by years of devastating warfare while, in comparison, per capita output of goods and services in the United States was four times as large in 1968 as in 1890 (a period of 78 years), and per capita disposable income three times as high in 1968 as in 1899. And in the decade from 1966 to 1975, real per capita GNP increased, according to conservative Western sources, by another 42 percent in the Soviet Union, as compared with a mere 17 percent in the United States (*CIA Handbook of Economic Statistics, 1977,* p. 35).

In 1921, the USSR produced roughly one-half of one percent of the industrial output of the world, at the time of the outbreak of World War II almost 10 percent, and by the mid-1970s the Soviet Union, with about 7 percent of the world's population, laid claim to producing one-fifth of the (by then many times greater) industrial output of the entire globe. Western assessments seem to roughly corroborate the Soviets' claim to their relative position in the world as an industrial power. . . . In any case, there is no doubt that the Soviet Union's industrial output is exceeded only by that of the United States and that she holds first place in Europe and either first or second in the world in the output of many industrial commodities essential for a great industrial power. . . .

The early 1960s was a period of considerable slackening of Soviet growth; and during the 1960s and the 1970s as a whole, Soviet economic progress was much slower than during the 1930s or the 1950s. But recurring Western predictions of economic crisis and impending economic disaster have proven wrong in the past and, if repeated, are likely to prove wrong again, at least in the foreseeable future.

One should perhaps still point out that Soviet economic progress during the past two decades has been achieved in the face of several consciously self-imposed macroeconomic decisions which, irrespective of any value judgment concerning their desirability, were bound to cause economic growth to slow down. First, both the average number of hours worked per week and the average number of days worked during the year have declined over the years and were considerably fewer towards the end of the 1970s than they had been in the 1950s; secondly, there was the conscious decision to place relatively greater emphasis than in the past on the consumers' goods sector; thirdly, defense expenditures have continued to grow, perhaps on the average by almost as much as the growth in GNP; and finally, the high rates of growth of fixed investments which during the 1950s had far exceeded growth rates in GNP were allowed to drop sharply during the 1960s so as to correspond roughly to growth in total output. And in recent years greater percentages of somewhat higher rates of investment have been directed into agriculture, which has less of an impact on future growth rates than investment in industrial construction, machinery, and equipment. . . .

There are many other achievements that could be added to those which have shown up in the figures presented above. In the supply of available medical and teaching personnel, for instance, the Soviets have exceeded the United States since the mid-1950s. Today, the USSR can boast of having fewer students per teacher and per 10,000 population, more hospital beds and almost 50 percent more physicians than the United States, claiming that her physician/population ratio (32.6 doctors per 10,000 population in 1975) is the highest in the world. As a result of improved nutritional and health standards, infant mortality rates have decreased spectacularly, from 273 per 1,000 live births in 1913 to 27.7 in the mid-1970s, and life expectancy has increased over roughly the same period from 32 to more than 70 years. . . . The Soviets have perhaps not gone far enough with their reforms, but their planning and administrative mechanism is no longer inflexible. Having proven their willingness to tamper with it, they will undoubtedly make further adjustments as called for by ever-changing economic conditions.

In the meantime, Soviet per capita and living standards are, to be sure, still far behind those of the principal Western market economies and even behind those of some of the more advanced socialist countries such as the GDR and Czechoslovakia. The overoptimistic goal of surpassing the United States in per capita output has proven unachievable within the short time span allowed for it. However, even Western analysts, with estimates of Soviet economic performance much lower than those of their Soviet colleagues, testify to the fact that the percentage difference has been narrowing rather consistently.

The record is available, for all who wish to examine it. With this record before it, the West would be well-advised not to underestimate the past performance nor the economic potential of the USSR. The United States is still ahead of the Soviet Union in total and per capita output, in consumption, and in living standards. But the Soviet Union has been steadily gaining on the United States. There may be disagreement as to exact percentage differences; but unless the trend of faster average growth rates in the USSR than in the United States is reversed, it is an arithmetically inevitable consequence that the economic gap will be closed sooner or later. The question is only when.

Production for Use, Not Profit

Alexander Guber

Development Accelerator

The Soviet Union today accounts for 20 percent of the world's industrial output. However, the volume of production is not among the main specific features of Soviet industry.

Socialist ownership is the main specific feature of Soviet industry. Industrial enterprises in the Soviet Union belong not to private owners or their associations but to the state, to the entire people. All the other specific features of Soviet industry stem from this main one.

Soviet industry comprises a single complex required to supply the needs of society and developing under a single national plan. Far from competing, its component parts complement each other. They produce what is needed by society and not simply what ensures maximum profit. Soviet industry knows neither crises, nor unemployment.

Abroad many do not regard the Soviet system as the best. Well, one is entitled to have an opinion. We in the Soviet Union believe in the advantages of our system, and consider it just and the most effective. We have every reason to believe so.

Industrial output in the USSR has increased 225 times over the 1917 level. Actually, this result has been achieved within some forty years, since about twenty years were taken up by wars imposed on our country and periods needed to restore the damage caused by those wars. Before the Great October Socialist Revolution (1917) Russia was increasingly lagging behind the leading capitalist countries, especially in the output of the key industries—those on which overall technical progress depended. Today, the Soviet Union is ahead of Great Britain, Federal Germany and France put together. That qualitative stride forward was made under socialism and owing to socialism. Our competitors in the economic field had every other development accelerator but this.

However, the low development level from which the world's first state of the workers and peasants started did not allow the Soviet Union to take up leading positions in all branches of industry. For instance, the Soviet automotive industry was in its infancy when motor cars were mass-produced in the West, their output numbering millions. Consider the progress in this field made by the Soviet Union since then. On the eve of the Second World War the USSR manufactured 5,500 passenger cars a year; in 1976 their output was 1.28 million.

The range of goods in the production of which the Soviet Union does not yet lead the world is shortening all the time. Evidence of that can easily be found in the statistical reports. Here are some relevant facts. Fifty years ago, France produced three times as much electric power as the Soviet Union (to say nothing of the other two leading European powers—Great Britain and Germany); and as for the United States' output, it was 25 times greater than the Soviet Union's. By the early 1960s, in power production the Soviet Union was ahead of the three West European powers put together, and it had caught up considerably with the United States: The U.S. power output was now only 2.5 times

Alexander Guber is a Soviet economic specialist. This excerpt from the author's Industry: Collective Owner, *published by Novosti Press Agency Publishing House, 1978, is reproduced with permission.*

greater—the gap had shrunk to one-tenth of what it was fifty years ago. In 1928 the United States produced 8.5 times as much steel as the Soviet Union; Great Britain and France—twice as much, and Germany—3.5 times as much. Today, the Soviet Union's steel output is far greater than that of the United States or of the three West European powers combined.

The Soviet Union's successes in the economic competition are, so to say, a by-product of its development. Not a single industrial enterprise was ever built and not a single economic programme was ever implemented expressly for the purpose of winning that competition. . . .

It was the policy of hostility towards Soviet government pursued by capitalist states, which resorted to armed intervention combined with an economic blockade, that compelled the USSR to take emergency measures and step up production in some branches decisive for attaining technological and economic independence and strengthening the country's defense capability. Soviet Russia herself had to organize the production of goods which normally it would have been simpler and cheaper to import. But she had been refused the sale of these goods, and so she was compelled to catch up with others and then go one better in order to survive. Back in 1919 the first contracts were signed with U.S. companies for delivery to the USSR of machines, footwear, food, and printing equipment. Unfortunately these contracts were never implemented because the State Department forbade U.S. companies to have any dealings with Moscow, and the Soviet representative who signed those contracts was expelled from the United States. . . .

Overcoming Imbalance

. . . History had placed the Soviet state in such conditions that it had to contend with certain imbalances in developing its economy. For a relatively long time, the scarcity of means and a constant threat of aggression did not allow the Soviet state to develop all branches of industry, and of national economy as a whole, in a balanced way. Whereas priority development of heavy industry is typical of socialist industrialization in general, the vital need to build it up within the shortest possible time and without any outside assistance compelled the Soviet state to do this with the means which in different circumstances could and should have been used to develop other sectors of social production, such as agriculture and industries producing consumer goods. The country was forced to accept imbalances, with a view to eliminating them in the future, relying on the heavy industry potential above all. . . .

It is an advantage of socialism that its economic system makes it possible both to foresee the need for changes and to implement them with comparative ease, specifically—by centralized redistribution of capital investments.

Immune to Energy Crises

In 1976 the Soviet Union's electric power output was 1,111,000 million kilowatt-hours. [See Figure 1.]

That means that within the last ten years or so, power generating facilities were put into operation with capacities greater than those built during all the preceding Soviet years. Equally high rates of growth are planned for the future.

Over 75 percent of the country's electric power is produced by fuel-burning stations. [See Table 1.]

FIGURE 1 Capacity of All Power-generating Plants (in million kilowatt-hours)

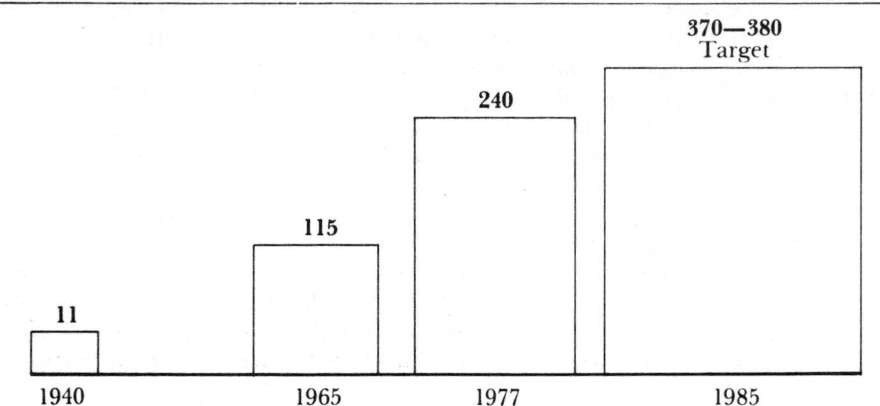

TABLE 1 Fuel Production

	1940	1965	1976
Oil (including gas condensate) (in millions of tons)	31.1	242.9	520
Natural gas (in thousands of millions of cubic meters)	3.2	127.7	321
Coal (in millions of tons)	165.9	577.7	711.5

These figures show why the USSR experiences no energy difficulties—why there is a steady supply of power and fuel, and no stoppage in the operation of enterprises, or central heating systems, or filling stations. . . .

It would be naive to try to explain the absence of energy difficulties in the Soviet Union merely by the abundance of the country's natural resources, although it is true that the USSR is richer in that respect than any other country of the world. While pre-1917 Russia had the same natural riches, she lagged far behind the leading capitalist powers in the extraction of power resources and generation of electricity. The transformation of the energy situation cannot be explained without considering socioeconomic factors. . . .

Let's make some comparisons between the USSR and the United States. In 1976, U.S. oil output shrank by 68 million tons compared with 1972, and gas output—by 82,000 million cubic metres compared with 1973. Within the same periods, the Soviet Union's output of oil grew by nearly 120 million tons, and of gas—by 84,500 million cubic metres. . . .

In planning, the country's entire economy is regarded as a single organism, and each industry—as an integral part operating not for the sake of making a profit for itself, but for the common weal. Hence the possibility to manoeuvre, to redistribute resources through the state budget, and consequently to develop the more promising sectors, which may not be the most profitable for the time being.

At present, oil and gas have, on the whole, substantial economic advantages over coal. Monopolies have used this circumstance in the competitive struggle, and in many countries have achieved a situation where coal production is marking time or has even been cut back. They deliberately ignore the fact that our planet is far richer in coal than oil and gas together, that at the present rate of oil extraction its reserves will not last much longer, and that, considering humanity's long-term interests, coal production and utilization should not be curtailed but developed in every way—as the Soviet Union is doing. . . .

A single power system guarantees the Soviet consumer from the disastrous consequences of such failures as the one that paralyzed New York some time ago. Although the United States has all the technical requisites for building such a system, it cannot create one because of the conflicting interests of rival companies. . . .

Planned, dynamic development of the Soviet fuel and power complex supplies the country's needs. The Soviet Union has no energy crisis, nor is there one in the offing. It is true that U.S. intelligence services predict that we shall have such a crisis. But they also predicted, after 1917, a near collapse of Soviet power, and the Soviet Union's defeat in the Second World War, and a prolonged monopoly of the United States in nuclear weapons. . . .

The Steel Basis

Modern industry is unthinkable without metal. So far no means of compensating for a weak iron and steel base has been found. That is why stepping up the production of iron, steel and rolled metal remains one of the Soviet state's chief concerns in the economic sphere. . . .

Like the fuel and power industries, the iron and steel industry is an important part of the national economic basis. [See Table 2.] The qualitative stride forward made by the Soviet metals industry brought it to first place in the world. . . .

Under capitalism the final say belongs to the market situation which determines the ups and downs of metals production and the level of employment in the metals industry. Under socialism everything is determined by a plan which takes due account of the needs of society. . . .

To comprehend how profoundly different the two economic systems are it is sufficient to compare the graphs showing metals production in the USSR and in any of the capitalist countries. In the first case we shall see a steady growth; in the second—abrupt fluctuations. On the average the Soviet Union has been increasing its steel output by five million tons a year; it has long outstripped many capitalist countries, and is getting farther and farther ahead of the United States. In the period of the tenth five-year plan (1976–1980) the output of the Soviet iron and steel industry will total 780 million tons, which is more than the combined output in the first six five-year plan periods. . . .

TABLE 2 Ferrous Metals Production (in millions of tons)

	1940	1965	1970	1976
Steel	18.3	91.0	116	145
Cast iron	14.9	66.2	85.9	105
Rolled iron	13.1	70.9	92.5	118

Catalyst of Progress

Speaking of industries which form the backbone of an advanced economy, one must name the chemical industry along with mechanical engineering, metal-making, and the power industry. The chemical industry and the petrochemical industry, are the biggest consumers of power, mineral raw materials, machines, instruments and other products turned out by nearly all the extractive and processing industries. At the same time, development of literally every sector of the national economy depends, in varying degrees, on the chemical industry. It is justly described as one of the most important motive forces of technical progress.

The rate of development of the Soviet chemical industry can be judged from the following facts. Pre-1917 Russia's peak output of mineral fertilizer was in 1913; she produced 90,000 tons. Germany's output then was 100 times greater, France's—33 times, and Britain's—nearly 20 times. Within a single day today, the Soviet Union produces 270,000 tons of mineral fertilizer, which is 26 percent more than the United States, nearly five times more than France, over six times more than Federal Germany, and 18 times more than Britain.

Within a decade (1966–1975), the output of mineral fertilizer in the USSR nearly trebled, and it was scheduled to increase another 60 percent by 1980. . . .

The highest rates of growth are imparted to industries which ensure the accomplishment of the principal economic task at a given stage. Raising agricultural production which, because of historical causes, came to lag substantially behind industrial production has been such a task over the last two decades. And it is being tackled, as it is always done in our country, on a nationwide scale. Capital investments are reallocated in favour of the agrarian sector; development of industries providing it with such things as fertilizers, pesticides and farm machinery is accelerated. A look at the statistics will show a simultaneous growth of these industries. . . .

Production for Consumption

The fact that Soviet industry develops at accelerated rates those of its branches which manufacture means of production is misinterpreted by many abroad. According to them, socialism, while commanding possibilities, unavailable to capitalism, for concentrating resources, can do a great deal as far as production of machines and power is concerned, but is organically incapable of solving the problem of the range and quality of consumer goods in a definitive way. Such a view is completely erroneous. Its exponents fail to discern many important points.

Not only light and the food industries work directly for consumption. In the USSR, 28.2 percent of the consumer goods is produced by branches of heavy industry. They also turn out about 80 percent of the cultural and household goods. That alone shows that it is inappropriate to try to correlate manufacture of means of production and production of consumer goods on the basis of a mechanical comparison of heavy, light and the food industries.

Furthermore, Soviet industry manufactures agricultural machines and equipment for light and the food industries, as well as for the trade and public catering services. Although such products are classified as means of production, it is easy to see that they serve the purpose of consumption.

Besides, whereas the share of consumer goods in Soviet export is not above 10 percent, in Soviet import it is about 40 percent. The mass of consumer goods on the internal market increases through foreign trade channels which it enters owing to Soviet export which consists mainly of machines, fuel and raw materials. In this way heavy industry branches help to meet the consumer demand.

Discussing the results which the Soviet Union has achieved in meeting the consumer demand, one must not disregard the fact that the country has had very little time at its disposal. The Soviet state has just turned sixty. As mentioned earlier, the country spent nearly two decades fighting wars imposed on it and recovering from the damage caused by those wars. During the remaining four decades the Soviet Government was not in a position to allocate sufficient means and resources for development of the consumer goods industries. . . .

In the obtaining situation the priority task was to ensure quantitative supply on the internal market, to eliminate the shortage of prime necessities. Since its resources were limited, the Soviet state faced this alternative: to give acceptable-quality goods to all or excellent-quality goods to a few. And although everyone was aware of the need to improve the quality and broaden the range of consumer goods, there was no real possibility to solve this problem conclusively.

Increasing the output of clothing required additional quantities of cotton, wool, synthetic fibre, dyes, equipment, etc. And to sell this produce new shops and warehouses were needed. The problem could be solved only in an integrated way.

Another consideration. A family of four living in one room could not afford to have much furniture. But when in the middle of the 1950s the country began building over two million apartments a year, demand for furniture skyrocketed. Likewise, demand for all durables shot up: people now had the floorspace where to put them and the money to buy them with, for their real incomes doubled every fifteen years.

Now that the shortage of consumer goods has been eliminated, problems of quality and range have advanced to the fore. Formerly, a customer came to the store to buy a refrigerator—any kind. Now he comes to buy a certain model he likes. The same is true of clothes, footwear, furniture, watches and all the rest. This marks a fundamentally new stage. Not all of its problems have been dealt with, but they are being tackled successfully and will be resolved before long.

It is not accidental that we call the tenth five-year plan "a quality and efficiency-oriented plan." A whole range of measures is being taken to improve the quality of entire industrial output. Special state bodies check on the quality of products to see whether they correspond to established standards, which are becoming higher and higher. A state system of quality assessment has been introduced. Under it industries, enterprises and workers responsible for the output of high-quality goods are rewarded, while those responsible for the output of outdated, unfashionable models or products of poor quality are punished, while manufacture of such products is discontinued. Control over quality is exercised at all levels and at all stages of production—from the development of a new article by the House of Fashions or a design bureau to its mass production.

We are not overoptimistic as to our accomplishments. Confirmation of that can easily be found in our newspapers and magazines, which are full of critical remarks addressed to industries producing consumer goods. But things are moving along, and we are optimistic about the future.

Our optimism rests on a firm foundation. Consider [Table 3 and Table 4].

[Table 3] does not include passenger cars. In 1940—5,500 cars were produced, in 1965—201,200 and in 1976—1,200,000. A spectacular rise in the output of motor cars, however, did not close the gap between the output of the Soviet automotive industry and

TABLE 3 Consumer Goods Manufacture

	1940	1965	1976
Woven fabrics (in millions of square meters)	3,320	7,498	10,280
Leather footwear (in millions of pairs)	212	486	724
TV sets (in thousands)	0.3	3,655	7,063
Household refrigerators (in thousands)	3.5	1,675	5,827

TABLE 4 Manufacture of Durables (per 100 families)

	1965	1976
Watches and clocks	319	469
Radio sets	59	81
TV sets	24	76
Household refrigerators	11	67
Washing machines	21	67
Vacuum cleaners	7	20

that of the leading capitalist countries. It must be made clear right from the start: we are not trying to catch up with the United States in that area, because we do not regard a privately owned car as a prime necessity. A developed system of public transport and low fares (the lowest in the world) enable Soviet citizens easily to do without a car of their own. Nor does the Soviet Union regard motor car production as crucial to the national prestige. We shall continue to raise the output of cars in our country, but not to the detriment of public transport, or the environment, or the fuels balance. In fact, we are trying to minimize the negative effects of the mass-produced car experienced in the West.

Unquestionably, these statistics are evidence of progress. Therefore, we find them gratifying. But this does not mean that we are content with the present level of development.

At the start of the current five-year plan, capacities put into service in the 1971–1975 period comprised one-third of the fixed productive capital of light and the food industries. By the end of the five-year plan period, [1980], mechanical engineering will increase its supply of the latest equipment to those industries by another 50 percent. In other words, we are witnessing a complete technical retooling of consumer goods production. . . .

A similar situation is observed in regard to consumer goods themselves. There was a time when the Soviet consumer bought clothes, footwear and other goods on sight just because they were made in Italy, or France, or Finland. True enough, they were better looking and more stylish than the corresponding Soviet-made articles. Since then the Soviet consumer has grown more demanding, and he appraises foreign-made goods critically, comparing them with Soviet-made ones, whose quality has been steadily improving and range broadening. Today, Soviet foreign trade organizations are compelled to reject a considerable part of the goods offered them for import, lest the consumer should do the same later on.

Chapter 15

SOVIET CENTRAL PLANNING: PROBLEMS AND PROSPECTS

While recognizing some of the successes of Soviet central planning, Alec Nove gives detailed consideration to its failures and deficiencies in recent decades. Keith Bush notes some difficulties in comparing Soviet and American production data and then evaluates Soviet Economic Growth.

Recent Economic Organization, Reorganization, Disorganization

Alec Nove

Khrushchev's Troubles: A Chronic Crisis of Planning

The fundamental problem that faced the planning system under Stalin's successors was this: centralized decision making could only encompass a portion of the multitude of decisions which, in any economy of the Stalin type, must be taken by the planner-administrators, and which, in the absence of any effective criteria other than plan-orders, logically cannot be taken elsewhere. Therefore many plans consisted of aggregated indicators (roubles of total output, or tons, or square metres), and many elements of the plan could be inconsistent with one another. For example, the supply plan frequently failed to match the production plan, the fulfilment of aggregated output targets was inconsistent with meeting user requirements; the labour, or wages, or financial plans were out of line with each other or with output plans, and so on. A large number of semianecdotal examples can readily be assembled to illustrate the resultant irrationalities. Steel sheet was made too heavy because the plan was in tons, and acceptance of orders from customers for thin sheet threatened plan fulfilment. Road transport vehicles made useless journeys to fulfil plans in ton-kilometres. Khrushchev himself quoted the examples of heavy chandeliers (plans in tons), and over-large sofas made by the furniture industry (the easiest way of fulfilling plans in roubles). New designs or new methods were avoided, because the resultant temporary disruption of established practices would threaten the fulfilment of quantitative output targets. It would indeed be a miraculous coincidence if the product mix which accorded with the requirements of the user also happened to add up to the aggregate total required by the plan. Of course, ideally, the aggregate total is made up of the separate requirements of all the users. But there is never time or information available for such perfect planning. The planners in fact proceeded on the basis of statistics of past performance.

Yet, with prices not even in theory capable of fulfilling their role as economic "signals," there was no other criterion than the plan. The central organs either themselves decided these plans, or laid down limits within which subordinate units could operate. Central decisions, though often incomplete and imperfect, were based on an assessment of what was needed. This in turn was based on political directives, past experience embodied in statistical returns, applications (indents) from below, and material balances designed to achieve an elementary input-output consistency. In the almost total absence of market

Alec Nove is an economist who has written extensively on Soviet affairs. This excerpt is from pp. 355–63, 364, 365, 366, 367, 368–72, 377–79 of his book, An Economic History of the USSR,*© Alec Nove, 1969, published by Penguin Books Ltd. and is reproduced with the permission of the author and publisher. It was updated by Mr. Nove in 1978.*

forces this combination of information flows, requests and directives constituted the foundation upon which economic activity rested.

This activity, highly complex in its nature, became more so as the economy grew, and then in a sense outgrew the centralization upon which it was built. Tasks had to be divided, between ministries administering industries, Gosplan and its numerous subdivisions (dealing with prices, investment policy, labour, supplies of key commodities), the Ministry of Finance, the State Committee on Construction, and so on. A further source of complication was the division of authority between government and party organs, at all levels. All this led to acute strain in the process of seeking to ensure coordination, and sometimes plans were inconsistent, or impossible to carry out *in toto*. In the key area of investment this took the form of chronic over-spreading of resources on too many projects (*raspylenie sredstv*), causing serious delays in completion. A contributory cause was that capital was provided free out of the state budget, there was no capital charge, and so subordinate authorities overapplied for it and started all they could in the hope of getting more.

Under Stalin the top priority of heavy industry was ruthlessly enforced. Errors and omissions were borne by the less important sectors. Hence persistent neglect of agriculture, and the fact that even the modest housing plans were never fulfilled, despite the notorious degree of overcrowding.

But under his successors this was no longer so. Housing, agriculture, consumers' goods, trade, all became matters of importance, even of priority. So the task of planning became more complicated, because a system based on a few key priorities resembling in this respect a Western war economy, could not work so effectively if priorities were diluted or multiplied.

Consumer demand, for so long ignored, became more important, as living standards improved and customers could exercise more choice. Some goods became unsaleable, either through poor quality or overproduction. Yet the system was not designed to respond to demand, whether from consumers or indeed from enterprises (e.g., for some particular item of equipment, or metal of precisely the desired quality). It was built to respond to orders from above, and for the achievement of large-scale investment projects and expanding the volume of production. The financial and price systems were well able to extract the surpluses needed to sustain high growth-rates.

The planners tried various expedients. They issued instructions that user demand should be met. They modified the bonus systems so that the achievement of purely quantitative targets should not be sufficient, that the assortment plan had also to be fulfilled, that costs had to be reduced, the wages plan not exceeded, and so on. They experimented with a kind of value-added indicator known as "normed value of processing." Each of these "success indicators" had its own defect, induced its own distortions. Thus, insistence on cost reduction often stood in the way of the making of a better-quality product. A book could be easily filled with a list of various expedients designed to encourage enterprises to act in the manner the planners wished, and the troubles to which each of them gave rise. The greater the number of indicators, the more likely it was that they would be inconsistent. Similarly, the greater the number of items and subitems planned and allocated by the centre, the greater the burden on the planners and the likelihood of error or delay. But, since the central plan was the basis of all activity, the absence of some item from the plan might have resulted in it not being provided. So efforts to reduce the number of centrally planned indicators tended to be futile. If, say, frying pans or electric irons were not in the plan, then they tended not to be produced, and productive capacity would be switched to make things in which the centre expressed an interest.

Errors in investment planning, shortfalls in technical progress, were to some extent offset, under Stalin, by unplanned movement of labour from the villages. In every plan period, except the second, more workers came to town than was envisaged. By the middle fifties there was much greater consciousness of the need for efficient utilization of resources, including the now scarcer labour resources, to meet the many competing needs. Matters were further complicated by labour's greater freedom of movement.

All these circumstances, and the liberating effect of Stalin's departure, led to a revival of economic thought. No longer barred from practical affairs, economists joined with the more intelligent planners in seeking new criteria—for investment decisions, for resource allocation by planners, and, last but not least, for decision making at enterprise level. The role of prices, of what came to be called "commodity-money relations," became a subject of lively discussion. Stalin's dictum that "the law of value" (affecting exchange relations) does not operate in transactions between state enterprises was rejected.

In the light of this situation the 1957 sovnarkhoz reform was a step in the wrong direction, or at best a step sideways. The essentials of the system were unaltered, in the sense that the plan was the sole effective operational criterion, plan fulfilment the only important source of managerial bonuses. (Profits, it is true, formed the basis of a "director's fund," renamed "enterprise fund," but it was of minor importance as an incentive to act.) Yet the abolition of the ministries removed a vital element in the chain of command. Any one of the 105 sovnarkhozy was unable to assess the needs of the other 104, unless these were conveyed to them by the centre. For how could an official in, say, Kharkov or Omsk know the relative importance of requests received from all over the country? In any case, the central allocation of key commodities was preserved, and indeed had to be reinforced to avoid confusion. But one can only allocate what is produced, and so the centre quickly found itself immersed in what amounted to production decisions too, but without the ministerial mechanism. Gosplan, the one body with the necessary information, lacked power and was deluged with work.

Yet enterprises were subordinated to sovnarkhozy, and the latter had only one independent criterion: the needs of their own regions. In the absence of clear orders to the contrary, they therefore allocated scarce resources to their own regions. Loud protests reached Moscow that established supply links were being broken. More and more items therefore had to be controlled by or through Gosplan. Similarly, investment funds under the control of sovnarkhozy were diverted to local needs, to the detriment of other regions. Evidently Khrushchev thought that the regional party secretaries would ensure that their sovnarkhozy enforced national priorities. This did not work out. The disease of "localism" (*mestnichestvo*) was diagnosed, officials blamed, dismissed, threatened with punishment (e.g., by the decree of 4 August 1958). The same complaints were afterwards repeated, since the defect was built into the system.

As the sovnarkhozy gradually lost effective power—in 1962 the Estonian sovnarkhoz controlled only 0.2 percent of the production of that republic—the enterprises found themselves virtually without a master, or rather with many masters, since production and supply plans reached them from several production and allocation departments at all-union and republican levels. It was fortunate that informal links of many kinds kept things more or less on an even keel most of the time. But some of these evidently worried the authorities, as they facilitated embezzlement, or just theft. The introduction on 7 May

1961 of the death sentence for a range of economic offences (as distinct from counterrevolutionary or treasonable activities) was a sign of alarm.

Organization, Reorganization, Disorganization

As the deficiencies of the 1957 reforms became apparent Khrushchev set about making administrative changes. To list and explain them all is impossible in the context of a general history. A bare list of main changes, affecting industry and construction, will be sufficient to demonstrate the confusion created in the process of trying to remedy confusion. They were part of a rather chaotic process of recentralization.

Firstly, a long list of state committees was created which by 1962 had very much the same designations as the defunct ministries, but they had no executive authority. Enterprises were not subordinate to them. They considered. They advised, especially on investment and technical policy. They could not order.

Secondly, Gosplan was again split. At all-union level perspective planning and research were made the responsibility of an Economic science council (*Gosekonomsovet*) in 1960. A division on a different basis was tried out in the large republics from 1961: Gosplan there was given the task of planning, republican sovnarkhozy the task of implementation of plans, including material supplies. Then, in November 1962, Khrushchev announced a similar change at the centre: Gosplan would plan particularly in the longer term, while a new body, the all-union sovnarkhoz, would implement plans. This division was not a happy one, and there was much criticism of parallelism. So, after an obscure struggle, there emerged in February 1963 a supercoordinator of the coordinators which was given the historically memorable name of VSNKh, but which seems to have achieved little in its short life.

Thirdly, sovnarkhozy were merged, reduced in number from over one hundred to forty-seven early in 1963. The four Central Asian republics were made into one sovnarkhoz, and a Russian was appointed to head it. There were also changes in sovnarkhoz powers: they lost construction, they gained local industry, previously under local Soviets. Other changes included the creation of large planning regions (seventeen for the whole country), which achieved little in practice.

Fourthly, the party itself was split in 1962, into industrial and agricultural sections, which caused much perplexity. So did the fact that the enlarged sovnarkhozy seldom coincided with the geographical divisions of the party, so on the one hand each half of the divided party was enjoined to supervise the economic activities within its jurisdiction, but on the other it was made organizationally difficult to do this. Khrushchev seems to have feared party officials' collusion in ''localism.'' Government organs were also, at provincial levels at least, to be split into two. This was a shock to party and state bureaucracies alike, and made no administrative sense.

By 1963 no one knew quite where they were, or who was responsible for what. Pungent criticisms were appearing in the specialized press. Planning was being disrupted.

Khrushchev added to the troubles of the planners by loud accusations of conservatism, and by pressing on them a chemical industry investment programme which threatened the whole balance of the economy, and extended to industry a typical Khrushchevian campaign of a type which had done harm in agriculture. Output was to be trebled in seven years. The targets he forced through were absurd and were promptly abandoned by his successors, though no one denied the desirability of substantially expanding the chemical industry. To make room for them, a new plan for 1964–65 scaled down many other plan targets, from steel to housing. Khrushchev's campaigning zeal threatened serious shortages of steel, of coal, of bricks. It was typical that sensible changes—such as the substitution of nonsolid fuels for coal, or prefabricated concrete for bricks—became much too drastic. Thus most brickworks were closed, 8,000 out of a total of 12,000, according to A. Birman (*Novy mir,* No. 1, 1967), causing grave shortages.

Further causes of trouble were the soaring expenses of the space and missile programme, and the sharp rise in military expenditure—by 30 percent in 1961, which represented a heavy call on scarce skills and specialist equipment.

Other reasons too, contributed to a slowdown in growth, which became quite noticeable especially after 1958. The rate of increase in investment greatly decreased, as the following figures amply demonstrate:

	(percent)
1958	+16
1959	+13
1960	+8
1961	+4
1962	+5
1963	+5

In 1963 and 1964, officially claimed industrial growth rates fell below 8 percent, the lowest peacetime figures except 1933. Owing to poor agricultural performance, the national income in 1963 is said to have risen by only 4.2 percent. This was when the CIA made news by claiming that the real figure was now down to 2.5 percent, or well below even the United States. The view became widespread that Khrushchev's handling of affairs did not help.

As strains developed, so investment controls became more stringent, and the housing programme, to which much publicity had been devoted, was cut back. Particularly severe cuts were imposed on private building as the figures [in Table 1] demonstrate.

Khrushchev indeed mounted a campaign against ownership of private cottages, which resulted in some confiscations. He seemed in his later years to have been pursuing a campaign against "bourgeois" property tendencies. He goaded on the planners and the management by loud-sounding promises about overtaking America within a few years, even by 1970, and promising to achieve some elements of full communism (free municipal housing, free canteen meals, free urban transport) by 1980. This was, no doubt, part of his effort to revive ideological fervour and inject dynamism into a system which, left to itself, was liable to fall victim to inertia. He made other promises too: a 35-hour week, the

TABLE 1 Urban House-building (million square metres of total space)

	State	Private
1960	55.8	27.0
1961	56.8	23.6
1962	59.8	20.7
1963	61.9	17.4
1964	58.9	16.2
1965	62.4	15.5

(*Source: SSSR v tsifrakh v 1965 godu,* p. 157.)

abolition of income tax, a minimum wage of 60 roubles, all by precise dates, at which they would not be implemented. (The 60-rouble minimum in fact came into force in 1968.)

Khrushchev's Agricultural Mismanagement

Agricultural output during the seven-year plan should have increased by 70 percent. [Table 2 shows] what in fact happened.

The 1963 and 1965 grain harvests were badly affected by adverse weather. But the picture as a whole was very disappointing, and was so treated by every Soviet analyst.

The following were the principal reasons for this—and speeches by Brezhnev and Matskevich made since Khrushchev's fall show that the Soviet leaders would not disagree with the analysis made below.

Firstly, the 1958 reform imposed excessive burdens on kolkhozes, which the procurement prices did not fully cover. They had to pay too much, and too quickly, for machinery. The result was to compel a cutback in investments and decline in payments to peasants. That there was a decline in pay after 1957 is fully admitted; its precise extent is still covered by statistical silence.

Secondly, the abolition of the MTS adversely affected maintenance by dispersing sophisticated equipment around kolkhozes, few of which possessed either the workshops or the skilled manpower to maintain or repair it properly. Many mechanics and tractor drivers had left the villages rather than become kolkhoz peasants. (The Repair Technical Stations provided for in the 1958 reform never got off, or rather on to, the ground.)

Thirdly, Khrushchev pressed campaigns upon the farms, using for this purpose the party machine, which interfered with little or no regard for local conditions, and did great damage. The list of campaigns and distortions is a long one. Maize was to be sown in areas in which the soil and climate were unsuitable, or where the necessary labour and machines were lacking, with miserable harvests as a result. Crop rotations were disrupted. Cattle was unnecessarily slaughtered to achieve spectacular short-term results in meat production, then permission to slaughter was withheld, to rebuild the herds, even if there was no point to it (other than a statistical point). . . .

Fourthly, as also in industrial planning, Khrushchev confused matters by repeated reorganizations. The 1958 reform had wiped out the MTS, and with it an important controlling mechanism. . . .

TABLE 2 Agricultural Output

	Total	Crops	Livestock
1958	100	100	100
1959	100.4	95	108
1960	103	99.4	107
1961	106	101	112
1962	107	101	115
1963	99	92	108
1964	113	119	106
1965	114	107	123
1965 plan	170	—	—

(*Source: SSSR v tsifrakh v 1965 godu,* p. 69.)

Fifthly, after 1957, output of many kinds of farm machinery actually fell. Apparently it was instinctively felt that the kolkhozes, as nonstate institutions, deserved a lower priority, and/or that the MTS had been oversupplied with equipment.

Sixthly, price relativities established in 1958 were in total conflict with the plan, especially the plan to expand the output of livestock products. Meat and milk prices were far too low, and Soviet economists had no difficulty in demonstrating that these items were produced at a loss. . . .

Finally, Khrushchev committed the grave error of attacking the private plots. We have seen earlier that suburban livestock owners had already been subjected to fiscal burden in 1956 but the drive began seriously to get under way in 1958 when Khrushchev made his speech to the effect that peasants in his birthplace, Kalinovka, had voluntarily sold their cows to the kolkhoz. He emphasized the word "voluntarily"; but soon enough thousands of party secretaries were exerting pressure on the peasants to do the same. . . .

The basic problems of agriculture were not, of course, Khrushchev's creation. He interfered, reorganized and campaigned too much, but he had inherited a generation of neglect and impoverishment and a system in which change could come only by order from above, since it treated peasant or even farm-managerial initiative with instinctive suspicion. . . .

Khrushchev's Fall

Khrushchev was dismissed in October 1964. The economic troubles just described were part-causes of his fall. His overambitious campaigning ("hare-brained schemes"), his exaggerated promises, his arbitrary methods, his disorganizing "reorganizations," were too much. Yet he did achieve considerable successes, especially in his first five years, and his defects are explicable by his background and experience. He was politically "educated" under Kaganovich, in the dramatic years of the early thirties. He inherited many perplexing problems, and his methods of tackling them belonged to a different epoch, and were now obsolete. He half understood the need and even the required direction of change, and often spoke of managerial autonomy in industry and agriculture, economic criteria, rational investment policy. He showed that he knew better than anyone how the bureaucratic apparatus of party and state could distort policy and paralyse desired initiative. But in the end he knew only the traditional methods.

Conclusion: Prospects and Assessment

Brezhnev and Kosygin succeeded Khrushchev. They undid what they (rightly) considered to be his wrong-headed reforms. They announced a relaxation of restrictions on the private ownership of livestock, higher agricultural prices (particularly for livestock products), better and guaranteed pay for peasants, lower prices for agricultural machinery and other inputs. The Ministry of Agriculture was restored to its former powers, with Matskevich, who had been sacked by Khrushchev, in charge. Better arrangements are being made for repairs and maintenance. The need for farm autonomy has been reasserted. The TPA have been converted into ordinary raion agricultural organs, the party district committees (raikomy) have been reconstituted. The unity of the party was likewise restored. . . . Various proposals—including the total abandonment of compulsory procurements—have been made and, so far, rejected. . . .

In industrial planning, the sovnarkhoz (regional) system of planning was ended in September 1965, the ministerial system put back in its place. VSNKh was abolished; Gosplan resumed sole authority for planning, under Baibakov, another who had been dismissed by Khrushchev. However, it was decided to preserve one advantage of the sovnarkhozy: regional interindustrial supply depots. These now come under the State Committee on Material Supplies, whose head, Dymshits, had been in charge of the USSR sovnarkhoz in the period 1962–65. A similar streamlining of the administrative machinery occurred in the republics. . . . There has been a large rise in minimum wages. The drive to increase supplies of consumers' goods and services has been complicated by the expansion of armaments spending.

While the organizational changes largely restored the pre-1957 situation, experience had taught Brezhnev and Kosygin that reforms are essential. They knew well that the planning system was not capable of meeting legitimate consumer demand, or of using or investing resources with necessary effectiveness. Sometimes a big relative rise in output of producers' goods was evidence of waste: it could simply be that an unnecessarily large number of intermediate products were used to make a given volume of consumers' goods. Neither efficiency nor welfare criteria are necessarily met by increased tonnages of steel, cement and machine-tools.

Efficiency was already a subject of vigorous discussion under Khrushchev. There were many schools of thought, but two principal reforming approaches can be identified. One, typified by Liberman and other industrial economists, argued for an extension of the profit motive and free contract, so that "what was good for society would be profitable for the enterprise." Others, notably Kantorovich, Novozhilov and the talented specialists in the Mathematical Economics Institute, looked for optimizing solutions through the use of programming techniques and computers. Reformers were concerned both with macroeconomic proportions and with microeconomic decision making. By and large, the traditional system was effective in making large-scale decisions and, once made, enforcing them. It was fairly efficient, too, at expanding basic industries and fuels, branches which are frequently monopolized or nationalized also in the West, suggesting that there are economies of scale and advantage in central control in the case of electricity, steel, cement and similar items. The system was well able to concentrate skills and materials on selected sectors of high priority, such as space research. But in other fields change is essential. The programming-and-computer school is well aware that the optimum which it is seeking is conditional upon microeconomic flexibility, since no computer will handle the information flows and decisions implied by the existence of upward of six million separate prices at present fixed at all-union or republic levels. There must be direct and effective links between customer and producer, and, surely, some price flexibility.

What should be the role of market forces? What should prices represent? Should they be free to vary? Who should fix them and on what principles? How far would it be possible to abandon the administrative allocation of resources between enterprises, and the regulation by planners of the output of every enterprise? Should free contract, based on profit considerations, determine what is produced? If so, what would be left of planning? What of the danger of monopolistic price increases? How can one avoid taking all major investment decisions centrally when, in absence of a capital market, investments are bound to be government-financed to a large degree? These are the kind of questions which are being debated. . . .

There has been some fascinating work in the field of the application of mathematical methods and programming, and Soviet economics has progressed rapidly from the dreary scholasticism of the Stalin era to the status by 1978 of a real and even exciting discipline, though there has been a long battle to overcome the resistance of vulgar-Marxist dogmatists. However, there still remains a wide gap between the recommendations of the more go-ahead economists and actual planning practice. Reforms introduced in 1965, which were to have granted wider autonomy to enterprise management and greater freedom to purchase inputs, have been to a considerable degree frustrated. Global planning indicators, many of them still in tons, continue to predominate over profits. Prices remain inflexible and based more or less on cost-plus, failing to reflect scarcity or utility. Centralization of planning remains virtually unaffected by reform so far. The principal attempt to improve matters has taken the form of the setting up of industrial associations (*obyedineniya*), through mergers of enterprises. This can simplify the task of central planners by reducing the number of units which they plan, but cannot resolve the deep-seated troubles of the system.

These troubles have shown themselves in reduced growth rates, in a tendency to underfulfil plans in many sectors of the economy and a sizeable growth of Soviet debts to the West. These debts have partly been incurred because of large-scale purchases of modern technology, and partly because the still slow and lopsided progress of agriculture has necessitated large-scale purchases of grain in the West in all but the most favourable weather years. A further complicating factor has been the burden on the Soviet Union of the arms race. While there are some branches of the economy where there have been impressive achievements, particularly in developing the oil and natural gas of Siberia, there has been increasing consciousness among the Soviet economic and political leadership of intractable obstacles in the way of making their system more efficient and raising labour-productivity to desired levels. The aging and conservative members of the Politbureau seem unable and unwilling to do more than tinker with the centralized system which they have inherited from Stalin.

Economic historians should note the high cost of elimination of all opposition. By this is meant not only the human cost, in the diversion to camps of unknown millions, of whom a high proportion were above average in intelligence, energy and technical knowledge. Heavy losses were imposed by the mere fact that exaggerated and impossible plans could not be criticized, even by experts, lest they be suspected of deviation. This certainly contributed a great deal to the excesses of the "leap forward" period, in industry and agriculture alike, and later also in China.

Yet the success of the Soviet Union, albeit by totalitarian and economically inefficient methods, in making of itself the world's second industrial and military power is indisputable. Therein lies its attraction to the "third world." Therein, too, may be found many lessons for economist and historian. What if, given Russia's whole historical experience and the irreversible fact of revolution, there was in fact no alternative path for her? By this is not meant that any one act of cruelty or oppression was in some sense predestined, but rather that modernization from above, by crude and sometimes barbarous methods, was rendered highly probable by the circumstances of the time. Might not some, or many, of the excesses, stupidities, errors, be part of the *cost* of industrializing in this manner? Most of the deformations of Soviet planning could be observed in the war economies of Western states. It did not follow that the wars should have been run on free-market principles. In this case at least, it must be conceded that the errors and omissions inherent in bureaucratic centralization were an integral part of the cost of running a war economy, and in this case at least most people accept the cost as justified. Oskar Lange did describe the "Stalin" economic system as "a war economy *sui generis*."

For what is a rational way of organizing the rapid development of a backward country? What content can be given to the word "rational"? Surely not the achievement of a purely economic optimum which, in any country, is rendered impossible by considerations of political feasibility and social circumstances. One cannot leave out of account the existence of classes and groups, the nature and qualities of the administrative machine, the ideology in the name of which the political leadership seeks to mobilize itself and the masses for the difficult task of changing society. Nor should the more purely military aspect be forgotten: to some extent Stalin really was engaged in building up the industrial base of a war economy in peacetime.

No doubt development economists will study Russian experience for many years. It abounds in lessons (and warnings) of the very greatest interest. They may well conclude that the political terror, the pace of economic development, the problem of capital accumulation and of the peasants were very intimately interconnected. A "softer" economic policy would have given more scope for the consideration of specifically economic efficacy, required fewer sacrifices, and so weakened the arguments for full-scale police terror. But a sense of danger contributed to the decision to go all out, to industrialize very quickly, to concentrate on heavy industry at any cost. Nor can one overlook the fact that there was no precedent, that bitter lessons had to be learned from experience, and that the Western economy was in sad disarray at the time when the "leap forward" was being effected. There was no easy path. The one chosen was not the result of accident or personal whim.

Historians may also conclude that the system, whatever its original logic or rationale, has for some time (literally) outgrown itself. If they are Marxists, they may speak of productive forces coming into contradiction with productive relations, necessitating change in the direction of a market economy. The Soviet development model will exercise, should exercise, considerable fascination. But many, including communists, who study its evolution, especially the key period which began in 1928, might well feel that somewhere in those years there was a wrong turning. And that no one should follow the trail blazed by Stalin, with its terrible sacrifices, unless some overriding set of circumstances makes other paths impracticable. It is said that one cannot make omelettes without breaking eggs. In that case, perhaps one should not make omelettes, if the menu happens to provide other choices. Perhaps it is Russia's tragedy that these choices were absent, and a measure of her achievement that, despite all that happened, so much has been built, and not a few cultural values preserved and handed on to a vastly more literate population.

Soviet Economic Growth: Past, Present, and Projected

Keith Bush

The 500 billion ruble question is, of course, how does the TsSU (The Central Statistical Agency) arrive at its valuations of Soviet and U.S. industrial and agricultural outputs? On this rather important topic, the customary methodological explanations leave certain questions unanswered. The problems of comparing Soviet with U.S. output levels, such as the structural dissimilarity, the differing patterns of preferences and resource availabilities and the divergences between ruble prices and dollar prices . . . will be familiar to our readers. Such considerations make any direct comparisons difficult and highly relative. Nevertheless, some of the following factors suggest that the TsSU's computations—for which no supporting data are apparently published—tend to overstate the Soviet output levels vis-a-vis those of the United States.

As far as industrial output is concerned, the consequences of a chronic seller's market upon the quality of so many products are amply evidenced not only by the complaints of domestic purchasers but also by the structure of the Soviet Union's foreign trade. When the gross output indicator serves as the prime criterion of performance and the yardstick for awarding moral and material incentives, then it is understandable if some inflation creeps in at all levels of reporting despite the existence of an extensive system of cross-checking. The degree of double-counting of intermediate products is probably greater than in economic systems which employ other prime criteria: in certain branches, for instance, even intraenterprise turnover is included in the value of gross output. Excessively high prices are set for "new" and "one-off" products, especially in the machine-building and metal-working industries. Expenditures incurred by several sectors in developing new products are included in the *val*. Greater prominence is accorded to the more material-intensive products. Indeed, under the existing system of normatives and economic stimulation, it is often advantageous for an enterprise to use expensive, high-grade materials where cheaper, low-grade inputs would suffice. How should one value a Soviet product which is made out of unnecessarily expensive material? The comparatively low degree of product specialization tends to inflate the gross output indicator. And so on. Of course, there also exist factors which tend to undervalue Soviet industrial output in relation to customary Western measurements, but these are felt to be less than forces working in the opposite direction. . . .

Further problems arise when comparing the values of the two nations' agricultural products. The double-counting of feed overstates the share of animal products. Of greater significance is the problem of prices. When valuing the Soviet gross agricultural product, the TsSU employs the actual prices paid to producers: these vary greatly by zone, season and between basic plan-quota and above-plan premium deliveries. What price does it use

Keith Bush is Director of Research of Radio Liberty in Munich. The first part of this material is reproduced with the permission of its author and of the journal in which it was published, Osteuropa-Wirtschaft, *no. 1, 1972 (Germany), and the balance, which follows the textual break, is reproduced with the permission of the author and of* Survey. *It appeared in vol. 23, no. 2 (Spring 1977–78), pp. 1–15.*

when valuing American farm output? Which rates of exchange does it employ? These are not divulged, yet they are clearly crucial. For instance, at the official rate of exchange, the all-union average basic procurement price for soft wheat is currently about 83 rubles a ton. In contrast, the offer price for U.S. No. 2 Soft Red Winter on November 17 at Rotterdam was $1.77 a bushel, (i.e., some $65 a ton). The average basic purchase price for beef in the USSR is roughly double its U.S. equivalent. Yet the average *realized* prices, (i.e., including the 50 percent above-plan bonus payments) are even higher. Standards of measurement differ greatly. The reported grain output figures contain as much as 15–20 percent excess moisture and admixtures when compared with Western measures, while the FAO sees fit to apply a 20 percent discount to Soviet meat production figures to bring these into line with Western data. Wool output is measured in terms of greasy weight, while cotton figures refer to seed or raw cotton rather than to lint. Many other divergences could be cited. . . . Interest in the "great economic race" is no bad thing. It may induce more citizens of the USSR to ponder on the ends to which Soviet economic power is applied. In the West, it may help to counter some of the more extreme arguments of the currently fashionable school of thought which decries economic growth per se. Many of the more eloquent spokesmen for this school, it should be noted, are already endowed with more than the average allotment of this world's riches.

The postwar period has witnessed sustained and extensive growth in the principal inputs into the Soviet economy. [Table 1] shows how fixed capital has risen at a higher rate than in most developed economies, while employment has grown even faster than the population of working age.

The growth record of the Soviet economy is compared with that of its major competitor (see Table 2 and Table 3).

Overall Soviet economic growth is still clearly subject to considerable annual fluctuations. In large part, these are attributable to the influence of the climate upon agricultural output which accounts for about one-fifth of the gross national product. However, with gross industrial output continuing to grow at a respectable rate, the Soviet economy has not emulated its U.S. competitor in undergoing a recession.

TABLE 1 The Soviet Economy—Growth of Inputs and Output, 1951-80 (average annual percentage rate of growth)

	1951-60	1961-70	1971-75	1976-80P
Inputs				
Net capital stock	9.4	8.1	7.9	6.5
Manhours	1.3	1.8	1.9	1.5
Land	2.4	0.4	0.8	0.5
Factor productivity	1.2	0.8	−0.6	1.5
Output				
GNP (Western concept)	5.8	5.1	3.7	5.0
National income produced (Soviet concept)	10.3	7.2	5.7	4.7

Sources: Drawn or derived from CIA, *Soviet Economic Problems and Prospects,* Washington, 1977, p. 10; *Narkhoz 75,* p. 56; *Pravda,* 27 Oct. 1976.

TABLE 2 Real Growth in Soviet and US GNP, 1951-77 (percentage growth)

	USSR	US
1951-1960 average annual	5.8	3.2
1961-1965 average annual	4.9	4.7
1966-1970 average annual	5.4	3.0
1971	3.9	3.0
1972	1.7	5.7
1973	7.5	5.3
1974	3.8	−1.8
1975	2.3	−2.0
1976 preliminary	3.7	6.2
1977 preliminary	3.1	4.9

Sources: Drawn or derived from CIA, *Handbook of Economic Statistics 1976,* Washington, 1976, p. 34; CIA, *Soviet Economic Problems and Prospects,* Washington, 1977, p. 2; *Pravda,* 28 Oct. 1976; *International Herald Tribune,* 17 Jan. 1977; *The Financial Times,* 26 Apr. 1977, *Pravda,* 15 Dec. 1977.

TABLE 3 The Great Economic Race (Continued) (in billions of 1975 US$)

Year	US	USSR	Absolute Difference	USSR as % of US
1950	679	223	456	33
1960	931	422	509	45
1970	1,359	719	640	53
1971	1,400	745	655	53
1972	1,480	758	732	51
1973	1,559	812	747	52
1974	1,530	847	683	55
1975	1,499	865	634	58
1976 preliminary	1,592	897	695	56
1977 preliminary	1,670	925	745	55

Note: Soviet GNP computed at US purchasing power equivalents.

Sources: Derived from CIA, *Handbook of Economic Statistics,* Washington, 1976, p. 31 and Table 2.

It may be seen that the Soviet economy, if viewed in terms of gross national product, was catching up with that of the U.S. at a rapid pace during the 1950s—a phenomenon which provoked no little concern in the latter country—but the rate of "catching up and overtaking" slowed during the 1960s. Since then, the United States has undergone the most severe recession since the 1930s, but the absolute gap between the U.S. and Soviet GNPs has nearly regained the highest level recorded in 1973 and the relation of the Soviet to the U.S. GNP appears to have stabilized at around 55 percent.

For the purpose of the computations given in Table 1, labour is weighted at 55.8 percent and capital at 41.2 percent of total factor costs in production, with land accounting for the residual of 3 percent. It will be seen that the inputs of labour and capital were maintained at a high level through 1975, yet the rate of growth of output (GNP) declined markedly. This diminution is attributable to a deterioration in factor productivity, (i.e., the effectiveness with which the primary inputs are utilized, from an annual average of + 1.2 percent in 1951–60 to − 0.6 percent in 1971–75.)

The reasons for this decline and for the fall-off of related inputs since the 1950s are many and varied. Some of them follow:

(a) The "catch-up" period after the Second World War was largely over by the end of the 1950s.

(b) The increasing complexities of the planning and management of a command economy were unalleviated by effective computerization.

(c) In this increasingly complex economy, administered prices posed an enhanced burden.

(d) Agricultural policy switched from a ruthless exploitation of the peasantry, from the tribute (*dan*) of the agricultural sector for the financing of forced-draft industrialization, to a growing support for this lagging sector from the rest of the economy. In addition to the highest relative and absolute farm price support bill in the world—the 1975 subsidy on meat and milk reportedly totalled nearly 19 billion rubles,[1] while the sum of all price supports related to agriculture is appreciably higher[2]—plus the allocation of 27 percent of new investment in the period 1976–80 to "the entire complex of agriculture,"[3] there is the vast albeit incalculable hidden cost of agriculture arising from the requisition of millions of industrial and transport workers and hundreds of thousands of trucks, tractors and other equipment each summer to help out with the harvest.

(e) The "great leap forward" of agriculture in 1953–58 could not be repeated in the 1960s. Some 30 million hectares of new land were brought under the plough during Khrushchev's Virgin Lands campaign. Most of the modest expansion of cultivated land during the 1960s has been offset by land lost to industrial and residential construction. Some of the more marginal virgin lands were withdrawn from cultivation during the 1960s. In response to the harvest shortfalls of the 1970s, almost every available piece of land has been cultivated, including fields due for clean fallow and the verges of roads, railroad tracks and canals.

(f) The workweek for all workers and employees was shortened from 47.8 hours in 1955 to 40.7 hours at present. Longer paid annual vacations were granted: these reportedly now average 19.3 workdays throughout the economy and 18.8 days in industry.[4]

(g) Virtually maximum labour participation has been attained. By 1970, 92.4 percent of the population of working age, including full-time students, were employed in the public sector, compared with roughly 76 percent of the equivalent category in the United States.

(h) Labour turnover has increased.

(i) With the exhaustion of the more accessible sites, exploitation has shifted to more remote and more expensive sources of raw materials.

(j) The voice of the consumer began to be heard, and her or his wishes had at last to be considered. It is perhaps easier to increase the output of pig iron than to increase the sales of fashionable shoes once a certain level of supply and of consumer sophistication has been attained.

(k) Repressed inflation has dampened incentive.

(l) Planners have been obliged, belatedly, to pay attention to environmental factors.

The Current Picture

Industry. Paradoxically, the USSR is the world's leading producer of iron ore, pig iron and steel, yet it spends much of its precious hard currency on imports of metal products; for example, nearly all of the pipe imported during 1976 at a total cost of three billion rubles (about $4 billion) came from the West.[5] This is attributable to a combination of factors: the prevailing supremacy of the *val* means that many steel products are unnecessarily heavy; the vast distances between the main fuel producing centres and the consuming regions demand an awful lot of pipe; Soviet technology in the field of rolled steel and pipe-making lags well behind that of the West, while any flaws are dramatically exposed in the climatic extremes of Siberia; and despite the chemicalization drive of the past fourteen years, metal is still frequently used where, in the West, chemically derived substitutes would be adopted. Predictably, the response of the Soviet authorities has been to issue decrees,[6] but massive imports are expected to continue in the foreseeable future.

Perhaps the greatest single problem confronting Soviet planners is the forthcoming oil crunch. According to CIA calculations, Soviet oil production is expected to peak, perhaps as soon as this year and certainly not later than in the early 1980s. The maximum level of output reached is likely to be between 550 million tons—just above the level attained in 1977[7]—and 600 million tons. However, maximum levels are not considered likely to be maintained for long. The Soviet oil industry has two basic problems: one of reserves and one of production. Barring an extremely unlikely discovery of a massive new field close to an existing field, new deposits will not be found rapidly enough to maintain acceptable reserves-to-production ratios, and those fields that account for the bulk of Soviet production are experiencing severe water encroachment. As a result, increasingly large quantities of water must be lifted for each barrel of oil produced, and high-capacity submersible pumps will be required if production declines are to be staved off even temporarily. Although some substitution of coal and gas for oil in domestic use will be possible in the long run, the effect of such substitution will be minimal in the short run. Neither hydroelectric power transmitted from the East nor the construction of nuclear power plants (mainly in the Western USSR) can be expected to afford much relief for more than a decade.[8] It might be noted that the CIA's sobering prognostications have been challenged, fuzzily by the Soviet media,[9] more concretely by other Western observers,[10] but now they have been partially confirmed by a Soviet spokesman.[11]

The ninth five-year plan for the period 1971–75 was unexampled in that it provided for a higher growth rate for Group B than for Group A industry. In the event, this reversal of the traditional priorities was never implemented; in the first year of the plan period, even before the first major setback of the 1972 harvest, Group A grew faster than Group B, and this ordering was subsequently maintained.[12] The tenth five-year plan for the period 1976–80 makes no pretence to such concessions to the consumer, even if its modest targets for Group B output are declared to be "minimum goals." In 1975, the share of Group A in total industrial production was reported by the TsSU to be 74 percent.[13] However, this proportion is understated in that the residual 26 percent for the value of Group B output is inflated by the above-average rates of profitability recorded by the food and light industries.[14] On the other hand, it can be, and has been, argued that heavy industry (especially the fuel and mining branches) supplies the bulk of Soviet exports to hard-currency markets and thus pays for the imports of consumer goods (such as grain and meat) together with the raw materials and machinery for their production. Moreover, Group A industry produces a growing share of all consumer goods, from a reported 18 percent in 1975 to a planned 22 percent in 1980.[15]

The decisive role in overall economic performance played by the agricultural sector was illustrated by the impact of the grain harvest shortfall of 1975. In its wake, industrial growth in 1976 was the lowest in peacetime history.

The leading growth branches in 1976–80 are scheduled to be chemicals, with a 10.2 percent, and machinery, with a 9.2 percent, planned average annual growth rate.[16] Both branches utilize appreciable inputs of Western technology, while one-third of the output of the machine-building and metal-working sector goes to defense. In this connection, the recent belittling of the impact of imported technology is somewhat misleading: consider, for instance, the repercussions of the Tol'yatti plant upon the Soviet economy and on Soviet society.

The level of mechanization and automation of Soviet industry and construction remains substantially behind that of most Western countries, with over one-half of industrial workers still engaged in manual labour. And despite the designation of the tenth five-year plan as "the plan of quality and effectiveness," with the quality-mix of output now employed as a principal success indicator, together with a plethora of decrees "decreeing" higher quality output,[17] there is little evidence to suggest that quality has replaced quantity (or the *val*) as the prime criterion of industrial performance.[18]

Agriculture. The Soviet Union is comparatively poorly endowed in terms of agricultural land and climate, and thus under any organizational system agricultural labour and agricultural productivity would probably be much lower than, say, in the United States or in Western Europe. But the recent setbacks in the face of an unwavering commitment of capital resources under the present leadership raise a whole series of nagging and legitimate questions. Just what is that one-third of the workforce up to? Can the planners maintain the share of scarce resources being allocated to that seemingly bottomless slough of despond? (In absolute terms, productive investment in agriculture in the USSR is currently estimated as being about five times higher than in the United States.[19]) Will a future Soviet leadership, that has no personal political capital invested in collectivization, dare to break down the gigantic *sovkhozes* and *kolkhozes* into more manageable subunits and give farmers meaningful operational autonomy?

In sharp contrast to his earthy and unpredictable predecessor, Brezhnev has been remarkably consistent in his agricultural policy. All of the major provisions of the March 1965 programme are still being implemented faithfully in 1978. Over one-quarter of total new investment will go to agriculture in 1976–80, including 40 billion rubles on land improvement programmes alone. Procurement prices have been repeatedly raised until they are among the highest in the world. Millions of new tractors, trucks and combines have been delivered to farms, whose inventories are gradually approaching the "optimal parks."[20] Feasibility studies are going ahead on grandiose plans to divert the flow of north-flowing rivers to the parched terrain of Central Asia, yet realization must be decades away. Livestock complexes are growing larger, although the sharp falling off of animal products coming to the market last year led the authorities to check the concentration drive and, instead, to display almost benevolent encouragement for the private livestock holdings. Finally, the record grain harvest of 1976 emboldened the planners to raise their sights somewhat: the new average output target for grain in 1976–80 is now 220.4 million tons (in place of 215–220 million tons) and for meat 16.0 million tons instead of 15.0–15.6 million tons.

Consumption. After a decade when per capita consumption grew both substantially (over 3 percent per annum) and visibly (e.g., new housing, motor cars, other consumer durables, soft goods and meat), the per capita consumption of all goods and services in 1976 rose by only one percent, largely attributable to a 3 percent drop in food consumption.[21]

In absolute terms, and by any static comparison with the West, living standards for the bulk of the Soviet population are wretchedly low. A juxtaposition of some of the salient indicators of the quality of life in the Soviet Union with those prevailing in the West puts Soviet conditions ahead only in respect to job security (admittedly most important), formal weekly working hours, the numbers of doctors and students per 10,000 of the population and the relation of noncontributory pension payments to final earnings. Soviet consumers are well behind when it comes to the purchasing power of their wages, the availability and quality of consumer goods and services, minimum wage, the rate of income tax on average earnings and below, the rates of indirect taxation (the turnover tax) on most consumer goods, food consumption and housing.[22]

The widespread and prolonged food shortages of 1975 and 1976 reportedly gave rise to isolated manifestations of popular discontent. For instance, absenteeism in Tula, when workers filed off the job so that they could shop in the better-stocked stores in Moscow, led in a roundabout route to the award of the title "Hero City." Baltic dockers staged go-slow strikes and refused to unload imported foodstuffs that were destined for the limited-access stores patronized by privileged members of Soviet society.[23] Four Latvian dockers were reportedly jailed for having struck in protest against meat shortages.[24] And a comprehensive survey of foodstuffs on sale in the state retail stores of Moscow—the best supplied city in the USSR—in May 1976 found no trace of, *inter alia*, poultry, carrots, coffee, pepper, butter, kefir, onions, potatoes, apples, lemons (or indeed any other tropical fruit), steak, cheese and cooking oil.[25]

While Soviet shoppers are occasionally confronted with overt retail price increases, such as those announced in January 1977 and again in March 1978,[26] they are well aware that the principal erosion in their purchasing power stems from covert inflation in the prices of "new" and "improved" products. The coveted Zhiguli offers a good example. The basic model is the VAZ-2101, which retails for 5,500 rubles. Subsequent and slightly improved models sell for much more: for instance, the VAZ-21011 now sells for 6,030 rubles, and the VAZ-2103 retails for 7,500 rubles.[27] Most aspiring car owners would, however, be perfectly happy, indeed ecstatic, with the cheapest model; after all, 5,500 rubles represents over three years' take-home pay for the average Soviet industrial worker.[28] But the majority of those on the waiting list cannot buy the VAZ-2101 any more, since the output of this model has been cut back (by nearly one-half in 1975), while the production of the 2103 and 21011 is rising rapidly.[29] What is more, most of the remaining VAZ-2101 output is earmarked for the markets of East and West Europe! This kind of creeping—or perhaps galloping—inflation can set the would-be driver back by a small fortune. And much the same kind of process may be observed for a whole range of consumer goods and services.

Most Soviet citizens are by now well aware that their living standards are markedly inferior to those prevailing in socialist neighbours such as Hungary, the GDR and Czechoslovakia, and that they are just not in the same league as those in the crisis-ridden and decaying capitalist societies of the West. However, particularly during the past twelve years or so they have been at least partially consoled by the realization of how much better off they are now than they or their parents were. Twenty years ago, for instance, most families shared apartments; now most families have their own front door. Fifteen years ago, a private motor car was an unattainable dream for most citizens; now practically everyone has at least a relation or an acquaintance who drives one. The consolation has been buttressed by the propagation and amplification by the Soviet media of the very real woes afflicting their Western counterparts in the shape of mass unemployment, inflation and declines in real incomes. But any prolonged and marked slowdown in the improvement in living standards, running counter to rising expectations, could switch attention from internal to external comparisons. And this could bring trouble.

Defence. After reappraisal, the CIA has revised its estimates of Soviet defence expenditure sharply upward. This revision is reportedly attributable to a reassessment of the efficiency of the defence sector and changes in pricing defence goods, together with the escalating costs of new and more complex weapons systems. The latest "best Western estimate" is: defence expenditures now absorb between 11 and 13 percent of the Soviet GNP; they have been rising by 4–5 percent annually in real terms during the past few years; this present upward momentum is likely to continue during the immediate future because of programmes already in motion; estimated dollar costs of Soviet defence exceeded U.S. outlays by some 40 percent in 1976 (30 percent if military retirement programmes are included); defence takes a large share of the products of major investment goods industries such as machine-building (one-third), metallurgy (one-fifth), chemicals (one-sixth) and energy (about one-sixth); defence has a heavy impact on high-technology areas where it has a priority claim on manpower and output.[30]

While the overall GNP was growing at annual rates of 4–5 percent, a defence bill that also increased at much the same pace was onerous but tolerable. But if the GNP growth rate slows to 3 percent or less, then clearly defence must increasingly preempt resources which would otherwise go to investment (i.e., future growth) and/or consumption.

Here again it should be recorded that the CIA's "new" estimates of Soviet defence expenditures are challenged by some Western observers as being still too low. One of the Agency's most vocal critics is W.T. Lee, who calculated defence to take 14–15 percent of the Soviet GNP in 1975 and who expected this burden to rise to over 20 percent by 1980.[31]

Foreign Trade. The volume and value of foreign trade has continued to grow at a faster rate than the GNP, so that it has an increasing impact upon domestic production and consumption. The most notable development in recent times in Soviet trade with its East European partners has been the growing dissatisfaction of the junior partners in Comecon with the inadequate supplies of Soviet oil and grain, together with a reported reluctance to participate in joint investment projects on Soviet territory to the extent desired by the host country. However, in any study of economic growth, attention should perhaps be focused on Soviet trade with the developed West, for the Soviet economy will have a continuing requirement for as much Western expertise and equipment as the Soviet hard-currency balance can afford and as the economy can absorb and diffuse. Both of these constraints are formidable, although only the former is quantifiable to any degree of accuracy.

After two years of large hard-currency deficits, the Soviet payments position improved somewhat in 1977. Moscow's net hard-currency debt is believed to have risen to about $17 billion. Approximately one-half of the USSR's hard-currency earnings in 1976 came from the export of crude oil and petroleum products to noncommunist countries. The Soviet debt service ratio (i.e., principal repayments on medium- and long-term debt) and interest payments on total debt as a share of merchandise exports) at the end of 1976 has been estimated at 26 percent.[32] Debt service is expected to rise to $3 billion in 1977 and to almost $4 billion next year.[33]

Reform. The reform of economic planning and management, unveiled by Premier Kosygin at the September 1965 plenum, was a sickly child from birth and never really recovered from the reaction of 1968. For all practical purposes, that particular reform is dead although it has not been officially buried. One of its prime features was a judicious mix of centralization and decentralization. Thus, while branch ministries recovered all of their previous powers and more, the individual enterprise was at the same time to be granted more autarky in its day-to-day operations. In practice, the decision-making powers of the enterprise manager were further eroded and circumscribed. This latter process has been accentuated and expedited with the grouping together of the already (by Western standards) large individual enterprises into gigantic production associations.

This organizational form was first introduced in 1961. It underwent an eclipse during the first flush of the implementation of the 1965 reform but has moved steadily forward since its endorsement at the 24th and 25th Congresses of the CPSU. It is currently scheduled to be adopted throughout industry by 1980, although at mid-1977 complaints were rife regarding foot-dragging in the creation and running of associations.[34] The already tenuous link between effort and reward for the mass of industrial workers and employees has been further obfuscated by the inevitable levelling that takes place in the vast conglomerates. In any case, wage increases have been held down in order not to exacerbate the existing degree of repressed inflation, and it looks as if higher productivity is to be induced not so much through higher wages as by means of exhortations, spurious ''Socialist Competitions'' and ''spontaneous'' pledges. In place of a realistic reform, a plethora of limited and local experiments is being tried out in industry and construction, including the ''Shchekino,'' ''Aksai,'' ''Zlobin,'' ''VAZ,'' and ''Belorussian'' models. But, as two distinguished observers pointed out recently on the pages of *Izvestiya,* despite the impressive successes recorded by these methods, their scale has been kept so modest that they have had little impact upon industrial growth and effectiveness.[35]

An authoritative pronouncement by no less than the head of the USSR Gosplan bore testimony to the demise of the spirit of the September 1965 reform. In March 1976, Baibakov wrote: ''At the bases of the successes of socialism's planned economy is the Socialist social structure and Socialist ownership of the means of production, which *wholly eliminates the influence of the law of the jungle and of market chaos.*''[36]

Roughly parallel developments with industry may be observed in the agricultural sector. Although many Soviet and Western critics might argue that a major source of weakness is the excessive size and unwieldiness of the basic production unit, with some *kolkhozes* encompassing over fifty villages separated by rivers and forests, the present trend is towards even larger interfarm organizations and agro-industrial complexes, although a ''pause'' was evidently decreed after the excesses of 1976.[37] At the same time, considerable leeway has been granted to some local authorities to experiment with variations on the theme of the normless *zveno*. This is a small team of farmers that is allocated a given area of land and some farm machinery for a period of several years and allowed to retain the ''surplus product'' after a given delivery target has been met.

The present climate of thought does not appear to be conducive to reform. Although at the very top, gerontocracy does not like change, the system's managers at the middle and lower levels surely realize that the Soviet command economy is extremely wasteful, inflexible and inefficient. Yet there are a host of objective constraints upon reform. For instance, economic reform threatens political control. Private enterprise offends ideology.

The untrammelled play of market forces would displace bureaucrats, cause disruption and give birth to mass unemployment. Large differentials in earnings would give rise to jealousy and discontent—perhaps shared misery is less disruptive? Planners' preferences would have to give way to consumers' choices, paving the way for "anarchy". Small wonder that the old men in the Kremlin have put reform on the back-burner and are leaving these painful decisions for their successors. They are also comforted in their caution by the less than impressive performance of the mixed market economies in recent years.

Prospects

With all of his failings, Khrushchev managed to detach himself on occasions from the day-to-day political hurly-burly to look ahead at the Promised Land of Full Communism. The principal monument to his visionary zeal, the Party Programme of 1961, has not been completely flushed down the memory hole, but it is seldom mentioned nowadays in polite society.

If his successors have a vision of future Soviet society, then they are keeping it to themselves and not sharing it with those who are most directly concerned, (i.e., the Soviet population.) Perhaps the inmates of the Kremlin are too preoccupied with their aches and ailments, plus the overwhelming mass of detail involved in reacting to daily pressures? In any case, the long-term plan for 1976–90, that was commissioned at the 24th Party Congress, has yet to be unveiled. Indeed, it is by no means certain that any final version of the current medium-term plan for 1976–80 will be published.

Notwithstanding the hazards involved in projecting the future of a society whose present is so obscured, it is quite possible to outline the rough parameters to economic growth over the next decade or so on the basis of some firm trends and some not-so-firm assumptions. The political and social implications of these growth projections are quite another matter where observers will clearly disagree and where one man's insight is just as good as, and no better than, that of his neighbour.

Table 1 showed how inputs of capital and labour into the Soviet economy were maintained at a high level from 1951 to 1975 and yet, owing to a fall in factor productivity, the rate of growth of output (i.e., GNP), declined. (The absolute decline in factor productivity growth of—0.6 percent in 1971–75 was attributable largely to the two exceptionally bad harvests of 1972 and 1975; without these, factor productivity would almost certainly have registered a gain, perhaps of around 0.5 percent.)

Inputs during the next decade or so may be predicted with a fair degree of probability. As far as capital stock is concerned, even if the current unrealistically low rates of retirement are retained, capital stock will not grow at much more than 6.5 percent per annum through 1980. And since new investment is planned to increase at an historically low average annual rate of 4.4 percent in 1976–80, this is bound to work itself out in a further reduction in growth of capital stock in the 1980s, probably to 5.5 percent per annum in 1981–85.

The prospects for the prime input, that of labour, are much gloomier. The number of man-hours worked has grown steadily from 1961 to 1975 at a steady 1.8–1.9 percent per annum. The employment ratio of 92.4 percent recorded by the 1970 census[38] represents virtually the maximum feasible (i.e., few more can be squeezed out of the private sector and those who are will merely offset the increased number of women staying home to bear and to care for children). All future employment growth must therefore stem basically from the natural increase in the population of working age (16–59 for men and 16–54 for women.) These future cohorts are already born and thus we can confidently predict that the population of working age will grow by an average of 1.6 percent in 1976–80 and by only 0.5 percent in 1981–85.[39] (The projection for the period 1986–90 is little different.)

The weight of the third input, land, is insignificant (3 percent) and the expansion of arable land in the foreseeable future is expected to remain at less than 0.5 percent per annum.

To sum up: if factor productivity grows at an average of 0.5 percent per annum in 1976–80, the GNP should increase at an annual average of around 4.0 percent. With the same growth in factor productivity in 1981–85, GNP growth will fall to about 3.1 percent.[40]

Yet even that 0.5 percent projected for factor productivity growth in 1981–85 could be too high. Some of the extraneous and domestic factors working against even this modest gain are:

(a) Most of the growth in increments to the labour force will take place in the non-Russian republics; in many of these, and especially in Central Asia, there has traditionally been resistance to migration to the cities and to the construction projects of the North.[41]

(b) By the mid-1980s, the USSR is expected to become a net importer of oil.

(c) Most of its hard-currency earnings will, it would seem, have to be earmarked for debt repayment and service plus oil imports from hard-currency suppliers, leaving little for the purchase of Western technology or grain.

(d) Large-scale cooperation or compensation ventures in Siberia may be hampered by the resistance of strongly conservative and nationalist elements in Moscow.

(e) Total indigenous energy supplies will taper off, with an anticipated growth of only about 1 percent per annum in 1981–85, compared with 5.4 percent in 1971–75 and 4.0 percent in 1976–80[42]; overall economic growth is usually closely akin to overall energy consumption.

(f) The period 1961–74 is believed by some observers to have represented a period of exceptionally favourable climate over the Soviet grain belt. Conversely, a return of more "normal" climate in the 1980s would lead to a lowering of yields.[43]

(g) The coming decade will witness a decline in the growth of educational attainment.

(h) To maintain the Soviet armed forces at their current strength, by 1985 or so it would be necessary to recruit about 85 percent of all 18-year olds. An increasing share of these will come from non-Russian nationalities.

(i) Will the defence lobby accept a slowdown in military expenditures in line with the decline in overall economic growth?

(j) Will the Soviet consumer tolerate a barely perceptible improvement in his still meagre living standards?

(k) Why should East European countries continue to supply most of their higher grade machinery, consumer durables and soft goods to the USSR when they cannot count on the Soviet oil and grain they need in repayment?

In the present perspective, five principal courses of action offer themselves to the Soviet leadership:

(a) Do nothing very much—this is apparently the option chosen by the present incumbents.

(b) Revert to the "Stalin model" of a high rate of growth of capital stock. This model was ruled out as being politically inviable for anyone but Stalin and the provisions of the tenth five-year plan suggest that the planners have conceded as much.

(c) Rely increasingly on the massive infusion and successful diffusion of Western technology and equipment: this is evident at present, but how will the USSR pay for it in the 1980s?

(d) Reduce the burden of defense—no sign of this yet.

(e) Institute meaningful reforms of planning and management—don't hold your breath.

But other options may also be open.

Notes

1. Pravda, *5 Jan. 1977.*
2. *See Vladimir G. Treml,* Agricultural Subsidies in the Soviet Union, *U.S. Department of Commerce, Washington, 1975.*
3. Pravda, *27 Oct. 1976.*
4. Trud *v.* SSSR, p. 241.
5. Vneshtorg 76, *p. 91.*
6. *The latest appeared in* Pravda, *28 July 1977.*
7. Vestnik statistiki, *No. 7, 1977, p. 90.*
8. *CIA,* Prospects for Soviet Oil Production, *Washington, Apr. 1977, p. 9.*
9. *For instance, Radio Peace and Progress in English for Asia, 15.30 GMT, 1 Aug. 1977.*
10. *See,* inter alia, Washington Post, *12 June 1977;* EastWest Markets, *25 July 1977;* The Times, *27 July 1977.*
11. Baltimore Sun, *19 Jan. 1978.*
12. *See this author's "Is the Ninth Five-Year Plan Consumer-Oriented?" in NATO,* Prospects for Soviet Economic Growth in the 1970s, *Brussels, 1971, pp. 83–90, and "Was the Ninth Five-Year Plan Consumer-Oriented?" in the follow-up volume published in 1975.*
13. Narkhoz 75, *p. 192.*
14. *28.7 percent and 24 percent respectively, against an industrial average of 15.8 percent:* Narkhoz 75, *p. 728.*
15. Sotsialisticheskaya industriya, *16 Mar. 1976.*
16. Pravda, *27 Oct. 1976.*
17. *See, for instance,* Ekonomicheskaya gazeta, *No. 3, 1977, p. 5 and* Pravda, *3 Feb. 1977.*
18. *Cf. RL 87/77, "New Success Indicators in Soviet Industry," 15 Apr. 1977.*
19. *JEC,* Allocation of Resources in the Soviet Union and China—1976, *Washington, 1976, p. 43.*
20. *See Radio Liberty Research Supplement,* Soviet Agriculture: Ten Years under New Management, *23 May 1975, pp. 10–14.*
21. *Perhaps for the first time since the war, ration cards were introduced for meat in some regions. A copy of such a card, believed issued in the Perm' Oblast' in late 1976, was reproduced in* Die Welt, *6 Aug. 1977.*
22. *See this author's "Soviet Living Standards: Some Salient Data" in NATO,* Economic Aspects of Life in the USSR, *Brussels, 1975, pp. 49–64 and "Retail Prices in Moscow and four Western Cities in May 1976," in* Osteuropa Wirtschaft, *No. 2, 1977, pp. 122–41.*
23. Die Welt, *2 June 1977.*
24. *See for example,* The New York Times, *31 Oct. 1976;* The Times, *1 Nov. 1976;* International Herald Tribune, *2 Nov. 1976; cf. AS 2742.*
25. *"Retail Prices in Moscow . . . ," op cit.*
26. Pravda, *5 Jan. 1977.*

27. *The latest retail prices are taken from the lottery lists in* Pravda vostoka, *21 Aug. 1977 and* Sovetskaya Rossiya, *2 Sept. 1977.*
28. *The calculations are spelled out in "Retail Prices in Moscow . . . ," op. cit.*
29. Za rulem, *No. 6, 1976, p. 7.*
30. *See CIA,* A Dollar Cost Comparison of Soviet and U.S. Defense Expenditures, *Washington, Jan. 1977; JEC,* Allocation of Resources in the Soviet Union and China, *Washington, June 1977; CIA,* Soviet Economic Problems and Prospects, *Washington, Aug. 1977.*
31. *W.T. Lee, "Soviet Defense Expenditures,"* Osteuropa Wirtschaft, *no. 2, 1976, and "Soviet Defense Expenditures in the 10 FYP," ibid. no. 4, 1977.*
32. *CIA,* USSR: Hard Currency Trade and Payments, 1977–78, *Washington, Mar. 1977, p. 17.*
33. *Ibid. p. 10.*
34. *See, for instance,* Pravda, *11 June 1977.*
35. Izvestiya, *23 June 1977.*
36. Sotsialisticheskaya industriya, *31 Mar. 1976 [emphasis supplied]; cf.* Pravda, *10, 11 and 12 Nov. 1977.*
37. *See* Pravda, *26 Oct. 1976; cf* Kazakhstanskaya pravda, *18 Nov. 1976;* Pravda vostoka, *26 Nov. 1976; Zarya vostoka, 2 Feb. 1977.*
38. *TsSU,* Chislennost', razmeshchenie, vozrastnaya struktura, uroven' obrazovaniya, natsional'ny sostav, yazyki i istochniki sredstv sushchestvovaniya naseleniya SSSR, *Statistika, Moscow, 1971, p. 33.*
39. *Godfrey Baldwin,* Projections of the Population of the USSR and Eight Subdivisions, by Age and Sex: 1973 to 2000, *p. 35.*
40. *5.5 × 41.2 + 0.5 × 55.8 + 0.5 × 3.0 yields 2.56 percent, to which is added factor productivity growth of 0.5 percent.*
41. *Murray Feshbach,* Prospects for Massive Out-Migration from Central Asia during the next Decade *(unpublished).*
42. *CIA,* Soviet Economic Problems and Prospects, *Washington, Aug. 1977, p. 8.*
43. *CIA,* USSR: The Impact of Recent Climate Change on Grain Production, *Washington, Oct. 1976.*

Chapter 16

ON THE TEMPO OF INDUSTRIALIZATION

The tremendous advances which have made the USSR the second-mightiest industrial nation in the world were achieved in an incredibly short period of time and with the imposition of tremendous hardships and sacrifices. Stalin and Brezhnev offer some explanations and justifications for the tempo involved, and Bertrand de Jouvenel raises some questions about the necessity for the sacrifices imposed. (While the de Jouvenel article was published in 1957 and is dated in some important respects, it continues to raise some fundamental questions that, whatever their merit, in this editor's opinion, are not raised as sharply elsewhere.)

On Soviet Industrialization

Joseph V. Stalin

Those Who Fall behind Get Beaten*

It is sometimes asked whether it is not possible to slow down the tempo somewhat, to put a check on the movement. No, comrades, it is not possible! The tempo must not be reduced! On the contrary, we must increase it as much as is within our powers and possibilities. This is dictated to us by our obligations to the workers and peasants of the USSR. This is dictated to us by our obligations to the working class of the whole world.

To slacken the tempo would mean falling behind. And those who fall behind get beaten. But we do not want to be beaten. No, we refuse to be beaten! One feature of the history of old Russia was the continual beatings she suffered because of her backwardness. She was beaten by the Mongol khans. She was beaten by the Turkish beys. She was beaten by the Swedish feudal lords. She was beaten by the Polish and Lithuanian gentry. She was beaten by the British and French capitalists. She was beaten by the Japanese barons. All beat her—because of her backwardness, military backwardness, cultural backwardness, political backwardness, industrial backwardness, agricultural backwardness. They beat her because to do so was profitable and could be done with impunity. Do you remember the words of the prerevolutionary poet: "You are poor and abundant, mighty and impotent, Mother Russia." Those gentlemen were quite familiar with the verses of the old poet.† They beat her, saying: "You are abundant," so one can enrich oneself at your expense. They beat her, saying: "You are poor and impotent," so you can be beaten and plundered with impunity. Such is the law of the exploiters—to beat the backward and the weak. It is the jungle law of capitalism. You are backward, you are weak—therefore you are wrong; hence, you can be beaten and enslaved. You are mighty—therefore you are right; hence, we must be wary of you. That is why we must no longer lag behind.

In the past we had no fatherland, nor could we have one. But now that we have overthrown capitalism and power is in our hands, in the hands of the people, we have a fatherland, and we will defend its independence. Do you want our socialist fatherland to be beaten and to lose its independence? If you do not want this, you must put an end to its backwardness in the shortest possible time and develop genuine Bolshevik tempo in building up it socialist system of economy. There is no other way. That is why Lenin said on the eve of the October Revolution: "Either perish, or overtake and outstrip the advanced capitalist countries."

We are fifty or a hundred years behind the advanced countries. We must make good this distance in ten years. Either we do it, or we shall be crushed. This is what our obligations to the workers and peasants of the USSR dictate to us.

But we have other, still more serious and more important, obligations. They are our obligations to the world proletariat. They coincide with our obligations to the workers and peasants of the USSR. But we place them higher. The working class of the USSR is part

From a speech at the First All-Union Conference of Managers of Socialist Industry, February, 1931.
†*Nekrasov, "Who Is Happy in Russia?" (1876)—Editor's note.*

of the world working class. We achieved victory not solely through the efforts of the working class of the USSR, but also thanks to the support of the working class of the world. Without this support we would have been torn to pieces long ago. It is said that our country is the shock brigade of the proletariat of all countries. This is a fitting definition. But this imposes very serious obligations upon us. Why does the international proletariat support us? How did we merit this support? By the fact that we were the first to hurl ourselves into the battle against capitalism, we were the first to establish a working-class state, we were the first to start building socialism. By the fact that we are doing work which, if successful, will change the whole world and free the entire working class. But what is needed for success? The elimination of our backwardness, the development of a high Bolshevik tempo of construction. We must march forward in such a way that the working class of the whole world, looking at us, may say: This is my vanguard, this is my shock brigade, this is my working-class state, this is my fatherland; they are promoting their cause, which is *our* cause, and they are doing this well; let us support them against the capitalists and promote the cause of the world revolution. Must we not live up to the hopes of the world's working class, must we not fulfill our obligations to them? Yes, we must if we do not want utterly to disgrace ourselves.

Such are our obligations, internal and international. As you see, they dictate to us a Bolshevik tempo of development.

I will not say that we have accomplished nothing in regard to economic management during these years. In fact, we have accomplished a good deal. We have doubled our industrial output as compared with the prewar level. We have created the largest-scale agricultural production in the world. But we could have accomplished more had we tried hard during this period really to master production, the technique of production, the financial and economic side of it.

In ten years at most we must make good the distance which separates us from the advanced capitalist countries. We have all the "objective" possibilities for this. The only thing lacking is the ability to take proper advantage of these possibilities. And that depends on us. *Only* on us! It is time we learned to take advantage of these possibilities. It is time to put an end to the rotten policy of noninterference in production. It is time to adopt a new policy; a policy adapted to the present times—the policy of *interfering in everything*. If you are a factory manager, then interfere in all the affairs of the factory, look into everything, let nothing escape you, learn and learn again.

Preparation for Defense*

What material potentialities did our country command before the Second World War? To help you examine this point, I shall have to report briefly on the work of the Communist Party in preparing our country for active defense.

If we take the figures for 1940, the eve of the Second World War, and compare them with the figures for 1913—the eve of the First World War—we get the following picture. In 1913 our country produced 4,220,000 tons of pig iron, 4,230,000 tons of steel, 29 million tons of coal, 9 million tons of oil, 21,600,000 tons of marketable grain and 740,000 tons of raw cotton. Those were the material potentialities with which our country entered the First World War. Such was the economic base of old Russia which could be drawn upon for prosecution of the war.

**The balance of this excerpt is from Stalin's speech delivered in Moscow on February 9, 1946.*

Now as regards 1940. In the course of that year our country produced 15 million tons of pig iron, or nearly four times as much as in 1913; 18,300,000 tons of steel, or nearly four and one-half as much as in 1913; 166 million tons of coal, or more than five and one-half times as much as in 1913; 31 million tons of oil, or nearly three and one-half times as much as in 1913; 38,300,000 tons of marketable grain, or nearly 17 million tons more than in 1913; 2,700,000 tons of raw cotton, or more than three and one-half times as much as in 1913. Those were the material potentialities with which our country entered the Second World War. Such was the economic base of the Soviet Union which could be drawn upon for prosecution of the war. The difference as you see is tremendous.

Such an unprecedented increase in production cannot be regarded as the simple and usual development of a country from backwardness to progress. It was a leap by which our Motherland was transformed from a backward into an advanced country, from an agrarian into an industrial country.

Five-Year Plans

This historic transformation was accomplished in the course of three Five-Year Plan periods, beginning with 1928, the first year of the First Five-Year Plan. Up to that time we had to concern ourselves with rehabilitating our ravaged industry and healing the wounds received in the First World War and the Civil War. Moreover, if we bear in mind that the First Five-Year Plan was fulfilled in four years, and that the fulfillment of the Third Five-Year Plan was interrupted by war in its fourth year, we find that it took only about thirteen years to transform our country from an agrarian into an industrial one. It cannot but be admitted that thirteen years is an incredibly short period for the accomplishment of such an immense task. . . .

Methods of Industrialization

By what policy did the Communist Party succeed in providing these material potentialities in the country in such a short time? First of all, by the Soviet policy of industrializing the country.

The Soviet method of industrializing the country differs radically from the capitalist method of industrialization. In capitalist countries industrialization usually begins with light industry. Since in light industry smaller investments are required and there is more rapid turnover of capital and since, furthermore, it is easier to make a profit there than in heavy industry, light industry serves as the first object of industrialization in these countries.

Only after a lapse of much time, in the course of which light industry accumulates profits and concentrates them in banks, does the turn of heavy industry arrive and accumulated capital begin to be transferred gradually to heavy industry in order to create conditions for its development.

But that is a lengthy process requiring an extensive period of several decades, in the course of which these countries have to wait until light industry has developed and must make shift without heavy industry. Naturally, the Communist Party could not take this course. The Party knew that a war was looming, that the country could not be defended without heavy industry, that the development of heavy industry must be undertaken as soon as possible, that to be behind with this would mean to lose out. The Party remembered Lenin's words to the effect that without heavy industry it would be impossible to uphold the country's independence, that without it the Soviet order might perish.

Accordingly, the Communist Party of our country rejected the "usual" course of industrialization and began the work of industrializing the country by developing heavy industry. It was very difficult, but not impossible. A valuable aid in this work was the nationalization of industry, and banking, which made possible the rapid accumulation and transfer of funds to heavy industry. There can be no doubt that without this it would have been impossible to secure our country's transformation into an industrial country in such a short time.

Agricultural Policy

Second, by a policy of collectivization of agriculture.

In order to do away with our backwardness in agriculture and to provide the country with greater quantities of marketable grain, cotton, and so forth, it was essential to pass from small-scale peasant farming to large-scale farming, for only large-scale farming can make use of new machinery, apply all the achievements of agronomical science and yield greater quantities of marketable produce.

There are, however, two kinds of large farms—capitalist and collective. The Communist Party could not adopt the capitalist path of development of agriculture, and not as a matter of principle alone but also because it implies too prolonged a development and involves preliminary ruination of the peasants and their transformation into farm hands. Therefore, the Communist Party took the path of the collectivization of agriculture, the path of creating large-scale farming by uniting peasant farms into collective farms.

The method of collectivization proved a highly progressive method not only because it did not involve the ruination of the peasants but especially because it permitted, within a few years, the covering of the entire country with large collective farms which are able to use new machinery, take advantage of all the achievements of agronomic science and give the country greater quantities of marketable produce. There is no doubt that without a collectivization policy we could not in such a short time have done away with the age-old backwardness of our agriculture.

The Role of Heavy Industry

Leonid Brezhnev

The . . . modification of the national-economic proportions does not mean that we are slackening our concern for heavy industry.

The Party's policy of ensuring the priority development of socialist industry, and principally its basis, heavy industry, has turned our country into a mighty power. It will be no exaggeration to say that only the consistent effectuation of this policy has enabled us to safeguard the gains of the socialist revolution, to end the centuries-long backwardness, to achieve gigantic economic, social and cultural progress.

High growth rates in heavy industry fully retain their importance in the present conditions.

They retain their importance principally because extended socialist reproduction, the possibilities and rates of future economic growth and the building of the material and technical basis of communism are all largely dependent on the successful development of heavy industry. Dependent on its work is the technical equipment of all spheres of the economy, the supply of material and technical resources for higher labour productivity.

They also retain their importance because without developing heavy industry we cannot maintain our defence capability at the level necessary to guarantee the country's security and the peaceful labour of our people. Much has been done in this respect in the past five years: the Soviet Army is now equipped with all types of modern sophisticated weaponry. The further development of the defence industry, its concrete work programmes, depend in many ways on the international situation. The Soviet Union is prepared to support realistic disarmament measures that consolidate peace and do not impair our security. At the same time we must be prepared for any possible turns in the train of events.

Lastly, the development of heavy industry is of special significance because, among other things, the basic tasks of improving the standard of living cannot be achieved without it. Heavy industry is to increase considerably the output of the means of production for the accelerated development of agriculture and the light and the food industries, for more housing, for further promotion of trade and community services.

That, precisely, is the ultimate purpose of heavy industry. In this connection, allow me to recall the words of V.I. Lenin: "In *the final analysis* the manufacture of means of production is necessarily bound up with that of articles of consumption, since the former are not manufactured for their own sake, but only because more and more means of production are demanded by the branches of industry manufacturing articles of consumption" (*Collected Works,* vol. 4, p. 163).

The Party is setting heavy industry yet another important task—to expand the manufacture of consumer goods directly in its own enterprises. For this all its branches possess considerable facilities. I should also like to mention the defence industry in the same context. Today, as much as 42 percent of its output is used for civilian purposes. By virtue of

Leonid Brezhnev is General Secretary of the CPSU Central Committee. This excerpt is from the Report of the Central Committee of the CPSU delivered at the 24th Party Congress, March 30, 1971.

its high scientific and technical level, its expertise, inventions and discoveries are of cardinal importance for all spheres of the economy.

Consequently, far from diminishing, the role of heavy industry is continuing to gain in importance in the present stage, because the set of immediate practical problems with which it deals is growing.

On the Character of the Soviet Economy

Bertrand de Jouvenel

Man is free to choose his purpose: but once wedded to a purpose, he is bound to the conditions of its fulfillment. The avowed purpose of the Soviet government is to bring Russian industrial power, in the shortest possible time, to parity with that of the United States. There is nothing specifically "communist" in this purpose. Indeed it stands in stark contradiction to the Marx-Engels picture of a communist economy which would not be concerned with building-up of capacities but with their full employment for the consumer satisfaction of the workers. . . .

It is worth stressing that the Soviet program is the conscious and systematic imitation of something which exists, but which was not brought about either consciously or systematically. Take, for instance, steel: steel capacity did not, in the United States, reach its successive levels because someone enjoying supreme power had decreed that steel capacity should reach such a level by such a date, but additions to capacity occurred in response to demands made upon it by steel-consuming industries, which, in turn, attuned their capacities to rising demand, ultimately consumer demand. There is no question in Russia of steel capacity growing under the prodding of demand: it must grow, period. Evidently if the growth of steel capacity is regarded as an end in itself, it can be best served by reserving all the steel presently produced for the building of more steel capacity.

At this writing, Bertrand de Jouvenel is a French political philosopher and economist, and author of On Power *and of* Sovereignty. *This selection is excerpted from the* Bulletin of the Atomic Scientists, *vol. 13 (November 1957), pp. 327–30. By permission of the publisher and the author. The reader should take note of the date of this piece which is a digest of a paper presented by the author some time earlier under the title "Some Fundamental Similarities between the Soviet and Capitalist Systems." The paper appeared in full in a volume entitled* The Soviet Economy, A Discussion, *published in London in 1956 by Secker and Warburg.*

This is, of course, driving things to the extreme; but it can serve at least to stress the orientation of Russian industry. Russian industry is, to a considerable degree, employed in producing industrial capacity. Of course every industrial nation has some part of its industrial plant engaged in producing plant and equipment. This is necessary in order that plant and equipment which wears down or becomes outdated can be replaced, and so that in every field the productive apparatus can be enlarged and improved.

But in Russia the production of plant and equipment has absolute priority, which is understandable enough, given the aim, which is to reach a stated level of productive capacity. According to the statistical publication which the Soviet government has recently brought out, industrial production in Russia consisted of consumer goods in the proportion of 66.7 percent in 1913, of 60.5 percent in 1928 (when total industrial production was no greater than in 1913, as far as one can tell on other authorities), and the proportion of consumer goods in total industrial production fell successively to 29.4 percent in 1955, the last figure given, producers' goods having risen to 70.6 percent of total industrial production. The Russian publication also gives indexes of growth of the two sectors of industry; all outside experts agree that these indexes are fantastically exaggerated, but the relation between the two indexes may presumably be trusted. From 1928 to 1955 it is claimed that the sector producing means of production multiplied its output almost thirty-nine times, while the sector producing consumer goods multiplied its own output only nine times.

The much faster expansion of the sector producing means of production has been obtained by a priority which is perhaps the decisive feature of the Russian economy. That sector, which bears the A label in Russian economic vocabulary (as against the B label for consumer goods industries) is bidden to produce means of production for itself instead of producing them for the consumer goods industries. The Soviet reasoning is that providing plant and equipment to consumer goods industries competes with providing the same to producer goods industries, and that the faster the A sector grows, the easier it will be for it then to fill out the voids existing in the plant and equipment of the consumer goods industries.

The logic of this reasoning cannot be attacked. It is quite true that the more steel that goes into not only motorcars but also the motorcar industries, the less there is available for building steel furnaces and hydraulic presses; and that the sooner you have a great deal of the latter, the easier you will find it to equip the motorcar industry.

Russian economic history from 1928 to date can be contrasted with American economic history up to 1914 as a thing different in kind: building as against growing. In the process of growth, the bones and the flesh develop together. In building, you first construct the skeleton, then you put on the flesh: that is the Russian formula—which is incidentally convenient for purposes of world power since it gives you means of war far in advance of your means of comfort.

Investment, Saving, and Political Structure

An economy is most easily understood if you analyze it in terms of concrete goods. The manpower of Russian industry has risen from less than 4 million in 1928 to approximately 18 million in 1956: this is about the same manpower as that of American industry. Russian industry however produces less of everything, and the difference in amounts produced is far more pronounced in consumer goods than it is in investment goods. There are indeed some investment goods which are produced in greater quantities in the USSR than in the United States. In other terms, the percentage of resources going into investment activities is much higher in Russia than in America. If this fact is formulated in the language of national financial accounting, we have to say that the rate of investment within the industrial product is very much higher in Russia than in the United States. . . .

Marx's critique of the capitalist system was based upon his postulate that the whole of added value belonged by right to the workers: and therefore the distribution of profits was an expropriation of the workers. It was an injustice, but at the same time it was necessary. Only through profits, as he clearly saw, could there be reinvestment, building up of the productive apparatus. Therefore this injustice would have to endure until the productive apparatus had been sufficiently built up. When no further capital investment was necessary, then the capitalist would become unnecessary. But he would not readily perceive his redundance; therefore he would have to be forcibly done away with. His redundance would be revealed by the fact that he would be able to find no productive employment for the capital arising out of profits: opportunities to invest would have withered away, and therefore his levy upon added value would be useless and nefarious, depriving the working consumers of the buying power needed to absorb rising production.

The historical necessity of the capitalist's disappearance was based primarily upon the postulate, widely prevalent in Marx's day, of the dwindling opportunities for productive investment: this is to be found in Ricardo. It was based on the assumption that capitalists would not allow workers to get directly or indirectly (through government redistribution) a rising share of added value. On the other hand, the capitalist was held necessary for the process of accumulation because Marx could not imagine (and here he was no doubt right) that the workers, if they received the whole of added value, would be willing to save a large part of it for investment.

The class struggle was regarded by Marx as a struggle over "value added," the workers wishing to obtain the whole of it and to apply it to consumption, the capitalists wanting to retain as much of it as possible, and to apply it to investment. The workers were bound to win this fight, but not as long as it was socially useful that accumulation should proceed. And therefore it was also a historical necessity that capitalists should retain their power to make profits as long as accumulation had to proceed.

Communism as Supercapitalism

When things are looked at from this angle, it becomes quite clear that the Soviet government plays the part of the capitalist as seen by Marx. Just as Marx pictured the capitalist, the government gives the workers the smallest possible share of "added value" and retains the largest possible share in order to apply it to investment. No doubt a true democracy of workers would, within an individual company, assign a far greater part of the financial product to wages, and, within the nation, address a far larger share of activities to consumption-serving activities. This tendency must be overcome in the interests of accumulation, and therefore there must be a despotic authority to do it.

No such thing was conceived by Marx. While this point cannot be stressed here, it may be mentioned that the term "dictatorship of the proletariat" was not understood by Marx to connote the strengthening of the state's power; the state, on the contrary, had to be destroyed root and branch, and by "dictatorship of the proletariat" Marx meant that workers' councils should be bound by no law until the liquidation of the privileged classes had been completed.

What interests us here however is simply the fact that in order to obtain rapid accumulation of productive assets, it is necessary to tilt the balance of power against the workers' eagerness to consume. This tilting was achieved in capitalist society, as Marx saw it, by the economic power of the capitalists, able to employ workers at a mere living wage. Why were they able to do so? As Marx saw it in England, there were three contributing factors: firstly, the rapid influx of candidates for industrial employment, due in small part to the rise in population and in major part to the flight from the fields. Secondly, because the capitalists owned the means of production and were free to give or deny employment: they held the whip-hand. Thirdly, they were able to do this because of the backing which the capitalists received from the state, which was a "class-state," the state of the capitalist class.

It is quite clear that in the capitalist countries of our day, there is no excess offer of manpower, thanks to policies of full employment. It is also clear that the government has ceased to be the wholehearted supporter of the employers as against the employees. Insofar as it departs from neutrality it does so in espousing the interests of the employees. Under such conditions, the ownership of the means of production does not give the capitalists the whip-hand over the workers, the power to dictate the share these will get.

On the other hand, we do find in Russia the precipitate influx of workers depressing the labor market which Marx observed in England in his day, and which led to the "hard times" described by Dickens. And we do find the solidarity between employers and government which Marx thought characteristic of capitalist society: this solidarity is based on the fact that the employers are the instruments of government, which is completely at one with them.

We are therefore tempted to conclude that Soviet communism as we see it today is a synthetic version of early industrial capitalism.

Are These Sacrifices Necessary?

A question, however, arises, which does not seem to have been asked in the leading circles of Soviet Russia: was it really necessary to reproduce, as it were systematically, all the most regrettable traits of capitalist growth, to condense and accentuate them? This is surely a relevant question, when Soviet economic development is imposed as a model upon the satellite European nations, accepted as a model by the leaders of Communist China, and suggested as a model for the underdeveloped countries of the world. . . .

But let us . . . make the questionable assumption that the basic equipment of the USSR could not have been built up to its present pitch in the given period of time by any other procedure than that which was adopted.[1] Then the discussion might turn upon the question whether so steep a rise by so arduous a path was a desirable thing.

Let us further assume that Russia persists in its procedure of rapid growth, and therefore catches up with the United States[2] in basic capacities by a certain date T, and in production of consumer goods by a certain later date T′. Is anyone ready to argue that the total welfare of the Russian people between the years 1928 and T′ will have been maximized by the procedure followed? Is it not far more plausible that the total welfare of the generations concerned would have been greater if a less arduous path had been followed?

It is natural to discount very distant satisfactions as against immediate satisfactions. Tinbergen has produced striking estimates of such discounting.[3] Acting as self-constituted "representatives" of the Russian people, the Soviet leaders seem to have turned things the other way round and to have set future satisfactions at a premium as against the present. But have they really reasoned in this manner? And have they not rather thought in terms of equalization of power?

For over a century, starting with Sismondi if not earlier,[4] there has been a ceaseless critique of capitalism, arguing that its unquestionable achievements in the building up of capacities were not worth the price paid in the uprooting and hustling of men, that in fact men would have been better off, and happier with a more leisurely pace of change than that forced upon them by capitalists and their sales pressure. It is interesting to find the communists enamored of the buildup achieved by the hated and despised capitalism, to the point of thinking that its speedy emulation justifies greater pressure upon men than was ever exerted under capitalism.

Notes

1. *We can note this analogy in respect of steel production: in Russia it rose from 4.5 million tons in 1928 to 45 million tons in 1955. In the United States it rose from 4.5 million tons in 1894 to 45 million tons in 1917.*
2. *As far as one thinks of consumer goods, one should, of course, picture the catching up as involving equalization of consumer goods per capita; if one thinks of power, then the catching up is to be thought of as merely the equality of productive capacities between the two nations, regardless of differences in population.*
3. *See Tinbergen's remarkable article in the* Economic Journal, *December 1956.*
4. *One might say that this critique starts with Rousseau's* Discourse on the Sciences and the Arts.

PART SEVEN

THE SOVIET SOCIAL SYSTEM: COMMUNITY, EQUALITY, WELFARE

The misfortune of despotism is not that it does not love people but that it loves them too much and trusts them too little.

Quoted by Ilya Ehrenburg in his *Memoirs*

There is only one heroism. That is to love life, one's own and the life of others.

Albert Camus

If we believe that men have any personal rights at all as human beings, they have an absolute right to such a measure of good health as society, and society alone, is able to give them.

Aristotle, 333 B.C.

Chapter 17

SELF-DETERMINATION AND EQUALITY OF NATIONS

One of the proudest boasts of the USSR is that "it has solved the national question—completely and finally." This thesis is elaborated by the distinguished Soviet editor, B.G. Gafurov, and challenged by the prominent American sociologist, Alex Inkeles. Despite their sharp differences, it is well to emphasize that, generally speaking, students of Soviet affairs credit the USSR, in the words of Alex Inkeles, with "substantial attainments" in the field of national relations.

It should be recalled that Lenin, as early as the turn of the century, supported recognition of "the equality of rights of all nationalities" including the right of self-determination. These "rights" were affirmed in the first program of the Party adopted in 1903, embodied in Soviet decrees after the Revolution, and appear in the Soviet Constitution. At the same time, it was Lenin's view that Marxism could not be reconciled with divisive, bourgeois nationalism, even in its "most 'just,' 'pure,' refined, or civilized" form. He confidently anticipated, as Professor Julian Towster explained in his pioneer study, *Political Power in the USSR,* that the proletariat, having attained power and eliminated oppression and friction, would induce the nations of the earth voluntarily to "draw together, fusing their different cultures and languages into one common culture and language," to constitute "one, unified community of mankind." "In place of any nationalism," Lenin wrote in 1913, "Marxism proposes internationalism—the amalgamation of all nations in a supreme unity."

Is there a basic inconsistency in Lenin's views? So some of the early Russian Marxists charged. And this, too, is the view of Professor Richard Pipes, author of *The Formation of the Soviet Union,* who maintains that Lenin's theory of self-determination was, in essence, an "endeavor to reconcile two sets of mutually exclusive premises: those derived from Marxism and those supplied by political realities." Lenin, as a "realist," assailed the Bolsheviks who anticipated that the proletarian power would abolish all borders and create a supranational state as visionaries seeking a "pure" instead of a "social" revolution. But, on the other hand, as a "Marxist," Lenin insisted that "the question of the right of self-determination" should not be confused "with the question whether the secession of this or that nation is expedient." The latter question must be decided by the Party "in each individual case entirely independently, from the viewpoint of the interests of the whole social development and of the interests of the proletariat's class struggle for socialism."

The careful reader will discern in the excerpt from the 1961 Program of the Communist Party—the third in its history—and in the article by Rein Taagepera some of the dualism to be found in Lenin's formulations on the national question.

The Solution of the National Question

B.G. Gafurov

For centuries the best minds of mankind both in the East and in the West dreamed of a brotherhood of peoples irrespective of nationality, race or color. But the grim reality of the old world barred the implementation of this dream.

In this connection I would like to start my lecture with a parable that is common in the East. Two tribes dwelt on two opposite banks of a river. For centuries they were at loggerheads with each other. Once, a peasant from the tribe dwelling on the right bank met a wizard who said to him: "I'll give you anything you wish, but under one condition—a member of the other tribe dwelling on the left bank of the river will receive twice as much." And the peasant answered: "Put out one of my eyes," wanting the wizard to put out both eyes of his counterpart in the other tribe. Such is the bitter tale of the formidable power of national enmity and hate that cripples human life.

As is known, in the last century two men—the Frenchman Arthur de Gobineau and the Germanized Englishman Houston Chamberlain—evolved a most elaborate argument to substantiate the theory that the northern, or the so-called Nordic race of the dolichocephalic, blond-haired and blue-eyed men, is the most superior of all existing human races, and because of merits inherent in it, is the natural master of all other races and, above all, of the colored ones. This theory was repeatedly lauded to the skies by various ideologists and politicians, and received its most finished and tragic manifestation in the policies of Hitlerism. History proved the antiscientific, reactionary and antipopular nature of this false theory. . . .

Even long before the October Revolution, Lenin and the Bolsheviks had worked out a comprehensive theoretical program on the national question in Russia. The main provisions of this program were: equality and sovereignty of all peoples of Russia; their right to free self-determination, including the right to secede; abolition of all national and religious restrictions and privileges; free development of national minorities and ethnographic groups.

Immediately after the victory of the October Revolution, the Communist Party set about to practically implement the program laid down on the national question. The Second All-Russian Congress of Soviets, on November 8, 1917, declared that it was the paramount task of Soviet power to insure to "all nations inhabiting Russia the genuine right to self-determination." The solicitude of the Leninist Party for the establishment of complete equality of all nations in our country found reflection in the Declaration of Rights of the Peoples of Russia adopted by the Soviet Government on November 15, 1917. The Declaration solemnly confirmed the sovereignty and equality of these peoples, their rights to self-determination including that to secede, abolished all national restrictions and privi-

B. G. Gafurov was, at this writing, director of the Institute of Oriental Studies and chief editor of its periodical, Sovremenniy vostok. *Mr. Gafurov has also been a member of the Central Committee of the Communist Party. The selection is from a lecture delivered to the Diplomatic Corps in Moscow on October 12, 1961.*

leges, guaranteed the all-around and free development of all nations and nationalities, however small. . . .

At a certain stage in the attainment of complete and all-round unity of the peoples of the country, the Eighth Congress of the Party [in 1919] recommended a federation of Soviet national republics. The federation was to be based on the well-known premise by V.I. Lenin who emphasized: "We want a voluntary union of nations; a union which would allow no coercion of one nation by another; a union which would be based on complete trust, clear awareness of fraternal unity and absolutely voluntary agreement. Such a union cannot be established at once; it should be built with the greatest possible patience and caution in order not to spoil everything, not to arouse distrust; to let distrust bred by centuries of landlords' and capitalists' oppression, of private property and enmity over its distribution and redistribution, be overcome." (V.I. Lenin, Letter to Workers and Peasants of the Ukraine, *Works*, vol. XXX, p. 269.) The Union of Soviet Socialist Republics established in 1922 was precisely such a voluntary alliance of nations. . . .

In the years of Soviet power the formerly backward, outlying areas of Russia have become prosperous industrial and agrarian republics. As a rule, the proportion of investments in the economy of the national republics exceeded the average for the Soviet Union as a whole, and this resulted in a quicker pace of their industrialization than that of the central areas of the country. The Communist Party radically changed the entire economics of the Soviet republics on the basis of socialism. It is particularly true regarding the Eastern republics of the USSR, where the working people made a direct transition from patriarchal and feudal relations and colonial slavery to socialism, by-passing the capitalist stage of development. . . .

In the course of socialist construction, achievements of historic significance were gained in the field of national relationships, their main characteristics being as follows:

1. The nationalities of the Soviet Union, which had not attained nationhood before the Revolution, have developed into nations under the banner of the Soviets. If previously history knew the process of development of nations on the basis of the development of capitalist relations, the experience of the Soviet Union proved that the development of capitalism is by no means an indispensable condition of the development into nations of nationalities that have not reached the stage of capitalism. Thus, for instance, the Tajik nationality, where prior to the October Revolution feudal relations prevailed, developed into a nation in this way.

   The process of development of nations in the Soviet Union had many peculiar and instructive features. Thus certain nationalities, speaking similar languages but historically self-determined a long time ago, developed into different nations (the Tartars, Bashkirs, Kazakhs and Kirghiz). On the other hand, nationalities speaking different languages but long brought together by history (the Persian-speaking Tajiks, the Pamirs peoples, Yazgulems, Yagnobs) developed into a single Tajik nation.
2. As a result of the effort of the Communist Party to eliminate economic and cultural inequality, there are no longer any backward nations in the USSR.
3. The greatest achievement in the solution of the national question was that national discord and enmity were replaced by fraternal friendship and cooperation of all nations and nationalities of the Soviet Union. History knows instances of peaceful coexistence of nations, of setting up of all kinds of unions between them, but the unity of Soviet socialist nations is essentially different from such alliances. The ob-

> jective basis of the union of Soviet nations is the socialist ownership of the implements and means of production, which is the dominant form of property in our land; socialist relations of production, which are the relations of cooperation and mutual assistance of people free from exploitation. It was the liquidation of the exploitation of man by man, the doing away with social strife in the land of Soviets, that ensured disappearance of national discord and establishment of friendship among all peoples of the USSR.

Of historic importance was also the fact that the biggest and, economically and culturally, the most developed nation—the Russian nation—which before the Revolution played the role of the ruling nation, now resolutely and selflessly gave up its former privileged position. Moreover, the Russian socialist nation made many efforts and sacrifices to help the formerly oppressed nationalities to develop into independent nations and to evolve their own statehood, economy and culture.

Tremendous successes and gains scored in the field of economic, political and cultural development of nations and nationalities of the Soviet Union support the claim that in the course of building a socialist society, the national question in our country has been solved completely and finally. All this was achieved as the result of tremendous work on the part of the Party, the Soviet Government and the entire Soviet people.

Let us remember that Russia herself was an underdeveloped country. To build industry, a great effort was needed. We did not have a rich uncle to depend on; everything had to be done by our own hands. But even at the height of the Civil War, when the country's economy was completely dislocated, Lenin ordered that machines and factory equipment be sent to the national republics. . . .

The degree of literacy was very low. In Tajikistan, for instance, there was only 0.5 percent literacy. Therefore, the elimination of illiteracy was an indispensable condition for the development of a new, advanced economy.

After the end of the Civil War, feudal relations and survivals of the tribal system, rules of feudal and tribal law (Adah, Sharia, etc.) proved a grave obstacle in the way of building up a new life in the national republics. . . .

Feudal survivals were completely eliminated on the basis of mass cooperation in agriculture. The land was given to the tiller. Collectivization transformed small-scale, backward farming into a large-scale mechanized branch of the economy. An end was put once and for all to impoverishment, famine and epidemics—three features of village life in the East before the Revolution.

To promote the development of the economy and culture, it was necessary to combat both great-power chauvinism and local nationalism. In the late twenties the main danger came from great-power chauvinism, against which the main blow of the Communist Party was directed. But local nationalism, too, did tremendous harm to the interests of the people. The Party always encouraged Russian Communists to fight against great-power chauvinism in the first place, and the local workers to combat local nationalism. The tremendous organizational and cultural work of the Party for the international education of the masses resulted in the strengthening of friendship among all nations.

In the USSR a man, preaching national discord and enmity, asserting the exclusiveness of one people and haughtily and contemptuously treating people of other nationalities, is bound to be severely condemned by the Soviet public. The laws of our state punish any encroachment on the rights of Soviet nations and nationalities. Combating great-power chauvinism and local nationalism, the Party fought against both: the ignoring of local national characteristics and the over-accentuating of them. . . .

Much had to be done in order to do away with the feudal attitude toward women. In the national republics, where the bulk of the population were Moslems, women had a very low status. Polygamy still existed there. In the areas with settled population, women had to wear all kinds of veils—*paranjas, chachvans* and *chadras*. They were 100 percent illiterate.

Women's departments and councils were set up by the Party committees and conducted a great project of enlightenment and education. In 1926–1927 a broad campaign was developed against the veil. Hundreds of courageous, open-minded women publicly burned their veils, calling upon other women to follow their example. Despite the furious resistance of feudal elements, who killed dozens of women, hundreds of thousands of women threw off the veil and joined the ranks of the builders of the new life.

I could tell you a lot of interesting things about the way we succeeded in getting rid of the custom of wearing the veil. In the thirties and forties there were people who insisted on laws and decrees being passed prohibiting the veil. But the Soviet Government refused to follow their advice, and chose the way of education and explanatory work. It often happened that at the meetings where women were told of the harm of the custom of wearing veils they would throw them off, but, coming back home, put them on again. And we realized that it was not enough to persuade only women and that men also had to be appealed to.

Special schools, courses and technical schools for women were opened in the national republics. In the cities where silk and cotton mills were built, many women, throwing off the veil, entered them as workers. The fight for the emancipation of women was bitter; it required great effort. But now we are proud of the fact that millions of women have become educated and aware members of society. Thousands of women who hold a doctor's or master's degree now work as specialists in industry, agriculture and the arts.

Extremely impressive are our gains in the field of social, economic and cultural transformation in the Soviet national republics. I would like to cite only a few examples to give you an idea of the scale of these changes: In Uzbekistan, which was formerly considered one of the backward regions of tsarist Russia, there are now 1,400 large industrial enterprises. Uzbekistan's industrial output is exported to more than 40 countries. . . .

Besides the Academy of Sciences, there are in Uzbekistan the Academy of Agricultural Sciences, two universities, 32 higher educational establishments, and 102 technical schools. Uzbekistan has more than double the number of students per thousand of population of France and Italy, and has outstripped the United States and Great Britain in this respect too. Forty years ago the Kirghiz people had no written language of their own. At present the republic has 80 students per 10,000 of population, considerably more than France, Belgium and Italy.

In Turkmenia there are 17 doctors per 10,000 of population, while in the United States the figure is 12, in Great Britian and France—11. Armenia, the formerly backward Transcaucasian land, has now become one of the most advanced Soviet republics as regards the level of economic and cultural development. At present it is a country of all-round electrification. In 1960 its per capita output of electricity was 1,478 kilowatt-hours (i.e., greater than that of Italy, Japan and Denmark.) When we turn to Armenia's neighbors on the opposite bank of the Araks, we find that Turkey generates 15 times less electricity and Iran 32 times less than Armenia. . . .

When numerous local specialists were trained and acquired the necessary experience, excessive centralization and supervision on the part of the Union government became unnecessary. . . . Important functions of the management of the huge economy were transferred to the local bodies. It is sufficient to mention that at present 94 percent of the over-all industrial output of the country comes from enterprises which are the responsibility of the Councils of Ministers of the union republics.

Now I would like to dwell briefly on certain other points. There are some people in the West who speak much about "Russification" of the USSR's national republics. They often base their allegations on the fact that Russian is taught in the higher educational establishments and that certain republics switched over to the Russian script.

The charge of "Russification" is, of course, wrong and does not reflect the real state of affairs. About 50 nationalities of the USSR got a written national language for the first time only after the October Revolution. Books and magazines are published in 89 languages of the peoples of the USSR. Even the nationalities numbering only 5 to 7 thousand people have their written languages and literatures. National opera and ballets are created, research works are written in national languages. Everything is being done in the Soviet Union to preserve and promote the development of national traditions. We collect and study rich collections of manuscripts of the peoples of the USSR. Hundreds of people are engaged in the collection and study of their folklore. Large-scale research is conducted in the fields of archaeology, ethnography and the classical literature of Soviet nations and nationalities.

The setup of the supreme legislative body of the country, the USSR Supreme Soviet, reflects the solicitude of the Soviet state for the needs and requirements of the peoples of the USSR. As is known, the Supreme Soviet consists of two chambers—the Soviet of the Union and the Soviet of Nationalities. All union republics, autonomous republics, autonomous regions, and national territories are represented in the Soviet of Nationalities. The union republics, irrespective of the size of their territory and population, send the same number of deputies to the Soviet of Nationalities, namely—25; and the autonomous republics, autonomous regions and national territories—11, 5 and 1 respectively.

A high-powered Economics Committee has been established in the Soviet of Nationalities. Its task is to ensure the proper solution of problems of economic, social and cultural construction in the republics in accordance with their national and economic characteristics.

I believe that these facts are sufficient to refute the charges of "Russification." Complete equality of languages has always been ensured in our country, and in the future national languages will be developed and perfected. The Program of the CPSU states that it is our task "to continue promoting the free development of the languages of the peoples of the USSR and the complete freedom for every citizen of the USSR to speak and to bring up and educate his children in any language, ruling out all privileges, restrictions or compulsions in the use of this or that language." By virtue of the fraternal friendship and mutual trust of peoples, national languages are developing on a basis of equality and mutual enrichment.

The friendship of our peoples has withstood all trials. It has to be admitted even by those whose outlook is very far from being communist. The well-known American social scientist E. Franklin Frazier, author of the book *Racial and Cultural Contacts in the Contemporary World,* published in 1957, wrote that if someone were to try to find an answer to the question of whether the Russian policy solved the national problem, he would have to note that during World War II, various peoples and nations remained loyal to the Soviet Union and fought enthusiastically to defend it. . . .

The USSR—a multinational state based on the friendship and brotherhood of nations—is a model of monolithic unity, indestructible strength and cohesion unprecedented in history. The peoples comprised in the Soviet Union cannot conceive of being separated;

they are full of inexhaustible vitality and creative power brought into being by the socialist system. The new Program of the Communist Party of the Soviet Union heralds the beginning of a new stage in the development of national relations in the USSR. . . .

The prophecies of the best minds of humanity, of great thinkers and poets about the era of equality and friendship of all nations have become true in the Soviet Union. It was not in vain that the Polish poet Mitskiewicz dreamed of "the future times when peoples, forgetting their quarrels, will unite as one great family." The bard of the Scottish people, Robert Burns, wrote of the day when all men will be brothers, and the great Arab thinker al Maari, who lived nine centuries ago, had a vision of a "pure land where human beings do not torture their like." These beautiful dreams have become a reality in our time, in our country.

Soviet National Policy in Perspective

Alex Inkeles

In the current atmosphere of "peaceful competition between systems," increasing emphasis is placed on the economic factor of production and consumption levels in comparisons of Soviet and non-Soviet achievement. In the process some observers have all but lost sight of the fundamental political, social and cultural characteristics that continue to differentiate the two systems. Among relevant issues one of importance is the status of the national and racial minorities in the Soviet Union. At a time when the Western democracies are granting full independent statehood to one after another of the formerly subject peoples of Africa and Asia, it seems particularly appropriate to inquire into the position of the Soviet minorities. Unfortunately, this subject has received less attention than it deserves, perhaps because many have uncritically accepted Moscow's claim that any issues of nationality and race have long since been successfully resolved. If this were true, Soviet policy would still merit close examination. The fact is, however, that despite some substantial attainments, the Soviet regime has far from solved the problem of minority status either to the satisfaction of the groups themselves or to the particular credit of the Soviet system.

In order to assess Soviet national policy intelligently, it is necessary to know certain distinctive historical and demographic facts about the minorities.

Alex Inkeles is the author of Public Opinion in Soviet Russia *and coauthor of* The Soviet Citizen. *This selection originally appeared in* Problems of Communism, *vol. 9 (May–June 1960), pp. 25–34, and is reproduced with permission.*

Population Patterns

While the Great Russians are the single largest group in the Soviet Union, they hold only a precariously slim margin of numerical superiority over the combined population of the national minorities. . . .

The minorities generally live in homogeneous and compact groups on the outer edge of the central land mass which is the territory of the Great Russians. This basic demographic structure persists despite a great increase in the dispersion of peoples—especially of Russians—into other nationality areas during World War II and its aftermath. The fifteen national republics strung around the outer borders of the Soviet Union constitute the overwhelming bulk, 80 percent or more, of the country's national minorities. In the northwest, the three Baltic republics include close to five million Latvians, Lithuanians and Estonians. On the western frontier there are some eight million Belorussians, and thirty-seven million Ukrainians who, when added to the Russians, give the Soviet Union its overwhelmingly Slavic majority. On the same frontier are two and a quarter million Moldavians, in the republic of the same name, and almost one and a half million Poles, who for obvious reasons have no identifying territorial unit. Further to the south and east, along the Black Sea and in the Caucasus, there are numerous nationalities distributed in a complex pattern of settlement. These include the Georgians, Armenians and Azerbaijanians, each in their own republic and each more than two and a half million strong—as well as several million Tatars. In Central Asia, the four republics of the Turkmen, Uzbeks, Tadzhiks and Kirghiz, along with the people of adjoining Kazakhstan, contribute some thirteen million Turkic people of Moslem faith. Other Moslems, living in areas further in from the border, include several million Volga Tatars and almost a million of the closely related Bashkirs. A neighboring area contains close to a million and a half Chuvash, a Christian and often Russianized remnant of the old Bolgar Empire on the Volga. Of the remaining larger nationalities, only the million and a quarter Mordvians and the two and a quarter million Jews are widely dispersed. . . .

Collectively, Russian groups constitute a median proportion of 13.5 percent of the population in the fourteen republics other than the RSFSR. In certain areas, however, the influx of Russians has been far greater. In Kazakhstan, for example, the Russians are now the most numerous group (43 percent) of the population; together with other Slavic residents, the Ukrainians and Belorussians, they constitute a majority of the republic. Thus, the Kazakhs have become a minority in the area presumably set aside for them as a national home, and by process over which they have had little say and less control.

Most of the important minorities represent separate and distinct nationalities, with their own language and literature, and in many cases an earlier history of independent existence as a nation-state. Their sense of separate identity is intensified by the fact that ethnicity is generally linked with religious identification, without the crosscutting of religion and race found in some lands. Thus, to be Russian is to be Orthodox, to be Polish, Catholic; Armenians are in the Armenian National Church and Georgians in the Georgian Church; and the Asiatic peoples, especially the Turkic, are overwhelmingly Moslem. It seems fairly clear that the last thing these people wish is the loss of identity as separate nationalities through absorption into the larger homogeneous culture of the Russian nation. Indeed, although there are often important historical ties which bind them to the center of Moscow, the nationalities seldom share much in common with other peoples of the Soviet Union beyond their minority status. How, then, did these diverse peoples all come together in common Soviet citizenship? The answer is not to be found, as in some other ethnically heterogeneous nations, in voluntary emigration or incorporation into

Russia. It must be sought in the history of Russian state policy going back many centuries.

Tsarist Expansionism

Following their subjugation by the Khans, the Russian people lived for centuries under the rule of the Tatar hordes, compressed into a modest area in central Russia and cut off from other major Slavic groups such as the Poles and Ukrainians, who were variously under domination by peoples from the West, Scandinavia and the Baltic. The starting point of Russian colonialism may be taken as 1552, when Ivan the Terrible took Kazan, and thus liquidated the Tatar Khanate. The expansion of the previously small Muscovite state thus began with the incorporation of large numbers of Turkic peoples, especially from along the Volga and its tributaries. About a century later a comparable major movement to the west was completed when the left-bank regions of the Dnieper were established as a protectorate, bringing Cossack and Ukrainian peoples under Russian hegemony. Peter the Great added the peoples along the coast of the Baltic Sea. In her turn Catherine the Great made further acquisitions in the west, including parts of Poland, and drove all the way to the Black Sea in the south. The Caucasus was added later, and most of the rest of Turkestan was acquired by Alexander II to complete the movement by the end of his reign in 1881.

This extraordinary territorial expansion was estimated to have proceeded at the rate of fifty square miles a day over a period of four hundred years, from the end of the fifteenth to the end of the nineteenth centuries. As pointed out earlier, it brought the Russians to the status of being a minority in the land they ruled. To speak of Russia as having a minority problem in the usual sense is therefore misleading. Russia was a huge colonial empire; but in distinction to the other empires of Europe, her colonial possessions were contiguous to the homeland. Thus she *incorporated* her possessions, her dependencies and satellites, within one continuous border, with the captive nations strung around the outer limits of the solid Great Russian core. It is impossible to understand the nationality problem in the Soviet Union without always keeping in mind that the Soviet regime inherited this ''prison of nations'' from the Tsars when it took power, and it had to operate within the framework thus set by history.

The Leninist Formula

In this situation, the Soviet regime has adopted an essentially dualistic attitude toward Tsarist expansionism: on the one hand, it has generally treated the conquest and incorporation of the minorities as an ''historically progressive'' policy; on the other hand, it has encouraged the myth that Tsarist treatment of the captive peoples was uniformly harsh, oppressive and reactionary, and that it was designed to destroy the character and individuality of the many groups which had come under the empire's sway. Actually Tsarist policy toward the subject minorities varied considerably at different times, depending on the political philosophy of the different rulers. It also varied with respect to different areas and groups. Most modern impressions of this policy tend to concentrate on the period of intensive suppression starting after the accession of Alexander III in 1881 and lasting until the revolution in 1905, after which a considerable liberalization again ensued. The depredations of Alexander's reign, especially the marked efforts at Russification and the virtual driving underground of local cultural movements, left a lasting mark not only on world opinion but on the national groups, and this fact was soon to be of great importance to the as yet unborn Soviet government.

Considering how obvious a source of grievance against the Tsarist regime here lay ready for exploitation, it is striking that the Bolsheviks were so slow to realize its potentialities as an instrument for shaking the old order. But their whole philosophy inclined them to gloss over the nationality problem. It was a basic belief of Marxists that the path of history would lead toward ever larger, more homogeneous, centralized, industrial, political units which in time would yield to a worldwide "proletarian" society. The slogan "the proletariat has no fatherland" expressed the belief that nationalism, patriotism, regionalism, and similar attachments were part and parcel of the social pattern of bourgeois capitalism, which would somehow be outlived and sloughed off once socialism and then communism came to the world. Lenin himself gave virtually no attention to the nationality problem until 1913, when he was forced to turn to it both because of the growing popularity of the Bauer-Renner program and because of his own growing awareness that the success of his plans must reckon with the fact of national loyalties and aspirations.

The Bauer-Renner program, conceived to meet the multinational situation facing the political parties in the Austro-Hungarian empire, proposed an unusual degree of autonomy for minorities in the conduct of their own affairs; had it been put into effect, it would have permitted a great multiplication of small and more-or-less exclusive national, religious and ethnic units. Lenin naturally viewed this program as a challenge to the principle of centralization which he had steadfastly espoused; but he was equally opposed to the alternative idea of federalism, again on grounds that it weakened the chances for the development of a truly international proletarian power. Forced to take a stand, he went to what he thought was the absolute heart of the matter, by basing his policy squarely *and exclusively* on the right of each nationality to so-called "self-determination." He was unwilling to consider any compromises which might weaken the power of a central Communist government. Any people or nation—theoretically, at least—had the right to secede from the larger society, but if it chose to remain it must accept the general system in its entirety, without demanding special status or privilege and without asking for a federal union:

> The right to self-determination is an exception to our general thesis, which is centralism. This exception is absolutely necessary in the face of the Black Hundred type of Great Russian nationalism. . . . But a broad interpretation may not be made of an exception. There is *nothing,* absolutely nothing here, and there must be nothing here, but the *right* to secede.

Lenin felt that this acknowledgment of the abstract "right" to secede was necessary as a political maneuver. But at the same time—in a contradiction that no amount of esoteric language could hide—he held that any attempt at *actual* secession would be retrograde, antiproletarian, bourgeois counterrevolution. He assumed, in short, that no one would want to *exercise* the right to secession should there be a proletarian revolution.

He proved completely wrong, although in this he had the company of most of the other political groups in Russia, all of whom inadequately assessed both the effect of Tsarist policy in hardening national feeling against *any* central Russian government, and the effect of the rapid social and cultural changes which were increasing national consciousness in many of the minority areas. In any event, the Bolshevik regime found, to its great embarrassment, that in most of the national areas of the former empire the local political leaders took their right of secession quite seriously. Even where complete separation was not their prime objective, the local leaders viewed themselves as equals with the leaders in Moscow, entitled on that basis to negotiate the nature of their nationality's participation in the new state.

The Bolsheviks did not hesitate to use the force of arms to meet this upsurge of independence, sending their Red Armies to regain control over most of the provinces of the former empire. Finland was allowed to slip away without any particular struggle, and Poland and the Baltic States were abandoned after unsuccessful military campaigns. But under the command of such well-known Communist figures as Frunze and Kuibyshev in Central Asia, Kirov and Ordzhonikidze in the north Caucasus, Kaganovich in Belorussia, and Mikoyan in Azerbaijan, almost all the other territories were recaptured by Soviet troops and turned over to the control of the local Communist parties, reliable subordinates of the central party apparatus in Moscow. The army which entered Georgia on February 16, 1921, and by February 25th once again placed the Communist flag over the capital Tiflis, fought the last major round in the effort to reintegrate the rebellious national areas.

The need for force to win back control of these areas brought home to the Soviet leaders the crucial nature of the nationality problem, and it is largely to this realization that we owe the particular forms which the so-called nationality policy of the Soviet Union has assumed. Rather than attempting to relate the explicit history of the policy, the writer will turn directly to a consideration of its overall features, giving the historical context as seems necessary. Perhaps the best approach is to pose four questions which would be important in evaluating the policy of any large-scale colonial power.

Self-Determination: A Paper Right

The first question in such an assessment would be: to what extent does the country's nationality policy provide for gradual transition to separate statehood for the major national minorities whose culture, history, and sociopolitical and economic maturity make them reasonable candidates for such status?

The attainment of a condition of self-government and national independence has come to be accepted as a fundamental goal and an inalienable right of people all over the world. Since World War II we have witnessed a tremendous sociopolitical movement as virtually all the major colonial dependencies of the former British Empire, and to a lesser but striking degree of the French Empire, have achieved national independence. . . .

Since the right of secession is constitutionally guaranteed in the Soviet Union, the right to pursue that goal would logically seem to follow. Yet even to advocate, let alone to work toward, the political independence of any area in the Soviet Union is unthinkable for the Soviet citizen. Such action is identified, both by law outside the constitution and by long practice of the secret police, as a counterrevolutionary crime against the state, warranting severe punishment. Almost every major purge trial has involved charges that the accused conspired to separate some national area from the Union. At various stages of Soviet history hundreds and thousands of officials, teachers, writers and other members of the intellectual classes of different national republics have been purged from the party and state apparatus, and/or sent into forced labor on charges of harboring "bourgeois nationalist leanings," the official term for identifying with the interests of one's national group and resisting abject subordination to the interests of the Moscow center.

In short, what the constitution says about the national question bears virtually no relationship to Soviet practice. Any lingering doubts on this score should have been destroyed by the action of the Soviet regime during World War II, when it simply erased from the map and from the face of the earth four autonomous socialist republics—the Volga German, the Crimean Tatar, the Kalmyk, and the Chechen-Ingush. Although there was an announcement in the case of the Volga Germans that this action was taken in the interest of national security, and a belated statement that the Chechen and Crimean Tatars had collaborated with the Germans, not even this much explanation was given with regard to the Kalmyks.

Not only were the republics liquidated as political entities, but their millions of people were dispersed to distant regions of the Soviet Union. There were wide repercussions and revulsion against this act; among others, Tito of Yugoslavia went so far as to accuse the Soviet Union of genocide. Certainly the indiscriminate mass dispersion of a whole population because of acts of individuals, no matter how numerous, violated basic standards of humanity and made a mockery of Stalin's assertion that "the national question and the problem of collaboration among nations have been settled better [in the USSR] than in any other multinational state." It was not until after Stalin's death that some members of these nationalities were rehabilitated and partially restored to their former status.

Cultural Survivals

The second broad question may be phrased: To what degree are the minorities permitted and facilitated in the free expression of their cultural heritage? First and foremost, this involves the right to use one's native tongue in all types of public and private communication and in the education of youth. Cultural expression also includes the preservation and further development of folk and tribal ways, including art forms, ceremonial and religious customs, the national costume, etc. In addition, some hold that free cultural expression should include the right to have economic and political forms of organization which are distinctive to a particular culture.

That the Soviet approach toward the cultural self-expression of the minorities has been unique is beyond doubt; whether it has been as liberal as is claimed is quite another question. The doctrinal explanation of Soviet policy rests in the distinction which is made between the content and the form of culture, expressed in the well-worn formula "national in form, socialist in content." In theory, this phrase means that the values and ideas of the socialist society should be uniform in every culture, though the means by which they are expressed may be—indeed, should be—of a traditional and indigenous nature. The vagueness of this formula, however, has left wide leeway in its application, and like most Soviet slogans it has become quite meaningless in practice. . . .

The outstanding survival has been the native languages. With one exception (Yiddish), the Soviet regime has made no attempt to eradicate local tongues; they are used in the educational system, in communications media, and in indigenous literature. Generally distinctive literary forms associated with the languages in such spheres as poetry, epic writing and drama have also been permitted. Another class of survivals which has suffered comparatively little interference is folk arts, including folk handicrafts and native art forms. Nor has there been much effort made to alter distinctive modes of native dress (except in the case of the Moslem veil for women, against which a rather successful campaign has been waged). These policies, it might be pointed out, parallel the practice adopted by most colonial powers.

If the Soviet attitude with respect to these several fundamentals of cultural expression has been generally permissive—and certainly represents a vast reform over the depredatory Russification efforts of Alexander III—there is nevertheless much on the record to indicate that tolerance extends only as far as it suits the interests of the central authorities. Even in the matter of language, Moscow's actions have in some cases profoundly affected an indigenous culture. Much is made of the fact that the Soviets provided alphabets for several dozen languages which previously could not be written down, paving the way for newspapers and other literature in these tongues. Less is known of the fact that the Soviet regime used its power, against the overwhelming opposition of the local population, to force the abandonment of the religiously-sanctioned Arabic script used by the millions of Soviet Moslems. Not once but twice they did this, first introducing the Latin alphabet, and then in 1939 substituting the Cyrillic. Even the Tsars never dreamed of attempting such a victory for Russian culture among their subject Moslems.

Folk literature and art, too, have been subjected to interference and suppression whenever Moscow chose to see in their various forms any manifestations of "bourgeois nationalism." Frequently the regime has seized on old or new folk writings, dramas, operas, etc., condemning them for deviation from the official line, forbidding their production, and taking reprisals against their authors. The writing or presentation of native history in particular has suffered from intervention by the authorities, who insist that the Tsarist subjugation of the nationality areas be treated as "historically progressive." Among many such acts of repression, one of the more glaring examples was the dissolution of the entire cultural apparatus of the Soviet Jews—including their native theater, newspapers, publishing houses and writers' association—during the postwar wave of officially-inspired anti-Semitism; despite regime claims that no discrimination is practiced, nothing has ever been done to rectify this situation.

All of the minority religions have, of course, been the object of repressive measures. The fact that these moves have, from a doctrinal point of view, been part of the Communist campaign against religious belief per se (including the Russian Orthodox faith) has made little difference to peoples whose religion and nationality are closely identified. For them, the attack on religion has been simply another example of the effort of an alien regime to encroach on indigenous cultural patterns and to shackle national development.

In short, the Soviet attitude toward "national forms" in the cultural sphere has been one of tolerance when—but only when—tolerance has not interfered with the ideological or practical needs of the regime.

System and Sacrifice

Outside of the specific areas of cultural expression mentioned above, few of the traditional ways of the minorities have been allowed to survive. In the political, economic, and generally the social spheres, the uniform institutions of Soviet society prevail in the form of the supreme ruling party, the bureaucratic administrative apparatus, the planned and centrally controlled industrial economy, the collectivized peasant agriculture, and the ubiquitous instruments of ideological indoctrination and control. Thus Soviet nationality policy has allowed no recognition of the fact that economic, political and social forms of organization may be distinctive and indeed crucial elements in a particular national culture.

The imposition of the Soviet system involved a social and cultural revolution throughout Soviet-held territory. Among the more settled European or Europeanized populations, whose culture was already somewhat geared to the patterns of industrial society, the process of Sovietization was highly disruptive, but no more so than for the majority of the Great Russians—and perhaps even less so in the case, say, of Armenian traders than of the Russian peasants. But among the peoples of the more isolated, underdeveloped areas—mainly in Asia—the depredations caused by Sovietization and the enforced departure from traditional ways were of enormous magnitude.

An outstanding example is the case of the Kazakh people. Before collectivization the Kazakhs were either nomads, who relied extensively on the use of horses on the great Central Asian steppe, or recently-settled cattle and sheep herders. Their whole way of life was regulated by and within the tribal structure, especially the clan system. The attempt blindly to impose the pattern of collectivization on these people in the early 1930s met with intensive resistance, leading to an open struggle with the regime. The loss of life was staggering. While some of the Kazakhs escaped with their herds over the border into Chinese Sinkiang, the huge decimation of the population during this period was mainly due to deaths in the fighting or through starvation. Census figures for 1926 and 1939 show that in the interim the Kazakh population dropped from 3.967 to 3.098 million, an absolute decline of 869,000, or 22 percent. . . . Moreover, in the course of the bitter struggle the greater part of the livestock on which the local economy had rested was lost, through retaliative slaughter on the part of desperate natives, neglect of the herds while the men were off fighting, or in minor part, through migration. Taking the stocks in 1928 as a base, by 1934 only 25 to 50 percent of the cattle, 13 percent of the sheep, and 12 percent of the horses remained.

Although the stark statistics above are from official sources, the Soviet regime has never put forward any explanation of this chapter of its history. Unfortunately the statistics are little known to the world, and are seldom weighed in the balance when glib estimates are made in praise of "enlightened" Soviet nationality policy. Yet this case represents a relentless fulfillment of Stalin's instruction to the Communist Party in 1923, when he urged that Turkestan—which included Kazakhstan—be transformed into a model republic because of its revolutionary significance for Soviet Russia's eastern policy. He declared: "We have to fulfill this task whatever the price, without sparing efforts and without shrinking from sacrifices. . . ." Stalin, certainly, could never be accused of having shrunk from sacrifices in Kazakhstan.

Equal Opportunity

Turning to the third question under consideration, to what extent is Soviet nationality policy nondiscriminatory—that is, to what extent does it offer members of the minority nationalities equal access to such benefits as the society provides for average citizens? Are opportunities for education, work, pay, social mobility, freedom of movement, and choice of residence the same for all or does the dominant group enjoy a favored status?

On the whole the record of the Soviet Union in these respects is good. The data which support this evaluation are based on republics as a whole, not on pure ethnic or national groups, so that the presence of large Russian and Ukrainian minorities in some of the national republics—and conversely of non-Russian minorities in the RSFSR—may distort the picture of Soviet accomplishment to some degree. Still, on the basis of a large number of indices, it seems clear that members of all nationalities (including the Great Russian) have received broadly equal treatment with respect to personal, economic, and social—if not political—opportunities. Allowance must be made, of course, for the fact that many of the minorities live in predominantly rural or backward regions whose development has expectably lagged behind that of more urban or industrial areas; however, the *relative* position of these groups has improved greatly since the prerevolutionary era.

Important among the indices considered here is the striking spread of literacy among all groups of the Soviet population. In the intercensus period from 1926 to 1939 the overall literacy rate in the Soviet Union rose from 51 to 81 percent. In certain national republics the low base at start made the rise much more dramatic. For example, in the Central Asian Tadzhik republic the rate of literacy increased from 4 to 72 percent, and in the Azerbaijan republic from 25 to 73 percent. The preliminary release on the 1959 census does not provide data on literacy by nationality, but since the All-Union rate is now reported to be 98.5 percent, it must be assumed that the nationality areas have continued to advance in this respect. While the Soviet definition of literacy is based on a very rudimentary level of learning, and while some area improvement can be attributed to the influx of Russian and other literates, the record of accomplishment is nevertheless substantial.

Data on improvements in education are closely related. In the area of the five Central Asian Republics (including Kazakhstan) there were in 1914–15 only 136,000 pupils in elementary and secondary schools, representing [an insignificant percentage of the number of pupils] in all Russia. By 1955–56 the parallel enrollment was 3.59 million, an increase by more than 25-fold; this figure constituted about 13 percent of the total student enrollment in the same grades, which is about the weight of the population of the Central Asiatic republics in the Soviet population as a whole. Similar progress has been made in higher education: whereas before the Revolution there were virtually no higher school establishments in these areas, by 1955 local institutions had an enrollment of 155,000 students, or about 9 percent of the total higher school population in the USSR.

There are many other ways in which the Soviet regime has accorded equal treatment to the minorities. Available data show that facilities such as libraries, medical clinics, movie and dramatic theaters, sports stadia, clubs, newspapers and journals, radio and television stations, etc., have been provided in the nationality area at close to the same per capita rate as in the Great Russian area.

The sum indication of such statistical evidence is that minority members (again, with the striking exception of Soviet Jews) do not suffer from any discrimination insofar as educational training, economic opportunity, and social benefits are concerned. This impression is supported by the testimony of Soviet refugees. . . .

Unequal Inopportunity

There was, however, one distinctive complaint voiced by those in the minority nationalities, and this on an issue of profound importance. The reader may have noted that all of the above examples of nondiscrimination have been confined to the economic and social spheres. In the political realm—in the structure of rule—a very different picture emerges. The crucial protest voiced in common by refugees from the minorities was that their people did not share equally in the direction of society and were not free to shape their culture along lines in keeping with native or indigenous traditions. Many saw themselves as still essentially vassals of a foreign power, as ruled by the alien Russian. The basis of these feelings is not just a matter of the sharp restrictions which, as we have seen, the regime places on the development of local nationalism. Just as important is the fact that the institutions of governance, both at the center and within the republics, have not included a proportionate representation of the minorities. The Communist Party has been predominantly a Russian party, with only a weak representation of the nationalities, while in the republics themselves the influence and indeed control of Russians and other outsiders sent in from Moscow have been painfully evident. . . .

The weakness of national representation has been evident not only at the top of the power hierarchy, but in the rank-and-file of the party. In proportion to population, the Communist Party is strongest in the predominantly Great Russian areas, weakest in the nationality regions. In Moscow and Leningrad, for example, the ratio of local to total party membership is more than twice that of local to total population; in republics like Tadjikistan the reverse applies. In fact, however, the disproportion is much greater, since within the nationality areas, the party is not only small but includes a substantial number of non-natives, preponderantly Russians. . . .

The fact that the party chief in the national areas has often been someone sent in from the outside has been perhaps the most important affront to national pride and symbol of the alien nature of the party. The best example in this respect is the Ukraine, where the First Secretary of the Communist Party has almost always been a non-Ukrainian, even though sometimes vaguely connected with the Ukrainian area or nationality. Kaganovich, who held the post in 1925–28, was a Russified Jew born in Belorussia. Kossior, who followed, was a Pole. The rest were Russians, and many never even learned to speak Ukrainian with fluency, despite the fact that it was the national tongue of some 40 million subjects. The only exception in the line was Khrushchev's chosen successor in the post—his Ukrainian assistant Kirichenko (who later rose to the Presidium but is now in disgrace).

Economic Development Policy

To pose the fourth and last question: has there been any economic exploitation of minority regions, by depletion of the land or other natural resources, by the carrying off of wealth produced in the area without sufficient compensation, or by the development of the region's economy in so special or limited a way as to subordinate it unduly to the productive needs and interests of the dominant majority?

In the Soviet case the answer to these questions is clear-cut: the regime's economic policy as a whole does not discriminate against the minority areas and their economic development in favor of the Great Russians. Soviet industrialization was, of course, based on forced savings, which the government extracted for investment at the cost of popular consumption. But the minorities were not asked to bear a disproportionate share of the resulting hardships of a depressed living standard. The burden fell on all; in fact, it might be argued that the Great Russian majority initially made the greater sacrifice in order to permit the development of the capital-hungry, economically backward areas.

One economist has estimated, for example, that while the all-Union living standard fell markedly during the 1930s, in the four republics of Central Asia (not counting Kazakhstan), it may actually have improved to a slight degree. At the time the local economy was undergoing rapid change, as indicated by the fact that industrial output, which had been negligible, multiplied between six and nine times over between 1928 and 1937. Such an increase could only have been accomplished by the substantial investment of capital drawn from other parts of the country and by the application of new technology. Such help was even more important to the agriculture of the region.

In the initial stage of European colonial development, substantial capital was invested in the colonies, but often only in order to create a one-crop economy that in the long run was economically disadvantageous to the local people. There was an element of this approach in the Soviet regime's insistence on the expansion of cotton acreage in Central Asia, usually at the expense of existing wheat crops. But the area was not treated simply as a vast cotton plantation for the rest of the Soviet Union. On the contrary, existing resources of other kinds were widely developed. A hydroelectric power industry was developed, the output of which increased 8.5 times over in the period 1928–37. Earlier virtually all cotton had been shipped to Russia to be made into textiles, which in turn had to be shipped back, but in the 1930s a substantial textile industry was established in Tashkent. Leather shoemaking was established to utilize the hides from the region's extensive herds. These efforts make it evident that capital was retained in the area and not syphoned off for accumulation at the center. The data already cited on the growth of education and other cultural and social facilities similarly indicate that a goodly share of the returns accrued from exploitation of the region's natural wealth was reinvested in raising standards in the region.

Although the central Asian case may be one of the more outstanding examples, it reflects the general pattern of Soviet policy in the economic development of backward areas. The allocation of investment during the process of economic expansion has not in any significant degree been guided by considerations of nationality, but rather by those of economic efficiency or the defense needs of the country. And the benefits—as well as the burdens—which have resulted from economic development have been more or less equally shared by all peoples of the Soviet Union.

A Summary View

The main features of Soviet nationality policy sketched above have been consistently manifested since at least the early 1930s. Although the program as a whole is often identified as "Stalinist" nationality policy, only minor modifications have taken place in the post-Stalin era. In line with the general relaxation of terror in the USSR, the most repressive policies vis-à-vis certain nationalities have been abandoned and some of the iniquities of Stalin's reign (e.g., the dispersion of the Chechen-Ingush, Kalmyks, and so on) have been rectified. . . .

In all other respects, however, the present leadership has followed the pattern of the past. On the credit side of the record, this has generally meant equality of social and economic opportunity for the individual of minority status. On the whole it has also meant equal treatment of national groups with regard to the exploitation of resources and economic development on the one hand, and to the elaboration of certain cultural institutions on the other.

Against these features other factors must be weighed. First, if equality of treatment has been the general rule in the above respects, the exceptions and departures have been numerous enough and in some cases so glaring as to demonstrate that the application of nationality policy remains a matter of arbitrary and expedient decision on the part of the regime. More important, however, are the moral and political issues which underly the question of minority rights. The basic fact—and no amount of achievement can obscure it—is that Soviet nationality policy has constituted a forceful imposition of social, political and economic forms by a powerful center upon a host of colonial subjects. If these people had little part in choosing their path of national development, they have as little freedom today to alter it.

National Relations in the Communist Stage

New Program of the Communist Party

*[**Editor's note:** The New Program of the Communist Party of the Soviet Union was adopted by the 22nd Congress on October 31, 1961. This is only the third program in the history of the Party; the others were adopted in 1903 (before it came to power) and in 1919. By its terms, it is designed "for the building of a communist society." The included excerpt reproduces the section of the program specifically concerned with "The Tasks of the Party in the Sphere of National Relations."]*

Under socialism nations flourish and their sovereignty is strengthened. The development of nations proceeds not along lines of strengthening national discord, national narrow-mindedness and egoism, as it does under capitalism, but along lines of their association, fraternal mutual assistance and friendship. The appearance of new industrial centers, the discovery and exploitation of natural resources, the plowing up of virgin lands and the development of all types of transport increase the mobility of the population and promote greater contact among the peoples of the Soviet Union. People of many nationalities live together and work in harmony in the Soviet republics. The boundaries between the Union republics within the USSR are increasingly losing their former significance, since all the nations are equal, their life is organized on a single socialist foundation, the material and spiritual needs of each people are satisfied to the same extent, and they are all united into one family by common vital interests and are advancing together to a single goal—communism. Common spiritual features deriving from the new type of social relations and embodying the finest traditions of the peoples of the USSR have taken shape in Soviet people of different nationalities.

Full-scale communist construction signifies a new stage in the development of national relations in the USSR in which the nations will draw still closer together and their complete unity will be achieved. The building of the material and technical base of communism is leading to still closer association of the Soviet peoples. The exchange of material and cultural wealth among nations is becoming more and more intensive, and the contribution of each republic to the common cause of communist construction is increasing. Obliteration of distinctions between classes and the development of communist social relations is intensifying the social homogeneity of nations and contributing to the development of common communist traits in their culture, ethics and way of living, to a further strengthening of mutual trust and friendship among them.

Reproduced, with permission, from The Current Digest of the Soviet Press, *vol. XIII (December 13, 1961), pp. 14–15. The new Communist Party Program appears in its entirety in* Current Soviet Policies—IV, *published by Columbia University Press from the translations of the* Current Digest.

With the victory of communism in the USSR, the nations will draw still closer together, their economic and ideological unity will increase and the communist traits common to their spiritual make-up will develop. However, the effacement of national distinctions, especially of language distinctions, is a considerably longer process than the effacement of class distinctions.

The Party approaches all questions of national relationships arising in the course of communist construction from the positions of proletarian internationalism and on the basis of unswerving application of the Leninist national policy. The Party permits neither the ignoring nor the overemphasis of national characteristics.

The Party sets the following tasks in the sphere of national relations:

(a) to continue the all-round economic and cultural development of all the Soviet nations and nationalities, ensuring their increasingly close fraternal cooperation, mutual aid, solidarity and closeness in all spheres of life and achieving the utmost strengthening of the Union of Soviet Socialist Republics; to make full use of and improve the forms of the national state system of the peoples of the USSR.

(b) in the economic sphere, to continue to pursue the line of comprehensive development of the economy of the Soviet republics; to ensure a rational geographical distribution of production and planned development of natural resources and to perfect the socialist division of labor among the republics, unifying and coordinating their labor efforts and properly combining the interests of the state as a whole and those of each Soviet republic. Since the expansion of the rights of the Union republics in economic management has yielded substantial favorable results, such measures may also be carried out in the future, with due regard to the fact that the creation of the material and technical base of communism will call for still greater interrelationship and mutual assistance among the Soviet republics. The closer the contact between nations and the greater the understanding of the countrywide tasks, the more successfully can manifestations of localism and national egoism be overcome.

For the successful accomplishment of the tasks of communist construction and the coordination of economic activities, interrepublic economic agencies (especially for such matters as irrigation, power grids, transport, etc.) may be set up in particular zones.

The Party will continue to follow a policy of ensuring the actual equality of all nations and nationalities with full consideration for their interests, devoting special attention to those areas of the country that are in need of more rapid development. Benefits growing in the process of communist construction must be fairly distributed among all nations and nationalities.

(c) to work for the further all-round flowering of the socialist culture of the peoples of the USSR. The vast scope of communist construction and the new victories of communist ideology are enriching the cultures of all the peoples of the USSR, cultures socialist in content and national in form. The ideological unit of the nations and nationalities is growing, and there is a rapprochement of their cultures. The historical experience of the development of socialist nations shows that national forms do not harden; they change, improve and draw closer together, shedding all obsolete features that conflict with the new living conditions. An international culture common to all the Soviet nations is developing. The cultural treasures of each nation are increasingly augmented by works of an international character.

Attaching decisive importance to the development of the socialist content of the cultures of the peoples of the USSR, the Party will promote their future mutual enrichment and rapprochement, the strengthening of their internationalist basis and thereby the formation of a future single worldwide culture of communist society.

While supporting the progressive traditions of each people and making them the possession of all Soviet people, the Party will in all ways develop new revolutionary traditions of the builders of communism, traditions common to all nations.

(d) to continue ensuring the free development of the languages of the people of the USSR and the complete freedom of each citizen of the USSR to speak and to rear and educate his children in any language, ruling out all privileges, restrictions or compulsions in the use of this or that language. In the conditions of the fraternal friendship and mutual trust of peoples, national languages are developing on a basis of equality and mutual enrichment.

The existing process of voluntary study of Russian in addition to the indigenous language has favorable significance, since it facilitates mutual exchange of experience and the access of each nation and nationality to the cultural achievements of the other peoples of the USSR and to world culture. The Russian language has, in effect, become the common medium of intercourse and cooperation among all the peoples of the USSR.

(e) to continue consistently applying the principles of internationalism in the field of national relations; to strengthen the friendship of peoples as one of the most important gains of socialism; to conduct an uncompromising struggle against manifestations and survivals of any kinds of nationalism and chauvinism, against trends of national narrow-mindedness and exclusiveness, idealization of the past and the veiling of social contradictions in the history of peoples, and against customs and ways that impede communist construction. The growing scale of communist construction calls for the continuous exchange of cadres among the nations. Any manifestations of national insularity in the rearing and employment of workers of different nationalities in the Soviet republics are impermissible. The elimination of manifestations of nationalism is in the interests of all nations and nationalities of the USSR. Each Soviet republic can continue to flourish and grow stronger only in the great family of fraternal socialist nations of the USSR.

The 1970 Census: Fusion or Crystallization of Nationalities?

Rein Taagepera

*[**Editor's note**: A new census was taken in 1979, but at this printing only incomplete results have been published. These show that between the 1970 and 1979 censuses, the Soviet Union's population grew by 20.7 million, reaching a total of 262.4 million persons; seven of the fifteen republics had a low rate of population growth, namely, Russia, the Ukraine, and Belorussia at 6 percent, Georgia and Latvia at 7 percent, Estonia at 8 percent, and Lithuania at 9 percent; two republics were in an intermediate growth position with Moldavia's increase of 11 percent and Kazakhstan's 13 percent; six republics showed*

This article is reprinted, with permission, from Soviet Studies, *vol. XXIII (October 1971), pp. 216–21.*

large increases in population, Azerbaidzhan 18 percent, Kirgizia 20 percent, Armenia 22 percent, Turkmenia 28 percent, Uzbekistan 30 percent, and Tadzhikiston 31 percent. In 1970, 11.3 percent of the country's population lived in the six republics with the most rapid rates of growth, but by 1979—accounting for 34.4 percent of the total population increase—their share rose to 13.2 percent.]

Are the various Soviet nationalities slowly fusing together or are they on the contrary crystallizing into ever more distinct nations? Or are some nationalities fusing while others are not? The purpose of this note is to comment on this much-discussed problem in the light of the recent census results.[1] Combined with the 1959 census, these results offer us for the first time since 1939 extensive data on the evolution of Soviet nationalities during a time interval which contains no catastrophic events.

In Soviet practice nationalities are defined primarily on the basis of language, and under East European conditions such a definition is reasonable. [See Table 1.] Accordingly, we will define fusion of nationalities as a general adoption of a common *lingua franca* for everyday use at work, in education and eventually in private life. Under Soviet conditions, the *lingua franca* would be the Russian which at times has been advertised in the Soviet press as the "second native tongue" of every Soviet citizen.[2] The contrary process of crystallization of separate nationalities will be defined as restricting the use of the *lingua franca* in the non-Russian areas to outside communication by a small élite, while developing a local work and education milieu overwhelmingly in the local language.

According to this linguistic criterion of fusion of nationalities, the following indicators are of interest. The *percentage of Russians* in the total population represents the fraction of the people who are fully committed to the *lingua franca* (except for a negligible 0.2 percent of Russians who consider a non-Russian language as their native tongue). Any increase in their percentage would be an unambiguous gain for fusion forces. The *percentage of linguistically assimilated non-Russians* represents the fraction of the people who are aware of their non-Russian origin and report a non-Russian nationality as their own at the census, in conjunction with reporting Russian as their effective everyday and intimate language ("native tongue"). The fusion of nationalities could be considered complete if and when all non-Russians reach that stage. The assimilated non-Russians may eventually start giving Russian not only as their language but also as their nationality. Finally, the *percentage of nonassimilated non-Russians who are fluent in Russian* is of interest. If this percentage is unusually high for a given nationality, it may indicate that the whole nationality is ready for assimilation. On the other hand, an extremely low percentage of people fluent in Russian should not be taken as a sign of national crystallization but rather as a sign of underdevelopment. Fusion and crystallization of nationalities both imply a high level of development, and under Soviet conditions a well-crystallized nation would require a fair number of people fluent in the *lingua franca*.

From 1959 to 1970 the Russians dropped from 54.6 percent to 53.4 percent of the total Soviet population, because of their decreasing birth rate. This development has been widely reported in the Western press. Yet this 1.2 percentage point decrease is of significance only if it is not compensated by an increased linguistic assimilation of non-Russians. In fact, there has been some such compensation. The percentage of those who declared Russian as their native tongue dropped only by 0.8 percentage points, from 59.5 percent in 1959 to 58.7 percent in 1970. The number of assimilated non-Russians grew from 10.0 to 12.8 million.[3] While the number of Russians grew by 13 percent and that of nonassimilated non-Russians by 18 percent, the number of assimilated non-Russians grew by 28 percent. The fusion was clearly in evidence during the 1960s. However, the fusion rate

TABLE 1 Size, Increase, and Fluency in Russian of Soviet Nationalities

Nationalities (in order of decreasing size)*	Linguistically Nonassimilated Population (millions)†		Population Increase 1959–70 %	% Fluent in Russian‡ 1970
	1970	1959		
Russians	129	114	13	99.9
Ukrainians	34.9	32.7	7	42.4
Uzbeks	9.1	5.9	54	14.7
Belorussians	7.3	6.7	9	60.8
Tatars	5.28	4.58	15	70.0
Kazakhs	5.20	3.66	42	42.6
Azerbaijani	4.30	2.87	50	16.9
Armenians	3.26	2.50	30	33.0
Georgians	3.19	2.64	21	21.7
Lithuanians	2.61	2.28	15	36.7
Moldavians	2.56	2.10	21	38.0
Tadzhiks	2.10	1.37	53	15.6
Turkmens	1.51	.99	53	15.6
Chuvashes	1.47	1.33	10	67.2
Kirgiz	1.44	.96	50	19.4
Latvians	1.36	1.33	2	47.5
Dagestani	1.32	.91	45	43.3
Germans	1.23	1.21	2	89.3
Mordvinians	.98	1.00	−2	84.5
Estonians	.96	.94	2	30.4
Bashkirs	.82	.61	34	80.5
Chechens	.60	.41	46	67.6
Udmurts	.58	.56	3	76.6
Maris	.55	.48	15	68.3
Ossetians	.43	.37	16	66.2
Komis	.40	.38	5	77.5
Jews	.38	.49	−22	92.1
Poles	.38	.62	−39	?
Buryats	.29	.24	21	72.0
Yakuts	.28	.23	24	43.3
Kabardinians	.274	.200	37	73.0
Bulgarians	.257	.257	0	80.5
Koreans	.245	.249	−2	73.4
Kara-Kalpaks	.228	.165	38	10.8
Ingushes	.154	.104	48	73.2
Tuvinians	.132	.099	34	39.4
Kalmyks	.126	.096	31	88.5
Karelians	.092	.119	−22	93.9
Balkars	.060	.042	43	73.5

*The list includes all nationalities which had a nonassimilated population of more than 0.2 million in 1970, and all titular nationalities of autonomous republics within the RSFSR.

†Calculated as product of the total number, and of the percentage of those who consider their national tongue as their native tongue, as given in the 1970 census report.

‡Calculated as the quotient of the percentage fluent in Russian and the fraction considering their national tongue as their native tongue. The figure for Poles comes to more than 100 percent (37/.325), suggesting a misprint.

was not sufficiently high to compensate totally for the widening birth-rate gap between the Russians and the non-Russians. The nonassimilated non-Russians have now reached the 100 million mark; 42 percent of them consider themselves fluent in Russian.

As far as union republics are concerned, the relative number of Russians decreased in all Asian republics, and in the RSFSR itself. In the case of Georgia even their absolute number declined. In the European republics the share of Russians increased, and the share of the titular nationalities of these republics declined, with the exception of Lithuanians.

There are wide differences in birth and assimilation rates between the various non-Russian nationalities. Table 1 shows the 1959 and the 1970 numerical strengths of the main Soviet nationalities, based on the criterion of native tongue. These values are hence lower than the ones explicitly shown in the census report. The 6.1 percent of the Soviet population who reported a native tongue different from their nationality are omitted from this table. (About 13 million of them reported a Russian native tongue, leaving almost two million people who are assimilated in a non-Russian direction, mostly presumably by union republic nations.) Table 1 also shows the relative population increase for various nationalities from 1959 to 1970, and the percentage of people of the given nationality and native tongue who are also fluent in Russian.

In Figure 1 population increase is plotted against fluency in Russian. It can be seen that the nationalities which have the highest population increases tend to be the least fluent in Russian. This trend might be expected, since a low knowledge of the Soviet *lingua franca* indicates limited scholarization, which often correlates with a high birth rate. Low or negative population increases for most nationalities which are highly fluent in Russian might also be expected, since high fluency in Russian is likely to lead to heavy assimilation losses. However, Figure 1 also shows an exception group of nationalities which are rapidly increasing in numbers and yet are highly fluent in Russian. These are mostly nations which suffered total deportation under Stalin, and were thus put into forced contact with Russians; the only other nationalities in this group are the Kabardinians (whose Balkar neighbours were deported) and the Bashkirs.[4]

Relative assimilation rates for various nationalities could be determined accurately only if their natural increase rates were known. These rates are not known for most nationalities. Under a number of simplifying assumptions, the known percentage of under-18-year-olds in national republics can be used to estimate the natural increase.[5] These estimates suggest heavy assimilation of all European ASSR nations, and also a considerable assimilation of Kalmyks, Buryats and Yakuts. Owing to high birth rates, the last three nationalities are still rapidly increasing in number, in spite of assimilation losses. It would seem from Figure 1 that a fluency in Russian ranging from 20 percent to 50 percent may be compatible with national crystallization, but that a more than 50 percent fluency in Russian is indicative of active fusion (except in the special case of forced-contact nationalities).

Union republic nations tend to be less fluent in Russian than the ASSR and diaspora nations which show the same population increase. With the exception of Belorussia, the fluency in Russian seems to be too limited to supply a basis for rapid linguistic assimilation. The average curve for union republic nations in Figure 1 may represent the path from underdevelopment to national crystallization, with widespread but not universal fluency in *lingua franca*. The average curve for the ASSR and diaspora nations, on the other hand, may represent the path from underdevelopment to eventual fusion.

In conclusion, the 1970 census results suggest that the Soviet leaders have been quite successful in establishing Russian as a *lingua franca,* except in Central Asia. But a clear-cut

FIGURE 1 Population Increase Plotted against Fluency in Russian

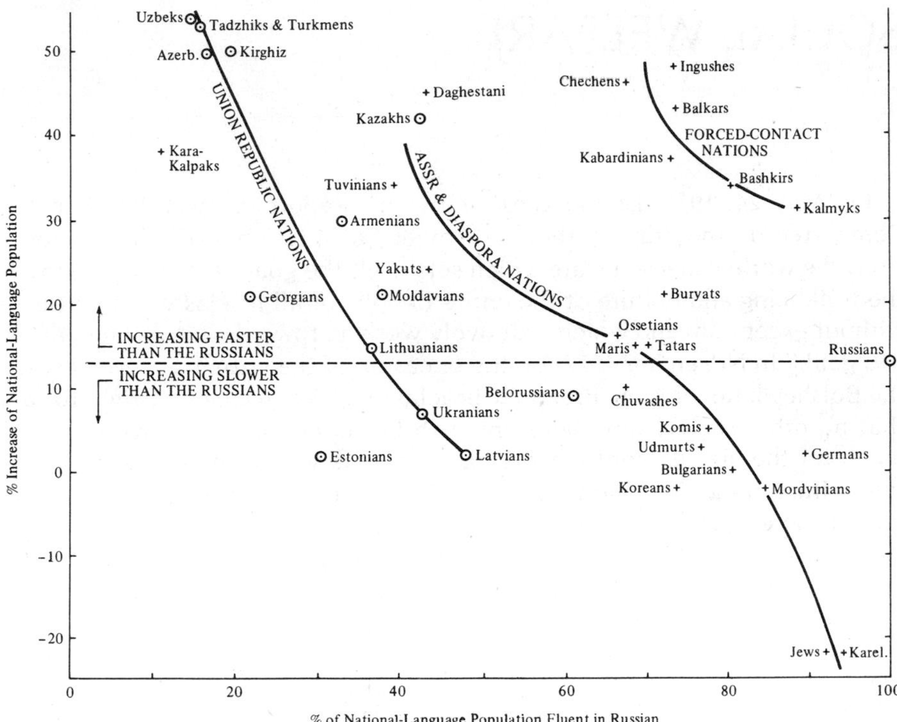

retreat of national languages on the local and private life level has taken place only in the European autonomous republics, and in the case of the diaspora nations. In all other regions, the fusion process has been slow at best, and a quiet crystallization of national languages is a definite possibility.

Notes

1. *Census data on national composition were first published in* Izvestiya, *16 April 1971. For this analysis the Estonian version in* Rahva Hääl, *17 April 1971, was used.*
2. *For example, T.A. Sarymsakov, "Know your second native tongue,"* Vestnik vysshei shkoly, *1964, no. 3.; S. Chekoeva, "Two native tongues,"* Uchitel'skaya gazeta, *12 March 1964.*
3. *To be exact, these figures represent the difference between the assimilated non-Russians and the 0.2 million counter-assimilated Russians. Close to 60 percent of the assimilated population were Ukrainians and Belorussians.*
4. *Tatars include Volga Tatars and the deported Crimean Tatars. Linguistic assimilation is not known for these groups separately. The total increase in number since 1959 (including the lingvistically denationalized Tatars) is 17 percent in the RSFSR and 33 percent in Central Asia and Kazakhstan.*
5. *For a list of percentages of under-18-year-olds in union and autonomous republics, see R. Taagepera, "National Differences within Soviet Demographic Trends,"* Soviet Studies, *vol. XX, no. 4 (April 1969), pp. 478–89. This percentage would correlate with nationality increase rates, if the titular nationalities predominate in their own republic, if birth rates have not changed markedly over the last decades, and if life expectancies do not deviate markedly from the Soviet average.*

Chapter 18

SOCIAL WELFARE

On May 24, 1977, Leonid Brezhnev in his Report to the CPSU Central Committee on the draft of the new Soviet Constitution said: "In its provisions the world will see a state which sets itself the goal of steady growth of the well-being and culture of the entire people, of all its classes and groups without exception, and which is actively working towards the attainment of this goal." In November 1977, on the occasion of the sixtieth anniversary of the Bolshevik Revolution, Brezhnev proclaimed, "We have every right to say that no other society anywhere on earth has done or could have done so much for the masses, for the working people, as socialism has done!" How the welfare interests of the Soviet people have in fact been served is the subject of the ensuing discussion.

Successes and Weaknesses

Bernice Q. Madison

At the close of the tsarist era, Russia was undoubtedly behind the other industrializing countries of Europe in all aspects of social welfare. At the beginning of the twentieth century none of these countries could be said to have done much toward alleviating the misery and suffering of its people, or preventing individual and family disorganization, but Russia was behind all of them—quantitatively, qualitatively, and philosophically. Her welfare efforts, in spite of their considerable size in absolute terms, had little impact on massive social problems deeply rooted in tradition, such as alcoholism, corruption, poverty, prostitution, vicious child labor practices, and illegitimacy. These massive problems were passed on to the Soviet regime. . . .

What can be considered the *major advances* in social welfare made during fifty years of Soviet power?

Indisputably, one major advance has been a steady broadening of the category of those with a legal right to comprehensive income assistance, and thus freedom from degrading means tests and humiliating charity. The movement toward the guarantee of a decent minimum income has been furthered by the all-inclusive nature of the coverage offered by social insurance, the rising level of insurance benefits, and the reduction in the number of people in the rural population with inadequate protection. If a citizen is a worker or employee or a dependent of a worker or employee, his assistance will come from the state social insurance system and will be paid for jointly by his employing establishment and the state; if he is a member of a collective farm or a dependent of such a member, his assistance will come from the collective farm system of social insurance and will be paid for jointly by the farm and the state; if he falls outside both of these groups and is in need, his assistance will be a flat grant financed from local revenues or placement in an institution in which he will receive complete support at state expense. These provisions protect him against most of the contingencies in industrial societies that interrupt, diminish, or cut off income.

Especially generous, from the point of view of eligibility and benefit rates, are provisions for expectant mothers. The privileged position of mothers and children in Soviet society is further strengthened by children's allowances, available for both urban and rural children. These allowances are granted because a decent income for families of all sizes cannot be guaranteed by a wage system based on the product of a man's labor and not on the size of his family. Flat assistance grants and institutional care—the catchall provisions underpinning social insurance—represent a recognition by the regime that an undeviating adherence to the "according-to-his-work" principle for income security purposes results in dire poverty for some to which they ought not to be abandoned. In all welfare arrangements (with the exception of institutional care), assistance is given in the form of money, so that beneficiaries retain the power to regulate their own affairs and are not set apart from the rest of the population by being deprived of the ability to make monetary transactions.

In sum, the Soviets have firmly established the general principle of public responsibility for income maintenance; they have discarded the old, inadequate poor laws and replaced them with a modern scheme of social security—a scheme based on the assumption that the role of social welfare institutions is to ensure individual fulfillment, rather than to treat the abnormal or pathological conditions found in modern society. During this transformation they have adhered to the fundamental idea that economic security can best be provided for the vast majority—the employable—by guaranteeing full employment through economic planning. On the other hand, they have recognized that eliminating the fear of income loss so that it is no longer a factor in promoting job stability and good workmanship creates the problem of maintaining incentive. Unwilling to rely on coercive measures, especially in the past decade, Soviet authorities have endeavored to use the provision of economic rewards to motivate workers to act voluntarily in the manner desired by the state, that is, to maintain and increase incentives that contribute to an upward productivity curve. Although this approach results in some injustices, care has been taken to produce an equitable situation for the majority, and the system now operates with no serious clash between the needs of the regime and the needs of the individual.

Another major advance is the creation of new social services, steadily extended to wider segments of the population and differentiated in accordance with individual needs. These services help people take greater advantage of what the society has to offer, and provide an institutionalized method for facilitating social adjustment and for intervening in cases of social dysfunction. They have been made more accessible by reducing costs to economically weak groups and by setting up facilities close to where people live. Consistent with their drive to lift the masses out of poverty, the Soviets have insisted that the main function of these services, as well as of the entire welfare system, is to make and keep people productive. Methods for achieving this objective have been formulated: they are addressed primarily to the rational elements in individual and social behavior, and utilize group relationships and work therapy as the major tools in treatment.

Services have been created for young and old, for the physically disabled and handicapped and the emotionally disturbed, for those whose maladjustments threaten society openly, and for those whose problems have more subtle injurious effects. On many occasions treatment methods are weakened by an excessive reliance on work and group pressures; on the whole, however, considerable success has been achieved by programs involving the aged, disabled, handicapped, delinquent, alcoholic, mentally retarded, and mentally ill. An impressive number of them are benefiting economically, physically, emotionally, and socially by being taught skills and placed in part-time and full-time jobs. Since 1930 it has been obligatory for employing establishments to hire them when directed to do so by welfare and educational authorities, and for the most part jobs for them have been plentiful. The desire to make these services more effective has led to a recognition of the need to individualize treatment programs, to strive for deeper therapeutic effects, and to develop capacities to handle interpersonal relations more successfully.

In social welfare administration, a number of important gains have been made. While state control of public welfare agencies and all allied voluntary groups exemplifies the totalitarian character of Soviet society, it has a positive side: the conviction that welfare services are too important to the general well-being to be left to the sporadic and uncertain activities of voluntary groups. All major social welfare functions have become part of the on-going responsibilities of state organs, are included in planning budgets, and are allotted resources on a regular basis. Social welfare agencies have come to occupy a permanent place within the structure of government. This has resulted from (and has contributed to) a clarification of functions. Administrative decentralization—a pronounced feature of the Soviet welfare scene—permits some control at the local level, but the Party remains the final determiner of policy. . . .

Planning in welfare has meant a more rational use of resources, avoidance of duplication of efforts, a steadier progress toward defined objectives, and less costly administration. It is widely supported by both welfare personnel and the citizenry. . . . Social welfare has become an integral part of the Soviets' scientifically oriented culture, in striking contrast to its place in the tradition-weighted, eternal-verities-oriented and superstition-laden era of the tsars.

Tied to the scientific approach is an emphasis on prevention. The effort to achieve an acceptable economic level and essential social services for all is in itself a preventive program of major proportions. There are also important efforts to create a more informed and more genuinely involved community. A more direct type of prevention is the concern shown for the well-being of mothers and children, a concern that starts from the time the child is conceived and continues until he reaches maturity; it takes in all aspects of his life, and its objective is to give him the opportunity to reach his full potential. The Soviet regime's willingness to devote extensive resources to the care, education, and upbringing of "defective" children (youngsters who at best can never be as productive as the nondefective) is an especially vivid proof of a desire to give all of the country's children a good start. The Soviets' accomplishments in raising women from their submerged state in tsarist times—economic, social, cultural, and legal—have been substantial. . . .

The transformations and achievements in social welfare since 1917 represent substantial progress: the metamorphosis of a backward, punitive system to one that compares favorably with those in other advanced countries. That this has been achieved in the relatively short period of fifty years, in the midst of rapid industrialization and of monstrously devastating social upheavals and wars, makes the transformation even more impressive. If continued, it will further enrich the lives of the people, make more genuine the guarantee of material and social aid, and increase the dignity of the individual in Soviet society.

What can be said about the *price that has been paid* for this progress? From the point of view of the masses, the price in human suffering has been enormous. One of the major reasons for this is that throughout the 1917–66 period, and to a lesser degree today, the working population has lived "under conditions characteristic of economically backward countries." Sums allocated for social insurance during the first twelve post-Revolutionary years were meager in the extreme. After the first five-year plan, greater resources became available, but welfare programs were severely limited by being subordinated to economic and production goals. The right to assistance in case of need was largely an empty promise, its irony underscored by the sporadic welfare handouts given only in cases of the most abject poverty, and even then only in trifling amounts. . . .

What are some of the *major weaknesses* of present-day Soviet welfare practice? One weakness is that social services by a responsible agency are not available at all for those confronted with certain kinds of social problems, such as difficulties that arise when childless married couples do not get along or, in the case of unmarried parents, from the lack of legal marital status. Welfare services are not uniformly available throughout the country. The rural population does not begin to receive the benefits and services that the urban population enjoys. Income-maintenance programs do not cover all losses of income, and the benefits they provide are often inadequate. For example, there is no unemployment compensation, because Soviet authorities insist that there is no unemployment as long as job openings in the economy as a whole exceed the number of workers available to fill them, as is the case in Russia today.[1] They refuse to recognize that people who are having a hard time finding employment are not helped by the availability of work in some distant place to which they are unable or unwilling to go.

In addition, as noted above, social insurance benefits are frequently inadequate. Current Soviet pensions are equal to only a fraction of the minimum wage and to an even smaller fraction of the average wage. It is clear that pensioners, on the average, are living below the standard they enjoyed before the loss of income against which they were insured.[2] This is especially true of survivors: the meagerness of their benefits belies the regime's alleged concern for large families, and underscores its use of the social insurance system to motivate people to work. The restrictive features of family allowances—with respect to extent of coverage and duration and amounts of benefits—make them least helpful to the most disadvantaged children.

These weaknesses in Soviet welfare practice indicate that so far Soviet ingenuity, limited by economic, political, and moral considerations, has failed to devise a system flexible enough to assure the meeting of all needs as a matter of right. Nor have the Soviets created a system that offsets through benefits the income inadequacies that existed during productive years. The benefit formula requires that benefits be calculated in relation to former earnings. Hence, people whose earnings were low receive low benefits, a hardship that is only partially relieved by the establishment of minimums below which no benefit is permitted to fall. This method of determining benefits, operative almost without interruption throughout 1917–68, has tended to perpetuate economic differences between population groups, which in turn have contributed to the formation of classes in a supposedly classless society. It is indeed a black mark against "socialist humanism" that to this day the Soviet public assistance program offers only the feeblest ministrations to needy persons excluded from social insurance, and to those whose insurance benefits are too low for them to maintain a decent standard of living. The silence with respect to this aspect of welfare administration, in contrast to the abundance of materials available concerning social insurance, is evidence of the Soviet regime's embarrassment over the fact that it has neither eliminated want nor devised a system for making it vanish when it appears. . . .

The social services provided for children reveal the contradictions in the regime's position concerning the family. On the one hand, it would like to remove an ever-increasing number of children from families to community institutions, because this would free mothers for work, would provide rearing by professionals rather than by parents, and would result in more children being raised as "new Soviet men" rather than as "individualists." On the other hand, it is faced with the fact that full-time institutional care is very expensive, and that "something irreplaceably valuable in the personality and moral development of the child" may be lost if the family's role in childrearing is drastically diminished. Parents, on the whole, want to keep their children with them (while at the same time they are eager for better facilities and services for their children), and many educators are not in agreement with the official ideology. How to give the child an upbringing that is social and collective and at the same time keeps the family intimately involved remains to be determined.

Administrative inefficiencies in Soviet welfare programs are apparent everywhere. Services often originate far away from the area or person they are intended for, adding to the frustrations of the poor and sick. Mistakes are not always rectified by the appeals machinery, especially when this involves the exercise of judgment on the part of incompetent administrators, which increases the possibility of unjust decisions. There are also evidences of rigidity, a tendency to ignore needs that have not been planned for, a failure to recognize genuine differences in individuals, and an adherence to outmoded ways of doing things.

Notes

1. *That fractional unemployment exists is not disputed. Enterprises shut down; staffs are reduced; people quit their jobs to find more suitable or more remunerative work, either on their own or at the request of management. However, the fact that there is no unemployment compensation undoubtedly has acted as an incentive to remain on the job or to actively seek new employment.*
2. *In Russia "no investments by individuals in the equities or debt obligation of industrial and commercial organizations are permitted, and wage and salary levels for rank-and-file workers are generally so low in comparison with living costs as to minimize the possibility of substantial savings of any type—home ownership, individual savings and insurance, and employer- or union-sponsored supplementary pensions. . . . Therefore, a pension that would be at all adequate would have to be quite close to full wages."*

Health Care

Boris Petrovsky

The Soviet state is the first in history to have assumed responsibility for the protection and improvement of the people's health, which is a public asset—"public property," as Lenin put it. A fundamentally new stage in the organization of care of public health set in with the Lenin decree (July 1918) establishing the Health Commissariat of the RSFSR as a unified managing and coordinating agency. The right to health protection is a law of socialist society. The socialist principles of health care are clearly reflected in policy documents of the Communist Party.

Public health is ensured through socioeconomic and medical measures and the integrated activities of government agencies, economic bodies and mass organizations directed towards labor protection—social insurance, social maintenance, modernization of communities, physical training on a mass scale, raising the people's cultural standard, and so on. The maintenance of medical institutions under the Health Ministry of the USSR cost over 9,000 million roubles in 1970.* Besides, substantial amounts are allocated by state and cooperative enterprises and the trade unions.

***Editor's note:** The reported figure for 1977 was 11,900 million roubles.*

At this writing, Boris Petrovsky is Minister of Health in the USSR. The article is reproduced, with permission, from World Marxist Review, *[© Progress Books], February 1971, pp. 52–54. Some statistical data have been updated from official Soviet sources by your editor.*

Medical care in our country is free and within everyone's reach.

The importance of prompt and competent medical aid is obvious, but prevention is more important still. The preventive orientation of our health services is a logical consequence of our view of medicine as both a natural biological and profoundly social science.

The ideas and problems of social hygiene and prevention are not alien to many progressive public leaders and medical workers abroad. But it is only in a socialist state that they can be dealt with adequately, being in complete harmony with the interests of the social system and the state.

Prevention in our country is the basis of work throughout the health services—in combating epidemics and infectious diseases, in maternity protection, in safeguarding the health of industrial workers and the rural population, in combating tuberculosis, nervous and mental disorders, etc.

Prevention and treatment, curative and sanitary measures have been synthesized best of all in specialized medical registration and checking centers. Combined with the district organization of medical care, it is the fundamental working method for both the specialized checking centers and other medical and preventative institutions. Extensive sanitary education of the people contributes to prevention.

A fundamental principle of the Soviet health services is the unity of medical science and care. Our medicine constantly equips physicians with up-to-date methods of prevention, diagnosis and treatment.

The main principles, forms and methods of organizing the health services at the present stage, as well as the rights and duties of citizens and medical workers, are set out in the "Fundamentals of Health Legislation of the USSR and the Union Republics" approved by the Supreme Soviet of the USSR in 1969.

An important index of our achievements is the considerable decline, in a comparatively short period of history, in the incidence of infectious diseases and mortality. Overall mortality in 1968 was one-fourth of the prerevolutionary rate. The drop in child mortality is even more striking; in 1969 the rate was 26 per 1000, whereas in 1913 as many as 269 out of every 1000 infants died before reaching the age of one. Life expectancy in the Soviet Union averages 70 years against 32 in prerevolutionary Russia.

Large-scale training of medical personnel is an indisputable achievement of the Soviet health system. In 1969 physicians and pharmeceutists were trained in 91 institutes, and intermediate medical personnel in 666 secondary medical schools. The Soviet Union has long ranked first in the world for the proportion of doctors. In 1969 it had a total of 642,500 doctors, or 26.6 doctors per 10,000 population.* Characteristically, many of the doctors in the Union republics are members of the respective nationalities.

A unified state sanitary and antiepidemic service is among our important achievements. It has a network of stations and research centers enabling it to maintain effective sanitary control.

We see it as one of our main tasks to extend the facilities of the health services by building modern multibranch and specialized hospitals and other medical institutions, as well as by enlarging those in existence. We attach special importance to the provision of medical transport. Our industry, drawing on progress in physics, chemistry, electronics and cybernetics, manufactures high-standard medical equipment, instruments and medicines.

Computerization and introduction of economico-mathematical methods in health planning and control are a major current challenge. We have already tackled it and will

Editor's note: *The reported figures at the end of 1978 were 923,000 doctors with a planned increase by the end of 1980 to the ratio of 35.7 per 10,000.*

keep up our effort over the coming years. Organizing work on scientific lines and cultivating medical deontology throughout are acquiring paramount importance. Other current problems are to improve the economic basis and planning of public health and to investigate the interconnection between economic and medical measures, for safeguarding and improving people's health benefits the economic condition of Soviet society.

An important long-range task is to extend the medical checkup system to the whole population. It can only be carried out gradually and must be preceded by extensive preparations and the elaboration of a proper methodological approach.

Personnel training will have a decisive effect on progress in the health services. We are steadily improving it. Now that an objective process of differentiation and specialization is going on in medicine, which has become a sophisticated branch of knowledge, we begin primary specialization in key fields at the medical school level.

Our medical science concerns itself especially with the treatment and prevention of cardiovascular diseases, malignant tumors and certain virus and infectious diseases in view of the imperative need for more effective methods of combating them.

A scientific task of the first importance is to carry forward such branches of medicine as immunology, endocrinology, allergology, medical genetics, anaesthesiology, reanimatology, geriatrics, aviation and space medicine and to extend transplant surgery meaningfully and consistently, without undue haste. However, we are not slackening attention to important theoretical aspects of medical science, specifically research into the structure and synthesis of proteins, hormones and vitamins, nor the effort to use new achievements in physics, chemistry and technology for medical purposes.

Social Security

Domna Komarova

Care of people is the main activity of our Communist Party. It is only natural, therefore, that every form of social security should receive serious attention in our country. The outstanding feature of Soviet social security is that it uses public funds only. This accounts for its advantages and determines its forms. In those capitalist countries where social security exists the working people must contribute their own money, as we know. In the United States this contribution amounts to 4.12 percent of the earnings, in France it is 6 percent and in the FRG, 13.5 percent.

Domna Komarova, when this was written, was Minister of Social Security in the RSFSR. The article is reproduced, with permission, from World Marxist Review, *[© Progress Books], February 1971, pp. 54–57. Some statistical data have been updated from official Soviet sources by your editor.*

Social security in the Soviet Union is a component of the state economic development plan. It is enjoyed by all citizens irrespective of sex, nationality, race or religion, whatever the nature of their jobs or the form of remuneration.

Social security and insurance absorb about two-fifths of the public funds total—an impressive amount. As much as 23,300,000 roubles will be spent on them this year.*

How are these funds spent?

To begin with, there is a uniform pensioning system encompassing all categories of workers. On reaching pension age blue- and white-collar workers are granted a pension equalling not less than 50 percent of the full amount of their latest monthly earnings, and in the case of low-paid categories the percentage varies from 80 to 100. Moreover, pensions are growing. Thus, minimum pensions for collective farmers and disabled ex-servicemen were raised as of January 1, 1968. Increases in pensions are also fostered by growing wages. The importance of this form of social maintenance will be seen in the fact that there are 41 million pensioners in the Soviet Union.†

Pension age in our country is among the world's lowest—60 years for men and 55 for women, irrespective of trade or profession. Account is also taken of people's capacity for work, and where they are employed. In the mining, chemical, iron and steel, textile or other industry in which working conditions are arduous or intensive and a hazard to health, men may retire on old-age pension at 55 or 50 and women at 50 or 45.

Monthly wages and salaries in the Soviet economy in 1969 averaged 117 roubles plus an average 41 roubles' worth of social benefits. In 1970 the pay average grew by 4.4 percent over 1969 and social benefits in cash and in free services, by 7.3 percent. ‡

The population gets free medical aid, free education and proficiency training, allowances, pensions, scholarships, paid leave, free or cut-rate accommodation in health and holiday homes. Had it not been for the benefits granted by the state, each family would have to pay almost three times as much rent as now, four to six times more for children in a kindergarten or nursery, and so on. . . .

It is interesting to note for comparison that in thirty-two countries no particular distinction is made in old-age pensioning between men and women: the required age is 65 for both men and women in the USA; 65 and 60, respectively, in Britain; 62 in Switzerland; 67 and 62 in Denmark; 60 in France, etc.

The seniority entitling one to an old-age pension on a universal basis is twenty-five years for men and twenty for women. We generally regard as part of seniority every form of socially useful work irrespective of its nature or length, or the length of intervals. Seniority requirements are much lower in the case of arduous jobs and minimal in the case of handicapped persons. In the event of an industrial accident or occupational disease a pension is granted regardless of length of service.

Geography, too, is taken into consideration. In the Far North it is enough to work for fifteen years, and in regions with a similar status twenty years, to be entitled to a pension. Mothers of large families and certain categories of disabled persons who retire on account of old age are granted an age reduction.

***Editor's note:** *The allocation for 1977 was 37,100 million roubles.*

†**Editor's note:** *The figure for 1979 was 47,000,000.*

‡**Editor's note:** *The monthly wage rose to 163.5 roubles by the end of 1979 (or $253.50 at the official exchange rate) with an additional 25 to 30 percent received in social benefits. The projected average wage for 1980 is 170 roubles.*

Pensioners may work if they wish. Those who work are employed with due regard to their health. This is all the more important, because to feel useful and perform moderately hard work helps restore health. Industrial enterprises have shops employing disabled persons affected with certain cardiovascular, mental, pulmonary and other diseases or disorders. Besides, they are taught new trades free of charge. In the Russian Federation alone there are forty-one vocational and eleven technical boarding schools. All pensioners are entitled to free medical treatment.

Nor do we in the Soviet Union forget those who cannot live in a family and need constant aid. They live in boarding houses providing board, medical care, recreational and other facilities. Social security agencies supply orthopedic footwear, prosthetic appliances and special transport. The manufacture of bioelectrically controlled artificial limbs designed under Professor B. Popov's direction promises to restore many handicapped persons to active service.

Allowances for temporary disability were increased as of January 1, 1968. Factory workers and other employees concerned receive full sick pay after eight years' service. Those with a job record of from five and under eight years are paid 80 percent of their earnings. Uniform sick pay conditions for collective farmers have been introduced throughout the country.

Sick pay is paid regardless of length of service; this applies equally in the case of expectant mothers. It follows that we have nothing like a ''waiting'' period, since allowances are paid even to persons temporarily incapacitated on the very first day of work. Nor is there any limit to the period during which an allowance is paid—other than recovery or until official retirement as an invalid. Seniority only affects the size of the allowance.

The role of public organizations, above all of the trade unions, is being increased in social security. Trade union organizations directly grant and pay temporary sick allowances and exercise control over the spending of pension funds. Their delegates sit as full-fledged members in commissions charged with granting pensions and other forms of social aid.

There is more to do, of course. The Communist Party and Soviet state plan further expansion of social security to cover in full the maintenance of the disabled and those incapacitated by old age.

Pensions Leaving Many Impoverished

Craig R. Whitney

Militsa Andreyevna has lived in a room 6 feet wide and 15 feet long for fifty-five of her eighty years. It is a scene of deprivation: a tiny bed, a single ceiling lamp tied over the rickety wooden table with a piece of string, a disorder of jars and bread and pieces of cheese in the drafty double window.

Her tea is accompanied by a spoonful of plum jelly, a slice of bread and inexpensive children's candy. She cannot afford more, for her old-age pension gives her 45 rubles a month to live on, $67.50 at the arbitrary official rate.

Putting Money Aside for Funeral

"The rent is only 2.50 rubles a month," she said, putting a comb in her wispy gray hair and donning a faded formal dress for three younger visitors. "Somehow I manage to put a little money aside, for my funeral," she added with a smile.

The problems of old age did not go away with the 1917 Revolution. Increasingly, they are being aired in the Soviet press and in the speeches and decisions of Soviet officials, some of whom often express a need to increase pensions.

Workers are constantly being assured that the state-run retirement plan, with its noncontributory pension payments, is the most advanced and generous in the world. Actually, the benefits, which average 50 to 55 percent of a retired worker's last monthly pay, lag far behind those in such capitalist European countries as West Germany, where old-age pensions have increased from year to year to keep up with the cost of living. Moreover, a Soviet pension, once set, is never increased, though retirement age is usually fifty-five for women and sixty for men.

Soviet official statistics say it takes 50 rubles a month, or $75, for a person to keep fed, clothed and housed. Yet the legal minimum is the pension Militsa Andreyevna receives, 45 rubles a month, and millions not entitled to full pensions get even less. The maximum monthly pension is 120 rubles, or $180.

Thirty million retired workers and farmers receive pensions, and 5.5 million continue working part time after they retire, according to the official figures. But not everyone who wants to can work and continue to receive a pension.

There is a retired barber who can, but only because he found a job selling ice cream at 75 cents a bar in a park—not so much because he needs the money but because he was bored. A retired factory worker earned money this fall selling mushrooms she had gathered in forests around Moscow—because, she said, her pension is not enough for her needs.

Craig R. Whitney is a New York Times *correspondent. This article by Craig R. Whitney, "Pensions in Soviet Leaving Many Elderly Impoverished,"* New York Times, *November 19, 1978.*

The complex rules, which allow some pensioners to go on working reduced hours at their jobs after retirement but make it impossible for others—economists, bookkeepers and designers, for example—to do so, may have outlived their usefulness. Recent analyses, including one in the Government daily *Izvestia,* suggest that this cannot continue in the face of a growing labor shortage. The Government was urged to allow pensioners who want to do so to go on working after retirement.

System Was Improved by Khrushchev

Before the basis for the current system was laid in 1956 during the tenure of Nikita S. Khrushchev, pensioners lived in something akin to poverty. Mr. Khrushchev recalled in his memoirs that he considered it unthinkable to reward dedicated labor with miserable pensions. After his own retirement, he related, he was approached on the street by old people grateful for the improvement.

Collective farmers were not even included in the system until 1964. Now they are about a third of the total and their minimums are even lower than those of industrial workers: 28 rubles a month.

Life in retirement under the Soviet system is, for millions, a time of reduced expectations, of doing without and of having to scrimp. For many, the only work available is menial. The elderly sell nearly all the newspapers and magazines distributed at kiosks the length and breadth of the country. They peddle ice cream and cigarettes in the parks of Moscow. They watch over the elevator entrances in most apartment buildings.

"What Is the Sense of That?"

A. Danilov, a retired music-school principal in Sochi, wrote to *Izvestia* last year to lament that he could not collect his pension and keep on working part time as a teacher. "The Social Security Department told me to find a job as an unskilled worker or a watchman," he complained, "but that would mean changing who I am. What is the sense of that?"

People do find other ways to survive.

"My aunt lives alone on 50 rubles a month," a scholar in Moscow said recently. "She never goes to the farmers' market because the prices are too high. She never eats meat. She gets by on tea, milk, cakes, cottage cheese, and her apartment rent is only 15 rubles a month. When she comes on the bus to visit me it costs only 4 kopecks. I offered to help and she told me no thanks. She does not think of herself as being poor. She just lives modestly."

The sectors of private enterprise that include the high-priced farmers' markets allow pensioners to supplement their incomes. The widow of a ship captain whose pension is 27 rubles lives in the country. In a small yard she keeps a couple of chickens for eggs, and she rents out a room, giving her a total of 50 to 60 rubles a month, on which she barely gets by.

Even though such an income is officially reckoned as subsistence level, it is difficult for foreigners used to higher standards to imagine how anyone can live on so little. In recognition of need, the average starting level was raised by 24 percent from 1970 to 1975, according to official figures, and Leonid I. Brezhnev, the Soviet leader, recently said pensions for collective farmers would be raised to city levels, but not until after 1980.

Among the aged, who can hear their Government's denunciations of the welfare and pension systems in the United States, the hidden poverty and quietly suffered deprivation are pervasive. According to the last census, in 1970, there were 36.2 million men and women of retirement age, with 23.7 million receiving old-age pensions. Today 30 million do, but even allowing for other explanations, there are still millions who receive nothing.

Camp Labor Does Not Count

Earlier this year a group of dissidents in Moscow did a study of the system to determine the most common victims of old-age poverty. Among those whose work does not count toward a pension, they found, are prisoners in labor camps—millions under Stalin, who died in 1953; handicraftsmen, who are not officially classified as blue- or white-collar workers; and collective farmers who retired before coverage was extended to them.

The group also found that people who had worked the twenty to twenty-five years required for entitlement to a full pension often got only a small fraction, less than 50 rubles a month. The conclusion was that "a considerable number of disabled Soviet citizens" and "a larger number of old-aged disabled people and children" got "such paltry pensions and allowances that they do not even have the means for subsistence by Soviet standards."

The explanation of how retired people—or the fully employed, for that matter—live on their earnings when these are clearly not enough to sustain life is not found in the official statistics. It can be seen in the petty corruption and subterfuges that exist in every sphere of Soviet life, sometimes out of sheer necessity.

A retired writer, for example, makes 120 rubles a month, the maximum pension, but acknowledges, "Of course we cannot get by on it."

He and his wife get the extra money they need by translating graduate theses and course papers for students who come to Moscow University from non-Russian republics and do not know Russian well. Such activity is illegal; if it was discovered, pensions would be canceled or cut.

But, as the writer said: "Nobody is clean in this country. There is even a curse about it in Soviet Georgia. 'May you be condemned to live on your salary!' The same thing goes for pensioners."

Public Education

Mikhail Prokofyev

Education for All

The level of literacy, the number of schools and pupils are basic indicators of the state of public education in a country and of its general cultural level. In the educational field prerevolutionary Russia was a backward country. The 1897 census showed that among people of over nine years of age only 28.4 percent could read and write.

On the outskirts of the Russian Empire inhabited by non-Russian peoples the situation was even worse. Among the Central Asian peoples—Uzbeks, Tajiks, Kirghiz and Turkmens—no more than 2 or 3 percent of the people were literate.

This immense Empire with a population of nearly 150 million had, according to the 1911 census, only 150 thousand teachers, 60 thousand of whom were instructors in theology, (i.e., priests). The total school enrollment was about eight million.

Long before the October Revolution the working masses demanded radical educational reforms and free compulsory schooling. But these just demands were ignored by the tsarist government.

The children of workers, peasants, artisans, small shopkeepers, etc., were not admitted to the Gymnasiums. "God be praised!" the Tsar exclaimed when he learned that nearly all peasants recruited into the army could not read.

According to estimates by tsarist officials, the magazine *Vestnik Vospitaniya* (Education Gazette) reported in 1866, it would take at least 180 years to wipe out illiteracy among Russia's male population and 300 years, among the women, and thousands of years in the country's outlying areas.

The 1917 October Revolution opened up an era of popular education. In November 1917, a few days after the victory of the Revolution, the Soviet Government defined the principles concerning public education in the country: education should be universal, free and compulsory for children of both sexes; teachers should be provided with the necessary material conditions for carrying out their work, etc.

Despite economic hardships caused by the Civil War and foreign intervention, the young Soviet republic tackled with great energy the question of public education. . . .

In 1930, universal and compulsory four-year schooling was introduced for all children aged eight years and over, and seven-year compulsory schooling for those living in industrial towns and districts and workers' settlements.

Large-scale construction of schools began, many teachers' training courses were opened and textbook publishing was stepped up. From 1930 on, the number of children enrolled in schools grew by 3–3.5 million a year.

In 1932, 7.6 million adults attended literacy classes and 6.5 million went to schools for the semiliterate. Literacy rose from 67 percent in 1930 to 90 percent in 1939. The number of people who could read and write continued to increase until illiteracy was completely eradicated.

Mikhail Prokofyev, at this writing, is USSR Minister of Education. This excerpt is from a pamphlet on "Public Education" published in the Soviet Union in 1971. Some statistical data have been updated from official Soviet sources by your editor.

When the Second World War broke out the Soviet Union held first place in the world in the number of students and schoolchildren. Enrollment in Soviet general schools was 20 percent higher than in Britain, Germany, France and Italy taken together.

The war and the nazi occupation inflicted immense damage on Soviet public education. In occupied areas the nazis burned down, wrecked and plundered 82 thousand schools with a total enrollment of 15 million, and destroyed 334 institutions of higher learning, hundreds of museums, thousands of libraries and cultural clubs.

But throughout the war on the territory not occupied by fascists, schools remained open. The Government continued to devote serious attention to public education and took important measures to carry out universal and compulsory education.

In the 1944–45 academic year, the school age was lowered from eight to seven years, bringing more pupils into the first form. War-ravaged schools were quickly rebuilt and supplied with equipment and teaching aids, and construction of new schools was begun on a large scale.

At the beginning of the 1960–61 academic year nearly 37 million pupils attended general schools. Today the country's 202,000 schools have an enrollment of 49 million pupils. . . .

The question of universal secondary education was considered in the Soviet Union before the Second World War. It was planned to introduce it first in cities and major industrial centres, then throughout the country. But, the war prevented the plans from being carried out.

How is universal secondary education being implemented in the Soviet Union? Today the number of young people who have finished the complete secondary school is steadily increasing. Over 60 percent of the young people who have completed the eight-year, daytime school go on to senior forms. Their numbers will rise in the years to come, and many more schools will have to be built. . . .

Basic Principles

The Soviet educational system is based on the following democratic principles:

State Support for Education. Since all schools and other educational institutions are set up, maintained and guided by the state, a uniform level of training, efficient planning, material security, a single curriculum and continuity are ensured. A state-supported system of education precludes disorganization, dependence on private or public charity, and the use of the school for commercial or other purposes which interfere with its proper functioning.

Equal Opportunities for all Peoples. People of all nationalities of the USSR have equal rights in enrolling in the country's educational establishments, and they may, if they wish, study in their native language, and receive an education on any level, including higher education, in their own republic.

Equality of Sexes. Boys and girls, young men and women study together in all Soviet schools and colleges. School-leavers of both sexes have the same opportunities, and girls are admitted to schools of higher learning on the same basis as boys. Male and female teachers draw the same salaries for the same work, and no difference is made in granting them pensions, seniority allowances, etc.

A Unified School System. In place of different types of schools which served different social groups in old Russia, there is a single, unified school system for all citizens of the USSR. We have no "dead-end" schools which rule out further education. There is complete continuity between all links and stages of the public education system.

Complete Separation of School and Other Educational and Training Institutions from the Church. In the USSR the church is separated from the state, and the school from the church. Education is based on freedom of conscience and a scientific, materialist outlook.

Broad Contacts between School and Society. Every school has a parents' committee elected by the parents themselves at the beginning of each academic year. Educational questions are widely discussed by the Soviet public. The trade unions, the Young Communist League and other public organizations, actively participate in the work of schools and other educational institutions. . . .

Stages of Education

Today the Soviet system of preschool and school education is as follows.

Kindergartens. From the very first the Soviet state made preschool education part of a unified system of education.

In 1914, Russia had only 275 preschool establishments, out of which 150 were kindergartens attended by 4 thousand children. After the October Revolution preschool education became a major concern of the state. In the period from 1918 to 1940 some 24 thousand kindergartens were built attended by over 1,170,000 children. During the Second World War the fascists destroyed and plundered many preschool institutions.

In the postwar period the number of preschool institutions rapidly increased. Damaged buildings were repaired, and new kindergartens, creches and medical institutions were built. In 1968, the country had some 100 thousand year-round state and collective farm preschool institutions attended by 9 million children and staffed by over 506,000 teachers and doctors; in the same year over 2.5 million children went to seasonal nurseries and specially organized kindergartens located in parks. . . .*

Eight-Year School. Incomplete secondary general school gives the pupils the fundamentals of general and polytechnical knowledge, instills in them industriousness and readiness to undertake socially useful activity. Here pupils aged seven to fifteen–sixteen years are also taught a sense of moral responsibility and given esthetic and physical training. Eight-year schooling was first introduced in 1958, and made compulsory in 1963 in place of the seven-year schooling. . . .

On completing the eight-year school, pupils sit for examinations and receive certificates entitling them to take a job or continue studying in a general secondary school, or in evening secondary schools for young workers and farmers, or in various vocational or specialized secondary schools.

***Editor's note:** *Between 1975 and 1978 the attendance in year-round preschool institutions had risen from 11,850,000 to 13,300,000 children.*

Complete Secondary School provides students with the necessary knowledge, habits in learning and skills for beginning higher education.

The curriculum includes literature, history, social science, economic geography, a foreign language, mathematics, physics, chemistry, astronomy, biology, draftsmanship and physical culture.

In the senior forms classes are conducted on a higher scientific level. Greater emphasis is placed on the practical application of knowledge. . . .

After Finishing Secondary School

An important role in educating the young is played by specialized secondary schools (technikums) and vocational schools. . . .

The system of vocational education provides for planned training of young skilled workers for various branches of the national economy. Vocational schools also give those whose speciality has become obsolete an opportunity to change professions. Vocational schools admit annually some 1,300,000 young people who have graduated from the eight-year or secondary school and wish to do production work.*

At urban vocational schools students study from one to three years, while at rural vocational schools—from one to two. The main emphasis is on mastering a chosen specialty. The students spend many hours working in the school workshop or at an enterprise. At the same time they are taught some special and general subjects, this helps them master their speciality. Vocational school graduates can enter a specialized secondary school or complete their education in a general secondary school for adults without leaving their jobs. After that they can enter any institute or university.

All students of vocational schools are supported by the state. In the 1968–69 academic year there were 5,000 vocational schools in the USSR with a total enrollment of 2 million.† Vocational schools train workers in 1,100 trades. Modern production requirements are fully taken into account. . . .

In industry, agriculture, various cultural, educational and medical establishments, a big contribution is made by workers with a secondary specialized education.

In the USSR there are 4 thousand specialized secondary schools and other secondary establishments with a total enrollment of some 4,300,000. . . .‡ Students at these schools receive state stipends.

Graduates of the eight-year school can enter specialized secondary schools immediately or after several years of work. Specialized secondary schools also have evening and correspondence departments where young people can study without leaving their jobs. The term of study is either three or four years. Some specialized secondary schools base their programmes on complete general secondary school and their term of study is shorter. . . .

A significant number of secondary school graduates go on to higher educational establishments. About one million students are admitted annually to institutes and universities (evening and correspondence departments included).

In the USSR there are three types of institutions of higher learning: the regular day department, evening department and correspondence department. The diplomas awarded by the three have identical value.

***Editor's note:** *In 1978–79, the vocational schools trained 3,800,000 young workers.*

†**Editor's note:** *In 1978, there were 6,600 vocational schools.*

‡**Editor's note:** *In 1978–79, 4,300 specialized schools had an enrollment of over 4,700,000 students, including 3,000,000 day-time, 500,000 evening, and 1,200,000 studying by correspondence.*

All Soviet citizens having a complete secondary education, irrespective of sex, nationality or social background, can enter any institution of higher learning in the country.

Altogether there are 794 institutions of higher learning in the country with a total enrollment of 4,500 thousand. In the USSR out of every 10,000 people 176 are students. In 1968, the country's institutes and universities graduated 511,400 young specialists. . . .*

Students studying successfully at regular day departments receive state stipends. Besides, the rectors have at their disposal special funds for helping those who need financial assistance (for instance, a student who has a family and cannot manage to live on the state stipend). Students receiving high marks in their studies are granted stipends which are 25 percent bigger than the usual stipend. . . .

Universities train specialists in the following fields: physics, chemistry, mathematics, mechanics, biology, geology, geography, philology, history, philosophy, economics, and law. Technical institutes train engineers in two hundred different fields.

Economists and trade and finance specialists are trained in institutes and universities as well as the engineering-economic departments of a number of technical institutes.

Those who wish to study law may enroll in law institutes or law departments at universities. Future teachers and doctors are trained in teachers colleges and medical institutes respectively. About fifty higher schools (half of these are musical) train workers in the arts. . . .

Correspondence and evening higher and secondary schools train specialists in nearly all fields. Large industrial enterprises and construction projects have evening and correspondence departments affiliated with correspondence and evening higher and secondary specialized schools.

All the students who do well in their work have the right to stop working and begin attending day lectures, to learn more about the theories and the methods of scientific and designing work.

***Editor's note:** *In 1978–79, there were 866 institutions of higher learning in the USSR with a total of over 5,000,000 students. By the end of that academic year, there were 12,500,000 persons in the USSR with a higher education.*

Chapter 19

THE POSITION OF WOMEN

What is the true status of women in the USSR? No honest observer can deny that, as Lotta Lennon affirms, "Much, indeed, has been achieved by and on behalf of Soviet women." William M. Mandel, a prominent American Soviet specialist, writing in the *American Behavioral Scientist,* maintains that because long ago the USSR "universalized" equal pay for equal work, women "earn 50-to-100 percent more than in any non-Communist country, relative to the general wage and salary scale in each." He adds, "The increase in women's earnings since the Revolution has been at least twice as high as that of men. It is on this broad social scale that the Soviet system is profoundly egalitarian." However, Lotta Lennon maintains that the Soviet Union's women "still appear to find themselves disadvantaged because of their sex," and Soviet writers, while emphasizing past progress and citing the "extensive program for improving women's working and living conditions" in the Tenth Five-Year Plan (1976–1980), agree that much remains to be done if women are to achieve true equality of status with men.

Women in the USSR

Lotta Lennon

Much, indeed, has been achieved by and on behalf of Soviet women, and it is with good cause that the USSR acclaims the feats of its female cosmonauts, jurists, engineers, teachers, and physicians. Nonetheless, on balance, the Soviet Union's 130 million women still appear to find themselves disadvantaged because of their sex.[1] Soviet sociologists, demographers, and journalists openly question whether Soviet women are truly emancipated, whether Soviet laws governing women's labor are observed, whether Soviet working wives and mothers have been able to cope with the stress of their dual roles, and whether the Soviet government has done enough to help women surmount the obstacles preventing them from accomplishing the heavy tasks which society has assigned them.

Soviet commentators decry the continuing underrepresentation of women in the managerial levels of all Soviet professions, even in professions where women comprise the vast majority of the total employment. And at the bottom rung of the social ladder, progress in relieving women of the burden of performing heavy manual labor in industry and agriculture has been slow, despite efforts at tightening enforcement of existing legal safeguards for working women. Soviet women generally remain locked in lower-paid professions and apparently have fewer chances than men to acquire the education, skills, and experience necessary to advance to the most remunerative and responsible positions. . . .

The production ethic so central to Soviet society contributes to women's inequality in another, related manner. Since the time spent in childbirth and infant-rearing (especially where there are inadequate state-run creches and nurseries) reduces the productive years a mother actually spends on the job, production-conscious managers tend to invest less in training working wives to perform skilled operations. Likewise, it does not seem desirable to the authorities to base long-term organizational plans on the promotion of married women to positions of great responsibility. . . .

A final, intangible factor which, Soviet observers admit, continues to block the all-round advancement of women is the tenacity of lingering male prejudices. Since these attitudes touch the psychological and historical roots of Russian behavior (and that of other Soviet nationalities), analysis of them is bound to be speculative. But they evidently affect women's status in society, particularly within the Soviet Communist Party (CPSU). While it may be tantamount to choosing sides in the debate over the historical precedence of the chicken or the egg, one is tempted to suggest that the trivial role accorded women in the party may itself underlie and explain the difficulties they experience elsewhere in Soviet society.

Women's Place

Despite the party's commitment to female emancipation—a policy which has unquestionably improved the lot of Soviet women in many spheres—leadership of the CPSU it-

This excerpt is taken from an article by the same title that appeared in Problems of Communism, *vol. XX (July-Aug. 1971), pp. 47–58. Ms. Lennon, as the context indicates, relied largely on Soviet sources. Most of her footnotes have been omitted. For details, see the original.*

self is unquestionably a male affair. This may reflect the impact on the party of what has been called Stalin's "strangely oriental attitude" toward women. Or it may be evidence of the persistence of the prejudices noted by Lenin in a 1920 letter to Clara Zetkin:

> Yes indeed, unfortunately, it is still true to say of many of our comrades, "Scratch a Communist and find a philistine. Of course, you must scratch the sensitive spot, their mentality as regards women . . . the old master-right of man still lives in secret."

Whatever the reason, there are no women in the CPSU Politburo, the apex of the CPSU hierarchy. Also, of the 467 members elected to the CPSU Central Committee and Central Auditing Commission at the 24th Party Congress this April, just 18 (3.7 percent) were women. Only 2 of the 26 persons on the current ruling Buro of the Komsomol—the Soviet youth organization—are women. In reality, very little has changed since 1956, when Premier Khrushchev complained to the 20th Party Congress that "many party and soviet [i.e., government] bodies exhibit timidity about putting women in executive posts. Very few women hold leading party and soviet positions, particularly as party committee secretaries."

Although the disparity is not as marked as in the top party echelons, women are also under-represented in the CPSU rank and file. There are 19 million more women than men in the USSR, and women labor alongside men in many occupations; yet there are only a little over 3 million women among the 14.5 million members of the Soviet Communist Party—about 21 percent. . . .

Turning from the party, in which fundamental policymaking power resides, to the top levels of government, we find that women have little voice in executive bodies. The duties of Ye Furtseva—Minister of Culture and the only woman among 95 men in the powerful USSR Council of Ministers—appear to have been limited in recent years to ceremonial duties such as opening festivals and competitions.[2] Women fare slightly better in the governments of the USSR's 15 constituent republics as can be seen in Table 1, compiled from a close reading of the Soviet press. . . .

Women fare somewhat better in the legislatures (also called "supreme soviets") of the 15 republics, where they account for 10 of 55 deputy chairpersons, according to a current tally. [See Table 1.] However, none serves as chairperson of a republic supreme soviet. It would appear that it is only at the lowest levels—the territory, region, town, and village soviets—that women deputies (comprising 43 percent of the total) have a real opportunity to affect decisions. Here the "showcase" function of serving on an elected body is much less in evidence than at the political summit, and women deputies—in close communication with their constituents—show considerable zeal in correcting local abuses.

Inequality in Employment

Outside the party and government, women are also conspicuously absent from higher-echelon positions, although they are heavily represented in middle-level jobs in many professions. The Soviet observer M. Sonin wrote in 1969:

> Even given an equal level of professional preparation, representatives of the stronger sex as a rule hold the managerial posts. How does one explain that while men comprise 15 percent of all medical personnel, they are 50 percent of all chief physicians and

TABLE 1 Women in the Councils of Ministers of the 15 Union Republics

Republic	Total No. Chairpersons and Dep. Chairpersons	Of Which Women	Total of Other Members	Of Which Women
Armenia	7	1	35	3
Azerbaidzhan	7	0	41	2
Belorussia	7	1	38	2
Estonia	6	0	31	1
Georgia	8	1	41	1
Kazakhstan	8	0	42	1
Kirgizia	7	1	32	2
Latvia	6	0	34	1
Lithuania	8	0	38	0
Moldavia	7	0	30	3
RSFSR	11	2	31	1
Tadzhikistan	7	1	36	1
Turkmenia	7	2	35	0
Ukraine	10	0	37	0
Uzbekistan	8	0	37	3
USSR Total	**114**	**9**	**538**	**21**

executives of medical institutions . . . ? In the overwhelming majority of cases, it is men who head departments, enterprises, and administrative agencies.

Regardless of the profession examined, female representation declines as the rank or level of the position rises.

This rule of thumb is particularly true for politically sensitive positions. In 1966, women comprised a mere 12.3 percent of the membership of the USSR Writer's Union, even when counting that organization's numerous female translators and minor poetesses. Among 573 Soviet radio, press and TASS commentators (a notch above the ordinary journalist) active in the same year, only eight were women.

In the field of science, Soviet women have made great strides since the days of the Bolshevik Revolution. By 1969 they comprised 39 percent of persons employed in scientific occupations, a proportion which is truly creditable by world standards. Yet in that year, only 10 percent of all professors, academicians and corresponding members of the USSR Academy of Sciences; 13 percent of all doctors of sciences (a super-Ph.D.); and 27 percent of all candidates of sciences (roughly equivalent to a Ph.D.) were women. No woman has ever held the post of president, vice-president, chief scientific secretary, or member of the Presidium of the USSR Academy of Sciences, nor has any woman served as a secretary or member of the ruling *buro* of any of the Academy's divisions. Moreover, the scholarly productivity of women scientists appears lower, judging from their proportional output of articles. Only one in seven women scientists defends a candidate dissertation, compared with one in three men scientists, and only one in 250 women scientists obtains a doctor of sciences, compared with one in 28 men scientists.

Likewise in industry, Soviet women have made significant gains but still find themselves disadvantaged in comparison with their male colleagues. Thus, at the end of 1963 women comprised 34 percent of the production leaders and specialists of industrial enterprises, but as shown in Table 2, they were heavily concentrated in such categories as tech-

TABLE 2 Share of Women in Responsible Positions in Industry: December 1963 (in percent)

Position	Share of Total
Enterprise directors	6
Chief engineers	16
Shop chiefs and their deputies	12
Chiefs of shifts, factory bays, sectors, shop labs, and their deputies	22
Chiefs of sections, offices, groups of plant services, workshops, labs, and their deputies	20
Engineers (with exception of engineer-economists, and engineer-rate-setters)	38
Technicians (except technician-rate-setters)	65
Foremen	20
Engineer-rate-setters, technician-rate-setters, rate-setters	62
Chief and senior bookkeepers	36
Engineer-economists, economists, planners, statisticians	70
All of above combined	**34**

Source: Zhenshchiny i deti v SSSR (Women and Children in the USSR), Moscow, Statistika, 1969, p. 102.

nician, economist, and rate-setter, and accounted for only 6 percent of enterprise directors. It should be noted that this table reflects the Soviet Union's own order of importance. Rate-setters, bookkeepers, planners, and economists in industry are predominantly clerical types with virtually no decision-making prerogatives. More recently, on Women's Day 1967, G. Ronina stated:

> Although they make up one-half of the industrial labor force contingent, women are employed as supervisors, shop chiefs, and in comparable leadership positions one-sixth to one-seventh as frequently as men.

This suggests that there had even been some downgrading of women in the four-year interim.

Such inequality appears to be even greater in rural areas, where *man*power has been chronically short and maldistributed. According to M. Gafarova, a woman heading a faculty of the Dushanbe Pedagogical Institute, "In many instances, work demanding manual labor falls to women, while the men work as accountants, section leaders and farm managers." Data from 1966 also revealed no women among the collective farm chairpersons of such important regions as Leningrad, Rostov, Sverdlovsk, Novosibirsk, and Omsk. As former Premier Khrushchev candidly admitted at a regional agricultural conference, "It turns out that it is the men who do the administrating and the women who do the work!"

Admissions Bias

How does one balance such facts against Soviet claims that as of November 1966 women comprised 58 percent of all specialists with higher or secondary specialized training? Accompanying Table 3 shows that women are heavily concentrated in the medical and educational professions, fields which enjoy less prestige than engineering or agronomy in the USSR.

TABLE 3 Women Specialists as a Percent of Total Specialists: November 1966

Category	Number	Share of Total
All Specialists	7,540,000	58
Specialists with higher education, of whom:	2,717,000	52
Engineers	545,000	30
Agronomists, zoo-technicians, and veterinarians	129,000	40
Economists	209,000	63
Doctors (except dentists with only secondary education)	375,000	72
Teachers and university grads (except geologists, doctors, economists, and lawyers), library and cultural workers	1,332,000	68
Specialists with secondary education, of whom:	4,823,000	63
Technicians	1,197,000	38
Agronomists, zoo-technicians, veterinary feldshers, and veterinary technicians	229,000	46
Planners and statisticians	478,000	75
Medical workers	1,423,000	93
Teachers, librarians, cultural workers	1,114,000	84

Source: Zhenshchiny i deti v SSSR (Women and Children in the USSR), Moscow, Statistika, 1969, pp. 97, 98, and 100.

The differential career patterns of Soviet women and men obviously reflect differential schooling, a phenomenon which still persists. True, Soviet women have made great strides in the area of education. For example, in the 1968–69 academic year, they accounted for 47 percent of all students of higher schools compared with only 28 percent in 1927–28. However, behind these impressive figures there still lurks a distinct bias against women in actual admission policies. Thus, in 1968–69 women comprised only 35 percent of students of higher schools of industry, construction, transportation, and communication, and 27 percent of students at higher schools of agriculture. The U.S. economist Norton Dodge in 1966 documented the existence of discrimination against women applicants to science faculties of Moscow University and identified one economic rationale underlying such a policy—the shorter productive life of women (because of early retirement, maternity, and domestic concerns), which makes it more rational to train a male than a female of the same aptitudes. S. Berezovskaia confirmed this discrimination in 1969: ". . . for young women, it is harder to gain entrance to higher educational institutions, even though they study and pass examinations just as well as young men." Similarly, M. Sonin noted:

> In institutes, for example, there are more male than female students, even though, as we recall, among secondary school graduates there are far fewer boys than girls. . . . The social consequences of such a disproportion are extremely negative.

As a result of the differential training of women and their continued high rate of participation in productive employment, a large segment of Soviet women end up in tedious manual jobs. Some 77 percent of the 56 million women employed in the Soviet labor force at the time of the 1959 Soviet census were engaged in the category of "physical" (as opposed to "mental") labor.[3] The majority of these were employed in agriculture, where some 90 percent of unskilled labor is female, according to one Soviet report. *Izvestia* of November 26, 1967, admitted that "the hardest and most monotonous" rural chores fall to women, and G. Ronina pondered why it was that women "haul feed bags or break up the sod with heavy crowbars while the men tally the output." The situation is hardly better in industry. Women are widely used as steel puddlers, coal shovelers, stevedores, cement workers, loggers and woodcutters, drillers, plasterers, snow removers, street-sweepers and ditchdiggers. Khrushchev himself complained:

> It is painful to see . . . our women, armed with crowbars, tamping down road ballast by hand.

Soviet men stubbornly defend "previously-won positions" in higher-paid, mechanized, skilled occupations of industry and agriculture. A hopeful sign of progress for women in this area was the February 1969 decree of the USSR Council of Ministers "On Wider Enlistment of Women to Participation as Skilled Labor in Agriculture." The measure specifically ordered modification of certain agricultural machinery for use by women and the designation of particular skilled agricultural jobs which are suitable for female employment.

Despite such gains, it is likely that Soviet women will continue to perform heavy and hazardous jobs in violation of the spirit, if not the letter, of Article 68 of the 1970 USSR Labor Code, which states:

> It is forbidden to employ women in heavy work, in work with harmful working conditions, or in jobs underground except for certain ones (nonmanual labor and work in health and other services).

Existence of such legislation is apparently no guarantee of enforcement. As one Soviet woman charged, such laws are "not always strictly observed, and public organizations frequently do nothing about it."

A clear example is provided in the area of mining. Karl Marx himself noted a hundred years ago that use of female labor in the mines had been forbidden in capitalist Great Britain prior to his writing of *Capital*. It is therefore ironic that in socialist Soviet Russia, where such use of women was outlawed in 1922, the practice still lingers. The official newspaper of the Soviet trade unions, *Trud*, reported on March 4, 1969, that some 20,000 women had "recently" been transferred to surface work in the Donbas and promised that in the "near future" all women "working in the mines" would be similarly shifted above ground. D. Shumsky indicated in 1966 that several thousand women were working in the ore mines of the Karaganda Basin and that many more were employed in other arduous or unhealthy jobs. One suspects that, although the 1970 Labor Code reiterates the 1922 proscription of the practice, women will continue to labor in Soviet mines, in part because of shortages of manpower for underground shifts. . . .

Women are drawn to hazardous and strenuous occupations by the supplemental pay and other fringe benefits accruing to these normally male jobs. One Soviet observer noted that wages in professions which are "specifically suitable for women" are so low that this is often a necessity. In general, however, women predominate among employees of the lowest-paying professions, as can be seen in Table 4. Wage conditions in education have apparently further deteriorated: in 1971 it was reported that the average monthly wage in education was 102.8 rubles while the national average wage had increased to 117 rubles a month. (The reader should also be reminded that the relatively large percentage of women

TABLE 4 Female Participation and Wage Scales in Soviet Labor Force Branches: 1967

Branch	Women as % of Total Employment	Rubles per Month
Science and scientific service	45	122.1
Construction	28	119.4
Transportation	24	115.5
Apparatus of government and economic administration and of cooperative and public organizations	58	112.7
Industry	47	112.0
Nationwide Average	50	103.4
Education	72	96.4
Credit and insurance	75	93.3
Health	85	82.2
Trade	74	82.2
Housing and municipal economy	51	78.7
Communications	66	78.1

Source: Narodnoe khoziaistvo SSSR v 1969 godu (National Economy of the USSR in 1969), Moscow, Statistika, 1970, p. 654.

in the category of "Apparatus" in Table 4 gives a misleading impression, for, as we have seen above, men predominate in the positions of true authority in the party and state apparatus, whereas women are concentrated in clerical jobs such as statistician, rate-setter, or even secretary-typist.)

Even when women work in higher-paying professions, they seem to find themselves at an economic disadvantage compared with men. A.G. Kharchev reported that the average wage of women in industry is well below that of men, a condition which he denounced as "economic and moral inequality." The veteran Soviet feminist V. Bilshay also noted that women in the economy earn lower salaries than men, and attributed this to the inferior skills of women.

Not only do women appear to end up in lower-paying branches of the labor force and lower-paying job categories, but many also end up working in piecework occupations where their earnings fall below the Soviet minimum wage of 60 rubles a month. *Komsomolskaia pravda* of June 17, 1970, printed a letter from a village hairdresser who earned 40 rubles a month—and that only because she was fortunate enough to work in a populous area. Publication of such letters is usually designed to draw attention to a widespread abuse. One may therefore infer frequent *de facto* violations of the minimum wage standard.

The burden of the wage disadvantages experienced by working women looms large when juxtaposed with the forces which drive women into the Soviet labor market in the first place. . . .

The Weight of the "Double Burden"

This brings us back to a problem briefly noted above—the phenomenon of the "double burden"—which is causing increasing concern. Many Soviet sociologists foresee deterioration of the physical and mental health of Soviet working women as a result of this "double burden'' and are concerned about the contribution of this situation to a declining Soviet birth rate. In a 1969 survey of Leningrad working women, 70 percent admitted they often felt fatigue on their jobs. Their illness rate was twice as high as that of working men. To the question, ''Is it difficult for you to combine family obligations with work on the production line?'' 44 percent answered ''bearable,'' 31 percent answered ''hard,'' and 25 percent answered ''very hard.'' . . .

One of the most serious consequences of the ''double burden'' from the Soviet point of view is a declining birth rate. Sociologists D. Valentei and G. Kisleva reported in 1969 that ''the overwhelming majority of families try to have one or a maximum of two children.'' As a result, they state, the birth rate fell from 24.9 per thousand in 1960 to 17.3 per thousand in 1968. Professor Kharchev was one of the first in the post-Stalin era to draw the link between the difficult conditions of Soviet women's lives and the lowered birth rate. More recently, R. Sagimbaeva, an associate of the Central Research Laboratory of the State Committee on Utilization of Labor Resources of the RSFSR Council of Ministers, explicitly stated:

> In the USSR, the fertility of working women is half that of the housewife. It is very difficult for women to both work and raise children. And often, if the choice is between working and raising children, women choose work.

. . . To counter the dropping birth rate, the authorities have steadily improved maternity benefits, most recently (in the 1970 Labor Code) giving a working mother, in addition to fifty-six days of paid leave both before and after giving birth, permission to take leave without pay until the child reaches one year of age, without prejudice to the mother's job rating. However, a whole nexus of other factors operates to discourage the raising of large families.

For example, Soviet experts make clear that men share the homemaking chores of women only slightly and that the government has been either unwilling or unable to develop sufficient appliances, consumer services, retail outlets, or child-care facilities to significantly ease this burden. According to one study, men spend 1 hour and 15 minutes daily on household-related matters compared to 4 hours and 20 minutes for women. The average Moscow woman spends ''a minimum of 50 percent of her [off-job] time shopping for groceries and cooking.'' Numerous commentators concur in the judgment that working women simply lack the time for civic work, personal development, improvement of job qualifications, or satisfaction of spiritual needs. The upshot is that the working woman ''turns into a wornout woman after 15–20 years of married life,'' according to A. Valentinov. . . .

In the matter of child-care facilities, the Soviet Union has made considerable progress since 1960, when the 4.4 million places in state-run nurseries and kindergartens (roughly comparable to the 1914 statistics!) could accommodate only 13 percent of Soviet children aged 1 to 6. By January 1970 the available places had more than doubled—to 9 million—but the existing capacity still fell short of meeting the needs of urban working mothers and, to an even greater extent, of working mothers in the countryside.[4] . . .

The overall impression which emerges from our examination of the status of women in the USSR is that, despite significant gains and even the achievement of genuine equality with men in some areas, there remains a wide gap between the myth of equality fostered by Soviet propagandists and the reality of women's life in the Soviet Union. In contemplating the possibilities for narrowing this gap, Soviet women must be aware that all the gains which they have registered to date were granted by the regime as pragmatic steps to increase efficiency and productivity, *not* in response to any effective articulation of demands by women themselves. Like all other Soviet citizens, women in the USSR have little chance to voice their complaints and demands, much less have a meaningful impact on the solution of everyday problems. In order to gain full equality, they must, in the words of one Soviet observer, become able "to insist on their legal rights and implement them." In today's Russia, as in Marx's Prussia, "complete emancipation is a *conditio sine qua non* for any partial emancipation." Much that impedes progress toward full liberation of women in Soviet Russia will be swept away only when all Soviet citizens gain full democratic rights.

Notes

1. *On January 1, 1970, there were 130.3 million females and 111.3 million males in the Soviet Union.*
2. *It might be recalled that Furtseva was also the* only *woman to rise to the top decision-making organ of the CPSU—she served as an alternate and then full member of the CPSU Presidium (the Khrushchev-era equivalent of the Politburo) during the years 1956–60.*
3. *The category "physical labor" covers anyone involved in the production, transportation, sale, or servicing of goods, and thus does not of itself imply manual labor. According to unpublished estimates of the U.S. Bureau of the Census, women continue to comprise roughly 50 percent of the total labor force, or upwards of 62 million. There is no current breakdown of this figure into "physical" and "mental" labor.*
4. *"Report of the Central Statistical Administration on Fulfillment of the 1969 Economic Plan,"* Izvestia, *Jan. 25, 1970. The Directives for the 1966–70 Five-Year Plan set a 1970 goal of 12,000,000 preschool places, which would meet the urban need "in the main" and "improve" the situation in rural areas (*Pravda, *Feb. 20, 1966). A Soviet survey in 1966 revealed that only 61 percent of children under age seven from families of mothers working in industry (i.e., predominantly in urban areas) attended preschool, with the comparable figure for children of white-collar working mothers at 71 percent. Of the 8,534,000 places available in 1966, 6,835,000 were in the cities compared with only 1,649,000 in the countryside (*Zhenshchiny i deti v SSSR, *p. 126). It is against this background that one must read the 1969 results.*

Women's Role at Work and at Play

M. Ya. Sonin

Soviet Editors' Note: The Basic Guidelines for the Development of the USSR National Economy in 1976–80 outline an extensive program for improving women's working and living conditions. Among the measures envisaged are the following:

—The introduction of partially paid leave for working women to enable them to care for children under the age of one year;

—The creation of greater opportunities for mothers to work part-time and at home;

—The expansion of the network of preschool institutions and extended-day schools and groups;

—The construction of day nurseries and kindergartens for 2.5 to 2.8 million children;

—An increase in the number of Young Pioneer camps; and

—The creation of conditions for reducing the amount of time spent on housework.

These measures should help solve such problems as the higher total work load that women bear—as compared to men—on the job and at home, the inadequate level of mechanization and automation, and the continued existence of strenuous working conditions and night shifts for women workers in some branches of the economy.*

In the USSR, 92 percent of all working-age women either work or study. Women are employed in all branches of the national economy, and they constitute 59 percent of all those who work with their minds.

In industry, the largest number of women work in machine building. Light industry—traditionally a female-dominated branch—has fallen to second place. In instrument making and electronics women make up 45 percent to 47 percent of the work force, and in precision machine building and the radio industry they constitute 65 percent to 75 percent of all workers. Women account for 10 percent of all chief specialists, 16 percent of all shop, shifts and section superintendents and assistants, and 26 percent of all department heads at enterprises.

Special mention should be made of women's involvement in science, education and public health. In 1975, 40 percent of all scientific workers and 70 percent of all teachers (including school administrators) and physicians were women.

This abstract of an article by Dr. Sonin, professor at The USSR Academy of Sciences' Economics Institute, Moscow, appeared in a specialized Soviet economics journal. Reprinted from The Current Digest of the Soviet Press, August 23, 1978, pp. 1, 3–4. *Translation copyright 1978 by* The Current Digest of the Soviet Press, *published weekly at The Ohio State University; reprinted by permission of the Digest.*

**Soviet Editors' Note ends here.*

Work and Family. The expansion of employment for women should be accompanied by concern for motherhood and women's all-round spiritual and physical development. Accordingly, the state gives considerable aid to women in the rearing of children. In 1975, 11.5 million children were enrolled in preschool institutions. Parents pay only one-fifth of the cost of maintaining children in day nurseries and kindergartens.

After the birth of a child, the mother has the right not to work for a year. In accordance with a decision of the 25th CPSU Congress, partial pay will be introduced for this period, which will count as uninterrupted work service. Specialists are discussing a proposal to offer women a two-year leave after the birth of a child, including one year without pay. There is also a proposal to increase the length of leaves with full or partial pay. The problems connected with such a proposal are clear if one bears in mind that there are 63.3 million working women and that over 4.5 million children are born each year.

But while the state can provide a wide array of consumer and cultural services, it cannot take over all household and child-rearing responsibilities, a considerable share of which must be borne by the parents. Much of the inequality in the division of labor between the sexes occurs here. Although men and women have equal rights, the responsibilities are not always divided equitably. Women have a much longer total working day—their jobs plus housework. This means that they have less free time.

One way to rectify this situation is to prepare men for family life and train them for what might be called physical labor in the family. Another solution is to have children help with household chores. While giving instruction in labor skills, preschool institutions and schools should pay more attention to housework; this would not only help to make children industrious and disciplined but also would do much to ease women's burden in the home.

The differences between the social roles taken by men and women are largely determined by differences in upbringing and vocational training, starting at a very early age. These patterns arose ages ago, took root and came to be considered natural. In principle, socialist society opposes the social inequality of women. But traditions are still quite strong, and they impede an equitable division of family labor and responsibilities between the sexes. [See Table 1.]

Education and Qualifications. Equality in the work place is another problem. On the average, women have slightly higher skills than men. But this is largely because women are employed in branches that require relatively high qualifications but pay relatively

TABLE 1 Distribution of Household Responsibilities within the Family

	% of Families in Which Given Work Is Done By:			
Type of Work	**Wife**	**Husband**	**Together**	**Other Family Members**
Shopping	61	3	19	17
Preparing breakfast	58	10	18	14
Preparing dinner	64	4	16	16
Picking up and washing dishes	10	17	39	34
General cleaning	32	12	39	17
Small repairs in the home	22	67	1	10
Washing and ironing	64	2	21	13
Paying bills	45	31	12	12

Source: A.G. Kharchev and S.I. Golod, "Women's Work and the Family (A Sociological Study)" [*Professionalnaya rabota zhenshchin i semya (sotsiologicheskoye issledovaniye)*]. Leningrad, 1971, p. 74.

poorly—education, public health, culture, etc. Still, the percentage of women doing unskilled physical labor is higher than that of men.

The emancipation of women from strenuous work is proceeding slowly. On the one hand, mechanization has not been introduced widely enough. On the other hand, women workers are not always interested in shifting to easier jobs, since this might mean lower pay and pension benefits.

The percentage of women working in services, particularly in trade, has grown considerably in recent years. But trade, especially in small, unmechanized grocery stores, requires a considerable amount of hard physical labor.

In recent years, the increase in the number of manual workers in industry has come almost exclusively from women. The share of women employed in such common undermechanized jobs as letter carriers, warehouse workers, goods examiners and distributors rose from 59 to 74 percent between 1959 and 1970. Women made up 84 percent of all letter carriers in 1970.

Women today have the same educational opportunities as men. In 1975 they constituted 54 percent of the students in specialized secondary educational institutions and 50 percent of the students in higher schools. But there are some difficulties here. It is women under thirty who are learning vocations and upgrading their skills, but these are also the years in which they establish families. As a result of this conflict, women lag behind men in the level of vocational skills. The declining birthrate is one response to this situation.

The system of elementary vocational training does not do enough to equalize qualifications. Retraining and advanced training, both on the job and during leave periods, are becoming increasingly important for women. In our view, women must be permitted to upgrade their vocational skills during working time, while continuing to receive their regular pay. This would give women an advantage over men. But only this approach can make it possible to raise labor productivity and to achieve true equality of the sexes in job skills.

Once More about Work. Work schedules deserve attention. The five-day workweek has made possible a considerable improvement in working and recreational conditions. However, this innovation has cut women's labor productivity, because evening shifts end late, at times when there is no public transportation to take the women home, and inconvenient schedules often prevent husbands and wives from spending their days off together. As a result, some women have expressed a desire to return to the six-day week. In some cases, this might be advisable.

The psychological climate in the production collective merits special consideration. Sometimes a man who is less qualified than his female subordinates is placed in charge of a women's brigade. Other psychological factors may be overlooked too. The head of a women's collective should possess not only work-related skills but also considerable tact and a basic understanding of psychology.

Some Proposals. To sum up, major "female" problems that require work at all levels are:

—vocational training and advanced training for women;
—improvements in working conditions for women; and
—upbringing work with men and children.

Other proposals worth consideration would allow women with young children to take one unpaid day off each month for family needs; give enterprises the right to alter schedules for women workers with families; and set up quotas for admitting girls to vocational-technical schools for training in a list of occupations drawn up by research organizations.

Chapter 20

LIVING STANDARDS IN GENERAL

From the available data, two close and astute observers of Soviet economic development, Paul R. Gregory and Robert C. Stuart, observed in *Soviet Economic Structure and Performance*, that while industrial wage differentials between high- and low-paid workers during the 1930s and early 1950s "were probably greater than in the United States," since the mid-1950s, "Soviet differentials have been narrowed substantially until they are now probably smaller than American differentials." They added that "When one considers the overall distribution of income among families as opposed to industrial wage income alone, it is fairly clear that income is distributed much more equally in the Soviet Union than in the United States." A Soviet economist, Gennadi Pisarovsky, supports this thesis while Murray Yanowitch, although agreeing that "there is little doubt that the period since the late 1950s has seen a reduction in money-wage and income differentials," concludes that substantial inequalities "in both money earnings and living standards parallel inequalities in power over the organization of the work process."

Living Standards: Imagination and Reality

Gennadi Pisarovsky

Living standards in the USSR are not yet so high as we would like it, but not at all so low as some people in the West imagine.

Double Underestimation

The standard of living is a capacious and complicated notion. But quite often it is interpreted one-sidedly. As a rule, one takes the amount of time which the Soviet and, say, the American worker must work to buy some goods, and proves on the basis of one rule of arithmetic that the working people in the USSR live much worse than those in the United States.

An unsophisticated reader is appealed to through this method by its simplicity and persuasiveness. But still there are four rules of arithmetic and, to put it mildly, it is not scientific to mechanically compare purchasing capacity in countries with different social systems.

People receive different wages in the USSR and in the United States: the Americans get much higher wages. But they spend them differently. [See Table 1.]

Addition to Arithmetic

Goethe said that figures did not rule the world, but they showed how the world was ruled. According to the International Labour Organization (ILO) the number of unemployed in the West ranges from 18.5 to 20 million. It makes little difference to any of them that according to statistics their average living standards are higher than those of a Soviet citizen. With hundreds of thousands of unoccupied flats, the people who cannot afford them do not care that per capita there are more dwellings in the United States or any other country than in the USSR.

Soviet people know that they face quite a few difficulties and problems. But they also know that today they live better than yesterday, and tomorrow they will live better than today.

At present, the average monthly wages and salaries of workers and employees in the USSR amount to 150 rubles, or 200 dollars according to the official rate of exchange. This is considerably less than in the United States. There are two or three working members in a Soviet family and, consequently, its budget amounts to approximately 300–450 rubles, or 400–600 dollars. Eighty percent of this sum (320–480 dollars) is spent on goods and services. Free flats as well as pensions, stipends, and other allowances should be added to the budget of the overwhelming majority of families.

The following appeared in Panarama, *a Soviet publication, on November 16, 1976. Reproduced with the permission of Anatoli Kandalintsev, Information Officer, The USSR Embassy, Information Department.*

TABLE 1 The Structure of Expenses by Families in the USSR and the USA (in %)

	A Family with Average Income		A Family with Minimum Income	
	USA	USSR	USA	USSR
Taxes	12	6	6	0
Housing	24	7	28	7
Transport	12	3	10	5
Insurance, savings, payments	7	3	4	1
Public health and child care	5	1	6	less than 1
Expenses on the purchase of goods and services	40	80	46	more than 86
Total	100	100	100	100

In the 10th Five-Year Plan, which was recently endorsed by the USSR Supreme Soviet session, the real incomes of the population are to grow by 21 percent. Experts have calculated that in 1980 an average Soviet family will, every month, buy 75–85 more rubles worth of goods and services (100–113 dollars) than in 1975 and 125–130 rubles (165–175 dollars) more than in 1970. What is more, this addition will be a "net" one; prices of commodities and the cost of services will remain stable.

No one in the Soviet Union makes a secret of the fact that the standard of living in the West, particularly in the United States, is higher than in our country. However, the welfare level in the USSR rises by 4–5 percent every year. As to the West, the extremely high growth rates of the cost of living and the skyrocketing taxes have led to the reduction of the population's real incomes. According to the Secretariat of the Organisation for Economic Cooperation and Development (OECD), the aggregate real incomes of the population of seven leading capitalist countries have gone down, on an average, by 1.3 percent during 1974–75. The incomes in the United States decreased by 2.6 percent in 1975 alone.

[Table 1] was calculated a few years ago by the American economist L. Turgeon. But even this table shows that a Soviet worker spends 80 percent of his wages on goods and services against 40 percent spent by an American worker. With such a difference in the structure of expenses, it is more than dubious to calculate the real buying capacity of the population in the USSR and the United States, proceeding from nominal wages. This method underrates at least by two times the real standard of living of the Soviet working people.

As regards the USSR, the table calculated by L. Turgeon, also reflects, in the main, the present situation, though it exaggerates the share of expenses on housing (approximately twice as much) and underrates the share of savings. As to the American part of the table, it needs to be substantially corrected. The share of noncommodity expenses of American families almost in all items (taxes, housing, medicine, transport) has increased by several points. In the past two years alone the cost of medical services in the United States went up by 25 percent. Rent also increased by 25 percent. Taxes, too, are increasing with unenviable steadiness. Despite curtailed employment in 1975, the total amount of income taxes in the United States grew by 6.9 percent.

On the other hand, the stability observed in the USSR is quite different: for example the price index now constitutes 99.6 points, against 1970. Taxes are not increasing: in the 1976 State Budget taxes are only 8.8 percent. Rent has been unchanged for nearly fifty years (since 1928), and together with communal services constitutes 3 to 4 percent of average family incomes. Public health in the USSR is free of charge; no matter how complicated the medical aid given, a patient pays nothing for it. All forms of education are also free, which fact, incidentally, was not reflected at all in the table calculated by L. Turgeon.

Social consumption funds are not taken into account either intentionally or because of ignorance. This is the part of the State Budget which is spent on free education, free medical aid, pensions, and other allowances with no payments and deductions from wages.

Differentiation of Incomes

Murray Yanowitch

What are some of the main patterns and approximate magnitudes of prevailing inequalities in Soviet money earnings and living standards? It should be stressed that what follows is not an attempt at a comprehensive survey of Soviet income structure. Our primary objective is to disclose the relative economic status of some of the principal social groups in Soviet society. Differences in money incomes are obviously not the only source of differential privileges in the Soviet Union. But with the increasing supply and variety of consumer goods and services in recent years, differences in monetary rewards can more readily be translated into differences in real income and distinct styles of life. . . .

The Nonegalitarian Reduction of Income Inequality

Beginning in 1931 and for approximately twenty-five years thereafter, wage policy pronouncements and discussions were almost invariably dominated by a single theme: the struggle against "egalitarianism" or "equality-mongering" (*uravnilovka*). Although wage policy during this period was not confined to widening the gap between high- and low-paid labor, there is unmistakable evidence of increased inequality in the distribution of wage income between the early 1930s and the late 1950s. Whatever its other functions—such as the consolidation of social privileges—the continuing denunciation of egalitarianism was a way of focusing attention on the need to utilize monetary incentives to promote the development of scarce skills and disciplined work habits. But like other policies of the period, the antiegalitarian campaign had all the earmarks of a frenzied struggle against "enemies." Egalitarianism was not only identified as a petty bourgeois

This excerpt from the author's Social and Economic Inequality in the Soviet Union *© 1977 by M.E. Sharpe, Inc. is reproduced with the permission of the publisher and author. The author's extensive footnotes have been omitted. Interested students should consult the original.*

and utopian socialist policy—which was bad enough—but it was also linked with more ominous forces: "Trotskyites, Zinovievites, Bukharinites, and other enemies of the people. . . ." Thus the theme of antiegalitarianism was an inseparable component of the whole "spirit" of the Stalinist epoch.

In contrast to the period of the prewar five-year plans and the early postwar years, there is little doubt that the period since the late 1950s has seen a reduction in money wage and income differentials. This is suggested both by official statements of policy as well as by Soviet empirical studies of income inequality. A gradual reduction in inequalities of economic status has now come to be regarded as a "natural" feature of Soviet economic and cultural development. Repeated increases in minimum wage levels, reduced ratios of highest-to-lowest basic wage rates, and essential stability of basic rates for the most highly paid groups of occupations have been characteristic of Soviet wage policy since the late 1950s and into the early 1970s. Some of the statistical evidence pointing to the implementation of a policy of reducing the gap between high and low income groups since 1956 is shown in Table 1.

Although the shrill antiegalitarian tone of the early planning years has been largely abandoned, the income narrowing policies of the more recent period are not typically presented as reflecting the introduction of new principles of wage and salary determination. . . .

Thus most recent discussions of wage differentials and inequalities in economic status have been contained within the bounds of traditional themes: "payment in accordance with work," the primacy of material incentives, the need to avoid egalitarian tenden-

TABLE 1 Selected Measures of Soviet Wage and Income Differentiation

Years	(1) Decile Coefficient of Wage Differentiation*	(2) Ratio of Average Wages of 10% Highest Paid to 10% Lowest Paid	(3) Decile Coefficient of Differentiation of Family Income†	(4) Leningrad: Ratio of Average Wages of 10% Highest Paid to 10% Lowest Paid
1956	4.4	8.1		
1959				4.6
1961				4.0
1964	3.7			3.7
1966	3.2		3.8‡	3.6
1968	2.7	5.1		3.3
1970	3.2		3.2	
1972				3.3
1975 (plan)	2.9	4.1		

*Ratio of the wage exceeded by 10% of workers and nonmanual employees to the wage exceeded by 90%

†Ratio of the income per capita exceeded by 10% of families to that exceeded by 90%

‡1965

Sources:

col. 1—G.S. Sarkisian, *Uroven', tempy i proportsii rosta real'nykh dokhodov pri sotsializma,* pp. 125, 132.

col. 2—L.E. Kunel'skii, *Sotsial'no-ekonomicheskie problemy zarabotnoi platy,* pp. 68–69.

col. 3—G.S. Sarkisian, *Dokhody trudiashchikhsia i sotsial'nye problemy urovnia zhizni naseleniia SSSR,* p. 134.

col. 4—N.M. Tikhonov, *Neobkhodimyi produkt v usloviiakh razvitogo sotsializma,* p. 169.

cies—all part of the heritage of the early planning years. But the intellectual climate of the late 1960s and early 1970s has also permitted some striking departures from customary formulations of the issue of economic inequality. Some of the ideas expressed during this period can only be interpreted as protests against privilege and criticisms of traditional practices governing income differentiation and work incentives. . . .

Perhaps even more significant was the attempt of some economists to argue that "distribution according to work" could not be an adequate guide to determining the earnings level of all occupational groups. It had to be supplemented by the "law of reimbursement of outlays of labor power." In the language of Marxian economics this meant that the incomes of even the lowest paid groups in the work force must be sufficient to cover "the cost of production and reproduction of labor power." This required a minimum level of compensation for all employed individuals, "independent of the share of their labor contribution to the creation of the social product." Such a level would not only meet the needs of sheer physical subsistence but would provide the minimum amenities required for cultural growth, work morale, and the "normal" reproduction of the work force. The implication was clear. The earnings of the lowest paid occupational groups (presumably determined in accordance with their "labor contribution") had been inadequate to cover the normal costs of production of labor power. Indeed, the very substantial increases required in minimum wage rates (from 40 rubles per month in 1965 to 70 rubles in the early 1970s) offered indirect testimony of the earlier prolonged neglect of "the law of reimbursement. . . ." Such increases could hardly be explained by changes in the "quantity and quality" of work performed by the lowest paid groups in the work force. . . .

The same can be said about some of the recent sociological literature on work attitudes. This has gone beyond the traditional one-dimensional identification of work incentives with "material interest," an identification that reduced the problem of work incentives to that of establishing a sufficiently differentiated structure of earnings. The new approach appeals for recognition of the fact that with a rise in educational attainments and general living standards there has been a "change in the structure of stimuli to labor." At the risk of trivializing a considerable body of literature in this area, we may summarize one of its principal themes as follows: The greater the "intellectual" and "creative" content of labor (the greater the scope for "self-supervision" and "self-organization"), the less important become the incentive effects of differentials in material rewards. . . .

Wage Differentiation in Industry: General Features

. . . The principal occupational categories distinguished in the official industrial labor statistics include workers, engineering-technical personnel, and employees (*sluzhashchie*). Each of these categories, of course, encompasses a highly heterogeneous composite of occupational titles. Engineering-technical personnel in industry, for example, include not only engineers and lower-level technicians but also plant managers and other high-ranking managerial personnel. The employees category in industry includes mainly low-ranking white-collar personnel in clerical and office jobs, but also embraces some groups requiring specialized training such as economists and accountants. Broadly speaking, the contrast between workers on the one hand and employees and engineering-technical personnel on the other may be regarded as a manual-nonmanual division within the industrial labor force, with engineering-technical personnel typically representing the higher-level nonmanual occupations ("specialists"). Soviet discussions frequently treat the relative wage positions of workers and engineering-technical personnel as symbolic of the gap between manual and higher-level "mental labor" in Soviet industry.

Perhaps the most clearly established trend in Soviet occupational wage structure is the steadily diminishing relative wage advantage of engineering-technical personnel over manual workers (see Table 2). While the average earnings of the former were more than double the wages of workers in the immediate prewar period, a continuing erosion of the money wage differential between these two groups reduced the earnings advantage of engineering-technical personnel to approximately 30 percent in the early 1970s. The earnings level of the clerical and office occupations in industry designated as "employees" has been below that of manual workers throughout most of the postwar period, standing at approximately 80–85 percent of workers' wages in recent years. . . .

The changing composition of the young people who enter the labor force as manual workers has also operated to raise the earnings of the latter closer to those of engineering-technical personnel. These new workers are no longer predominantly rural migrants or even the children of rural migrants eager to obtain whatever nonagricultural jobs might be available. An increasing proportion are secondary-school graduates who aspire to admission to higher educational institutions and are reluctant to accept the many semiskilled and unskilled workers' jobs which remain to be filled in the Soviet economy. The need for industrial enterprises to attract and retain such workers has also contributed to a reduction in the relative wage advantage of engineering-technical personnel.

The traditional Soviet policy of unbalanced economic development, with its markedly unequal priorities for different economic sectors, has also had a distinctive impact on the occupational earnings differentials we are considering here. One of the familiar manifestations of the highly uneven pattern of Soviet economic development has been substantial inequalities in earnings between all occupational groups employed in heavy industry on the one hand and light and food industry on the other. Although these inequalities have recently been reduced, they remain considerable. . . . For a particularly privileged group of workers such as coal miners, average earnings are higher than those received by engineering-technical employees in most industries. Thus differences between "low" and "high" earnings do not simply mirror the difference between employment in manual workers' versus nonmanual specialists' occupations. Although our discussion has been confined to industrial employment, it should be obvious that both the working class and the intelligentsia (in its official definition as "specialists" in mental labor) are highly fragmented social entities. . . .

TABLE 2 Average Monthly Wages of Workers, Engineering-Technical Personnel, and Employees in Soviet Industry

	Average Monthly Wages (in rubles)				
Years	Workers	Engineering-Technical Personnel	Employees	Wages of Engineering-Technical Personnel in % of Workers'	Wages of Employees in % of Workers'
1955	76.2	126.4	67.8	166	89
1960	89.8	133.0	73.2	148	82
1965	101.7	148.4	85.8	146	84
1970	130.6	178.0	111.6	136	85
1973	145.6	184.9	118.5	127	81

Sources: Tsentral'noe statisticheskoe upravlenie, *Trud v SSSR,* pp. 138–39; *Narodnoe khoziaistvo SSSR v 1973 g.,* p. 586.

Urban Strata: Earnings and Living Standards

. . . The extent of female representation differs markedly among the various occupational strata. It is highest in unskilled manual jobs and the simpler office and clerical occupations, where the female share is in the neighborhood of four-fifths or more. In the Tatar Republic women also predominate among personnel in "skilled mental work," which in this area includes teachers and doctors—traditional female work roles—along with engineering and accounting positions. But the highest positions in the occupational spectrum—"managerial personnel"—as well as skilled workers' jobs, are largely staffed by men. . . .

One of the principal limitations of the Soviet studies of urban strata on which we have drawn is that they fail to distinguish the specific positions to be found at the poles of the occupational hierarchy and thus tend to understate the range of inequality in earnings. As noted earlier, the average earnings of the highest-paid strata appear to be only some two to three times those of the lowest. But this comparatively low ratio reflects, at least in part, the heterogeneous collection of jobs included in Shkaratan's top-ranking occupational stratum: "managerial personnel" (in the Leningrad studies the latter is a composite of shop chiefs, department heads, and plant directors). A closer estimate of the magnitude of the earnings gap between polar groups in these studies is suggested by the fact that individuals in the upper 10 percent of the earnings distribution of "managerial personnel" were paid some three to four times the average wages received by the lowest-skilled manual and nonmanual groups.

The range of inequality is further extended when we consider the privileged position (in terms of monetary rewards) of two "elite" groups at the upper extreme of the occupational hierarchy: directors of industrial enterprises and scientists at research institutes. Enterprise directors are frequently paid at "personal rates" (*personal'nye oklady*). These rates are literally "personal" in the sense that they are not established for a particular job title but for individuals with "outstanding knowledge and experience" in their field. Soviet sources make it clear that "personal rates" (set in excess of officially authorized "occupational rates") are a "mass phenomenon" for directors of large industrial enterprises. The earnings of scientists at research institutes may be taken as representing the economic status of an "elite" group outside industrial employment. If we examine jointly the "personal rates" of factory directors, the earnings of particular categories of Leningrad scientists, Shkaratan's occupational groups in Leningrad machinery plants, and the minimum rates of plant cleanup personnel (*uborshchitsy*), we may derive a closer approximation of the extremes in economic status which prevailed in major Soviet urban centers during the late 1960s and early 1970s (see Table 3). Such a comparison, although certainly not embracing the highest incomes received in the Soviet Union, obviously reveals a much wider range of inequality than anything we have cited thus far. Thus the monthly "personal rates" of factory directors and the earnings of department heads in scientific research institutes were some four to five times the earnings of low-skilled industrial employees and "junior" scientific personnel, and some seven to eight times the legal minimum basic wage rate (the rate at which plant cleanup personnel were paid). It is also clear that there was a wide earnings gap between the "masses" of nonmanual specialists and those in higher-level managerial and administrative positions. . . .

Thus far we have relied largely on earnings differentials as indicators of inequalities in the economic status of occupational strata. To what extent are the various strata characterized by inequalities in living standards and style-of-life differences as these are reflected in such indicators as housing characteristics and possession of selected consumer durable goods? . . . Not only the Leningrad studies but several others make it apparent that ac-

TABLE 3 Monthly Wages* of Selected Occupational Groups, Leningrad, 1967-68, 1970

Occupational Groups	Monthly Wages (in rubles)
Scientific personnel of research institute, 1967/68†	
Head of department	422
Head of laboratory	366
Senior scientific associate	261
Junior scientific associate	92
Groups employed in industrial enterprises, 1970‡	
Directors of "large industrial enterprises"	450–500
Managerial personnel	191
Engineering-technical personnel and other "specialists" in nonmanual work	132
Skilled manual workers	141
Unskilled manual workers	106
Clerical, office employees	90
Cleanup personnel	60

*All figures except for directors of enterprises and cleanup personnel are monthly earnings. For these two groups the figures are for "personal rates" and minimum basic rates respectively.

†The figures for scientists apply to the D.I. Mendeleev All-Union Scientific Research Institute of Metrology. We have taken an average of 1967 and 1968 since the figures fluctuate rather markedly from year to year.

‡The figures for all groups except directors are cited in our sources as applicable to machine-building enterprises. The figure for directors appears in a 1973 publication, and we assume it was in effect in 1970. The figure for cleanup personnel was authorized in 1968, and we assume it was still in effect in 1970.

Sources: Some of the figures are taken directly or derived from Table 2.4. [See original.] Others are from Leningradskii ordena Lenina i ordena trudovogo krasnogo znameni gosudarstvennyi universitet imeni A.A. Zhdanova, *Khozraschet v sovremennykh usloviiakh upravleniia promyshlennost'iu,* p. 110; L.E. Kunel'skii, *Zarplata, dokhody, stimulirovanie,* p. 29; S.V. Sharutin, "Some Problems of Improving the Organization of Wages of Engineering-Technical Personnel," in Uchenye zapiski kafedr obshchestvennykh nauk vuzov Leningrada, politicheskaia ekonomiia, Issue XIV, *Raspredelitel'nye otnosheniia sotsializma i ikh razvitie na sovremennom etape,* p. 132.

cess to separate apartments is considerably more frequent among nonmanual specialists than among working-class families. In some studies the inequalities in this respect are striking, certainly greater than can be accounted for by occupational differences in money earnings or per capita income. Thus a 1970 survey of "typical cities" found that more than four-fifths of engineering-technical personnel lived in separate apartments, while the comparable figure for manual workers was approximately one-third. . . .

In most of the studies available to us, information on the distribution of consumer durables among social groups appears in the form of holdings of selected goods by broad occupational categories: workers and engineering-technical personnel, or workers and several subgroups within the broad "mental labor" category, but usually excluding the upper and lower extremes of the occupational hierarchy. Evidence from a variety of such studies suggests that certain types of consumer durables were more or less uniformly distributed among these broad occupational groups in the late 1960s and early 1970s, at least within given urban communities. This common core of goods included items like sewing machines, radios, and television sets. Substantial inequalities appeared, however, in the possession of other items, particularly equipment designed to aid in housework: washing machines, vacuum cleaners, refrigerators. For example, in the Urals studies of industrial enterprises in the late 1960s (the findings in other areas could be used to illustrate the same point), the proportions of manual workers owning these items were reported as follows: refrigerators—20 percent, washing machines—57 percent, vacuum cleaners—11 percent; among technical specialists the proportions were 56 percent, 82 percent, and 37 percent, respectively.

Such inequalities, were not a simple reflection of differences between social groups in money earnings or income per capita. The fact is that manual and nonmanual strata—particularly when the latter category is confined to employees with higher education—are often distinct cultural groups whose differing value systems are reflected in differential patterns of consumption of goods other than "necessities," even when their income levels are essentially similar. . . .

The increasing accessibility and variety of consumer goods, housing facilities, and "cultural" goods have created new opportunities for social differentiation, opportunities for translating even reduced inequalities in monetary rewards and substantial differences in educational levels and "value orientations" (to use a favorite Soviet term) into distinct modes of life. It is here that the contrasting characteristics of manual strata and nonmanual "specialists" may assume the form of a major social division in urban communities.

A Note on Rural Income Differentiation

The relatively depressed economic status of the Soviet rural population as a whole, and of the collective farm peasantry in particular, have long been recognized in both Western and Soviet literature on urban-rural differentials in living standards. But to some extent the focus on the relative backwardness of the Soviet rural community has obscured the existence of substantial social and economic differentiation in the countryside. To state the obvious—whatever may have been the case in the early years of collectivization—the Soviet rural community is not now a homogeneous mass living in equally shared deprivation. Despite the socialization or "cooperativization" of land and the comparatively limited scope for the division of labor inherent in agricultural operations, the Soviet countryside is characterized by large inequalities in economic status rooted in differing work roles in the production process. . . .

Even when farm managers cannot be distinguished as a separate group, a considerable spread is apparent between the earnings of the top and bottom of the occupational ladder. In most of the areas studied the earnings of the highest-paid occupational groups (managers and specialists combined, or personnel in "skilled mental labor") were more than three times the earnings of farm laborers; in the studies of the Belorussian and Tatar Republic collective farms the earnings ratios of these groups approached 4:1. . . .

Some idea of the spread in earnings between the mass of farm laborers and this managerial group is provided by information on the average yearly pay of collective farm chairmen and common laborers in the Ukraine in 1970. The earnings of these groups and several others in the collective farm work force were reported as follows (in rubles per year):

collective farm chairmen	2,700
chief specialists	1,935
work brigade leaders, heads of livestock departments	1,268
agronomists	1,260
tractor operators, motor vehicle drivers	1,081
office and store-keeping personnel	780
common laborers	531

Thus the "socialized sector" (or in its official designation, the "cooperative sector") of Soviet agriculture admittedly generates an earnings spread on the order of 5:1 between its top managerial stratum and the mass of the farm work force in laborers' jobs, as well as a highly differentiated earnings structure between "middle management" and technical specialists on the one hand and farm laborers. . . .

Although we have focused chiefly on money earnings, available evidence on strata differences in material conditions of life only reinforces the picture of deep divisions in the economic status of rural social groups. Thus farm administrators and specialists (in a Moldavian study of 1970) were reported to have roomier and better-equipped housing quarters for their smaller families. In some of the areas studied by Arutiunian in 1967 there were striking inequalities in the possession of household amenities. For example, in state farms of the Krasnodar Territory refrigerators were owned by 44 percent of managers and specialists and 4 percent of laborers; in Kalinin Region the figures for ownership of washing machines were 69 percent and 11 percent, respectively. The frequency of ownership of these items on collective farms was generally lower, but the degree of inequality was of the same order or even greater. The ownership of TV sets among rural strata was also highly uneven (generally 3:1 or more in favor of managers and specialists). Obviously the distribution of these few items in a scattering of sample studies is a crude indicator of differences in overall levels of living, but it is sufficient to illustrate the highly unequal distribution of symbols of recent progress in the material well-being of the Soviet countryside. It seems clear that inequalities in both money earnings and living standards parallel inequalities in power over the organization of the work process. This is one meaning of "distribution in accordance with labor."

Chapter 21

MOTIVATIONS AND LIMITATIONS

Some years ago the editor of *Problems of Communism* stated that "within recent years the USSR has made notable progress, as compared with the past, in meeting some of the basic needs of its long-deprived population." He then posed a series of questions to which Alec Nove addressed himself and which provided the basis for a number of the ensuing comments. It seems appropriate to reproduce those questions:

> What is the significance of the Soviet leaders' seeming preoccupation with material welfare? How is it to be explained? Is the regime truly abandoning its traditional overwhelming emphasis on heavy industrial growth, which has for many decades reduced the satisfaction of consumer needs to a place—at best—of secondary importance? If the proportion of consumer goods vs. producers' goods is indeed changing in favor of the former, if we are witnessing a shift from "socialist accumulation" to "socialist abundance," does this not of necessity imply a fundamental transformation of the economic structure of the Soviet Union, as well as of its political system and political goals? Or are we to conclude that a totalitarian system is quite compatible with a relatively "enlightened" consumer-oriented economy?

In the following article, Robert J. Osborn considers whether welfare in the Soviet Union has been "a function of other purposes," particularly military purposes, or an understandable attempt to balance military capacity and consumer satisfaction. In the final essay, Harry Schwartz asks and answers: "What's Communism? Is It Being Achieved?" While much of this material may on its face appear dated, in your editor's judgment it retains its essential cogency. Most of what is said of Khrushchev would apply to his successors.

Guns and Butter

Robert J. Osborn

Western theories of totalitarianism have treated welfare as a function of other purposes rather than as a purpose in its own right. One of the best known of these theories, that of Carl J. Friedrich and Zbigniew K. Brzezinski, relegated economic goals of every variety to a position far subordinate to the overriding cluster or syndrome of political goals. The vitality of the industrial process, they wrote, is the key to political success, and the distribution of rewards is of minor significance, for "what is decisive is the overpowering reality of totalitarian central control by the dictator and his party."[1] Promises of future abundance—the welfare component of a totalitarian regime's chiliastic claims—are instrumental in establishing and building the regime, but are not in themselves a goal or operating principle. W.W. Rostow, the economist and former White House policy planner, pointed out that a minimum level of economic welfare is necessary in order to maintain a labor force and avoid any rebellion which might result from desperation. The same considerations, he concluded, may lead to a rising level of welfare, the "increasing minimum" which is necessary in order to sustain growth of a type which was at first achieved by "mining" existing human resources to the utmost.[2] . . .

Alec Nove, a British economist, pointed out that judging consumption to be merely instrumental to heavy industry and weapons simply is not meaningful because this begs the question. "One could reverse it," he wrote, "and say that they devote as much as possible to improving the citizen's lot, subject to the necessary investment in heavy industry and weapons. . . . Is the glass half-full or half-empty?"[3]

Alfred G. Meyer of the University of Michigan argued that the Soviet industrialization drive has commingled means with ends. Referring to communist systems generally, he singled out "entrepreneurship as the overriding motive force of Communist rule; that means that the chief aim (or, perhaps, the chief effect) of communism is perhaps the promotion of industrialization." Secondary aims and effects include "strict consumer austerity, dictatorial rule, and an ambitious attempt to reeducate peasants and other preindustrial cultures for the twentieth century and the industrial way of life." These aims change in time, of course, and in the case of the Soviet Union Meyer even stands prepared to argue that there has been in fact "a succession of political systems differing from each other in purpose, structure, and functioning."[4] . . .

Why were these choices made, and why are they being upheld over decades? Here Rostow shifted from a substantive criterion to a procedural criterion: High national security allocations can be sustained only as long as the Soviet leaders are able to convince themselves and their population of "the case for hostility, for the secret police, and for austerity"; but in the face of an effective arms control agreement "the case for democracy and welfare would be overwhelming." Full entry into the age of high mass consumption, for which Soviet society is now technically, educationally, and psychologically ready, is delayed ("the regime is straining to hold the dam") because the leadership is trying to

Reprinted, with permission, from Robert J. Osborn, Soviet Social Policies: Welfare, Equality, and Community, *© The Dorsey Press, Homewood, Ill., 1970, pp. 18, 22-24, 25.*

convert its present economic maturity into world primacy. The leadership's choice represents not only an unnecessary denial of the goals of welfare and/or mass consumption, according to Rostow, but an economic strategy appropriate only to the transition from the earlier "takeoff" stage to the stage of economic maturity.[5]

Here too, the reader who seeks clear comparisons of national purpose in a cross-national comparison of defense expenditure levels and the share of defense expenditure in the GNP is invited to look at the figures.[6] He will soon realize that information about defense expenditures by other industrialized nations outside of the two great powers does not give a meaningful background against which to measure these two giants. They are in a league of their own, and the one clear policy which emerges from a look at long-term Soviet military expenditures is the Soviet Union's determination to stay in this league. If one thing stands out in these figures it is that the nations which have spent more than 10 percent of their GNP on national defense are mainly the smaller nations whose security has been under some kind of direct threat. During the 1960s the two nuclear giants followed next in this list with expenditures of 8 to 10 percent, which if correct would mean a Soviet arms budget considerably smaller than that of the United States. If one takes instead the proportion of GNP per capita which is spent on defense, the United States is in the lead according to most calculations of Soviet GNP and military expenditure levels. The Soviet Union would not have equalled the U.S. level in this respect even by spending an overall 20 percent of GNP on armaments, which Rostow suggests was being spent in the 1950s. Any yardstick one chooses is ambiguous, therefore.

Another criticism of Soviet defense expenditures is that Moscow has been striving to equal our defense outlays in absolute terms, using a GNP which by the mid-1960s had just attained half the size of the American GNP (by most American calculations) or at most was a bit over three-fifths of ours (by official Soviet calculations). It is one thing, the argument goes, for a country to maintain a first-class nuclear striking force which can afford great consumer prosperity on top of it; it is another thing for a country to try to equal this force which in so doing has to depress its people's living standards far below the economy's potential for maintaining satisfactory standards. Here the reader is invited to take still another look at the GNPs of other countries to see which ones devote an even greater portion of their output to armaments than do the two titans. To try to pass judgment on their allocation decisions is to try to pass judgment on who is justified in feeling very nervous about national security: objective criteria just do not exist. As between the two superpowers, the search for a justification for the present military expenditures of both or either must start with the old insoluble problem of who started the cold war. So what a judgment based on the Soviet Union's smaller GNP boils down to is that nations less rich than the United States have no business trying to rival us in military strength.

Americans are probably more tempted than others to see the choice between guns and butter as a clear choice resting on clear alternatives. Our attitude is influenced by the fact that until World War II, our security choices did not involve drastic consequences one way or another. For most of the history of our country, up to 1941, U.S. leaders were free to choose or reject important military outlays: a two-ocean navy, the geographical extension of the U.S. security interests into Latin America and the Pacific, and the defense of Western Europe during 1914–17 and again in 1939–41. The alternative to these choices was not insecurity in any immediate sense, but only the restriction of our security concept to the safety afforded by two oceans. . . .

Soviet commentators contend that the military establishments of a number of Western powers were used from 1917 on to deny the Soviet Union normal economic relations with much of the world's territory. In their view, post-1945 Soviet political gains can justifiably be sustained through high security outlays in support of expanded economic ties. Soviet promotion of the "camp of socialism" idea from 1946 on has embraced the idea of a socialist sphere of trade through which the Soviet Union could overcome its handicaps in maintaining economic relations with the nonsocialist world.

For all these reasons, no sure criterion of national purposes may be found in the familiar assumption that a nation which greatly enlarges its military outlays at a time when its security is not immediately threatened is choosing military power as its primary purpose. It would be safer to assume that the value choices which great powers make have sometimes been choices between lesser or greater effort in enlarging their resources in *both* military capacity and consumer satisfactions. . . . In short, Rostow's charge that the Soviet Union made a senseless, externally needless and internally disadvantageous choice in devoting a substantial part of its GNP to military purposes, must remain an impression rather than a verifiable statement.

Notes

1. *C.J. Friedrich and Z.K. Brzezinski,* Totalitarian Dictatorship and Autocracy, *2d ed. (New York: Praeger, 1956), p. 244.*
2. *W.W. Rostow et al.,* The Dynamics of Soviet Society *(New York: Mentor, 1954), pp. 80–89.*
3. *Alec Nove,* Was Stalin Really Necessary? *(London: Allen and Unwin, 1964), p. 234.*
4. *Alfred G. Meyer, "The Comparative Study of Communist Political Systems,"* Slavic Review *XXXVI:1 (March, 1967), pp. 6–7.*
5. *Rostow, op. cit., 1960, pp. 132–33.*
6. *These are handily summarized for the 1950s in Russett, 1964, pp. 79–80, and for the 1960s in Institute for Strategic Studies,* The Military Balance 1968-69, *pp. 55–56.*

Social Welfare in the USSR

Alec Nove

As some critics see it, the Soviet state is exclusively an organ of oppression. The motivations of its leaders, they believe, are to be found solely in the pursuit of world revolution, of national aggrandizement, of personal power—or of all these at once. The attitude of the Soviet leaders toward their own people is often represented as if it were mainly in-

Alec Nove is the author of numerous studies on the Soviet economy. This selection is from "Social Welfare in the USSR," Problems of Communism, *vol. IX (Jan.-Feb. 1960), pp. 1–10. By permission.*

spired by the objective of keeping the mass of Soviet citizens on the lowest possible living standard consistent with the necessity of providing minimum work incentives.

Hence such critics are inclined to view all Soviet measures which seem to increase public welfare as ''concessions'' wrung from a reluctant regime by irresistible force of circumstance or popular pressure. It is but a short step from this view to the conclusion that such measures are, in themselves, proof of the regime's weakness or instability. If more was done to improve welfare in the first years after Stalin's death, these critics might argue, it was only because the struggle for power among Stalin's successors was undecided, and because the police apparatus had lost much of its capacity to intimidate. Inversely, now that Khrushchev has become unquestioned boss, they should logically expect a return to the old ways.

The purpose of the present article is to inquire into the validity of such interpretations of the ''welfare'' aspect of Soviet rule. But it is necessary first of all to define the area of discussion. To take a negative approach, the author does not propose to discuss such matters as wage rates and consumer goods production. It is acknowledged fact that real wages in the Soviet Union have been rising slowly but steadily, that peasant incomes and retail trade turnover have gone up, and that the present Soviet leadership has declared its intention to continue this process through the period of the Seven-Year Plan (1959–65). It is also true that the upward trend in these areas is highly relevant to welfare in the general sense and should be duly noted. In the present paper, however, attention will be concentrated rather on activities of a more direct ''public welfare'' nature, i.e., on the various social services (health, education, etc.), on housing and such other state measures as affect the everyday life of Soviet citizens. . . .

*[**Editor's note:** Because so much of the statistical data on welfare benefits in the USSR are covered in the preceding chapters, the portion of the Nove article dealing with such data, which appeared in earlier editions of this book, has been omitted.]*

Motivations of Recent Policy

This, then, is the actual Soviet record in social welfare. It suggests, first of all, that even under Stalin's rule much attention was paid to the expansion and improvement of health services and education, and fairly generous rules adopted in regard to such things as sickness benefits and paid vacations. In the late 1930s, however, some steps backward were taken, particularly affecting hours of labor, maternity leave, and the worker's right to change his occupation, and it was only after Stalin's death that moves got underway to restore the conditions which had prevailed until the mid-1930s. In the last few years, the record shows, much more has been or is being done to improve old-age pensions and disability pay, to reduce working hours, to build more housing, and to provide more consumer services, even though the Soviet citizen certainly still has—and probably will continue to have—much to complain about.

Only the willfully blind will refuse to take all this seriously. But more than *what* has been done, the vital question is *why* has it been done, and what significance, if any, do these developments have from the standpoint of assessing the nature of the Soviet system? No single, definitive answer is possible of course, but here, for what they may be worth, are a few thoughts on the subject.

While it is arguable that the Soviet rulers do as little as possible for the citizen in order to devote the largest possible share of national resources to heavy industry and weapons, such a formulation begs the question. One could reverse it and say that they devote as much as possible to improving the citizen's lot, subject to the necessary investment in heavy industry and weapons—which would sound better from the Soviet point of view, but mean equally little. Is the glass half-full or half-empty? In any case, neither formulation explains why more is being done for the Soviet citizen today than in the past.

One relevant factor may simply be that the USSR is now powerful enough economically to permit the diversion of an increasing amount of resources to the satisfaction of the needs of its citizens, without curtailing ambitious plans for the expansion of heavy industry. To carry out the first Five-Year Plan (1928–32), Stalin found it necessary to reduce living standards drastically, but it would be foolish to take this to be what lawyers term "evidence of system." It is obviously no part of Communist ideology to make people poorer; on the contrary, communism lays great stress on abundance. The "abundance" of communism may well be—in the author's opinion it definitely is—a meaningless, even nonsensical concept, but it surely was the intention of all Soviet leaders, including even Stalin, to raise living standards at some future date, once the painful sacrifices of "primitive accumulation" were no longer necessary. The Soviet citizen was, and still is, denied adequate housing, but it would be a mistake to conclude that the leadership believes in bad housing in the same sense that it believes in the undesirability of private peasant enterprise. Soviet leaders have been willing to sacrifice a generation, to neglect urgent needs for years, but it would be patently foolish to represent them as favoring poverty and hardship as such. They surely would concede, and even advocate, improvements in popular welfare if doing so would not interfere with the pursuit of their basic aims.

Before leaving the subject of ideology, two other points are worth making. One is the enormous attention which Communists always pay to education: however they may twist its content to suit their purposes, they have invariably lavished resources on its development, whether under Stalin or under his successors. It is true that this effort is due, in part, to the urgent need of developing technical skills, but this is far from the whole explanation. Indeed, the promise made at the 20th Congress to extend full-time secondary education to all went far beyond practical necessities, and its implementation even tended to aggravate social tensions, which was one reason for Khrushchev's subsequent counter-reforms.

The second point is the great importance, from the standpoint of Communist ideology, of appearing to be doing something to improve the lot of the working masses. Even when nothing or little is actually being done, the party leaders must of necessity claim to be acting in that direction. Too great a contrast between words and deeds, however, can lead to general cynicism, as in fact it did under Stalin. Khrushchev is now engaged in an evident effort to revive the fervor of the party and to replace passive bureaucratism with initiative. It is reasonable to suppose, therefore, that with this aim in view he wants to show that the party is genuinely doing something to carry out its promises to the people.

One example of this ideological influence is the regime's insistence, for political reasons, on cheap bread and low rents even when these are economically irrational and administratively inconvenient. Thus, Khrushchev recently reasserted the *political impossibility* of raising bread prices despite the fact that, at these prices, it pays to feed bread rather than regular cattle feed to private livestock. In short, cheap bread is essential to the party's outward picture of itself.

The Role of Incentives

Other factors, too, have a bearing on the regime's attitude in regard to welfare. For a number of reasons too complex to be analyzed here, the functioning of the Soviet economy is coming to depend more on incentives and less on compulsion. Prisoners can be kept working even when forced to live in overcrowded barracks on a minimum diet, but unless there is some emergency to spur them, free men work better when they can expect to live better by greater effort. To achieve the leadership's ambitious plans, better work, more efficient organization, more initiative at the grass roots are all objective necessities. To some extent, of course, this was also true under Stalin and was acted upon, as evidenced by the lavish rewards given to Stakhanovites. But few analysts question that there has been a shift toward much *greater* reliance on incentives in recent years, paralleled by a scaling down of the number and powers of the police. To give but one of many examples of how this works in practice, the author, during a tour of the Soviet Union, was shown a new apartment block in Kiev, which he was told was being erected by the building industry for its own workers because, now that they could change employment without incurring criminal penalties, they would not remain in the industry "unless we replaced the barracks and hostels with decent housing."

Of course, people's attitudes and expectations are relevant to the efficacy of incentives as well as to political stability. The more the Soviet Union boasts of its great technical progress, of its Sputniks and moon rockets, of its equality with or superiority over the United States in weapons, the more impatient its citizens become with their backward living conditions, and the less reasonable it seems to them that nothing drastic is done to improve them. Confronted by such a popular state of mind, an intelligent leadership is likely to see the wisdom of taking some action to satisfy it.

The increasing range of contacts between Soviet citizens and foreigners plays a dual role in this process. Many more Soviet citizens are now learning at first or second hand how the other side lives, and this affects their own expectations. Then, too, with the increasing flow of foreign visitors to Russia, it must certainly appear politically advantageous to the leadership to impress them with higher standards of living. This is much more than a matter of impressing unsophisticated tourists from the West, who can if necessary be fobbed off with Potemkin villages. Much more important are the thousands of students and others from underdeveloped countries, as well as from the Soviet Union's own allies, who actually spend some time living among the Russians and cannot help learning the truth. Khrushchev is well aware that relative living standards will play an important role in the world impact of the two opposed systems.

Some Points of Logic

For all its simplicity, one should not overlook still another point: Khrushchev wants to be popular. He may genuinely care to reduce poverty, or he may be acting on the basis of cold political calculation—it does not matter which. He may even aspire to go down in history as the man who brought prosperity to the Soviet people—on the foundations laid by his grim predecessor. There are some Western observers who seem to shy away from even considering such motives possible, as if to do so would label them as pro-Soviet. This is clearly an illogical attitude. What is primarily objectionable about the Soviet system is its totalitarian character, its lack of intellectual and political freedom; and this character is not directly affected by the shortening of working hours or the provision of a separate apartment for every family.

It is indeed true that certain features of the Soviet economy are inconsistent with the proper satisfaction of consumer demand. It may also be true that the ultimate logic of a better-educated and materially more satisfied citizenry is incompatible with the totalitarian one-party state.

Why the Changes?

Solomon M. Schwarz

What is this force which, especially in the last decade, has so deeply influenced the development of the Soviet Union and—to remain within the frame of Mr. Nove's topic—has made the improvement of public welfare so necessary and, indeed, so unavoidable? The answer may be reduced to a simple formula: *the USSR has become a modern industrial state, but the great majority of its working population lived until recently, and to a lesser degree continues to live today, under conditions characteristic of economically backward countries.* It is this simple yet fundamental fact—perhaps *the greatest internal contradiction of Soviet life*—which in the past few years has, with "irresistible force," influenced the entire course of development in the USSR. And it is this contradiction which has engendered not only economic and social but, to some degree, even political adjustments to the conditions and requirements of a modern industrial society.

Again confining our analysis to Mr. Nove's topic, it is important to point out that a modern industrial state can function properly only if it possesses a working class that enjoys a relatively high standard of living, tolerable working conditions, and access to educational opportunities. Ineluctably, a modern working class will also demand more and more freedom. These are not merely social imperatives finding their expression in social tensions and pressures: they are also economic imperatives—that is, necessary preconditions for the required rise in the quality and productivity of labor. It is these economic imperatives which, as will be shown, have played the most important role in recent developments.

A few examples will illustrate this point. They are taken not from the field of social welfare *stricto sensu*—i.e., not from the field of "fringe benefits," in popular American terminology—but from the general area of labor relations, where the causalities of the development appear more clearly.

Throughout the 1930s, that is, during the first decade of intensive Soviet industrialization, Russian workers were subjected to extraordinary strains which became even more exacerbated during World War II. To further industrial development under general conditions of misery and deprivation, the Soviet government provided relatively better conditions for a small number of highly skilled workers, thus in effect creating a privileged class at the expense of the vast majority of the population. The policy of extreme wage-differentiation, which would have been unthinkable in any advanced industrial country, was for many years hailed as a true expression of socialism in action—in contrast, of course, to the "capitalist wage policy," supposedly based on the "levelling" principle. In the last decade, however, this wage policy became more and more of a handicap to further industrial development, making impossible a rational organization of labor. Its continuation caused a creeping demoralization, an increasing tendency to resort to ruses and stratagems of all sorts—in short, a situation harmful to labor and management alike.[1] In 1956 this unique "socialist" wage policy was finally buried, and the Soviet authorities set about reorganiz-

Solomon Schwarz is the author of The Jews in the Soviet Union *and of* Labor in the Soviet Union. *The selection is from* Problems of Communism, *vol. IX (Jan.-Feb. 1960), pp. 10–12. By permission.*

ing the wage system, cutting down the extraordinary high earnings of some privileged workers, and raising the wages of the underprivileged ones. . . .

One more example. Under Stalin, Soviet labor relations came to be based not on a free labor contract but on compulsion. The development in the direction of greater compulsion was climaxed by a decree of the Supreme Soviet of the USSR, dated June 26, 1940, which deprived employees of the right to terminate their employment of their own volition, invested managers with virtually unrestricted power to hire and fire at will, and made not only unauthorized departure but even lateness in reporting for work (by as little as twenty minutes!) subject to criminal punishment. In the postwar years, however, the Soviet leadership came to realize the impossibility—and, from a practical standpoint, the undesirability—of keeping the entire working population in a straitjacket, and it gradually relaxed its labor practices—characteristically, without issuing any open instructions to this effect. It was not until three years after Stalin's death, in April 1956, that the basic provisions of the 1940 decree were finally rescinded.[2] To quote Mr. Nove, "the functioning of the Soviet economy is coming to depend more on incentives and less on compulsion." This, indeed, is the essence of *any* modern industrialism, to which the Soviet system can no longer claim exception.

The need to adjust Soviet realities to the imperatives of modern industrialism is thus the *main* cause of the recent development of social welfare in the USSR. Yet one more factor should also be mentioned, namely, *the change of generations,* the importance of which must not be underrated. Those who were children at the beginning of World War II are now in their early and middle thirties. Those who were in their teens are now in their late thirties. Together with their juniors, they comprise the most active segment of the working population, the great majority in the newly developed eastern areas. With the exception of the 1948–53 period, which embraced the so-called *"Zhdanovshchina,"* the hysterical "vigilance" campaign of 1952, and the ominous "doctors' plot" in January 1953, the Soviet youth and young adult population of today have grown up in a relatively relaxed political atmosphere. The horrors of the prewar decade are relatively unfamiliar to them. In their feelings, in their thoughts, in their attitudes they differ considerably from their elders—those who were psychologically mutilated during the long years of unmitigated terror. The urgent needs and demands of these young people—voiced or still in the process of germination—create those social pressures which, in addition to the economic imperatives described above, are exercising such a profound influence on the evolving Soviet system.

Notes

1. *On this subject, see "Blat Is Higher than Stalin!," by Joseph Berliner,* Problems of Communism, *January–February 1954.*
2. *A thorough examination of this development will be found in "Recent Trends in Soviet Labor Policy," by Jerzy G. Gliksman,* Problems of Communism, *July–August, 1956.*

Facts and Polemics

Bertram D. Wolfe

The Historical Framework

Most writing on the Soviet era suffers from a lack of consideration of the earlier history of Russia; the history of the postwar upsurge of other war-ruined countries such as Germany and Japan; and the history of industrialization in general.

Thus our whole perspective on the rate of recovery and industrial expansion in post-World War II Russia is altered if we stop to consider the faster rate of recovery and expansion of, let us say, Germany and Japan during the same period.

Or again, in examining the Soviet Union's rate of industrial growth, we get a fresh perspective if we examine the history of the sudden march of other countries into industrialism. Thus in the period 1860–1900, Russian industrial productivity increased more than seven times, German almost five times, French two and one-half times, English a little over twice. When we attempt to evaluate Soviet industrial growth at various periods, we must regard it in the context of these comparative figures.

It is no less interesting to examine the standard of living during the industrial upsurge in Tsarist Russia. There were two distinct periods so far as labor was concerned. In the decade of the 1890s, the upsurge of industry was accompanied, and in fact partly achieved, by a fall in the standard of living. But in the next decade, the still more stormy advance was accompanied by a *rise* in the standard of living. May this not be characteristic of the earlier and later phases of industrialism under any sociopolitical system?

The same applies to such "welfare" features as health. When Mr. Nove retreats from the comparative figure on doctors (of little meaning, incidentally, unless we define the degree of training) to the sounder "nevertheless a great deal has certainly been done to spread hygiene, combat epidemics, and reduce infant mortality," is it not incumbent on us to remember that medical progress is fatefully easier and cheaper than industrial progress, and that this generalization on hygiene, epidemics and infant mortality applies even to the most underdeveloped countries?[1]

Again, does not advancing industrialism—under any "system"—require more literate, better-trained workers? In the Khrushchev era, for the first time in the history of the Soviet Union, there is a shortage of the rural "reserve" population which hitherto has made up any deficiency of capital investment per worker and productivity per worker. Does this not make mandatory more capital investment per head? And more "investment" in the training of "human capital"? Do not these questions on the historical framework of industrialization take precedence over an examination of the special role of totalitarianism in shaping industrialization?

When Mr. Nove comes to the proportions of the national product devoted to consumers' goods on the one hand and "power" goods (means of production plus military might) on the other, his question ("Is the glass of water half-full or half-empty?") is any-

Bertram D. Wolfe is author of Three Who Made a Revolution; Khrushchev and Stalin's Ghost; *and* Communist Totalitarianism. *This selection is from* Problems of Communism, *vol. IX (Jan.–Feb. 1960), pp. 12–13. By permission.*

thing but helpful. For if we compare a society that devotes three-fourths of its GNP to consumption and one-fourth to expansion of production with a society that reverses these fractions, then the question of whether the glass is one-fourth full or three-fourths full is far from meaningless to those who drink.

Totalitarianism and the Motives of the Rulers

Mr. Nove says that the "purpose" of the article is to inquire into the validity of some interpretations of the interrelations between the sector devoted to "welfare" and the sector devoted to the expansion of power. But some of the "interpretations" he chooses seem to border on the fatuous.

Thus his first target (sentence one) is those "who see the Soviet state as exclusively an organ of oppression." But is it not ABC that we are dealing with the greatest managerial and ownership state in all history? If there are any serious students of Soviet affairs who do not know that, do we need all of Mr. Nove's statistical ammunition on "welfare" when we can dispose of it by the simple reminder that a state which seeks to own and run everything must be primarily an organ of the administration of the economy itself?

In sum, I find the factual material which Mr. Nove has assembled highly useful. His interpretation of the facts he has assembled is weakened by the failure to put them into the perspective of the history of modern industrialization, and of the features common to industrializing societies whatever their political form—republic, monarchy, limited despotism and totalist despotism.

As for the polemical framework, it is scarcely worthy of the material he has been at pains to assemble. The analysis of the nature of totalitarianism is an even more difficult subject, and one on which far less progress has been made than on the analysis of industrialization—or, for that matter, on the problems of how much of the Soviet product is devoted to the expansion of "power," and how much to "welfare." Indeed, it is even difficult to decide such a simple question as the degree to which such a "welfare" feature as health is also a "power" problem, for does not any modern state need healthy soldiers, schooled workingmen, and at least some measure of mass acceptance of things as they are?

Note

1. *This is the source of the "population explosion" in underdeveloped countries.*

Reply to My Critics

Alec Nove

I am very grateful to those who criticized my article "Social Welfare in the USSR." . . .

I did not examine "the historical framework of industrialization," or specifically "the special role of totalitarianism in shaping industrialization," to the apparent dissatisfaction of Mr. Wolfe (from whom I quote these phrases), because I was not asked to write about them, though I do indeed take these things very seriously in their proper context.

His more relevant criticisms puzzle me, because I very largely agree with him. He accuses me of failing to see that totalitarian "power" considerations could be consistent with increased attention to welfare. Yet the basic implication of my entire article . . . was that a shift to more welfare can be explained "without assuming a basic change in the political and ideological motivations of the ruling Communist Party and its leaders." Certainly, given the general situation confronting them and the various technical, social and political factors involved, the party leadership is wise, from its own point of view, in sharply increasing welfare appropriations. To say so is the clear purpose of the final sentence of my article. Then what is Mr. Wolfe attacking? The dichotomy between "power" and "welfare" is not of my making; it is surprisingly common among the less thoughtful critics of Soviet policies. It is certainly not "bordering on the fatuous" (his words) to point out that many in the West still believe the propaganda stereotype to the effect that Soviet leaders pursue power to the constant and deliberate detriment of welfare. It is important to note that this interpretation leads logically to seeing the provision of more pensions or houses, or relaxation of labor restrictions, as *signs of political weakness,* because they are taken to represent reluctant yielding to pressure from below. This view is thought by many to be held to this day by Dr. Adenauer, and to have been held by Mr. Dulles. I believe these arguments to be wrong, and note with pleasure that Mr. Wolfe agrees with me.

I am also delighted to find Mr. Wolfe saying that the Soviet state "must be primarily an organ of the administration of the economy itself." If I had made so sweeping a generalization, I would have been accused of *déformation professionnelle,* perhaps not altogether unjustly. Mr. Wolfe also criticizes me for failing to see that increased welfare goes with developing industrialization. Yes, to some extent it does, and references to this (*e.g.*, in connection with education) did appear in my article. Firstly, however, the fact remains that in relation to national income the Soviet Union spends far more on health, education and so on, than highly industrialized Western countries do, and it is therefore wrong to assume that her present rate of spending is in some sense economically predetermined, regardless of political decision or system of government; secondly, *pace* Rostow, it is possible to argue that the USSR, as distinct from Western countries, can hold down living standards despite achieving a high level of industrialization—therefore we cannot assume what must be proved; and, thirdly, long-term tendencies inherent in establishing a rela-

This selection is from Problems of Communism, *vol. IX (May–June 1960), pp. 49–51. By permission.*

tionship between industrial society and welfare cannot help to explain an important shift in policy of which the most significant developments were concentrated into the years 1956–59. Less "basic," more prosaic, reasons must be considered. . . .

I have very little disagreement with Mr. Solomon Schwarz. He stresses the tension caused by the contrast between backward living standards and modern industrial technology, and indeed I made the same point in my paper. The resultant social attitudes and expectations are part of the situation to which the Soviet leadership seeks to adapt its policy. In that sense, there is indeed a species of unorganized pressure from below, since failure to respond would lead to tension and perhaps trouble. Yet the process is rightly described by Mr. Schwarz as due more to what he calls "economic imperatives": the leaders find that it is necessary and right, from their point of view, to act in the way they do. In *this* sense, they do not make "concessions," which suggests a forced compromise, any more than a sensible general who feeds his men properly makes a "compromise" with the troops. . . .

Whether improved living standards would contribute to lessening of tension and of totalitarian ideology is a matter which [some] rule out of court. Indeed, the experience of Nazi Germany shows that an educated and technically advanced country can be totalitarian. This disposes of anyone's delusion about some *inevitable* development toward freedom, but surely there is more to be said. If Soviet totalitarianism is historically connected with social tensions, if the size and power of the police had some relation to the scale on which people were compelled to do things they disliked, then the increased attention to welfare and the decrease in the powers of the police are also connected. It needs fewer police to supervise an increase than a decrease in wages. While none of this leads necessarily to the solution of any international or internal problem, evolution in this direction can surely be taken seriously as a ground for hope. . . .

Undeniably, Khrushchev has a greater possibility of neglecting public opinion, or of molding it, than has any Western statesman. Undoubtedly, in some last-resort situation, he would sacrifice nonpriority objectives to the survival of party power. But, looking at the present situation realistically, is it really useful to say that he could at any time reverse his welfare policies? Aside from anything else, why on earth should he?

What's Communism? Is It Being Achieved?

Harry Schwartz

"The Congress of the Builders of Communism" is the name the Soviet press has given to the Twenty-second Congress of the Soviet Communist Party. No Communist party gathering anywhere has ever before been labeled as being of such high importance from the point of view of Communist ideology. The reason is simple: no previous Communist party conclave has ever met explicitly to consider and approve a program which promises specifically to build the ideal Communist society of tomorrow. The meeting had as the central item on its agenda the draft of a new party program promising exactly that, and ending with the words:

"The party solemnly proclaims: the present generation of Soviet people shall live under communism!"

The historic nature of that promise deserves to be underlined. For more than a century Marxists have used the concept of the Communist Utopia purely as a propaganda weapon to attack the capitalist system and to win converts. Now the party that rules one of the two richest and most powerful nations on earth has gone on record that it intends to deliver the goods—to realize ideal communism—within the lifetime of most present-day Soviet citizens.

All this presents an occasion to explore two key questions: What do the Russians mean by "communism"? How close are they to attaining that state?

At the very outset, one is struck by a curious fact: for all the many decades of discussion and propaganda about communism, nowhere is there any clear, simple and generally accepted blueprint explaining exactly what a Communist society would be like. And the more one searches the literature, the more one suspects that there has been a kind of unspoken agreement among Communist theoreticians through the generations to leave the idea as vague as possible.

Karl Marx never supplied any detailed scheme in the millions of words he wrote. In "The Communist Manifesto," for example, he began by asserting, "A specter is haunting Europe—the specter of communism," but he never bothered to define communism beyond the statement that the "theory of the Communists may be summed up in the single sentence: abolition of private property."

The nearest Marx ever came to a definition was in his "Critique of the Gotha Program," in which he talked of two stages of communism, the first immediately after a successful revolution, and the second or higher phase, which he described this way:

> In a higher phase of Communist society, after the enslaving subordination of individuals under division of labor, and therewith also the antithesis between mental and

Harry Schwartz is an economist, specializing on Soviet affairs, and author of Russia's Soviet Economy *and of* The Red Phoenix. *The article originally appeared in* The New York Times Magazine, *Oct. 15, 1961, and is reproduced with the permission of the author and the newspaper.*

> physical labor has vanished; after labor, from a mere means of life, has itself become the prime necessity of life; after the productive forces have also increased with the all-round development of the individual and all the springs of cooperative wealth flow more abundantly—only then can the narrow horizon of bourgeois rights be fully left behind and society inscribe on its banners: from each according to his ability, to each according to his needs!

For almost a century that brief paragraph has dominated all discussion of communism—a system whose propaganda image has been presented as the final realization of abundance, equality, justice and freedom for all. Such vagueness had the advantage of permitting each individual to read into the idea of communism all that he personally hoped and wanted for a better future. . . .

The new Communist party program in the Soviet Union . . . shares the vagueness shown by Marx. It states:

> Communism is a classless social system with one form of public ownership of the means of production and full social equality of all members of society; under it, the all-round development of people will be accompanied by the growth of productive forces through continuous progress in science and technology; all sources of public wealth will gush forth abundantly, and the great principle "From each according to his ability, to each according to his needs" will be implemented. Communism is a highly organized society of free, socially conscious working people in which public self-government will be established, a society in which labor for the good of society will become the prime vital requirement of everyone, a necessity recognized by one and all, and the ability of each person will be employed to the greatest benefit of the people.
>
> A high degree of Communist consciousness, industry, discipline and devotion to the public interest are qualities typifying the man of Communist society.

But even that latest formula is obviously still vague, so the orders have gone out to Soviet theoreticians to come up with something more concrete. The result has been to make plain how cloudy the whole business is.

Some Soviet writers declare that personal property will continue to exist under communism—clothing, books and the like. Others deny that personal property of any kind is compatible with communism. The top Soviet theoretician, Academician S.G. Strumlin, has drawn a picture of Communist society as one in which people live together in communal dwellings of 2,000 to 3,000 people each, within ten-minute walks of where they work. Others have assailed this picture as obsolete, insisting that "communism" can be built without "communes." The debate goes on.

Yet even amid all the cloudiness of current Soviet thinking about the perfect Communist future, certain points are clear and can be used as a basis for trying to judge how close the Soviet Union now is to the ultimate communist society. Let us look at four vital points in this matter.

(1) *Communist society will have to be one of great abundance so that all needs can be met.*

Soviet spokesmen have shown an awareness of the potential insatiability of human desires. They have stated bluntly that they do not envisage communism as a state in which everyone can have all the automobiles, houses, yachts and trips around the world he wants. Instead, they talk about the "reasonable needs" of people, implying that it is intended to set up a system of norms— so many pounds of meat, so many suits of clothes and the like—defining what people are entitled to.

But even on such limited terms, Soviet spokesmen have admitted that it would require more production than that of the United States at present to meet the requirements for Communist "abundance."

On this score it is evident that the Soviet Union is still far from the Communist ideal. By Premier Khrushchev's own admission, the Soviet Union still does not have anything like enough housing, enough food, enough clothing, enough durable consumer goods to meet its people's needs.

Moreover, the new Communist party program concedes that even if its ambitious economic plan for the next twenty years is fulfilled, full Communist abundance will not have been reached, although by 1980 the USSR was planning to produce more than twice as much as the United States produces now [1960]. There is, of course, no assurance that these ambitious production plans will be achieved.

Just how far behind the United States—let alone a state of Communist abundance—the Soviet Union is may be seen from a few statistical comparisons. In 1960, for example, the United States produced three times as many eggs per person as did the Soviet Union, more than twice as much meat per person and 70 percent more grain per person. Soviet production of automobiles last year was only equal to about one week's normal production of the United States passenger-car industry. Soviet production of cotton cloth—the basic clothing material in that country—was only about half that of the United States per person.

Putting all the available material together, it seems safe to say that the standard of living in the United States is on the average almost three times as high as that in the Soviet Union.

(2) *Communist society will have to be inhabited by people moved by motives different from those the West knows.*

Work in that society, the Soviet blueprint holds, will be "the prime vital requirement of everyone." Moreover, the amount and quality of work people will do in that society will apparently have no relationship to their income, so that apparently the citizens of the Communist society will not require incentives. Are the Soviet people anywhere near such a highly developed sense of social obligation and social responsibility as this requirement suggests?

For the moment, at least, the answer seems to be clearly in the negative. The Soviet wage system contains substantial inequalities of payment, aimed deliberately at rewarding those who work hard and have the most skill while giving the least payment to those who work poorly and have little or no skill. At the beginning of this year, Premier Khrushchev underlined the importance of the incentives in modern Soviet society by blaming the failures in agricultural production in part on the failure to reward the hardest-working peasants generously enough in comparison with their fellows who worked poorly.

Moreover, it is clear that the Soviet Union contains an appreciable number of persons whose main object in life seems to be to get along with as little work as possible, or at least as little honest work as possible. The tightening up of Soviet law this past year testifies to this. A campaign has been waged against "idlers" and "parasites" who disdain honest factory or farm labor but make their living in the black market. Such unsavory characters can now be exiled from their places of residence. Another recent revision of Soviet law makes it possible to apply the death sentence to counterfeiters, to persons who embezzle large amounts of state property, to speculators in foreign currency and the like. Several such death sentences have already been handed down.

All in all, the picture of the ordinary Soviet citizen that is recorded daily in the Soviet press is hardly one to suggest a population of near-paragons who have almost reached the level of selflessness that perfect communism seems to assume. Rather, the picture that emerges is one of human beings just as subject to the pull of self-interest, to laziness and to the desire for easy, sometimes illicit, gain as those of other lands.

(3) *Communist society is one in which there will be "full social equality of all members of society."*

How near to perfect equality is Soviet society today? Not very near at all, any candid inspection of the Soviet scene suggests. The real income of a top Soviet official, writer or scientist is on a level with that of an average resident of Westchester County; at the bottom of the Soviet economic system there are millions living at a poorer level than the American who receives unemployment insurance.

Inequality of power is even more marked than economic inequality. There is no analogue in our society for the contrast between the political power of Premier Khrushchev and the complete political powerlessness of the average Soviet citizen. Further, it must be remembered that in each sphere of Soviet life—in each province, city, town and district—there tends also to be a hierarchy of power in which the man at the top makes the key decisions to which those below must submit.

These inequalities in contemporary Soviet life have led inevitably to sharp social inequality. A standard target for Soviet satire is the upper-class mother who is appalled when her son or daughter comes home and announces he or she plans to marry the offspring of an ordinary worker. Soviet college students, and their parents, tend to look down upon proletarians doomed to lives in the factory or on the farm, and upper-class Soviet families pull every string possible—and sometimes pay expensive bribes—to avert the awful calamity represented by the failure of a son or daughter to enter the university.

It is true that Premier Khrushchev has sought to combat some of the most extreme aspects of inequality. He has reduced some of the highest salary categories and raised minimum wages. He has introduced the requirement that most high school graduates work for two years before entering the university full-time. He has denounced the wire-pulling and bribery that upper-class parents use to get their not-overly-bright children into the university.

But his own liking for the good things of life—for Italianmade clothes, American pens and foreign hunting equipment—has set an example that others in important positions have not ignored. And his obvious favoring of his son-in-law Alexei Adzhubei, who is now editor-in-chief of *Izvestia,* has given an example of the use of power that is much more vivid than are his words denouncing such practices.

(4) *The Communist society is to be composed of "free" people.*

How free are the Soviet people today? Not very free. The dictatorship of the Communist party not only is strong now, but is apparently envisaged as continuing indefinitely. The demand that the press, radio, schools, theatre and the like adhere to the party line is no less insistent than it was in Stalin's time. And the identification of political opposition with subversion continues unchanged.

It is true that there has been some parting of the Iron Curtain under Khrushchev. A small fraction of the Soviet people is allowed to go abroad these days, some even to the capitalist West. Jamming of foreign broadcasts is less frequent than it was in Stalin's day, and there is greater access to foreign writing. But all of these concessions are far from being what "free men" have a right to expect.

Soviet society today, one must conclude, is a long way from the Communist Utopia. It is still a poor civilization inhabited by people who are moved by self-interest rather than by idealistic concern for others. Soviet society is shot through with many different kinds of inequality and its citizens are far from free.

Undoubtedly, the Soviet Union is likely to make much material progress over the next decades, so that . . . the Soviet people should be able to live much better than they do now. But anything approaching the kind of abundance genuine communism assumes seems far out of reach.

Even more out of reach, it would appear, is the kind of selflessness that the official picture of communism calls for. Whether that ideal of selflessness is ever realized in any society is doubtful indeed.

As for the inequality rife in the Soviet Union, it is based in part upon the dictatorial character of the regime and in part simply upon natural inequalities of talent.

Finally, the lack of freedom of Soviet people is a necessity of the Communist party dictatorship and could be ended only by removal of that dictatorship—something Khrushchev and his colleagues do not envisage at all.

The conclusion seems inevitable that whatever kind of society the Soviet Union will have in 1980 or later it will not be the ideal communism Marx had in mind but was careful never to spell out. But there is nothing to stop the Communist rulers of the Soviet Union—if they are still in power—from calling whatever society they may have then "communism." After all, one of the powers a dictatorial regime enjoys is the power to decide what words mean, and that power has been exercised by the Soviet regime for many years.

AFTERWORD

Never had the heritage of the past been more sharply, more sweepingly or more provocatively rejected [as by the Bolshevik Revolution]; never had the claim to universality been more uncompromisingly asserted; never in any previous revolution had the break in continuity seemed so absolute. . . . But presently tradition begins to unfold its power as an antidote to change. . . . The process may be a matter of a few years or a few generations. But, broadly speaking, the greater the distance in time from the initial impact of the revolution, the more decisively does the principle of continuity reassert itself against the principle of change.

Edward Hallett Carr

Far from having spent itself, the dynamic of the revolution seems to be growing; and after a period during which it is overlaid by the patterns of Russian tradition, it reasserts itself all the more powerfully. . . .

Isaac Deutscher

Marxism, as an intellectual system and a Weltanschauung, is dead. What survives are movements and governments which use the tatters of its ideology as a justification for autocratic rule, whether the autocracy be that of a military elite, a technocratic elite, a party elite—or a mixture of all three.

Irving Kristol

Whatever the communist may do, he feels guided by principles insofar as he wants to work for the proletarian revolution and for socialism. Meanwhile, whatever his strategies, the communist can remain a Marxist as long as he keeps analyzing his environment in Marxist terms. Whatever he does, Marxism remains a guide to his action as long as it guides his thinking.

Alfred G. Meyer

Chapter 22

MARXIST THEORY AND SOVIET PRACTICE

By way of conclusion, it is appropriate to again give consideration—in light of actual Soviet practice—to the relation such practice bears to Marxist theory. Parenthetically, it may be noted that, as Robert L. Heilbroner recently observed, Marx's thought continues to exert "a fascination that has survived a hundred debunkings, 'disproof,' and disillusionments to reassert itself as *the* great challenge whose measure must be taken by everyone seeking to understand the social condition of mankind." [Author's emphasis.] But, historic connection apart, has Marxist theory profoundly affected or influenced the policies of the Soviet leaders? There is a school of thought, typified by Nicholas P. Vakar, which maintains that Marxism, "long ago emptied of meaning, has become, like any official piety, perfectly adaptable." More specifically, according to W.W. Rostow in *The Dynamics of Soviet Society*, Soviet policies and practices have been primarily and essentially a consequence of a single-minded effort by Soviet leaders to maintain their own absolute internal power over Russian society and extend their power vis-à-vis the external world. In Rostow's view, what is left of Marxism is what has been found useful "to support the maintenance and enlargement of power by the regime at home and abroad."

Other Western scholars have agreed that Marxist theory in actual practice and in important respects has been subordinated to or abandoned for other compulsions or considerations. They have nonetheless attributed significant influence to its continuity and impact on policy. Representative of this position is Julian Towster who, in the opening words of his pioneer study *Political Power in the USSR*, asserted, "So great is the stress placed upon the interrelation of theory and practice in the Soviet state that an understanding of its operative constitutional order would lack coherence without due attention to avowed theory." Your editor agrees with this conclusion and has attempted to support and document it in the reading selection that follows.

Whatever the merit of either position, Marxist theory is so deeply embedded in the ethos of Soviet society that even the process of attenuation requires obeisance. It has, as Edward Hallett Carr makes clear, "the status of a creed which purports to inspire every act of state power and by which every such act can be tested and judged."

The Role of Theory

Samuel Hendel

An important question is what, if any, has been and continues to be the significance of Marxist theory for an understanding of the Soviet system. The fact is that, although far-reaching changes have occurred in the USSR since the death of Stalin, there has been little reconsideration of the conception, long and generally favored in the West, that however variously Soviet history may be explained or appraised, commitment to Marxist theory on the part of Soviet leaders forms little or no relevant part of that explanation or appraisal. For some observers of the Soviet scene, Marxism is constantly being revised or discarded, but never appears to exist or exert influence. For others, like Daniel Bell, the ideology of Marxism has been "exhausted."

Denigration of the impact of Marxist theory on Soviet practice is understandable in light of the wide disparity between myth and reality in the USSR. It is undeniable that certain ideological goals that found expression in the writings of Marx and Engels, however officially rationalized, have been abandoned, perverted, or attenuated. This process was begun by Lenin himself. Time and again, the Soviet leaders subordinated theory as they yielded to other drives and exigencies. Even loyalty to certain Marxist principles was punished as a crime, when it conflicted with the prevalent official orthodoxy. But time after time, when the complete demise of theory as a guide to practice had been assumed or predicted, it showed a persistence, or a renaissance, and a vitality and influence that cannot, in my judgment, reasonably be denied. This has been true not only with respect to policies pursued, but also those debarred. I am convinced, for example, that, despite great flexibility, before the Soviet regime could embrace or disregard *certain* policies, it would first have to completely destroy its own birth certificate and ideological title deeds. . . .

Preliminarily, it must be pointed out that, contrary to the focus of much recent discussion, evaluation of the interrelationship of *Marxist* theory and Soviet practice is properly and essentially concerned only with *internal* rather than external policy. There is little that one can glean, even by indirection, from a reading of Marx (as distinguished from Lenin, Stalin, Khrushchev, and Brezhnev) about Soviet policies suitable to the "coexistence" of socialist and capitalist countries. Marx expected socialist revolutions to mature more or less simultaneously in advanced industrial countries; but in any event, once revolution had taken hold in any one country, he believed the force of its example and momentum would soon prove overwhelming.

Foreign policy apart then, what evidence and reasoning support the thesis that in significant respects Marxist theory, *qua* theory, played and continues to play an important role in influencing Soviet practice? To deal with this inquiry, it will be useful, first, to give consideration to several leading formulations which, directly or indirectly, have sought to evaluate this interrelationship.

This excerpt (updated 1980) is from "The Soviet Union: The Search for Theory" in William G. Andrews, ed., European Politics I: The Restless Search *(D. Van Nostrand Co., Inc., © 1966), pp. 216–240. It is reproduced here by permission. For footnote references, the original should be consulted.*

The "Naked Power" Thesis. The most detailed, systematic, and probably the most influential formulation of this thesis appeared some years ago in W.W. Rostow's *The Dynamics of Soviet Society,* which purported to synthesize much of the available knowledge of Soviet society, and was meant to assist the makers of American policy. Mr. Rostow's central thesis, "the concept of the priority of power," is that whenever conflict arose, the Soviet leaders, beginning with Lenin, chose "the power of their own political group" as against Marxist doctrine, revolutionary goals, the aims and traditions of the progressive movement, or the majority will of the people. While priority of power drew support from elements of Marxist doctrine and from Russian history and geography, "the inner core of consistency in the story of the Russian Communists is the priority they were prepared to give to the maintenance and expansion of their own power. . . ." Specifically, with regard to theory, what remains of Marxism is what has been found useful "to support the maintenance and enlargement of power by the regime at home and abroad." In a more recent study, *The Stages of Economic Growth,* Mr. Rostow postulates that "*the* motive" (my emphasis) of "Communist political economy" is "the maintenance and extension of the elite's power" which exercises its dictatorship over the majority "in terms of its own interests."

Just how the "priority of power" thesis is applied to the USSR is often a study in argument by selected instances and fiat assertion. These techniques enable Mr. Vakar to draw the sweeping conclusion that "the goal" that the Soviet leaders "talk about exerts no perceptible attractive or compulsive force on them as practical politicians. . . . it points them in no direction they would not otherwise choose." Or consider Mr. Rostow's technique. When Stalin opposed rapid industrialization and collectivization, which were being urged by other Bolsheviks in the mid-1920s, this was essentially because "Stalin was concentrating his attention on the problem of achieving and consolidating his dictatorship, and he used his growing power to restrain accelerated industrialization until his dictatorship was secured." When, on the other hand, in 1928–9, Stalin embarked on these measures, this was "a decision by a personal ruler, who had fully consolidated his position, to increase his hold over his own domain and to enlarge the strength and power his state might exercise in the world arena." And, when Stalin called a temporary halt in 1930 to the tempo involved, it was because to maintain power he was "forced" to do so. On this basis, Mr. Rostow simply cannot lose for, in whatever direction a Soviet leader moves, it is postulated à priori that he is motivated exclusively by personal power drives.

What we are offered in the Rostow-Vakar thesis is a version of Soviet history as pervasive, oversimplified, and misleading in its own way as the materialist conception of history is in another. This view enables the Communist Party of the Soviet Union, in its New (1961) Program, to maintain that a bourgeois republic, "however democratic," inevitably constitutes "a machine for the exploitation and suppression of the vast majority of the working people by a handful of capitalists." As for social welfare legislation, and even the welfare state itself, these are no more than devices to preserve the capitalist system and mask its exploiting character. "The vaunted 'welfare,' " we are told, "is welfare for the magnates of finance capital, and torment and suffering for hundreds of millions of working people."

The absurdity of crude Marxist formulations regarding the structure and uses of power in many countries of the West is apparent. What we tend to ignore, however, is that the Western view of the USSR also frequently suffers from crude oversimplifications which, turning Marxism upside down, see in the Soviet state exclusively an organ for exploitation and oppression and reduce complex motivations to some monistic explanation such as "the priority of power."

This is not to deny that Soviet history may be explained, *in significant part,* in terms of a personal, dictatorial power drive, however rationalized. (This is in striking contrast to Marx's expressed "aversion from any cult of the individual" and from "anything tending to foster irrational beliefs in authority.") Some of its clearest manifestations are found in the destruction of all opposition parties, the tawdry internecine battles among the Bolsheviks, the deliberate rewriting and falsification of Soviet history, and the cynical manipulation of all mass media to glorify and discredit particular leaders and causes. But it seems to me erroneous to elevate the power struggle from its role as an important and necessary part of a complex explanation of Soviet history to the status of virtual self-sufficiency. If one were seeking, for example, to explain the prewar history of Germany, would it be correct to reduce the complex amalgam to the manic propulsions for power that guided Hitler? There is wisdom in Harold Laski's statement that "the impulses of men are never referable to any single source."

Even the "amoral" Machiavelli, who sought to construct a science of power by abstracting politics from ideology (and ethics), necessarily failed because in the real world ends and means are not wholly separable; and because politics is a system of controls inevitably based, in good part, on a system of values. . . .

The "End" of Ideology. Perhaps it is unconscious recognition of these considerations that leads some Sovietologists to cast Marxism out the front door only to readmit it, at least a little, through a side door. Thus Robert V. Daniels, for example, categorically asserts that in the USSR, "Theory does not guide practice, but it is manipulated to justify it after the fact." However, in the same piece he says, "From Lenin's time on, the Communist leaders have been active men, not philosophers; they have found in Marx's doctrine a more-or-less comfortable rationalization for what they *wanted to do* or *felt should be done.*" And elsewhere he writes, "Marxism in Russia has from the very beginning neatly fit Marx's own definition of ideology as 'false consciousness'—a set of ideas used without concern for truth or consistency to rationalize the *interests* and *aims* of a particular social group." (My emphasis.)

Now, there is a palpable ambiguity here. Are the "interests" and "aims" of the leaders and what they "wanted to do" and felt "should be done" all self-consistent and compatible? Would not the "aims" and conceptions of "what should be done" have been molded, in significant part at least, by the Marxist philosophy in which they have been educated and nurtured? What men "should" do, Professor Robert M. MacIver has said, is always expressive of a myth complex, that is, a given ideology. To put it more concretely, if the aims of the leaders (consciously and unconsciously influenced by Marxist conceptions) are to achieve Marxist ends (which they may, in any event, genuinely regard as inevitable), would not their "aims" at times conflict with their "interests?" If this is so, how can it be categorically asserted that "theory does not guide practice" at all!

Or consider Daniel Bell's position. He argues, on the one hand, that the old ideologies, Marxism foremost among them, have been "exhausted," that is, "have lost their 'truth' and their power to persuade." As for the specific merits of communism, "the content of that doctrine has long been forgotten by friends and foes alike." Yet, on the other hand, as Bell himself has recognized in his provocative "Ten Theories in Search of Reality," ideology cannot be disposed of in quite so cavalier a fashion. Thus, he states that "Every society, every social organization, lives for certain goals which in considerable measure are dictated by its ideology." While he then goes on to argue that with the advent of Khrushchev, practical considerations rather than ideology seem to determine policy in important fields, tellingly he concludes that at some point some essential aspects of the regnant ideology must be maintained, for "without a central belief system with some continuity, disintegrative opinions begin to spread. . . ."

The Coming "Triumph" of Ideology. It is one thing, however, to recognize the continuing importance of the revolutionary dynamic; it is quite another to maintain, as Isaac Deutscher does, that "Marxism has entered into the very core of national consciousness" and that "whatever its mutations Marxism remains the mainstream of Soviet thought." Guided by this proposition, Deutscher insists that the working class "cannot possibly remain content with the administrative-ideological limitations of the post-Stalinist reform" and is eventually bound "to give a distinctive proletarian meaning and content to the current ideas and slogans of democratization." We are told that "the social and cultural advance tends to make the masses aware of the fact that they are deprived of political liberties and are ruled by an uncontrolled bureaucracy. In coming years this will impel them to seek freedom of expression and association, even if this should bring them into conflict with ruling bureaucracy." In an earlier study Deutscher had concluded that "the balance of domestic factors favors a democratic regeneration of the regime."

Deutscher appears to have moved to another extreme and permitted his own Marxist determinism to carry him beyond the established facts of industrialization and collectivization, urbanization, mass education, increase in social welfare, and relaxation of the dictatorship to insist that the process of change cannot be halted or aborted (except for temporary setbacks) short of the realization of a democratic socialist society truly in the image of Marx. Liberalization has probably gone so far, gathered so much support, and aroused such expectations as to make it extremely difficult to revert to a form of Stalinist totalitarianism. But the evidence from Soviet experience in particular, or human experience in general, seems insufficient to warrant Deutscher's far-reaching optimistic prediction.

The Durability of Soviet Despotism. It is noteworthy that Leonard Schapiro, for one, based upon essentially the same developments, found that "the trend of the past few years in the Soviet Union has been in the direction of benevolent despotism rather than towards a free society." Neither greater prosperity nor industrial development, he stated, was likely to affect this pattern so long as the party preserves its monopoly of power. In fact, increased benefits may make the system more acceptable, and thus more durable.

Bertram Wolfe, in even more categorical fashion, insists that "the durability of Soviet despotism" derives from the nature of modern totalitarianism, which is based upon a powerful and self-perpetuating framework enabling it to absorb changes (both intended and forced) so that "they tend to remain *within-system* changes in an enduring system." (Wolfe's emphasis.) To the argument that totalitarianism is incompatible with the complexity of modern industry and advanced technology, he counters that "Germany adopted totalitarianism when it was the paramount country of Europe in industry and technology."

The Role of Ideology in the USSR Today

It is, I believe, highly significant that each of these projections—whether based essentially on the priority of power, the force of tradition, the dynamic of Marxism, or the within-system durability of totalitarianism—although arguable, is far from demonstrable.

What is even more important is that in each case there appears to be substantial evidence and logical bases for alternative and even contradictory theses.

"The function of history," J.B. Bury has written, "is to belie prophets." Thus, history has dealt harshly with the assumption, particularly prevalent after World War I, that liberal democracy of the Anglo-Saxon pattern was the final product of enlightenment, a system toward which all societies would naturally tend. This was true, Laski once argued, because "men who have once tasted power will not, without conflict, surrender it." But, authoritarianism in one form or another, as George F. Kennan reminds us, has throughout the ages been the normal lot of mankind. So, also, Marx's confident assumption of the inevitable triumph of socialism in the advanced industrial countries was confounded by his own oversimplified analysis of the nature and "contradictions" of capitalism. It is curious to observe how so many who reject Marxist determinism, as grounded upon inadequate understanding of the complexities of capitalism, substitute a determinism of their own so confidently charting the direction of Soviet society.

There is, I fear, no escape—no matter how appealing and beguiling our quest for simplicity—into a universal formula which either totally accepts the integral relationship of Marxist theory and Soviet practice or totally rejects it. Every attempt to do so, whether by Soviet leaders or apologists or by Soviet critics, in the end runs afoul of stubborn realities. There is no substitute for painstaking theoretical, historical and logical analyses—doctrine by doctrine, case by case.

Limitations of space make it possible only to suggest an appropriate method. And since the case *against* the impact and continuity of Marxist theory is better known in the West, I am concerned principally with the opposing one. Before I proceed with the latter, in order to make it clear that evidence moves in both directions, I cite a few illustrations (without attempting substantiation) of the *disparity* and *discontinuity* of Marxist theory and Soviet practice. Specifically, in my judgment, Lenin's conceptions of the role of the Party, both in prerevolutionary theory and in postrevolutionary practice constituted significant departures from Marxism. In practice, too, the dictatorship of the Communist Party (which in Lenin's day became rule by an oligarchy and, under Stalin, one-man rule) bore and, despite some dispersion of power since Stalin, bears no relation to the Marxist conception of the dictatorship of the proletariat. Closely linked to this conception was Marx's doctrine of the withering away of the state—an ideal professed by Marx in his very early writings. The failure of the Soviet state to wither away, in the face of the claim that the USSR has already achieved socialism, a classless society and, according to the New Party Program, "a state of the entire people" (itself a formulation in conflict with basic theory)—however rationalized—is in fundamental contradiction with Marxist theory.

Contrariwise, what evidence supports the proposition that key Marxist doctrines (however modified or distorted in practice) have nonetheless, in a truly vital sense, maintained basic and significant meaning, and exercised important and continuing influence on the operative Soviet order? In this connection consideration is given to three Marxist conceptions of fundamental importance.

Socialized Property. In the Communist Manifesto, Marx and Engels wrote that "the distinguishing feature of communism" is "the abolition of bourgeois property," a system based "on class antagonisms, on the exploitation of the many by the few." They added, "In this sense, the theory of the Communists may be summed up in a single sentence: Abolition of private property."

A powerful argument may be made (as Erich Fromm, for example, does) that Marx, in seeking the end of capitalism, was essentially concerned not with maximizing production, but with the "full and free development of every individual," and that his "idea" was "deformed and corrupted" by the Communists. Or, as put by Robert Tucker, what Marx had sought was "the spiritual regeneration of man" and "to end human alienation by changing the world." . . . The fact, however, cannot be gainsaid that—from a *Marxist* point of view—the basis for the development of unalienated man was the abolition of private ownership of means of production and the substitution of common ownership, a planned economy, and production for use rather than for profit. Insofar as the USSR corresponds to this conception, and it surely does in substantial degree, it may be said, in a real and meaningful sense, to derive from and to have been influenced by Marxism. . . . And, what is more, these institutions are so fundamentally rooted in the beliefs of the people and their leaders that, for the foreseeable future, they are as unlikely to be abolished as is the basic system of private property in the United States.

It is true that dictatorial controls in the USSR mean that the Marxist scheme, particularly in its conception of socialist democracy, has not been realized. This lack of freedom, in turn, affects and limits the common ownership of property, but—and this is critical to understanding—it does not negate it. Milovan Djilas, for example, goes too far when he maintains that, in effect, the Communist political bureaucracy owns the nationalized property because it "uses, enjoys, and disposes" of it. While their controls give the bureaucrats important and special benefits, so long as marked fluidity prevails and national property may not be inherited, the privileges of the party leaders fall far short of ownership as Malenkov, Molotov, and Khrushchev discovered.

Not only does the fundamental organization of the economy reflect the Marxist scheme, but the strength of ideology is shown by frequently stubborn adherence to doctrine at the expense of rationality and efficiency. For example, much waste and neglect would be eliminated or reduced, and incentives increased, if small producers and traders were permitted to operate on a personal profit basis. The storekeeper and the restaurateur, among many others, would have compelling motives to reduce labor and other costs while improving service. But to permit private profit would mean a return to private enterprise, and this is ideologically unacceptable.

Consider another case. Planners in the USSR, basing themselves on Marx's proposition that only labor creates value, were ideologically debarred from imposing an interest charge for the use of capital. If used, it would serve as a means of efficient allocation and rationing of scarce capital and tend to set rational limits to the amounts of capital which planners would find it attractive to use in projected plants. But, as Professor Robert W. Campbell writes, "the Russians have been unable to use this simple approach because it is contradictory to the Marxist theory of value." And, despite the fact that, as Nicolas Spulber points out, "the labor theory is a poor tool for tackling problems of rational allocation of resources, it was called upon to serve as a normative principle of valuation."

It is true that recently the Russians have succeeded, in part, in getting around the difficulty by using certain other devices, but these are not entirely satisfactory substitutes. So also, recent measures for a system of plant (not individual) "profit" incentive, interest on capital, a new pricing system to reflect more accurately labor and material costs and stimulate production of new items, fines for delivery delays, and other techniques are designed to improve the planning system, not to replace it. In any event, ultimate intrusion of elements of rationality into the planned economy is akin to the fact that welfare state measures are permitted to alter our free enterprise system without destroying it.

Adaptations and modifications in both systems do not mean that beliefs or ideologies are lacking in force. On the contrary, continuing adherence to essentials, and the time lag required to make sensible modifications, suggest that theory, *qua* theory, plays an important role in guiding practice in both cases. But this is more particularly true within a relatively closed, doctrinaire society like that of the USSR.

Agriculture presents an even clearer and more dramatic example of the compulsions of theory. Now, it must first be said that there are many explanations for the failure of the USSR to achieve the repeatedly promised high level of agricultural production. These include the infertility of much Soviet land; inadequate rainfall; lack of mechanization, storage, and transport facilities; and heavy dependence on the labor of women and children—but surely a primary factor is the basic inadequacy of the system of collectivization itself. It simply does not give the peasant sufficient incentive to produce abundantly.

This failure is pointed up by the vitality of the private farm sector. Although it covers only an insignificant part of the total agricultural land and sown area, this sector, according to official Soviet statistics, contributes a heavily disproportionate share of the total output of many important foods such as vegetables, potatoes, meat, milk, and eggs. In August 1977, an article in *Literaturnaya Gazeta* pointed out that personal, auxiliary farming accounts for "about 28% of gross agricultural output." By contrast, the figures for labor productivity, the care of livestock, and vegetable and fruit produce in the public agricultural sector are so incredibly poor as to be almost unbelievable. Soviet leaders have, in fact, repeatedly admitted the comparative inefficiency of Soviet agriculture. . . . Typically, the Russian Republic Minister of Trade stated in *Planovoye Khozyaistvo* in July 1978 that "substantial amounts of potatoes, vegetables and fruits grown on farms never reach consumers or reach them in poor condition. For example, every year the Russian Federation's state trade network receives over 1 million tons of substandard or damaged produce. Such produce regularly amounts to 12% to 17% of all deliveries." So, also, an article in *Trud* on September 3, 1977 noted that "last fall 16% of the potatoes that the consumers' cooperative in Bryansk Province procured to ship to other provinces were substandard, (i.e., mechanically damaged, diseased, or beginning to rot). But since the farms' contracts with the consumer cooperatives make no mention of quality, and since substandard potatoes count toward the farms' plan fulfillment, the growers have no interest in improving the quality of the potatoes they sell." It further observed, "In many other countries improvements in potato-harvesting machinery are aimed at reducing damage to the crop, but in the Soviet Union improvements are aimed solely at increasing the machines' productivity, which tends to result in an even higher rate of damage to the harvested crop."

Why, then, in the face of these difficulties, does the USSR reject private enterprise in small-scale industry, commerce, and agriculture? While it has been argued that internal power drives or practical considerations "converged" with ideology to make socialized property desirable, the explanation is hardly convincing. The Communists were committed to achieving this goal as a central, unalterable aspect of a creed for which many had languished in Tsarist prisons. It seems more reasonable to suppose that the collectivization program in particular, with its loosing of a hornet's nest of opposition and concomitants of ruthless discipline, belt tightening, and even famine, involved serious, calculated risks to *personal* power to serve the ends of preservation and extension of the *socialist* system.

Furthermore, it was not possible, once recovery from the ravages of war and civil war had been achieved, for any Bolshevik leader, who aspired to achieve or hold power, to oppose in principle or delay nationalization of property—just as it is impossible today for any such leader to seek to dismantle or fundamentally alter the collectivist industrial and agricultural systems in the USSR. And this is true despite the fact that, in specific regard to agriculture, as Alex Inkeles and Raymond A. Bauer have shown in their probing study of the USSR (based mainly on interviews with Soviet refugees), "nothing approaches the directness, simplicity and pervasiveness of hostility toward the collective farm system. Only 2 percent of the sample had no opinion on this subject. All groups without distinction and virtually unanimously wanted it eliminated. On a direct question, nine-tenths of the entire sample said flatly that the *kolkhoz* should be abolished and all the land distributed." . . . Nonetheless, as Alec Nove has said, "the maintenance of the collective principle against private farming has become an unchallengeable dogma."

Materialism. Fundamental to Marxism is its materialist philosophy which rejects supernaturalism in any form, insisting that "The material, sensuously perceptible world to which we ourselves belong is the only reality" and that "the ideal is nothing more than the material world reflected by the human mind and translated into terms of thought." In this view, "It is not religion that creates man but man who creates religion," which serves as "the opium of the people." Lenin characterized this dictum as "the cornerstone of the whole Marxist view on religion" and insisted that "We shall always teach a scientific world outlook." On the other hand, purely as a matter of tactics, he was not always prepared "to put the religious question in the forefront."

Similarly, Lenin's successors have pursued the antireligious campaign with varying degrees of intensity at various times, but the convictions and goals have never been altered and the campaign has never been fully relaxed. During World War II, to be sure, the regime, while engaged in a life and death struggle, felt it necessary to make some concessions to the religious sentiments of the people, particularly in the villages. These concessions served also to appease allies and promote pan-Slavic support.

By 1947, only two years after the end of the war, however, the official Komsomol journal again called for an "aggressive ideological struggle" against those who did not recognize "the incompatibility of religious convictions and membership in the Komsomol," and by 1950, *Science and Life* flatly announced that "Marxism-Leninism and religion are as irreconcilable as materialism and idealism."

That this irreconcilability is a fundamental premise of Soviet society today is manifest in many ways. It is reflected, despite some concern with methods, in the New Party Program adopted in October 1961. It is propagated and urged on a variety of fronts: in Party and youth organizations; in special associations and conferences; in films, and television and radio programs; in books, articles, and editorials; and, perhaps, most important and pervasive, in the educational system. . . . The whole campaign was intensified when the Communist Party Central Committee in 1964 announced a new, extensive and coordinated program to eradicate religion from every aspect of Soviet life. On August 18, 1971, *Pravda* proclaimed editorially that the destruction of religious views is "the most important condition for forming the new man."

It is possible to argue that the antireligious campaign in the USSR is not *basically* a matter of ideological commitment, but an aspect of a power struggle. The church, after all, had bitterly opposed the revolution. If given a free hand to propagate its views, it might become an opposing center of power. But the argument is not very persuasive. The leaders of the USSR were schooled in and, there is no reason to doubt, believe in Marxist materialism. Apart from making temporary and tactical retreats—dictated by immediate exigencies—they seem determined to spread materialist doctrine even at some risk to Communist and personal power.

It is reasonable to suppose that if the Party came to terms with the church, already rendered thoroughly subservient under pervasive surveillance, it might well serve to make the leaders more acceptable to the masses. Other rulers have known how to use and bend the state religion for their purposes. Why not the Communists? That the church might prove agreeable is not at all to be excluded. On Easter of 1972, Aleksandr Solzhenitsyn in a Lenten letter sent to Patriarch Pimen of Moscow and All the Russias commented that "The Russian Church has its indignant opinion on every evil in distant Asia or Africa, yet on internal ills—it has none—ever" and he added "A church dictatorially ruled by atheists is a sight not seen in two thousand years." Of course, no Communist could make a real accommodation with the church without risking ouster. But this is simply another way of saying that personal power and position, in this instance, depend upon continuing commitment to fundamental Marxist materialism.

The evidence is clear, too, that ideology and philosophical criteria, such as materialism, have often been invoked in the USSR, with harmful consequences to Soviet scientific progress. One of the best known examples was the whole controversy over Lysenkoism. Under pressure from the lay Central Committee of the Communist Party, the Presidium of the Academy of Science, in 1948, found it necessary to hold that "Michurin's [Lysenko's] materialist direction in biology is the only acceptable form of science, because it is based on dialectical materialism and on the revolutionary principle of changing Nature for the benefit of the people." . . . Similarly, Einstein's theory of relativity, which seemed to Soviet philosophers to have elements of the metaphysical or mystical, was, as early as 1938, described by the Astronomical section of the USSR Academy of Sciences as "counterrevolutionary."

Now it is true that within the USSR, Lysenko's biological theories are no longer the *only* acceptable form of science, and that many experimental scientists ignored the postulates of the philosophers with respect to Einstein's theory. It should be observed, however, that Marxist theory dictated (or appeared to dictate) scientific theory and how considerable—in face of error and risks to progress—was its force, at least for a time. And basic philosophical theory continues to maintain its importance as a point of general reference and frequently retarding influence. The New Party Program, for example, provides that "In an age of rapid scientific development, the working out of the philosophical problems of contemporary natural science, on the basis of dialectical materialism as the only scientific method of cognition, acquires greater urgency." . . .

If, as suggested by some quoted earlier in these pages, the Soviet leaders are practical and/or power-driven men, with no real theoretical commitment, then the scientific area would seem to be the least congenial (and most damaging to *their own purposes*) for the intrusion of philosophical ideas, which they value little or not at all. Yet the record makes abundantly clear that, again and again, adherence to certain Marxist principles by Soviet leaders retarded social progress, engendered unnecessary hardship, and made their own positions less, rather than more, secure.

Egalitarianism. A fundamental theoretical "end" of Marxism is the realization of a thoroughly egalitarian society. It was Marx's view that, in the socialist phase, the economic system would provide payment to its workers "proportioned to the labor they supply," and equality would consist "in the fact that measurement is made with an equal standard, labor." But true equality would be achieved only in the higher, Communist phase, "after the productive forces have also increased with the all-round development of the individual, and all the springs of cooperative wealth flow more abundantly.'' Then would the standard prevail, ''From each according to his ability, to each according to his needs.''

In the aftermath of the Bolshevik Revolution, equality to its uttermost limits was the order of the day. As David J. Dallin wrote:

> Everything that stood in the way of equality was to be abolished, at once, completely: that was the spiritual crux of the November revolution and of the ideology of the early period of the Soviet regime. Equality in consumption and strict rationing were to eliminate inequality in the distribution of food supplies. The floor space of houses and apartments was carefully measured and the available space equally distributed among the population. . . .

In this period of war ''Communism,'' wages tended toward equality. By 1921, workers of widely varying qualifications, skill, or performance, received nearly equal wages. But this equality, extorted from an economy of want and scarcity (a base that made a travesty of Marx's vision), had to be abandoned to restore the ravaged economy. Under N.E.P., the traders and small entrepreneurs were invited back and peasants given the right to sell their products in the free market. The inevitable effect was marked differentiation in income. With the ebbing of revolutionary élan and under conditions of poverty, higher earnings provided the strongest incentive to more productive and skilled work for the working class as well. By June 1931, Stalin was decrying ''the consequences of wage equalization,'' which deprived unskilled workers of incentive to become skilled workers and led to heavy turnover in labor. ''In order to put an end to this evil,'' he said, ''we must abolish wage equalization and discard the old wage scales.''

In typical fashion, Stalin sought to make a virtue of what may well have been a necessity. What is more, he carried the inequalities far beyond the needs, or even utility, of the case. Accordingly, in 1934, Stalin characterized the views of those who ''think that socialism calls for equalization, for levelling the requirements and the individual lives of the members of society'' as ''petit-bourgeois views of our leftist blockheads.'' With regard to their ''one time'' attempt to organize industry to provide equal compensation for skilled and unskilled workers, he added: ''You know what harm these infantile equalitarian exercises of our 'left' blockheads caused our industry.''

More inequality became the fashion and the cry. As a consequence, the piecework wage became the prevailing system, and gross disparities developed between the earnings of the skilled and unskilled so that Soviet labor law provided for seventeen wage gradations, with the highest paid eight times as much as the lowest. At the same time, Stalin instituted ruthless and draconic measures of labor discipline. And, in 1940, a decree was issued requiring payment of tuition fees for upper secondary and higher education.

In light of these developments, it was quite generally predicted in the West that egalitarianism had been permanently and irrevocably abandoned as a goal of Soviet policy. Quite typical was the statement of Arthur Koestler that a survey of the trends in the USSR ''contradicts the alleged temporariness of these expedients and reveals a continuous and coherent movement in a direction opposed to fundamental principles of socialism.''

Consequently, it is noteworthy that with postwar recovery and further progress in building a high industrial base, a number of measures were adopted to restore greater equality. These included currency devaluation (which had a particularly adverse effect on high income groups as well as black marketeers), the ending of the tuition system (making education generally available to the talented, at all levels, without tuition fee), an increase in minimum wages and pensions, extension of the pension system to farm workers, special tax concessions for low-income groups, and reduction in the use of the piecework system—all of which have been of special and substantial benefit to those at the bottom of the economic scale. Labor benefited, too, from a shorter work week and from reform and liberalization of the labor code. In addition, the Soviet people for many years have had access to cultural opportunities and to hospital and medical facilities on a widespread and generally egalitarian basis. While, as Murray Yanowitch pointed out in these pages, substantial inequalities in money earnings and living standards persist in the USSR, these disparities may well be largely explained by the continuing and pervasive need to spur lagging productivity with material incentives. With increasing production, particularly in consumer goods, it is not improbable that there will be a further erosion of inequalities in incomes and living standards (as, concededly, has generally been the case since the late 1950s).

While motivation does not alter the facts involved, it does bear upon the role of ideology and prospects for the future. Some Western observers have explained the Soviet program of popular education and other welfare measures, as W.W. Rostow does, "mainly as a reflex to its power goals." Or, as put by Solomon M. Schwarz, "The need to adjust Soviet realities to the imperatives of modern industrialism is thus the *main* cause of the recent development of social welfare in the USSR." (Schwarz's emphasis.) In a similar vein, Bertram Wolfe queried, "Does not advancing industrialism—under any system—require more literate, better-trained workers?"

There is, I believe, little doubt that increased welfare is an important and, in the long run, indispensable concomitant of developing industrialization. But, as Alec Nove pointed out in a carefully documented analysis, "the fact remains that in relation to national income the Soviet Union spends more on health, education and so on, than highly industrialized Western countries do, and it is therefore wrong to assume that her present rate of spendng is in some sense economically predetermined, regardless of political decision or system of government. . . ." More recently (1966), Frederick C. Barghoorn, in general a rather severe critic of the Soviet Union wrote that, "In some aspects of community policy, such as public health services and medical care for the citizenry, the Soviet record, considering the difficulties which had to be overcome before the present level could be achieved, is brilliant." (Parenthetically, in July 1978, Joseph A. Califano, Jr., U.S. Secretary of Health, Education and Welfare, commented that President Carter "is deeply concerned that the present health care system fails to serve millions of Americans. More than 20 million have no health insurance; another 65 million face potential bankruptcy because of the lack of insurance protecting them against catastrophic medical expenses, and many citizens receive substandard medical care.") Under the circumstances, is it not reasonable to assume that while the motivations for social welfare in the USSR may be varied and complex, the egalitarianism suggested in Marx's vision of a socialist society—a vision in which the Soviet leaders, like the Soviet people, have been educated and reared—may form a real and important element in the composite?

As for the future, the New Party Program, adopted October 31, 1961, promised that by 1980 national income would rise by 400 percent, agricultural production would attain two and a half times its then volume, that the disparity between high and low incomes would be steadily reduced; and that a variety of free benefits, services, and facilities would be provided to such extent that "public consumption funds would total about half of the aggregate real income of the population." The program further promised that by 1980

"Soviet society will come close to a stage where it can introduce the principle of distribution according to needs. . . ." Less extravagant projections were made in the definition of goals in the Directives for the Ninth Five-Year Plan for 1971–1975 and for the Tenth Five-Year Plan for 1976–1980 and are likely to be reflected in its forthcoming Eleventh Five-Year Plan for 1981–1985.

In light of the continued emphasis on heavy industry, the great deficiencies of collectivized agriculture, imbalances of the Soviet economy, chronic shortages, the slowdown of economic growth and the record of broken promises, it seems highly improbable that the USSR will achieve the overall production goals of the New Party Program within the forseeable future. Industrial output for 1979, according to official Soviet sources published in 1980, grew by only 3.4 percent, against a projection of 5.7 percent. Add the recalcitrance of human nature and it is extremely doubtful that the Soviet Union will "come close" to realizing the ultimate Marxist conception of distribution according to need—which, in any event, may be visionary and utopian.

On the other hand, barring war, there is little reason to doubt that the Soviet Union, despite the recent slowdown from its former comparatively high rates of economic growth, will be able, in the next several decades, to make slower but continuing progress toward the realization of many of the economic and welfare goals outlined in its New Party Program and Five-Year Plans. These plans are consistent in conception and formulation with *certain* fundamental Marxist egalitarian principles and it seems to me fatuous to believe that Marxist ideology, per se, has played and will play no real or substantial part in their implementation.

Conclusions

The conclusions of this essay will not appeal to those who are attracted to tidy and monistic explanations. Soviet leaders may in the future, as they have in the past, subordinate Marxism and the welfare of the Russian people to a variety of considerations and pressures. Certain Marxist doctrines have been attenuated, perverted, deferred, and, in some instances, discarded. But the whole truth is far more complicated than is suggested by those who ascribe little or no importance to the continuity and influence of Marxist theory. It would, in fact, be most surprising if Marxist ideology had little or no hold on Soviet leaders. They have been nurtured in the Marxist creed since birth, and have been advanced, in many instances, because of uncritical loyalty to it. As for the people, while no doubt much apathy and cynicism prevail among them, it remains true that they exhibit a "peculiarly Soviet style of thinking, and of formulating problems," and "seem to absorb a good deal of the 'metaphysics' of Marxism." As Inkeles and Bauer conclude from their study of Soviet attitudes:

> It is impossible to be exposed to a system of propaganda as all-pervasive and monopolistic as that of the Soviet regime and escape without some influence. The areas where greatest influence was exerted were precisely those our knowledge of human learning points to, namely the basic values of the individual and the implicit dimensions of this thought. . . .

In early 1980, a former Soviet sociologist and pollster, Dr. Vladimir Shliapentokh, who has emigrated to the United States, commented in a news conference that "You shouldn't underestimate the devotion of the [Soviet] population to the dominant values."

Paradoxically, some who argue that a fundamental *ideological* cleavage exists between the West and the USSR at the same time refuse to endow the Soviet ideology with any content. But, as R.N. Carew Hunt has said, "the movement would not be the force it has become were there not in every country men and women who sincerely believe in the ideas behind it, which form collectively what we call its ideology. To represent this ideology as a species of opium with which the Soviet leaders contrive to lull the people while taking care never to indulge in it themselves is to attribute to them an ability to dissociate themselves from the logic of their system—an ability which it is unlikely they possess."

Even in the areas where distortion or perversion of Marxism has manifestly taken place, it is revealing to observe how the "old truths" persist so that a measure of relaxation promptly brings people to the fore who seek to restore Marx's true meaning and purpose. Typical is that group of intellectuals in the USSR today, whose attitude was perhaps best expressed by Yevtushenko's statement that "those who speak in the name of Communism but in reality pervert its meaning are among its most dangerous enemies, perhaps even more dangerous than its enemies in the West," and in the poem of Boris Slutsky: "Time to bring the dreams to pass. Yes, with neither doubt nor hesitation—To get to work and bring the dreams to pass."

I conclude that the USSR is most rationally explained as a complex and unique interpenetration and amalgam of Marxist ideology and a host of other forces including the compulsions of expediency and power, the old Russian tradition, and the recalcitrance of the human condition. As such, it is *sui generis* and defies monistic interpretation and characterization. To maintain that because departures from Marxism have been far-reaching in some areas, Marxism cannot possibly have *any* continuing impact or significance is to insist upon the absolute indivisibility of Marxist doctrine—a test we would be unable to apply to other doctrines. By so rigorous a standard, it would be impossible to explain the coexistence of democracy and slavery in the United States for nearly one hundred years, or the coexistence of Christianity (and other religions) and un-Christian-like autocracy for nearly two thousand years.

If this conclusion is sound, the task of evaluating Soviet society is extraordinarily complicated and challenging. It is necessary, as A.N. Whitehead suggested, to "seek simplicity, and distrust it." One must avoid the temptation to compress, to find symmetry and consistency unjustified and unsupported by the complexities of the real Soviet world. One must take account of and grapple with all the significant forces and pressures acting and interacting to mold Soviet reality, including both the revolutionary and antirevolutionary dynamic. Above all, one must recognize that oversimplification of the "socialist" world will no more contribute to true understanding than oversimplification of the "capitalist" world. As E.H. Carr has truly said, "the *homo politicus* who pursues nothing but power is as unreal a myth as the *homo economicus* who pursues nothing but gain."

APPENDIX

CONSTITUTION (FUNDAMENTAL LAW) OF THE UNION OF SOVIET SOCIALIST REPUBLICS

The Great October Socialist Revolution, made by the workers and peasants of Russia under the leadership of the Communist Party headed by Lenin, overthrew capitalist and landowner rule, broke the fetters of oppression, established the dictatorship of the proletariat, and created the Soviet state, a new type of state, the basic instrument for defending the gains of the revolution and for building socialism and communism. Humanity thereby began the epoch-making turn from capitalism to socialism.

After achieving victory in the Civil War and repulsing imperialist intervention, the Soviet government carried through far-reaching social and economic transformations, and put an end once and for all to exploitation of man by man, antagonisms between classes, and strife between nationalities. The unification of the Soviet Republics in the Union of Soviet Socialist Republics multiplied the forces and opportunities of the peoples of the country in the building of socialism. Social ownership of the means of production and genuine democracy for the working masses were established. For the first time in the history of mankind a socialist society was created.

The strength of socialism was vividly demonstrated by the immortal feat of the Soviet people and their Armed Forces in achieving their historic victory in the Great Patriotic War. This victory consolidated the influence and international standing of the Soviet Union and created new opportunities for growth of the forces of socialism, national liberation, democracy, and peace throughout the world.

Continuing their creative endeavours, the working people of the Soviet Union have ensured rapid, all-round development of the country and steady improvement of the socialist system. They have consolidated the alliance of the working class, collective-farm peasantry, and people's intelligentsia, and friendship of the nations and nationalities of the USSR. Socio-political and ideological unity of Soviety society, in which the working class is the leading force, has been achieved. The aims of the dictatorship of the proletariat having been fulfilled, the Soviet state has become a state of the whole people. The leading role of the Communist Party, the vanguard of all the people, has grown.

In the USSR a developed socialist society has been built. At this stage, when socialism is developing on its own foundations, the creative forces of the new system and the advantages of the socialist way of life are becoming increasingly evident, and the working people are more and more widely enjoying the fruits of their great revolutionary gains.

It is a society in which powerful productive forces and progressive science and culture have been created, in which the well-being of the people is constantly rising, and more and more favourable conditions are being provided for the all-round development of the individual.

It is a society of mature socialist social relations, in which, on the basis of the drawing together of all classes and social strata and of the juridical and factual equality of all its na-

Adopted on October 7, 1977.

tions and nationalities and their fraternal co-operation, a new historical community of people has been formed—the Soviet people.

It is a society of high organisational capacity, ideological commitment, and consciousness of the working people, who are patriots and internationalists.

It is a society in which the law of life is concern of all for the good of each and concern of each for the good of all.

It is a society of true democracy, the political system of which ensures effective management of all public affairs, ever more active participation of the working people in running the state, and the combining of citizens' real rights and freedoms with their obligations and responsibility to society.

Developed socialist society is a natural, logical stage on the road to communism.

The supreme goal of the Soviet state is the building of a classless communist society in which there will be public, communist self-government. The main aims of the people's socialist state are: to lay the material and technical foundation of communism, to perfect socialist social relations and transform them into communist relations, to mould the citizen of communist society, to raise the people's living and cultural standards, to safeguard the country's security, and to further the consolidation of peace and development of international co-operation.

The Soviet people,

guided by the ideas of scientific communism and true to their revolutionary traditions,

relying on the great social, economic, and political gains of socialism,

striving for the further development of socialist democracy,

taking into account the international position of the USSR as part of the world system of socialism, and conscious of their internationalist responsibility,

preserving continuity of the ideas and principles of the first Soviet Constitution of 1918, the 1924 Constitution of the USSR and the 1936 Constitution of the USSR,

hereby affirm the principles of the social structure and policy of the USSR, and define the rights, freedoms and obligations of citizens, and the principles of the organisation of the socialist state of the whole people, and its aims, and proclaim these in this Constitution.

I. PRINCIPLES OF THE SOCIAL STRUCTURE AND POLICY OF THE USSR

Chapter 1 The Political System

Article 1. The Union of Soviet Socialist Republics is a socialist state of the whole people, expressing the will and interests of the workers, peasants, and intelligentsia, the working people of all the nations and nationalities of the country.

Article 2. All power in the USSR belongs to the people.

The people exercise state power through Soviets of People's Deputies, which constitute the political foundation of the USSR.

All other state bodies are under the control of, and accountable to, the Soviets of People's Deputies.

Article 3. The Soviet state is organised and functions on the principle of democratic centralism, namely the electiveness of all bodies of state authority from the lowest to the highest, their accountability to the people, and the obligation of lower bodies to observe the decisions of higher ones. Democratic centralism combines central leadership with local initiative and creative activity and with the responsibility of each state body and official for the work entrusted to them.

Article 4. The Soviet state and all its bodies function on the basis of socialist law, ensure the maintenance of law and order, and safeguard the interests of society and the rights and freedoms of citizens.

State organisations, public organisations and officials shall observe the Constitution of the USSR and Soviet laws.

Article 5. Major matters of state shall be submitted to nationwide discussion and put to a popular vote (referendum).

Article 6. The leading and guiding force of Soviet society and the nucleus of its political system, of all state organisations and public organisations, is the Communist Party of the Soviet Union. The CPSU exists for the people and serves the people.

The Communist Party, armed with Marxism-Leninism, determines the general perspectives of the development of society and the course of the home and foreign policy of the USSR, directs the great constructive work of the Soviet people, and imparts a planned, systematic and theoretically substantiated character to their struggle for the victory of communism.

All party organisations shall function within the framework of the Constitution of the USSR.

Article 7. Trade unions, the All-Union Leninist Young Communist League, co-operatives, and other public organisations, participate, in accordance with the aims laid down in their rules, in managing state and public affairs, and in deciding political, economic, and social and cultural matters.

Article 8. Work collectives take part in discussing and deciding state and public affairs, in planning production and social development, in training and placing personnel, and in discussing and deciding matters pertaining to the management of enterprises and institutions, the improvement of working and living conditions, and the use of funds allocated both for developing production and for social and cultural purposes and financial incentives.

Work collectives promote socialist emulation, the spread of progressive methods of work, and the strengthening of production discipline, educate their members in the spirit of communist morality, and strive to enhance their political consciousness and raise their cultural level and skills and qualifications.

Article 9. The principal direction in the development of the political system of Soviet society is the extension of socialist democracy, namely ever broader participation of citizens in managing the affairs of society and the state, continuous improvement of the machinery of state, heightening of the activity of public organisations, strengthening of the system of people's control, consolidation of the legal foundations of the functioning of the state and of public life, greater openness and publicity, and constant responsiveness to public opinion.

Chapter 2 The Economic System

Article 10. The foundation of the economic system of the USSR is socialist ownership of the means of production in the form of state property (belonging to all the people), and collective farm-and-co-operative property.

Socialist ownership also embraces the property of trade unions and other public organisations which they require to carry out their purposes under their rules.

The state protects socialist property and provides conditions for its growth.

No one has the right to use socialist property for personal gain or other selfish ends.

Article 11. State property, i.e. the common property of the Soviet people, is the principal form of socialist property.

The land, its minerals, waters, and forests are the exclusive property of the state. The state owns the basic means of production in industry, construction, and agriculture; means of transport and communication; the banks; the property of state-run trade organisations and public utilities, and other state-run undertakings; most urban housing; and other property necessary for state purposes.

Article 12. The property of collective farms and other co-operative organisations, and of their joint undertakings, comprises the means of production and other assets which they require for the purposes laid down in their rules.

The land held by collective farms is secured to them for their free use in perpetuity.

The state promotes development of collective farm-and-co-operative property and its approximation to state property.

Collective farms, like other land users, are obliged to make effective and thrifty use of the land and to increase its fertility.

Article 13. Earned income forms the basis of the personal property of Soviet citizens. The personal property of citizens of the USSR may include articles of everyday use, personal consumption and convenience, the implements and other objects of a small-holding, a house, and earned savings. The personal property of citizens and the right to inherit it are protected by the state.

Citizens may be granted the use of plots of land, in the manner prescribed by law, for a subsidiary small-holding (including the keeping of livestock and poultry), for fruit and vegetable growing or for building an individual dwelling. Citizens are required to make rational use of the land allotted to them. The state, and collective farms provide assistance to citizens in working their small-holdings.

Property owned or used by citizens shall not serve as a means of deriving unearned income or be employed to the detriment of the interests of society.

Article 14. The source of the growth of social wealth and of the well-being of the people, and of each individual, is the labour, free from exploitation, of Soviet people.

The state exercises control over the measure of labour and of consumption in accordance with the principle of socialism: "From each according to his ability, to each according to his work." It fixes the rate of taxation on taxable income.

Socially useful work and its results determine a person's status in society. By combining material and moral incentives and encouraging innovation and a creative attitude to work, the state helps transform labour into the prime vital need of every Soviet citizen.

Article 15. The supreme goal of social production under socialism is the fullest possible satisfaction of the people's growing material, and cultural and intellectual requirements.

Relying on the creative initiative of the working people, socialist emulation, and scientific and technological progress, and by improving the forms and methods of economic management, the state ensures growth of the productivity of labour, raising of the efficiency of production and of the quality of work, and dynamic, planned, proportionate development of the economy.

Article 16. The economy of the USSR is an integral economic complex comprising all the elements of social production, distribution, and exchange on its territory.

The economy is managed on the basis of state plans for economic and social development, with due account of the sectoral and territorial principles, and by combining centralised direction with the managerial independence and initiative of individual and amalgamated enterprises and other organisations, for which active use is made of management accounting, profit, cost, and other economic levers and incentives.

Article 17. In the USSR, the law permits individual labour in handicrafts, farming, the provision of services for the public, and other forms of activity based exclusively on the personal work of individual citizens and members of their families. The state makes regulations for such work to ensure that it serves the interests of society.

Article 18. In the interests of the present and future generations, the necessary steps are taken in the USSR to protect and make scientific, rational use of the land and its mineral and water resources, and the plant and animal kingdoms, to preserve the purity of air and water, ensure reproduction of natural wealth, and improve the human environment.

Chapter 3 Social Development and Culture

Article 19. The social basis of the USSR is the unbreakable alliance of the workers, peasants, and intelligentsia.

The state helps enhance the social homogeneity of society, namely the elimination of class differences and of the essential distinction between town and country and between mental and physical labour, and the all-round development and drawing together of all the nations and nationalities of the USSR.

Article 20. In accordance with the communist ideal—"The free development of each is the condition of the free development of all"—the state pursues the aim of giving citizens more and more real opportunities to apply their creative energies, abilities, and talents, and to develop their personalities in every way.

Article 21. The state concerns itself with improving working conditions, safety and labour protection and the scientific organisation of work, and with reducing and ultimately eliminating all arduous physical labour through comprehensive mechanisation and automation of production processes in all branches of the economy.

Article 22. A programme is being consistently implemented in the USSR to convert agricultural work into a variety of industrial work, to extend the network of educational, cultural and medical institutions, and of trade, public catering, service and public utility facilities in rural localities, and transform hamlets and villages into well-planned and well-appointed settlements.

Article 23. The state pursues a steady policy of raising people's pay levels and real incomes through increase in productivity.

In order to satisfy the needs of Soviet people more fully social consumption funds are created. The state, with the broad participation of public organisations and work collectives, ensures the growth and just distribution of these funds.

Article 24. In the USSR, state systems of health protection, social security, trade and public catering, communal services and amenities, and public utilities, operate and are being extended.

The state encourages co-operatives and other public organisations to provide all types of services for the population. It encourages the development of mass physical culture and sport.

Article 25. In the USSR there is a uniform system of public education, which is being constantly improved, that provides general education and vocational training for citizens, serves the communist education and intellectual and physical development of the youth, and trains them for work and social activity.

Article 26. In accordance with society's needs the state provides for planned development of science and the training of scientific personnel and organises introduction of the results of research in the economy and other spheres of life.

Article 27. The state concerns itself with protecting, augmenting and making extensive use of society's cultural wealth for the moral and aesthetic education of the Soviet people, for raising their cultural level.

In the USSR development of the professional, amateur and folk arts is encouraged in every way.

Chapter 4 Foreign Policy

Article 28. The USSR steadfastly pursues a Leninist policy of peace and stands for strengthening of the security of nations and broad international co-operation.

The foreign policy of the USSR is aimed at ensuring international conditions favourable for building communism in the USSR, safeguarding the state interests of the Soviet Union, consolidating the positions of world socialism, supporting the struggle of peoples for national liberation and social progress, preventing wars of aggression, achieving universal and complete disarmament, and consistently implementing the principle of the peaceful coexistence of states with different social systems.

In the USSR war propaganda is banned.

Article 29. The USSR's relations with other states are based on observance of the following principles: sovereign equality; mutual renunciation of the use or threat of force; inviolability of frontiers; territorial integrity of states; peaceful settlement of disputes; non-intervention in internal affairs; respect for human rights and fundamental freedoms; the equal rights of peoples and their right to decide their own destiny; co-operation among states; and fulfilment in good faith of obligations arising from the generally recognised principles and rules of international law, and from the international treaties signed by the USSR.

Article 30. The USSR, as part of the world system of socialism and of the socialist community, promotes and strengthens friendship, co-operation, and comradely mutual assistance with other socialist countries on the basis of the principle of socialist internationalism, and takes an active part in socialist economic integration and the socialist international division of labour.

Chapter 5 Defence of the Socialist Motherland

Article 31. Defence of the Socialist Motherland is one of the most important functions of the state, and is the concern of the whole people.

In order to defend the gains of socialism, the peaceful labour of the Soviet people, and the sovereignty and territorial integrity of the state, the USSR maintains armed forces and has instituted universal military service.

The duty of the Armed Forces of the USSR to the people is to provide reliable defence of the Socialist Motherland and to be in constant combat readiness, guaranteeing that any aggressor is instantly repulsed.

Article 32. The state ensures the security and defence capability of the country, and supplies the Armed Forces of the USSR with everything necessary for that purpose.

The duties of state bodies, public organisations, officials, and citizens in regard to safeguarding the country's security and strengthening its defence capacity are defined by the legislation of the USSR.

II. THE STATE AND THE INDIVIDUAL

Chapter 6 Citizenship of the USSR: Equality of Citizens' Rights

Article 33. Uniform federal citizenship is established for the USSR. Every citizen of a Union Republic is a citizen of the USSR.

The grounds and procedure for acquiring or forfeiting Soviet citizenship are defined by the Law on Citizenship of the USSR.

When abroad, citizens of the USSR enjoy the protection and assistance of the Soviet state.

Article 34. Citizens of the USSR are equal before the law, without distinction of origin, social or property status, race or nationality, sex, education, language, attitude to religion, type and nature of occupation, domicile, or other status.

The equal rights of citizens of the USSR are guaranteed in all fields of economic, political, social, and cultural life.

Article 35. Women and men have equal rights in the USSR.

Exercise of these rights is ensured by according women equal access with men to education and vocational and professional training, equal opportunities in employment, remuneration, and promotion, and in social and political, and cultural activity, and by special labour and health protection measures for women; by providing conditions enabling mothers to work; by legal protection, and material and moral support for mothers and children, including paid leaves and other benefits for expectant mothers and mothers, and gradual reduction of working time for mothers with small children.

Article 36. Citizens of the USSR of different races and nationalities have equal rights.

Exercise of these rights is ensured by a policy of all-round development and drawing together of all the nations and nationalities of the USSR, by educating citizens in the spirit of Soviet patriotism and socialist internationalism, and by the possibility to use their native language and the languages of other peoples of the USSR.

Any direct or indirect limitation of the rights of citizens or establishment of direct or indirect privileges on grounds of race or nationality, and any advocacy of racial or national exclusiveness, hostility or contempt, are punishable by law.

Article 37. Citizens of other countries and stateless persons in the USSR are guaranteed the rights and freedoms provided by law, including the right to apply to a court and other state bodies for the protection of their personal, property, family, and other rights.

Citizens of other countries and stateless persons, when in the USSR, are obliged to respect the Constitution of the USSR and observe Soviet laws.

Article 38. The USSR grants the right of asylum to foreigners persecuted for defending the interests of the working people and the cause of peace, or for participation in the revolutionary and national-liberation movement, or for progressive social and political, scientific or other creative activity.

Chapter 7 The Basic Rights, Freedoms, and Duties of Citizens of the USSR

Article 39. Citizens of the USSR enjoy in full the social, economic, political and personal rights and freedoms proclaimed and guaranteed by the Constitution of the USSR and by Soviet laws. The socialist system ensures enlargement of the rights and freedoms of citizens and continuous improvement of their living standards as social, economic, and cultural development programmes are fulfilled.

Enjoyment by citizens of their rights and freedoms must not be to the detriment of the interests of society or the state, or infringe the rights of other citizens.

Article 40. Citizens of the USSR have the right to work (that is, to guaranteed employment and pay in accordance with the quantity and quality of their work, and not below the state-established minimum), including the right to choose their trade or profession, type of job and work in accordance with their inclinations, abilities, training and education, with due account of the needs of society.

This right is ensured by the socialist economic system, steady growth of the productive forces, free vocational and professional training, improvement of skills, training in new trades or professions, and development of the systems of vocational guidance and job placement.

Article 41. Citizens of the USSR have the right to rest and leisure.

This right is ensured by the establishment of a working week not exceeding 41 hours, for workers and other employees, a shorter working day in a number of trades and industries, and shorter hours for night work; by the provision of paid annual holidays, weekly days of rest, extension of the network of cultural, educational and health-building institutions, and the development on a mass scale of sport, physical culture, and camping and tourism; by the provision of neighbourhood recreational facilities, and of other opportunities for rational use of free time.

The length of collective farmers' working and leisure time is established by their collective farms.

Article 42. Citizens of the USSR have the right to health protection.

This right is ensured by free, qualified medical care provided by state health institutions; by extension of the network of therapeutic and health-building institutions; by the development and improvement of safety and hygiene in industry; by carrying out broad prophylactic measures; by measures to improve the environment; by special care for the health of the rising generation, including prohibition of child labour, excluding the work done by children as part of the school curriculum; and by developing research to prevent and reduce the incidence of disease and ensure citizens a long and active life.

Article 43. Citizens of the USSR have the right to maintenance in old age, in sickness, and in the event of complete or partial disability or loss of the breadwinner.

This right is guaranteed by social insurance of workers and other employees and collective farmers; by allowances for temporary disability; by the provision by the state or by collective farms of retirement pensions, disability pensions, and pensions for loss of the breadwinner; by providing employment for the partially disabled; by care for the elderly and the disabled; and by other forms of social security.

Article 44. Citizens of the USSR have the right to housing.

This right is ensured by the development and upkeep of state and socially-owned housing; by assistance for co-operative and individual house building; by fair distribution, under public control, of the housing that becomes available through fulfilment of the programme of building well-appointed dwellings, and by low rents and low charges for utility services. Citizens of the USSR shall take good care of the housing allocated to them.

Article 45. Citizens of the USSR have the right to education.

This right is ensured by free provision of all forms of education, by the institution of universal, compulsory secondary education, and broad development of vocational, specialised secondary, and higher education, in which instruction is oriented toward practical activity and production; by the development of extramural, correspondence and evening courses; by the provision of state scholarships and grants and privileges for students; by the free issue of school textbooks; by the opportunity to attend a school where teaching is in the native language; and by the provision of facilities for self-education.

Article 46. Citizens of the USSR have the right to enjoy cultural benefits.

This right is ensured by broad access to the cultural treasures of their own land and of the world that are preserved in state and other public collections; by the development and fair distribution of cultural and educational institutions throughout the country; by developing television and radio broadcasting and the publishing of books, newspapers and periodicals, and by extending the free library service; and by expanding cultural exchanges with other countries.

Article 47. Citizens of the USSR, in accordance with the aims of building communism, are guaranteed freedom of scientific, technical, and artistic work. This freedom is ensured by broadening scientific research, encouraging invention and innovation, and developing literature and the arts. The state provides the necessary material conditions for this and support for voluntary societies and unions of workers in the arts, organises introduction of inventions and innovations in production and other spheres of activity.

The rights of authors, inventors and innovators are protected by the state.

Article 48. Citizens of the USSR have the right to take part in the management and administration of state and public affairs and in the discussion and adoption of laws and measures of All-Union and local significance.

This right is ensured by the opportunity to vote and to be elected to Soviets of People's Deputies and other elective state bodies, to take part in nationwide discussions and referendums, in people's control, in the work of state bodies, public organisations, and local community groups, and in meetings at places of work or residence.

Article 49. Every citizen of the USSR has the right to submit proposals to state bodies and public organisations for improving their activity, and to criticise shortcomings in their work.

Officials are obliged, within established time-limits, to examine citizens' proposals and requests, to reply to them, and to take appropriate action.

Persecution for criticism is prohibited. Persons guilty of such persecution shall be called to account.

Article 50. In accordance with the interests of the people and in order to strengthen and develop the socialist system, citizens of the USSR are guaranteed freedom of speech, of the press, and of assembly, meetings, street processions and demonstrations.

Exercise of these political freedoms is ensured by putting public buildings, streets and squares at the disposal of the working people and their organisations, by broad dissemination of information, and by the opportunity to use the press, television, and radio.

Article 51. In accordance with the aims of building communism, citizens of the USSR have the right to associate in public organisations that promote their political activity and initiative and satisfaction of their various interests.

Public organisations are guaranteed conditions for successfully performing the functions defined in their rules.

Article 52. Citizens of the USSR are guaranteed freedom of conscience, that is, the right to profess or not to profess any religion, and to conduct religious worship or atheistic propaganda. Incitement of hostility or hatred on religious grounds is prohibited.

In the USSR, the church is separated from the state, and the school from the church.

Article 53. The family enjoys the protection of the state.

Marriage is based on the free consent of the woman and the man; the spouses are completely equal in their family relations.

The state helps the family by providing and developing a broad system of childcare institutions, by organising and improving communal services and public catering, by paying grants on the birth of a child, by providing children's allowances and benefits for large families, and other forms of family allowances and assistance.

Article 54. Citizens of the USSR are guaranteed inviolability of the person. No one may be arrested except by a court decision or on the warrant of a procurator.

Article 55. Citizens of the USSR are guaranteed inviolability of the home. No one may, without lawful grounds, enter a home against the will of those residing in it.

Article 56. The privacy of citizens, and of their correspondence, telephone conversations, and telegraphic communications is protected by law.

Article 57. Respect for the individual and protection of the rights and freedoms of citizens are the duty of all state bodies, public organisations, and officials.

Citizens of the USSR have the right to protection by the courts against encroachments on their honour and reputation, life and health, and personal freedom and property.

Article 58. Citizens of the USSR have the right to lodge a complaint against the actions of officials, state bodies and public bodies. Complaints shall be examined according to the procedure and within the time-limit established by law.

Actions by officials that contravene the law or exceed their powers, and infringe the rights of citizens, may be appealed against in a court in the manner prescribed by law.

Citizens of the USSR have the right to compensation for damage resulting from unlawful actions by state organisations and public organisations, or by officials in the performance of their duties.

Article 59. Citizens' exercise of their rights and freedoms is inseparable from the performance of their duties and obligations.

Citizens of the USSR are obliged to observe the Constitution of the USSR and Soviet laws, comply with the standards of socialist conduct, and uphold the honour and dignity of Soviet citizenship.

Article 60. It is the duty of, and a matter of honour for, every able-bodied citizen of the USSR to work conscientiously in his chosen, socially useful occupation, and strictly to observe labour discipline. Evasion of socially useful work is incompatible with the principles of socialist society.

Article 61. Citizens of the USSR are obliged to preserve and protect socialist property. It is the duty of a citizen of the USSR to combat misappropriation and squandering of state and socially-owned property and to make thrifty use of the people's wealth.

Persons encroaching in any way on socialist property shall be punished according to the law.

Article 62. Citizens of the USSR are obliged to safeguard the interests of the Soviet state, and to enhance its power and prestige.

Defence of the Socialist Motherland is the sacred duty of every citizen of the USSR.

Betrayal of the Motherland is the gravest of crimes against the people.

Article 63. Military service in the ranks of the Armed Forces of the USSR is an honourable duty of Soviet citizens.

Article 64. It is the duty of every citizen of the USSR to respect the national dignity of other citizens, and to strengthen friendship of the nations and nationalities of the multinational Soviet state.

Article 65. A citizen of the USSR is obliged to respect the rights and lawful interests of other persons, to be uncompromising toward anti-social behaviour, and to help maintain public order.

Article 66. Citizens of the USSR are obliged to concern themselves with the upbringing of children, to train them for socially useful work, and to raise them as worthy members of socialist society. Children are obliged to care for their parents and help them.

Article 67. Citizens of the USSR are obliged to protect nature and conserve its riches.

Article 68. Concern for the preservation of historical monuments and other cultural values is a duty and obligation of citizens of the USSR.

Article 69. It is the internationalist duty of citizens of the USSR to promote friendship and co-operation with peoples of other lands and help maintain and strengthen world peace.

III. THE NATIONAL-STATE STRUCTURE OF THE USSR

Chapter 8 The USSR—A Federal State

Article 70. The Union of Soviet Socialist Republics is an integral, federal, multinational state formed on the principle of socialist federalism as a result of the free self-determination of nations and the voluntary association of equal Soviet Socialist Republics.

The USSR embodies the state unity of the Soviet people and draws all its nations and nationalities together for the purpose of jointly building communism.

Article 71. The Union of Soviet Socialist Republics unites:

the Russian Soviet Federative Socialist Republic,
the Ukrainian Soviet Socialist Republic,
the Byelorussian Soviet Socialist Republic,
the Uzbek Soviet Socialist Republic,
the Kazakh Soviet Socialist Republic,
the Georgian Soviet Socialist Republic,
the Azerbaijan Soviet Socialist Republic,
the Lithuanian Soviet Socialist Republic,
the Moldavian Soviet Socialist Republic,
the Latvian Soviet Socialist Republic,
the Kirghiz Soviet Socialist Republic,
the Tajik Soviet Socialist Republic,
the Armenian Soviet Socialist Republic,
the Turkmen Soviet Socialist Republic,
the Estonian Soviet Socialist Republic.

Article 72. Each Union Republic shall retain the right freely to secede from the USSR.

Article 73. The jurisdiction of the Union of Soviet Socialist Republics, as represented by its highest bodies of state authority and administration, shall cover:

1. the admission of new republics to the USSR; endorsement of the formation of new autonomous republics and autonomous regions within Union Republics;
2. determination of the state boundaries of the USSR and approval of changes in the boundaries between Union Republics;
3. establishment of the general principles for the organisation and functioning of republican and local bodies of state authority and administration;
4. the ensurance of uniformity of legislative norms throughout the USSR and establishment of the fundamentals of the legislation of the Union of Soviet Socialist Republics and Union Republics;
5. pursuance of a uniform social and economic policy; direction of the country's economy; determination of the main lines of scientific and technological progress and the general measures for rational exploitation and conservation of natural resources; the drafting and approval of state plans for the economic and social development of the USSR, and endorsement of reports on their fulfilment;
6. the drafting and approval of the consolidated Budget of the USSR, and endorsement of the report on its execution; management of a single monetary and credit system; determination of the taxes and revenues forming the Budget of the USSR; and the formulation of prices and wages policy;
7. direction of the sectors of the economy, and of enterprises and amalgamations under Union jurisdiction, and general direction of industries under Union-Republican jurisdiction;
8. issues of war and peace, defence of the sovereignty of the USSR and safeguarding of its frontiers and territory, and organisation of defence; direction of the Armed Forces of the USSR;
9. state security;
10. representation of the USSR in international relations; the USSR's relations with other states and with international organisations; establishment of the general procedure for, and co-ordination of, the relations of Union Republics with other states and with international organisations; foreign trade and other forms of external economic activity on the basis of state monopoly;
11. control over observance of the Constitution of the USSR, and ensurance of conformity of the Constitutions of Union Republics to the Constitution of the USSR;
12. and settlement of other matters of All-Union importance.

Article 74. The laws of the USSR shall have the same force in all Union Republics. In the event of a discrepancy between a Union Republic law and an All-Union law, the law of the USSR shall prevail.

Article 75. The territory of the Union of Soviet Socialist Republics is a single entity and comprises the territories of the Union Republics.

The sovereignty of the USSR extends throughout its territory.

Chapter 9 The Union Soviet Socialist Republic

Article 76. A Union Republic is a sovereign Soviet socialist state that has united with other Soviet Republics in the Union of Soviet Socialist Republics.

Outside the spheres listed in Article 73 of the Constitution of the USSR, a Union Republic exercises independent authority on its territory.

A Union Republic shall have its own Constitution conforming to the Constitution of the USSR with the specific features of the Republic being taken into account.

Article 77. Union Republics take part in decision-making in the Supreme Soviet of the USSR, the Presidium of the Supreme Soviet of the USSR, the Government of the USSR, and other bodies of the Union of Soviet Socialist Republics in matters that come within the jurisdiction of the Union of Soviet Socialist Republics.

A Union Republic shall ensure comprehensive economic and social development on its territory, facilitate exercise of the powers of the USSR on its territory, and implement the decisions of the highest bodies of state authority and administration of the USSR.

In matters that come within its jurisdiction, a Union Republic shall co-ordinate and control the activity of enterprises, institutions, and organisations subordinate to the Union.

Article 78. The territory of a Union Republic may not be altered without its consent. The boundaries between Union Republics may be altered by mutual agreement of the Republics concerned, subject to ratification by the Union of Soviet Socialist Republics.

Article 79. A Union Republic shall determine its division into territories, regions, areas, and districts, and decide other matters relating to its administrative and territorial structure.

Article 80. A Union Republic has the right to enter into relations with other states, conclude treaties with them, exchange diplomatic and consular representatives, and take part in the work of international organisations.

Article 81. The sovereign rights of Union Republics shall be safeguarded by the USSR.

Chapter 10 The Autonomous Soviet Socialist Republic

Article 82. An Autonomous Republic is a constituent part of a Union Republic.

In spheres not within the jurisdiction of the Union of Soviet Socialist Republics and the Union Republic, an Autonomous Republic shall deal independently with matters within its jurisdiction.

An Autonomous Republic shall have its own Constitution conforming to the Constitutions of the USSR and the Union Republic with the specific features of the Autonomous Republic being taken into account.

Article 83. An Autonomous Republic takes part in decision-making through the highest bodies of state authority and administration of the USSR and of the Union Republic respectively, in matters that come within the jurisdiction of the USSR and the Union Republic.

An Autonomous Republic shall ensure comprehensive economic and social development on its territory, facilitate exercise of the powers of the USSR and the Union Republic on its territory, and implement decisions of the highest bodies of state authority and administration of the USSR and the Union Republic.

In matters within its jurisdiction, an Autonomous Republic shall co-ordinate and control the activity of enterprises, institutions, and organisations subordinate to the Union or the Union Republic.

Article 84. The territory of an Autonomous Republic may not be altered without its consent.

Article 85. The Russian Soviet Federative Socialist Republic includes the Bashkir, Buryat, Daghestan, Kabardin-Balkar, Kalmyk, Karelian, Komi, Mari, Mordovian,

North Ossetian, Tatar, Tuva, Udmurt, Chechen-Ingush, Chuvash, and Yakut Autonomous Soviet Socialist Republics.

The Uzbek Soviet Socialist Republic includes the Kara-Kalpak Autonomous Soviet Socialist Republic.

The Georgian Soviet Socialist Republic includes the Abkhasian and Adzhar Autonomous Soviet Socialist Republics.

The Azerbaijan Soviet Socialist Republic includes the Nakhichevan Autonomous Soviet Socialist Republic.

Chapter 11 The Autonomous Region and Autonomous Area

Article 86. An Autonomous Region is a constituent part of a Union Republic or Territory. The Law on an Autonomous Region, upon submission by the Soviet of People's Deputies of the Autonomous Region concerned, shall be adopted by the Supreme Soviet of the Union Republic.

Article 87. The Russian Soviet Federative Socialist Republic includes the Adygei, Gorno-Altai, Jewish, Karachai-Circassian, and Khakass Autonomous Regions.

The Georgian Soviet Socialist Republic includes the South Ossetian Autonomous Region.

The Azerbaijan Soviet Socialist Republic includes the Nagorno-Karabakh Autonomous Region.

The Tajik Soviet Socialist Republic includes the Gorno-Badakhshan Autonomous Region.

Article 88. An Autonomous Area is a constituent part of a Territory or Region. The Law on an Autonomous Area shall be adopted by the Supreme Soviet of the Union Republic concerned.

IV. SOVIETS OF PEOPLE'S DEPUTIES AND ELECTORAL PROCEDURE

Chapter 12 The System of Soviets of People's Deputies and the Principles of Their Work

Article 89. The Soviets of People's Deputies, i.e. the Supreme Soviet of the USSR, the Supreme Soviets of Union Republics, the Supreme Soviets of Autonomous Republics, the Soviets of People's Deputies of Territories and Regions, the Soviets of People's Deputies of Autonomous Regions and Autonomous Areas, and the Soviets of People's Deputies of districts, cities, city districts, settlements and villages shall constitute a single system of bodies of state authority.

Article 90. The term of the Supreme Soviet of the USSR, the Supreme Soviets of Union Republics, and the Supreme Soviets of Autonomous Republics shall be five years.

The term of local Soviets of People's Deputies shall be two and a half years.

Elections to Soviets of People's Deputies shall be called not later than two months before the expiry of the term of the Soviet concerned.

Article 91. The most important matters within the jurisdiction of the respective Soviets of People's Deputies shall be considered and settled at their sessions.

Soviets of People's Deputies shall elect standing commissions and form executive-administrative, and other bodies accountable to them.

Article 92. Soviets of People's Deputies shall form people's control bodies combining state control with control by the working people at enterprises, collective farms, institutions, and organisations.

People's control bodies shall check on the fulfilment of state plans and assignments, combat breaches of state discipline, localistic tendencies, narrow departmental attitudes, mismanagement, extravagance and waste, red tape and bureaucracy, and help improve the working of the state machinery.

Article 93. Soviets of People's Deputies shall direct all sectors of state, economic, and social and cultural development, either directly or through bodies instituted by them, take decisions and ensure their execution, and verify their implementation.

Article 94. Soviets of People's Deputies shall function publicly on the basis of collective, free, constructive discussion and decision-making, of systematic reporting back to them and the people by their executive-administrative and other bodies, and of involving citizens on a broad scale in their work.

Soviets of People's Deputies and the bodies set up by them shall systematically inform the public about their work and the decisions taken by them.

Chapter 13 The Electoral System

Article 95. Deputies to all Soviets shall be elected on the basis of universal, equal, and direct suffrage by secret ballot.

Article 96. Elections shall be universal: all citizens of the USSR who have reached the age of 18 shall have the right to vote and to be elected, with the exception of persons who have been legally certified insane.

To be eligible for election to the Supreme Soviet of the USSR a citizen of the USSR must have reached the age of 21.

Article 97. Elections shall be equal: each citizen shall have one vote; all voters shall exercise the franchise on an equal footing.

Article 98. Elections shall be direct: deputies to all Soviets of People's Deputies shall be elected by citizens by direct vote.

Article 99. Voting at elections shall be secret: control over voters' exercise of the franchise is inadmissible.

Article 100. The following shall have the right to nominate candidates: branches and organisations of the Communist Party of the Soviet Union, trade unions, and the All-Union Leninist Young Communist League; co-operatives and other public organisations; work collectives, and meetings of servicemen in their military units.

Citizens of the USSR and public organisations are guaranteed the right to free and all-round discussion of the political and personal qualities and competence of candidates, and the right to campaign for them at meetings, in the press, and on television and radio.

The expenses involved in holding elections to Soviets of People's Deputies shall be met by the state.

Article 101. Deputies to Soviets of People's Deputies shall be elected by constituencies.

A citizen of the USSR may not, as a rule, be elected to more than two Soviets of People's Deputies.

Elections to the Soviets shall be conducted by electoral commissions consisting of representatives of public organizations and work collectives, and of meetings of servicemen in military units.

The procedure for holding elections to Soviets of People's Deputies shall be defined by the laws of the USSR, and of Union and Autonomous Republics.

Article 102. Electors give mandates to their Deputies.

The appropriate Soviets of People's Deputies shall examine electors' mandates, take them into account in drafting economic and social development plans and in drawing up the budget, organise implementation of the mandates, and inform citizens about it.

Chapter 14 People's Deputies

Article 103. Deputies are the plenipotentiary representatives of the people in the Soviets of People's Deputies.

In the Soviets, Deputies deal with matters relating to state, economic, and social and cultural development, organise implementation of the decisions of the Soviets, and exercise control over the work of state bodies, enterprises, institutions and organisations.

Deputies shall be guided in their activities by the interests of the state, and shall take the needs of their constituents into account and work to implement their electors' mandates.

Article 104. Deputies shall exercise their powers without discontinuing their regular employment or duties.

During sessions of the Soviet, and so as to exercise their deputy's powers in other cases stipulated by law, Deputies shall be released from their regular employment or duties, with retention of their average earnings at their permanent place of work.

Article 105. A Deputy has the right to address inquiries to the appropriate state bodies and officials, who are obliged to reply to them at a session of the Soviet.

Deputies have the right to approach any state or public body, enterprise, institution, or organisation on matters arising from their work as Deputies and to take part in considering the questions raised by them. The heads of the state or public bodies, enterprises, institutions or organisations concerned are obliged to receive Deputies without delay and to consider their proposals within the time-limit established by law.

Article 106. Deputies shall be ensured conditions for the unhampered and effective exercise of their rights and duties.

The immunity of Deputies, and other guarantees of their activity as Deputies, are defined in the Law on the Status of Deputies and other legislative acts of the USSR and of Union and Autonomous Republics.

Article 107. Deputies shall report on their work and on that of the Soviet to their constituents, and to the work collectives and public organisations that nominated them.

Deputies who have not justified the confidence of their constituents may be recalled at any time by decision of a majority of the electors in accordance with the procedure established by law.

V. HIGHER BODIES OF STATE AUTHORITY AND ADMINISTRATION OF THE USSR

Chapter 15 The Supreme Soviet of the USSR

Article 108. The highest body of state authority of the USSR shall be the Supreme Soviet of the USSR.

The Supreme Soviet of the USSR is empowered to deal with all matters within the jurisdiction of the Union of Soviet Socialist Republics, as defined by this Constitution.

The adoption and amendment of the Constitution of the USSR; admission of new Republics to the USSR; endorsement of the formation of new Autonomous Republics and Autonomous Regions; approval of the state plans for economic and social development, of the Budget of the USSR, and of reports on their execution; and the institution of bodies of the USSR accountable to it, are the exclusive prerogative of the Supreme Soviet of the USSR.

Laws of the USSR shall be enacted by the Supreme Soviet of the USSR or by a nationwide vote (referendum) held by decision of the Supreme Soviet of the USSR.

Article 109. The Supreme Soviet of the USSR shall consist of two chambers: the Soviet of the Union and the Soviet of Nationalities.

The two chambers of the Supreme Soviet of the USSR shall have equal rights.

Article 110. The Soviet of the Union and the Soviet of Nationalities shall have equal numbers of deputies.

The Soviet of the Union shall be elected by constituencies with equal populations.

The Soviet of Nationalities shall be elected on the basis of the following representation: 32 deputies from each Union Republic, 11 deputies from each Autonomous Republic, five deputies from each Autonomous Region, and one deputy from each Autonomous Area.

The Soviet of the Union and the Soviet of Nationalities, upon submission by the credentials commissions elected by them, shall decide on the validity of Deputies' credentials, and, in cases in which the election law has been violated, shall declare the election of the Deputies concerned null and void.

Article 111. Each chamber of the Supreme Soviet of the USSR shall elect a Chairman and four Vice-Chairmen.

The Chairmen of the Soviet of the Union and of the Soviet of Nationalities shall preside over the sittings of the respective chambers and conduct their affairs.

Joint sittings of the chambers of the Supreme Soviet of the USSR shall be presided over alternately by the Chairman of the Soviet of the Union and the Chairman of the Soviet of Nationalities.

Article 112. Sessions of the Supreme Soviet of the USSR shall be convened twice a year.

Special sessions shall be convened by the Presidium of the Supreme Soviet of the USSR at its discretion or on the proposal of a Union Republic, or of not less than one-third of the Deputies of one of the chambers.

A session of the Supreme Soviet of the USSR shall consist of separate and joint sittings of the chambers, and of meetings of the standing commissions of the chambers or commissions of the Supreme Soviet of the USSR held between the sittings of the chambers. A session may be opened and closed at either separate or joint sittings of the chambers.

Article 113. The right to initiate legislation in the Supreme Soviet of the USSR is vested in the Soviet of the Union and the Soviet of Nationalities, the Presidium of the Supreme Soviet of the USSR, the Council of Ministers of the USSR, Union Republics through their highest bodies of state authority, commissions of the Supreme Soviet of the USSR and standing commissions of its chambers, Deputies of the Supreme Soviet of the USSR, the Supreme Court of the USSR, and the Procurator-General of the USSR.

The right to initiate legislation is also vested in public organisations through their All-Union bodies.

Article 114. Bills and other matters submitted to the Supreme Soviet of the USSR shall be debated by its chambers at separate or joint sittings. Where necessary, a bill or other matter may be referred to one or more commissions for preliminary or additional consideration.

A law of the USSR shall be deemed adopted when it has been passed in each chamber of the Supreme Soviet of the USSR by a majority of the total number of its Deputies. Decisions and other acts of the Supreme Soviet of the USSR are adopted by a majority of the total number of Deputies of the Supreme Soviet of the USSR.

Bills and other very important matters of state may be submitted for nationwide discussion by a decision of the Supreme Soviet of the USSR or its Presidium taken on their own initiative or on the proposal of a Union Republic.

Article 115. In the event of disagreement between the Soviet of the Union and the Soviet of Nationalities, the matter at issue shall be referred for settlement to a conciliation commission formed by the chambers on a parity basis, after which it shall be considered for a second time by the Soviet of the Union and the Soviet of Nationalities at a joint sitting. If agreement is again not reached, the matter shall be postponed for debate at the next session of the Supreme Soviet of the USSR or submitted by the Supreme Soviet to a nationwide vote (referendum).

Article 116. Laws of the USSR and decisions and other acts of the Supreme Soviet of the USSR shall be published in the languages of the Union Republics over the signatures of the Chairman and Secretary of the Presidium of the Supreme Soviet of the USSR.

Article 117. A Deputy of the Supreme Soviet of the USSR has the right to address inquiries to the Council of Ministers of the USSR, and to Ministers and the heads of other bodies formed by the Supreme Soviet of the USSR. The Council of Ministers of the USSR, or the official to whom the inquiry is addressed, is obliged to give a verbal or written reply within three days at the given session of the Supreme Soviet of the USSR.

Article 118. A Deputy of the Supreme Soviet of the USSR may not be prosecuted, or arrested, or incur a court-imposed penalty, without the sanction of the Supreme Soviet of the USSR or, between its sessions, of the Presidium of the Supreme Soviet of the USSR.

Article 119. The Supreme Soviet of the USSR, at a joint sitting of its chambers, shall elect a Presidium of the Supreme Soviet of the USSR, which shall be a standing body of the Supreme Soviet of the USSR, accountable to it for all its work and exercising the functions of the highest body of state authority of the USSR between sessions of the Supreme Soviet, within the limits prescribed by the Constitution.

Article 120. The Presidium of the Supreme Soviet of the USSR shall be elected from among the Deputies and shall consist of a Chairman, First Vice-Chairman, 15 Vice-Chairmen (one from each Union Republic), a Secretary, and 21 members.

Article 121. The Presidium of the Supreme Soviet of the USSR shall:

1. name the date of elections to the Supreme Soviet of the USSR;
2. convene sessions of the Supreme Soviet of the USSR;
3. co-ordinate the work of the standing commissions of the chambers of the Supreme Soviet of the USSR;
4. ensure observance of the Constitution of the USSR and conformity of the Constitutions and laws of Union Republics to the Constitution and laws of the USSR;
5. interpret the laws of the USSR;

6. ratify and denounce international treaties of the USSR;
7. revoke decisions and ordinances of the Council of Ministers of the USSR and of the Councils of Ministers of Union Republics should they fail to conform to the law;
8. institute military and diplomatic ranks and other special titles; and confer the highest military and diplomatic ranks and other special titles;
9. institute orders and medals of the USSR, and honorific titles of the USSR; award orders and medals of the USSR; and confer honorific titles of the USSR;
10. grant citizenship of the USSR, and rule on matters of the renunciation or deprivation of citizenship of the USSR and of granting asylum;
11. issue All-Union acts of amnesty and exercise the right of pardon;
12. appoint and recall diplomatic representatives of the USSR to other countries and to international organisations;
13. receive the letters of credence and recall of the diplomatic representatives of foreign states accredited to it;
14. form the Council of Defense of the USSR and confirm its composition; appoint and dismiss the high command of the Armed Forces of the USSR;
15. proclaim martial law in particular localities or throughout the country in the interests of defence of the USSR;
16. order general or partial mobilisation;
17. between sessions of the Supreme Soviet of the USSR, proclaim a state of war in the event of an armed attack on the USSR, or when it is necessary to meet international treaty obligations relating to mutual defence against aggression;
18. and exercise other powers vested in it by the Constitution and laws of the USSR.

Article 122. The Presidium of the Supreme Soviet of the USSR, between sessions of the Supreme Soviet of the USSR and subject to submission for its confirmation at the next session, shall:

1. amend existing legislative acts of the USSR when necessary;
2. approve changes in the boundaries between Union Republics;
3. form and abolish Ministries and State Committees of the USSR on the recommendation of the Council of Ministers of the USSR;
4. relieve individual members of the Council of Ministers of the USSR of their responsibilities and appoint persons to the Council of Ministers on the recommendation of the Chairman of the Council of Ministers of the USSR.

Article 123. The Presidium of the Supreme Soviet of the USSR promulgates decrees and adopts decisions.

Article 124. On expiry of the term of the Supreme Soviet of the USSR, the Presidium of the Supreme Soviet of the USSR shall retain its powers until the newly elected Supreme Soviet of the USSR has elected a new Presidium.

The newly elected Supreme Soviet of the USSR shall be convened by the outgoing Presidium of the Supreme Soviet of the USSR within two months of the elections.

Article 125. The Soviet of the Union and the Soviet of Nationalities shall elect standing commissions from among the Deputies to make a preliminary review of matters coming within the jurisdiction of the Supreme Soviet of the USSR, to promote execution of the laws of the USSR and other acts of the Supreme Soviet of the USSR and its Presidium, and to check on the work of state bodies and organisations. The chambers of the Supreme Soviet of the USSR may also set up joint commissions on a parity basis.

When it deems it necessary, the Supreme Soviet of the USSR sets up commissions of inquiry and audit, and commissions on any other matter.

All state and public bodies, organisations and officials are obliged to meet the requests of the commissions of the Supreme Soviet of the USSR and of its chambers, and submit the requisite materials and documents to them.

The commissions' recommendations shall be subject to consideration by state and public bodies, institutions and organisations. The commissions shall be informed, within the prescribed time-limit, of the results of such consideration or of the action taken.

Article 126. The Supreme Soviet of the USSR shall supervise the work of all state bodies accountable to it.

The Supreme Soviet of the USSR shall form a Committee of People's Control of the USSR to head the system of people's control.

The organisation and procedure of people's control bodies are defined by the Law on People's Control in the USSR.

Article 127. The procedure of the Supreme Soviet of the USSR and of its bodies shall be defined in the Rules and Regulations of the Supreme Soviet of the USSR and other laws of the USSR enacted on the basis of the Constitution of the USSR.

Chapter 16 The Council of Ministers of the USSR

Article 128. The Council of Ministers of the USSR, i.e. the Government of the USSR, is the highest executive and administrative body of state authority of the USSR.

Article 129. The Council of Ministers of the USSR shall be formed by the Supreme Soviet of the USSR at a joint sitting of the Soviet of the Union and the Soviet of Nationalities, and shall consist of the Chairman of the Council of Ministers of the USSR, First Vice-Chairmen and Vice-Chairmen, Ministers of the USSR, and Chairmen of State Committees of the USSR.

The Chairmen of the Councils of Ministers of Union Republics shall be *ex officio* members of the Council of Ministers of the USSR.

The Supreme Soviet of the USSR, on the recommendation of the Chairman of the Council of Ministers of the USSR, may include in the Government of the USSR the heads of other bodies and organisations of the USSR.

The Council of Ministers of the USSR shall tender its resignation to a newly elected Supreme Soviet of the USSR at its first session.

Article 130. The Council of Ministers of the USSR shall be responsible and accountable to the Supreme Soviet of the USSR and, between sessions of the Supreme Soviet of the USSR, to the Presidium of the Supreme Soviet of the USSR.

The Council of Ministers of the USSR shall report regularly on its work to the Supreme Soviet of the USSR.

Article 131. The Council of Ministers of the USSR is empowered to deal with all matters of state administration within the jurisdiction of the Union of Soviet Socialist Republics insofar as, under the Constitution, they do not come within the competence of the Supreme Soviet of the USSR or the Presidium of the Supreme Soviet of the USSR.

Within its powers the Council of Ministers of the USSR shall:

1. ensure direction of economic, social, and cultural development; draft and implement measures to promote the well-being and cultural development of the people, to develop science and engineering, to ensure rational exploitation and conservation of natural resources, to consolidate the monetary and credit system, to pursue a uniform prices, wages, and social security policy, and to organise state insurance and a uniform system of accounting and statistics; and organise the management of industrial, constructional, and agricultural enterprises and amalgamations, transport and communications undertakings, banks, and other organisations and institutions of All-Union subordination;
2. draft current and long-term state plans for the economic and social development of the USSR and the Budget of the USSR, and submit them to the Supreme Soviet of the USSR; take measures to execute the state plans and Budget; and report to the Supreme Soviet of the USSR on the implementation of the plans and Budget;
3. implement measures to defend the interests of the state, protect socialist property and maintain public order, and guarantee and protect citizens' rights and freedoms;
4. take measures to ensure state security;
5. exercise general direction of the development of the Armed Forces of the USSR, and determine the annual contingent of citizens to be called up for active military service;
6. provide general direction in regard to relations with other states, foreign trade, and economic, scientific, technical, and cultural co-operation of the USSR with other countries; take measures to ensure fulfilment of the USSR's international treaties; and ratify and denounce intergovernmental international agreements;
7. and when necessary, form committees, central boards and other departments under the Council of Ministers of the USSR to deal with matters of economic, social and cultural development, and defence.

Article 132. A Presidium of the Council of Ministers of the USSR, consisting of the Chairman, the First Vice-Chairmen, and Vice-Chairmen of the Council of Ministers of the USSR, shall function as a standing body of the Council of Ministers of the USSR to deal with questions relating to guidance of the economy, and with other matters of state administration.

Article 133. The Council of Ministers of the USSR, on the basis of, and in pursuance of, the laws of the USSR and other decisions of the Supreme Soviet of the USSR and its Presidium, shall issue decisions and ordinances and verify their execution. The decisions and ordinances of the Council of Ministers of the USSR shall be binding throughout the USSR.

Article 134. The Council of Ministers of the USSR has the right, in matters within the jurisdiction of the Union of Soviet Socialist Republics, to suspend execution of decisions and ordinances of the Councils of Ministers of Union Republics, and to rescind acts of ministries and state committees of the USSR, and of other bodies subordinate to it.

Article 135. The Council of Ministers of the USSR shall co-ordinate and direct the work of All-Union and Union-Republican ministries, state committees of the USSR, and other bodies subordinate to it.

All-Union ministries and state committees of the USSR shall direct the work of the branches of administration entrusted to them, or exercise inter-branch administration, throughout the territory of the USSR directly or through bodies set up by them.

Union-Republican ministries and state committees of the USSR direct the work of the branches of administration entrusted to them, or exercise inter-branch administration, as a rule, through the corresponding ministries and state committees, and other bodies of Union Republics, and directly administer individual enterprises and amalgamations of Union subordination. The procedure for transferring enterprises and amalgamations from Republic or local subordination to Union subordination shall be defined by the Presidium of the Supreme Soviet of the USSR.

Ministries and state committees of the USSR shall be responsible for the condition and development of the spheres of administration entrusted to them; within their competence, they issue orders and other acts on the basis of, and in execution of, the laws of the USSR and other decisions of the Supreme Soviet of the USSR and its Presidium, and of decisions and ordinances of the Council of Ministers of the USSR, and organise and verify their implementation.

Article 136. The competence of the Council of Ministers of the USSR and its Presidium, the procedure for their work, relationships between the Council of Ministers and other state bodies, and the list of All-Union and Union-Republican ministries and state committees of the USSR are defined on the basis of the Constitution, in the Law on the Council of Ministers of the USSR.

VI. BASIC PRINCIPLES OF THE STRUCTURE OF THE BODIES OF STATE AUTHORITY AND ADMINISTRATION IN UNION REPUBLICS

Chapter 17 Higher Bodies of State Authority and Administration of a Union Republic

Article 137. The highest body of state authority of a Union Republic shall be the Supreme Soviet of that Republic.

The Supreme Soviet of a Union Republic is empowered to deal with all matters within the jurisdiction of the Republic under the Constitutions of the USSR and the Republic.

Adoption and amendment of the Constitution of a Union Republic; endorsement of state plans for economic and social development, of the Republic's Budget, and of reports on their fulfilment; and the formation of bodies accountable to the Supreme Soviet of the Union Republic are the exclusive prerogative of that Supreme Soviet.

Laws of a Union Republic shall be enacted by the Supreme Soviet of the Union Republic or by a popular vote (referendum) held by decision of the Republic's Supreme Soviet.

Article 138. The Supreme Soviet of a Union Republic shall elect a Presidium, which is a standing body of that Supreme Soviet and accountable to it for all its work. The composition and powers of the Presidium of the Supreme Soviet of a Union Republic shall be defined in the Constitution of the Union Republic.

Article 139. The Supreme Soviet of a Union Republic shall form a Council of Ministers of the Union Republic, i.e. the Government of that Republic, which shall be the highest executive and administrative body of state authority in the Republic.

The Council of Ministers of a Union Republic shall be responsible and accountable to the Supreme Soviet of that Republic or, between sessions of the Supreme Soviet, to its Presidium.

Article 140. The Council of Ministers of a Union Republic issues decisions and ordinances on the basis of, and in pursuance of, the legislative acts of the USSR and of the Union Republic, and of decisions and ordinances of the Council of Ministers of the USSR, and shall organise and verify their execution.

Article 141. The Council of Ministers of a Union Republic has the right to suspend the execution of decisions and ordinances of the Councils of Ministers of Autonomous Republics, to rescind the decisions and orders of the Executive Committees of Soviets of People's Deputies of Territories, Regions, and cities (i.e. cities under Republic jurisdiction) and of Autonomous Regions, and in Union Republics not divided into regions, of the Executive Committees of district and corresponding city Soviets of People's Deputies.

Article 142. The Council of Ministers of a Union Republic shall co-ordinate and direct the work of the Union-Republican and Republican ministries and of state committees of the Union Republic, and other bodies under its jurisdiction.

The Union-Republican ministries and state committees of a Union Republic shall direct the branches of administration entrusted to them, or exercise inter-branch control, and shall be subordinate to both the Council of Ministers of the Union Republic and the corresponding Union-Republican ministry or state committee of the USSR.

Republican ministries and state committees shall direct the branches of administration entrusted to them, or exercise interbranch control, and shall be subordinate to the Council of Ministers of the Union Republic.

Chapter 18 Higher Bodies of State Authority and Administration of an Autonomous Republic

Article 143. The highest body of state authority of an Autonomous Republic shall be the Supreme Soviet of that Republic.

Adoption and amendment of the Constitution of an Autonomous Republic; endorsement of state plans for economic and social development, and of the Republic's Budget; and the formation of bodies accountable to the Supreme Soviet of the Autonomous Republic are the exclusive prerogative of that Supreme Soviet.

Laws of an Autonomous Republic shall be enacted by the Supreme Soviet of the Autonomous Republic.

Article 144. The Supreme Soviet of an Autonomous Republic shall elect a Presidium of the Supreme Soviet of the Autonomous Republic and shall form a Council of Ministers of the Autonomous Republic, i.e. the Government of that Republic.

Chapter 19 Local Bodies of State Authority and Administration

Article 145. The bodies of state authority in Territories, Regions, Autonomous Regions, Autonomous Areas, districts, cities, city districts, settlements, and rural communities shall be the corresponding Soviets of People's Deputies.

Article 146. Local Soviets of People's Deputies shall deal with all matters of local significance in accordance with the interests of the whole state and of the citizens residing in the area under their jurisdiction, implement decisions of higher bodies of state authority, guide the work of lower Soviets of People's Deputies, take part in the discussion of matters of Republican and All-Union significance, and submit their proposals concerning them.

Local Soviets of People's Deputies shall direct state, economic, social and cultural development within their territory; endorse plans for economic and social development and the local budget; exercise general guidance over state bodies, enterprises, institutions and organisations subordinate to them; ensure observance of the laws, maintenance of law and order, and protection of citizens' rights; and help strengthen the country's defence capacity.

Article 147. Within their powers, local Soviets of People's Deputies shall ensure the comprehensive, all-round economic and social development of their area; exercise control over the observance of legislation by enterprises, institutions and organisations subordinate to higher authorities and located in their area; and co-ordinate and supervise their activity as regards land use, nature conservation, building, employment of manpower, production of consumer goods, and social, cultural, communal and other services and amenities for the public.

Article 148. Local Soviets of People's Deputies shall decide matters within the powers accorded them by the legislation of the USSR and of the appropriate Union Republic and Autonomous Republic. Their decisions shall be binding on all enterprises, institutions, and organisations located in their area and on officials and citizens.

Article 149. The executive-administrative bodies of local Soviets shall be the Executive Committees elected by them from among their deputies.

Executive Committees shall report on their work at least once a year to the Soviets that elected them and to meetings of citizens at their places of work or residence.

Article 150. Executive Committees of local Soviets of People's Deputies shall be directly accountable both to the Soviet that elected them and to the higher executive and administrative body.

VII. JUSTICE, ARBITRATION, AND PROCURATOR'S SUPERVISION

Chapter 20 Courts and Arbitration

Article 151. In the USSR justice is administered only by the courts.

In the USSR there are the following courts: the Supreme Court of the USSR, the Supreme Courts of Union Republics, the Supreme Courts of Autonomous Republics, Territorial, Regional, and city courts, courts of Autonomous Regions, courts of Autonomous Areas, district (city) people's courts, and military tribunals in the Armed Forces.

Article 152. All courts in the USSR shall be formed on the principle of the electiveness of judges and people's assessors.

People's judges of district (city) people's courts shall be elected for a term of five years by the citizens of the district (city) on the basis of universal, equal and direct suffrage by secret ballot. People's assessors of district (city) people's courts shall be elected for a term of two and a half years at meetings of citizens at their places of work or residence by a show of hands.

Higher courts shall be elected for a term of five years by the corresponding Soviet of People's Deputies.

The judges of military tribunals shall be elected for a term of five years by the Presidium of the Supreme Soviet of the USSR and people's assessors for a term of two and a half years by meetings of servicemen.

Judges and people's assessors are responsible and accountable to their electors or the bodies that elected them, shall report to them, and may be recalled by them in the manner prescribed by law.

Article 153. The Supreme Court of the USSR is the highest judicial body in the USSR and supervises the administration of justice by the courts of the USSR and Union Republics within the limits established by law.

The Supreme Court of the USSR shall be elected by the Supreme Soviet of the USSR and shall consist of a Chairman, Vice-Chairmen, members and people's assessors. The Chairmen of the Supreme Courts of Union Republics are *ex officio* members of the Supreme Court of the USSR.

The organisation and procedure of the Supreme Court of the USSR are defined in the Law on the Supreme Court of the USSR.

Article 154. The hearing of civil and criminal cases in all courts is collegial; in courts of first instance cases are heard with the participation of people's assessors. In the administration of justice people's assessors have all the rights of a judge.

Article 155. Judges and people's assessors are independent and subject only to the law.

Article 156. Justice is administered in the USSR on the principle of the equality of citizens before the law and the court.

Article 157. Proceedings in all courts shall be open to the public. Hearings *in camera* are only allowed in cases provided for by law, with observance of all the rules of judicial procedure.

Article 158. A defendant in a criminal action is guaranteed the right to legal assistance.

Article 159. Judicial proceedings shall be conducted in the language of the Union Republic, Autonomous Republic, Autonomous Region, or Autonomous Area, or in the language spoken by the majority of the people in the locality. Persons participating in court proceedings, who do not know the language in which they are being conducted, shall be ensured the right to become fully acquainted with the materials in the case; the services of an interpreter during the proceedings; and the right to address the court in their own language.

Article 160. No one may be adjudged guilty of a crime and subjected to punishment as a criminal except by the sentence of a court and in conformity with the law.

Article 161. Colleges of advocates are available to give legal assistance to citizens and organisations. In cases provided for by legislation citizens shall be given legal assistance free of charge.

The organisation and procedure of the bar are determined by legislation of the USSR and Union Republics.

Article 162. Representatives of public organisations and of work collectives may take part in civil and criminal proceedings.

Article 163. Economic disputes between enterprises, institutions, and organisations are settled by state arbitration bodies within the limits of their jurisdiction.

The organisation and manner of functioning of state arbitration bodies are defined in the Law on State Arbitration in the USSR.

Chapter 21 The Procurator's Office

Article 164. Supreme power of supervision over the strict and uniform observance of laws by all ministries, state committees and departments, enterprises, institutions and organisations, executive-administrative bodies of local Soviets of People's Deputies, collective farms, co-operatives and other public organisations, officials and citizens is vested in the Procurator-General of the USSR and procurators subordinate to him.

Article 165. The Procurator-General of the USSR is appointed by the Supreme Soviet of the USSR and is responsible and accountable to it and, between sessions of the Supreme Soviet, to the Presidium of the Supreme Soviet of the USSR.

Article 166. The procurators of Union Republics, Autonomous Republics, Territories, Regions and Autonomous Regions are appointed by the Procurator-General of the USSR. The procurators of Autonomous Areas and district and city procurators are appointed by the Procurators of Union Republics, subject to confirmation by the Procurator-General of the USSR.

Article 167. The term of office of the Procurator-General of the USSR and all lower-ranking procurators shall be five years.

Article 168. The agencies of the Procurator's Office exercise their powers independently of any local bodies whatsoever, and are subordinate solely to the Procurator-General of the USSR.

The organisation and procedure of the agencies of the Procurator's Office are defined in the Law on the Procurator's Office of the USSR.

VIII. THE EMBLEM, FLAG, ANTHEM, AND CAPITAL OF THE USSR

Article 169. The State Emblem of the Union of Soviet Socialist Republics is a hammer and sickle on a globe depicted in the rays of the sun and framed by ears of wheat, with the inscription "Workers of All Countries, Unite!" in the languages of the Union Republics. At the top of the Emblem is a five-pointed star.

Article 170. The State Flag of the Union of Soviet Socialist Republics is a rectangle of red cloth with a hammer and sickle depicted in gold in the upper corner next to the staff and with a five-pointed red star edged in gold above them. The ratio of the width of the flag to its length is 1:2.

Article 171. The State Anthem of the Union of Soviet Socialist Republics is confirmed by the Presidium of the Supreme Soviet of the USSR.

Article 172. The Capital of the Union of Soviet Socialist Republics is the city of Moscow.

IX. THE LEGAL FORCE OF THE CONSTITUTION OF THE USSR AND PROCEDURE FOR AMENDING THE CONSTITUTION

Article 173. The Constitution of the USSR shall have supreme legal force. All laws and other acts of state bodies shall be promulgated on the basis of and in conformity with it.

Article 174. The Constitution of the USSR may be amended by a decision of the Supreme Soviet of the USSR adopted by a majority of not less than two-thirds of the total number of Deputies of each of its chambers.

SELECTED BIBLIOGRAPHY

"Revolutions," once wrote Leon Trotsky, who made no small contribution to both the art and the commentary, "are always verbose." This is unquestionably true of the Bolshevik Revolution and of its historical and philosophical background, about which probably more has been written than about any other revolution in the troubled history of humankind. Under the circumstances, this bibliography is necessarily limited and, to an extent, personal. To facilitate further study, however, I have in the first instance listed some fuller bibliographical sources and, secondly, divided the remaining selections under several broad rubrics.

Bibliographies and General Sources

Allworth, Edward. *Soviet Asia: Bibliographies*. Praeger, New York, 1975.

The American Bibliography of Russian and East European Studies. Indiana University Press, Bloomington, 1957, annually.

Grant, Steven A. *Scholars' Guide to Washington, D.C. for Russian/Soviet Studies*. Smithsonian Institution Press, Washington, D.C., 1977.

Grierson, Philip. *Books on Soviet Russia, 1917–1942: A Bibliography and a Guide to Reading*. Methuen, London, 1943.

Hnik, Thomas, ed. *European Bibliography of Soviet, East European and Slavonic Studies, Vol. 1: 1975*. University of Birmingham, England, 1977.

Horak, Stephan M. *Junior Slavica: A Selected Annotated Bibliography of Books in English on Russia and Eastern Europe*. Libraries Unlimited, Rochester, N.Y., 1968.

———. *Russia, the USSR, and Eastern Europe: A Bibliographic Guide to English Language Publications, 1964–1974*. Edited by Rosemary Neiswender. Libraries Unlimited, Littleton, Colo., 1978.

Horecky, Paul L., ed. *Russia and the Soviet Union*. University of Chicago Press, Chicago, 1965.

Jones, David L. *Books in English on the Soviet Union, 1917–1973*. Garland Publishing, New York and London, 1975.

Mickiewicz, Ellen, ed. *Handbook of Soviet Social Science Data*. Free Press, New York, 1973.

Nerhood, Harry W., ed. *To Russia and Return: An Annotated Bibliography of Travelers' English-Language Accounts of Russia from the Ninth Century to the Present*. Ohio State University Press, Columbus, 1969.

Shaffer, Harry G. *Periodicals on the Socialist Countries and on Marxism*. Praeger, New York, 1977.

U.S. Library of Congress. *Half a Century of Soviet Serials, 1917–1968: A Bibliography and Union List of Serials Published in the USSR*. Library of Congress, Washington, D.C., 1968.

History

Bialer, Seweryn, ed. *Stalin and His Generals: Soviet Military Memoirs of World War II*. Pegasus, New York, 1969.

Browder, R.P., and A.F. Kerensky, eds. *The Russian Provisional Government, 1917 Documents*. Stanford University Press, Stanford, Calif., 1961.

Carr, E.H. *A History of Soviet Russia*. Multi-volumed. Macmillan, New York, 1951–1976.

Chamberlin, William H. *The Russian Revolution, 1917-1921.* 2 vols. Macmillan, New York, 1935.
Clarkson, Jesse D. *A History of Russia.* Random House, New York, 1969.
Daniels, Robert V. *The Conscience of the Revolution.* Harvard University Press, Cambridge, Mass., 1960.
______. *A Documentary History of Communism.* Random House, New York, 1960.
Florinsky, Michael T. *Russia: A History and an Interpretation.* 2 vols. Macmillan, New York, 1955.
Haimson, Leopold H. *The Russian Marxists and the Origins of Bolshevism.* Harvard University Press, Cambridge, Mass., 1955.
______, ed. *The Mensheviks: From the Revolution of 1917 to the Second World War.* University of Chicago Press, Chicago, 1974.
Keep, John L.H. *The Russian Revolution: A Study in Mass Mobilization.* Norton, New York, 1976.
Klyuchevsky, V.O. *A History of Russia.* 2 vols. Dutton, New York, 1931.
MacKenzie, David, and Michael W. Curran. *A History of Russia and the Soviet Union.* Dorsey Press and Irwin-Dorsey Ltd., Homewood, Ill., 1977.
Pipes, Richard. *The Formation of the Soviet Union.* Harvard University Press, Cambridge, Mass., 1954.
Pokrovskii, M.N. *History of Russia from the Earliest Times to the Rise of Commercial Capitalism.* International, New York, 1931.
Reed, John. *Ten Days That Shook the World.* Modern Library, New York, 1935.
Robinson, Geroid T. *Rural Russia under the Old Regime.* Macmillan, New York, 1949.
Steinberg, Isaac N. *In the Workshop of the Revolution.* Rinehart, New York, 1953.
Sukhanov, N.N. *The Russian Revolution, 1917: A Personal Record,* Oxford University Press, Oxford, 1955.
Trotsky, Leon. *The History of the Russian Revolution.* University of Michigan Press, Ann Arbor, 1955.
Ulam, Adam B. *A History of Soviet Russia.* Praeger, New York, 1976.

Philosophy

Berdyaev, Nicolas. *The Origin of Russian Communism.* Geoffrey Bles, London, 1948.
Feuer, Lewis S., ed. *Basic Writings on Politics and Philosophy by Karl Marx and Friedrich Engels.* Doubleday Anchor Books. Garden City, N.Y., 1960.
Hook, Sidney. *Towards the Understanding of Karl Marx.* John Day, New York, 1933.
Hunt, R.N. Carew. *The Theory and Practice of Communism.* Macmillan, New York, 1957.
Jaworskyj, M., ed. *Soviet Political Thought: An Anthology.* Johns Hopkins University Press, Baltimore, Md., 1968.
Lenin, V.I. *Selected Works.* 12 vols. Cooperative Publishing Society of Foreign Workers in the USSR, Moscow, 1934.
Marcuse, Herbert. *Soviet Marxism.* Columbia University Press, New York, 1958.
Marx, Karl. *Capital.* 3 vols. Kerr, Chicago, 1909.
______. *Selected Works.* 2 vols. International, New York, 1942.
______ and Frederick Engels. *Selected Correspondence.* International, New York, 1942.
Meyer, Alfred G. *Leninism.* Harvard University Press, Cambridge, Mass., 1954.
______. *Marxism.* Harvard University Press, Cambridge, Mass., 1954.
Somerville, John. *Soviet Philosophy.* Philosophical Library, New York, 1946.
Stalin, Joseph, *Problems of Leninism.* Foreign Languages Publishing House, Moscow, 1953.
Tucker, Robert C., ed. *The Lenin Anthology.* Norton, New York, 1975.
Utechin, S.V. *Russian Political Thought.* Praeger, New York, 1964.

Biography

Berlin, Isaiah. *Karl Marx.* Oxford University Press, New York, 1959.

Cohen, Stephen F. *Bukharin and the Bolshevik Revolution: A Political Biography, 1888–1938.* Knopf, New York, 1973.

Deutscher, Isaac. *The Prophet Armed: Trotsky, 1879–1921.* Oxford University Press, New York, 1954.

______. *The Prophet Unarmed: Trotsky, 1921–1929.* Oxford University Press, New York, 1959.

______. *The Prophet Outcast: Trotsky 1929–1940.* Oxford University Press, New York, 1963.

______. *Stalin.* Oxford University Press, New York, 1967.

Fischer, Louis. *The Life of Lenin.* Harper & Row, New York, 1964.

Khrushchev, Nikita S. *Khrushchev Remembers.* Little, Brown, Boston, 1974.

Medvedev, Roy A., and Zhores Medvedev. *Khrushchev: The Years in Power.* Columbia University Press, New York, 1976.

Payne, Robert. *The Life and Death of Lenin.* Simon and Schuster, New York, 1964.

Rühle, Otto. *Karl Marx.* Viking Press, New York, 1929.

Shukman, Harold. *Lenin and the Russian Revolution.* Putnam's, New York, 1967.

Trotsky, Leon. *Stalin.* Harper, New York, 1941.

Ulam, Adam B. *Stalin: The Man and His Era.* Viking Press, New York, 1973.

Wolfe, Bertram D. *Three Who Made a Revolution.* Dial Press, New York, 1948.

Resources and Development

Baransky, N.N. *Economic Geography of the USSR.* Foreign Languages Publishing House, Moscow, 1956.

Baykov, Alexander. *The Development of the Soviet Economic System.* Harvard University Press, Cambridge, Mass., 1946.

Bergson, Abram. *Economics of Soviet Planning.* Yale University Press, New Haven, Conn., 1964.

______. *Soviet Post-War Economic Development.* Almqvist & Wiksell International, Stockholm, 1974.

Berliner, Joseph S. *Factory and Manager in the USSR.* Harvard University Press, Cambridge, Mass., 1957.

______. *The Innovation Decision in Soviet Industry.* MIT Press, Cambridge, Mass., 1976.

Brodersen, Arvid. *The Soviet Worker.* Random House, New York, 1966.

Cohn, Stanley H. *Economic Development in the Soviet Union.* Heath, Lexington, Mass., 1970.

Cressey, George B. *Soviet Potentials: A Geographical Appraisal.* Syracuse University Press, Syracuse, N.Y., 1961.

Dobb, M. *Soviet Economic Development Since 1917.* Routledge and Kegan Paul, London, 1958.

Granick, David. *Management of the Industrial Firm in the USSR.* Columbia University Press, New York, 1954.

______. *The Red Executive: A Study of the Organization Man in Russian Industry.* Doubleday Anchor Books. Garden City, N.Y., 1961.

Gregory, Paul R., and Robert C. Stewart. *Soviet Economic Structure and Performance.* Harper & Row, New York, 1974.

Hodgman, Donald R. *Soviet Industrial Production, 1928–1951.* Harvard University Press, Cambridge, Mass., 1954.

Hutchings, Raymond. *Soviet Science, Technology, Design: Interaction and Convergence.* Oxford University Press, 1976.

Jasny, Naum. *The Socialized Agriculture of the USSR*. Stanford University Press, Stanford, Calif., 1949.
______. *Soviet Industrialization, 1928–1952*. University of Chicago Press, Chicago, 1960.
Kaser, Michael. *Soviet Economics*. McGraw-Hill, New York, 1970.
Katkoff, V. *Soviet Economy, 1940–1965*. Dangary, Baltimore, Md., 1961.
Lane, David. *The Socialist Industrial State: Towards a Political Sociology of State Socialism*. Westview Press, Boulder, Colo., 1976.
Lydolph, Paul E. *The Climates of the Soviet Union*. Elsevier Scientific Publishing Company, Amsterdam and New York, 1977.
Miller, Margaret. *Rise of the Russian Consumer*. Institute of Economic Affairs, London, 1965.
Nove, Alec. *An Economic History of the USSR*. Allen Lane, London, 1969.
______. *Political Economy and Soviet Socialism*. George Allen and Unwin, London, 1979.
______. *The Soviet Economic System*. George Allen and Unwin, London, 1977.
Shaffer, Harry G., ed. *Soviet Agriculture: An Assessment of its Contribution to Economic Development*. Praeger, New York, 1977.
Sherman, H.J. *The Soviet Economy*. Little, Brown, Boston, 1969.
Spulber, Nicolas. *The Soviet Economy*. Norton, New York, 1962.
Stalin, Joseph. *Economic Problems of Socialism in the USSR*. International, New York, 1952.
Turgeon, Lynn. *The Contrasting Economies*. Allyn and Bacon, Boston, 1963.
______, and Abram Bergson. *Prices of Basic Industrial Goods in the USSR*. The Rand Corporation, Santa Monica, Calif., 1957.
Volin, Lazar. *A Century of Russian Agriculture: From Alexander II to Khrushchev*. Harvard University Press, Cambridge, Mass., 1970.
Yevenko, I.A. *Planning in the USSR*. Foreign Languages Publishing House, Moscow, n.d.

Law and Politics

Barghoorn, Frederick C. *Politics in the USSR*. Little, Brown, Boston, 1966.
Bauer, Raymond A., Alex Inkeles, and Clyde Kluckhohn. *How the Soviet System Works*. Harvard University Press, Cambridge, Mass., 1956.
Berman, Harold J. *Justice in the USSR*. Vintage Books, New York, 1963.
Cocks, Paul, et al., eds. *The Dynamics of Soviet Politics*. Harvard University Press, Cambridge, Mass., 1976.
Daniels, Robert V. *The Nature of Communism*. Random House, New York, 1962.
Denisov, A., and M. Kirichenko. *Soviet State Law*. Foreign Languages Publishing House, Moscow, 1960.
Djilas, Milovan. *The New Class*. Praeger, New York, 1957.
Fainsod, Merle. *Smolensk under Soviet Rule*. Harvard University Press, Cambridge, Mass., 1958.
Feldbrugge, F.J.M., ed. *Encyclopedia of Soviet Law*. 2 vols. Oceana Publications, Dobbs Ferry, N.Y., 1973.
Hammer, Darrell P. *USSR: The Politics of Oligarchy*. Dryden Press, Hinsdale, Ill., 1974.
Hazard, John N., and Isaac Shapiro. *The Soviet Legal System*. 3 vols. Oceana Publications, Dobbs Ferry, N.Y. 1962.
Hough, Jerry F., and Merle Fainsod. *How the Soviet Union Is Governed*. Harvard University Press, Cambridge, Mass., 1979.
Johnson, E.L. *An Introduction to the Soviet Legal System*. Methuen, London, 1969.
Juviler, Peter H. *Revolutionary Law and Order: Politics and Social Change in the USSR*. Free Press, New York, 1976.
______, and Henry W. Morton, eds. *Soviet Policy Making*, Praeger, New York, 1967.

Lane, David. *Politics and Society in the USSR*. Random House, New York, 1971.
Meyer, Alfred G. *The Soviet Political System: An Interpretation*. Random House, New York, 1965.
Moore, Barrington, Jr. *Soviet Politics—The Dilemma of Power*. Harvard University Press, Cambridge, Mass., 1950.
______. *Terror and Progress, USSR*. Harvard University Press, Cambridge, Mass., 1954.
Morton, Henry W., and Rudolf L. Tökés, eds. *Soviet Politics and Society in the 1970s*. Free Press, New York, 1974.
Osborn, Robert J. *The Evolution of Soviet Politics*. Dorsey Press, Homewood, Ill., 1974.
Ploss, Sidney, ed. *The Soviet Political Process*. Ginn, Lexington, Mass., 1971.
Schapiro, Leonard. *The Communist Party of the Soviet Union*. Random House, New York, 1971.
______. *The Origin of the Communist Autocracy*. Harvard University Press, Cambridge, Mass., 1977.
Sharlet, Robert. *The New Soviet Constitution of 1977: Analysis and Text*. King's Court Communications, Brunswick, Ohio, 1978.
Skilling, Gordon H., and Franklyn Griffiths, eds. *Interest Groups in Soviet Politics*, Princeton University Press, Princeton, N.J., 1971.
Tatu, Michel. *Power in the Kremlin*. Collins, London, 1969.
Taubman, William. *Governing Soviet Cities: Bureaucratic Politics and Urban Development in the USSR*. Praeger, New York, 1973.
Towster, Julian. *Political Power in the USSR, 1917-1947*. Oxford University Press, New York, 1948.
Trotsky, Leon. *The Revolution Betrayed*. Doubleday, Doran, New York, 1937.
Vyshinsky, Andrei Y. *The Law of the Soviet State*. Macmillan, New York, 1948.

Disaffection and Dissent

Beck, F., and W. Godin. (pseuds.) *Russian Purge and the Extraction of Confession*. Viking Press, New York, 1951.
Bukovsky, Vladimir. *To Build a Castle—My Life as a Dissenter*. Viking Press, New York, 1979.
Conquest, Robert. *The Great Terror*. Macmillan, New York, 1968.
Fisher, Alan. *The Crimean Tatars*. Hoover Institution Press, Stanford, Calif. 1978.
Grigorenko, P.G. *The Grigorenko Papers: Writings by General P.G. Grigorenko and Documents on His Case*. Westview Press, Boulder, Colo., 1976.
Levytsky, Boris. *The Uses of Terror: The Soviet Secret Police*. Coward, McCann and Geoghegan, New York, 1972.
Mandelstam, Nadezhda. *Hope Abandoned*. Atheneum, New York, 1974.
Medvedev, Roy A. *Let History Judge*. Knopf, New York, 1971.
Sakharov, Andrei D. *Sakharov Speaks*. Edited by Harrison E. Salisbury. Knopf, New York, 1974.
Solzhenitsyn, Aleksandr I. *The Gulag Archipelago, 1918–1956: An Experiment in Literary Investigation, I–II*. Harper & Row, New York, 1974.
______. *The Gulag Archipelago, 1918–1956: An Experiment in Literary Investigation, III–IV*. Harper & Row, New York, 1975.
Tökés, Rudolf L., ed. *Dissent in the USSR: Politics, Ideology and People*. Johns Hopkins University Press, Baltimore, Md., 1975.

Soviet Society in General

Atkinson, Dorothy, et al., eds. *Women in Russia*. Stanford University Press, Stanford, Calif. 1977.

Barghoorn, Frederick C. *Soviet Russian Nationalism*. Oxford University Press, New York, 1956.

Bauer, Raymond A. *The New Man in Soviet Psychology*. Harvard University Press, Cambridge, Mass., 1952.

Brown, Deming. *Soviet Russian Literature Since Stalin*. Cambridge University Press, New York, 1978.

Field, Mark G. *Doctor and Patient in Soviet Russia*. Harvard University Press, Cambridge, Mass., 1957.

______. *Soviet Socialized Medicine*. Free Press, New York, 1967.

Goldhagen, E., ed. *Ethnic Minorities in the Soviet Union*, Praeger, New York, 1968.

Halevy, Zvi. *Jewish Schools under Czarism and Communism: A Struggle for Cultural Identity*. Springer Publishing, New York, 1976.

Hendel, Samuel, and Randolph L. Braham, eds. *The USSR after 50 Years: Promise and Reality*. Knopf, New York, 1957.

Hollander, Paul, ed. *American and Soviet Society: A Reader in Comparative Sociology and Perception*. Prentice-Hall, Englewood Cliffs, N.J., 1969.

______. *Soviet and American Society: A Comparison*. Oxford University Press, New York, 1973.

Inkeles, Alex. *Social Change in Soviet Russia*. Harvard University Press, Cambridge, Mass., 1968.

Kochan, Lionel, ed. *The Jews in Soviet Russia Since 1917*. Oxford University Press, New York, 1970.

Kolkowicz, Roman. *The Soviet Military and the Communist Party*. Princeton University Press, Princeton, N.J. 1967.

Mace, David R., and Vera Mace. *The Soviet Family*. Doubleday, New York, 1963.

Madison, Bernice. *Social Welfare in the Soviet Union*. Stanford University Press, Stanford, Calif. 1968.

Mandel, William M. *Soviet Women*. Doubleday Anchor Books, Garden City, N.Y., 1975.

Meisel, James, and Edward Kozera. *Materials for the Study of the Soviet System*. George Wahr, Ann Arbor, Mich., 1953.

Osborn, Robert. *Soviet Social Policies*. Dorsey Press, Homewood, Ill., 1970.

Sacks, Michael P. *Women's Work in Soviet Russia: Continuity in the Midst of Change*. Praegar, New York, 1976.

Shaffer, Harry G. *The Soviet Treatment of Jews*. Praeger, New York, 1974.

Smith, Hedrick. *The Russians*. New York Times Book Company, New York, 1976.

Struve, Gleb. *Russian Literature under Lenin and Stalin, 1917–1953*. University of Oklahoma Press, Norman, Okla., 1971.

Tobias, Henry J. *The Jewish Bund in Russia from Its Origins to 1905*. Stanford University Press, Stanford, Calif., 1972.

Weinberg, Elizabeth A. *The Development of Sociology in the Soviet Union*. Routledge & Kegan Paul, London and Boston, 1974.

Yanowitch, Murray. *Social and Economic Inequality in the Soviet Union*. M.E. Sharpe, 1977.